DEAD SOULS

THE REAVEY TRANSLATION
BACKGROUNDS AND SOURCES
ESSAYS IN CRITICISM

W.W. NORTON & COMPANY, INC.
also publishes

THE NORTON ANTHOLOGY OF ENGLISH LITERATURE
edited by M. H. Abrams et al.

THE NORTON ANTHOLOGY OF AMERICAN LITERATURE
edited by Nina Baym et al.

THE NORTON ANTHOLOGY OF WORLD MASTERPIECES
edited by Maynard Mack et al.

THE NORTON ANTHOLOGY OF LITERATURE BY WOMEN
edited by Sandra M. Gilbert and Susan Gubar

THE NORTON ANTHOLOGY OF MODERN POETRY
edited by Richard Ellmann and Robert O'Clair

THE NORTON ANTHOLOGY OF POETRY
edited by Alexander W. Allison et al.

THE NORTON ANTHOLOGY OF SHORT FICTION
edited by R.V. Cassill

THE NORTON FACSIMILE OF
THE FIRST FOLIO OF SHAKESPEARE
prepared by Charlton Hinman

THE NORTON INTRODUCTION TO LITERATURE
edited by Carl E. Bain, Jerome Beaty, and J. Paul Hunter

THE NORTON INTRODUCTION TO THE SHORT NOVEL
edited by Jerome Beaty

THE NORTON READER
edited by Arthur M. Eastman et al.

THE NORTON SAMPLER
edited by Thomas Cooley

and the

NORTON CRITICAL EDITIONS

NIKOLAI GOGOL

DEAD SOULS

THE REAVEY TRANSLATION
BACKGROUNDS AND SOURCES
ESSAYS IN CRITICISM

-»» «‹-

Edited by

GEORGE GIBIAN

CORNELL UNIVERSITY

W. W. NORTON & COMPANY

New York   London

The editor would like to express his warm thanks to John Benedict, Tanya Mairs, and Marian Johnson of W. W. Norton and Company.

ISBN 0-393-95292-4 {PAPER}
ISBN 0-393-01736-2 {CLOTH}

Copyright © 1985 by W. W. Norton & Company, Inc.
All rights reserved.

Published simultaneously in Canada by
Penguin Books Canada Ltd,
2801 John Street, Markham, Ontario L3R 1B4.

PRINTED IN THE UNITED STATES OF AMERICA.

Library of Congress Cataloging in Publication Data
Gogol', Nikolaï Vasil'evich, 1809–1852.
　Dead souls.
　Translation of: Mertvye dushi.
　Bibliography: p. 585
　1. Gogol', Nikolaï Vasil'evich, 1809–1852—Translations, English.
2. Gogol', Nikolaï Vasil'evich, 1809–1852. Mertvye dushi—Addresses,
essays, lectures. 3. Gogol', Nikolaï Vasil'evich, 1809–1852—Criticism
and interpretation—Addresses, essays, lectures. I. Gibian, George. II.
Title.
PG3333.M4　1984　　891.73'3　　84-8027
ISBN 0-393-95292-4

W. W. Norton & Company, Inc., 500 Fifth Avenue,
New York, N. Y. 10110
W. W. Norton & Company Ltd., 37 Great Russell Street,
London WC1B 3NU

1 2 3 4 5 6 7 8 9 0

Contents

Preface   vii

Illustration: Gogol's frontispiece design for *Dead Souls*   ix

The Text of *Dead Souls*

Backgrounds and Sources

A Chronology of Gogol's Life   410

Gogol's "Four Letters to Divers Persons Apropos
      Dead Souls"   411

From Gogol's Letters   424

    To A. S. Pushkin. October 7, 1835.   424

    To V. A. Zhukovsky. November 12, 1836.   424

    To S. T. Aksakov. December 28, 1840.   426

    To P. A. Pletnev. January 7, 1842.   427

    To N. Ya. Prokopovich. April 9, 1842.   430

    To A. V. Nikitenko, April 10. 1842.   430

    To A. S. Danilevsky. May 9, 1882.   431

    To V. Zhukovsky. June 26, 1842.   432

    Addressee unknown. About July 20, 1842.   433

    To S. T. Aksakov. August 18/6, 1842.   434

    To A. O. Smirnova. July 25, 1845.   436

    To N. M. Yazykov. May 5, 1846.   437

Ranks in Tsarist Russia   437

Essays in Criticism

    Robert A. Maguire • [The Legacy of Gogol Criticism]   441

    V. G. Belinsky • Chichikov's Adventures,
      or *Dead Souls:* Gogol's Epic Poem   453

    Alexander I. Herzen • Diary Entries on *Dead Souls*   458

    Donald Fanger • *Dead Souls:* The Mirror and
      the Road   459

    Yuri Mann • On the Two Opposing Structural
      Principles of *Dead Souls*   482

    V. V. Gippius • An Introduction to *Dead Souls*   489

    Andrei Bely • The Figure of Fiction in *Dead Souls*   517

    Vladimir Nabokov • Our Mr. Chichikov   531

    Edmund Wilson • Gogol: The Demon in the
      Overgrown Garden   542

v

Simon Karlinsky • [Portrait of Gogol as a
  Word Glutton]   546
Dmitry Čiževsky • Gogol: Artist and Thinker   558
Viktor Shklovsky • The Literary Genre of
  Dead Souls   564
M. M. Bakhtin • Verbal Art and the Folk
  Culture of Laughter   569
Yuri M. Lotman • The Problem of Artistic Space
  in Gogol's Prose   577
Selected Bibliography   585

Preface

Gogol has had a varied reception in Russia and abroad. Few authors' works have been interpreted in so many different ways as *Dead Souls* and Gogol's other writings have by successive generations of critics.

His contemporaries considered him a humanitarian who saw life in Russia as it really was, criticized abuses, and called for pity for humble, downtrodden "little people." Some were put off by what they regarded as unseemly humor; others were attracted by it. Later, Gogol came to be viewed as a great "realist" and father of the Russian novel. "We have all come out from under Gogol's 'Overcoat' " is a famous although apocryphal remark attributed to Dostoevsky.

Radicals reproached Gogol for the religious, conservative opinions that he expressed in his later years; some even abhorred him. On the other hand, some symbolists at the end of the nineteenth century saw in him their spiritual and artistic ancestor.

The twentieth century brought revivals of the socially conscious interpretation of Gogol and a return to the "realistic" conception of his work. The formalist critics and scholars studied his works as masterpieces of artistic composition and analyzed his devices and techniques. The influence of Franz Kafka and World War I led to emphasis on Gogol's grotesquerie. Western "literature of the absurd" found spiritual and artistic kinship in Gogol, as did the existentialist movement around World War II.

Those who valued literary art as primarily a playful magician's sleight of hand rediscovered Gogol's arabesques —his curlicues and his tangential, zany comedy. Vladimir Nabokov, author of a slim book on Gogol, was the most prominent spokesman of this school of thought. The generation of Kurt Vonnegut led to still another revival of interest—in the mixture of naturalism with bizarre fantasy that it found in *Dead Souls*.

The present edition reprints George Reavey's translation of *Dead Souls*, with a few emendations and changes and with additional footnotes. The background materials include extracts from Gogol's letters and from his *Selected Passages from Correspondence with Friends*. The anthology of critical and scholarly essays presents samples of a variety of Russian criticism, both nineteenth- and twentieth-century. Several of the pieces have never been published in English before.

The selection of Western criticism aims at making available examples of the best of comments and analyses, as well as presenting a cross section of the different approaches taken to *Dead Souls*. Some are by well-known critics and writers (Vladimir Nabokov, Edmund Wilson); others, by specialists and scholars.

Quotations from *Dead Souls* in the critical essays reprinted here have been left in such versions as were used by authors or were freshly translated in the Russian essays, instead of being replaced by the George Reavey version, since the points being made might have been weakened if a different translation had been substituted. Uniformity of translation has seemed less important than the force of the critical argument.

The editor owes particular thanks to many friends and graduate students. Thomas Seifrid, Geoffrey Packer, and Robert Sorenson did the translations from the Russian; Joan Mack, Sally Keyel, and Diane Williams prepared the manuscript; Robert MacDonald, an undergraduate student, suggested places in the text of *Dead Souls* needing annotation in footnotes. Donald Fanger, author of the outstanding recent book *The Creation of Nikolai Gogol*, made excellent suggestions of critical materials to be included in this edition.

As Robert A. Maguire has written in his preface to his book, *Gogol from the Twentieth Century*, Gogol has been "irresistible to critics of all temperaments, styles, and philosophies; indeed, much of the history of Russian literary criticism could be written around the opinions generated by him. He has been proclaimed a realist and a fantast; a subtle student of the human heart and a creator of cardboard characters; a revolutionary and a reactionary; a monger of the lewd and a hierophant of the sublime; a pathological liar and an honest anatomist of the soul; a self-promoter and a self-immolator; a typical Russian and a typical Ukrainian; a narrow nationalist and a universal genius; a jejune jokester and a tragic poet."

It is our hope that this edition will bring new readers to the humorous, artful, and phantasmagoric art of Nikolai Gogol.

GEORGE GIBIAN

This intricate design is attributed to Nikolai Gogol himself.
Meant as a front wrapper, it was reproduced as the frontispiece
in the first edition of the novel in 1842. The illustrations that it
contains allude to several places in the text of the book, as well
as the title (skulls = dead souls?). The relative size of the letter-
ing of the various lines is also significant. They read in English:

CHICHIKOV'S ADVENTURES

or

DEAD SOULS

A POEM

by N. Gogol

1842

COPYRIGHT ACKNOWLEDGMENTS

Gogol's "Four Letters": From Jesse Zeldin, ed. and trans., *Selected Passages from Correspondence with Friends*, by N. Gogol (1969). Pages 96-110. Reprinted by permission of Vanderbilt University Press.

Gogol's Letters: From Carl R. Proffer, ed., *Letters of Nikolai Gogol*, translated by Carl R. Proffer in collaboration with Vera Krivoshein. Copyright 1967. Reprinted by permission of the University of Michigan Press.

Robert A. Maguire: From Robert A. Maguire, ed. and trans., *Gogol from the Twentieth Century*. Copyright © 1974 by Princeton University Press. Excerpts, pp. 3-16, reprinted by permission of Princeton University Press.

Donald Fanger: Reprinted by permission of the publishers from *The Creation of Nikolai Gogol* by Donald Fanger. Cambridge, Mass.: Harvard University Press, copyright © 1979 by the President and Fellows of Harvard College.

Vladimir Nabokov: From Vladimir Nabokov, *Nikolai Gogol*. Copyright © 1944 by New Directions. Copyright © 1982 by Vera Nabokov and Dimitri Nabokov, Trustees of the Article Third B Trust.

Edmund Wilson: Edmund Wilson, "Gogol: The Demon in the Overgrown Garden," from *The Nation*, December 6, 1952. Reprinted by permission of *The Nation*.

Simon Karlinsky: Simon Karlinsky, "Portrait of Gogol as Word Glutton, with Rabelais, Sterne and Gertrude Stein as Background Figures," from *California Slavic Studies*, vol. 5 (1970), 170-85. Copyright © 1970 by The Regents of the University of California, reprinted by permission of the University of California Press.

Dmitry Čiževsky: Dmitry Čiževsky, "Gogol: Artist and Thinker," from *The Annals of the Ukrainian Academy of Arts and Sciences in the U.S.*, vol. III, Spring 1952, nos. 22-4. Reprinted by permission of the Ukrainian Academy of Arts and Sciences in the U.S.

The Text of

Dead Souls

Translated by George Reavey

PUBLISHER'S NOTE

The present translation is based upon the edition of **Dead Souls** *published in Moscow in 1937 by the State Publishing House. The Soviet editors restored the passages cut out by the Tsarist censor, which were not published in pre-revolutionary editions. The translation of Part II is founded upon the tenth edition (Tikhonravy's), which contains the original draft as corrected in manuscript by the author.*

EDITOR'S NOTE

The word "soul" (dusha) in nineteenth-century Russia also carried the secondary meaning of "serf." Gogol plays on the two meanings of the word in the title and at various places in the novel.

PART I

CHAPTER I

A FAIRLY smart, medium-sized chaise[1] on springs rolled through the gates of an inn of the provincial town of N. The chaise was of the kind favoured by bachelors of the class of retired lieutenant-colonels, staff-captains and landowners with no more than about a hundred serfs to their name—in short, by all who are usually dubbed the 'middling gentry'. The gentleman lolling back in the chaise was neither dashingly handsome nor yet unbearably ugly, neither too stout nor yet too thin; it could not be claimed that he was old, but he was no stripling either. His arrival in the town created no stir and was not marked by anything out of the ordinary. But two Russian peasants, who were loitering by the door of a pothouse opposite the inn, ventured on a few remarks which referred, however, more to the turn-out than to the person in it. 'Just look,' said one of them, 'what is that for a wheel! D'you think, if it had the luck, a wheel like that would ever get to Moscow?' 'It'd get there, all right,' the other replied. 'But it wouldn't reach Kazan,[2] I bet.' 'It wouldn't reach Kazan,' the other agreed. On that the conversation ended. Just then, as the chaise was driving up to the inn, a young man strolled past, attired in white dimity trousers, very narrow and very short, and a swallow-tailed coat with some pretensions to fashion which disclosed a shirt-front fastened with a bronze pin of Tula[3] design in the shape of a pistol. The young man swung round, inspected the turn-out, clutched his cap as a gust of wind was threatening to blow it away, and strolled on his way.

As the chaise rattled into the courtyard, the gentleman

1. A lightweight carriage.
2. A town on the river Volga about 450 miles east of Moscow.
3. A town about a hundred miles south of Moscow, famous for its metalworking industries.

was greeted by a waiter of the inn—or floorman, as such waiters are called in Russian inns—who was so quick and agile that it was quite impossible to distinguish his features. He came dashing out promptly, with a napkin slung over his arm, a lanky figure wearing a cotton jacket, the waist of which was almost level with the nape of his neck, swept back his hair, and briskly conducting the traveller upstairs by way of a long wooden gallery, showed him the room vouchsafed to him by the Almighty. The room was of the ordinary sort, just as the inn was of an ordinary sort. In fact, it was the kind of inn to be found in all provincial towns where, for a couple of roubles a night, travellers are assigned to a room in which cockroaches peer out of all the corners, like dried prunes, and which usually has a door giving on the next room—a door always barricaded with a dressing-table, at the back of which some neighbour is stationed, a quiet and taciturn man who is yet excessively inquisitive and eager to discover all possible details about the new arrival. The façade of the inn was like its interior: it was very long and had two storeys; the lower floor was of dark-red brick, not stuccoed, dirty enough as it was but grown even more grimy in consequence of an intemperate climate; the upper floor was painted in the eternal shade of yellow; and on the ground floor there was an assortment of shops retailing horse-collars, rope and cracknels. In the corner of one of the shops—indeed right in the window of it—sat a vendor of spiced and honeyed drinks next to a red copper samovar. His face was quite as red, and from afar one might have fancied that, if one of them had not had a pitch-black beard, two samovars were standing in the window.

While the new arrival was inspecting his room, his belongings were brought in: first and foremost, a white leather trunk, a little the worse for wear and exhibiting evidence of having seen much travel. This trunk was carried in by Selifan, the coachman, a squat fellow in a sheepskin coat, and Petrushka, the footman, a small man aged about thirty, wearing a loose-fitting and well-worn coat that had obviously been part of his master's wardrobe. He had a very flat nose, thick lips, and a surly enough expression. After the trunk a small mahogany dressing-case was carried in, inlaid with patterns of Karelian[4] birch; also a boot-tree and a roast chicken wrapped in blue paper. When all these had been set down, Selifan, the coachman, went off to the stables to attend to the horses while Petrushka, the footman, began to make himself at home in the small ante-chamber. This was an extremely dark kennel in which he had already had time to deposit his topcoat and, with it, a peculiar smell of his own—a smell that was also common to the sack in which he kept his toilet accessories and which he brought in later. In this kennel he fixed up a narrow three-legged bed against the wall, covering it over with the semblance of a small mattress which was squashed as flat as a pancake and perhaps quite as greasy. This he had succeeded in extracting from the innkeeper.

While the servants were fussing about, the gentleman made for the parlour. Every traveller has a very good notion of the nature of these parlours: the walls are always the same and covered in oil paint, discoloured near the top by smoke and stained below in patches by the backs of innumerable travellers—more especially by the backs of the merchants of the neighbourhood who repair here on market days in sixes and sevens to sip their customary two glasses of tea. There was the same grimy ceiling, the same sooty chandelier with a multitude of pendant glass drops that quivered and tinkled each time the waiter ran across the worn linoleum flourishing boisterously a tray piled with as many glasses of tea as there are birds on the sea-shore. There was the same display of oil-paintings on the walls, in short, the sameness was all pervasive; the only note of difference was provided by a picture portraying a nymph with breasts so enormous that the reader has never seen the like. Such freaks of nature are to be met with, however, in some historical paintings which have been brought to Russia no one knows when, whence or by whom, but sometimes by some of our noble amateurs of art who have acquired them in Italy on the advice of their guides.

4. Karelia is a region in northwestern Russia, close to Finland, rich in birch forests.

The gentleman threw off his cap and unwound a rainbow-coloured woollen scarf such as wives are in the habit of knitting with their own hands for their husbands, furnishing them at the same time with suitable injunctions as to how they should wrap themselves. Who knits them for bachelors I cannot tell. God knows! I never wore such scarves. After unwinding his scarf, the gentleman ordered dinner to be served to him. While they were plying him with various dishes common to all inns, such as cabbage soup with pasties[5] that had been kept for weeks specially for travellers, calf's brains with peas, sausages and cabbage, roast chicken, salted cucumber, the invariable sweet puffs and always serviceable tartlets—while all these things were being served up to him either just warm or quite cold, he encouraged the waiter to gossip at random and to tell him who it was that had formerly kept the inn and who kept it now, whether it brought much profit and whether the proprietor was a notorious scoundrel? To this the waiter replied with the customary: 'Oh yes, sir, a great rogue!' As in enlightened Europe, so nowadays in enlightened Russia, there are many worthy people who cannot forbear, when dining at an inn, from chatting with the waiters and even jesting at their expense.

However, the visitor's questions were not all idle; he was extremely meticulous in his enquiries as to who was the governor of the town, who the president of the court, who the prosecutor; in short, he did not pass over a single official of any importance. With an even greater minuteness, almost bordering on sympathy, he enquired after all the leading landowners, asked how many peasant souls each of them owned, how far they lived from town, what sort of characters they had and how often they came to town. He probed carefully into the state of the region: were there any epidemics in the province, any typhus or any sort of deadly fevers, smallpox, and the like; and this he did in such detail that there was obviously more in it than mere curiosity. The gentleman's

5. Small baked dumplings, usually filled with ground meat, which Russians like to eat with soup.

manner was quite imposing and he blew his nose extremely loudly. It was a mystery how he did it, but his nose sounded like a trumpet. This apparently quite guileless trait inspired the greatest respect in the tavern waiter who, each time he heard the trumpet call, tossed his hair back, straightened his spine more respectfully, and, bending down his head, asked whether the traveller required anything.

After dinner, the gentleman sipped a small cup of coffee and settled himself on the sofa, propping his back with a cushion, such as is to be found in Russian taverns, usually stuffed with something very like bricks or cobblestones instead of resilient wool. Then he began to yawn and asked to be taken to his room where he lay down and slept for a couple of hours. After his rest, he wrote out at the request of the tavern servant his rank, his Christian name and his surname on a piece of paper so that it might be communicated, as behoved, to the police. As he went downstairs, the waiter spelled out the following: 'Collegiate Councillor,[6] Pavel Ivanovich Chichikov, landed proprietor, travelling on private business.'

While the waiter was still spelling out the syllables, Pavel Ivanovich Chichikov set out on a tour of the town. Its appearance evidently satisfied him, for he found it in no way inferior to other provincial towns: the yellow façades of the stone buildings were a perpetual eyesore and the wooden houses were of a nondescript grey. The houses were of one, two, or one and a half storeys, and they all had their entresol[7] which was very beautiful in the opinion of the provincial architects. In places these houses looked lost in the midst of a street as spacious as a field and with endless wooden fences; in others, they were bunched together, and there was more bustle and coming and going of people. Here and there one saw faded posters advertising biscuits and boots, and oc-

6. Sixth of fourteen ranks in the 1722 Table of Ranks of Peter I; the civilian equivalent of colonel in the army. The eight highest ranks in the civil service automatically became members of the nobility; only noblemen could own (and buy) serfs. When Fenya, Korobochka's servant, asks Chichikov who he is, he answers, "A nobleman" (p. 42). See *Ranks in Tsarist Russia,* pp. 437–38 below.

7. A structure like a dormer, or half-story, added between the stories to the upper half of a house.

casionally a sign with a pair of faintly delineated blue trousers on it and the name of some Arsaw[8] tailor; or a shop displaying peaked caps and forage caps, with a signboard above it, *Vassily Feodorov, Foreigner*;[9] or a poster showing two billiard-players in evening dress such as is worn only by guests on the stage who make their appearance in the last act. The billiard-players were portrayed in the act of playing, their arms turned out and their legs askew, as if they had just been executing an *entrechat*. Beneath all this was written: 'Here is the Establishment.' In places stalls were set out in the street with nuts, soap, and honey-cakes very like the soap; elsewhere a chop-house under the sign of a goodly fish with a fork stuck in it. Most frequently of all one caught sight of the faded Imperial arms, the double-headed eagle, which has since been replaced by the laconic inscription 'Beerhouse.' Everywhere the roadway was in bad shape.

Chichikov peeped into the town garden, consisting of some frail trees, which had taken root badly and which were supported from below by triangular props very beautifully covered in green oil paint. Although these trees were no higher than bulrushes, it had been said of them in the local newspapers, when the illuminations were described, that: 'our town has been beautified, thanks to the solicitude of the municipal authorities, by a garden of spreading, shady trees, the source of coolness on sultry days,' and that 'it is touching to observe how the hearts of the citizens quivered in an excess of gratitude and poured out torrents of tears by way of thankfulness to the town governor.'

Having questioned a watchman in some detail how he might reach, if need be, the Cathedral, the courts, and the governor's house, he set off to have a look at the river, which flowed through the centre of the town. On the way, noticing a theatrical bill nailed to a pole, he tore it off so that he might study it at leisure when at home,

---

8. The fashionable tailors often came from Warsaw. In Russian dialect the initial consonant is often dropped [*Translator's note*].

9. Vassily Feodorov is a very Russian name and surname, and so it's surprising to see it followed by the designation "Foreigner."

stared fixedly at a lady of attractive appearance who was walking along the wooden pavement followed by a boy in military uniform with a bundle in his hand; and once more casting his eyes round everything, as if to imprint the locality firmly on his memory, he made straight off towards his room, being assisted up the stairs by one of the tavern servants. Having drunk his fill of tea, he sat down at the table, ordered a candle to be brought to him, pulled out the bill from his pocket, moved it into the candle-light and began to read, screwing up his right eye a little as he did so. The bill had nothing of great note in it: it announced a drama by Kotzebue[1]; the part of Rolla was to be played by G. Poplevin and that of Cora by Zyablova, while the rest of the cast was even less distinguished. However, he read through all the names, reached the price of the stalls and discovered that the bill had been printed in the printing-house of the provincial administration. He then turned the bill over in case there might be something on the back of it, but finding nothing, he rubbed his eyes, folded the bill with care and put it in his box, into which he liked to stow away any odd thing that came to hand. The day was concluded by a portion of cold veal, some sour cabbage soup and a sound sleep—sleep like a suction pump, as folk say in some parts of the spacious Russian Empire.

The whole of the following day was set aside for visits. The new-comer made a round of all the high officials. He paid his respects to the governor, who resembled Chichikov himself in being neither stout nor thin; he wore the order of St. Anna[2] round his neck, and it was even whispered that he had been recommended for the star;[3] he was, however, a good soul and sometimes did embroidering on tulle. Then Chichikov called on the vice-governor and later visited the prosecutor, the president of the court, the chief of police, the farmer of the

1. August Friedrich von Kotzebue (1761–1819), a German playwright who lived in Russia at various times and was most popular in the early years of the nineteenth century.

2. One of the important Russian decorations, established in 1735. Only

the highest, first rank of the Order of St. Anna was worn around one's neck; the second, third, and fourth had to be worn in one's buttonhole.

3. Order of Stanislas, still higher than the first rank of St. Anna.

vodka revenues, the superintendent of the imperial factories. . . . What a pity it is so difficult to remember all the mighty of this world. But suffice it to say that the new-comer displayed an extraordinary zeal in making his calls: he even paid his respects to the medical inspector and the town architect. And then he sat a long while in his chaise, wondering whom else he might visit, but there were no more leading officials left in the town.

In conversing with these potentates, he showed himself an adept in flattering each of them in an artful way. He hinted to the governor quite casually that to enter his province was like coming to Paradise, that the roads were everywhere of velvet, and that a government which appointed such a wise dignitary was deserving of the highest praise. He said something very flattering to the chief of the police about the night-watchmen of the town. And while talking to the vice-governor and the president of the court, who were as yet only state councillors,[4] he delighted them greatly by twice addressing them in error as 'Your Excellency.' As a consequence of this, the governor invited him that same evening to an at-home; other officials followed suit, one inviting him to dinner, another to join him in a game of Boston,[5] and a third to tea.

The stranger appeared reticent about himself; when he did say anything, he showed a marked discretion and was prone to indulge in platitudes, his talk on these occasions assuming a somewhat literary flavour. In this world he was but an insignificant worm, he said, and unworthy of having any great attention lavished upon him. In his time he had undergone many trials; he had suffered in the cause of justice while in the service, he had many enemies, some of whom had even made attempts on his life and, wishing now to find a haven of rest, he was seeking a place where he might settle. Having reached this town, he had considered it his bounden duty to pay his respects to its leading dignitaries.

4. The fifth highest rank in the Table of Ranks. (The four highest ranks were equivalent to the rank of general and rated the appellation "Your Excellency.")

5. A card game allegedly originating in Boston and introduced to Europe by Benjamin Franklin. Most popular at the end of the eighteenth and beginning of the nineteenth centuries.

That was all that the people of the town ever learnt about this new personage, who did not fail to put in a prompt appearance at the governor's evening party. His preparations for the party occupied him over two hours, and here it transpired that the stranger's close attention to his toilet was of a most uncommon kind. After a brief after-dinner nap, he asked for the washing things to be brought, and took an extremely long time to rub and soap his cheeks, propping out each in turn from inside with his tongue as he did so, then, snatching a towel from the servant's shoulder, he applied it to every part of his rubicund face, beginning behind his ears and snorting first of all a couple of times straight into the servant's face. Then facing a looking-glass, he donned a shirt-front, plucked two hairs out of his nose, and immediately after that appeared attired in a sprigged, cranberry-coloured swallow-tailed coat. Having dressed himself in this fashion, he drove in his carriage along the wide, interminable streets, lit up by a faint glow in windows here and there. However, the governor's house was illuminated as though for a ball; there were calashes[6] with lanterns, two gendarmes in the drive, coachmen shouting in the distance; in short, everything was as it should be.

The intense glare of the candles, the lamps and the ladies' gowns, made Chichikov screw up his eyes for a moment as he set foot in the room. Everything was bathed in light. Black tail-coats flashed and flitted singly and in swarms here and there, like so many flies buzzing round the bright whiteness of a sugar loaf in the hot month of July, when some old housekeeper is breaking the loaf up into glittering lumps by an open window; the children gather round and look on inquisitively at the movements of her horny hands wielding the hammer, while the aerial squadrons of flies, upborne on the light air, dart in boldly as if they were masters of the domain and, profiting by the dazzling sun and the feeble eyesight of the old woman, they swarm round the tasty lumps singly or in

6. A light two-horse carriage with space for four inside, an outside seat for the driver, and a folding top.

throngs. Already satiated by the abundance of summer, which proffers tasty dishes at every step, they fly here not to gorge but only to display themselves, to saunter up and down the sugar pile, to rub their back or front feet together or, stretching out their front feet, to rub them both together over their heads, spin round and wing away, and then fly back again in fresh irritating squadrons. Chichikov had barely time to take in the scene before the governor had grasped him by the arm and introduced him to his wife. The new arrival was not at a loss here either: he paid her a compliment that was most becoming in a man of middle age whose rank was neither too exalted nor too lowly. When the couples of dancers formed and pressed everyone else back against the walls, he stood gazing at them very attentively for a minute or two. Many of the ladies were well dressed and according to fashion, others were wearing whatever the Lord had thought fit to send to a provincial town. Here as elsewhere, the men were of two sorts. The slightly built ones hovered in the vicinity of the ladies; and some of them looked as if they might well have come from Petersburg, judging by their carefully and tastefully brushed side-whiskers, their good-looking and very smoothly shaved oval faces, and the easy manner in which they approached the ladies, spoke to them in French and made them laugh. The other sort were either stout or resembled Chichikov in being neither too plump nor too thin. These latter looked askance at the ladies and stepped out of their way, looking around them to see whether the servants were getting the card tables ready for whist. Their faces were full and round, some of them even had warts and others were pock-marked. They did not wear their hair in tufts or curls, nor in the devil-may-take-it manner of the French; their hair was either closely cropped or licked back while their features were more rounded and rugged. These were the official dignitaries of the town.

Alas! In this world stout men know better than thin men how to manage their affairs. The thin ones are more often employed on special missions, or are merely 'on the staff', scurrying hither and thither; their existence is somehow too slight, airy and altogether insubstantial. The stout ones are never to be found filling ambiguous posts, but only straightforward ones; if they sit down anywhere, they do so solidly and firmly, so that though their position may creak and bend beneath them, they never fall off. They have no love of superficial brilliance; their evening dress is not so well cut as that of the thin ones, but, on the other hand, their coffers are full of divine blessings. At the end of three years, a thin man will not have a serf left out of pawn; while without any fuss a stout one will have acquired a house, in the name of his wife, somewhere on the outskirts of the town, and then another house elsewhere, a village near to the town, and afterwards a larger village and all that goes with it. In the end, having served God and his Tsar, and won general respect, the stout one will retire from service, migrate and set up as a landowner, a fine Russian gentleman and host, and so live on and live well. After him, as is the Russian custom, his thinner heirs will quickly dissipate the paternal fortune in foreign travel.

It cannot be disguised that such were the reflections that preoccupied Chichikov as he gazed on the company, and the result of them was that he joined the clan of the stout ones, in the midst of whom he recognized many faces that were already familiar to him. There was the prosecutor with his exceedingly black brows and a left eye that had a tendency to blink slightly, as if he were saying: 'Come along, brother, come to the next room. I have something to say to you!' He was, however, a man of serious and taciturn mien. There was the postmaster, a squat but witty man, who was a philosopher into the bargain; and the president of the court, a most circumspect and amiable man. All these greeted him as an old acquaintance, and he responded to their greetings by bowing a trifle aloofly but not without amiability. He next made the acquaintance of a most courteous and civil landowner, Manilov, and of the rather boorish-looking Sobakievich,[7] who began by treading on his foot and saying: 'I beg your pardon!'

---

7. "Manilov": The name is cognate with the root of the verbs *manit'* and *zamanit'*— "to entice, attract." *Sobaka* means "dog" in Russian.

When a card for whist was thrust upon him, he accepted it with the same polite bow. They sat down at a card-table and did not rise till supper-time. There was an end to all talk, as happens when people finally become engrossed in a sensible occupation. Although the postmaster was extremely loquacious, his face likewise assumed a look of intelligence as soon as he had picked up the cards, and biting his lower lip he preserved that tense expression all through the game. Whenever he played a court-card, he thumped the table, interjecting if it were a queen: 'There goes the old priest's wife,' and if it were a king: 'There goes the Tambov moujik.'[8] And the president would mutter, 'I've got him by the whiskers. I've got him!' Sometimes, as the cards hit the table, they stimulated the players to exclamations such as, 'Well, I never!' 'Diamonds, is it!' Or they provoked odd reactions, such as 'Hearts!' 'Heartburn!' 'Spadefull!' 'Spadille!' 'Spadefoot!' 'Spadone!' or simply 'Spille!' Such were the names which the company were accustomed to bestow on the various suits. At the end of the game, they argued as usual, noisily enough, and our traveller joined in, but he did so artfully, making it obvious to all that he was arguing and preserving his good humour at the same time. He never said 'You led,' but always 'You were good enough to lead and I had the honour to beat your two,' and more in the same strain. In order to propitiate his opponents still further, he would invariably hold out to them his silver and enamel snuff-box, at the bottom of which they could see two violets placed there for the sake of fragrance.

The traveller's attention was especially drawn to Manilov and Sobakievich, the two landowners previously mentioned. He promptly informed himself about them, drawing the president and the postmaster aside to question them. Some of his questions proved his thoroughness as well as his curiosity; for he began by enquiring how many peasant souls each of them possessed, and what was the condition of their estates, only later asking their

8. Proverbial for a peasant *(muzhik)* from a remote rural area; Tambov is a small town in Russia, southeast of Moscow.

Christian names and surnames. Very soon he had succeeded in captivating them completely.

Landowner Manilov was far from being an elderly
man; he had eyes as sweet as sugar and he screwed them
up whenever he laughed; he was in ecstasies over
Chichikov. He shook hands with him very warmly and
pressed him to do him the honour of visiting his domain
which, according to him, was only some ten miles from
the town boundaries. Chichikov responded to this by
inclining his head most politely, shaking him warmly
by the hand, and saying that he was not only ready to do
so, but would consider it a sacred duty. Sobakievich also
said, rather laconically, 'I beg you to visit me also.' As
he did so, he scraped back a foot, which was shod in a
boot of such gigantic proportions that it would have been
difficult to find another such anywhere, particularly in
these days when *bogatyrs*[9] or champions are beginning to
grow scarce in Russia.

On the following day Chichikov went off to dine and
spend the evening with the chief of police. There, after
dinner, from three o'clock in the afternoon onwards,
they sat down to a game of whist which lasted until two
in the morning. Here, incidentally, he made the acquaintance of Nozdrev,[1] a landowner of some thirty years of
age, a sprightly young fellow, who began to address him
familiarly as *thou* after the first few words. Nozdrev was
on the most intimate terms with the chief of police and
the prosecutor, addressing them also as *thou*; yet, when
they sat down to play for high stakes, those two officials
watched his play most closely and scrutinised almost
every card he put down.

Chichikov spent the following evening with the president of the court, who received his guests, including two
ladies, in a rather greasy dressing-gown. Then he passed
an evening with the vice-governor, attended a large
dinner at the tax-farmer's[2] house and a small one at the

9. A *bogatyr* was a legendary hero
of Russian medieval songs and
poems.
1. *Nos* means "nose" in Russian;
nozdrya means "nostril."
2. *Otkupshchik:* someone who had

purchased from the government the
right to collect taxes in a certain
region in return for keeping a commission often amounting to 50% of
what he collected; usually a very rich,
influential man.

prosecutor's—this latter, however, was quite on a par with the big one—and also a buffet lunch given by the mayor of the town after mass; and this, too, was the equal of a dinner. In short, he had not an hour to himself, and returned to his inn only for sleep.

The new-comer was somehow always able to find his feet, and he proved himself worldly and experienced. He could always converse on any topic; if it was a question of a stud farm, he was quite in his element; if there was talk of pedigree dogs, he was full of information on the subject: if some criminal case were under discussion, he demonstrated that he was no stranger to legal wiles; if there was an argument about billiards, he was at no loss either; if philanthropy was mentioned, he spoke eloquently about it, and tears even started to his eyes; he was well versed in the art of distilling spirits and in their properties; and from his comments on customs officials and civil servants it might have been thought that he was himself one of them. The way in which he succeeded in imparting an air of gravity to all this and in preserving decorum was remarkable. He spoke neither too loudly nor too softly, but just at the right pitch. In brief, whichever way one looked at him, he was a reputable man. All the officials were delighted with the new arrival. The governor was heard to say that he was a well-intentioned person; the prosecutor, that he was an able man; the colonel of gendarmes, that he was a learned man; the president of the court, that he was an informed and respectable man; the chief of the police, that he was a respectable and amiable man; the chief's wife, that he was a most courteous and obliging person. Even Soba-kievich, who rarely ventured to say anything good of anyone, observed to his spindly wife as he got into bed beside her after returning at a late enough hour from town: 'My little dove, I spent the evening with the governor and dined with the chief of police. I met Pavel Pavlovich Chichikov, a collegiate councillor—a most charming man!' Whereupon his spouse replied, 'H'm!' and gave him a push with her foot.

Such was the very flattering opinion which was formed

of him in the town; and this opinion persisted until such time as an odd peculiarity or undertaking of his or, as they say in the provinces, a 'passage,' of which the reader will soon learn more, threw the whole town into a state of consternation.

CHAPTER II

THE new-comer had been in the town for over a week, driving about to evening parties and dinners, and having, as they say, a very pleasant time. At last he resolved to pay a few calls out of town and to visit, as he promised, the landowners Manilov and Sobakievich. This step was perhaps dictated by another and more material reason, a more serious and immediate motive. . . . But the reader will learn about all this gradually and in due course if he has enough patience to read right through this very long narrative which will flow ever more broadly and spaciously as it nears its end and climax.

Selifan, the coachman, had his orders to harness the horses and to get the familiar chaise ready early in the morning, while Petrushka was instructed to stay at home and keep an eye on the room and the trunk. It will not be out of place for the reader to make the acquaintance of our hero's two bondsmen. Although they are not of course prominent, nor even characters of the second or third degree, and although the mainspring and plot of this poem do not function for their benefit and have only the slightest reference to them, the author is nevertheless inordinately fond of every kind of detail and, although he is a Russian, in this respect at least he wishes to be as precise as any German. His intention, however, need not take up too much time or space since it is not necessary to add much detail to what the reader already knows, namely, that Petrushka used to walk about in a rather loose-fitting brown coat off his master's peg, and had, as is usual with people of his calling, a large-sized nose and thick lips. By nature he was reserved rather than loquacious; he even had a noble urge for enlightenment, that is, for reading books without paying much heed to their content. It was a matter of absolute indifference to him whether he was reading about the adventures of an infatuated hero, a simple primer, or a prayer-book: he perused all these books with equal attention; if a treatise on chemistry had been slipped in front of him, he would not have disdained it. What pleased him was not so much what he read as just reading or, rather, the process of reading, the fact that letters were always composing some sort of word, which sometimes meant the devil only knows what. His reading was chiefly accomplished in a reclining position in the ante-room, on the bed and on the mattress which in consequence became as squashed and as thin as a mill-cake. Apart from his passion for reading, he had two other characteristic peculiarities: he slept without undressing, just as he was, in the same coat; and he always carried about with him a peculiar atmosphere, a special ripe and cheesy smell of his own. As a result, he had only to set up his bed somewhere, even in a room uninhabited hitherto, and to bring his overcoat and belongings there, for that room at once to give the impression of having been lodged in for a good ten years.

Being extremely sensitive and sometimes even pernickety, Chichikov frowned as he caught a sniff of this air in the morning, shook his head and admonished Petrushka with 'I say, brother, the devil take you, you're sweating, aren't you? Why don't you go to the baths!' But Petrushka made no answer to this and at once tried to busy himself with one thing or another, either by going up to brush one of his master's swallow-tailed coats or simply by tidying the room. What was he thinking about as he held his tongue? Maybe he was saying to himself, 'You're a beauty too. Ain't you tired repeating one and the same thing a score of times?' God knows, it is hard to discover what a household serf may be thinking when his master takes him to task. Anyhow, for a start, this much may be said of Petrushka.

Selifan, the coachman, was a different sort of man. . . . But knowing as he does by experience how unwilling they are to acquaint themselves with low society, the author has a bad conscience in taking up so much of the readers' time with people of base origin. Such is the Russian: he is passionately desirous to hob-nob with anyone a rank above him, and considers a bowing acquaintance with a count or a duke as more beneficial to him than any more intimate friendship. The author has even some misgivings for his hero who is no more than a collegiate councillor. Aulic councillors, perhaps, will not be loath to know him, but those who have already attained a general's rank, these, God knows, will only deign, perhaps, to cast one of those contemptuous glances which are proudly thrown by men at everything that crawls and fawns at their feet. Worse still, they may display a deadly indifference for the author. But however distressing this or that may be, it is time to return to our hero.

Thus, having issued all the necessary orders the night before, he got up very early in the morning, washed and sponged himself from head to foot—a thing he did only on Sundays and that day happened to be a Sunday—and having shaved himself so as to make his cheeks as smooth as satin, he donned his sprigged, cranberry-coloured, swallow-tailed coat and then a greatcoat lined with bear, descended the staircase, supported now on this side and now on that by the tavern servant, and then climbed into the chaise. The chaise thundered out of the gates and into the street. A priest who was going by doffed his hat while several urchins in soiled shirts held out their hands, mumbling, 'Please help an orphan, gentleman!' Noticing that one of them was expert at stealing a ride on the foot-board, the coachman took a crack at him with his whip, and off went the chaise bumping over the cobbles. It was a relief when the black and white barrier [3] was seen looming in the distance, for it was a sign that the cobbled roadway was coming to an end like any other suffering; and so, after having struck his head several times violently against the frame of the carriage, Chichikov at last found himself being wafted over softer ground.

No sooner had the town receded than both sides of the

3. The limits of Russian towns were marked by road barriers similar to those that now exist at the national borders of European countries.

road began to provide the usual stuff and nonsense of descriptive writers: tree-stumps, fir-groves, the low scanty bushes of saplings, the charred trunks of old pine-trees, wild heather, and the like nonsense. They drove past villages stretched out like a piece of string, resembling in their structure a stack of logs, covered over with grey roofs which had under them carved-wood ornamentation in pattern very much like the embroidery on hand-towels. A few peasants sat about on benches in front of the gates, wearing their sheepskin coats and yawning as usual. Peasant women with solid faces and tightly fastened bosoms were gazing out of the upper windows; out of the lower windows a calf would be staring or a pig would be thrusting its short-sighted snout. In short, the view was quite a familiar one. Having passed the tenth milestone, Chichikov remembered that, according to Manilov, his village should be hereabouts, but the eleventh milestone flew by without any sign of the village; and if two peasants had not come by, he would hardly have succeeded in hitting the mark. On being questioned as to the whereabouts of the village Zamanilovka, the peasants doffed their caps, and one of them, the brighter of the two, who had a forked beard, replied, 'Manilovka maybe, but not Zamanilovka.'

'All right, Manilovka.'

'Manilovka! Well, when you push on another mile or so, there it will be, that is to say, straight to the right.'

'To the right?' the coachman repeated.

'To the right,' said the peasant. 'That will be the road to Manilovka; but there is no Zamanilovka. That's what it's called, I mean to say, its name is Manilovka, but there is nothing like Zamanilovka here. Up there on a hill you will see the house, a stone house it is, two whole storeys, that's the squire's house, I mean, that's where the gentleman himself lives. And that's Manilovka for you, but there's no Zamanilovka here at all, and never was.'

They drove on in search of Manilovka. After driving over a mile, they came on a turning into a cross-country road, but even when they had covered another mile or two there was still no sign of a two-storied house. Then

Chichikov remembered that, when a friend invites you to visit him in a village a mere ten miles away, it is always at least a good twenty miles off.

The situation of Manilovka was anything but alluring. The squire's house stood in an exposed position, on a height open to all the winds that might care to blow; the slope on which it stood was covered with short turf. Scattered over it in the English fashion were two or three beds planted with lilac-bushes and yellow acacias; five or six birch-trees in small clumps raised up their fine-leaved scanty crests here and there. Beneath two of them a summerhouse was visible, with its flat green cupola, azure wooden columns, and an inscription, 'The Temple of Solitude and Meditation.' Lower down was a pond overgrown with weeds, no novelty this in the English gardens of the Russian landed gentry. At the foot of this eminence, and along part of the slope itself, the dark patches of grey timber huts could be seen and, for reasons known only to himself, our hero instantly began to count them and made them add up to over two hundred. Nowhere among them was there a tree or any vegetation growing; there was only the timber of the houses and piles of logs everywhere.

The view was enlivened by two peasant women who, gathering up their skirts as in a painting and tucking them in on all sides, were wading up to their knees in the pond, dragging in their wake a ragged net in which could be seen two struggling crabs and a glistening roach. It looked as if the women were engaged in a dispute and were abusing each other. To one side, in the distance, a pine forest showed up darkly and gloomily blue. Even the weather fitted into the scene perfectly: the day was neither limpid nor cloudy, but of a sort of bright-grey hue such as is discoverable only on the old uniforms of garrison soldiers, a peaceful enough army except when somewhat drunk on Sundays. To complete the picture, a cock was not wanting, that harbinger of fickle weather who, despite the fact that his head was drilled right through by the beaks of other cocks as a consequence of his notorious philandering, crowed most lustily and even flapped his wings that looked as frayed as an old mat.

As Chichikov was driving towards the courtyard, he noticed the master of the house himself standing on the steps, dressed in a green shalloon[4] coat, holding his hands over his eyes like an umbrella the better to distinguish the approaching carriage. As the chaise drew nearer the steps, his eyes lit up and he smiled broadly.

'Pavel Ivanovich!' he exclaimed at last, as Chichikov was getting out of the chaise. 'So you have just remembered us.'

The two friends hugged and kissed each other most warmly, and Manilov conducted the visitor indoors. Although they did not take long to cross the vestibule, the hall and the dining-room, let us try and see if we cannot profit somehow by this interlude and say a few words concerning the master of the house. But here the author must confess that such an undertaking is very difficult. It is far easier to portray characters of greater dimensions. In such cases, you simply throw handfuls of paint at the canvas—black burning eyes, beetling brows, foreheads furrowed in wrinkles, a black or a scarlet cloak, like fire, thrown over a shoulder, and the portrait is ready. But as for all these gentlemen, of whom there are so many in the world and who are very like each other in appearance—when you come to look at them, you will perceive a multitude of elusive peculiarities—and they are terribly hard to portray. Great concentration is required here in order to force all their fine and almost imperceptible traits into relief, and, generally speaking, one is obliged to make an eye already expert in the science of interrogation far more deeply penetrating.

Only God, perhaps, could have described Manilov's character. There is a breed of men known as the just so's, the neither this nor that, 'Cockney Albert, rustic Hodge,' as the proverb says. Maybe, Manilov was of their kidney. In appearance, he was a good-looking man; his features were not unpleasant, but it seemed that this pleasantness had too much sugar in it; his manners and turns of speech

4. A light woolen fabric.

suggested the pursuit of favours and profitable acquaintances. His smile was seductive, his complexion fair and his eyes blue. After a minute's conversation with him, you could not fail to say, 'What a kind and pleasant person!' The next minute you would say nothing, and the third you would exclaim, 'The devil! What kind of a man is this?' And you would move away from him; if you did not, you would be overwhelmed by a deadly spleen. You would fail to extract from him a single lively or even arrogant word, such as you might hear from anyone when touching on a subject which affected him.

Each man has his passion: one concentrates on borzoi dogs;[5] another believes that he is a great lover of music and is wonderfully sensitive to its most profound passages; a third is a past-master in revelry; a fourth in playing a role one inch above his measure; a fifth, more bounded in his desire, sleeps and dreams in order to show off in the company of an imperial aide-de-camp to his friends, acquaintances and even strangers; a sixth has sleight-of-hand and is imbued with the supernatural desire to turn down the corner of an ace of diamonds or a two; while the hand of the seventh itches to establish order somewhere, to insinuate itself near the face of a station-master or a coachman—in short, everyone has a peculiar quality of his own, but Manilov had nothing. He spoke little when at home and, for the most part, reflected and pondered, but what he was thinking about only God knew.

It could not be said that he was preoccupied with the management of his estate, for he never even drove out into the fields, and his affairs seemed to run themselves. Whenever his steward said, 'It would be as well, sir, to do this and that,' he usually answered, 'Yes, that's not a bad idea,' smoking his pipe the while, a habit acquired when serving in the army, where he was regarded as the most modest, sensitive and cultured of officers. 'Yes, not at all a bad idea,' he would repeat. Whenever a peasant came to him and, scratching the back of his head, said, 'Master, give me leave to get an outside job, to pay off

5. A breed of Russian hunting dog.

my taxes,' Manilov invariably answered 'Go,' and
puffed at his pipe; and it never entered his head that the
peasant was merely off on a drunken spree. Sometimes,
as he stood on the steps gazing at the courtyard and the
pond, he used to say what a good idea it would be if a
subterranean passage could be tunnelled from the house,
or a stone bridge built across the pond with shops on each
side of it and tradesmen sitting in them retailing small
wares required by the peasants. As he said this, his eyes
looked particularly sweet and his face assumed an expression of great contentment; however, none of these
projects ever came to anything.

There was always some book lying about in his study,
marked on page fourteen, which he had been reading
persistently for over two years. In his house there was
always something lacking. His drawing-room contained
some fine furniture covered in showy silk which must
have cost him quite a sum; but there was not enough of it
for two of the armchairs, and these stood covered simply
in matting; for a period of several years, however, the
master of the house had always warned his guests in the
following words, 'Please do not sit on these chairs. They
are not ready yet.' Another room was entirely bare of
furniture, although he had said a few days after his wedding, 'Darling, we must see to it to-morrow that some
furniture at least is put into this room.' In the evening
a very impressive candlestick of dark bronze, with three
graces and a dandy mother-of-pearl shield, was set on the
table, side by side with a plain brass cripple of a candlestick, lame, crooked and all stained in tallow, but neither
the master, nor the mistress, nor the servants appeared
to notice this.

His wife. . . . However, they were perfectly satisfied
with each other. In spite of the fact that more than eight
years had elapsed since their marriage, they always used
to press upon each other various titbits such as a slice of
apple, a sweet or a nut, and address each other in touch-
ingly tender tones—'Open your little mouth, darling,
here is a morsel for you.' Of course, on these occasions,
the little mouth would open very gracefully. They always

planned surprises for each other's birthdays, for example, a glass-bead case for a toothbrush. And very frequently, as they sat on a sofa, for no apparent reason at all he would put down his pipe and she her work, if she chanced to be holding it at the time, and they would exchange such a long and languishing kiss that one might easily have smoked a small whiff while it lasted. In brief, they were what is called happy.

We must note in passing that there were many other things to be done about the house besides exchanging prolonged kisses and springing surprises; and a multitude of questions could well be asked. For instance, why was the cooking in the kitchen managed so stupidly and unsystematically? Why was the larder so empty? Why was the housekeeper a thief? Why were the servants untidy and drunken? Why did the whole of the domestic staff sleep so unmercifully and gossip the rest of the time? But all these are base subjects and Madame Manilova was well brought up. As we know, a good bringing up is imparted in young ladies' boarding-schools. And as we also know, these three principal subjects constitute the foundation of human virtue: the French language, which is indispensable to domestic bliss; the pianoforte, essential for providing pleasant moments for a husband; and finally, matters of personal domestic utility such as the knitting of purses and other surprises. However, in our day especially, there have been various changes and improvements in these methods; it depends a great deal on the sense and ability of the boarding school keepers. In some boarding schools matters are so organized that the piano comes first, the French language next and the domestic part last. In others the order is reversed, and the domestic part comes first, that is, the knitting of surprises, followed by the French language and then the piano. The methods vary. It will not be out of place to remark that Madame Manilova . . . but I confess that I am very afraid of talking about ladies, and besides, it is time to return to our heroes, who have already been standing for some minutes before the drawing-room door, entreating each other to take precedence.

'Pray, oblige me, do not put yourself out on my account. I shall follow you,' Chichikov said.

'No, Pavel Ivanovich, no—you are my guest,' Manilov insisted, pointing to the door.

'Do not be embarrassed, I beg you. Pray, proceed,' Chichikov persisted.

'You must excuse me, I cannot permit such a charming and cultured guest to walk behind me.'

'Why cultured? Pray proceed.'

'No, I beg of you. You must go first!'

'But why should I?'

'Well, just because,' said Manilov with an ingratiating smile.

At length, the two friends entered the door sideways and together, squeezing each other slightly in the process.

'Allow me to present my wife to you,' said Manilov. 'My love, this is Pavel Ivanovich!'

Then Chichikov had a clear view of the lady whom he had completely failed to notice when exchanging compliments with Manilov in the doorway. She was pretty and dressed becomingly. A morning dress of pale-hued silk sat well on her; her slender wrist made a hurried movement as she flung something on the table and then clutched an embroidered cambric handkerchief in her hand. Then she got up from the sofa on which she had been sitting. It was not without pleasure that Chichikov went up to kiss her hand. Speaking with a slight rolling of her *r*'s, Madame Manilova told him that he had delighted them greatly by his visit and that not a day passed without her husband remembering him.

'Yes,' said Manilov, 'she would keep asking me, "And why isn't your friend coming?" "Patience, love, he will come!" And so at last you have deigned to visit us. A real pleasure you have done us, it's a real May day, a union of true hearts. . . .'

On hearing that they had already got as far as the union of true hearts, Chichikov felt slightly embarrassed and replied modestly that he owned no resounding name or even any notable rank.

'You have everything,' Manilov interrupted him with

the same ingratiating smile. 'You have everything, and even more.'

'What impression did our town make on you?' said Madame Manilova. 'Have you had an agreeable stay?'

'It's a very fine town, a beautiful town,' Chichikov replied. 'And I have spent my time most pleasantly: the society there is very affable.'

'And what do you think of our governor?' asked Madame Manilova.

'A most estimable and obliging person, isn't he?' interjected Manilov.

'Absolutely true,' exclaimed Chichikov, 'a most estimable man. And how he has mastered his duties and how he understands them! I wish there were more people like him.'

'And how well he knows how to receive people and how considerate he is,' added Manilov with a smile, almost closing his eyes with delight, like a cat whose ears are tickled slightly.

'A most considerate and agreeable person,' continued Chichikov. 'And what a craftsman! I could never even have supposed that. How well he embroiders his patterns. He showed me a purse he made: few ladies are as expert.'

'And what a nice man the vice-governor is, isn't he?' said Manilov, again half-shutting his eyes.

'Really, a most worthy man,' replied Chichikov.

'And, pray, how does the chief of police impress you? A most agreeable man, is he not?'

'Extremely agreeable, and how knowledgeable and well read! We played whist in his house together with the prosecutor and the president till cock-crow. A most estimable man.'

'Well, and what do you think of the wife of the chief of police?' asked Madame Manilova. 'A most charming woman, isn't she?'

'Oh, I think she is one of the most delightful women I know,' replied Chichikov.

After this they did not fail to mention the president of the court and the postmaster; and in this fashion they enumerated almost all the officials of the town who without exception turned out to be most estimable people.

'Do you always live in the country?' Chichikov at last ventured a question in his turn.

'Mostly in the country,' replied Manilov. 'Sometimes, however, we go to town, but mainly to mix in cultured society. One would grow wild, you know, if one lived all the time in seclusion.'

'Very true, very true,' said Chichikov.

'Of course,' continued Manilov, 'it would be quite another matter if one had a suitable neighbour, if, for example, there were someone with whom one could have a chat about friendship and good breeding, or study some sort of science, to stir the mind a little and, as it were, let off steam . . .' He was on the point of adding something, but noticing that he was growing long-winded he only waved his hand in the air and went on. 'Then, of course, the country and solitude would have many charms. But there is absolutely no one. . . . From time to time one merely reads *The Son of the Fatherland*.'[6]

Chichikov was in complete agreement with this, and he added that there was nothing more agreeable than to lead a secluded life, enjoy the spectacle of nature and occasionally read some book. . . .

'But you know,' Manilov interjected, 'all the same, if one has no friend with whom one may share . . .'

'Oh, how right, how very right you are!' interrupted Chichikov. 'What are all the treasures in the world worth then! "If you have no money, have good company," as a certain wise man said.'

'And do you know, Pavel Ivanovich!' said Manilov, with an expression that was not only sweet but downright hypocritical, not unlike a medicine which a cunning society doctor has sweetened unmercifully in the hope of pleasing a patient. 'Then you feel a sort of, as it were, spiritual enjoyment. . . . Just as now, for example, when chance has brought me the fortune, as you might

---

6. A political, historical, and literary journal of conservative leanings.

say, the unequalled fortune of chatting with you and enjoying your agreeable conversation. . . .'

'I protest! What kind of agreeable conversation? I am an insignificant person, and no more,' replied Chichikov.

'Oh, Pavel Ivanovich, will you allow me to be frank with you. . . . I would gladly give half of all I possess if I could only acquire some of your qualities.'

'On the contrary, for my part I would consider it the greatest . . .'

It is difficult to say what point this mutual outpouring of feelings would have reached, had not the servant entered at that moment and announced that the meal was served.

'I humbly beg you,' said Manilov. 'You will excuse us if our dinner is not of the kind served in great houses and capital cities, we have only the traditional Russian cabbage soup, but we offer it in all sincerity. I beg you . . .'

Thereupon they argued again for a while as to who should take precedence and, in the end, Chichikov sidled into the dining-room.

Two boys, Manilov's sons, were already standing in the dining-room; they were of an age when children are allowed at table but are still seated in high chairs. Their tutor, who bowed and smiled politely, stood by them. The mistress of the house seated herself near the soup tureen; the visitor was placed between the master and the mistress, and a servant tied napkins round the children's necks.

'What darling children,' said Chichikov, glancing at them. 'And how old are they?'

'The eldest is eight, and the youngest was six only yesterday,' replied Madame Manilova.

'Themistoclous!'[7] said Manilov, turning to the eldest, who was trying to free his chin from the napkin which the footman had fastened round it. Chichikov raised his brows slightly on hearing this partly Greek name, to which for some unknown reason Manilov had added the

---

7. Pretentious (and corrupted) ancient Greek name. Themistocles was an Athenian general and statesman.

suffix of *ous*, but he at once made an effort to regain his usual composure.

'Themistoclous, tell me, which is the finest city in France?'

The tutor now concentrated his whole attention on Themistoclous and looked as though he would jump right into his eyes; but he settled back again quietly and nodded his head when Themistoclous said, 'Paris'.

'And which is our finest city?' Manilov questioned him again.

The tutor concentrated once more.

'Petersburg,' replied Themistoclous.

'And what other?'

'Moscow,' answered Themistoclous.

'You clever little boy,' was Chichikov's reaction. 'Well I never . . .' he went on, instantly turning to Manilov with a look of some surprise. 'I must tell you that this child has great ability.'

'Oh, but you don't know him yet,' replied Manilov. 'He has a great deal of wit. Now the younger one, Alcides,[8] is not so quick; but the other, if he comes across anything, an insect or a beetle, he's on the alert at once; he will follow after it and investigate. My design is to get him into the diplomatic service. Themistoclous,' he continued, turning to him again, 'would you like to be an ambassador?'

'Yes, I would,' answered Themistoclous, chewing a piece of bread and wagging his head.

At that moment the footman, who was stationed behind him, wiped the ambassador's nose and it was well that he did so, for otherwise a largish superfluous drop would have dripped into the soup. The conversation at table turned on the pleasures of a retired life, interrupted from time to time by the hostess's comments on the theatre and the actors of the town. The tutor kept a close watch on the speakers, and when he noticed that they were about to laugh, he opened his mouth instantaneously and guffawed. He probably had a sense of gratitude and

8. One of several names for Hercules, the Greek mythological half-god, famous for his physical strength.

wished to repay his employer in this way for the good treatment he received. On one occasion, however, his face assumed a stern look and he rapped the table severely, staring at the children sitting opposite him. That was timely, for Themistoclous had bitten Alcides' ear, and the latter, with his eyes screwed up and his mouth open, was about to burst out crying in the most lamentable fashion; but realizing that he might lose a course if he did so, he restored his mouth to its former position and began tearfully to gnaw at a mutton bone which made his cheeks shine with grease. The hostess turned to Chichikov very frequently, saying, 'But you are not eating anything, you have taken much too little.'

To which Chichikov replied each time, 'I am most obliged. I have eaten my fill. An agreeable conversation is better than any dish.'

They had already risen from table. Manilov was exceedingly pleased and, with his hand on his friend's back, was about to conduct him in this way to the drawing-room when the visitor suddenly declared with a most significant look that he would like to discuss one very essential matter with him.

'In that case, permit me to take you to my study,' said Manilov, and he led him to a small room with windows giving on a darkling blue forest. 'This is my nook,' said Manilov.

'A pleasant little room,' said Chichikov as he looked round it. The room was really not unpleasant: its walls were painted an azure-greyish blue. There were four chairs, an armchair, a table on which lay the book with the marker to which we have already had occasion to refer, several sheets of scribbled paper, but above all there was plenty of tobacco. It was there in various forms, in packets and containers, and finally just in a heap on the table. Heaps of pipe-ash were also strewn over both window-sills and swept not without deliberation into very neat rows. It was obvious that this was one of Manilov's pastimes.

'May I ask you to take a seat in this armchair,' said Manilov. 'You will find it more restful.'

'If you will allow me, I shall sit in the chair.'

'Give me leave not to allow that,' said Manilov with a smile. 'I have already assigned this armchair for our visitor. Whether you like it or not, you will have to sit in it.'

Chichikov sat down.

'Allow me to offer you a pipe.'

'No, I don't smoke,' replied Chichikov affectionately and with a look of regret.

'How is that?' said Manilov also affectionately and with a look of regret.

'I am afraid, I never formed the habit. They say a pipe dries one up.'

'Forgive me if I remark that that is a prejudice. I even maintain that to smoke a pipe is much healthier than to take snuff. There was a lieutenant in our regiment, a splendid fellow and a most cultured man, who not only never parted from his pipe, but kept it in his mouth even at table and, if I may say so, everywhere else. He is now already forty and a bit over, but, thank God, to this day his health could not be better.'

Chichikov remarked that such things do indeed occur and that there are many things in nature which are inexplicable even to the broadest minds.

'But allow me first of all to make a request. . . .' He said this in a voice which had in it an echo of something strange or almost strange, and on saying it he glanced behind him for some curious reason. For some unknown reason Manilov also looked round. 'How long is it since you were good enough to hand in your census list?'

'It was quite a way back. I can't even remember.'

'And have many of your peasants died since that time?'

'I couldn't say. I should think we had better ask the steward. Hey, there, you fellow, call the steward, will you! He should be here to-day.'

The steward appeared. He was a man of about forty who shaved his face, wore a frock-coat and apparently led a very tranquil life, for his full face was all puffy, and his yellow skin and small eyes showed that he enjoyed only too well the comfort of feather-beds and downy pillows. It was clear at once that he had followed in the steps of all landowners' stewards: he had started as a boy about the house who could read, then he married one Agashka, a housekeeper and the lady's favourite, became a house-steward himself and later on a steward of the estate. Having become a steward, he conducted himself of course as do all stewards: he consorted and kept company with the village folk who were better off, augmented the taxes levied on the poorer households and, never getting up before nine in the morning, waited for the samovar to boil and then drank tea.

'Listen, my good fellow, tell us, how many of our peasants have died since the last census?'

'What? How many? Why, many have died since those days,' said the steward, giving a hiccup and raising his hand like a shield to his mouth.

'Yes, I confess, I thought so myself,' interposed Manilov. 'Yes, a great many must have died!' Here he turned to Chichikov and added, 'Exactly so, a great many. . . .'

'In what sort of numbers, for instance?' asked Chichikov.

'Yes, in what numbers?' Manilov caught him up.

'How can I tell the number? For it is not known how many died. No one counted them.'

'Yes, precisely,' said Manilov turning to Chichikov, 'I also had assumed a high mortality; it is quite unknown how many died.'

'Will you please check them,' said Chichikov. 'And make a detailed list of all their names.'

'Yes, of all their names,' repeated Manilov.

The steward replied, 'Yes sir!' and went out.

'And for what reason do you require this?' Manilov asked as soon as the steward had gone.

This question appeared to embarrass the visitor, judging by the tense expression which settled on his face and even made him blush; this was the result of an attempt to express something that would not quite fit into words. And indeed, Manilov was soon to hear such strange and extraordinary things as had never yet been heard by human ears.

'You ask me for the reason? It is simply that I should

like to buy the peasants. . . .' said Chichikov coming to a halt and leaving his sentence unfinished.

'But pray, may I enquire,' said Manilov, 'how do you wish to buy these peasants, with land or simply for removal, without land?'

'No, it's not that I want the peasants alive,' said Chichikov, 'I'd rather have them dead. . . .'

'What? Excuse me . . . I am a little hard of hearing, I thought I heard you say a very strange thing.'

'It is my intention to acquire dead peasants but only such as have been registered as living according to the last census,'[9] said Chichikov.

Manilov let drop his long pipe and gaped for some minutes with his mouth wide open. The friends, who had been discussing the delights of friendly intercourse, remained motionless, fixing each other with their eyes, like those portraits which in olden days used to be hung facing each other on each side of a mirror. At length, Manilov picked up his pipe and stared down into Chichikov's face, trying to catch some sign of a smile on his lips or of a jest, but nothing of the sort was discernible; on the contrary, Chichikov's expression was, if anything, graver than usual. Then it occurred to him that his visitor might have suddenly taken leave of his senses, and he stared at him fixedly in some alarm. But Chichikov's eyes were perfectly clear; they revealed no wild or restless fire such as flashes in the eyes of madmen, and his demeanour was decent and perfectly composed. Think as he might how to behave or what to do, he could hit on nothing better than to blow a thin spiral of smoke out of his mouth.

'And so I should like to know whether you can transfer such peasants as are not alive in reality but only alive relatively speaking and in accordance with the legal forms—transfer them or do whatever seems best to you?'

But Manilov was so embarrassed and confused that he only stared at him.

9. A census of serfs was held at wide intervals. The last one before the action of *Dead Souls* was the seventh, in 1815. (The eighth took place in 1833.) A head tax had to be paid yearly by the owner for all serfs until the next census, even if some had died in the meantime. A purchase of a serf transferred the tax obligation to the new owner.

'It seems to me that you are embarrassed,' remarked Chichikov.

'I? No, it's not that,' said Manilov, 'but I cannot . . . er . . . quite grasp . . . excuse me . . . Of course, I did not have the opportunity of receiving such a brilliant education as is observable in your every gesture; I am lacking in the high art of expression. . . . Perhaps, here . . . in this explanation you have just ventured to make . . . there is a hidden meaning. . . . Perhaps you were good enough to express yourself thus for the sake of verbal harmony?'

'Not at all, not at all,' Chichikov explained, 'I intend my statement to mean exactly what I said, that is to say, I mean the peasants who are really dead. . . .'

Manilov was completely baffled. He felt that he must do something, pose a question, but which question—the devil alone knew! He ended finally by blowing out some more smoke, this time through his nostrils instead of through his mouth.

'And so, if you have no objections, with God's help we can set about to prepare a deed of purchase,' said Chichikov.

'What? A deed of purchase for the dead souls?'

'Not quite!' said Chichikov. 'We shall have it on record that they are living as, indeed, they are according to the census register. I am in the habit of observing the civil laws, although I have suffered as a result when in the service, so you will excuse me, but in my eyes duty is always sacred. I am dumb when confronted with the law.'

These last words appealed to Manilov, but he failed nevertheless to get to the bottom of the matter and, instead of replying, began to suck his pipe so violently that it started to wheeze like a bassoon. It seemed as though he wished to extract from it some opinion concerning such an unheard of event; but the pipe only wheezed, and that was all.

'You may have some doubts, perhaps?'

'Oh, I assure you, not at all. I am not saying that I have any, what might be called, critical prejudice against you. But may I ask whether there may not be something in this undertaking or rather, if I may so express myself, in this negotiation, something not quite corresponding with the civil regulations and the future prospects of Russia?'

Hereupon Manilov, moving his head slightly, looked very significantly into Chichikov's face, displaying in all his features and in his compressed lips such a profound expression as may never have been seen on a human face except, perhaps, on that of some too clever minister and, even so, only when he was confronted by some brain-seeking problem.

But Chichikov simply replied that such an undertaking or deal was in no way inconsistent with the civil regulations and the future prospects of Russia, adding a moment later that the Treasury would even profit by it, for it would pocket the legal dues.

'You think so?'

'Yes, I do, I think it would be a good proposition.'

'Ah, if it is a good thing, then I have nothing against it,' said Manilov, now completely reassured.

'It only remains now to agree on a price. . . .'

'What? On a price?' exclaimed Manilov, and he paused. 'You do not suppose that I shall accept any money for souls that have, in a certain way, ended their existence. If such a, so to speak, fantastic wish ever entered your head, then for my part, I shall transfer them to you in a disinterested spirit and take the deed of purchase on myself.'

It would have been a blot on the chronicler of these events had he failed to record the delight which filled the visitor as he heard these words of Manilov's. Although usually grave and dignified in his bearing, he could hardly resist capering about, a performance indulged in by people only in moments of extreme joy. He swivelled round so abruptly in his armchair as to split the woollen material covering the back of it, and Manilov stared at him in some perplexity. Overcome with gratitude, he at once gave vent to so many expressions of thanks that Manilov grew confused and very red in the face, made a negative movement with his head and finally said that it was a mere trifle, that he only wished to give him some proof of his affection and of that magnetic affinity which united their souls, whereas the souls of the dead were in some respects absolutely worthless.

'They are not worthless at all,' said Chichikov, squeezing his hand.

Then he allowed a very deep sigh to escape him. He seemed in a mood to disclose his heart; and it was not without emotion and expressiveness that he finally uttered the following words:

'If you only knew the service you have rendered me, a man without home or family, by this so-called worthless gift. Yes, in reality, what have I not suffered? Like some bark struggling in a tempestuous sea. . . . What oppression and persecution have I not endured? What sorrow have I not tasted? And what for? All because I respected truth, a clean conscience, and because I aided the helpless widow and the wretched orphan. . . .'

As he said this, he wiped away a tear with his handkerchief.

Manilov was deeply moved. The two friends pressed each other's hands for a long while and gazed raptly into each other's eyes which showed a glimmer of tears. Manilov would not let go our hero's hand and continued to press it so warmly that the latter was at a loss how to rescue it. At last, quietly disengaging it, he said that it would not be a bad thing to make out the deed of purchase as soon as possible, and that he himself must be off to town.

'What? You are thinking of going already?' said Manilov, coming to himself suddenly and looking almost alarmed.

At that moment Madame Manilova entered the study.

'Lizanka,' said Manilov pitifully, 'Pavel Ivanovich is thinking of leaving us.'

'Because we have bored Pavel Ivanovich,' she replied.

'Madame,' exclaimed Chichikov, laying his hand on his heart, 'it is here I shall preserve the memory of the delightful time I have spent with you! And believe me, no bliss could be greater than that of staying with you, if not in the same house then, at least, in the near vicinity.'

'But you know, Pavel Ivanovich,' said Manilov, to

whom this notion appealed very much, 'it would indeed be an excellent idea to live thus together, under one roof, or under the shade of some elm-tree, to philosophize and plumb the depths!'

'Oh, that would be paradise,' said Chichikov, sighing. 'Farewell, Madam,' he continued, approaching to kiss her hand. 'Farewell, my deeply respected friend! Do not forget my request!'

'Oh, you may rest assured!' replied Manilov. 'Our separation will not last more than two days.'

They all came out into the dining-room.

'Bye-bye, my little ones!' said Chichikov, catching sight of Alcides and Themistoclous who were playing with an already armless and noseless wooden hussar.[1] 'Bye-bye, my darlings. Excuse me for not bringing you any presents, but I confess that I had no idea even of your existence; but now, when I come again, I shall make a point of it. I shall bring you a sword. Would you like one?'

'Yes, I would,' replied Themistoclous.

'And you shall have a drum. Wouldn't you like a drum?' he continued, bending over Alcides.

'A dlum,' answered Alcides in a whisper, dropping his head.

'Very good, I shall bring you a drum. A fine drum, you'll see, all turrrr-ra-tra ta ta, ta ta ta. . . . Bye-bye, my pet! Bye-bye,' and then he kissed him on the head and turned to Manilov and his spouse with the sort of laugh which is always used to make parents realize the innocent nature of their children's desires.

'But do stay, Pavel Ivanovich!' said Manilov when they were already on the steps. 'Just look at those clouds.'

'They are tiny clouds,' replied Chichikov. 'By the way, do you know the way to Sobakievich's? I did want to ask you about that.'

'If you will give me leave, I shall tell your coachman at once.'

Hereupon Manilov was as obliging as ever and gave the coachman the proper directions, and he even went so far as to forget to address him once with the familiar *thou*.

1. A cavalry soldier.

On hearing that he was to miss two turnings and take the third one, the coachman said, 'We shall hit it, your honour.' And so Chichikov departed, accompanied by much bowing and waving of handkerchiefs on the part of the excited Manilovs.

For a long time Manilov stood on the steps, following the receding chaise with his eyes, and he was still standing there puffing away at his pipe after it had passed out of sight. At length he went inside, sat down and pondered, very glad in his heart that he had been able to afford his guest some slight pleasure. Then his thoughts imperceptibly concentrated on other subjects, and were transported into God alone knows what regions. He was thinking of the happiness of friendship, of how fine it would be to live together with some friend on the banks of a river, and he began to construct a bridge over this river, then a vast house with a high belvedere[2] from which even Moscow would be visible and where, sitting in the open air in the evenings, his friend and he might discuss some agreeable topic. Then he pictured Chichikov and himself arriving in splendid carriages at some social gathering, where they confounded everyone by the amiability of their manners, and he imagined that the Tsar, on learning of their great friendship, had promoted them both to be generals; his fancy grew so lively that eventually he could not even follow it himself. Suddenly Chichikov's strange request disturbed his day-dreaming. He found the idea of it peculiarly difficult to absorb; however much he turned it over in his head, he could not see any sense in it; and so he sat on puffing away at his pipe until it was time for supper.

CHAPTER III

MEANWHILE Chichikov was in the best of humours as he sat back in the chaise which had been rolling along the highway for some time. From the preceding chapter we are clear as to the main theme of his tastes and inclina-

---

2. A lookout or porch built on top of a building, particularly to give on a beautiful view.

tions, and it is no wonder that he was very soon engrossed in it body and soul. The surmises, calculations and notions, reflected in his face, were to all outward appearance most agreeable, for they left frequent traces of a satisfied smile. Preoccupied with his thoughts, he paid no attention to his coachman who, also content with the reception accorded him by Manilov's domestics, was addressing most decided comments to the dapple-grey side-horse harnessed on the right. This dapple-grey was mighty cunning and only pretended to be pulling his weight, whereas the bay in the centre and the fallow-bay on the left-hand side, which had been nicknamed the Assessor because it had been acquired from one, both laboured with a good heart—so much so that even their eyes showed signs of the pleasure they were deriving.

'Cunning, are you! You wait, I'll double-cross you!' said Selifan as he stood up and whipped the lazybones. 'Learn to work, you German pantaloon! The bay's a respectable horse, he does his duty, I'd willingly give him an extra feed of oats, because he's a respectable horse, and the Assessor, too, he's a good horse. . . . Hie! Why are you shaking your ears? Listen, idiot, when you're spoken to! I shan't teach you nothing wrong, you lout. Look where he's crawling!' Thereupon he applied the whip again, muttering, 'Hie, you barbarian! You cursed Bonaparte, you!' Then he shouted at them all, 'Gee up, you darlings!' and whipped them up all three, not by way of punishment but just to show that he was pleased with them. Having given them that pleasure, he addressed the dapple-grey again: 'Do you think you can hide your behaviour from me? No, you must live in truth if you want to be respected. Now the folk we just visited were good people. It's a pleasure to talk to a good man; with a good man I'm friends always, the best of chums, whether it be to drink a cup of tea or eat a morsel—with pleasure, I say, if he's a good man. A good man, he has everyone's respect. Now take our master, everyone respects him, because, do you hear, he was in the government service, he's a collegiate councillor. . . .'

Reasoning in this way, Selifan in the end embarked on the most remote and abstract allusions. If Chichikov had been listening, he would have learnt many details concerning himself; but he was so engrossed in his own theme that it required a loud clap of thunder to make him sit up and look about him: the whole of the sky was entirely clouded over and the large drops of rain were sprinkling the dusty highway. Finally, another clap of thunder resounded more loudly, nearer this time, and the rain suddenly poured out as from a bucket. First of all, coming at an angle, it beat on one side of the carriage frame, and then on the other; next, changing its tactics, it came down absolutely vertically, drumming straight on the top of the chaise; and in the end, the spray began to drench his face. This obliged him to pull the leather curtains, which had two small round windows cut out in them to permit a view of the landscape, and he ordered Selifan to drive faster.

Interrupted in the middle of his discourse, Selifan grasped that this was indeed no time to dawdle; he fetched out a sort of ragged grey cloth from beneath his seat, pulled it on, seized hold of the reins and yelled at the *troika*,[3] which was barely advancing under the pleasurable sensation induced by his moralizings. But for the life of him Selifan could not recall whether he had made two or three turnings. Thinking it over and remembering something of the road, he divined that he had missed a great many turnings. But as a Russian will always know what to do in a critical moment, without wasting time on further reflection, he turned to the right, into the first road he came across, admonished his horses with a 'Gee up, dear friends!' and set off at a gallop without much thought of where the chosen road would land him.

The rain, however, seemed likely to continue for quite a while. The dust of the road was quickly kneaded into mud, and every moment the horses found it more difficult to haul the chaise. Chichikov was already beginning to be seriously perturbed at catching no glimpse as yet of Sobakievich's village. According to his calculations, they should have been there long ago. He kept peering out of the windows but the darkness was quite blinding.

'Selifan!' he called at last, leaning out of the chaise.

3. A Russian sled pulled by three horses.

'What, master?' replied Selifan.

'Will you look and see if there is no village nearby?'

'No, master, it's nowhere to be seen!'

Thereupon, waving his whip, Selifan started up a song that was no song but something very drawn out and endless. Everything went into it: all the inciting and exhortatory cries with which horses are regaled from one end of Russia to the other; adjectives of every stock without discrimination, just as they happened to fall on his tongue. And thus it was that he even began to dub the horses 'secretaries.'

Meanwhile Chichikov could not help noticing that the chaise was rocking from side to side and jolting him violently; this made him feel that they had left the road and were probably bumping over a harrowed field. Selifan seemed to have grasped this too, but he said not a word.

'Where are you driving? What sort of a road is this, you rogue?' asked Chichikov.

'What's to be done, master, in this weather? I can't see my whip even, it's that dark.'

Having said this, he swung the chaise round at such an angle that Chichikov was forced to hold on with both hands. It was only then that he realized that Selifan had been having a spree.

'Hold it, hold it, you'll overturn us!' he shouted at him.

'No, master, how could I overturn you?' said Selifan. 'It's a bad thing to overturn anyone, I know it. I shan't overturn you at all.'

Then he began to pull the chaise gently round. He pulled and pulled, and finally heaved it over completely on one side. Chichikov sprawled in the mud on his hands and feet. However, Selifan did bring the horses to a stop, although they would have stopped in any case out of sheer exhaustion. Such an unexpected accident quite amazed him. Crawling off his seat, he took up his stand in front of the chaise, with his arms on his hips, while his master was wallowing in the mud and striving to crawl out of it. After reflecting for a moment, he ejaculated 'Well I never! it's overturned!'

'You're as drunk as a cobbler,' Chichikov exclaimed.

'No, master, how could I be drunk? I know it's bad to be drunk. I only had a word with a friend, because I like having a chat with a good man, there's nothing bad in that; and we had a bite together. A helping of food is no offence; one can have a bite with a good man.'

'And what did I tell you the last time you got drunk? Ah? Have you forgotten?' said Chichikov.

'No, your honour, how could I have forgotten? I know my business. I know it's a bad thing to get drunk. I had a talk with a good man, because . . .'

'I'll give you such a thrashing, you'll know how to talk to a good man!'

'Azh your grace de-zhires,' answered Selifan, completely acquiescent. 'If it's a thrashing, then let it be a thrashing; I've no objections. Why not a thrashing, if it's deserved, that's what a master's will is for. A thrashing's all right when a peasant takes liberties, order must be preserved. If it's deserved, then thrash away. Why shouldn't one?'

The master was completely at a loss what to reply to this reasoning. But in the meantime it seemed that fate had decided to intervene and take pity on them. There was the sound of a dog barking in the distance. Chichikov was overjoyed and ordered the horses to be whipped up. The Russian driver has a good intuition in place of eyes, and that is why he often rushes along with his eyes shut but always gets somewhere. Although he could not see a jot, Selifan directed the horses so unerringly to the village that they stopped only when the shafts of the chaise struck a fence and there was decidedly nowhere further for them to go. Through a thick blanket of drenching rain Chichikov could only perceive something that looked like a roof. He despatched Selifan to find the gates, and this no doubt would have taken a long time had it not been customary in Russia to keep savage dogs instead of porters; these announced his arrival with such piercing barking that he put his fingers to his ears. A light glimmered in one of the windows and, as its misty beam reached the fence, our travellers were able to make out the gates. Selifan started to knock at them loudly and, very soon, opening a wicket, a figure appeared wrapped in a loose peasant coat, and both master and servant heard a hoarse peasant woman's voice saying:

'Who's knocking? Why are you prowling at this hour?'

'We're travellers, mother, will you let us spend the night here?' Chichikov asked.

'There's a quick-foot for you,' said the old woman, 'and to arrive at this time of night! This is no inn for the likes of you, a lady lives here.'

'What's to be done, mother? You see we've lost our way. We can't sleep out in the steppe in such weather.'

'Yes, it's a dark night, and the weather couldn't be worse,' added Selifan.

'Shut up, you fool,' said Chichikov.

'And who are you?' asked the old woman.

'A nobleman, mother.'

The word 'nobleman' forced the old woman to reflect a little.

'Wait a bit, I shall tell my lady,' she said.

In a couple of minutes she was back again with a lantern in her hand. The gates were unlocked. A light glimmered in another window. Driving into the court-yard, the chaise pulled up in front of a small house which it was difficult to distinguish clearly in the darkness. Only half of it was lit up by the light coming from the windows; in its beam a large puddle could be seen in front of the house. The rain was pattering loudly on the wooden roof and cascading down in babbling streams into a tub. In the meantime, the dogs were barking in every pitch and key: one of them, his head uplifted, was howling so continuously and with so much effort that he might have been earning God alone knows what salary; another was clipping it off hastily like a sacristan. In between them, like a front-door bell, rang out a scrambling soprano voice, probably a puppy's, and all these were finally capped by a bass voice, that of a grandfather, maybe, endowed with a sturdy dogged nature; for he was as husky as a contrabasso in a choir when a concert is at its height and the tenors are standing on tiptoe from passionate desire to utter a high note and everybody strains aloft with head uplifted, while he alone, tucking his unshaven chin into his tie, squatting almost to the ground, lets out a note at which the very window-panes shake and rattle. From the barking of the dogs' choir alone, composed as it was of such musicians, one might have concluded that the village was of a goodly size; but our chilled and drenched hero thought of nothing but his bed. The chaise had not come to a full stop before he leapt out on the steps, stumbled, and almost fell. At that moment a woman, younger than the preceding one but very like her, made her appearance. She conducted him to a room. Chichikov cast a couple of quick glances round him: the room was hung with ancient striped wall-paper; on the walls were pictures of some variety of birds; between the windows hung several small, antique mirrors in dark frames of garlanded leaves, and behind each mirror a letter, an old pack of cards or a stocking had been tucked; there was a wall-clock with flowers painted on its dial. . . . Chichikov was too exhausted to notice anything more. He felt his eyes glueing together as if they had been smeared in honey.

A minute later in came the mistress of the house, an elderly woman in a sort of sleeping cap that had been hurriedly donned, and with a piece of flannel round her neck, evidently one of those motherly women and small proprietresses, who complain of bad harvests, losses, hold their head slightly perched to one side, and yet amass money little by little in striped canvas bags stowed away in various drawers. The silver roubles will be put in one bag, the half-roubles in another, and the twenty-five kopeck pieces in a third, although at first sight the chests of drawers would seem to contain nothing but linen, night-gowns and skeins of thread, as well as some ripped-up cloak put by there for fashioning into a dress later on, if the old one should happen to get scorched while holiday cakes and fritters are being baked, or if it should happen simply to wear out. But the dress will not get scorched or wear out, for the old crone is thrifty, and the cloak is destined to lie on there in its ripped-up state and be passed according to her will and testament, to some niece of hers together with all the other odds and ends.

Chichikov apologized for the trouble caused by his unexpected arrival. 'Not at all, not at all,' said the mistress of the house, 'God brought you here in this weather! It's a proper upset, a real blizzard, you ought to have a bite to eat after the journey, but it's too late for cooking anything.'

The old crone's words were interrupted by such a strange hissing noise that the guest took fright; the room might have been full of snakes; but looking up, he was reassured, for he saw immediately that it was only the wall-clock trying to strike the hour. The hissing was at once followed by a wheezing and, straining with all its might, the clock at last struck the hour of two with a sound resembling someone beating a cracked earthenware pot with a stick; after this the pendulum resumed its quiet clicking swing to right and left. Chichikov thanked the lady, and told her that he did not require anything, she must not put herself out, he wanted nothing but a bed; but he was curious to know into what parts he had strayed and how far it was from the estate of the landowner Sobakievich. To this the old woman replied that she had not even heard of that name and no such landowner existed.

'But at least you must know Manilov?' said Chichikov.

'And who is Manilov?'

'A landowner, my dear Madam.'

'No, I have never heard of a landowner of that name.'

'Who are the landowners in the neighbourhood then?'

'Brobov, Swinin, Kanapatyev, Harpakin, Trepakin, Pleshakov.'

'Are they well to do or not?'

'No, father, there are none here who are too rich. Some own twenty souls, some thirty, but as for owning a hundred souls, we have none here.'

Chichikov perceived that he had strayed into a regular wilderness.

'Is it far from town?' he enquired.

'Forty miles it would be. I am sorry there is nothing for you to eat, but maybe you would like some tea?'

'Thank you, my dear lady, I would like nothing better than a bed.'

'It's very true, after a journey like that you would be wanting to have a good rest. You can lie down here, on this sofa. Hey, Fenya, fetch a feather-bed, pillows and the sheets. What weather God has sent us! and the thunder—I have had a candle lit in front of the icon all night. Oi, father mine, you've got your side and back all muddy like a boar! Where did it please you to soil yourself so?'

'Glory be to God, that I only soiled myself! I must be grateful for not getting my ribs broken.'

'Holy Saviour! What agony! Would you be wanting your back to be rubbed?'

'Thank you, thank you. Don't put yourself out, only please give instructions for my clothes to be dried and cleaned.'

'Do you hear, Fenya!' said the mistress of the house, turning to the woman, who had met him on the porch with a candle and who had already brought the feather-bed and, after pummelling its sides, let loose a whole flood of feathers all over the room. 'Take the gentleman's *kaftan* and what's under it, and dry them in front of a fire first, as you used to do for the deceased master, and afterwards rub them well and beat them out.'

'It shall be done, lady!' said Fenya as she spread the sheet over the feather-bed and set out the pillows.

'Well, there's the bed ready for you,' said the mistress of the house. 'Fare thee well, father, a good night's rest I wish you. Will you not be wanting anything? Maybe you are accustomed, father, to have your feet rubbed for the night. My deceased one could not fall asleep without it.'

But the guest declined to have his feet rubbed. As soon as the lady had gone out, he hastened to undress and to give Fenya all his stripped-off trappings, the lower as well as the upper parts. Wishing him also a good night's rest Fenya carried off these damp accoutrements. When he was alone, he glanced, not without satisfaction, at the bed which almost reached to the ceiling. Fenya was obviously quite a hand at beating up feather-beds. When he had climbed on a chair and then scrambled into the bed, it sagged almost to the floor beneath his weight, and the feathers, which he had ousted from their confinement, flew into all the corners of the room. Snuffing the candle, he pulled a calico coverlet over himself and, curling up under it like a ring, he instantly fell asleep.

When he awoke next morning it was already fairly late. Through the window the sun was shining straight into his eyes and the flies, which but yesterday had been drowsing peacefully on the walls and ceiling, now all turned their attention to him. One of them perched on his lips, another on his ear, a third was aiming to land on his very eye, while still another was incautious enough to settle in the vicinity of his nostrils; sleepily he sniffed it right into his nose. This made him sneeze violently—and this was the real cause of his awakening.

On glancing round the room, he now perceived that not all the pictures represented birds: in between them hung a portrait of Kutuzov[4] and an oil-painting of some old gentleman in a uniform trimmed with red facings such as were the fashion in the days of the Emperor Paul.[5] The clock hissed out again and struck ten; a woman's face peeped through the doorway, and vanished as quickly, for in his desire to get some more sleep Chichikov had thrown aside absolutely all his bed-clothes. The peering face struck him as familiar. He tried to remember who it could be and at length recollected that it was the mistress of the house. He donned his shirt—his clothes, already dry and brushed, were lying nearby. Having dressed himself, he approached the mirror and sneezed again so loudly that a turkey-cock, which had ventured near the window that almost reached the ground, suddenly burst out into rapid gibberish, wishing probably

4. Mikhail Illarionovich Kutuzov (1745–1813), who figures prominently in Tolstoy's *War and Peace,* was a commanding general in the Napole- onic Wars and a great Russian popu- lar hero.
5. Born 1754, ruled Russia from 1796 to 1801.

to bid him good-day; Chichikov returned the compliment by swearing at him. Then he went up to the window and began to inspect the landscape; the window overlooked a chicken-farm—at least, he saw that the narrow yard was teeming with fowl and every kind of domestic animal. There was no counting the turkeys and hens; through their midst a cock was stalking with great deliberation, shaking his comb and turning his head sideways as if listening to something. There was also a sow with her family; as she scraped in a heap of garbage the sow in passing swallowed a chicken and, without even noticing it, continued unconcernedly to gobble up the water-melon rinds. This small yard or chicken-farm had a wooden fence round it, and beyond stretched a row of garden plots planted with cabbages, onions, potatoes, beetroot and other household vegetables. In among them were apple-trees and other fruit-trees, with nets hung over them for protection against magpies and sparrows; the latter were flitting from one end to the other in oblique clouds. To keep them off, a number of scarecrows had been set up on long poles with hands outstretched; one of them had a bonnet belonging to the mistress of the house perched on top of it. Beyond the orchards were the peasants' huts; and although dispersed and not concentrated in regular streets, they bore evidence, as Chichikov observed, of the well-being of the inhabitants. They were properly maintained: the decayed roofing had been replaced by new planks; the wickets were nowhere askew; and in the peasant sheds facing him he noticed in some an almost new cart and in others as many as two. 'Her village is not so small,' he said to himself, and he at once decided to cultivate the lady and get to know her better. He peeped through a crack in the door and, seeing her seated at the tea-table, went in to join her with a cheerful and affectionate look.

'Good-day to you, little father. And how did you rest?' said the mistress of the house, getting up from her seat. She was better clad than on the previous day, and wore a dark dress; she had discarded her sleeping-cap, but she still had a piece of stuff wound around her neck.

'Oh, excellently, excellently,' answered Chichikov as he sat down in the armchair. 'And you, mother?'

'Very badly, father.'

'How so?'

'Insomnia. My hips ache all the time, and my leg, above the ankle, is just gnawing.'

'That will pass, that will pass, mother. You must not think about it.'

'Give God, it may pass. And I have been rubbing it with lard and applying turpentine too. And what will you have in your tea? There is some cherry-brandy in the flask there.'

'That wouldn't be bad at all, mother, we'll try the cherry-brandy.'

The reader will have already noted, I think, that, for all his affectionate manner, Chichikov was talking to her in a much freer way than to Manilov, and did not stand on ceremony. It is appropriate to say here, that if, in Russia, we have not quite caught up with foreigners in some respects, we have far outstripped them in behaviour. It is impossible to enumerate all the shades and refinements of our intercourse. A Frenchman or a German will take an age to grasp or will even fail altogether to understand all these peculiarities and distinctions; he would be inclined to address a millionaire or small tobacconist in much the same terms, although in his soul he would of course be fawning on the former. With us it is quite different: we have experts in sophistry who will sing quite a different tune in front of a landowner with two hundred souls and one with three hundred; quite differently again in front of one having three hundred souls and another possessing five hundred, and even more differently in front of one having five hundred souls and one owning eight hundred—in short, were you to count up to a million there would be no lack of shades. Let us suppose, for example, that there is a chancellery, not here but in some imaginary state, and that this chancellery has, let us suppose, a chief. I beg you to glance at him as he sits among his subordinates—from fear you would not dare utter a word! Pride and good birth, much else, are they not written on his face? It only remains to pick up a brush and paint him: a Prometheus, a veritable Prometheus![6] He peers like an eagle, and advances smoothly, with assurance. That same eagle, as soon as he quits his office and comes near the study of his own chief, scurries along like some startled grouse, with a wad of papers under his arm. In society or at an evening party, if everyone is of a minor rank, Prometheus will preserve his Promethean identity, but should the company be of a higher grade, this Prometheus will undergo a metamorphosis such as even Ovid[7] could not contrive: he will prove a mere fly, less even, no more than a grain of sand! 'But that is not Ivan Petrovich,' you will say, staring at him. 'Ivan Petrovich is of bigger build, while this man looks small and thin; the former talks loudly, in a deep voice sometimes, and never laughs, while the latter is the devil knows what: he twitters like a bird and keeps sniggering all the time.' You approach him, have a good look at him, and in fact he turns out to be Ivan Petrovich! 'That's how it is!' you will think to yourself. . . .

However, it is time to return to our characters. As we have seen, Chichikov had decided not to stand on ceremony; and thus, picking up a glass of tea in both hands and pouring some cherry-brandy into it, he started to discourse as follows:

'You have a tidy little village here, mother. How many souls have you got?'

'Souls? Why some eighty thereabouts,' said the old lady. 'But the misfortune of it is the times are hard, last year there was such a bad harvest, God help us.'

'Your peasants, however, look a healthy lot and their huts are well built. But may I ask you your surname! I am afraid I was a little distraught . . . what with this arrival in the middle of the night. . . .'

'Korobochka. My husband was a collegiate secretary.'[8]

---

6. Classical god of fire, regarded as the bringer of the first civilization (fire) to human beings.
7. Latin poet (43 B.C.–?A.D. 17), author of the *Metamorphoses,* about mythological transformations of human beings into gods, plants, or animals.
8. "Korobochka": *Korobka* is Russian for "box" (suggestive of containers where she hides away her property). "Collegiate secretary": tenth of the fourteen ranks.

'I am most obliged to you. And what is your Christian name and your father's name?'

'Nastasya Petrovna.'

'Nastasya Petrovna? An excellent name that. My aunt, my mother's sister, is also called Nastasya Petrovna.'

'And what is your name?' she asked. 'You are probably a tax-assessor?'

'No, mother,' answered Chichikov with a smile. 'Most certainly not an assessor. I am just travelling on my own business.'

'You must be a buying agent then! What a pity it is that I have already sold all my honey to the merchants so cheaply. I think you might have bought it from me at a good price.'

'But I would not have bought the honey.'

'What else then? Hemp? I haven't got much hemp left either, only some thirty pounds or so.'

'No mother, I am after other wares. Tell me, have your peasants been dying off?'

'Och, little father, eighteen of them!' said the old lady, sighing. 'And such fine fellows too, hard workers all of them. It's true, there were a lot of births after that, but what are they worth—all small fry, and the tax-assessor, he came along and told me to pay tax on every one of them. Last week my blacksmith got burnt up, such a handy man and he was a locksmith into the bargain.'

'You don't mean you had a fire here, mother?'

'The Lord preserved us from such a calamity, a fire would have been worse: no, he set himself on fire. Something caught fire inside of him, he had been drinking too much, he was all wrapped in a blue flame, he smouldered and smouldered, and then turned as black as coal. And what a handy smith he was! And now I cannot drive out at all, there is no one to shoe the horses.'

'It was God's will, mother!' said Chichikov with a sigh. 'There is no denying the wisdom of God. . . . Will you give them to me, Nastasya Petrovna?'

'Whom do you mean, father?'

'Why, all these dead peasants.'

'But how can I give them to you?'

'Oh, quite simply. Or, if you please, sell them to me. I shall give you money for them.'

'But how can I? I don't see the sense of it. Will you be wanting to dig them out of the earth?'

Chichikov perceived that the old lady was quite off the mark and that he would have to explain what it was all about. In a few words he demonstrated to her that the transfer or purchase would only figure on paper and that the souls would be registered as living.

'And what do you need them for?' said the old lady, looking goggle-eyed at him.

'That's my affair.'

'But they are dead!'

'But who is saying that they are alive? Being dead, they are a loss to you: you are paying taxes on them, but I shall relieve you of all worry and payment. Do you understand? And not only will I relieve you, but I shall also pay you fifteen roubles on top of it. Well, is it clear now?'

'I really don't know,' said the old lady hesitatingly. 'I have never yet traded in dead folk.'

'I should think not! It would have been almost a miracle if you had been selling them to anyone. Maybe you think there is really some profit to be got out of them?'

'No, I don't think that. What profit can there be in them? There can be no profit. The only thing that worries me is that they are already dead.'

'Well, isn't she a hard-headed woman!' thought Chichikov to himself. 'Now listen, mother. Just reason it out well: you are being ruined. You are paying taxes for them as though they were alive. . . .'

'Och, father, don't talk about it!' she interrupted him. 'Only three weeks ago I paid over a hundred-and-a-half, and I had to grease the assessor's palm too.'

'Well, you see, mother. And now try and imagine that you will not have to grease the assessor's palm any longer because it is I who will have to pay for them; I, and not you; I assume all the responsibilities. I shall even pay for the title-deed, do you understand that?'

The old lady looked thoughtful. She could see that the

affair really looked profitable, but it was too novel and unprecedented. And that made her very alarmed lest this agent might not cheat her in some way; he had arrived God alone knows whence, and at night into the bargain.

'Well, mother, what about it? Shall we shake hands on it?' urged Chichikov.

'But really, father, I have never had occasion to sell dead folk—only living ones. Three years ago I let Protopopov take two girls for a hundred roubles each, and he was very grateful for them, they turned out to be fine workers: they can weave napkins.'

'But we're not talking about the living. I am enquiring about the dead.'

'Really, I am afraid of incurring some loss just in the beginning. Maybe you are deceiving me, father, and they . . . they may be worth more.'

'Now look here, mother. . . . What are you thinking of! What can they be worth? Just look at them: they are nothing but dust. Do you understand that? Dust only. Take any useless, cast-off thing, some rag, for example, it will have a price: it will at least be bought for a paper-mill, but as for them they are of no use whatever. I ask you, what use are they?'

'That's true enough, that's exact. They are no use at all. Yes, but one thing only makes me hesitate and that is the fact that they are dead.'

'Blast her, what a blockhead!' Chichikov exclaimed inwardly, already beginning to lose his temper. 'Try and agree with her! She's made me sweat, the hag!' And indeed, pulling out a handkerchief from his pocket, he began to wipe the perspiration from his brow. However, Chichikov fumed in vain: many a respectable and official personage turns out to be a perfect Korobochka in practice. Once something has been knocked into his head, there is no arguing with him; however many demonstrations, clear as daylight, you might offer, everything will bounce back from him like a rubber ball from a wall. Having mopped his brow, Chichikov resolved to try and see if he could not bring her to reason in another way.

'Either you do not wish to understand my words, mother,' he said, 'or you are talking like that on purpose just for the sake of arguing. . . . I am giving you the money: fifteen roubles in notes. Do you understand? That's money, isn't it? You would not find that in the street. Well, tell me now frankly how much did you sell your honey for?'

'Twelve roubles for two-score pounds.'

'Another small sin on your soul, mother. You did not sell it for twelve roubles.'

'I swear to God, I did.'

'But look here now. That was honey. It may have taken you a whole year, maybe, to gather it with care, trouble and toil; you had to travel about, to catch the bees, to feed them for a whole winter in your cellar, but dead souls are not of this world. They required no effort from you, it was by the will of God only that they forsook this world, thus bringing loss to your household. For all your effort and toil you realized twelve roubles for three stones[9] of honey, but in this case you are getting for nothing, as a gift, not twelve but fifteen roubles, and you are getting them not in silver but in blue currency notes.'

After such persuasion, Chichikov had almost no doubt but that the old dame would finally surrender.

'That's true,' she replied. 'But I am only an inexperienced widow! I had better consider it a while. There will surely be other merchants too, and I shall be able to compare prices.'

'Shame on you, shame, mother! It's quite disgraceful! Just think what you are saying. Who else would dream of buying them? What use would they be to anyone?'

'But maybe they would prove useful in the household on some occasion,' retorted the old lady, and stopping in the midst of her sentence she looked open mouthed at him to see what he would reply.

'Dead men in a household! That's a fine one! They might perhaps frighten sparrows in your orchard in the night-time?'

9. I.e., forty-two pounds. A stone (English measure of weight) equals fourteen pounds.

'The Lord be with us? What things you do be saying!' said the old woman crossing herself.

'Where else would you have put them? Incidentally, the bones and graves, all that you can keep; the transfer will only be on paper. Well, what about it? Answer me at least!'

The old lady grew thoughtful again.

'What are you thinking about, Nastasya Petrovna?'

'To tell the truth, I don't know what I'd better do. I'd rather sell you some hemp.'

'What's hemp got to do with it? If you don't mind, I'm asking about something quite different, and you thrust hemp at me! Hemp is hemp, I shall come another time and buy hemp. Well, what do you think, Nastasya Petrovna?'

'Oh Lord, they are queer sort of wares, quite unprecedented.'

At this point, Chichikov finally lost his patience, banged the chair on the floor and told her to go to the devil.

 The old lady was extraordinarily frightened of the devil. 'Oh, don't mention him, God forbid!' she exclaimed, turning pale. 'Only three days back, in the night, I dreamt of the evil one. After prayers, I thought I would tell my fortune at cards, but God sent him along, it seems, to punish me. And so disgusting he was to see too; and his horns were longer than a bull's.'

'I am amazed you don't dream of dozens of them. It was only out of Christian pity that I wished . . . on seeing a poor widow, needy and worried. . . . But may the plague take you and the whole of your village. . . .'

'Oh, what expressions you do use,' cried the old dame, staring at him in alarm.

'I can't find enough words where you are concerned! You're just like some mongrel—not to use a bad word—that's lying on hay it won't eat itself, and won't let anyone else eat either. By the way, I should like to buy some of your other produce too, for I am in charge also of official contracts. . . .'

This was a lie, uttered by chance and without any deep

reflection, but it unexpectedly hit the mark. The official contracts produced a strong impression on Nastasya Petrovna—at least, she said in an almost soliciting tone:

'Why are you so angry and heated? Had I known you were irascible, I would not have contradicted you at all.'

'There are plenty of reasons to be angry! The whole thing is not worth an egg-shell, and here am I losing my temper about it!'

'Well then, if you please, I am ready to let you have them for fifteen roubles in currency notes! Only you must do something, father, about those contracts: if you should be wanting rye flour, buckwheat, or any cattle, then please do not pass me by. . . .'

'No, mother, I shall not pass you by,' he said, wiping the abundant perspiration off his face. He asked whether she had a solicitor or any friend in town to whom she might entrust the task of drawing up the deed and seeing to all the rest. 'Why of course, there is the archpriest's son who is employed in the courts,' said Korobochka. Chichikov requested her to write out a warrant for him and, to save her extra trouble, he took it upon himself to compose it.

'It would be a fine thing,' Korobochka thought to herself meanwhile, 'if he would purchase my flour and cattle for the Treasury,[1] I must put him in a good humour. There is some dough left over from yesterday, I must go and tell Fenya to make us some oatcakes; and it would be just as well to put on an egg pie, we do them well here, and they do not take much time.' The mistress of the house went out to put her plan for the pie into operation and, very likely, to add to it some other products of home baking and cooking. In the meantime, Chichikov passed into the drawing-room, where he had spent the night, in order to fetch the necessary papers from his box. In the drawing-room everything had been tidied long ago, the sumptuous feather-bed had been removed, and a table had been laid in front of the sofa. Setting his box down on it, he relaxed for a while as he still felt himself bathed in perspiration as in a river: every stitch he wore,

1. For the Imperial Russian Government.

beginning with his shirt and ending with socks, was quite damp. 'Ah, she has done me in, the accursed beldam,' he exclaimed after a short rest and he then opened his box.

The author is convinced that there are readers so inquisitive that they would like to learn all about the internal structure of the box. By all means! Why should we not satisfy them? Here then is its internal structure: right in the centre was a compartment for soap, and next to it some five or six narrow partitions for razors; then came square nooks for the sand-box and the inkstand, a chiselled groove for quills, sealing-wax and all the other long things; afterwards all sorts of compartments, with or without lids, for the shorter things—these were filled with visiting cards, funeral, theatre, and other notices, which were kept there as souvenirs. The whole of the upper part of the box with all its compartments could be lifted out, and underneath a space was revealed, heaped with sheaves of papers; lastly there was a small, secret money drawer which could be pulled out from one of the sides of the box. Its master invariably opened and shut the drawer so quickly that it was impossible to judge how much money it contained. Chichikov at once got busy and, having sharpened his quill, began to write. At that moment the mistress of the house came in.

'It's a nice box you have there, father,' she said, sitting down by his side. 'You must have bought it in Moscow.'

'In Moscow,' Chichikov replied, continuing to write.

'I guessed that: the workmanship there is always good. Some three years ago my sister brought me some warm winter boots from Moscow for the children: very solid stuff, it's still wearing. Oh, look at all that stamped paper you've got!' she continued, glancing into the box. And in fact there was no lack of stamped paper there. 'You might give me a sheet! I am rather short of it; just in case I have to make an application to the courts and I haven't any left.'

Chichikov explained to her that it was not that sort of paper, and that it was intended for deeds of purchase, not petitions. However, to quieten her, he gave her a sheet worth about a rouble. He then asked her to sign the letter he had drafted and to provide him with a brief list of her peasants. It turned out that this land-owning lady kept no notes or lists, but knew almost all the details by heart; and he at once made her dictate them to him. Some of the peasants astounded him by the names they bore, and even more by their nicknames, so that, on hearing them, he paused each time before writing them down. He was particularly struck by one of them—Pyotr Saveliev—Blast-the-Trough, and he could not help remarking. 'What a long one!' Another had the word Kirpich or 'Brick' attached to his name of 'Korovy,' which meant cow, and yet another was called simply 'Ivan-the-Wheel.' As he was finishing his writing, he sniffed a little air into his nostrils and caught a promising whiff of something fried in butter.

'I humbly beg of you to have a bite,' said the mistress of the house. Chichikov looked round and saw that the table was already set with mushrooms, pies, fritters, cheese-cakes, pancakes, and mill-cakes with all kinds of things baked on top of them, such as onion, poppy, curds, smelt, and every sort of other thing.

'And here is the egg pie,' said the mistress.

Once he had moved nearer to the egg-pie and eaten a good half of it, Chichikov praised it. In reality, it was tasty enough and, after all his toil and trouble with the old dame, it struck him as even more appetizing.

'And the pancakes?' asked the mistress.

By way of reply Chichikov rolled three pancakes together, and after dipping them in melted butter, directed them into his mouth, wiping his lips afterwards with a napkin. Having repeated this action three times, he asked the mistress to give orders to have his horses harnessed. Natasya Petrovna at once despatched Fenya to see to this, telling her at the same time to bring some more hot pancakes.

'Your pancakes are very tasty, mother,' said Chichikov, applying himself to a steaming new lot.

'Yes, they do them well in my house,' said the mistress. 'But the trouble is that the harvest was a bad one, the flour is not so very good. . . . And why are you in such a hurry?' she enquired, noticing that Chichikov had picked up his cap. 'The horses are not harnessed yet.'

'They'll be harnessed, mother, they'll be harnessed. My folk don't waste time.'

'And please don't forget about the contracts.'

'I shall not, I shall not,' said Chichikov as he made for the hall.

'And do you buy lard too?'

'Why not? I do buy it, only later.'

'I shall have a stock of lard about Christmas time.'

'We'll buy it, we'll buy it, we'll buy everything, the lard too.'

'Maybe you require feathers? I shall be having feathers round about St. Philip's day.'[2]

'Very well, very well,' said Chichikov.

'You see, father, your chaise is not here yet,' she said as they came out on the porch.

'It will be here soon, very soon. But can you tell me now how to find the highway?'

'How am I to explain it?' said the old lady. 'Explaining is complicated, there are a great many turnings: I had better send a girl with you to show you the way. Very likely you'd have a place for her to sit down next to the coachman or somewhere.'

'Of course.'

'Yes, maybe I shall send a girl with you; she knows the way. Only look here, you must not drive off with her. I have already lost one girl in that way when some merchants were passing through.'

Chichikov convinced her that he would not make off with the girl and, thus reassured, Korobochka began to inspect all there was to be seen in the yard: she stared at the housekeeper as she was carrying a wooden dish full of honey from the storehouse, at a peasant entering the gateway, and so gradually slipped back into her household routine.

But why spend so much time over Korobochka? Whether it is a question of Korobochka or Manilov, and

2. The St. Philip's Fast started on November 1. In central Russia it was the usual time to slaughter poultry.

whether their households are well organized or not—
what does it matter! That is not so wonderful. Joy will
instantly turn to gloom if we dawdle too long over it,
and then God knows what might come into one's head.
One might even begin to wonder whether Korobochka's
place in life is really so low in the infinite scale of human
perfection. Is the abyss really so great that separates her
from any sister of hers, who may be cloistered out of reach
—within the walls of some aristocratic mansion with its
fragrantly smelling, wrought-iron staircases, glittering
brass, mahogany and carpets—yawning over an unfinished book as she sits expecting the visit of some witty
society caller who will give her scope to shine and to utter
her oft-digested platitudes. And as the fashion goes, her
platitudes will entertain the town for a whole week—
these empty thoughts of hers unconcerned with anything
in her own house or on her estates, which have gone to
rack and ruin as a result of her ignorance of household
affairs, but concerned rather with attempts being made to
change the present government of France or with the
latest trends in the now most fashionable Catholic
Church. But what does it all matter! Do not let us pause
here! Why talk about it? And yet why, in the midst of
such thoughtless and careless moments, does another
stream of ideas occur in a flash? Laughter has barely
time to fade on people's faces before they are transformed
and lit up by another light. . . .

'Here's the chaise, here's the chaise!' exclaimed
Chichikov as he caught sight of it approaching at last.
'You blockhead, why have you been so long? I can see
you haven't come to yet after yesterday's bout.'

Selifan made no reply to that.

'Farewell mother! But where is the girl?'

'Hey, Pelageia,' said the old lady to a girl of about
eleven standing near the porch, in a homespun dress and
with bare feet which, at some distance, could easily have
been mistaken for boots so crusted were they with mud.
'Show the master the road.'

Selifan helped the girl up on the driver's seat; as she
stepped on the footrest, she first of all soiled it in mud

and then climbed up and took her place beside him. After her, Chichikov himself stepped on the footrest and, tilting the chaise to the right as he did so, for he was quite a weight, finally settled himself and said: 'Ah! It feels good now! Farewell, mother!' The horses started off.

Selifan was well disciplined for the rest of the way and also most attentive to his duties; this only happened with him after some indiscretion or a bout of drunkenness. The horses looked amazingly glossy. One of the horse-collars, which until then had almost always looked ragged with the tow peeping from under the leather, had been cleverly patched up. He preserved a dogged silence, whipped the horses, and refrained from addressing any lectures to them, although the dapple-grey would have liked naturally to hear something instructive. But the normally verbose coachman held the reins slackly and his whip flicked over their backs for the sake of form only. This time those gloomy lips of his gave vent only to monotonous and unpleasant exclamations, such as, 'Gee up, you crow! Yawn, would you!' and nothing else. Even the bay horse and the Assessor were dissatisfied at not once hearing any words of endearment or respect. The dapple-grey felt some most unpleasant blows land on his spacious quarters. 'What's bitten him!' he thought to himself, twitching his ears a little. 'He knows, he does, how to hit! He doesn't use his whip right on one's back, but picks the spot where it hurts most, now he will singe one's ears, now he will give one's belly a welt.'

'To the right is it?' With that dry question Selifan turned to the girl sitting beside him, pointing with his whip to the road which the rains had turned all black and muddy and which stretched between the refreshed, bright-green fields.

'No, no. I'll tell you when,' replied the girl.

'Is that it?' said Selifan as they got nearer.

'That's where it is,' replied the girl, pointing with her finger.

'Well, well,' Selifan muttered. 'But that is to the right. She doesn't know what's right and what's left.'

Although it was a very fine day, the ground had become so muddy that, scooping it up, the wheels of the chaise were soon covered with it as with felt, and this weighed down the carriage quite a lot: moreover, the soil was clayey and unusually sticky. With one thing and another, they did not get out of the locality before midday. They would have found even that difficult without the girl, for many roads spread out on all sides of them, like netted crabs when they are spilled out of a sack, and Selifan would have been obliged through no fault of his own to drive aimlessly about. But soon the girl pointed to a structure which was outlined darkly in the distance, saying, 'There's the highway.'

'And the building?' asked Selifan.

'A tavern,' she replied.

'Well, now we can find our way,' said Selifan. 'Off you go.'

He stopped and helped her to get down, muttering through his teeth, 'Ah, you blackfoot!'

Chichikov gave her a brass farthing, and she set off back on her own, well satisfied with her ride.

CHAPTER IV

WHEN they drew level with the tavern, Chichikov ordered the chaise to be stopped. He had two reasons for doing so: to rest the horses, and to fortify himself by having a bite to eat. The author must confess that he is envious of the appetite and capacity of this sort of folk. He attaches no significance at all to the highfalutin gentry living in Petersburg and Moscow, who spend their time imagining what they may eat next day and what to contrive for dinner the day after, and who sit down to that dinner only after swallowing a pill—those in fact who gobble oysters, sea-spiders and other monstrosities, and then repair for a cure to Carlsbad or the Caucasus. No, these gentry never roused his envy. But the middling gentry who ask for a plateful of ham at one stage of their journey, a sucking pig at the next, and a portion of sturgeon at the third, or for some baked sausage with onion, and then, as if it were the most natural thing in the world, sit down at table no matter at what hour and tuck into a sterlet soup followed by patties or cabbage pie with fish, till their appetite is completely satisfied—these are the gentry whom heaven has incomparably endowed! Not one of these highfalutin gentlemen would dream of sacrificing instantly half of his peasants and half of his estates, mortgaged or not, and with all improvements foreign and Russian, for the sake of being able to boast of a stomach such as is the property of the middling gentry; but the trouble is that no sum less than the equivalent of an estate, with or without the latest improvements, suffices to procure them a stomach of such capacity.

The grimy wooden tavern received Chichikov beneath its narrow hospitable eaves which were supported by turned wooden columns not unlike antique church candlesticks. The tavern was something like a Russian peasant's hut on a large scale. It had cut ornamental cornices of fresh wood round the windows and under the roof, offering a bright and charming contrast to the dark walls; and on the shutters were painted jugs with flowers.

On mounting a narrow wooden staircase he came upon a spacious hall just as a creaking door was being opened and a stout old woman in variegated satins emerged and said, 'This way, please!' The room contained all those old friends whom it is the lot of everyone to meet in small wooden taverns, of which there are not a few set up along the highways—namely, a frost-rimed samovar, smoothly scraped pine-wood walls, a three-cornered cupboard with tea-pots and cups in one corner, gilt porcelain eggs dangling on blue and red ribbons in front of the icons, a cat with a recent litter, a mirror that reflected back four eyes instead of two and a sort of flat bun instead of a face; and finally, bundles of fragrant herbs and cloves in the vicinity of the icons, all so dried up that anyone attempting to smell them could only sneeze.

'Have you any sucking pig?' With this question Chichikov turned to the old woman.

'We have.'

'With horse radish and sour cream?'

'With horse radish and sour cream.'

'Bring it along!'

The old woman went off to rummage about and came back with a plate, a napkin so stiff with starch that it stood up like dried bark, a knife with a faded bone handle and a blade as narrow as a penknife's, a two-pronged fork, and a salt-cellar which would not stand straight on the table.

As was his habit, our hero at once engaged her in conversation and asked her whether she managed the tavern herself or whether there was a proprietor, what their income was, whether they had sons living with them, whether the eldest son was a bachelor or married, and what his wife was like, had she a large dowry or not, and had the father-in-law been satisfied or had he been angry at receiving so few presents at the wedding. In short, he omitted nothing. It goes without saying, that he was curious enough to find out what landowners lived in the vicinity and he discovered that there were all kinds: Blokhin, Pochitayev, Mylonoy, Colonel Cheprakon, and Sobakievich.

'Ah! You know Sobakievich?' he asked, and learnt at once that the old woman knew not only Sobakievich but also Manilov, and that in her opinion Manilov was a little grander than Sobakievich. He would not hesitate to order a boiled chicken and some veal into the bargain; if there were sheep's liver, he would ask for it as well, and what only would he not try, whereas Sobakievich would order just one thing, eat it all up, and even ask for a second helping for the same price.

As he was talking and helping himself to the sucking pig, of which only a last morsel now remained, there was a rattle of wheels as a carriage drew up by the tavern. Peeping out of the window, he saw a light chaise and harnessed to it a *troika* of goodly horses. Two men were just getting out of the chaise. One of them was tall and fair; the other short and swarthy. The fair one had on a dark blue Hungarian jacket, the swarthy one merely a striped Caucasian dress. In the distance another small carriage could be seen, empty and drawn by a shaggy-maned foursome with ragged collars and roped-in harness. The fair one at once mounted the steps while his swarthy companion lingered behind, looking for something in the chaise, chatting with the servant and waving at the same time to the carriage in the rear. His voice struck Chichikov as being familiar. While Chichikov was staring at the swarthy man, the fair one had time to find the door and open it. He was a tall man with a pinched face, slightly the worse for wear as they say, and a ginger moustache. From his tanned complexion one might have concluded that he had been through fire and smoke—if not that of gunpowder, then at least of tobacco. He bowed politely to Chichikov, who returned the compliment. Very likely, only a few minutes would have sufficed for them to have become engrossed in conversation and to have struck up an acquaintance-ship because the initial steps had already been taken. Both had simultaneously expressed their pleasure at the fact that the dust on the highway had been completely quelled by yesterday's rain and that it was now pleasant and cool for driving; but then his swarthy companion came in, pulling off his cap and throwing it on the table, and ruffling his black hair with a youthful gesture. He was a not badly built fellow of middle height, with full rosy cheeks, teeth as white as snow and whiskers as black as pitch. He was as fresh as milk; it seemed as though his face was simply beaming with health.

'Ba, ba, ba!' he suddenly exclaimed, spreading out his arms at the sight of Chichikov. 'What brings you here?' Chichikov recognized Nozdrev, with whom he had dined at the prosecutor's and who had instantly become on such a good footing with him as to call him *thou* although he had given him no pretext for this.

'Where have you been?' asked Nozdrev, and continued without waiting for an answer, 'I've come from the fair, brother. You may congratulate me: I've been skinned to the bone! Would you believe it, never in my life have I been had like this. Just look, I've come back on those common hacks! Just look out of the window!' On saying this he bent Chichikov's head down so that it nearly struck the window-frame. 'Look at them, just rubbish! Those accursed nags barely managed to get me here, I finally got into his chaise!' As he said that, Nozdrev pointed to his companion. 'But you don't know each other yet? My brother-in-law, Mizhuyev! We talked about you the whole of the morning. "Well, look," I said, "we may meet Chichikov." Ah, if you only knew, brother, how I've been had! Would you believe it, I not only blewed four good trotters, but everything else as well. I haven't got a watch-chain left on me, to say nothing of a watch. . . .' Chichikov glanced at him and saw that it was indeed true: he had neither watch nor chain. It even struck him that one of his whiskers was a shade smaller and a trifle less thick than the other. 'If I had twenty roubles left,' continued Nozdrev, 'twenty, no more, I'd win it all back, and on top of winning it back, as I'm an honest man, I'd put a cool thirty thousand into my pocket-book.'

'You said that at the time,' retorted the fair one. 'And when I gave you fifteen roubles, you lost them at once.'

'I shouldn't have lost them! Honest, I shouldn't have! Had I not been stupid, I really wouldn't have. If I hadn't doubled on the seven, I might have broken the bank.'

'But you didn't,' said the fair one.

'I didn't because I doubled at the wrong moment. You think that major of yours plays well, do you?'

'Well or not, he skinned you.'

'What matter!' said Nozdrev, 'I'll skin him too. Just let him try and play doublet, then I'll see. I'll see what sort of a player he is. But despite it all, it was a magnificent spree for the first few days, brother Chichikov! To tell the truth, the fair was an excellent one. The merchants themselves say there had never been such a throng. Everything I brought from the village was sold most profitably. Ah, brother! What a spree! Even to remember it now . . . the devil take it! I mean to say, it's a great pity you weren't there. Just imagine, there was a dragoon regiment quartered three miles out of town. Would you believe it, how many officers there were, forty no less. . . . And when we started drinking, brother. . . . Staff-captain Potzeluyev . . . he's a fine chap! Moustaches like that, brother! He calls bordeaux bawdikins. "Bring me some bawdikins," he says. And lieutenant Kuvshinikov. . . . Ah, brother, what a charming man! He is quite a rake. We were with him all of us. And the wine Ponamarev let us have! I must tell you that he is a rogue, you can't buy anything in his shop: he puts all kinds of filth into the wine—sandalwood, burnt cork and even elderberry; but if you get a bottle from his back room, the one he calls the "special", well then, brother, you are in the empyrean. The champagne we had would make the governor's brand taste like *kvas*.[3] Imagine, not just *clicquot* but clicquot *matradura*, which means extra fine clicquot. And he also brought out a bottle of French wine labelled "Bonbon." And the fragrance of it! The bouquet and everything you wish. What a spree! . . . After us some duke arrived and sent for champagne, but there was not a bottle left in town, the officers had drunk it all. Would you believe it, over dinner I alone drank seventeen bottles of champagne.'

'Come now! You couldn't drink seventeen bottles,' remarked the fair one.

'Honestly, I tell you I did,' replied Nozdrev.

'You can say what you like, but I tell you, you couldn't drink even ten.'

'What will you bet me that I couldn't?'

'Why should I bet?'

'Come on, stake that gun you bought in town.'

'I don't want to.'

'Come on, put it on, just try!'

'I don't want to try.'

'You'd have no gun left just as you have no cap left. Ah, brother Chichikov, I must say I regret you were not there. I know you and lieutenant Kuvshinikov would have been inseparable. How well you would have got on with him. He is not like the prosecutor or any of those codgers in our town, who quake in their shoes for every penny. He is ready to take on any game. Ah, Chichikov, why didn't you come along! You are a pig, really you are, not to have come, you cattle-drover! Kiss me now, I'm

---

3. *Kvas:* a popular, nonalcoholic Russian drink made of fermented bread. "Clicquot": a brand of champagne.

fond to death of you! Look, Mizhuyev, fate has brought the two of us together. What is he to me, or I to him? He has arrived God knows from where, and I live here ... And the carriages, brother, there were quantities and quantities of them. I tried my luck at the fortune-wheel and won two jars of cream, a porcelain cup and a guitar; then I staked again and lost, damn it, six silver roubles into the bargain. And what a flirt that Kuvshinikov is! We went together to nearly all the balls. At one of them there was a woman all dressed-up, in ruche and knick-knacks, and just what wasn't there on her. . . . The devil I said to myself! But Kuvshinikov, he's that sort of a creature, sat down by her side and paid her such compliments in French. . . . Would you believe it, he doesn't let the common women slip him either. He calls that picking strawberries. And the wonderful fish and sturgeon there was! I've got a sturgeon with me, lucky I thought of buying it while I had money. And where are you making for?'

'Oh, just to see a man,' said Chichikov.

'Why worry? Throw him overboard! Come along with me instead!'

'I really can't, I have business.'

'Business! Tell me another! Ah, you, busy Ivanovich!'

'I really have got business and important at that!'

'I bet you are lying! Well, tell me, whom are you going to see?'

'If you want to know, Sobakievich.'

At this Nozdrev burst out laughing. His laughter had that bell-like quality only possessed by a fresh and healthy man, who reveals a row of teeth as white as sugar, whose cheeks quiver and shake, and whose guffaws wake a neighbour two doors away, in another room, making him jump up and exclaim goggle-eyed, 'He's bats!'

'Is there anything funny about that?' asked Chichikov, a little displeased by this laughter.

But Nozdrev went on laughing as loudly as ever, stuttering: 'Have mercy, or I'll burst!'

'There is nothing funny about it. I promised to visit him,' said Chichikov.

'But you won't enjoy it when you do get there. He's an

old skinflint! I know your character, you'll be out of your element if you imagine you'll be able to have a gamble and a good bottle of "Bonbon." Listen, brother, send Sobakievich to the devil, come along with me. I'll treat you to such a sturgeon! Ponamarev, the creature, bowed and scraped, and told me there was not another one like it in the whole of the Fair. But he's a swindler if there ever was one. I told him so to his face: "You", I said, "you and your agent, you're both rogues." And he laughed, stroking his beard. Kuvshinikov and I lunched every day in his shop. Ah, brother, I forgot to tell you. I know you won't lag behind now, but I won't part with it for ten thousand roubles, I warn you. Hey, Porphyry!' he shouted to his man as he went up to the window. The latter was holding a knife in one hand and a crust of bread with a slice of sturgeon on it in the other—a piece which he had chanced to slice off as he was taking something out of the chaise. 'Hey, Porphyry!' Nozdrev was shouting, 'bring me that puppy! What a puppy!' he continued turning to Chichikov. 'It was stolen. His master would not part with him for anything. I had offered him my bay mare which, you remember, I got from Khvostyrev in exchange. . . .' Chichikov, however, had seen neither the bay mare nor Khvostyrev.

'Master, will you not have something to eat?' asked the old woman approaching Nozdrev at that moment.

'Nothing. Ah, brother, what a spree it was! However, give me a glass of vodka. What sort have you?'

'Aniseed,' replied the old woman.

'Well then, aniseed,' said Nozdrev.

'A glass for me too!' said the fair one.

'In the theatre a villainous-looking actress was singing like a canary! Kuvshinikov, who was sitting beside me, he says, "Brother, why not pick a few strawberries." There must have been at least fifty booths at the fair, I think. Fenardi turned somersaults for four hours on end.' At this point Nozdrev accepted a glass from the old woman, who made a low bow to him. 'Ah, bring it here!' he shouted, seeing Porphyry entering with the puppy. Porphyry was dressed like his master, in a kind of long

Asiatic coat lined with cotton wool and looking a bit greasy.

'Bring him here, put him down on the floor!'

Porphyry set the puppy down on the floor. Stretching itself out on its four paws, it began to sniff the ground.

'Here's the puppy!' said Nozdrev, picking it up by the scruff of its neck. The puppy let out a pitiful moan.

'But you haven't done what I told you to do,' said Nozdrev, turning to Porphyry and examining the puppy's belly closely. 'You didn't think of combing him?'

'But I did comb him.'

'Why these fleas then?'

'I can't say. Maybe they hopped on to him in the chaise.'

'You're lying, that's what you're doing, it just didn't occur to you to comb him, and, idiot, you have passed on to him some of your own fleas. Now just look at that, Chichikov, look at his ears, now feel them.'

'Why should I? I can see quite well. A good breed!' replied Chichikov.

'No, come on, feel them, feel the ears!'

Chichikov obliged and fingered the puppy's ears, adding, 'Yes, he'll make a good dog.'

'And do you feel how cold is his nose? Go on, feel it with your hand.' Not wishing to offend him, Chichikov touched the nose too, saying, 'A good scent!'

'A real bulldog,' continued Nozdrev. 'I confess I have been looking for one for a long time. Here, Porphyry, take him away.'

Holding the dog under the belly, Porphyry carried it off to the chaise.

'Listen, Chichikov, you simply must come along with me, it's only five miles from here, we shall be there in a trice, and then, afterwards, by all means make your call on Sobakievich.'

'And why not?' thought Chichikov to himself. 'I will go along with Nozdrev. He is no worse than the others, he is a man like them, and he has lost at cards into the bargain. One can see he is ready for anything and, there-

fore, one may get something out of him for nothing.'
'If you please, let us go,' he said, 'but only I must not
overstay, time is money.'

'Well, my dear fellow, that's fine! That's excellent!
Wait, let me kiss you for that.' Thereupon Nozdrev
and Chichikov embraced. 'Excellent, we shall drive off,
the three of us!'

'No, pray excuse me,' said the fair-haired one, 'I must
go home.'

'Nonsense, nonsense, brother, I won't let you go.'

'I tell you, my wife will be angry, and now you can
use Chichikov's chaise.'

'No, no, no! You musn't dream of going.'

The fair-haired man was one whose character at first
sight seemed to have a streak of obstinacy. Before one has
time to open one's mouth such men are already bent on
quarrelling and they never seem to agree with anything
that contradicts their way of thinking, they never dream
of calling a stupid man clever, and above all, they never
agree to dancing to another man's tune; but in the end
their character always betrays a weak spot and they will
invariably agree to what they had repudiated, they will
call the stupid man clever, and they will go tripping
merrily to another man's tune; in short, they will start on
the level and end up on the crook.

'Nonsense!' said Nozdrev in reply to the fair-haired
one, putting his cap on for him, and the fair-haired one
followed them out.

'You haven't paid for the vodka, sir,' said the old
woman.

'Ah, very well, very well, mother. I say, in-law, will
you pay this, please. I haven't a penny in my pocket.'

'How much is it?' asked the brother-in-law.

'Only twenty kopecks in all,' said the old woman.

'You're putting it on. Give her half of that, it will be
quite enough.'

'It's too little, sir,' the old woman said, but she nevertheless accepted the money gratefully and ran to open the
door for them. She had suffered no loss because she had
asked four times as much as the vodka normally cost.

The travellers took their seats. Chichikov's chaise drove side by side with the one in which Nozdrev and his brother-in-law were sitting, and they could therefore converse quite freely on the way. Nozdrev's small carriage followed drawn by skinny common hacks which were always lagging behind. In it were Porphyry and the puppy.

Since the conversation in which the travellers indulged is of no great interest to the reader, we shall do better to say a few words about Nozdrev, who is destined perhaps to play a not unimportant part in our poem.

The reader is certainly familiar to some extent with Nozdrev's personality. There are quite a few such people one has met. They are known as happy-go-lucky fellows, they have a reputation of being good comrades in childhood and at school, yet in spite of it all they are quite often involved in painful scrapes. Their faces always have an air of frankness, directness and daring. They are quick to strike up a friendship and, before you have had time to look round, they are already treating you like a bosom friend. Their friendship has an air of permanency; but almost invariably their new friend will fall out with them on the very evening of their festive meeting. They are great talkers, men-on-the-spree, devil-may-care fellows, and always in the public eye. At the age of thirty-five Nozdrev might have been eighteen or twenty: he loved a spree. Marriage had not changed him in the least, especially as his wife had soon passed into the other world, leaving him with two children for whom he had no use at all. He kept, however, a good-looking nanny to take care of the children. Gifted with a keen sense of smell for anything in the nature of market-fairs or balls for miles round—for he would not stay at home for more than a day—in a twinkling of an eye he would transport himself to the spot, start an argument and cause confusion at the gaming tables, for like all men of his kind he had a passion for cards. As we have already seen in the first chapter, his card play was not altogether clean nor above reproach, for he was a master of subterfuge and other subtle devices, and his game frequently culminated in another sort of play: he would either be kicked or have his side-whiskers pulled, with the result that he sometimes came home with only one side-whisker left and a very sparse one at that. But his plump and healthy cheeks were so well fashioned and had so much vital sap in them that his whiskers sprouted anew and even better than ever. What was even more strange, and a thing which could only happen in Russia, he would in a short while be meeting again those very same friends who had pummelled him—meeting them as if nothing had ever occurred; he would be at his ease and so would they.

In a sense Nozdrev was an historical character. There was always some 'history' attached to any gathering at which he assisted. Something always happened: either he would have to be conducted from the room by gendarmes or his own friends would be obliged to push him out. If nothing of the kind happened, then inevitably something else out of the ordinary would occur: either he would get so tight at the refreshment bar that he could only roar with laughter, or he would tell such whoppers that his own conscience would prick him. And he used to indulge in lies without any necessity: he would suddenly spin a yarn about some horse he had with a pink or light-blue coat, or some nonsense of the sort, so that the people he was talking to would leave him, saying, 'That's a fisherman's tale, my lad.' There are some people who have an urge to do the dirty even on their closest friends and very often without any good reason for it. Sometimes even a man of rank and respectable appearance, wearing an order on his breast, will press your hand warmly, discuss with you some profound subject requiring reflection, and then before you have had time to look round he will be saying something nasty about you in your hearing. And he will do it as any collegiate registrar might do, and not like a man who has an order pinned on his breast and who is discussing a subject that needs pondering: you are taken aback and are so amazed that you can only shrug your shoulders. Nozdrev had this strange passion. The more friendly you became with him, the more certain he was to turn against you: he would spread such a rumour about you that it would be hard even to imagine it; he would upset a wedding or a business deal without at all considering himself your enemy. On the contrary, if he were to meet you again by chance, he would display every sign of friendship and even say, 'Why don't you ever visit me?' In many respects Nozdrev was a man of many parts, that is to say, he could turn his hand to anything. Within a minute he would suggest going with you anywhere, to the edge of the world if need be, express his willingness to take part in any enterprise or to embark on any kind of exchange. Guns, dogs, horses—all these he would be ready to barter not so much with any idea of making profit out of them but out of sheer high spirits and a natural restlessness of character. If he had the good fortune to come across some simpleton at a fair and to fleece him, he would at once buy up a heap of anything he saw in the shops: horse-collars, fumigating candles, kerchiefs for the nanny, a stallion, raisins, a silver wash-basin, holland linen, fine wheaten flour, tobacco, pistols, herrings, pictures, a grindstone, earthenware pots, boots and china, for as much money as he had on him. However, this junk rarely ever reached home, most of it was lost that very day to some other lucky gambler, and he sometimes even had to part with his own pipe and tobacco-pouch, or on occasions with his four-in-hand, carriage and coachman, and he was then obliged, wearing a short jacket or Caucasian coat, to go in search of some friend who might give him a lift back home. That was Nozdrev! Perhaps it will be said that he is a shoddy character and that no Nozdrevs exist in these days. Alas, those who say so are wrong. It will take a long while yet for characters like Nozdrev to become extinct. They are still to be found everywhere in our midst, though they have changed their clothes; but people are thoughtless and unperceptive, and they believe that the man himself has changed once he has donned a new suit.

In the meantime the three carriages rolled up to the door of Nozdrev's house. No preparations had been made for their reception. Some wooden trestles had been set in the middle of the dining-room and standing on them were two peasants whitewashing the walls and intoning a monotonous song; the floor was all spattered with whitewash. Nozdrev at once sent the peasants away and ran into the next room to give his orders. The visitors heard him giving his instructions to the chef; as he did so Chichikov, who was already feeling the pangs of hunger, realized that they would not sit down at table before five o'clock. On returning, Nozdrev conducted his guests on a tour of the village and within two hours he had shown them absolutely all there was to be seen. To begin with, they inspected the stables where they saw two mares, one a dapple-grey and the other a chestnut, then a bay stallion which was not anything to look at but Nozdrev swore that he had bought it for ten thousand roubles.

'You did not pay ten thousand for him,' said the brother-in-law.

'I swear to God I did,' said Nozdrev.

'You can swear as much as you like,' replied the brother-in-law.

'I am ready to bet that I did!' said Nozdrev.

But the brother-in-law had no wish to bet.

Then Nozdrev showed them round his empty stalls which had formerly contained some good horses. In the stables they also saw a goat which, according to an old superstition, it was considered essential to keep together with the horses; apparently it was on the best of terms with them, for it was quite at ease walking about under their bellies. Then Nozdrev took them along to see a wolf-cub, which was chained up. 'Here's the wolf-cub,' he said, 'I feed him on raw meat on purpose. I want him to be a real beast!' They went to inspect the pond in which, according to Nozdrev, there were fish of such dimensions that it required two men to pull one of them out, but his relative had some doubts on the subject. 'I am going to show you a pair of fine dogs,' said Nozdrev. 'Their black flesh is of astonishing vigour and their coat is all needles!' And he led them towards a beautifully constructed little house with a garden surrounded by a fence. On entering the yard they saw all sorts of dogs, of all breeds and colours: dark-brown, black and tan, black and white, brown and white, red and white, black-eared and grey-eared. . . . They had a great variety of names, many of them in the imperative mood: Shoot, Swear, Flutter, Fire, Cross-eye, Blot, Finish-off, Darling, Reward, Guardian. Nozdrev might have been their father and they his children: they all flew to meet him and to greet the visitors, with their tails in the air according to canine rules of etiquette. Some dozen of them put their paws on Nozdrev's shoulders. Swear showed his affection for Chichikov and licked him on the mouth so that he was obliged to spit out at once. They had a look at these dogs which were astonishing for their vigour of 'black flesh' and their fine breed. Next they went to inspect a Crimean bitch which was already blind and, according to Nozdrev, due to peg out very soon; but some two years back she had been a very fine bitch: they inspected her and found that she was unquestionably blind. Then they went to see the water-mill; it had an iron ring missing, the ring on which the upper stone rests as it turns rapidly on its axle or 'flutters' as Russian peasants so expressively say. 'We shall soon come to the smithy!' said Nozdrev. As they walked on they did indeed come across the smithy and they solemnly surveyed it.

'That field over there,' said Nozdrev, pointing to it, 'is teeming with hares; you can't see the ground for them; the other day I caught one myself by the hind legs.'

'You couldn't catch a hare with your hand,' the brother-in-law remarked.

'But I did, I did!' Nozdrev replied. 'And now,' he said, turning to Chichikov, 'I shall show you the boundaries of my lands.'

Nozdrev led his visitors across a field which in many places was full of stumps. The visitors had to thread their way through fallow land and ploughed earth. Chichikov began to feel weary. The ground was low-lying and in places their boots squelched through water. At first they took care and stepped gingerly, but seeing that this was no advantage they trudged ahead without bothering to pick their way through the mud. Having covered a good distance, they did in fact perceive the boundary line which consisted of a wooden post and a narrow ditch. 'Here is the boundary!' Nozdrev announced. 'Everything on this side of it is mine, and on that side too. That forest over there and everything beyond it, are all mine.'

'Since when has that forest become yours?' the brother-in-law enquired. 'Did you buy it recently? It wasn't yours before.'

'Oh, I bought it recently,' Nozdrev replied.

'How did you manage to buy it so quickly?'

'Oh, I bought it the day before yesterday, and I gave quite a lot for it too.'

'But you were at the fair then.'

'Ah, stupid! Can't one be at the fair and buy land at the same time! Well, I was at the fair, but my steward did the buying.'

'You don't say so!' said the brother-in-law, but all the same, he looked doubtful and shook his head.

The visitors wended their way back over the same nasty road. Nozdrev conducted them to his study which had no signs in it of what is usually to be found in such places, namely, books and papers; the walls were hung only with swords and there were two guns, one worth three hundred and the other eight hundred roubles. The brother-in-law only shook his head as he stared round him. Next they were shown some Turkish daggers, one of which had engraved on it by mistake the name of its maker: Master Savely Sibiryakov. The visitors were then shown a hurdy-gurdy. Nozdrev played a tune for them. The tune was not unpleasant but in the middle of it something must have gone wrong, for the mazurka ended on a song— 'Malbrook s'en va-t-en guerre',[4] and that in turn finished most unexpectedly on the note of a long-familiar waltz. Nozdrev had already stopped turning the handle, but one of the pipes was so irrepressible that it continued to wheeze away for a long time by itself. After this they were

---

4. "Malbrook [the Duke of Marl-borough] goes off to war": a French song popular all over Europe, refer-ring to the English duke, ancestor of Winston Churchill.

introduced to various tobacco pipes of wood, clay or meerschaum, smoked and unsmoked, in chamois leather and without, a chibouk with an amber mouthpiece recently won at cards, a tobacco-pouch embroidered by a countess who had fallen head over heels in love with Nozdrev somewhere at a posting station and whose hands were, according to him, most subtly *superfluous*, a word evidently signifying the height of perfection for him.

After a helping of sturgeon they sat down to the table at about five o'clock. It was clear that food was not Nozdrev's main interest in life; no great importance was attached to the dishes, some of which were burnt and others undercooked. The chef evidently relied on inspiration and put in whatever came to hand: if pepper were near he would put in some peper; if cabbage was to hand, he would put that in; he added milk, ham, peas—in short, whatever turned up; and he was concerned only that it should be hot, not bothering about the taste. On the other hand, Nozdrev plied the wines: before the soup had been served he had already poured out a large glass of port and another one of Haut Sauterne for his guests, for in provincial and district capitals simple Sauterne is not to be found. Then Nozdrev called for a bottle of Madeira. 'No Field-marshal ever tasted a better one,' he said. The Madeira certainly burnt their mouths, for the merchants were well versed in the tastes of the country gentry and doctored it unmercifully with rum and sometimes even with ordinary vodka, hoping for the best from a Russian stomach. Nozdrev followed this up by ordering a special bottle which, so he said, consisted of a mixture of Burgundy and champagne. He poured it out with great application into the glasses on either side of him— those of his brother-in-law and Chichikov; but Chichikov happened to notice that he did not help himself to the same extent. That put him on guard, and whenever Nozdrev turned to speak to his brother-in-law or was filling his glass, he immediately emptied his own glass into his plate. In a short while rowan-berry liqueur appeared on the table. According to Nozdrev it was as smooth as cream, but to their surprise it smelled strongly of corn-brandy. Afterwards they drank a balsam the name of which it was hard to remember and even the host kept giving it different titles. The dinner was long over and the wines had all been tasted, but the company was still at table. Chichikov was loath to broach his main subject in front of the brother-in-law. After all the brother-in-law was a stranger and what he had to say made a friendly *tête-à-tête* necessary. Not that his fellow guest would have proved dangerous, for he appeared to have had his fill, and more than enough—his head was already nodding as he sat in his chair. Realizing himself that he was in a perilous state, he began to say that he wished to go home, but he spoke in such a drawling and listless voice that, as the Russian expression has it, he might have been pulling at a horse's collar with a pair of tweezers.

'No, no, I won't let you go!' said Nozdrev.

'No, don't embarrass me, my dear friend. I must go, I really must go,' the brother-in-law was saying. 'You'll only embarrass me otherwise.'

'Fiddlesticks! We shall arrange a game of cards in a moment.'

'No, brother, you can play if you like, but my wife is waiting for me. I must tell her about the fair. I really must give her that pleasure. No, you mustn't keep me.'

'You can send her to blazes.... As if you had anything important to do with her!'

'But she is such a good and faithful wife! And the things she does for me . . . you wouldn't believe it. It brings tears to my eyes. No, don't keep me. I shall be a decent man and go. I must go, honestly I must.'

'Let him go. Why keep him?' Chichikov said to Nozdrev in a low voice.

'Why keep him indeed?' said Nozdrev. 'For the life of me I hate these softies!' But aloud he said: 'The devil take you, go away and spoon, you sap!'

'Now, don't you call me a sap,' the brother-in-law replied. 'I owe my life to her. She is such a nice and dutiful wife, and she is so sweet to me . . . it brings tears to my eyes. She will ask me what I saw at the fair and I must tell her, she's such a darling.'

'Well, go then and tell her a pack of lies! Here's your cap.'

'No, you really mustn't talk of her like that. If I may say so, you offend me, she's such a darling.'

'Well then, get out and go to her quickly.'

'Yes, brother, I shall go. You must excuse me for not staying. I'd love to stay but I can't.' The brother-in-law was a long time making his excuses and hardly noticed that he was already in his carriage, out of the gates and driving through the open fields. It must be supposed that his wife heard but few details of the fair.

'What a pig!' Nozdrev exclaimed as he stood by the window watching the departing carriage. 'There he goes rolling along! His trace-horse is not a bad one. I've been wanting to snaffle it for some time. But there is no way of coming to an understanding with him. He's a sap, a simple sap!'

They went back to the room. Porphyry brought candles and Chichikov noticed that Nozdrev was holding a pack of cards which had appeared as if by magic.

'Well now,' said Nozdrev, pressing the sides of the pack with his fingers and making it bend so that the wrapper cracked and fell apart. 'Well, to pass the time I shall put three hundred roubles in the bank.'

But Chichikov pretended not to hear and, as if he had just remembered something, exclaimed: 'Ah, before I forget, I have a favour to ask you.'

'What favour?'

'You must first promise to oblige.'

'But what is it?'

'You must promise first!'

'If you like.'

'On your word?'

'On my word of honour.'

'Now this is what I should like to ask you. You probably have a lot of peasants who died but are still on the census register.'

'Why, of course. What about them?'

'Will you transfer them to me, in my name.'

'Why do you want them?'

'Oh, I need them.'

'What for?'

'Oh, I just need them. . . . That's my affair. In short, I need them.'

'You have something up your sleeve, I can see. Tell me what it is.'

'I've nothing up my sleeve. I couldn't have over such a trifle.'

'Why do you want them then?'

'How inquisitive you are! You'd like to touch and feel any old rag, and to smell it into the bargain!'

'And why don't you want to tell me?'

'And what would it profit you to know? It's just a fancy of mine.'

'Well then, I shan't oblige until you tell me!'

'That's not very fair of you. You gave me your word and now you are backing out.'

'As you like, but I shan't oblige until you tell me.'

'What should I tell him?' Chichikov thought to himself, and, after reflecting for a moment, he declared that he needed the dead souls in order to acquire a more solid standing in society, and, as he had no large estates, in the meantime he could do with a few souls. . . .

'You're lying, lying!' said Nozdrev without letting him finish. 'You're lying!'

Chichikov realized that he had not been very clever and that his pretext was a fairly weak one.

'Well, let me tell you straight out,' he said, pulling himself together. 'Only you must not tell anyone. I have decided to get married. But I must tell you that my fiancée's father and mother are very ambitious folk. That's the rub. I'm not too pleased at getting entangled. They insist that the bridegroom have at least three hundred souls and I am some one hundred and fifty short. . . .'

'You're lying, lying!' Nozdrev shouted again.

'Now this time,' said Chichikov, 'I have not lied even that much,' and he pointed with his thumb to the top of his little finger.

'I'll stake my head that you are lying!'

'Now you are being offensive! What am I indeed! Why must I be lying?'

'But I know you very well. You're a great rascal, if I may say so in a friendly way! If I were your chief, I'd have you hanged on the first tree.'

Chichikov took offence at this remark. He disliked any expression savouring of coarseness or affecting his dignity. He would not even allow any expressions of familiarity towards him unless they came from a personage of so exalted a rank that he could not resent them. So now he was quite seriously offended.

'Honest to God, I'd have you hanged,' Nozdrev repeated. 'I am telling you that quite openly, not in order to offend you but just in a friendly sort of way.'

'There is a limit to everything,' said Chichikov with dignity. 'If you want to show off in this way, then do it in a barracks.' But as an afterthought, he added: 'If you don't want to make a present of them to me, sell them then.'

'Sell them! But I know you. You're a rogue. You wouldn't give much for them?'

'You're a fine fellow too! Just look at you! Are they made of diamonds or what?'

'There you are. I knew you'd say that.'

'Really! You are behaving like a Jew! You should make a present of them to me.'

'Now listen, to prove that I am not one of your bloodsuckers, I shall not charge you anything for them. If you buy a stallion from me, I shall give you them for nothing.'

'But, pray, what do I need with a stallion?' said Chichikov, genuinely astonished at this offer.

'Why don't you? I paid ten thousand for the stallion and I am offering him to you for four thousand.'

'But why do I need a stallion? I don't keep a stud farm.'

'But listen, you don't understand. I'll only take three thousand from you now, and you can pay the other thousand later.'

'But I don't need the stallion, bless him!'

'Well then, buy the chestnut mare.'

'I don't need a mare either.'

'For the mare and the grey horse you saw in the stable I shall take only two thousand from you.'

'But I don't want any horses.'

'You can sell them. At the first fair they will give you three times as much.'

'You had better sell them yourself if you are convinced that you will make three times as much on them.'

'I know that I shall make a profit, but I should like you to make some too.'

Chichikov thanked him for his kind intention and declined to have anything to do either with the grey horse or the chestnut mare.

'Well then, buy a few dogs. I'll sell you a couple of dogs that will make your flesh creep! With great whiskers and a coat as stiff as a brush. You couldn't imagine how barrel-shaped their ribs are, and their paws are like velvet, they don't leave a trace.'

'What do I want with dogs? I don't hunt.'

'But I should like you to have dogs. Listen, if you don't want dogs, then buy my hurdy-gurdy, a wonderful hurdy-gurdy. It cost me a thousand and a half, honestly it did. I shall let you have it for nine hundred.'

'But what do I need with a hurdy-gurdy? I am not a German to go dragging along the road with it, hat in hand!'

'But it's not that kind of hurdy-gurdy. It's an organ; just have a look at it: it's all mahogany. I'll show it to you again!' Hereupon, catching hold of Chichikov by the hand, Nozdrev started to pull him towards the study; and however much Chichikov dug his heels in or assured him that he remembered what it was like, he was obliged to hear once more how Marlborough went to the wars.

'If you don't want to pay cash for it,' said Nozdrev, 'this is what we shall do. Now listen to me. I shall give you the hurdy-gurdy and as many dead souls as I can find, but you will give me in exchange your chaise and three hundred roubles thrown in.'

'That's a fine deal! And how do you think I shall travel?'

'I shall give you another chaise. Come along to the shed and I'll show it to you! You will only have to get it painted and it will be a wonderful chaise.'

'Phew! He's possessed!' Chichikov thought, deciding to

dispense at any cost with all these chaises, hurdy-gurdies, and dogs of various breeds with their unimaginable barrel-shaped ribs and velvety paws.

'Well now, take them all, the chaise, the hurdy-gurdy and the dead souls!'

'I don't want them!' Chichikov said once more.

'Why don't you want them?'

'Because I don't, and that's that.'

'Now what sort of fellow are you! I see that one simply can't get together with you as friend or comrade. . . . One can see a mile off that you are a dual personality!'

'Do you take me for a fool? Now just think it over yourself. Why should I acquire anything I don't need?'

'That's no argument, if you please. Now I know you inside out. You're a rogue, that's all. But listen, if you like we'll play it out in cards. I'll stake all the dead souls and the hurdy-gurdy too.'

'To stake it all on cards means submitting to chance,' Chichikov answered, but he could not help glancing at the cards Nozdrev was holding. It looked as though both packs had been tampered with and the markings on them roused his suspicions.

'Why is it a question of chance?' Nozdrev asked. 'There's no chance about it! If you only have luck on your side, you will win the very devil. There it goes! There's luck!' he exclaimed as he began to deal in the hope of provoking Chichikov. 'There's luck! There's luck! Simply bursting with it! There's that damned nine on which I've staked all! I had a feeling it would betray me and I said to myself as I closed my eyes: "Betray me and be damned."' As Nozdrev was saying this Porphyry brought in a bottle. But Chichikov resolutely declined either to play or to drink.

'Why don't you want to play?' Nozdrev asked.

'I don't feel like it. And to tell you the truth, I am no great lover of cards.'

'Why aren't you?'

Chichikov merely shrugged his shoulders and said: 'Because I'm not.'

'You're no good!'

'That can't be helped. God made me so.'

'You're just a sap! I used to think that you were a decent enough chap, but you have no manners. One simply can't talk to you as to a friend . . . there is no frankness or sincerity about you! You are just like Sobakievich, a regular knave!'

'But why are you abusing me? Is it my fault that I do not play? If you are so put out over a trifle, sell me just the souls and nothing else.'

'The devil's horns, that's all you'll get! I would have let you take them for nothing, but now you shan't have them at all! I wouldn't give them to you for three kingdoms. You're a sharper, a filthy chimney-sweep! From now on I do not wish to have anything more to do with you. Porphyry, go and tell the stable-boy to stop giving his horses oats. Hay is good enough for them!'

This conclusion was utterly unexpected.

'I wish I had never seen you,' Nozdrev added.

However, in spite of this tiff, the host and his guest had supper together, but this time there were none of those exotic drinks on the table. A bottle of Cyprian wine was all they had, and it was very like vinegar. After dinner Nozdrev conducted Chichikov to a room where a bed had been prepared for him and said: 'There's your bed, I don't want even to say good-night to you!'

After Nozdrev had left him, Chichikov was in a disagreeable frame of mind. He blamed and scolded himself inwardly for having come here and wasted his time. But he blamed himself even more for having broached the affair to Nozdrev and for having acted as rashly as a child might have done or a fool, for the affair was not the sort that could be safely confided to a man like that. . . . Nozdrev was a good-for-nothing, who might tell a pack of lies, embroider on the theme, and spread heaven knows what rumour or slander. . . . He had made a mistake, a bad mistake. 'I'm simply an idiot,' he said to himself. His sleep was troubled. Some tiny but persistent insects kept biting him most painfully and he was obliged to scratch himself violently with all his fingers on the affected spots, saying as he did so: 'The devil take you and Nozdrev as well!' He woke up early. The first thing he did on putting on his dressing-gown and boots was to cross the yard, call in at the stables, and order Selifan to get the chaise ready at once. On his way back he ran into Nozdrev, who was also in a dressing-gown and with a pipe between his teeth.

Nozdrev greeted him in a friendly way and enquired how he had slept.

'Not too well,' Chichikov replied drily.

'As for me,' said Nozdrev, 'I've been seeing such horrors that it would be too depressing to tell you, and this morning my mouth feels as if a squadron of cavalry had spent the night there. Just imagine, I dreamt that I had been given a thrashing. Oi, oi! And just imagine who it was? You'll never guess. It was staff-captain Potzeluyev and Kuvshinikov.'

'Yes,' thought Chichinov to himself. 'It's a pity they don't really give you a drubbing.'

'They did indeed! and quite painful it was too! And when I wakened, the devil take me if I hadn't really got an itch. Those witches of fleas no doubt. Well, go and get dressed now, I'll come along in a minute. I must just go and give that man of mine a talking to.'

Chichikov retired to his room to wash and dress himself. When he emerged into the dining-room a tea service and a bottle of rum were already set out on the table. The room still bore traces of yesterday's dinner and supper: it did not seem as if it had been swept at all. The floor was littered with crumbs and there was even tobacco ash on the tablecloth. The master of the house was not long in making his appearance and under his dressing-gown he wore nothing but a bare and bearded chest. Holding his chibouk in one hand and sipping his tea, he was a good subject for any painter who hated pomaded gentlemen or those who are all curled as on hairdressers' signboards or those again who have their hair cut slickly.

'Well, what do you think?' asked Nozdrev after a moment's silence. 'Shall we play for the souls?'

'I have already told you that I am not going to play. To buy them is another matter. I'm quite willing to buy them.'

'I don't want to sell them. It wouldn't be a friendly

act. I don't intend to skin money off any damn thing.
To win at cards that's another matter. Let's just have one
game!'

'I told you I won't.'

'What about bartering them then?'

'I don't want to.'

'Look here then, let us play a game of draughts. If you
win, you can have them all. I have a lot of serfs who need
deleting from the register. Hey, Porphyry, bring along
the draughtsboard!'

'You needn't trouble, I refuse to play.'

'But this is not cards. There is no question of chance
or deception here. I even go so far as to warn you
that I can't play at all. Perhaps you will give me a
start?'

'Why shouldn't I have a try?' Chichikov thought to
himself. 'I used to be a good hand at draughts, and it's
hard to get up to any tricks in this game.'

'As you like, so be it. I shall play.'

'You'll stake a hundred roubles against the souls!'

'Why a hundred? Fifty's enough!'

'That's not much of a stake. I had better throw in a
puppy of sorts or a gold seal for a watch-chain.'

'By all means!' said Chichikov.

'What start will you give me?' Nozdrev asked.

'And why should I do that? Certainly not.'

'You must give me two moves at least.'

'I shan't do anything of the sort. I am bad at the game
myself.'

'We all know how badly you play!' Nozdrev sneered
as he moved a piece.

'It's ages since I've handled draughts!'[5] said Chichikov
as he also moved a piece.

'We all know how badly you play!' Nozdrev repeated
as he moved the piece and at the same time pushed forward another with the edge of his sleeve.

'It's ages since I've handled. . . . Hey, hey, what's this
you're up to? Put it back!' cried Chichikov.

'What?'

5. The game usually called "checkers" in the United States.

'Why that piece,' Chichikov said; and at the same time caught sight of another one right under his nose on the point of being converted into a queen. God alone knows where it had sprung from. 'No,' said Chichikov getting up, 'one can't play with you. That's not the way to play, with three pieces at once!'

'Why with three? That was a mistake. One was moved accidentally, I shall put it back.'

'And where did the other one come from?'

'Which other one?'

'The one that's creeping up to be a queen.'

'Well, well, don't you remember?'

'No, I don't. I counted all the moves and I don't remember it at all. You've only just moved it. Its place is over there.'

'Why should it be there?' said Nozdrev, blushing. 'You're imaginative, that's what you are!'

'You're the imaginative one, but you're not very successful at it.'

'Whom do you take me for?' Nozdrev asked. 'You don't imply that I would stoop to cheating?'

'I don't take you for anyone, but from now on I shall never play with you.'

'No, you can't refuse,' shouted Nozdrev, getting heated. 'The game is begun!'

'I have the right to refuse because you are not playing properly, not like an honest man.'

'No, you are lying. You can't say that!'

'No, you are lying yourself.'

'I did not cheat and you can't refuse to go on. You must finish the game!'

'You can't force me to do so,' replied Chichikov coldly and, going up to the draughtboard, he swept all the pieces in a heap.

Nozdrev flared and advanced upon Chichikov, forcing him to retreat a couple of paces.

'I shall force you to play! It doesn't matter your having mixed up the pieces. I remember all the moves. We shall put them back as they were.'

'No, I have finished. I shall not play with you.'

'So you don't want to play with me?'

'You know yourself that it is impossible to play with you.'

'But come and tell me now straight: you don't want to play?' Nozdrev was saying as he continued to advance upon Chichikov.

'No, I don't!' Chichikov declared and, just to be on the safe side, he raised both his hands nearer to his face, for the situation was fast getting out of hand. This precaution was timely, for Nozdrev took a swing with his arm. . . . One of our hero's plump and pleasing cheeks might well have been smirched with indelible dishonour, but luckily he warded off the blow, seized Nozdrev firmly by the wrists and held him tightly.

'Porphyry! Pavlushka!' Nozdrev bawled in a rage as he struggled to free himself.

On hearing him shout, Chichikov, in order to avoid making the domestics witnesses of this charming scene, and realizing also that there was no sense in holding him any longer, let go his wrists. At that moment Porphyry entered, followed by Pavlushka, a sturdy lad, with whom it would have been unprofitable to try his strength.

'So you refuse to finish the game?' said Nozdrev. 'Answer me straight!'

'It is impossible to finish the game,' said Chichikov, casting a glance at the window. Through it he saw his chaise, which was ready for the journey, and Selifan who seemed to be waiting for a summons in order to drive up to the porch, but there was no way of escaping from the room. The doorway was blocked by the two hefty fools of serfs.

'So you don't want to finish the game?' Nozdrev repeated, his face burning as if on fire.

'I would have if you had played like an honest and decent person. But as it is, I cannot.'

'So you cannot, you scoundrel! You can't when you see you are losing! Go on, give it to him!' he yelled, beside himself, to Porphyry and Pavlushka and, as he did so, he seized hold of his cherrywood chibouk. Chichikov turned as pale as a sheet. He tried to say something but felt his lips moving without a sound.

'Give it to him!' Nozdrev bellowed, dashing forward
with his cherrywood chibouk, all flushed and perspiring
as if he were storming an unassailable fortress. 'Give it to
him!' he shouted in a voice that might have been used by
some desperately brave lieutenant as he yelled, 'Forward,
lads!' when leading a detachment of soldiers to the
assault—a lieutenant already so well known for his reck-
lessness that orders had to be given to hold him back from
the fray. But the lieutenant is already carried away by
martial ardour, his head is in a swirl, the image of
Suvorov haunts him and he presses on to great deeds.
'Forward, lads!' he cries, dashing forward and paying no
heed to the thought that he may be acting contrary to the
general plan of attack, that countless rifles may be levelled
at him from the unassailable and soaring battlements of
the fortress, that his impotent detachment of soldiers may
be blown sky-high, and that the bullet is already speeding
which will shut his strident mouth. But if Nozdrev looked
like a desperately brave and rash lieutenant storming a
fortress, then the fortress he was attacking did not at all
look unassailable. On the contrary, the fortress was so
frightened that it had cold feet. The serfs had already
torn away the chair with which he was hoping to defend
himself and, with eyes half-closed, more dead than alive,
he was preparing to take the brunt of Nozdrev's Cir-
cassian chibouk, and heaven alone knows what would
have happened to him, if the fates had not decided to
spare the ribs, shoulders and all the other parts of our
well-bred hero. But of a sudden the sound of tinkling bells
rang out, a trap rolled up to the door, and the deep
snorting and laboured breathing of a steaming *troika*
could be heard. Involuntarily they all glanced out of
the window: a man with moustaches and wearing a
jacket of half-military cut was stepping out of the trap.
After making a few enquiries in the hall he at once
entered the room before Chichikov had time to recover
from his fright and the pitiable condition to which he had
been reduced.

'May I enquire which of you is Mr. Nozdrev?' the
stranger said, staring with some perplexity first at Nozdrev, who was standing with the chibouk in his hand, and

then at Chichikov, who had barely begun to pull himself together.

'May I enquire first of all whom I have the honour of addressing?' asked Nozdrev as he took a few steps towards him.

'I am a captain of the police.'

'And what can I do for you?'

'I have come to inform you that you are under arrest pending your trial.'

'Rubbish! What's the charge?' said Nozdrev.

'You were mixed up in an affair which resulted in landowner Maximov being birched while he was drunk.'

'That's a lie! I have never seen landowner Maximov.'

'My dear sir! I should like you to know that I am an officer. You may say such things to your servants but not to me!'

Without waiting to hear what Nozdrev would reply to that, Chichikov promptly grabbed his hat and, slipping behind the captain's back, made his way to the front door, climbed into his chaise, and ordered Selifan to drive for all he was worth.

CHAPTER V

OUR hero had had the fright of his life. Though the chaise was rolling along at top speed and Nozdrev's village had long disappeared from sight behind the fields, the sloping ground and the hillocks, he still kept looking back in trepidation as if he were expecting to be overtaken. He was breathing heavily and when he tried to lay his hand on his heart, he felt it fluttering like a quail in a cage. 'Well, he's made me sweat! What a fellow!' Hereupon he wished Nozdrev all the ills he could think of; nor did he stint a few bad words. What else do you expect? He was a Russian and in a rage too. Besides, it was no joking matter. 'Whatever you may say,' he told himself, 'if the police-captain had not turned up, I might never have seen the light of day again! I should have burst like a bubble in the water without leaving a trace, with no descendants or future children to whom I might have bequeathed a fortune and honour!' Our hero was very concerned about his descendants.

'He was a bad 'un, that gent!' Selifan was thinking to himself. 'I haven't seen the like of him yet. I'd spit on him for that! Better not feed a man than leave the horses without fodder, for a horse likes his oats. That's his victuals: just as we have our sustenance, so oats are his victuals.'

The horses likewise seemed to entertain a poor opinion of Nozdrev: not only the bay and Assessor but even the dapple-grey seemed out of spirits. Though he always got the worst of the oats and Selifan never filled the manger without first exclaiming, 'Ah, you rogue!' still they were oats and not simply hay; he chewed them with satisfaction and often thrust his muzzle into his companions' mangers, to check up on the quality of their sustenance, especially when Selifan was out of the stable; but on this occasion there had only been hay—it was too bad! Everyone had a grouse.

But soon they were interrupted in their expressions of annoyance in a sudden and quite unexpected way. All of them, not excluding the coachman, roused themselves and grasped the situation only when a carriage drawn by six horses was right upon them and almost over their heads. The cries of the ladies seated in the carriage, the abuse and the threats of the other coachman resounded: 'Ah, you swindler, didn't I shout to you? Turn right, you crow, turn right! Are you drunk, or what?' Selifan felt a twinge of conscience, but as a Russian dislikes having to acknowledge his guilt in front of others, he at once snapped back with an air of dignity: 'And why were you going so fast? Did you leave your eyes pawned in a tavern or what?' When he had got that off his chest, he began to back the horses so as to get them clear of their entanglement in an alien harness but he met with little success. With curiosity the dapple-grey was sniffing at his new-found friends who now closed him in on either side. Meanwhile the ladies in the carriage gazed at all this with an expression of alarm on their faces. One was an old lady, the other a young girl of sixteen, with golden hair ravishingly and cunningly brushed back over her small head. The pretty oval of her face showed up roundly like a newly laid egg and had all the transparent whiteness of one when, all fresh and still warm, it is held up to the light by a prying housekeeper's swarthy hand and the rays of the beaming sun penetrate it: her delicate ears also glowed transparently, suffused by the warm transpiercing light. Moreover, the alarm imprinted on her parted lips, the tears in her eyes, were so captivating that our hero stared at her for some minutes without paying any attention to the mess in which the coachmen and horses were involved. 'Get back there, you Nizhny-Novgorod crow!' the other coachman was shouting. Selifan tugged at the reins, the other did the same, the horses backed slightly and then got entangled in the traces again. In this situation the dapple-grey showed such pleasure in his new acquaintance, that he would do nothing to get himself out of this fix into which the fates had unexpectedly thrust him and, putting his muzzle on the neck of his new friend, he seemed to be whispering something in his very ear, some frightful nonsense no doubt, because it made the new-comer twitch his ears.

The peasants from a village, which was fortunately nearby, had already hastily arrived on the scene of this commotion. Since a spectacle of this sort was a real godsend to a peasant, the equivalent of a newspaper or club to a German, there was a great crowd of them soon gathered near the carriage, and only the old women and little children were left in the village. The horses were unharnessed; the dapple-grey was given a few pushes on the muzzle and made to back; in short, the horses were separated and led apart. But whether it was out of pique at being parted from their friends or simply from obstinacy, the other horses would not budge, however much the coachman might whip them, and they stood there as if rooted to the ground. The interest and excitement of the peasants reached an incredible pitch. They interrupted each other with their counsels: 'Andriushka, you go and look after the trace-horse, the one on the right, while uncle Mityai mounts the shaft-horse! Come, get on it, uncle Mityai!' Uncle Mityai, a lean and long-legged peasant with a red beard, scrambled up on the shaft-horse and had all the appearance of a village belfry or, better still, of a crane such as is employed to draw water from a well. The coachman plied his whip but to no purpose; uncle Mityai was no help at all. 'Stop, stop,' the peasants kept shouting. 'You get on the trace-horse, uncle Mityai, and let uncle Minyai mount the shaft-horse!' Uncle Minyai, a broad-shouldered peasant with a beard as black as pitch and a belly that looked like a giant samovar in which honey posset is brewed for a whole marketful of frozen folk, willingly straddled the shaft-horse, which almost sank to the ground under his weight. 'Now they'll go!' yelled the peasants. 'Go on, give it to him, give it to him! Give that one, the bay, a crack with the whip! Why's he wriggling like a spent mosquito?' But when they perceived that no progress was being made, that no spurring on did any good, then uncle Mityai and uncle Minyai both mounted the shaft-horse while Andriushka got on the trace-horse. At last, his patience exhausted, the coachman chased away both uncle Minyai and uncle Mityai, and it was just as well that he did so, for the horses were now giving off as much steam as if they had covered a stage without drawing breath. He gave them a minute to recover themselves and then of their own accord they set off.

While all this was going on, Chichikov was staring very closely at the young lady. He made several attempts to start a conversation with her but somehow it did not catch on. But now the ladies drove off, the pretty head with the fine features, and the slender waist, vanished like some vision, and all that was left was the highway, the chaise, the familiar *troika*, Selifan, Chichikov, and the bare expanse of the fields around them. In every walk of life, whether among the coarse, rough and ragged, untidily mouldering ranks of the lower orders, or among the uniformly frigid and tediously tidy higher orders—in every condition of life a man is likely to behold at least once in his life a vision unlike anything he has ever seen before, which for once rouses in him feelings entirely unlike those he is destined to experience all the rest of his days. At times a gay and radiant joy irradiates every life however much it may be woven of the sorrows common to mankind, just as sometimes a glittering carriage with golden harness, picturesque horses and the flashing shimmer of glass, will unexpectedly rush through some wretched out-of-the-way village, which had till then seen only country carts; and for a long time afterwards the peasants will stand about with gaping mouths and un-covered heads, though the wonderful carriage has long since swept by and vanished from sight. In the same way, this fair-haired girl had also most unexpectedly appeared in our narrative and vanished again. Had some youth of twenty been there in Chichikov's place, and had he been a hussar, a student, or simply a young man about to embark on a career—Heavens, what feelings would not have awakened, stirred and spoken in his heart! For a long time he would have stood there on the same spot, all his senses numbed, with his eyes fixed vacantly into space, oblivious of the road, the chidings in store for him, the reproofs for his delay, oblivious of himself, his duty, the world and everything in it.

But our hero was already middle-aged and of cautious, tempered character. He also grew thoughtful and re-flected, but his pondering was more positive, less irrespon-sible, and to some extent even well founded. 'A goodly wench,' he said, opening his snuff-box and taking a pinch of snuff. 'But what is her chief virtue? It lies in the fact, as it seems, that she has just come out of some boarding-school or institute, that there is nothing feminine about her, nothing of what makes all women so repulsive. At present she is like a child, everything about her is simple, she says what comes into her head, laughs when she feels like it. She might be moulded in any way—either into a miraculous or a worthless person. Most likely the latter! Only wait till the mammas and aunties take her in hand. Within a year they will fill her with so many feminine wiles that her own father would not recognize her. Hence will spring conceit and affectation; she will begin to twist and turn within a groove of injunctions; she will rack her brains and puzzle over whom she ought to address, in what way and for how long, and whom she may deign to look at; every minute of the day she will be afraid of saying more than she ought; she will finally get so involved that she will turn into an inveterate liar and become the devil knows what!' At this juncture Chichikov paused for a while before adding: 'It would be interesting to know who she is. And what her father is. A rich landowner of respectable character or simply a well-intentioned man with some capital acquired in the service? Now supposing this girl had a dowry of some two hundred thousand, she might make a very tasty morsel. She might, so to speak, make the right man very happy.' The two hundred thousand suggested such an attractive picture to his imagination that he began inwardly to regret that, during the incident with the carriage, he had not enquired of the postilion or coachman the names of these travellers.

Soon, however, his thoughts were distracted at the sight of Sobakievich's village and concentrated again on his usual theme. The village impressed him as being a fairly large one; to the left and right of it, like two wings, one of darker and the other of lighter hue, lay two forests, one of birch and the other of pine; in the middle was a wooden house with a mezzanine, a red roof and dark grey or, more correctly, natural-coloured walls, the sort of house that is usually built in Russia for military settlers or German colonists. It was obvious that, while building it, the architect had constantly to take into account the tastes of the owner. The architect was a pedant and strove for symmetry, while the owner thought only of convenience and, evidently for this reason, had boarded up all the windows at one side, and in their place had a small one cut out, very likely to illumine a dark storeroom. The pediment likewise was not quite in the centre despite the architect's striving to make it so, for the owner had ordered one of the side columns to be removed with the result that only three columns remained instead of the intended four. The yard was enclosed by a sturdy and disproportionately thick wooden fence. It seemed as if the landowner was much concerned about solidity. The stable, sheds and kitchens were constructed of thick and solid beams to withstand many centuries. The peasants' huts were also wonderfully well built: the walls were plain, without fretwork or other fancies, but everything was solidly and properly fashioned. Even the well was made of that strong oak which is usually reserved for windmills and ships. In short, everything he saw was stable and substantial in a forceful and clumsy style.

As he drove up to the porch, he noticed two faces which were peeping out of the window almost simultaneously: one was a woman's, long and narrow as a cucumber, crowned with a cap; the other a man's, broad and round as the Moldavian pumpkins, which go by the name of *gorlyanki* from which Russians make balalaikas—light two-stringed balalaikas, the boast and joy of some smart twenty-year-old lad, saucy-eyed and jaunty, winking an eye and whistling at the white-breasted and white-throated maidens who gather round to listen to his soft-stringed twanging. The two faces peeped out and vanished as quickly. A lackey in a grey jacket with a light-blue stand-up collar came out on the steps and conducted Chichikov into the hall where the master of the house was already expecting him. On seeing his visitor, he said abruptly, 'Please come in,' and led him inside.

As Chichikov took a sidelong glance at Sobakievich, the latter seemed to him on this occasion to be very like a medium-sized bear. To complete the resemblance he was wearing a dress-coat of an entirely bearish hue with long sleeves, his trousers were long too, he lurched from side to side as he walked, and he was continually treading on other people's feet. His face had a tempered and glowing look such as is to be seen on a copper penny. We know there are many such faces in the world to whose symmetry nature has paid little heed, disdaining the use of any such fine tools as files or gimlets, and the like, having simply gone about it straight from the shoulder: one swing of the axe and the nose would appear, another and the lips, one turn of the drill and the eyes would emerge, and so, without any finish, nature will cast this product out into the world: 'He lives!' Sobakievich had just such a rugged and amazingly fashioned countenance: he held it lowered rather than erect, never turning his head at all and, by virtue of this rigidity, rarely looked at anyone he was addressing but invariably stared either at the corner of the stove or at the door. As they were entering the dining-room, Chichikov glanced at him again from under his brows: he was a bear, there was no getting away from it, a bear! To make this strange resemblance even more convincing, he was called Mikhail Semyonovich.[6] Since he was aware of Sobakievich's habit of treading on other people's feet, Chichikov moved his own cautiously and gave him the right of way. The master of the house seemed to be aware of this sin and at once asked him, 'Have I inconvenienced you?' But Chichikov thanked him and assured him that so far he had suffered no inconveniences.

When they were in the drawing-room Sobakievich pointed to the armchairs and again said, 'Please!' As he sat down, Chichikov glanced at the walls and the pictures hanging on them. They were all of heroes, Greek war-leaders portrayed full length, Mavrocordato in red trousers and uniform, with spectacles on his nose, Miaoulis and Kanaris.[7] All these heroes had such thick calves and incredible moustaches that they made one shudder. Among these mighty Greeks, for some unknown reason, hung a portrait of Bagration,[8] a lean and gaunt figure, with tiny flags and cannons below, in the narrowest of frames. Next to him was the Greek heroine, Bobelina,[9] one of whose legs seemed to be larger than the whole body of the sort of dandy that crowds our drawing-rooms nowadays. Since he was strong and healthy himself, it looked

6. A Russian folk name for a bear.
7. Mavrocordato (1791–1835), the chief leader of the Greek revolt against the Turks; Andreas-Vokos Miaoulis (1768–1835), a Greek admiral in the war against the Turks; Constantine Kanaris (1790–1877), a Greek statesman who fought against

the Turks.
8. Prince Peter Bagration (1765–1812), a Georgian general who fought in the war against Napoleon.
9. An Albanian woman who equipped three naval ships at her own expense and fought alongside the Greeks against the Turks; murdered in 1825.

as though the master of the house intended to have his room adorned with representations of people equally strong and healthy. A cage hung by the window, near Bobelina, and out of it peeped a thrush of a dark hue speckled with white; he also was very like Sobakievich. The host and his guest had barely time to remain silent for two minutes when the drawing-room door opened and in came the lady of the house, who was very tall and wore a cap adorned with home-dyed ribbons. She was dignified in her bearing and held her head as erect as a palm-tree.

'This is my Feodolya Ivanovna,' said Sobakievich.

Chichikov went up to kiss Feodolya Ivanovna's hand, which she almost pushed into his mouth. As she did so, he had the opportunity to note that her hands had been washed in cucumber brine.

'My sweet, may I present to you Pavel Ivanovich Chichikov,' Sobakievich continued. 'I had the honour of making his acquaintance at the governor's and the post-master's.'

Feodolya Ivanovna begged him to take a seat, saying also 'Please!' and making a motion with her head like that of an actress playing the role of a queen. Then she sat down on the sofa, pulled a merino shawl over herself and settled back into a state of perfect immobility.

Chichikov raised his eyes again and once more saw Kanaris with his thick calves and endless moustaches, Bobelina and the caged thrush.

For almost a full five minutes they all remained silent; the only sound was a knocking which came from the thrush as he pecked the wooden bottom of the cage while angling for bits of grain. Once again Chichikov glanced round the room and all it contained—everything was solidly in its place, everything looked extremely clumsy and bore a strange resemblance to the master of the house.

In a corner of the drawing-room stood a pot-bellied walnut bureau on four very awkward legs looking like the very image of a bear. The table, the armchairs, the chairs, all these were as heavy and restless in appearance as they could be; in short, every object, every chair, seemed to be saying, 'I am a Sobakievich also!' or 'I am very like Sobakievich!'

'We were talking about you last Thursday at the president's, at Ivan Grigoryevich's,' said Chichikov at last, realizing that no one was predisposed to start the conversation. 'We spent a very pleasant evening there.'

'Yes, I was not at the president's that day,' answered Sobakievich.

'What a fine man he is!'

'Whom do you mean?' asked Sobakievich, staring at the corner of the stove.

'The president.'

'Well, maybe, he seems so to you. He's a freemason[1] but you wouldn't find a bigger fool anywhere.'

Chichikov was slightly puzzled by this somewhat curt definition, but regaining his composure he went on: 'Of course, every man has his weaknesses, but take the governor, for example, he's a delightful person!'

'The governor a delightful person?'

'Yes, isn't he?'

'He's the biggest bandit of them all!'

'What? The governor a bandit?' exclaimed Chichikov, who completely failed to understand how the governor could qualify to be a bandit. 'I confess that I would never have suspected it,' he continued. 'But permit me to observe that his behaviour completely contradicts your assumption; on the contrary, there is a great deal of kindness in him.' Hereupon, by way of proof, he referred to the purses which the governor had embroidered with his own hands and alluded in laudatory terms to the amiable expression of his face.

'He has the face of a bandit!' said Sobakievich. 'Give him a knife and let him loose on the highway, he'd cut your throat, he'd do it for a few coppers! He and the vice-governor—a fine pair both of them, Gog and Magog,[2] that's what they are.'

1. Freemasons were members of a secret, religio-moral, often progressive or radical international organization, mainly consisting of prominent persons and intellectuals.

2. "Gog": a cruel and evil biblical prince; "Magog": the name of his nation—proverbial for terror-inspiring entities.

'I can see that he's not on good terms with them,' thought Chichikov to himself. 'I'll try talking to him about the chief of police. I believe they are friends.' 'As for myself,' he said, 'I confess that I like the chief of police best of all. His is a straightforward and open character; one can see from his face that he is a warm-hearted man.'

'A rogue!' replied Sobakievich coolly. 'He'd betray and deceive you, and then have dinner at your expense! I know them all: they are all rogues, the whole town is like that. One rogue on top of another, all out to catch rogues. They're all Judases. The prosecutor is the only decent man among them; and to tell the truth, even he is a swine.'

After these appreciative though somewhat brief biographies, Chichikov realized that there was no point in mentioning any of the other officials, and then he remembered that Sobakievich did not like speaking well of anyone.

'Well, my sweet, shall we go and dine?' said Madame Sobakievich to her husband.

'Please!' said Sobakievich. Whereupon, going up to the table which was laid with *zakouski*,[3] the host and his guest drank their glasses of vodka as was fitting, and tasted the *zakouski* as was the custom throughout the length and breadth of Russia in town and village alike, that is to say, they first sampled all those salted and other stimulating heaven-sent appetizers, and then passed on to the dining-room; the lady of the house bore ahead of them like a paddling goose. A small table was laid for four. The fourth place was very soon taken by a person—it is difficult to determine what she was exactly, a married lady or a spinster, a relative or a housekeeper, or simply someone living in the house—without a cap, aged about thirty, wearing a bright scarf. In the world there are some persons who exist not as objects but as incidental specks or spots *on* an object. They always sit in one place, hold their heads in the same way, so that one is almost ready to accept them as pieces of furniture and to imagine that from birth their lips had uttered no word; but somewhere in the maid's quarters or in the pantry it will be quite a different story!

3. Russian for "snacks."

'The cabbage soup is very good to-day, my sweet!' said Sobakievich, swallowing a spoonful of it and helping himself to a huge portion of *nyanya*, a well-known dish which is served with cabbage soup and is made up of sheep's stomach, stuffed with buckwheat, brains and sheep's trotters. 'You wouldn't get a *nyanya* like this in town,' he continued, turning to Chichikov, 'there you'd be served with the devil knows what!'

'The governor's table is not at all bad,' said Chichikov.

'But do you know what goes to make it? You wouldn't eat any of it, if you did.'

'I don't know what it's made of, I can't judge, but the pork cutlets and the boiled fish were excellent.'

'You only imagined that. I know what they buy on the market. That scoundrel of a cook they have, the one who learnt from a Frenchman, he'd buy a cat, skin it and then serve it up in place of a hare.'

'Fie, what disagreeable things you do say,' said Madame Sobakievich.

'I can't help it, my sweet. That's the way they go about things. I'm not to blame for that, am I? All the odd bits that our Akulka throws away, if I may say so with your permission, into the refuse heap, they put into their soup! Yes, into their soup! that's where it goes!'

'You're always saying things like that at table,' Madame Sobakievich again protested.

'You can't accuse me of such behaviour, my dear,' said Sobakievich. 'But I tell you straight out that I refuse to eat filth. I wouldn't touch a frog even if you crust it over with sugar, and I won't touch oysters either; I know what an oyster is. Now take the mutton for example,' he went on, turning to Chichikov. 'Why, it's a saddle of mutton with buckwheat! It's no fricassée such as they make up in gentlemen's kitchens out of mutton which has been lying about on a market stall for at least four days! It's these German doctors and Frenchmen who have invented all that; I'd have them strung up, the whole lot of them! The diet they have invented, a hunger-cure, that's what it is! They imagine that because they are thin-blooded, they can manage a Russian stomach! No, that's no good, it's pure fabrication, it's all . . .' At this point

Sobakievich even shook his head angrily. 'They chatter away about enlightenment, enlightenment, and their enlightenment is just—a fig! I'd have used another word, but it wouldn't sound decent at table. Now I do things differently. When there's pork, put the whole pig on the table; when there's mutton, bring along the whole sheep, when there's goose, the whole goose! I'd rather eat only two dishes, but have my fill of them as the soul dictates.' Sobakievich confirmed this in practice: he swept half of the saddle of mutton on to his plate, ate it up, gnawed it, and sucked it to the very last bone.

'Yes,' Chichikov reflected, 'he's no fool.'

'With me things are different,' Sobakievich was saying as he wiped his hands on a napkin, 'I don't do things like any Plyushkin: he's got eight hundred souls but dines worse than any of my shepherds!'

'Who is this Plyushkin?' Chichikov enquired.

'A rogue,' Sobakievich answered. 'He's such a codger you'd find it hard to believe it. The convicts have a better time of it in prison than he: he has starved all his folk to death.'

'You don't say so!' exclaimed Chichikov with some interest. 'You were saying that his folk die off in great numbers?'

'Like flies they do.'

'Like flies? You don't say so? And may I enquire if he lives very far from you?'

'About four miles.'

'Four miles!' Chichikov exclaimed and he even felt his heart fluttering slightly. 'But is it to the right or left as one drives out of your gates?'

'I don't advise you even to know the way to that dog!' said Sobakievich. 'It would be more pardonable to visit the lowest den rather than him.'

'Oh, I wasn't enquiring for any particular reason, but just because I am interested to know all kinds of places,' was Chichikov's reply.

The saddle of mutton was followed by curd cakes, each one of which was much larger than a plate, then a turkey as big as a calf, stuffed with a variety of good things, such as eggs, rice, kidneys and heaven knows what else, all of them heavy on the stomach. On that the dinner came to an end; but when they got up from table, Chichikov felt about three stones heavier. They went into the drawing-room where a saucer of jam had already been prepared for them—it was neither of pear, plum nor of any sort of berry—and they did not touch it. The lady of the house went out to fetch some more saucers of jam. Profiting by her absence, Chichikov turned to Sobakievich who was sprawling back on an armchair, grunting after such a copious repast and emitting inarticulate sounds while he crossed himself and every other minute politely put his hand over his mouth. Chichikov turned to him with these words:

'I should like to talk to you about a certain matter.'

'Here is some more jam!' said the lady of the house returning with a saucer. 'It's radish made with honey!'

'We'll taste it afterwards!' said Sobakievich. 'You go to your room now. Pavel Ivanovich and I will take off our coats and rest awhile!'

The lady had already expressed her readiness to have feather-beds and pillows fetched, but the master of the house told her, 'Don't bother, we can rest in the arm-chairs,' and she departed.

Sobakievich put his head to one side slightly as he got ready to hear what it was all about.

Chichikov's approach was somewhat oblique. He began by touching on the affairs of the whole Russian state and spoke appreciatively of the extent of the em-pire, saying that even ancient Rome was not so spacious, and that quite rightly foreigners were amazed. . . . Soba-kievich was listening to him with his head down. And Chichikov went on to remark that, according to the exist-ing state of affairs in this empire, which had no equal in glory, the souls of departed peasants registered on the census list were treated as though they were among the living until the next census, so as not to complicate the routine by a multitude of trifling and useless enqui-ries and so burden unnecessarily the already complex machinery of government. . . . Sobakievich was still listening with bowed head . . . and for all the justice of this arrangement it often proved a burden to many of the landowners, for it obliged them to pay taxes as though for a living thing, and so, as he had a feeling of personal respect for Sobakievich, he was partly prepared to take on himself this really onerous obligation. With respect to the main objective Chichikov expressed himself very cautiously: he did not refer to the souls as being dead but only as non-existent.

As before, Sobakievich was listening to him with lowered head, and his face disclosed nothing resembling an expression. It was as though his body were completely devoid of soul or, if he had a soul, it dwelt in some other region—as was the case with Koschey[4] the Deathless, whose soul dwelt somewhere beyond the mountains and was enclosed in a shell so thick that, whatever stirred at the bottom of it, made no impression whatsoever on the surface.

'And so . . . ?' said Chichikov, waiting not without some emotion for the answer.

'You are in need of dead souls?' enquired Sobakievich with great simplicity, without any show of surprise, as if they had been talking about bread.

'Yes,' Chichikov replied, and he again toned down the expression by adding, 'non-existent ones.'

'We'll find some. Why not?' said Sobakievich.

'If you do find any, you will doubtless . . . be glad to get rid of them?'

'If you please, I am willing to sell them,' said Sobakievich, who had already raised his head a little and had grasped that the purchaser probably had some profit in mind.

'The devil take him,' thought Chichikov to himself. 'This fellow is ready to sell before I have even hinted at the idea!' But aloud he said, 'And what might your price be? The article is, indeed, of a sort . . . it is even strange to discuss prices. . . .'

'Well, not to be exorbitant, I'll ask you a hundred roubles a piece!' said Sobakievich.

4. A mythical old man in Russian folk literature who knows the secret of longevity.

'A hundred!' Chichikov exclaimed, opening his mouth and staring at him as if he were not sure whether he had heard aright or whether Sobakievich's tongue had taken a wrong turn as a result of its unwieldy nature and had pronounced the wrong word.

'Why? is that too much for you?' enquired Sobakievich, and then added, 'And what would your price be?'

'My price! We've probably made a mistake or failed to understand each other. We have overlooked the nature of the article. For my part, and I am quite sincere about it, I think eighty kopecks would be a very fine price for them!'

'Eighty kopecks? That's absurd.'

'I can't help it. In my opinion, they're not worth more.'

'But I am not selling bast-shoes.'

'But you would have to agree that they are not living people either.'

'So you imagine that you have found a fool who would sell you a registered serf for eighty kopecks?'

'But excuse me, why do you call them registered serfs? They have been dead a long time, all that remains of them is some impalpable sound. However, not to prolong this conversation, I am prepared to go to a rouble and a half, but I can't give you more.'

'Are you not ashamed to offer such a sum? You are merely bargaining, name a real price!'

'I can't, Mikhail Semyonovich, believe me, I can't. What's impossible is impossible,' Chichikov was saying, but he added another half rouble all the same.

'Why are you being so stingy?' Sobakievich demanded. 'It's cheap at the price. A rogue would cheat you, sell you some worthless rubbish instead of souls, but mine are as juicy as ripe nuts, all picked—they are all either craftsmen or sturdy peasants. Now just consider this: there is Miheyev, the wheelwright, the carriages he made were always on springs. And it wasn't like Moscow work either, good for an hour only, but quite solid, and he'd do all the lining and the varnishing himself!'

Chichikov was about to open his mouth and remark that Miheyev was no longer among the living, but just at that moment Sobakievich had reached the high pitch of oratory and he was borne upon a flow of words:

'And Probka Stepan, the carpenter? I stake my head on it that you wouldn't find another peasant like him. And the strength of him! Heaven alone knows what they would have given him to serve in the guards, he was over seven foot high!'

Chichikov was again about to remark that Probka was not among the living, but Sobakievich was evidently well and truly launched; from him flowed such torrents of speech that he had no alternative but to listen.

'There is Milyushkin, the bricklayer! He could put up a stove in any house. There is Maxim Telyatnikov, the shoemaker: the touch of his awl was enough to make a pair of boots, and you'd thank him for boots like that; and he was as sober as a judge. And Yeremei Sorokoplekhin! Why, he's worth the whole bunch of them, he used to trade in Moscow and brought me in as much as five hundred roubles a year in labour-exemption tax alone. That's the kind of folk they are! It's not the quality you'd get from some Plyushkin or other.'

'But excuse me,' Chichikov intervened at last, astonished at this flood of seemingly endless eloquence, 'why enumerate all their qualities? There's no sense in it, they are all dead folk. You might as well prop a fence with a dead body, as the proverb has it.'

'Yes, of course, they are dead,' said Sobakievich, coming to himself and remembering that they were really dead; then he added: 'If it comes to that what about the folk who are counted among the living now? They are not much good. They are flies, not men.'

'But still they do exist. Your other folk are but a dream.'

'A dream? I don't agree. I'll tell you what Miheyev was like; you won't find many like him. A regular engine of a man—too big to get into this room. No, he was no dream! And he had more strength in his shoulders than any horse; where else, I ask you, would you have come across a dream like it!' As he uttered these last words, he

turned towards the portraits of Bagration and Kolokoteones[5] which were hanging on the wall, as often
happens to people engaged in conversation when one of
them suddenly, for some unknown reason, will address
himself not to his companion but to some third person, a
complete stranger, who has chanced to come in, from
whom, as he well knows, he will get no answer, opinion,
or confirmation, but on whom he will nevertheless fix his
gaze as if appealing to him as an intermediary; and, embarrassed at first, the stranger will not know whether to
offer an opinion on a matter about which he is in complete ignorance or whether to stop only in a polite sort of
way before taking his leave.

'No, I cannot give you more than two roubles,' Chichikov protested.

'If you like, that I may not be accused of asking too
much or of not wanting to be obliging—if you like, I shall
charge you seventy-five roubles a soul, only in banknotes,
and because we know each other!'

'Does he really think me a fool?' thought Chichikov to
himself, and he then added aloud: 'It seems to me that
we are engaged in a theatrical performance or comedy,
otherwise I find it difficult to explain. . . . You seem to be
a fairly intelligent man, you show evidence of education.
The goods we are discussing are worth—just that! What
are they worth? Who wants them?'

'But you're trying to buy them, and that means they
are wanted.'

Chichikov bit his lip and found no appropriate
answer. He broached his family circumstances, but Sobakievich retorted quite simply:

'There is no need for me to know the circumstances:
I don't interfere in family affairs, that is your own business. You have need of souls, and I am selling them to
you, and you will regret it if you don't buy them.'

'Two roubles,' said Chichikov.

'Yes, that's what Jacob's magpie cried about all and
sundry, as the proverb says. Now you've got these two

5. Teodor Kolokoteones (1770–1843), a leader in the Greek wars of independence against the Turks.

roubles into your head and can't get them out. Why don't you name a real price?'

'He's the very devil,' thought Chichikov to himself, 'I'll have to add another half rouble, by way of a sop.' 'Very well, I'll give you another half rouble.'

'Very well, I'll name my final price: fifty roubles! True, it will be a loss to me, you wouldn't get such fine folk cheaper anywhere!'

'What a *kulak*!'[6] Chichikov said to himself and then went on to speak aloud, though with a certain sadness. 'But really . . . the way you go about it one might think this was a serious business; but I could get them for nothing elsewhere. Anyone else would part with them willingly and they would be glad to get rid of them. Only a fool would hang on to them and pay tax on them!'

'But do you realize that purchases of this sort, and I am telling you this in confidence since we are friends, are not always permissible, and if I or anyone else were to talk about it such a person would have little security with regard to contracts or, indeed, any profitable transaction.'

'So that's what he's at, the scoundrel!' Chichikov thought, and he at once said coolly: 'As you wish, I'm not buying them out of any necessity as you imagine, but just for a personal whim. Two and a half roubles, that's as far as I shall go. Good-bye!'

'There's no flustering him, he's obstinate!' Soba-kievich thought. 'Well, God bless you, give me thirty roubles and take them!'

'No, I see that you are not keen to sell. Good-bye!'

'But allow me, allow me!' said Sobakievich, keeping a grip on Chichikov's hand and treading on his foot, for our hero had forgotten to take due care, and now as punishment he was obliged to hiss and jump about on one leg.

'I beg your pardon! I seem to have upset you. Please, will you sit down here! Please!' Hereupon he made him take a seat in one of the armchairs and he did this rather deftly, just as a bear might have done who had been trained in the art of turning somersaults and miming answers to such questions as 'Now show us, Misha, what

6. A rich, grasping peasant (derived from the Russian word for "fist").

peasant woman do in a steam bath?' or 'Misha, how do little boys steal peas?'

'I'm really wasting my time, I must be off.'

'Do stay a little, I'll tell you something nice in a moment.' Hereupon Sobakievich sat down close to him and whispered with a show of secrecy into his ear: 'Shall we make it a quarter?'

'You mean twenty-five roubles? No, no no, I wouldn't even give you a quarter of a quarter, not a penny more!'

Sobakievich was silenced. Chichikov was also silent. The silence lasted for about two minutes. Eagle-nosed Bagration stared down at this transaction with the greatest of attention.

'And what would your final price be?' Sobakievich asked at last.

'Two and a half.'

'Truly, your human soul is like a boiled turnip. You might at least offer me three roubles!'

'I can't do it.'

'Well, there's nothing to be done with you. Very well! It's a loss, but such is this dog's life. I cannot resist obliging a friend. I suppose I'll have to have a deed of purchase made out to get everything straight.'

'Of course.'

'Well, and I suppose I shall have to go into town.'

So the deal was concluded. They decided they must go to town next day and complete the deed of purchase. Chichikov asked for a list of the peasants. Sobakievich readily agreed to this and, going up to his bureau, began to make out a list in his own hand not only naming the peasants but commenting on their praiseworthy qualities.

As he had a moment's respite and found himself standing behind Sobakievich, Chichikov occupied himself in scrutinizing his spacious frame. When he looked at his back, which was as broad as that of a squat Vyatka horse,[7] and at his feet, which were like curb-stones, he could not help exclaiming inwardly: 'Ough, God has been lavish to you! As they say, you're badly cut but strongly sewn! . . . Were you born such a bear or was it the life in the wilds,

---

7. A draft horse. Vyatka is a small town in Russia, northeast of Moscow and now called Kirov.

the work on the land and the dealings with peasants, that made you bearish and, in that way, the sort of person they call a fist of a man or a *kulak*? But no: I believe you would have been the same even though you had been brought up in the best fashion, had been properly put into circulation and dwelt in Petersburg instead of in the wilds. The whole difference consists in this, that now you stuff away half a saddle of mutton with buckwheat and follow it up with a curdle-cake the size of a plate, whereas otherwise you would have been eating some sort of cutlets with truffles. Now you have peasants under your authority: you manage to get on with them and, of course, you would not be too harsh with them, for they belong to you and you would be worse off if you did maltreat them; otherwise you would have had officials under you, whom you would have kept on the run as soon as you had grasped the fact that they were not your serfs, or you would have dipped into the public funds! Yes, once a *kulak* always a *kulak*! And even if one were to unclench one or two fingers of the *kulak*'s clenched fist, it would be still worse. Now even if he did acquire a slight, superficial acquaintance with some branch of knowledge, he would see to it, as soon as he occupied a superior post, that those who really had a smattering of knowledge should feel his weight. Yes, and maybe he would say afterwards, "Ah, let me show you what I can do!" And he would lay down the law in such a way that many would not find it to their taste. . . . Ah, if every one were a *kulak*! . . .'

'The list is ready,' said Sobakievich, turning round.

'Ready? May I have it?' He ran his eyes over it and was astonished at its accuracy and neatness: not only were the craft, quality, age and family circumstances of these peasants minutely detailed, but there were special comments in the margin as to their conduct and sobriety, in a word, it was a beautiful document to look at.

'And now, if you please, an advance!' said Sobakievich.

'Why do you want an advance? You will get the money in town in a lump sum.'

'It's the custom you know,' Sobakievich retorted.

'I don't know if I can manage it, I haven't brought enough money with me. Here's ten roubles, if you like.'

'What's the good of ten! Give me fifty, at least!'

Chichikov was on the point of declining further, but Sobakievich affirmed so positively that he must have the money that he pulled out another note, saying as he did so:

'As you like, here's another fifteen, that makes twenty-five. May I have a receipt?'

'And why do you want a receipt?'

'It's always better to have one. In a bad hour anything might happen.'

'Very well, but let me have the money!'

'Why do you want the money? I've got it here in my hand! As soon as you write out the receipt you will have it immediately.'

'But, pray, how am I to make out a receipt without first seeing the money?'

Chichikov let Sobakievich take the notes. Approaching the table and putting the fingers of his left hand over them, he then scribbled with his other hand on a bit of paper a statement to the effect that he had duly received an advance of twenty-five roubles in banknotes for the sale of the souls. Having finished writing this, he examined the banknotes once more.

'The paper is rather worn!' he said, raising one of the notes to the light. 'It's a bit torn too, but that doesn't matter so much between friends.'

'What a *kulak*!' Chichikov thought to himself. 'And a regular beast into the bargain!'

'And you wouldn't be wanting any of the female sex?'

'No, thank you.'

'I wouldn't charge you much for them. Only a rouble a piece for friendship's sake.'

'I have no need of the female sex.'

'Well, if you don't need them, there's no point in pressing it. There is no accounting for taste: some are fond of the priest, others of his wife, as the proverb says.'

'May I also ask you to keep our deal to yourself,' Chichikov said.

'But of course. It's no business of anyone else; whatever

takes place between good friends should remain between them, as part of their mutual friendship. Good-bye! I am grateful to you for your visit; I beg you not to forget to come again: if you have an hour to spare, come along and dine with us, and pass the time. Maybe an occasion for rendering each other a service will present itself again.'

'Well, well!' Chichikov thought to himself as he settled back in the chaise. 'He's skinned me—two and a half roubles for a dead peasant, that devil of a *kulak*!'

He was highly displeased with Sobakievich's behaviour. After all, he was an acquaintance, they had met at the governor's and at the house of the chief of police, and yet he had behaved like a complete stranger and had extorted money for nothing! When the chaise had driven out of the yard, he looked back and saw Sobakievich still standing on the steps and watching to see, so it seemed, which direction his guest would now take.

'The scoundrel, he is still standing there!' he ground through his teeth and he ordered Selifan, who had turned the horses towards the peasant huts, to drive in such a way as to hide the chaise from that side of the land-owner's house. He wished to pay a visit to Plyushkin whose folk were dying like flies according to Sobakievich's account, but he did not desire his intention to be known. When the chaise was on the outskirts of the village, he beckoned to the first peasant they came across shouldering a large log which he had picked up somewhere on the road and which, like some industrious ant, he was carrying back home.

'Hey, grey-beard! Which is the way to Plyushkin's so as not to drive past the squire's house?'

It looked as if the peasant found this a difficult question.

'Don't you know?'

'No, I don't sir.'

'Well, well! And you boast of grey hairs! Don't you know the skinflint Plyushkin, the one who feeds his folk badly?'

'Oh, that patched-up . . .!' the peasant cried. The substantive he used was a very appropriate one but not one suited for polite conversation, and for that reason we shall omit it. However, as we may guess, it was a very telling expression, for, although the peasant had long been lost sight of and much ground had been covered, Chichikov still chortled to himself as he lolled back in the chaise. Russian folk like strong expressions! Find a just description of anyone, it will stick to him through thick and thin and go down to posterity; he will drag it with him when he is in the service and, when he retires, to Petersburg or to the edge of the world. And however much he may try and ennoble his nickname later, even though he induce scriveners for a consideration to trace it back to an ancient princely house, naught will avail: the nickname will raise its own croaking voice, like a crow, and proclaim clearly the nest out of which the bird had flown. A pointed word, once it is spoken or written, cannot be cut away with an axe. And everything that comes out of the depths of Russia is pointed enough, for there we find no German, Finnish or any other variety of tribes, but only the indigenous native, the quick and boisterous Russian mind which does not fumble in any pocket for a word, does not brood over it like some hen, but sticks it on at once, like a passport to be carried about forever; there is no point then in adding the sort of a nose you have or lips—you have already been drawn in a single trait from head to foot!

Just as a countless multitude of churches and monasteries with their cupolas, domes and crosses, is dispersed throughout holy, pious Russia, so a countless multitude of tribes, generations, peoples, flocks together in a shimmer of colours and erupts over the face of the earth. And each of these peoples, bearing within itself the pledge of its powers, its fulfilment and its other divine gifts, has made an original contribution in its own words which, when they are used to designate some object and give expression to it, reflect some aspect of the people's character. The words of the Briton will suggest heart-searching and a sagacious knowledge of life; the Frenchman's brief-spanned words will scintillate like a gay dandy and then burst like a bubble; inventively the German will ponder his own intellectually meagre words which are not comprehensible to every one; but there is no word so expansive, so lively in character, so directly bursting out of the heart itself, so surging and tremulous, as the pointedly spoken Russian word.

CHAPTER VI

In former days, a long time ago, in the years of my youth, in the years of my irrevocably vanished childhood, I used to experience a feeling of joy whenever I came for the first time to any strange place: it made no difference whether it was a hamlet, a lowly township, a large village or a settlement, the inquisitive eyes of a child picked out much that was curious about them. Every building, everything that bore the impress of some observable peculiarity, everything arrested my attention and amazed me. Whether it was a government house, built of stone and in the usual style with half the windows blind, standing all by itself amid a cluster of one-storied roughly hewn log-houses belonging to the common folk; or the round cupola or straight steeple, all covered with sheets of white metal, rising above a new church whitewashed as bright as snow; or a market; or some neighbouring dandy come to town; nothing of all this was lost upon my fresh and impressionable mind as I thrust my head out of my travelling cart and stared at the unusual cut of some jacket and at the wooden cases of nails, of sulphur glowing yellow from a distance, of raisins and of soap, all of which could be glimpsed through the door of a grocer's together with jars of stale Moscow sweets. And I would stare at the infantry officer who was walking to one side and who had drifted here God alone knows from what province, at the boredom of this provincial scene, and at the merchant in the green greatcoat who flashed past in a racing droshky; and as I did so my thoughts travelled with them and shared in their wretched existence. If a local official went by, I asked myself at once where he was going? Was he going to spend the evening with some other official, or was he off home where he might lounge for half an hour on his front door-step till it grew quite dark before sitting down to an early supper with his mother, wife, his sister-in-law and the whole family? And I asked myself what they could be talking about while a servant-maid in a necklet or a boy in a thick jacket was coming in, after the soup, bringing a tallow candle in a home-made candlestick that had seen service these many years. When nearing some landowner's village, I used to eye with curiosity the tall, narrow, wooden belfry or the dark and spacious outlines of the old wooden church. From afar, through the green foliage, the red roof and the white chimneys of the landowner's house beckoned me enticingly, and I waited impatiently until the gardens which shaded it on both sides would part and reveal its then—alas, then!—by no means vulgar appearance; and from it I tried to guess what sort of a person the landowner was, whether he was stout, whether he had sons or a full complement of six daughters with laughing girlish voices, games and, as always, the youngest a beauty, whether they all had black eyes, and whether the old man was of a hearty disposition or as brooding as the last days of September when he consulted the calendar and bored the young folk with talk of rye and wheat.

Now I feel quite indifferent when I drive through any new village and it is with indifference that I watch its dreary exterior. To my chilled gaze it looks uninviting and no longer amuses me; and what in bygone years would have provoked a lively animation in my face, laughter and a flow of words, now merely passes me by, and my unmoving lips preserve an impartial silence. Oh, my youth! Oh, my spontaneity!

While Chichikov was turning over and inwardly chuckling at the nicknames bestowed on Plyushkin by the peasant, he failed to notice that the chaise had reached the centre of a spacious village with a multitude of huts and streets. However, a formidable jolt, caused by a wooden roadway in comparison with which the town cobbles were as nothing, very soon made him sit up and take note. These wooden planks rose and fell like piano keys, and an imprudent driver acquired either a bump on the back of

his head or a bruise on his forehead, or it might happen that
he would bite off a goodly portion of his own tongue with
his teeth. He could not help noticing a strange air of decay
about all these village buildings: the wood of the huts was
old and weather-beaten; many of the roofs let in the
draught like a sieve; some consisted only of the ridge on top
and rib-like supports on the sides. It looked as if the house-
holders themselves had stripped them of their stuffing and
beams, arguing, and very rightly so, that, as huts in these
parts are not roofed for wet weather and as it does not
rain on fine days anyhow, there is no point in trying to
shelter in them, when there is plenty of room in the gin-
shop or on the highway—in short, wherever you like.
Some of the windows in the huts had no glass, others were
stuffed with a rag or an old coat; the little balconies with
railings, which for some unknown reason are built under
the roofs of many Russian huts, were all askew and had
grown grimy in a way that was not even picturesque. In
places enormous stacks of corn stretched in rows behind
the huts, and it was apparent that they had been standing
there for quite a time; in hue they resembled old, badly-
baked bricks, and all kinds of weeds were growing on top
of them while a shrubbery sprouted in their midst. The
corn was evidently the master's.

As the chaise twisted and turned, two village churches
could be distinguished in close proximity, sometimes to
the right and sometimes to the left, peeping out from
behind the stacks and the tumbledown roofs. One of them
was an abandoned wooden church and the other a stone
one with yellow walls stained and cracked. Then the
landowner's mansion came into view, at first in parts and
then as a whole, when the chain of huts came to an end
and gave place to an open space of orchards and cabbage
patches ringed by a low and partly broken fence. That
strange castle, which was long, disproportionately long,
had all the appearance of a chronic invalid. In some places
it was one-storied, in others two-storied; upon its dark
roof, which provided an uncertain shelter for its age,
two belvederes were stuck facing each other; both of them
were sagging and innocent of the paint which had once

covered them. In places, the walls of the house revealed the bare laths under the plaster and, as was apparent, had suffered a great deal from all kinds of intemperate weather, rains, gales and the fickleness of autumn. Only two of the windows remained uncovered, the rest were shuttered or boarded up. But even these two windows were only half-uncovered, for one of them had a triangular piece of dark blue sugar paper pasted over it.

An old and spacious garden, which stretched behind the house and into the country beyond the village, though overgrown and neglected, alone seemed to refresh this rambling village; and its wild landscape was the only highly picturesque feature of the place. The intertwining tops of the trees, branching out in unhampered freedom, pressed upon the skyline in green clouds and wavy, leaf-quivering cupolas. The huge, white trunk of a birch-tree, which had lost its crest in a gale or storm, rose up out of that green thicket and towered roundly in the air like a straight and glittering marble column; the slanting jagged top, which crowned it instead of a capital, was set darkly, like a cap or a black bird, against its snowy whiteness. Having smothered the bushes of elder, mountain-ash and hazel below it, and then run full length along the top of the hedge, strands of hop climbed and twined half-way up the broken birch-tree. Having got half-way they hung down and twisted round the tops of other trees or just hung in the air, tying themselves in slender and clinging knots, easily swayed in the breeze. In places, the green thickets fell apart, illumined by the sun, and revealed the unlighted chasms between them, gaping like great dark jaws, all plunged in shadow. In those dark depths could just be seen a narrow path, tumbledown railings, a sagging summer-house, a decaying and hollow trunk of a willow tree, and tufts of sedge protruding in a thick stubble from behind the withered willow, its leaves and twigs all dried up in the dense thicket of this terrible tangle, and a young branch of a maple stretching out its green paw-like leaves to one side, with the sun, heaven alone knows how, peeping under one of them and transforming it suddenly into a transparent and fiery patch shining miraculously in that thick gloom. On one side, at the very extremity of the garden, several tall aspens, towering above the other trees, raised up high in the air huge crows' nests on their quivering tops. Some of them had broken but not completely severed branches hanging down together with their withered leaves. In short, it was glorious, beyond the contriving of nature or art alone, but possible only when they join forces, as happens when nature gives a final touch to man's accumulated and frequently senseless labour, lightening the heavy masses, eliminating a crudely-felt symmetry and man's unimaginative elaboration of it, through which peeps an undisguisedly naked design, nature imbuing with a miraculous warmth everything that was created in the cold light of calculated purity and precision.

After rounding one or two corners, our hero found himself at last in front of the house, which now looked even more depressing. The crumbling wood of the fence and of the gates was already covered over with a green mould. The yard was crowded with buildings—servants' quarters, barns and underground storehouses, all obviously going to rack and ruin; nearby, to the left and right of them, could be seen gateways leading into other yards. Everything bore evidence of the fact that once upon a time there had been a prosperous estate here, but now everywhere was an air of gloom. There was nothing to add animation to the scene, neither doors being opened nor folk coming out, no bustle, no household flurry! Only the main gates were open, and that was because a peasant had just driven through them in a cart covered over with sacking, and he had appeared as though expressly to animate this moribund place; at any other time, the gates would have been firmly shut, for a gigantic padlock hung there on an iron hook. Near one of the buildings Chichikov soon noticed a figure engaged in an altercation with the peasant who had just arrived. It took him quite a while to distinguish whether the figure was that of a man or woman. The dress it had on was quite indefinable, very like a woman's dressing-gown; on its head was a conical cap such as is worn by country servants; only the voice seemed too husky to be a woman's. 'Oh, a female!' he thought to himself, but at once added: 'Oh, no!' Finally, 'Of course it's a female!' he said after further, closer scrutiny. The figure was also staring intently at him. It seemed as though a visitor were a rare bird, for she scrutinized not only him but also Selifan and the horses from tail to head. From the keys hanging at her girdle and the way she took the peasant unceremoniously to task, Chichikov concluded that she must be the housekeeper.

'Tell me, my good woman,' he said as he got out of the chaise, 'is the master . . . ?'

'Not at home,' the housekeeper interrupted him, and then a minute later added: 'What do you want?'

'I have business.'

'Go in!' she said, turning her back upon him, which was all covered in flour and showed a large tear in her skirt.

He set foot in a dark, wide hall, the breath of which chilled him like a cellar. From the hall he emerged into a room which was also dark, with a glimmer of light showing through a big crack at the foot of the door. On opening this door, he at last came out into the light and was amazed at the disorder which confronted him. It was as though the floors of the house were being washed and all the furniture had been stacked there in the meantime. One of the tables had a broken chair standing on it and next to it a clock with a motionless pendulum, to which a spider had already affixed a cobweb. Here was also a cupboard leaning against the wall, full of old silver, decanters and china. On the bureau, inlaid with a mosaic of mother-of-pearl, which had fallen out in places, leaving brown holes filled with glue, lay a great assortment of all kinds of things: a heap of closely written bits of paper held down by a marble paper-weight with a little egg-shaped handle on top, all green with age, an ancient book in a leather binding with red chasing, a lemon shrivelled to the size of a hazel-nut, the broken-off arm of a chair, a wine-glass with some liquid in it and three

flies, covered with a letter, a piece of sealing-wax, a bit
of an old rag picked up somewhere, two ink-stained
quills, all burnt out as though from consumption, and a
toothpick grown so yellow with age that its owner had
probably cleaned his teeth with it before the French had
marched on Moscow.[8]

The walls were packed with pictures hung anyhow.
There was a long faded engraving of some battle, with
great big drums, yelling soldiers in three-cornered hats
and drowning horses, set in a glassless mahogany frame
with narrow strips of bronze and bronze discs at the
corners. Half the wall was taken up with an enormous,
blackened oil-painting, representing flowers, fruit, a cut
water-melon, a boar's head and a duck hung upside
down. From the ceiling in the middle of the room a
chandelier was suspended in a homespun bag, so dusty
that it resembled the cocoon of a silkworm. In a corner of
the room lay a heap of coarser ware which was unworthy
to take its place on the table. It was difficult to make out
what was in the heap, for the dust was so abundant that
anyone who touched it came to have hands that looked
as though they had dusty gloves on them; a piece of a
broken wooden spade and an old boot-sole were the most
prominent objects sticking out of the pile. It could not
have been argued that this room was inhabited by any
living creature if an old and worn night-cap lying on the
table had not suggested that possibility. While Chichikov
was examining this strange array, a side door was opened
and in came the same housekeeper whom he had met in
the yard. But now he perceived that it was a house-
steward rather than a housekeeper: at least, a housekeeper
would not shave, but the figure confronting him did
shave and infrequently at that, for the whole of his chin
and the lower part of his cheek looked like a wire brush
such as is used for cleaning horses. Assuming an enquiring expression, Chichikov waited patiently for the house-
steward to speak. The house-steward on his part also
waited for Chichikov to speak. Finally, astonished at this
strange suspense, Chichikov resolved to enquire:

8. An allusion to the Napoleonic invasion of 1812.

'Where is the master? Is he in his room?'

'The master is here,' said the house-steward.

'Where is he then?' Chichikov asked.

'Are you blind or what, my good sir?' said the house-steward. 'Can't you see? I'm the master!'

At this our hero involuntarily stepped back and stared fixedly at him. He had had occasion to see all sorts of folk such as neither the reader nor I are ever likely to see; but he had never seen anyone like this. His face was in no way out of the ordinary; it might almost have been that of any other gaunt old man except that his chin was unusually prominent, and this made him cover it with a handkerchief each time he spat out; his small eyes had not yet lost their fire and scurried about under his arching brows, like mice when, thrusting their pointed noses out of their dark holes, with their ears pricked up and their whiskers quivering, they look around them to make sure that a cat or a mischievous boy is not lying in wait for them, and suspiciously sniff the very air. His garb was far more remarkable. There was no means or way of telling what went to the making of his dressing-gown: the sleeves and lapels had grown so dirty and greasy that they looked like boot leather; at the back there were four tails instead of two, and out of them dangled tufts of cotton wool. It was also impossible to make out what he had tied round his neck: a stocking, a garter or a stomach-belt, but it was certainly not a cravat. In short, if Chichikov had met him so attired at the entrance of a church, he would in all likelihood have given him a copper coin. For be it said in our hero's favour that his heart was compassionate and that he could not resist giving a farthing to a beggar. But the man now facing him was no beggar but a landowner. He owned over a thousand souls, and few could be found who had so much bread stored in grain, flour, or simply in stacks of corn, such storehouses, barns and drying sheds heaped with such quantities of linen, cloth, cured and uncured sheepskins, dried fish, and every kind of vegetable. If anyone had peeped into his work-yard, where a stock of various woods and utensils had been got ready but had never been used, he might have imagined himself wafted to the wood-ware market in Moscow, where bustling mothers-in-law make their daily pilgrimage, with their cooks trailing behind them, to effect their household purchases, and where white mounds of every kind of wooden articles fitted together, turned, dovetailed, wickered, lie about—barrels, mincers, tubs, buckets, vessels with spouts and without spouts, loving cups, linden-bark baskets, boxes in which peasant women dump their filaments and other waste, hampers of thin flexible aspen wood, pots of plaited birch-bark and much else serving the use of the rich and poor alike in Russia. One might well ask what need Plyushkin had of such a heap of articles? A whole lifetime would not have sufficed to make use of them even if his estate had been twice as large—but it all seemed too little for him. Not satisfied with what he had, he used daily to stalk the streets of his village, peeping under the little bridges and planks, and everything he came upon, whether it was an old sole, a bit of a peasant woman's dress, an iron nail, a piece of broken earthenware, he carried them all off home and put them in the pile which Chichikov had noticed in the corner. 'He is out fishing again!' the peasants used to say when they saw him stalking his prey. And as a matter of fact, there was no need to sweep the street after he had gone down it. If a visiting officer happened to lose a spur, it instantly found its way to the notorious pile. If a careless peasant woman happened to forget her bucket at the well, he would grab it too. However, if a peasant were to catch him in the act, he would not argue but return his prize; nevertheless there was no redress if ever it got into the pile—he would swear that the article was his, bought at a certain date from someone, or that it had been left him by his grandfather. He used to pick up anything he saw on the floor of his room, a piece of sealing wax, a bit of paper, a feather, and put it all away on his desk or on the window-sill.

And yet once upon a time he had been a model proprietor! He had a wife and family, and many a neighbouring landowner had called on him and stayed to dinner in order to hear him talk and learn from him the elements of economy and thrift. There was a pace and rhythm about the work on his estate: the wind-mills and fulling mills were in motion, the cloth factories, the carpenters' lathes, and the spinning mills were all busy; the master's keen eye allowed nothing to slip by and, like a diligent spider, he used to scurry about inquisitively and nimbly from one end to the other of his proprietary web. No great intensity of feeling was observable in his face but his eyes suggested intelligence; experience and knowledge of the world characterized his talk, and it was a pleasure to listen to him. His courteous and talkative wife was famed for her hospitality; the guests would meet two charming daughters, both fair and fresh as roses; a sprightly son would come running out and kiss everyone, little caring whether they liked it or not. All the windows in the house were kept open to let in the light. The entresol was inhabited by the French tutor, who shaved to perfection and who was much given to shooting: he would usually turn up with a few woodcock or wild-duck for dinner, but sometimes he would only bring sparrows' eggs from which he would have an omelette made for himself, for no one else in the house would touch them. The entresol also housed a compatriot of his, the governess of the two daughters. At table the master of the house would wear a slightly worn but tidy frock-coat with sleeves all in order and no visible patches. But then the good lady of the house died; and he inherited the keys and with them the everyday management of the house.

Plyushkin then grew restless and, like all widowers, he became more suspicious and stingier. He could not entirely rely on his eldest daughter, Alexandra Stepanovna, and rightly so, for it was not long before she eloped with the staff-captain of a cavalry regiment, whom she then hastily married in some village church, knowing that her father entertained a strange prejudice against all officers, whom he regarded as gamblers and wasters. The father cursed her but did not bother to pursue her. The house grew emptier still. The master's miserly traits became more pronounced, and these were further emphasized as his wiry hair began to grey. The French tutor departed when it was time for the son to take up service. The governess was sent away because it seemed that she was not altogether guiltless in the affair of Alexandra Stepanovna's elopement. On being sent to a provincial town to take up a post in the department of justice, a good service in his father's opinion, the son got a commission in a regiment instead and, only after obtaining it, wrote to his father asking him for money to equip himself; and not unnaturally all he got was a fig, as the common folk say. Finally, his last remaining daughter died, and the old man was left alone as watchman, guardian and master of all his riches. His solitary life only fed his avarice which, as we know, has the appetite of a wolf and grows more insatiable the more it devours. With every minute the human feelings, of which he never had a great store, diminished, and every day some part of that tottering wreck crumbled away. Then, as though to confirm his prejudice against army officers, his son lost heavily at cards; he cursed him heartily and never took any more interest in his fate. Every year more windows were boarded up until, at last, only two remained uncovered; and, as the reader has seen already, one of these was glued over with paper. Every year he increasingly neglected important parts of his estate while his petty attention was concentrated on bits of paper and feathers which he used to collect in his room; he became more uncompromising with the dealers who used to come and buy his produce; the dealers bargained and bargained, and finally gave him up, saying that he was a devil rather than a man. The hay and corn rotted, the stocks and stacks turned to manure only good for cabbage growing, the flour in the cellars turned to stone and had to be chopped and chipped; it was terrifying to touch the cloth, linen and household materials, for they crumbled to dust. He had already himself forgotten what he had, and all he remembered was the cupboard in which he kept a decanter with the remains of some liqueur in it, and the mark he had made to prevent anyone helping himself to it, and also where he kept his quill and sealing-wax.

Meanwhile the revenues poured in as before: the peasants had to contribute as much as ever, the peasant women had to bring in their usual share of nuts while the cloth-weavers had to weave quite as much as before; and all this was stored and went to rack and ruin, while Plyushkin himself turned into a walking ruin. Alexandra Stepanovna paid two or three visits in an attempt to see whether she could prevail on him to give her anything; her campaigning life with the staff-captain was apparently not as full of attractions as it had seemed before the wedding. However, Plyushkin forgave her and he even let his small grandson play with a button which he picked from the table, but he did not give his daughter any money. Another time Alexandra Stepanovna arrived with two children and brought him a cake for tea and a new dressing-gown, for the one he was wearing not only pricked her conscience but made her downright ashamed. Plyushkin fondled both the children, sat them on his knees, the one on the right and the other on the left, and rocked them as if they were riding on horseback; he accepted the cake and the dressing-gown, but gave his daughter nothing at all, and on that Alexandra Stepanovna departed.

Such was the landowner who stood facing Chichikov! It must be said that the like of him is to be rarely met in Russia, where everything tends to expand rather than to contract. And the type is all the more astounding when it is to be found living side by side with a landowner of quite different character, given to spreading himself out to the full breadth of Russian rashness and lordly ways and, as they say, scorching his way through life. At the sight of such a man's dwelling the fictitious traveller will stop and gape, wondering what sort of a prince had unexpectedly taken up his abode among the smaller fry of landowners: the white stone buildings look like palaces with their multitude of chimneys, belvederes and turrets, ringed by a flock of wings and lodges for accommodating visitors. There is everything there. Theatres, balls; all night the garden is illuminated and hung with lamps, and filled with thundering music. Half the province is there, all dressed up and gay, strolling about under the trees, and no one in this violent light feels it strange and menacing when, out of the dark shadows, a branch juts out dramatically into the artificial light, stripped of its bright greenery, while in that light the night sky looms above harsher and darker still, and twenty times more menacing; and with their far rustling leaves plunging ever deeper into the unawakening gloom, the austere tree tops express their indignation at this gaudy glitter lighting up their roots below.

Plyushkin had been standing there for some minutes without uttering a word, while Chichikov was feeling so distracted by the appearance of the landowner and everything he saw in the room that he did not venture to speak either. For a long time he could think of no words in which to explain the reason for his visit. He was about to express himself somewhat in this style, that he had heard of Plyushkin's virtues and rare spiritual qualities, and had thought it his duty to pay his personal respects; but he thought better of it and felt that he might be exaggerating. On casting another sidelong glance at everything that was in the room, he sensed that the words 'virtues' and 'rare spiritual qualities' might be fittingly replaced by the words 'economy and order'. Therefore, transforming his speech in this way, he said that, having heard a great deal about his economy and rare ability to manage his estates, he regarded it as his duty to make his acquaintance and pay his personal respects to him. Of course, he might have quoted a better reason, but nothing else occurred to his mind.

In answer to this Plyushkin muttered something between his lips—he had no teeth—but what exactly he said was not certain. It was probably something like this: 'The devil take you and your respects!' But as hospitality is so honoured among us that even a miser will not violate its laws, he went on to add a trifle more distinctly: 'I humbly beg you to take a seat!'

'I have had no guests here for a long time,' he went on, 'and to be frank with you I don't see much point in them. It's quite indecent the way folk visit one another and neglect their estates . . . and one is expected to feed their horses into the bargain! I have had my dinner already, my kitchen is small and in a state of disrepair, the chimney is falling to pieces, one might start a fire if the stove were heated.'

'So that's how it is!' Chichikov thought to himself. 'It's just as well I had a bite of cheese-cake and a portion of mutton at Sobakievich's.'

'And to make it worse, there is hardly a wisp of hay in the whole place!' Plyushkin continued. 'And, indeed, how is one to save any? There isn't much land, the peasants are lazy, they don't like work and only like drinking. . . . If I'm not careful, I'll end up as a beggar in my old age!'

'But I have been told,' said Chichikov modestly, 'that you have over a thousand souls.'

'Who told you that! You ought to have spat in his face, whoever it was! Some jester, no doubt, who wanted to pull your leg. A thousand souls, that's what they say, but just try and count them, it wouldn't amount to much! In the last three years a cursed fever has killed off quite a heap of peasants.'

'But tell me did it kill off many?' Chichikov exclaimed sympathetically.

'Yes, quite a lot.'

'And may I enquire how many?'

'About eighty.'

'You don't say so?'

'I wouldn't lie, would I?'

'May I ask you another question: I suppose these souls are still on the last register?'

'I wouldn't mind that,' said Plyushkin, 'but since the last census there is a collection of some hundred and twenty of them.'

'Really? A hundred and twenty?' exclaimed Chichikov, and he even gaped slightly in his astonishment.

'I'm too old to tell lies: I'm in my seventh decade!' said Plyushkin. He appeared to have taken offence at that almost joyful exclamation. Chichikov made a mental note that such lack of sympathy for other people's sorrows was indeed not quite decent, and so he immediately gave vent to a sigh and declared that he sympathized.

'But sympathy is not a thing you can put in your

pocket,' said Plyushkin. 'Now I have a neighbour, a captain, the devil alone knows where he comes from, he says he is a relative of mine. "Uncle, uncle," he calls me, and kisses my hand, and when he starts sympathizing you might as well close your ears, he howls so much. He has such a red face: he is strong on brandy. Very likely he squandered all his money when he was in the army, or some actress filched it from him, and so he is all sympathy now!'

Chichikov tried to explain that his sympathy was of a different kind from the captain's, and that he was ready to prove it, not in words but in deeds. And coming straight to the point, without any beating about the bush, he declared his readiness to take on himself the obligation to pay dues on all those peasants who had so unfortunately died. The offer, it seems, completely stunned Plyushkin. His eyes popped out, he gaped at him for a long while and finally enquired: 'Why, have you served in the army?'

'No,' Chichikov replied cunningly enough, 'I used to be in the civil service.'

'In the civil service?' Plyushkin repeated and began to chew his lips as if he were masticating something. 'But how's that? Won't you lose on it?'

'I am ready to suffer some loss for your sake.'

'Ah, little father, benefactor!' exclaimed Plyushkin, failing to notice in his joy that a small lump of snuff not unlike coffee grounds was most unpicturesquely dangling from his nostrils and that, coming undone, his dressing-gown revealed a costume of none too respectable appearance. 'What comfort you have brought an old man! O Lord, O Lord! O ye saints!' . . . Plyushkin could say no more. But after a minute, the joy, which had suddenly illumined his wooden face, vanished as quickly as if it had never been there, and his face once more assumed an anxious look. He even mopped his face with a handkerchief and, rolling it up into a ball, began to dab his lip with it.

'How are you going to arrange it then, if I may enquire without offending you? Will you pay the dues for them every year? And will the money be paid to me or into the Treasury?'

'This is what we shall do: we shall draw up a deed of purchase as if they were alive and you had sold them to me.'

'Yes, a deed of purchase,' said Plyushkin as he began to think it over and chew his lips again. 'A deed of purchase, why, that's an extra expense. The clerks have no conscience. In days past you could get away with half a rouble in copper and a bag of flour, but now they expect a cartload of groats and a red note thrown in. I don't know why somebody doesn't look into the matter; or at least say a few words to them about it! You can do a lot with a word. Whatever anyone may say, one can't resist a salutary word.'

'I think *you* might!' Chichikov thought to himself, and he immediately told Plyushkin that out of respect for him he was ready to take on himself even the cost of the deed of purchase.

On hearing that Chichikov was taking this expense upon himself, Plyushkin concluded that his guest was an utter fool and was only pretending when he claimed to have been in the civil service—it was more likely that he had been in the army and had been gadding about with actresses. Nevertheless, he was unable to hide his joy and he showered all kinds of blessings not only on Chichikov but also on his offspring, without bothering to enquire whether he had any or not. Going up to the window, Plyushkin drummed on the glass and shouted, 'Proshka!' A minute later someone could be heard running noisily into the hall, bustling about and making scraping noises with his boots. At last the door opened and in came Proshka, a boy of thirteen, wearing a pair of boots so large that he almost stepped out of them as he walked. The reason why Proshka wore such large boots can be explained at once: Plyushkin kept only one pair of boots for all of his servants, however numerous they were, and they always stood in the hall. Any servant, who had been summoned to the master's quarters, usually did a bare-foot dance across the yard, but donned the boots in the hall before entering the room. On departing he once more discarded the boots in the hall and then went off on his own soles. If anyone happened to look out of a window on an autumn day, and especially in the morning when the ground was a little frozen, he would have seen the servants making such leaps as could hardly be equalled by the most vigorous ballet dancer.

'Just look at his mug!' Plyushkin said to Chichikov, pointing to Proshka's face. 'He's as dumb as wood. But only try and leave anything lying about, he'd pinch it at once! Well, why have you come, fool, tell me that?' Here he fell silent for a time and Proshka responded with silence. 'Put on the samovar, do you hear! And take this key, give it to Mavra so that she can go to the storeroom: there is a rusk of a cake Alexandra Stepanovna brought, it's somewhere on the shelf, it can be served for tea! . . . Stop, where are you going? Idiot, that's what you are! Is the devil tickling your feet or what? Now, you listen first: the rusk surely has gone mouldy on top, so let her scrape it with a knife but tell her not to throw away the crumbs, they'll do for the chickens. And as for you, don't you put your nose inside the storeroom or I shall— you know what I'll do—give you a spanking with that birch-broom, just for the taste of it! You have a fine appetite now, and a birching will make it finer still! Now just try and enter the storeroom, I'll keep watch from the window here. One can't trust him an inch,' he continued, turning to Chichikov after Proshka had departed, boots and all. Then he started to stare at Chichikov suspiciously. He began to find his extraordinary generosity improbable and he thought to himself: 'The devil alone knows, he may be just a braggart, like all these wastrels. He may be just lying and lying, to have something to talk about and to get some tea, and then he may just beat it!' Therefore, out of caution and in order to test him, he suggested that it would not be a bad idea to arrange the deed of purchase as soon as possible, for there was little certainty about human beings: a man may be alive one day and dead the next.

Chichikov showed himself ready to complete the arrangements that very minute if necessary, and asked only that the list of peasants should be prepared.

This reassured Plyushkin. It could be seen that he was cogitating something, and so he was, for, picking up the keys, he approached the cupboard, and opening the door, fumbled for a long time in among the glasses and cups. Finally, he said, 'Why, I can't find it, but I had a fine liqueur somewhere if they haven't drunk it all! Such thieves, these folk! This is it, maybe?' In his hands Chichikov perceived a decanter, which was all covered in dust as if in a woollen jersey. 'My deceased wife made it,' Plyushkin continued, 'that rascally housekeeper almost threw it away and she did not even put a stopper in it, the slut! It was full of beetles and all kinds of creatures, but I took them all out and it's pure now. I'll pour you out a glass.'

But Chichikov tried to decline such a liqueur, saying that he had already eaten and drunk.

'You have eaten and drunk already!' said Plyushkin. 'Yes, of course, one can easily tell a man of good breeding: he does not eat but has had his fill; but take some of these swindlers, why, however much you feed them. . . . There's the captain, for example: "Uncle," he says, "will you give me something to eat!" He has probably not a bite left at home, and that is why he gads about! So, you need a little list of all these parasites? That's all right, I have already noted all of them down on a special piece of paper so as to have them struck out at the next census.'

Plyushkin put on his spectacles and began to rummage among his papers. As he was undoing all kinds of packets, he regaled his guest with such a shower of dust that the latter sneezed. At last, he pulled out a piece of paper which had been scribbled all over. The peasants' names were dotted about it like flies. Every possible sort was there: Paramons, Pimens and Pantelymons, and even one Grigory Never-Get-There. There were over a hundred and twenty in all. Chichikov smiled on seeing such a multitude. Pocketing the piece of paper, he remarked to Plyushkin that he would have to go into town to complete the transfer.

'To town? But how can I? . . . How can I leave the

house? My folk are all either thieves or rogues: in one day they would strip the place clean and not leave even a nail to hang a coat on.'

'Is there nobody you know?'

'Somebody I know? All my friends have either died or we have fallen out. Ah, but to be sure, I have some-one!' he exclaimed. 'Why, there is the president, he even visited me in days gone by. Of course, I know him! We were lads together, we used to climb all the fences to-gether! Of course, I know him! I know him very well! Should I write to him?'

'Certainly, write to him.'

'Of course I know him! We were friends at school.'

And suddenly a sort of beaming warmth passed over that wooden face, expressing not so much feeling as a pale reflection of it, and as a phenomenon this was not unlike a drowning man unexpectedly reappearing on the surface amid the joyful shouts of the crowd gathered on the bank of a river. But vainly do his brothers and sisters throw a rope into the water and wait for the drowning man's back or exhausted arms to appear again—he has shown himself for the last time. After that all is darkness, and the still surface of the elements bespeak an even greater void and terror. So it was with Plyushkin's face: the instant of feeling was succeeded by an even more callous and meaner mask.

'There was a sheet of clean paper on the table,' he said. 'Where has it got to? What rogues my servants are!' He then began to scratch on the table and under it, rum-maging everywhere until at last he called out: 'Mavra! Mavra!' At his call a woman came in holding a plate, and on it was the rusk which is already familiar to the reader. The following conversation took place between them:

'You bandit, where have you put that piece of paper?'

'Honestly, master, I haven't seen it, except for the small piece with which you were good enough to cover the glass.'

'But my eyes tell me that you have snaffled it.'

'But why should I snaffle it? It's no use to me; I have no grammar.'

'You're lying, you gave it to the sacristan: he has a smattering of things, so you took it to him.'

'But he knows where to get some himself if he wants it. He hasn't seen your bit of paper!'

'You just wait: on the Day of Judgment the devils will roast you for that on their iron forks! You wait and see how they'll roast you!'

'And why should they roast me if I haven't touched that piece of paper? They might do it for some other woman's failing, but no one has yet accused me of stealing.'

'But I tell you the devils will roast you! They will say, "Here, that's for you, you dishonest woman, for cheating your master!" Yes, they will roast you all right!'

'And I'll tell them they're wrong! Honest, I'm not to blame, I didn't take it. . . . But there it is lying on the table. You're always too quick in blaming people!'

And indeed Plyushkin then saw the sheet of paper and he paused for a moment, chewing his lips, before saying: 'Well, why are you so excited! You're a conceited creature, that's what you are!—You only have to say a word to her and she gives a dozen back!—Go now and bring a light for me to seal a letter. Just a moment, you'll bring me a tallow candle; they melt too quickly, there's only loss from them. You'd better bring me a chip!'

When Mavra had gone, Plyushkin sat down in an armchair, picked up a quill, and, moving the sheet of paper about for a long time, cogitated whether there was any way of saving a piece of it, but, convincing himself at last that it was impossible, he dipped the quill into the inkstand full of a mouldy liquid and a quantity of flies, and began to write, scrawling letters that were like notes of music, bridling every now and then the impetuosity of his hand which was apt to gallop all over the paper, setting down one niggard line after another, and thinking to himself not without regret that a lot of white margin would still be left.

To what depths can man fall to be so low, petty and nasty! How he can alter! And is this really true? There is truth in everything and man can become anything.

The fiery youth of to-day would start back in horror if he were shown his own portrait in old age. As you emerge from your tender youthful years and embark upon the austere and harsh years of manhood, take with you on your journey, take with you all those human emotions which you will never recover once you leave them behind! Imminent old age is a menace and a terror, for it never returns or gives anything back! The grave is more charitable than old age, for on the grave shall be written: 'Here lies a man!' But there is nothing to be read in the cold and callous features of inhuman senility.

'And do you happen to have a friend or so?' Plyushkin enquired as he folded the letter. 'Someone in need of runaway serfs?'

'So you also have runaway serfs?' Chichikov promptly asked, all attention now.

'That's the trouble, I have. My brother-in-law made a few investigations: he says all trace has been lost of them, but he's an army man, only good at clinking his spurs; but if one were to take the matter up with the courts. . .'

'And how many of them would there be?'

'Oh, about six dozen.'

'You don't say so?'

'Yes indeed! Not a year passes but some of them take to their heels. They're a greedy crowd, from doing nothing they have taken to drink, and I haven't anything left to eat myself. . . . I'd take anything you gave me for them. Tell your friend that: if he'd only round up a dozen of them, he'd get a good living out of it. You know, a registered serf is worth fifty roubles.'

'No, we shan't let any friend of ours get even a sniff at them,' said Chichikov to himself; and then he went on to explain that it would be impossible to find such a friend and the expense involved would come to more than it was worth; for one would have to trim the tails of one's coat to satisfy the courts; but if Plyushkin was really so hard-pressed, why then out of sympathy he was prepared to give him . . . but it was such a trifle that it was hardly worth mentioning.

'And how much would you give?' asked Plyushkin,

turning Jewish, for his hands began to quiver like mercury.

'I'd give you twenty-five kopecks a soul.'

'And how will you pay? Cash down?'

'Yes, cash down.'

'But out of consideration for my poverty won't you give me forty kopecks for each?'

'My most respected sir!' Chichikov said. 'I'd gladly give you not only forty kopecks but five hundred roubles. I'd do it very gladly because I see that you are a most worthy and kind old man and that your misfortune is due entirely to the kindness of your heart.'

'That is so! Honestly, it's so!' Plyushkin declared, dropping his head and shaking it vigorously. 'It's all the fault of my generosity.'

'You see, I have guessed your character. So why wouldn't I pay you five hundred roubles a soul, but . . . I haven't got the means. Now, five kopecks, if you like, that I can add, so that each soul would then work out at thirty kopecks.'

'Well, it's your will, my good sir, but you might throw in another two kopecks.'

'Why not? Certainly. How many souls are there? Seventy you said, I think?'

'No. There are seventy-eight to be exact.'

'Seventy-eight, seventy-eight, at thirty kopecks each, that makes . . .' Our hero paused to think for a second, not more, and then he suddenly said: 'That will make twenty-four roubles ninety-six kopecks!' He was strong in arithmetic. At once he made Plyushkin write out a receipt and handed over the money, which the latter accepted with both hands and carried over to his desk most cautiously as though it were some sort of liquid that he was afraid of spilling. On reaching the desk, he looked over the money once again and then put it away with extreme care into one of the drawers where, in all probability, it was fated to lie buried until such time as Father Carp and Father Polycarp, the two village priests, would come to bury him to the indescribable joy of his brother-in-law and daughter and even, perhaps, the captain who claimed to be a relative. Having put the money away,

Plyushkin slumped down in an armchair, winded, as it were, of talking-matter.

'Are you about to depart?' he asked, noticing that Chichikov had made a slight motion as if to pull a handkerchief out of his pocket.

This question reminded Chichikov that it really was time to be going.

'Yes, it's time to go!' he pronounced, stretching out for his hat.

'But the tea?'

'No, thank you, I'd better have tea with you some other time.'

'But I ordered the samovar to be put on. I must own that I am no great tea-drinker: it's an expensive drink, and the price of sugar has also gone up unmercifully. Proshka! We don't want the samovar now! Take the rusk and give it back to Mavra, do you hear! Tell her to put it back in the same place, but no, let me have it, I had better put it away myself. Well, good-bye, my good sir, God bless you, and please give the letter to the president. Yes, let him read it, he's an old friend of mine. Why, we were at school together!'

Thereupon, this strange apparition, this shrunken old man, conducted him from the yard and ordered the gates to be shut; then he made a round of all his storehouses to check whether the watchmen were in their places, standing at all the corners and beating with wooden spades on empty barrels instead of on the usual sheet iron;[9] after that he peeped into the kitchen where, under the pretext of verifying whether the servants' food was eatable, he had a good helping of cabbage soup and buckwheat; and, having scolded each one of them for being a thief and a good-for-nothing, he returned to his room. When he found himself alone, it occurred to him that he ought to thank his guest in some way for his unexampled generosity. 'I shall make him a present of a pocket watch,' he thought to himself. 'It's a good, silver watch, not one of your pinchbeck or bronze ones, a little out of order

---

9. Russian watchmen usually beat on metal objects while patrolling the grounds.

but he'd have it repaired. He's a young man still, and he needs a pocket watch to impress his young lady! Or no,' he added, after a moment of reflection, 'I had better leave it to him on my death, in my will, so that he may remember me.'

But our hero was in the best of spirits even without the watch. This unexpected gain was like manna from heaven. And in reality, whatever you may say, here were not only dead souls but also runaway serfs, in all over two hundred of them! Of course, he had a presentiment when driving up to Plyushkin's village that he would get something out of it, but such profit as this he had never expected. All along the road he was unusually gay: he whistled, blew through his fist as if it were a bugle, and finally indulged in a song which was so extraordinary that Selifan himself listened and listened to it until, with a shake of his head, he said: 'See how the master's singing!'

It was already dusk when they reached town. The light and shadows were so intermingled now that the very objects seemed fused. The black and white barrier assumed a nebulous colour; the sentinel's whiskers seemed to grow out of his forehead above his eyes and he did not appear to have a nose at all. The thundering noise and the jolts gave one to understand that the chaise was driving along the cobbled roadway. The street lamps had not yet been lit, there were as yet only occasional glimmers of light in the windows while, in the side-streets and alleys, scenes and conversations were going on such as are inseparable from this hour of the day in all towns, where lots of soldiers, cab-drivers, workers, are in the habit of forgathering and where creatures of a special kind in the shape of ladies, in red shawls and boots worn on stockingless legs, flit about the crossroads like bats. But Chichikov had no eyes for them and he even did not notice a number of thin officials with canes who were returning home, very likely after a stroll in the country. From time to time there was the sound of women's voices raised in exclamations, such as 'You are lying, drunken sot! I never allowed him any familiarity!' or 'Don't brawl, you ruffian, come along to the police-station. I'll show you there. . . .' In short, the sort of phrases which would scald some dreamy twenty-year-old youth as he was returning on his way back from the theatre, with his head full of images of a Spanish street, a nocturnal sky, and a beautiful woman with a guitar and curling locks. What only has he not got in his head? What dreams? He is in high heaven and is paying a call on Schiller[1]—when suddenly, like thunder, the fatal words are uttered above his head, and he discovers that he is treading the earth again, somewhere near Sennaya[2] square or some low tavern; and so once more he is sucked back into the round of everyday life.

At last, with a leap and a jolt, the chaise seemed to come to rest in a ditch by the gates of the hotel. Chichikov was greeted by Petrushka, who was holding the skirts of his coat with one hand to prevent them flying apart while with the other he helped his master down. The waiter also came running out with a candle in his hand and a napkin slung over his shoulder. It was hard to say whether Petrushka was pleased to see his master, but anyhow he and Selifan exchanged winks, and for once his usually glum expression appeared more cheerful.

'You have been away quite a while,' said the waiter as he lighted Chichikov up the stairs.

'Yes,' said Chichikov, when he had mounted the stairs. 'And how are you getting on?'

'Quite well, thank God!' answered the waiter, bowing. 'Yesterday an army lieutenant arrived and took Room Sixteen.'

'A lieutenant?'

'I don't know exactly. He's from Ryazan, he has bay horses.'

'Very well, very well! Try and be as smart next time!' said Chichikov and went into his room. As he passed through the outer room he sniffed the air and said to Petrushka: 'You might have opened the windows at least!'

---

1. Johann Friedrich von Schiller, (1759–1805), a German Romantic poet.

2. The Haymarket, a shabby square in St. Petersburg.

'But I did open them,' said Petrushka, telling a lie. However, his master knew that he was lying but he did not wish to contradict him. He felt quite worn out after the journey. Ordering himself a very light meal, consisting only of some sucking-pig, he undressed forthwith and, creeping under the quilt, he fell into a deep and sound sleep, a wonderful sleep, such as is the privilege of those fortunate people who know nothing of hæmorrhoids or fleas, or of any over-developed intellectual faculties.

CHAPTER VII

HAPPY is the traveller who, after a long and boring journey with all its chills, sleet, mud, drowsy overseers at posting-stations, jingle of bells, stoppages, altercations, drivers, blacksmiths and all sorts of riff-raff on the road, beholds at last the familiar roof and the glimmer of lights rushing to meet him. Then he will picture the familiar rooms, the joyful cries of the folk running out to greet him, the noise and the running footsteps of his children, and the gentle soothing words interspersed with passionate kisses that have the power to erase all sad thoughts from his memory. Happy the family man with a home of his own, but woe to the bachelor!

Happy the writer who, avoiding boring and repulsive characters, as well as those that astound one by their painful reality, is drawn to characters that embody the highest values of humanity; the writer, who, from the great whirlpool of everyday models, has selected only a few exceptions, who has never once pitched his lyre in a lower key, has never deigned to descend to the level of his poor, insignificant fellow creatures, but without touching the earth has concentrated entirely on his own images so elevated and remote from it. His fine lot is doubly to be envied: he is of the family of ordinary men; and yet his fame resounds far and wide. He has clouded men's eyes with the smoke of illusion; he has flattered them wondrously, obscuring the sadness of life and showing them man as a thing of beauty. All hasten and rush applauding in the wake of his triumphant chariot. They salute him as a great universal poet, soaring high above all the other geniuses of the world as the eagle soars above the other high-flying birds. At the sound of his name alone impulsive, youthful hearts are seized with trembling; tears gleam responsively in every eye. . . . He has no equal in power—he is a god!

But such is not the lot, and quite different the destiny, of the writer who has ventured to bring into the open what is ever before men's eyes, all those things which the indifferent gaze fails to perceive, the whole horrid and shocking slimy mess of trifling things which have clogged our life, the whole depth of those chilly, split-up, every-day characters who swarm upon our bitter and dreary path on earth, and with the firm power of a relentless chisel to dare and present them roundly and clearly for the benefit of all! It is not for him to receive the applause of the people, to behold the grateful tears and the unanimous enthusiasm of souls he has stirred; no girl of sixteen, giddy and impelled by heroic enthusiasm, will fly into his arms; he will find no oblivion in his own sweet numbers; and last of all, he will not escape the judgment of his contemporaries, that hypocritically callous judgment, which will brand his cherished creations as mean and insignificant, will assign him a despicable niche among writers who have affronted humanity, will attribute to him the qualities of his depicted heroes, will rob him of heart and soul and the divine fire of genius. For contemporary judgment does not admit that the telescope pointed at the sun and the microscope recording the movements of unnoticed insects are equally wonderful; contemporary judgment does not recognize that great spiritual depth is required to illuminate a picture drawn from despised life and to make of it the pearl of creation; for contemporary judgment does not allow the high laughter of delight a worthy place side by side with lofty lyrical emotion, nor admit the great gulf between it and the grimaces of a circus bard! No, contemporary judgment does not allow that, and will turn it all to the censure and disadvantage of the unrecognized writer; without sympathy, without response, without compassion, he will be left standing alone in the middle of the road like a homeless wayfarer. Hard is his lot and bitter the solitude he will experience.

For a long time to come I am destined by the magic powers to wander together with my strange heroes and to observe the whole vast movement of life—to observe it through laughter which can be shared by all and through tears which are unknown and unseen! And far off still is that time when the dread whirlwind of inspiration will spout in another stream out of a head swathed in holy terror and in gleams, when in confusion and tremor men will hear the majestic thunder of other declamations. . . .

But let us be off! Let us be off! Away with invading wrinkles and the harsh twilight that falls upon a face! Without hesitation let us plunge into life with all its hollow noise and jingle of bells, and let us see what Chichikov is about.

As he woke up, Chichikov stretched his arms and legs and felt that he had had a good rest. After lying for a couple of minutes on his back, he snapped his fingers and remembered with a joyful face that he had now close on four hundred souls. At once he jumped out of bed without even looking at his face, which he sincerely loved and of which the chin was apparently the most attractive feature, for he was in the habit of boasting about it in front of friends, especially at times when he was shaving. 'Just look,' he would say, stroking his chin, 'see what a chin I've got; it's quite round.' But on this occasion he did not glance either at his chin or face, but simply pulled on his boots just as he was—his morocco boots with multi-coloured patterns of all sorts such as are to be found selling briskly in the town of Torzhok,[3] thanks to the Russians' love of ease—and attired in Scottish fashion only in a shirt, forgetting his dignity and what was owed

3. A town between Moscow and St. Petersburg which used to have several factories that manufactured leather goods.

to middle age, he gave two leaps across the room, deftly striking his heels on the calves of his legs. Then he at once got down to business: he rubbed his hands in front of his box with the same glee that an unbribable district judge, who has set out to conduct a case, will feel at the sight of a good lunch, and he quickly took some papers out of it. Wishing to avoid delay and bring the matter to a head as quickly as possible, he had decided to draw up the deeds of purchase himself, to write them out and copy them, and so save the expense of a clerk. He was well versed in legal phraseology: in a bold hand he put down the year eighteen-hundred and something, following it up in a smaller hand with So-and-so, landowner, and the rest. Within two hours everything was ready.

Afterwards, when he looked over these lists—at the names of peasants who had once been really peasants, who had toiled, ploughed, got drunk, driven their carts, cheated their masters, or had simply been good peasants —he was overcome by a strange and to him incomprehensible emotion. Each of the scrawls seemed to have a special character of its own and in this way the peasants themselves acquired a character of their own. Those belonging to Korobochka had almost all of them character sketches and nicknames. Plyushkin's list was distinguished by its brevity of expression: quite often only the initial letters of their names appeared, followed by dots. Sobakievich's register was astonishing for its extraordinary completeness and detail: not one of the peasants' qualities was omitted; of one it was said that he was a 'good carpenter' while another was described as 'intelligent and sober'. It was also detailed who their father was and who their mother, and how they conducted themselves; of one, Fedotov, it was noted that 'his father was unknown and he was born of the serving girl Capitolina, but was of good behaviour and no thief'. This variety of detail made it all very animated: it seemed as if the peasants were alive but yesterday. As he stared at their names, Chichikov was moved and said with a sigh: 'Oh Lord, how many of you there are scrawled here! And what did you do, my dear hearts, in your day?

How did you rub along?' Involuntarily his eyes rested on
one name. It was that of the Pyotr Saveliev Blast-the-
Trough, of whom the reader has heard already and
who once belonged to Korobochka. He could not resist
saying again: 'Ah, what a daddy-long-legs, he has
sprawled all over the page! Whether you were a craftsman or a common peasant, I wonder what sort of death
took you? Was it in a gin-shop? Or did a clumsy cart run
over you when you were drowsing in the middle of the
road? Stepan Probka, carpenter and a model of sobriety!
Ah, yes, that is the Probka who was a *bogatyr*, a champion,
and fit to be a guardsman! Why, he must have trudged
through all the provinces with his axe in his belt and his
boots slung over his shoulder, eating a farthing's worth
of bread and two farthings' worth of dried fish, but I
wager he used to bring back a hundred roubles or so in
silver in his bag each time, or, if it were a note, he'd sew
it up in his sackcloth trousers or stick it into his boot. I
wonder where you met your death? Did you mount up
under a church cupola to make an extra rouble; or maybe you clambered up the cross and, slipping from the
crossbeam, hit the ground while some uncle Mihey
standing by scratched his head and said: "Ah, Vanya,
you've done it this time!" and, slinging a rope round himself, scrambled up in your place. Then there is Maxim
Telyatnikov, the shoemaker. Ha, a shoemaker! Drunk as
a shoemaker, so the proverb has it. I know you, I know
you, my fine fellow; if you like, I shall relate the whole
of your life-story. You were apprenticed to a German,
who had a common table for the lot of you, beat you on
the back with a strap for carelessness and never let you
out of doors to gad about; you turned out to be no ordinary shoemaker but a miracle, and the German could
not praise you highly enough when he was talking to his
wife or a friend. And how did this apprenticeship end?
"I'll get me my own house now," you said. "And I
shan't be like the German who counts every penny, I'll
get rich all at once." And so compounding with your
master for a goodly sum, you started up a shop, collected
a lot of orders and set to. You got hold of some rotten

leather thrice as cheap and made twice as much on each boot, true enough, but then your boots all went to pieces in a couple of weeks and you got a good rating for it. And so your shop lost its customers and off you went sousing and rolling about the streets, saying: "No, it's a bad world! There's no living to be made by a Russian, it's all these Germans in the way!" But what's this for a peasant—Elizaveta Vorobey. Well, I'm damned, a woman! And how did she get here? That swine of a Sobakievich must have played a fast one on me!'

Chichikov was quite right: it was a woman. How she got there was a mystery, but her name was so artfully scrawled that, at a distance, it might have been mistaken for that of a man and the name even had a hard ending, that is to say, it read Elizavet instead of Elizaveta. However, he was not to be taken in and he struck the name out at once. 'Grigory Never-Get-There! What sort of a man were you? Did you set up as a driver and, procuring a *troika* and a tilt-cart, renounce your home and native lair forever, and spend the rest of your days driving merchants to the market-fairs? Did you give up your soul on the road? Or was it your own friend who did you in over some plump and red-cheeked soldier's wife? Or did some forest tramp like the look of your leather mittens and your *troika* of squat but sturdy horses? Or maybe, after lying thinking and thinking on your plank-bed, you suddenly went off to the gin-shop and, after that, right through the ice of a river, and that was all that was remembered of you? Ah, you Russian folk! You don't like dying in your beds!

'And what about you, my doves?' Chichikov continued as his eyes strayed on the names of Plyushkin's runaway serfs. 'You're still alive, but what's the use of you! You might as well be dead! And where have your fast feet carried you now? Was it so bad with Plyushkin? Or is it of your free will that you stalk the forests and rob travellers? Are you in jail or have you been ploughing for another master? Eremey Karyakin, Nikita Volokita,[4] his

4. "Volokita" is also the colloquial term for a vagabond, a wanderer, someone who does not have a house of his own.

son Anton Volokita, a family of lazybones—one can see by their very nicknames how fast they ran! Popov was attached to the household and must have been literate: I bet he did not take to the knife but did his thieving like a gentleman. But being without a passport you must have been caught by a captain of the police. You put a good face on it when examined. "Whose are you?" says the captain, profiting by this occasion to address a rude word or two to you. "Landowner So-and-So's," you answer briskly. "What are you doing here?" says the captain. "I've compounded," you reply without hesitation. "Where's your passport?" "My present master, Pimenov, has it." "Call Pimenov." "Are you Pimenov?" "Yes, I am Pimenov." "Has he given you his passport?" "No, he never gave me any passport." "Why are you lying?" says the captain, ejaculating a strong word. "Exactly so," you answer smartly, "I did not give it to him because he came home late, but I gave it into the keeping of Antipe Prohorov, the bell-ringer." "Call the bell-ringer!" "Did he give you a passport?" "No, I never got a passport from him!" "Why are you lying again?" says the captain, fortifying his speech with some more curses. "I did have it," you say promptly, "but maybe, it seems, it looks like as if I might have dropped it on the way." "And why did you steal that soldier's coat?" the captain demands, cursing you again. "And the trunk with the copper coins you took from the priest?" "I never did it," you say, unmoved, "I have never been mixed up with stealing." "Then why was the coat found among your things?" "I can't say: most likely, someone put it there." "Ah, you brute, you brute!" cries the captain, shaking his head and holding his sides. "Get the foot-stocks on him and off with him to jail!" "As you please, sir, with pleasure," you reply. And then, pulling out a snuff-box, you hand it round amicably to the two veterans who are busy hammering on your stocks, and you enquire of them whether they have been long retired and in what campaigns they have fought. And so you live in jail until your case comes to court. And then the court decides to have you moved from Tsarevokokshaisk to a jail elsewhere; and there it is further decreed to have you transported to some place called Vessiegonsk; and you pass from jail to jail, and say to yourself when you see your new habitation: "No, the Vessiegonsk jail is cleaner, there's room for a game of skittles here and more company!"

'Abakum Fyrov! What about you? Where are you knocking about? Have you taken to the Volga? And have you grown fond of a free life among the barge-haulers? . . .' At this point Chichikov paused and reflected. What was he thinking about? Was he pondering on the lot of Abakum Fyrov? Or was he reflecting upon himself as every Russian is apt to do, whatever his age, rank or condition, when he thinks of life in its broadest and most rollicking sense. And indeed, where is Fyrov now? He leads a carefree and boisterous life on a corn wharf,[5] bargaining with the merchants. With ribbons and flowers on their caps, the band of barge-haulers makes merry as they bid farewell to their women-folk and wives, who look tall, well-built, and bedecked with necklets and ribbons. There is singing and dancing; the whole square is agog as, in the midst of all this shouting, swearing and cries of encouragement, the porters hook on some twenty-five stone to the haulers' backs and then noisily tip oats and grain into the deep holds of the barges; and all over the square pyramids of sacks are to be seen piled up like cannon balls, and the whole arsenal of grain will look huge until it has all been loaded into the barges and carried away in endless Indian file together with the spring ice. Then will be the time for you, barge-haulers, to work your fill! And just as before you made merry or went on a rampage, so now you will toil and sweat, hauling away in unison to that one chant, which is as endless as Russia herself!

'Aha! It's midday!' exclaimed Chichikov at last, glancing at his watch. 'Why have I got stuck? If only I had been doing something useful, but here I've been building castles in the air and dreaming. What a fool I am!' Having expressed himself thus, he changed from his

5. A pier on the river Volga for loading grain shipments, often the place of free merrymaking by handlers of barges and others.

Scottish costume into a European one, tightened the buckle of his belt over his rotund belly, sprayed himself with eau-de-cologne, picked up his warm cap, thrust his papers under his arm, and set off to the civil courts to legalize his deeds of purchase. He was in a hurry, not because he was afraid of being late—the president was an old acquaintance and could prolong or shorten an interview at will, like Homer's ancient Zeus who lengthened days or lent quick-falling nights whenever it was judicious to cut short the disputes of the heroes he loved or to give them more light in which to finish their fighting—but he felt impelled to bring the matter to an end as soon as possible; until that was accomplished he had a sense of unease and discomfort; in spite of himself he was haunted by the thought that the serfs in question were not altogether real and that in such cases it was always better to get the burden off one's shoulders as quickly as possible.

He had barely set foot in the street, lost in his thoughts and wrapped at the same time in a bearskin covered with brown cloth, when at the very next corner he ran into a gentleman also attired in a bearskin covered with brown cloth and wearing a warm cap with ear-flaps. The gentleman hailed him: it was Manilov. At once they put their arms round each other and remained in that position for about five minutes. The kisses they showered on each other were so powerful that their front teeth ached for the rest of the day. Manilov's joy was so pronounced that his nose and lips were all that remained of his face—his eyes disappeared entirely. For the next quarter of an hour he held Chichikov's hand in both of his until it grew terribly hot. In the most agreeable and delicate way he related how he was flying to embrace Pavel Ivanovich: this speech was crowned with a compliment such as was becoming only for a maiden whom one has invited to a dance. Chichikov opened his mouth, uncertain as yet how to thank him, when suddenly Manilov pulled out a paper from under his fur-coat, a piece of paper rolled up into a pipe and tied with a pink ribbon.

'What is that?'

'The serfs.'

'Ah!' Chichikov at once unrolled the paper, glanced over it, and was amazed at the beautiful and tidy handwriting. 'What fine writing,' he said, 'there will be no need to copy it. And there's a border round it! It's quite artistic! Who did it?'

'Well, you musn't ask,' said Manilov.

'You?'

'My wife.'

'Heavens! I'm really embarrassed for giving you so much trouble.'

'It's no trouble at all when it's a question of Pavel Ivanovich.'

Chichikov acknowledged this with a bow. Learning that he was on his way to the courts, Manilov expressed his readiness to accompany him. The friends set off together arm in arm. Whenever they came across any incline, hillock or step, Manilov supported Chichikov and almost lifted him off the ground, interjecting with an amiable smile that he would not on any account permit Pavel Ivanovich to stumble. At a loss how to express his gratitude, Chichikov felt self-conscious and awkward as any calf. Exchanging mutual compliments, they finally reached the square which contained the building they sought: it was a large, three-storied, stone house as white as chalk, no doubt to symbolize thus the purity of soul of those who exercised their various callings within it: the other buildings in the square did not compare in size with this stone house. Among them were a sentinel's box with an armed sentinel standing by, two or three cab stations and, finally, the fences, which stretched far and wide with the usual sort of scribbles and drawings scrawled on them in coal and chalk; there was nothing more to be found in this isolated or, as it was sometimes called, lovely spot. From the second- and third-floor windows the incorruptible heads of some of the votaries of Themis[6] peeped out, only to withdraw instantly, most likely on the entry of their chiefs.

The friends flew rather than ascended the stairs, because Chichikov hurried his steps in order to avoid

6. Greek goddess of justice, represented as holding scales.

Manilov's support while Manilov flew ahead to try to prevent Chichikov from overtiring himself, and for that reason both were much out of breath when they set foot in the dark corridor. Neither the corridors nor the offices struck them as very clean. In those days little heed was paid to cleanliness, and what was dirty remained dirty without any pretensions to an attractive appearance. Themis received her guests, just as she was, in negligée and dressing-gown. The various offices through which our heroes trekked ought to be duly described, but the author has always fought shy of such places. If ever he happened to pass through them, even when they were at their best and noblest with an array of polished floors and tables, he tried to run past as quickly as possible with eyes meekly lowered and fixed on the floor, and as a result he has no idea whatever how anything prospers and flowers there. Our heroes caught sight of a great deal of paper, some in rough draft and some blank, many bowed heads, thick necks, dress coats, frock coats of a provincial cut and even one light-grey jacket, which stood out sharply and leaned to one side as its owner screwed his head sideways almost touching the paper—he was writing out boldly and with a flourish some protocol of land recovered as a result of a lawsuit, or the inventory of an estate sequestrated by a peaceful landlord who lived on it without qualms while the courts pursued their investigations, begot and reared children, and even had grandchildren there. Intermittently voices could be heard giving vent hoarsely to such expressions as: 'Fedosey Fedoseyich, will you pass me case No. 368!' or 'You are always mislaying the lid of the office inkpot!' At times a more majestic voice, no doubt that of a chief, rang out imperiously: 'Here, copy that! Otherwise your boots will be taken off and you'll be locked in for six days on hard rations.' There was a great deal of pen-scratching and the noise of it was like the passage of several carts loaded with brushwood through a forest several feet deep in withered leaves.

Chichikov and Manilov went up to the first desk, at which sat two officials of youthful age, and enquired of them: 'May we ask who deals here with deeds of purchase?'

'What is it you want exactly?' asked both clerks, turning round.

'I should like to put in an application.'

'And what have you bought?'

'I should first of all like to know where this matter of deeds of purchase is dealt with, here or in another office?'

'But tell us first what you bought and the price, and then we shall tell you, it's impossible otherwise.'

Chichikov gathered at once that the officials were merely inquisitive and, like all young officials, they wished to endow their office with greater weight and consequence.

'Listen, dear friends,' he said, 'I know very well that all affairs having to do with deeds of purchase are concentrated in one office and that is why I am asking you to tell me where it is, but if you don't know your own organization then we shall ask someone else.' The officials made no reply to this, but one of them pointed to a corner of the room where an elderly man was sitting and marking some papers. Chichikov and Manilov made their way past the other desks towards him. The old man was very much engrossed.

'May I enquire,' asked Chichikov, bowing, 'whether you deal with deeds of purchase?'

The old man raised his eyes and said with deliberation:

'No, we don't deal with deeds of purchase here.'

'Where then?'

'In the Deeds Section.'

'And where is that?'

'That's Ivan Antonovich's department.'

'And where is Ivan Antonovich?'

The old man pointed to the other end of the room. Chichikov and Manilov set off towards Ivan Antonovich. Ivan Antonovich had already sized them up but he had at once stuck his nose into his papers.

'May I enquire,' asked Chichikov with a bow, 'whether you deal with deeds of purchase?'

Ivan Antonovich appeared not to have heard and made no reply as he studied his papers. It was apparent that he was a man of reasonable age and no young chatterbox or gad-about. He was well over forty, with black, thick hair; the whole middle of his face jutted out and concentrated in his nose; in short, it was the sort of face that is commonly known as a 'jug snout'.

'May I enquire if this is the deeds section?' Chichikov persisted.

'This is it,' said Ivan Antonovich, turning away his 'jug snout' and starting to scribble again.

'My affair is as follows: I have bought a number of peasants from various landowners in this district: I have the deed of purchase, it's only a question of the formalities now.'

'And are the sellers here?'

'Some are here, I have an authorization from others.'

'And have you brought an application?'

'Yes, I have. I should like . . . I am in a hurry. . . . Could you not, for example, have it all ready to-day?'

'To-day! Impossible!' said Ivan Antonovich. 'I shall have to make some enquiries and find out whether there is nothing against it.'

'However, to speed up the matter, there is Ivan Grigorievich the president, who is a friend of mine. . . .'

'Ivan Grigorievich is not the only one; there are others too,' Ivan Antonovich retorted severely.

Chichikov took the hint and said: 'The others will not be losers either; I have been in the service, I know. . . .'

'Well, go and see Ivan Grigorievich,' Ivan Antonovich advised in a kindlier voice. 'Let him give the order and the affair will not be delayed.'

Chichikov pulled out a note and put it down in front of Ivan Antonovich, who, without appearing to notice it, covered it over with a book. Chichikov was about to point it out to him, but Ivan Antonovich nodded his head as much as to say that he was quite aware of it.

'He'll take you along to the president!' said Ivan Antonovich with a nod of his head. One of the votaries who was standing by and who had been sacrificing so zealously to Themis that both elbows of his sleeves had burst, revealing the lining beneath, for which good offices he had in his time been awarded the rank of collegiate registrar, now attached himself to our heroes just as Virgil had once offered his services to Dante,[7] and led them to the inner sanctum which was furnished only with spacious armchairs; and there, at a desk, behind a coat of arms and two thick volumes, sat the president, all alone like the sun. The new Virgil was so awed by this sanctum that he did not venture to set foot in it and retreated, displaying a back as ragged as an old mat with a feather stuck to it. On entering the sanctum they perceived that the president was not alone—Sobakievich was there too, masked by the coat of arms.[8] The visitors' arrival gave rise to exclamations and the presidential armchair was moved noisily aside. Sobakievich also got out of his chair and, long sleeves and all, became visible from all sides. The president took Chichikov in his arms and the room echoed to their kisses; they enquired after each other's health; it turned out that they both had an ache in their back and this was at once ascribed to a sedentary life. It seemed that Sobakievich had already informed the president of the sale, for the latter began to congratulate Chichikov much to the latter's immediate confusion, since he was now openly faced with both Sobakievich and Manilov with whom he had concluded his deals separately. However, he thanked the president, and, turning at once to Sobakievich, asked him:

'And how are you?'

'There's nothing to complain of, thank God,' said Sobakievich. And true enough there was little to complain of; for sooner might a lump of iron catch cold, and cough, than this marvellously formed landowner.

'Yes, you were always famed for your health,' said the president, 'and your deceased father was also a strong man.'

7. In Dante's *Divine Comedy*, the Latin poet Virgil serves as a guide to Dante during a trip through Hell. 8. According to a decree by Peter I, every governmental court office was obliged to have in it a three-sided mirror surmounted by an eagle (symbol of the monarchy) and three decrees setting forth the rules of the court.

'Yes, he used to stalk bears all by himself,' answered Sobakievich.

'It seems to me,' pursued the president, 'that you could also tumble a bear if you wished to try.'

'No, I couldn't,' replied Sobakievich. 'The old man was stronger than I am.' And with a sigh he continued: 'No, folk are not the same these days. Now take my life, what sort of a life is it? There isn't much to it. . . .'

'And why isn't your life a thing of joy?' enquired the president.

'It's no good, no good,' said Sobakievich, shaking his head. 'Judge for yourself, Ivan Grigorievich: I'm in my fiftieth year now and have never been ill; if only I had had a sore throat, an abscess or a boil. . . . No, it's no good! I'll have to pay for it one day.' And here Sobakievich sank into a melancholy.

'What a man!' Chichikov and the president thought, simultaneously. 'Just imagine what he's grumbling about!'

'I have a letter for you,' said Chichikov as he took Plyushkin's letter from his pocket.

'From whom?' enquired the president and, opening the envelope, he exclaimed: 'Ah! from Plyushkin. Is he still leading his frozen existence? What a fate! Once upon a time he was a very clever and rich man! But now . . .'

'A dog,' said Sobakievich. 'A rogue. He's starving all his folk to death.'

'Certainly, certainly,' declared the president when he had finished the letter. 'I shall act for him. When would you like to complete the formalities, now or later?'

'Now,' said Chichikov. 'I shall even ask you, if it is possible, to do it to-day, because I am planning to leave the town to-morrow. I have the deeds of purchase and the application with me.'

'That's all very well, but say what you like, we are not going to let you go so easily. The formalities will be completed to-day, but you must stay on with us for a while. I shall give the order now,' he said, opening the door of the office which was chock-a-block with officials who looked like industrious bees scattered about their combs, if a honeycomb can in anyway be compared with an office. 'Is Ivan Antonovich there?'

'Yes, sir,' a voice replied.

'Will you ask him to come in!'

The 'jug's snout', Ivan Antonovich, who is already familiar to the reader, made his appearance in the sanctum and bowed respectfully.

'Will you take all these deeds, Ivan Antonovich. . . .'

'And please don't forget, Ivan Grigorievich,' Sobakievich interjected, 'you will have to have witnesses, at least two for each party. Send at once for the prosecutor. He is not a busy man and you will very likely find him at home; Zolotuha, the attorney, a real extortioner, does all the work for him. The medical inspector is also a man of leisure and probably at home, if he has not gone off to play cards somewhere, and there are a lot more within reach—Truhachevsky, Begushkin, and their like, who have nothing better to do than get in the way!'

'That is so, that is so,' the president agreed, and he immediately had a messenger despatched after them.

'May I ask you another favour?' said Chichikov. 'Would you please send for the agent of a lady landowner with whom I have also concluded a deal—he is the son of Father Cyril, the head priest, and he is in your service.'

'Why, of course, we shall send for him too!' said the president. 'Everything will be done and I would ask you not to make any presents to my subordinates. My friends should not have to pay.' Having said that, he at once gave an order to Ivan Antonovich, which the latter evidently did not like very much. The deeds of purchase apparently made a good impression on the president, especially when he had grasped that they amounted to some hundred thousand roubles. For some minutes he gazed into Chichikov's eyes with an expression of great satisfaction and then finally said: 'So that's how things are! In this way, Pavel Ivanovich, you have acquired property.'

'I have,' said Chichikov.

'Very good that, very good!'

'I am quite aware that I could not have done anything

better. Whatever you may say, a man's goal is uncertain unless he has set his foot firmly upon a sound foundation rather than on some wilful chimera of youth.' Here he set about castigating the younger generation, and deservedly so, for its liberalism. But curiously enough there was no conviction in his words, it was as if he had said to himself: 'Ah, brother, you are lying, and how you are lying!' He did not even look at Sobakievich and Manilov, for fear of catching some disapproving expression on their faces. But his fear was vain: Sobakievich's face did not register a flicker, while Manilov, rapt by his phrases, only nodded his head in approving delight, sinking into an attitude commonly adopted by lovers of music whenever a soprano outdoes the violinist himself and emits a note of such high pitch that even a bird cannot compete with it.

'But why don't you tell Ivan Grigorievich what exactly you have acquired,' put in Sobakievich. 'And you, Ivan Grigorievich, why do you not enquire what it is? Why, they are worth their weight in gold, these folk! Just think, I have sold him my coach-maker, Miheyev.'

'You don't say so?' said the president. 'I know this Miheyev, a fine coach-builder he is too; he once repaired my droshky. But excuse me, how can that be. . . . Didn't you tell me that he was dead? . . .'

'Who? Miheyev dead?' said Sobakievich coolly. 'It was his brother who died. He himself is very much alive and is in better health than ever. A short while back he made me a chaise the equal of which you would not find in Moscow. He really should be working only for the Tsar.'

'Yes, Miheyev is a fine craftsman,' said the president. 'I am surprised you parted with him.'

'But it's not Miheyev alone! There is Probka Stepan, the carpenter, Milushkin, the bricklayer, Maxim Telyatnikov, the shoemaker, they are all gone, I've sold them all.' And when the president asked why he had parted with these folk, essential for the household and the workshops, Sobakievich answered with a wave of his hand: 'Oh, just out of foolishness, I'll get rid of them, I said, and I did so like a fool!' Then he hung his head as if repenting, and added: 'Grey hairs have not taught me any sense.'

'But may I ask, Pavel Ivanovich,' enquired the president, 'how is it that you are buying peasants without the land? Or is it for transplantation?'

'Yes, for transplantation.'

'Well, that is a different matter. And where?'

'Oh. . . . In the Kherson province.'[9]

'Ah, there is fine land there!' said the president, and he spoke very favourably of the luxuriant vegetation in that region.

'And have you plenty of land there?'

'Quite enough. As much as the peasants I have purchased will be able to look after.'

'Is there a river or pond on your estate?'

'A river. However, there is also a pond.' On saying this, Chichikov accidentally glanced at Sobakievich and it struck him that, although not a muscle of Sobakievich's face moved, there was written on it: 'Oh, now you're lying! I very much doubt if you have a river and a pond, to say nothing of any land!'

While they continued to converse, the witnesses began to arrive: the prosecutor with his blinking eyes, the medical inspector, Truhachevsky, Begushkin and the rest of those who, according to Sobakievich, only got in the way. Many of them were quite unknown to Chichikov: the gaps were filled by some of the officials. Not only the son of Father Cyril, the head priest, but the head priest himself, was fetched. Each of the witnesses signed himself according to his worth and rank, some scrawling their names and titles backwards, some slantwise and others almost upside down, setting down letters that had not even been seen in the Russian alphabet. Ivan Antonovich conducted himself most efficiently, the deeds of purchase were registered, stamped, recorded in a register or wherever it had to be, a half per cent. was deducted as well as the amount for a notice in *The Gazette*, and

9. A province adjoining the Black Sea north of the Crimea, newly acquired by Russia after wars with Turkey; settlement of peasants was encouraged in this area, which was called "New Russia."

Chichikov got away with the minimum of expense. The president even gave orders that only half the dues should be collected from him while the other half was in a manner unbeknown put down to the account of some other petitioner.

'And so,' said the president when it was all over, 'it only remains to "sprinkle" the deal.'

'Delighted,' said Chichikov. 'It's up to you to fix the time. It would be a sin if I did not uncork two or three bottles of fizz for the pleasure of such an agreeable company.'

'No, you misunderstand us: we shall provide the fizz,' said the president. 'It's our duty, our obligation. You are our guest: we shall entertain you. Do you know what, gentlemen! Let us do it now: let us all go just as we are, to the chief of the police. He is a miracle-worker, he only has to wink an eye when passing a fishmonger or a wine-cellar and we shall make a fine meal of it! And a game of whist into the bargain!'

No one could refuse this suggestion. At the very mention of the fish-stalls the witnesses felt a growing appetite; they at once picked up their caps and hats and the audience was at an end. As they were passing through the outer office, Ivan Antonovich or 'jug's snout', as he was called, bowed respectfully and said to Chichikov in a low voice:

'You've bought a hundred thousand roubles' worth of peasants, but you have only given me twenty-five roubles for my pains.'

'But what sort of peasants are they?' Chichikov whispered back. 'They are a pretty worthless lot, not worth half of that.' Ivan Antonovich understood that he had to deal with a firm character and would get no more.

'And how much did you pay Plyushkin for each soul?' Sobakievich whispered in his other ear.

'And why did you include Vorobey?' Chichikov retorted.

'Which Vorobey?' asked Sobakievich.

'The female, of course. Elizavet Vorobey, you even added a hard sign[1] at the end.'

---

1. Chichikov, as usual in purchasing serfs, was buying only adult male serfs. "Hard sign": a letter in the Russian alphabet.

'No, I did not include any Vorobey,' Sobakievich declared, walking off to join some of the other members of the party.

The whole company arrived at last in a crowd at the house of the chief of police. This official was really a miracle-worker: as soon as he heard what it was all about, he immediately summoned a policeman, a dashing young fellow in glittering boots, and apparently whispered only two words in his ear, adding: 'Do you understand?' and in a trice, while some of the guests were settling down to whist, the table in the other room was laid with a great spread of white sturgeon, salmon, pressed and fresh caviare, herrings, stellated sturgeon, assortments of cheese, smoked tongue, and further varieties of sturgeon, which had all been brought from the fish market. To these were added other items from the household larder and tit-bits from the kitchen: a fish-head pie filled with the trimmings of a three-hundred-pound sturgeon, another pie of mushrooms, then fried-pastries, butter-cakes, and fritters. The chief of police was in a sense the father and benefactor of the town. He treated the citizens as though they were all members of his family, and he kept his eye on the shops and the market-hall as though they were his own larder. In general he kept his place, as they say, and mastered his profession to perfection. It was hard to decide whether he had been created for his post or the post for him. He had arranged things so ably that he drew double the income of any of his predecessors and at the same time preserved the affection of the whole town. The merchants in particular liked him greatly for not being proud: and, true enough, he stood godfather to their children, fraternized with them and, though he skinned them too, he somehow did it with unusual dexterity; he would slap a man on the back, laugh with him, give him tea, promise to call on him and play a game of draughts, enquire about all his affairs and how he was getting on. If he heard that a child had fallen sick he would recommend a medicine—in short, he was a grand fellow! Whenever he went out driving and issued his orders, he would find time to slip a word to someone or other: 'Well, Miheyich, we must finish our game one day.' 'Yes, Alexei Ivanovich,' the other would reply, taking off his hat, 'we must.' 'Well, Ilya Paramonich, do come and see my trotter, we'll have a race between yours and mine; we'll try him out.' The merchant, who was crazy about trotting horses, smiled back at this with particular favour, as they say, and, stroking his beard, said: 'We'll try him out, Alexei Ivanovich!' Even the shopmen, who were accustomed at such times to stand about with their caps off, exchanged pleasurable glances as if wishing to say: 'Alexei Ivanovich is a fine man!' In short, he had succeeded in winning universal popularity and in the merchants' opinion: 'Alexei Ivanovich would never betray you even though he does line his pockets.'

Noticing that the meal had been set out, the chief of the police suggested to his guests that they should finish their game of whist after luncheon, and they all proceeded into the room from which a pleasant smell had been emanating and tickling their nostrils, and into which Sobakievich had already been peeping after observing a sturgeon on a large dish set to one side. After drinking a glass of vodka of a darkish olive colour such as is to be found only in those transparent Siberian stones from which seals are cut in Russia, they closed in on the table from all sides with forks in their hands and began to exhibit, each of them, their characters and inclinations, one favouring caviare, another sturgeon, and a third cheese. Sobakievich, ignoring all these trifles, settled down to his sturgeon and, while the others were drinking, talking and eating, finished it off in some quarter of an hour, so that when the chief of police remembered about it and said: 'Gentlemen, and what do you think of this creation of nature?' he perceived, on going up to it with a fork, followed by the rest of the company, that the tail of the creation was all that remained. In the meantime Sobakievich pretended that he was in no way to blame for this and concentrated on a plate of small dried fish which was some distance off. Then, full of sturgeon, Sobakievich sat back in an armchair and took no more to drink or eat, only half-closing and blinking his eyes.

The chief of police evidently did not like to stint his wine: there was no end of toasts. As the reader may guess, the very first toast was proposed in honour of the new Kherson landowner, the next for the welfare of his serfs and their happy transplantation, then to the health of his beautiful future wife—a toast that made our hero break into a pleasant smile. The company now surrounded Chichikov and began to plead with him to stay at least a fortnight longer in town: 'No, Pavel Ivanovich, say what you will, a fleeting visit like that only cools the hut, as they say! No, you must spend a little time with us! We'll marry you off, isn't that so, Ivan Grigorievich? We'll marry him off, won't we?'

'Of course, we will!' exclaimed the president. 'However much you may resist, we shall marry you off nevertheless! No, once you are here, you must not complain. We don't like trifling.'

'Well, and why should I resist?' said Chichikov with a smile. 'Marriage is too attractive to resist provided there is a bride.'

'Certainly there will be a bride! Why shouldn't there be? There will be everything, everything you like! . . .'

'Well, then . . .'

'Bravo! He's staying!' they all shouted. 'Viva, hurrah, Pavel Ivanovich! Hurrah!'

They all came up to clink glasses with him and Chichikov clinked with every one of them. 'No, no, again!' shouted those who were excited and they all clinked glasses again; then they came up for a third round, and a third time they clinked glasses. In a short while they were all extraordinarily merry. The president, who was the most charming of men, embraced Chichikov several times when at his gayest and called him from the heart: 'My soul! my mummy dear!' and snapping his fingers he started to dance round him singing that well-known song: 'Hey, you this and that, Kamarinsky [2] peasant lad.' After the champagne, they uncorked some bottles of Tokay, which put more spirit into them and still further cheered up the company. They entirely forgot about the

---

2. A lively, comic Russian folk dance.

whist; they argued, shouted and talked about everything
—politics, military affairs, they gave vent to free thoughts
for which at other times they would have thrashed their
own children. In passing, they resolved a multitude of the
most complex problems. Chichikov had never felt himself so happy and he already saw himself as a real Kherson landowner, talked about various improvements he
was going to introduce, the three-field system, the happiness and beatitude of two kindred souls, and he began to
read aloud to Sobakievich Werther's epistle in verse to
Charlotte,[3] at which the latter merely blinked his eyes as
he lay back in the armchair, for after that sturgeon drowsiness was his sole preoccupation. It occurred to Chichikov that he was letting himself go too much, so he asked
for a carriage and availed himself of the prosecutor's
droshky. As luck would have it, the prosecutor's coachman was an old hand at the game, for he drove the horses
with one hand only and supported the gentleman with
the other. In this wise, in the droshky, he reached the
hotel where for a long while he babbled a great deal of
nonsense about a comely bride, Kherson villages, and
capital funds. Selifan was even given instructions to
assemble all the transplanted serfs in order to make a roll
call of them all. Selifan listened to all this for a long while
in silence and then left the room, saying to Petrushka:
'Go along and undress the master!' Petrushka started to
pull off his master's boots, almost jerking him on the
floor as he did so. But at last the boots were off, the master
was properly undressed, and after twisting and turning
for a time in the bed, which creaked unmercifully, he
drowsed off like a real Kherson landowner.

In the meantime Petrushka had carried his master's
trousers and his shot cranberry-coloured coat into the
passage; slinging them over a wooden coat-stand he
began to whip them with a crop and to brush them,
raising enough dust to fill the whole corridor. As he was

3. The hero of a novel (1774) by
Johann Wolfgang von Goethe (1749–
1832), the famous German writer.
Werther falls in love with Charlotte,
a married woman, and commits sui-
cide. Chichikov probably read not
Goethe, but a popular poem by the
Russian poet V. I. Tumansky, pub-
lished in 1819, entitled "Werther to
Charlotte, an Hour before His
Death."

about to take them down he happened to look over the balustrade and to see Selifan returning from the stables. Their eyes met and they understood each other: their master was asleep and here was a chance for them to go off somewhere. After taking the trousers and the coat back into the bedroom, Petrushka at once went downstairs, and they set off together without so much as a word about their destination and gossiping on the way about quite extraneous matters. They did not stroll far: in fact, they only crossed the road to a house standing opposite the hotel. Here they passed through a low and grimy glass door leading into a sort of cellar where all sorts of folk were already sitting at wooden tables: some of these folk were shaved and others not, some were in sheepskins, some in Russian shirts only, and a number had frieze overcoats. Heaven alone knows what Petrushka and Selifan did there, but an hour later they emerged holding each other by the hand and observing perfect silence, taking the greatest care of each other and manœuvring each other round any corners. Hand in hand, without letting go, they took a whole quarter of an hour to clamber up the stairs until, in the end, they succeeded and reached the top. Petrushka paused for a while before his narrow bedstead, trying to figure out how he could lie down most comfortably, and finally sprawled right across it with his feet pressed against the floor. Selifan lay down on the same bed, rolling his head on Petrushka's belly and quite forgetting that he should be sleeping elsewhere—either in the servants' quarters or in the stables near the horses. They both fell asleep instantly and gave vent to unbelievably raucous snores, to which the master from next door responded with a thin nasal whistling. Soon everything grew quiet and the hotel was enveloped in a fast slumber; only one window still showed a glimmer of light, coming from a room in which a lieutenant from Ryazan[4] was staying, who was evidently a great lover of boots, for he had already ordered four pairs and kept trying on a fifth. Several times he came near the bed intending to take them off and to lie down,

4. A town on the river Oka, approximately 110 miles southeast of Moscow.

but he could not force himself to do so: the boots were, of course, excellently made and for a long while yet he kept raising his foot and examining the wonderfully turned heel.

CHAPTER VIII

CHICHIKOV's affairs became a topic of conversation. The town was full of rumours, opinions and arguments as to whether it was a profitable thing to buy up peasants for transplanting elsewhere. From the debates it was clear that many of the disputants had a perfect grasp of the subject. 'Of course, there's no doubt about it,' some said. 'The lands in the south are good and fertile. But how will the peasants manage without water? There are no rivers there.'

'Lack of water is not the worst, Stepan Dmitrievich, but transplantation itself is not a very reliable proposition. You know what peasants are: if you plant them on strange land and expect them to till the earth without anything to hand, without home or household effects, they will simply run away as sure as two and two make four. It would be like looking for a needle in a haystack to find them again.'

'No, Alexei Ivanovich, I protest, I protest. I disagree with what you say, that Chichikov's peasants would run away. A Russian can adapt himself to anything and get used to any climate. Why, if you send him even to Kamchatka and give him only a pair of warm mittens, he'll smack his hands together, pick up an axe and start making a hut for himself.'

'But, Ivan Grigorievich, you have missed an important point: you haven't asked what Chichikov's peasants are like. You have quite overlooked the fact that a landowner would not sell off his best peasants; you can chop my head off if Chichikov's peasants are not thieves and drunkards, wastrels and rowdies.'

'You're right, you're right, I agree. It's quite true; no one would sell their best folk and so Chichikov's lot must be drunkards. But you must take into account that there is a moral to that: they may be good-for-nothing now, but they may of a sudden turn into excellent material when transplanted. Life and history have afforded many such examples.'

'Never, never,' said the superintendent of the state factories. 'Believe me, such a thing is impossible. Chichikov's peasants will now have two powerful enemies to contend with. The first of these is the proximity of the Little Russian[5] provinces where, as you know, there is no restriction on the sale of vodka. I assure you that within a fortnight they will drink themselves silly. Their other enemy is the habit of vagrancy they will have acquired in the process of transplantation. That is, unless Chichikov keeps a close watch on them, disciplines them, and sends them packing at the slightest provocation; and it's not enough to rely on someone else, he must see to it himself, and be ready to cuff and kick them whenever necessary.'

'Why should Chichikov have to cuff them himself? Couldn't he get a steward to do it for him?'

'Where are you going to find a steward? Aren't they all rogues?'

'If they are rogues, it's because their masters allow them to become so.'

'That's right,' many assented. 'If a master knew anything at all about management and how to pick his men, he would always have a good steward.'

But the superintendent maintained that you could not get a good steward under five thousand roubles. The president objected that you could find one for three thousand. Whereupon the superintendent retorted: 'Where would you find him? Not under our nose, is he?' To this the president replied: 'No, not under our nose, but right here in the district. I have Pyotr Samoylovich in mind: he's the right man to look after Chichikov's peasants.'

Many were seriously concerned with Chichikov's dilemma and much perturbed at the difficulties of transplanting such a multitude of peasants; they even began

5. A term used in the nineteenth century for "Ukrainian."

to worry lest a revolt might break out among such unruly folk as Chichikov had bought. But the chief of police gave it as his opinion that there was no danger of a revolt, that there was the captain of police to deal with such eventualities, and that even if the captain did not stifle this trouble himself but only sent a subordinate, that would be enough to ensure that the peasants reached their new destination. Many suggestions were offered as to how to extirpate the spirit of rebellion which was rife among Chichikov's peasantry. These suggestions were of all kinds: some smacked overmuch of military harshness and severity, and leant too heavily on the side of punishment; others, however, stressed leniency. The postmaster remarked that Chichikov was now faced with a sacred obligation, that he could in a sense become a sort of father to his peasants and even introduce some beneficial enlightenment into their midst; and in passing he referred with unstinted approval to the Lancastrian system of mutual education.[6]

Such were the arguments and opinions current in the town; and many persons, stirred by sympathy, went as far as to impart some of their counsels to Chichikov, even suggesting that an escort might be formed to ensure the safe arrival of the peasants at their destination. Chichikov thanked them for their advice and told them that in case of need he would have recourse to it, but he flatly turned down the idea of an escort, holding it to be unnecessary, for, as he said, the peasants he had acquired were of exemplary docility, they were quite disposed to be transplanted, and there was no possibility of rebellion among them.

However, all these debates and arguments produced an unexpected but exceedingly pleasant result for Chichikov. Rumour had it that he was more or less of a millionaire. As we have seen from the very first chapter, the town folk had already taken Chichikov to their heart, but after this rumour they took him to their bosom even more closely. To speak the truth, they were all kindly

6. A system of mass instruction developed by English educator Joseph Lancaster (1778–1838); Lancaster advocated using children to teach other children.

folk, they lived in concord and treated each other as friends, and their talk was marked by a special kind of good-nature and intimacy, as exemplified in: 'My dear friend, Ilya Ilyich!' . . . 'Listen, brother mine, Antipator Zaharievich!' . . . 'That's a tall one you're telling me, mummy darling, Ivan Grigorievich!' . . . When talking to the postmaster, Ivan Andreyevich, they always tacked on 'Sprechen Sie Deutsch, Ivan Andreutsch?'[7]. . . In short, it was very much of a family atmosphere. Some of them were not without education: the president knew Zhukovsky's *Lyudmilla* by heart. This was still a great novelty, and he used to recite many passages of it with great accomplishment, especially this one: 'The plains are drowsed, the forest sleeps.' And the way he uttered the syllable 'choo' seemed really to evoke the drowsy plains; and to make the imitation even more perfect, he used to close his eyes as he did so.[8] The postmaster dabbled more in philosophy and was a diligent reader even at night of Young's *Night Thoughts* and Eckartshausen's *The Key to the Mysteries of Nature*, from which he used to copy very long passages, though no one ever knew what they meant.[9] However, he was a wit, flowery in his speech, and he loved, as he admitted, to embellish his language. And he did adorn it with a multitude of little clauses, such as: 'my dear sir . . . what's his name . . . you know . . . you understand . . . you can imagine . . . relative so to say . . . to a certain degree . . .' and other suchlike phrases of which he had sackfuls. He also embellished his speech most successfully by winking or closing one eye, and this helped to give many of his expressions a satirical turn. The others were also more or less enlightened folk: some read Karamzin,[1] some the *Moscow Gazette*, while

---

7. German for "Do you speak German?"

8. Vasily Zhukovsky (1783–,852), a famous Russian Romantic poet and translator. The exclamation "choo!" occurs in the line after "the forest sleeps." The poem and this word were famous in the 1820s because of the unusual, bizarre sound "choo," as unexpected and puzzling in the Russian original as in English; the poem was much admired by senti-mental, provincial Russians.

9. Edward Young (1683–1763), an English poet famous for his gloomy reflective works and a member of the so-called Graveyard School of poetry. Karl von Eckartshausen (1752–1808), German author of the religio-mystical work *Mystical Nights of the Key to the Secrets of the Miraculous* (1791).

1. A prominent Russian writer (1766–1826).

others did not read anything at all. Some were of a species known as 'bolsters', that is to say, men who required the help of a boot on their posterior to make them rise up to anything. Others were just 'slugs', used to lying perpetually on their sides, and it was even a waste of time to kick them: they would not get up in any case.

As to respectability, they were quite reliable folk, as we know, and there were no consumptives among them. They were all of a species upon whom their wives, in the seclusion of their intimate life, bestowed such endearments as 'little goblet,' 'fatty,' 'tubby,' 'blacky,' 'kiki,' 'zou-zou,' and the like. In general, they were kindly and very hospitable, and anyone who had partaken of their hospitality or spent an evening playing whist with them became one of them; and that was all the more true of Chichikov who, armed with his enchanting qualities and manners, had really mastered the great secret of pleasing. They took such a liking to him that he was puzzled how to escape their clutches. On all sides he heard them saying. 'But do stay another week, just another week with us, Pavel Ivanovich!' In short, he was like a babe in arms for them. But incomparably more striking was the impression (a perfect subject for astonishment!) that Chichikov made on the ladies. To explain this it would be necessary to say a great deal about the ladies themselves and the society in which they moved, and to describe, as they say, in vivid colours their spiritual qualities; but the author finds that very difficult. On the one hand, he is unable to do so because of the boundless respect which he feels for the spouses of the higher officials; and on the other . . . on the other, he finds it just too difficult. The ladies of the town of N. were . . . but no, I simply cannot go on; I feel a sort of shyness stealing over me. The most remarkable thing about the ladies of the town of N. was . . . How strange! My quill just will not move; it is as though it were full of lead. Let us leave it at that: their characters evidently ought to be described by someone who has a wider range and a brighter assortment of colours on his palette, while we shall content ourselves with a word or two about their appearance and their most superficial features.

The ladies of the town of N. were what is termed 'presentable': and in this respect one would have no hesitation in regarding them as models for all others. In the matter of deportment, good tone, the observance of etiquette, a multitude of subtle conventions and, above all, that of following fashion to its minutest details—in all these things they were ahead even of the ladies of Petersburg and Moscow. They dressed with great taste, and drove about town in carriages, as the latest mode decreed, with a footman swaying behind in livery and gold braid. A visiting card was held most sacred even though it might only be a name scribbled on a playing card—a two of clubs or an ace of diamonds. It was on account of this that two great friends and relatives had a decisive quarrel, simply because one of them had failed to pay a return call. And however much their husbands and relations tried to reconcile them later, it turned out to be quite impossible to achieve just that one thing in a world where everything else is possible, namely, to reconcile two ladies who had fallen out over a neglected visiting card. And so the two ladies remained in a state of 'mutual indisposition' as local society expressed it. There were a great many violent scenes enacted too, over the question of precedence, and these sometimes inspired in their husbands a sense of generous knight-errantry. Of course they did not have recourse to duels since they were civil servants, but instead they tried to trip one another up whenever possible; and that, as we know, is often harder to bear than any duel. The ladies of the town of N. were very strict in their morals, and they were full of noble indignation against all corruption and temptation; they were merciless in their punishment of any kind of weakness. If anything in the nature of a 'triangle' did make its appearance among them, a veil was drawn over it, and no inkling was given of its existence; dignity was preserved and the husband himself was so well primed that, even if he happened to get wind of it, he answered briefly and sensibly in the words of the proverb: 'Why should anyone worry if a godmother sits out with a godfather?'

Moreover, it is fitting to add that the ladies of the town of N., like many Petersburg ladies, were distinguished by their unusual care and propriety in the use of words and expressions. They could never be heard saying: 'I blew my nose, I am perspiring, I spat.' Instead, they expressed themselves in this manner: 'I relieved my nose' or 'I had recourse to my handkerchief.' In no circumstance might one say: 'That glass or that plate stinks.' And it was even out of the question to say anything which might give the slightest hint of this; they used to say instead: 'That glass is misbehaving,' or something of the kind. To ennoble the Russian language still further, almost half of its words were banished from their current conversation, and so they often had to fall back on French; but the use of French was quite a different matter, for it permitted them to employ words which were far coarser than those we have mentioned above. So this is all we can say, speaking superficially, of the ladies of the town of N. If we were to delve deeper, many other things would come to light; but it is most dangerous to delve too deeply into ladies' hearts. And so let us continue, restricting ourselves to our superficial impressions.

Until lately the ladies had discussed Chichikov very little, although they had given him full marks for his pleasant social manner; but after rumour had designated him as a millionaire they discovered other qualities in him. The ladies were not at all self-interested; the *word* was to blame, the word millionaire and not the millionaire himself; the *word* itself, in fact; for in its very sound apart from any idea of a bag full of money, there is something compelling, something that influences people, be they rogues or just the average sort of good folk; in short, this word influences every one. The millionaire has the advantage of being able to observe meanness in its pure and disinterested state, and based on no calculation; many know very well that they will not get anything out of him and have no right to it anyhow, but they will go out of their way to cross his path, to smile at him, to take off their hat to him, to use all possible means to get invited to dinner at a house to which they know that he is coming. It cannot be said that the ladies indulged in this tender regard out of servility; however, in many of the drawing-rooms it began to be said that, although Chichikov was not so handsome as all that, he was nevertheless a fine figure of a man, and that it would not do if he were a little fatter or stouter. And as an afterthought to this it was added, somewhat insultingly, with regard to thin men, that they were nothing but toothpicks.

Many new dresses were to be seen among the ladies' toilettes. There was a crowd, almost a crush of people in the market-hall; it was like a promenade, so many were the carriages that drove up. The merchants were amazed to see that several rolls of cloth, which they had brought back with them from the market-fair and which they had not succeeded in selling owing to the high price, were suddenly in demand and were being snapped up in a rush. During mass at church one lady was observed to have such a wide hoop round the bottom of her dress that it made the dress blow out half-way across the aisle, and a police sergeant who happened to be there ordered the public to move further away, nearer to the porch, so as to prevent my lady's dress being crumpled. Chichikov himself could not help noticing that he was the centre of extraordinary attention. One day on returning home he found a letter lying on his table: who brought it and whence it came was a mystery; the tavern servant merely said that it had been brought and orders had been given not to mention the author. The letter opened decisively, in this manner to be exact: 'Yes, I must write to you!' Then it went on to speak of a secret affinity of souls: that truth was punctuated with a number of dots which took up almost half a line. Next followed several reflections so remarkable for their justice that we consider it almost essential to quote them: 'What is our life? A valley where sorrow dwells. What is the world? A crowd of people who have no feelings.' Then the writer mentioned that she was bedewing the lines with tears for a tender mother, who departed this life some twenty-five years ago; Chichikov was asked to find a refuge in the desert and to forsake forever the city where men suffocate for lack of air behind stifling barriers; the letter ended on a note of resolute despair and was rounded off with these verses:

> *Two turtle doves will draw*
> *You to my chilly bier,*
> *And coo there till you saw*
> *That I died in tears.*

The last line did not scan, but that did not matter: the letter was written in the spirit of those times. There was no signature: neither Christian name nor surname, neither the name of the month nor the date. But in a postscriptum it was added that his own heart should divine the writer, and that she would be present in person next day at the governor's ball.

This intrigued him enormously. There was so much of the mysterious and provoking in the anonymous letter that he read and re-read it a second and third time, and then at last he said: 'It would be curious to know who she is!' In short, it was evidently developing into a serious affair. He pondered about it for over an hour, then spreading out his hands and bowing his head, he said: 'The way it's written, it's quite a curly sort of letter!' It goes without saying that the letter was then folded and put away in his box beside a theatre bill and a wedding invitation which had lain there in the same place and position for the last seven years. A little while later he was, indeed, brought an invitation to the governor's ball —almost a routine in the chief provincial towns. Wherever there is a governor, there must be a ball, otherwise he would lose the love and respect of the nobility.

At once all other considerations were put aside, and his attention was concentrated on getting ready for the ball, for he had every reason to look forward to it with excitement. As a result, never perhaps since the creation of the world did a man spend so much time on titivating himself. A whole hour was devoted to the sole object of examining his face in the mirror. An attempt was made to communicate to it a variety of different expressions:

now a look of gravity and importance, now one of respect tinged with a smile, now one simply of respect without a smile; the mirror received several bows accompanied by inarticulate sounds somewhat resembling French words, although Chichikov knew no word of French. He gave himself a number of pleasant surprises, winking an eye and twitching a lip, and he even did something with his tongue; in short, what may one not do when one is left alone, with a feeling of being handsome and a conviction into the bargain that no one is peeping through the keyhole? At length he chucked himself slightly under the chin and said: 'What a little dial!' and began to dress. His pleasurable mood persisted while he dressed; pulling on his braces or knotting his tie, he scraped and bowed most adroitly and, although he never danced, he ventured to make an *entrechat*.[2] This *entrechat* produced a small and harmless effect: the dressing table shook and a brush fell from the table.

His arrival at the ball created an extraordinary stir. Everyone who was there swung round to greet him— one with cards in his hand, another cutting short a conversation at its most interesting point, just as he had uttered: 'And the lower district court answers to this. . . .' But what it was to answer had already been tossed aside as the speaker hastened to greet our hero. 'Pavel Ivanovich! Oh, heavens, Pavel Ivanovich! My dear Pavel Ivanovich! Most honourable Pavel Ivanovich! My dear soul, Pavel Ivanovich! Here is our Pavel Ivanovich! May I embrace you, Pavel Ivanovich! Bring him here, let me kiss my dear Pavel Ivanovich!' Chichikov felt himself in more than one embrace at the same time. He had barely succeeded in scrambling out of the president's arms when he was already in the grip of the chief of police; the chief of police passed him on to the medical inspector; the medical inspector handed him on to the contractor, the contractor to the architect. . . . The governor, who was talking to the ladies at the time and holding in one and the same hand a chocolate-wrapper

2. A dance leap in which the feet touch each other several times before touching the ground.

and a spaniel, threw these down on the floor as soon as he perceived Chichikov, and the dog yelped; in short, his arrival brought unusual joy and delight. There was not a face which did not reflect either joy or, at least, universal pleasure. So officials' faces might look when their posts are being inspected by a visiting superior: after the first fear has passed, they see that he is pleased with much and that he has even allowed himself a joke, that is, to utter a few words with a pleasant smile. His subordinates gather round him and laugh twice as much in reply; hearty laughter comes from those who have, in fact, heard his words but indistinctly; and finally a policeman who has been standing on the edge of it all near the door, who has never laughed in his life before, and who a minute earlier had shaken his fist in the face of the crowd —even he, according to the unalterable laws of reflection, gives expression to a sort of smile, although this smile is more like the contortion of someone about to sneeze after a good pinch of snuff.

Our hero responded to each and all, and had a sensation of being unusually smart: he bowed to left and right of him, a bit sideways as was his wont but entirely at his ease, and everyone was enchanted by it. The ladies at once clustered round him in a glittering garland and brought with them whole clouds of every kind of scent: one breathed roses, another spring and violets, a third smelt of mignonette. Chichikov could only prick up his nose and sniff the scented air. A vast display of taste had gone into their attire: the muslins, satins, chiffons, were of such pale fashionable shades that they defied description (such was their refinement!). Bows and bouquets fluttered here and there in most picturesque disorder— though much care had gone to the creation of that disorder. Their light head-pieces just managed to cling to their ears and seemed to say: 'Look out, I shall fly off. A pity I can't take the beauty with me!' The waists were tightly laced and most agreeably shaped (it must be noted that in general the ladies of the town of N. tended to be on the plump side, but they laced themselves so artfully and had such charming manners that their plumpness was hardly noticeable). They had gone to unusual trouble to think out and plan all the items of their attire; their necks and shoulders were left bare just as much as was necessary and no more; each one revealed her possessions to the point only where she was convinced that they might prove the downfall of man. The rest was hidden away with extraordinary taste: either some light ribbon of a neckband, as dainty as the pastry known as 'kisses', ethereally encircled the neck, or tiny crenellated edges of fine batiste known as 'modesties' peeped out from under the dress at the shoulders. These modesties concealed in front and behind that which could not bring about man's downfall but which made one suspect that the road to perdition lay precisely there. The long gloves did not quite reach the sleeves but intentionally left bare those glamorous parts of the arms above the elbow which in many cases were of an enviable plumpness. The kid gloves of some of them had split in the effort to pull them on as far as possible; in short, it was as if everything bore the label: 'This is not the provinces, this is a capital city, this is Paris!' Only in places was some indescribable cap to be observed or some peacock feather contrary to all fashion. But there was no escaping such things, which are in the nature of a provincial capital: it is bound to trip up somewhere or other. As Chichikov stood facing them, he was thinking to himself: 'Now who could be the writer of that epistle?' But as he thrust his nose out, it came up against a whole swirling battery of elbows, cuffs, sleeves, fragrant chemisettes and dresses. The gallop had reached its climax: the postmaster's wife, the police captain, a lady with an azure feather, the Georgian prince Chiphayhilidzev, a Petersburg official, a Moscow official, the Frenchman Coucou, Perhunovsky, Berebendovsky—all these were swirling madly round. . . .

'There goes the province!' said Chichikov as he retreated. As soon as the ladies had returned to their seats, he began to scan their faces in the hope that the expression of one of them might reveal the author of the letter. But it was quite impossible to recognize the author from the expression either of their faces or their eyes, though

everywhere there was noticeable a barely revealed something, so subtle and so finely shaded, oh, how finely
shaded! . . . 'No,' Chichikov said to himself, 'women are
such creatures. . . .' Here he waved his hand in despair.
'There's simply no point in talking about it. Just try and
describe or translate all that you see passing over their
faces, all that subtle play and all those hints, and you
would surely fail. Their eyes alone are such an infinite
territory that, once you have got there, you would forget
your own name! There would be no way of pulling yourself out, not even with a hook. Just try for example to
describe the glitter of them—the humidity, the velvet
and sweetness of them. God alone knows, what cannot be
found among them! Harsh qualities and soft, and quite
voluptuous ones too, or, as some say, indulgence or no
indulgence, but the greater the indulgence, the more it
will catch the heart and the more it will play on your soul
as with a violin bow. No, there is no finding the right
words. It's the posh half of the human species, that's
what it is.'

Sorry! I believe our hero has just let slip a vulgar word.
What is to be done? Such is the writer's predicament in
Russia! However, if a word off the streets has got into
the book, it is not the writer's fault but rather that of
readers who belong to higher society. It is from them that
you will not hear a single decent Russian word, whereas
they are so generous with French, German and English
words that you will have more than enough of them, and
in using them they will take care to preserve every possible
kind of pronunciation, drawling through their nose when
speaking French, chirping like a bird and even looking
like one when talking in English—and laughing into the
bargain at anyone who is unable to look like a bird; but
they have nothing Russian to contribute except, perhaps,
some log hut in the Russian peasant style which they will
put up out of patriotic sentiment on their country estate.
Such are the readers of the best society and such are all
those who hang on their skirts and claim to belong to that
society! And yet how exacting they are! They insist that
an author should write in the strictest, purest and noblest

language; in short, they expect the Russian language to drop from the clouds, already refined, and that it should come naturally to the lips, so that all they have to do is to open their mouth and stick out their tongue. It goes without saying of course that the feminine half of the human species is very wise; but it must be confessed that our respected readers are even wiser.

In the meantime Chichikov was much perplexed in trying to make out which of the ladies was the author of the epistle. Having attempted to concentrate his gaze even more, he noticed on the ladies' part something which seemed to promise both hope and sweet torment to the heart of a poor mortal, and he finally said: 'No, there is no way of guessing!' This did not however dispel the happy mood in which he found himself. He exchanged easily and deftly a few pleasant words with some of the ladies, going up to one and then another with short stilted steps or, as they say, with 'mincing steps' as do old dandies on high heels, who are known as 'mousy little stallions' and who are always to be found strutting in front of the ladies. Having taken one or two mincing turns to the right and to the left of him, he would scrape his foot either in the form of a short tail or a comma. The ladies were very pleased, and they not only discovered a great many agreeable and amiable qualities in him, but even began to discern a majestic expression on his face, a martial and military look, such as women are known to adore. Finally, they began to quarrel slightly on his account. Observing that he was usually to be found standing by the door, some of the ladies vied with each other to secure a seat in that vicinity, and when one of them happened to be the first on the spot, this almost resulted in an unpleasant incident; and such impudence appeared extremely disgusting to many of those who were trying to achieve the same.

Chichikov became so engrossed in his conversation with the ladies, or rather the ladies so absorbed him and so turned his head with their chatter, compounded of the most abstruse and subtle allegories which required a great deal of decyphering and even made him sweat—that he entirely forgot to do his duty and pay his compliments to the lady of the house. He only remembered about it when he heard the voice of the governor's wife who had already been standing for some minutes beside him. With an amiable shake of her head and in a voice both affectionate and playful she said: 'Ah, Pavel Ivanovich, so here you are! . . .' I am unable exactly to convey her words, but whatever she said was most agreeable and was spoken in the spirit in which ladies and cavaliers converse in the novels of our society writers, who love to describe drawing-rooms and to boast of their familiarity with high tone, and implying something of this nature: 'Have they really conquered your heart so much as to leave no room in it, not even a nook, for those you have so mercilessly forgotten?' Our hero at once turned round and was about to reply to the governor's wife in a style very likely in no way inferior to that employed in the fashionable novels by the Zvonskys, Linskys, Lidins, Gremins[3] and all the other smart officers, but happening to raise his eyes, he stopped of a sudden as though he had been bludgeoned.

The governor's wife was not standing there alone. On her arm was a young girl of sixteen, with a fresh complexion and fair hair, with delicate and well-modelled features, a pointed chin, and a charmingly oval face such as a painter might have chosen as a model for a Madonna and such as was rarely to be found in Russia, where everything tends to be spacious—everything there is, whether it be the hills, the forests and the steppes, or faces, lips and feet. She was the same blonde whom he had met by chance on the highway when driving away from Nozdrev's and when, owing to the stupidity of coachmen or horses, their carriages had so strangely met and become entangled, and uncle Mityai and uncle Minyai had undertaken to disentangle the affair. Chichi-

3. The names are meant to sound like those of heroes of Romantic works of the period. "Gremin": The idealized hero of a Romantic tale by Alexander Bestuzhev-Marlinsky (1797–1837), *The Test*. The name Gremin was later used by the librettist of Tchaikovsky's opera *Eugene Onegin* (who happened to be Modeste Tchaikovsky, the composer's brother) for the husband of the heroine, Tatiana. In Pushkin's work, which served as the source for the opera, the husband is not named.

kov was so taken aback that he could not utter any
sensible word, only muttering the devil knows what, a
thing that neither Gremin, Zvonsky nor Lidin would
have allowed themselves to do.

'You don't know my daughter yet?' said the governor's
wife. 'She has just finished her schooling.'

He replied that he had the fortune to make her acquaintance in an unexpected manner; he attempted to
add something more but did not succeed. Having said a
few further words, the governor's wife moved away with
her daughter to the other end of the room where she
conversed with other guests while Chichikov remained
rooted to the spot, like a man who has sauntered out gaily
into the street for a stroll, with eyes disposed to take
everything in, but who has suddenly come to a full stop,
remembering that he has forgotten something. There is
nothing sillier than such a person: in an instant his carefree expression forsakes him, he struggles to remember
what he has forgotten. Was it a handkerchief? No, the
handkerchief is in his pocket. Was it his money? He has
the money also in his pocket. He seems to have everything
on him; and yet an unknown spirit is whispering in his
ears, 'You have forgotten something!' And so there he is
staring confusedly and vacantly at the passing throng, the
rushing carriages, the shakos and the rifles of a regiment
marching by, some signboard, unable to distinguish any
of it. In the same way, Chichikov was suddenly abstracted
from everything around him.

In the meantime a stream of hints and questions, all
imbued with subtlety and amiability, poured out at him
from the ladies' fragrant mouths. . . . 'May we, wretched
earth-bound creatures, be permitted to be bold enough to
ask you what you are thinking about?' 'Where are the
happy hunting grounds of your thoughts?' 'Is it permissible to enquire what lady has plunged you into this
sweet valley of meditation?' But Chichikov was decidedly
inattentive in his replies, and these agreeable phrases
were drowned as in water. He was even so uncivil as to
quit them and proceed to another part of the room in
order to spy out the whereabouts of the governor's wife

and her daughter. But it seems that the ladies were not to be put off in this fashion; each one of them was inwardly resolved to employ every means so perilous for our hearts and to concentrate all her best devices to this end. It may be noted that some of the ladies—I say some and not all—display a failing when they become aware of any good feature about themselves, be it the forehead, the mouth or the hands; they immediately conclude that this feature will be the first to strike anyone and that everyone will say at once: 'Just look, look! What a perfect Grecian nose she has!' or 'What a charming classical forehead!' And if one of them has fine shoulders, she is convinced that all the young men will be completely bowled over with admiration and will keep on repeating whenever she goes by: 'Ah, what wonderful shoulders she has!' without as much as looking at her face, hair, nose or forehead, or, if they do, they would think it was something alien to her. This is how some of the ladies think. Each of them has taken a secret oath to be as ravishing as possible when dancing and to display her excellencies to the full. While waltzing, the postmaster's wife let droop her head so voluptuously that it indeed gave the impression of something unearthly. One very amiable lady who had come with no idea of dancing because she had developed a slight 'incommodity' in the shape of a corn on her right foot as a result of which she was even obliged to wear plush boots, could not resist the temptation and took a few turns in these plush boots, just to discourage the postmaster's wife from thinking too highly of herself.

But none of this produced the desired effect upon Chichikov. He did not even notice the swirling ladies, but was continually rising on tiptoe to stare over people's heads in the hope of catching sight of the entrancing blonde. He squatted down, too, peering in between shoulders and backs until he perceived her at last sitting beside her mother, above whose head an oriental turban with a feather was majestically swaying. It looked as though he intended to take them by storm. Whether it was the effect of spring or whether someone was pushing him from behind, he pressed forward with determination and regardless of any obstacles. The spirit tax-collector[4] received such a shove from him that he staggered, just managing to retain his balance on one foot, which saved him from knocking down a whole row of people; the postmaster also stepped back and stared at him with astonishment mixed with subtle irony; but Chichikov did not even glance at them. He had eyes only for the fair damsel in the distance who was pulling on her long gloves and doubtless dying to set foot on the parquet floor. Four pairs of dancers had already taken the floor and were knocking off a mazurka; their heels were smashing away on the parquet, and the staff-captain was labouring body and soul, with hands and feet, tossing such capers as no one would even have dreamt of achieving. Chichikov darted past the mazurka dancers, almost treading on their heels, and he made straight for the spot where the governor's wife was sitting with her daughter. His actual approach to them, however, was timid; he did not mince his steps or move like a dandy; he even showed signs of confusion, and all his movements were a trifle awkward.

It cannot be said with any certainty that our hero was overcome by the feeling of love; it is even doubtful whether gentry of that sort, that is to say, those who are neither too fat nor yet too thin, are capable of love, but taking everything into consideration there was something strange here, something of a nature he could hardly explain. It seemed to him, as he afterwards confessed, that the whole of the ball with all its hum and noise grew very remote for a few minutes; the strings and the brass were strident echoes somewhere behind the mountains, and everything was clouded in a mist resembling a carelessly painted field in an oil-painting. The delicate features of the entrancing fair damsel were the only clear and well-defined object emerging from the background of that nebulous, slovenly painted field. All he saw was her rounded oval face, her slender, very slender, figure, such as girls preserve for a few months after leaving school,

4. The Russian government had a monopoly on alcohol and imposed a tax on sales of alcohol. It was possible to purchase the right to collect these taxes for the government; in return, one was allowed to keep a large part of them.

her white and almost plain dress, which sat lightly and gracefully on her youthful, well-proportioned form and showed to advantage its pure lines. She seemed to resemble a toy of sorts carved with precision out of ivory. And she alone emerged white, transparent and luminous, from that blurred and dense crowd of people.

Apparently that does sometimes happen. Apparently even men like Chichikov are transformed into poets for a few moments in their life: though the word 'poet' would be an exaggeration here. But at least he felt himself something of a young man, a hussar almost. Noticing an empty chair in their vicinity he at once occupied it. The conversation did not go smoothly at first, but after a time it took on life and even began to gather momentum. . . . Here, however, to our regret, we must note that sedate men and those occupying important posts are a trifle clumsy in their converse with ladies; the real masters of this art are lieutenants and certainly not anyone above the rank of captain. How they manage it, God alone knows! There seems to be little wisdom in the conversation, but the young lady they are addressing rocks in her chair for laughter. Your civil councillor,[5] on the other hand, will indulge in heaven alone knows what for a conversation, he will either say that Russia is a very spacious country or he will let fall a compliment which is not unwitty but has something very bookish about it; or if he happens to make a joke he will laugh incomparably more at it than the young lady who is listening to him. We have drawn attention to this so that the reader might understand why it was that the fair young lady began to yawn in the middle of our hero's talk. Our hero quite failed to notice this as he went on telling her a great many pleasant things such as he was accustomed to say in similar situations in various places, namely: in the province of Simbirsk, in the house of Sofron Ivanovich Bezpechny, where dwelt his daughter Adelaida Sofronovna and her three sisters-in-law, Maria, Alexandra and Adelheida Gavrilovna; at the house of Feodor Feodorovich Prekroyev in the province of Ryazan; in that of Flor

5. Councillor of State, fifth of the fourteen ranks.

Vassilievich Pobiedonosny in the province of Pienza and
at his brother's, Pyotr Vassilevich's, where dwelt his
sister-in-law, Katerina Mikhailovna and her second
cousins Rosa and Emilya Feodorovna; and in the province of Vyatka, at the house of Pyotr Varsonofyevich,
where dwelt the sister of his betrothed, Sofia Rotislavna
and her two half-sisters Sofya and Maklatura Alexan-
drovna.

The ladies were highly displeased with Chichikov's
conduct. One of them deliberately walked past him in
order to make him sit up, and she even carelessly brushed
against the fair damsel with the flounce of her dress while
at the same time tugging at her fluttering scarf in such a
way as to make it fly into her face; at that moment, too,
one of the ladies standing behind him let drop a sharp
and acid observation which the scent of her violet per-
fume could not muffle. But Chichikov either did not hear
it or he pretended not to hear it, and that was a mistake,
for value must be attached to ladies' opinions. He came
to regret it afterwards but it was already too late.

This feeling of indignation, for which there was every
justification, was reflected in many faces. However great
may have been Chichikov's standing in society as a
millionaire and as one who had a martial and military
appearance, there are certain things which ladies will
never forgive anyone, whoever he may be; and when that
is the case, one may as well write off one's loss! However
weak and helpless a woman's character in comparison
with a man's, there are occasions when she shows herself
firmer than any man or anything else in the world. The
unintentional neglect shown by Chichikov had even the
effect of restoring that harmony between the ladies which
had been undermined by their rivalry for a seat near the
door. They began to discover veiled sarcasms in some of
his casual and dry observations. To make things worse,
one of the young gentlemen extemporized some satirical
verses on the dancers, and, as we know, no provincial
ball is ever complete without them. These verses were at
once attributed to Chichikov. The indignation grew, and
in various parts of the room the ladies began to speak of

him in the most unfavourable way. As for the poor schoolgirl, she was absolutely annihilated and her doom was sealed.

Meanwhile our hero was about to get the shock of his life. While the fair damsel was yawning and he was embroidering on various incidents for her benefit and had even referred to the Greek philosopher Diogenes,[6] Nozdrev emerged from an adjoining room. Whether he had burst out from the buffet bar or from the small green drawing-room where the play was more hazardous than ordinary whist, whether he had come of his own volition or had been pushed out of there, he arrived all gay and beaming, dragging the prosecutor by the arm: he must have been dragging him along for some time, because the poor prosecutor's thick eyebrows were turning here and there as though seeking a way of escape from that comradely, arm-in-arm peregrination. It was really unbearable. Having gulped some courage from two cups of tea not unmixed of course with rum, Nozdrev was spouting the most appalling lies. On catching sight of him from afar, Chichikov was even resolved to make a sacrifice, that is, to abandon his vantage point and to remove himself as quickly as possible: their encounter portended no good. But as ill luck would have it, the governor materialized and gave expression to his great joy at finding Pavel Ivanovich; he stopped him and asked him to arbitrate in an argument he was having with two ladies as to whether woman's love was durable or not. In the meantime Nozdrev had spotted him and was making straight for him.

'Ah, you Kherson landowner, you Kherson landowner!' he was shouting as he approached, roaring with laughter till his cheeks, fresh and pink as a spring rose, quivered and shook. 'Well! Have you been doing a good trade in the dead ones? But you did not know, Your Excellency,' he yelled, turning to the governor, 'that he trades in dead souls. Honest, he does! Listen, Chichikov! I am telling you this out of friendship, we are all friends of yours here, and His Excellency is here too, I say I'd have you hanged. Upon my soul, I would!'

6. Ancient Greek philosopher who despised riches and social conventions.

Chichikov simply did not know where he stood.

'Believe me, Your Excellency,' Nozdrev continued, 'when he said to me, "You must sell me your dead souls," I burst with laughter. When I came here I was told that he had bought three million roubles' worth of peasants for transplantation. Transplantation indeed! Why, with me he was bargaining over the dead! Listen Chichikov, you're a pig, that's what you are. And His Excellency is here, isn't that so, prosecutor?'

But the prosecutor, Chichikov, and the governor himself were thrown into such confusion that they found no reply, and Nozdrev carried on tipsily without paying any attention to them: 'As for you, you, you . . . I shan't leave you till I find out why you were buying those dead souls. Listen, Chichikov, you are ashamed, aren't you? You know that you have no better friend than myself. And here is His Excellency, isn't that so, prosecutor? Your Excellency, you would not believe how attached we are, that is, if you were to say, and I was standing here, and you were to say: "Nozdrev, tell me honestly whom do you put greater store by—your father or Chichikov?" I would reply: "Chichikov, honestly. . . ." Allow me, my dear, to paste a *baiser*⁷ upon you. You must permit me, Your Excellency, to kiss him. Yes, Chichikov, don't resist. Allow me to imprint one little kiss on your snow-white cheek!'

Nozdrev with his *baiser* was given such a push that he almost landed on the floor: everyone gave him a wide berth and stopped listening to him; but his words about the purchase of the dead souls had been uttered so loudly and had been accompanied by such boisterous laughter, that they had attracted the attention even of those who were at the far end of the room. This bit of information struck every one as so strange that they all stood gaping with a sort of wooden and stupidly enquiring expression on their faces. Chichikov noticed that many of the ladies winked at each other with spiteful and biting smiles on their faces; some of them exchanged ambiguous glances, and this further increased his confusion. Every one was

7. French for "kiss."

aware that Nozdrev was a notorious liar, and it was nothing new to hear him indulge in utter nonsense. But just look at us poor mortals, for example. It is hard to understand what we are made of. However trivial a piece of news may be, as long as it is news your ordinary mortal will make a point of communicating it to another if only for the sake of being able to say: 'Look now, what false rumours are abroad!' And the other mortal will gladly lend his ears, although afterwards he will say: 'But this is absolute falsehood, not worth the slightest attention!' Yet on saying that, he will at once go in search of a third in order to retail it to him and then exclaim together with him in noble indignation: 'What an absolute lie!' And so this lie is bound to make the round of the town, and all the mortals, however many of them there may be, will have their fill of chatter about it before they admit that it was not worthy of their attention and not worth while discussing.

This apparently absurd incident markedly upset our hero. However stupid the words of a fool may be, yet they may sometimes suffice to put a wise man out of countenance. He began to feel awkward and ill at ease; it was as though he had stepped with brightly polished boots into a nasty, stinking puddle; in a word, it was most disagreeable! He tried not to think about it, he attempted to distract his thoughts, to amuse himself he sat down to a game of whist but everything went wrong: he revoked twice, and forgetting that it was not right to trump in the third place, he let go his whole hand and foolishly threw away the game. The president found it difficult to understand that Pavel Ivanovich, who had such a good and subtle understanding of the game, could commit such errors and even lure his king of spades under the axe, a card upon which, to use his own expression, he had relied as upon God. The president, the postmaster and even the chief of police indulged of course in a few jests at the expense of our hero. They asked him whether he was not in love and told him that they were quite aware that his heart had a slight limp and who it was that had wounded it. But however much he laughed and jested back, he drew little comfort from it. At supper he was also in no state to relax despite the fact that the company at table was a very agreeable one and that Nozdrev had long ago been shown out, for even the ladies had at last noticed that his behaviour was exceeding the bounds of propriety. In the middle of a cotillon he had sat down on the floor and had started to grab hold of the dancers' skirts, which, as the ladies said, was really going too far.

The supper was a gay one. In a background of triple candelabras, flowers, sweets and bottles, all the faces shone with a look of carefree pleasure. The officers, the ladies, the tail-coated civilians, were all as amiable as they could be to the point of mawkishness. The men would leap up from their chairs and run to relieve a waiter of some dish which they would then present with extraordinary adroitness to the ladies. One colonel even served up some dish of sauce to a lady on the blade of his drawn sword. The gentlemen of respectable age among whom Chichikov was sitting were disputing loudly and following up each weighty word with a bite of fish or beef mercilessly dipped in mustard. They were arguing about subjects in which he always took part, but he felt more like a person who has been exhausted and shaken by a long journey and whose mind is incapable of thought or of any display of interest in anything. He did not even stay to the end of the supper but departed long before he was accustomed to do on such occasions.

Back in that room which is already familiar to the reader, that room which had a dressing table barricading the door and cockroaches peeping out of corners, he was as uncomfortable in mind and spirit as the armchair in which he sat. His heart felt heavy and confused, and there was a gaping void in it. 'May the devil take you all whoever invented these balls!' he was saying in his heart. 'Why that foolish merriment? The province is suffering from bad harvests and the prices have gone up, and here they are indulging in balls! What a joke! They put on all their female finery! To think of it, some of them had a thousand roubles' worth of rags on them! And all squeezed out of the peasants or, worse still, at the expense of their own conscience. We know why they take bribes and play fast and loose with their conscience. To get a wife, a shawl or some frills or whatever they are called. And why do they do it? Oh, simply that some upstart Sidorovna might not say that the postmaster's wife was wearing a better dress! And that's where the thousand roubles goes! They go shouting, "A ball, a ball, it will be gay!" But a ball is just nonsense, neither in the Russian spirit nor part of Russian nature. The devil only knows what it is: a grown up and mature man will suddenly leap out all dressed in black, all plucked and fitted as tightly as a little demon, and off he goes twirling with his legs. And you find some of them capering about like a little goat to right and left, even when engaged in a serious conversation with another person. . . . It's all monkey-tricks, just monkey-tricks! The fact that a Frenchman is as much of a child at forty as at fifteen is a good enough excuse for them to imitate him! Really . . . after every ball it is as though one had sinned: one does not even want to remember it. One's head is as empty as after talking to some society light: he will talk of everything, touch slightly on every imaginable topic, will repeat anything he has culled from books gracefully and colourfully. But what do you remember after it all? You realize afterwards that you would have had a more profitable time talking to an ordinary merchant who at least knows his own business properly. What can you squeeze out of a ball like that? Now suppose that a writer got it into his head to describe that scene as it was? Wouldn't there be as little sense to it in a book as in life? What is its nature? Is it ethical or unethical? It is simply the devil knows what! You would just spit and shut the book!'

Such were Chichikov's critical opinions of balls in general; but at bottom there was apparently another reason for indignation. His principal grief was not at the ball but at the fact that he had tripped up, that he had of a sudden been put in a false position, that he played a strange and ambiguous part. Of course, when he looked at it in the light of reason, he saw that it was all nonsense, that there was no significance in a foolish word, especially now that the affair had blown over as it should. But man is a strange creature! Chichikov was much aggrieved at the lack of regard towards him among those whom he did not respect and whom he sharply criticized for their vanity and sartorial display. He felt all the more sad when, on analysing the matter clearly, he realized that he was himself partly to blame. However, his anger did not turn against himself, and in that he was right. We are all prone to go easy on ourselves and to look round for a scapegoat on whom we may unburden our ill humour, on some servant for example, some subordinate official who may happen to come in, a wife, or finally, a chair that can be thrown the devil knows where, at the door itself maybe, so that its back and arms are broken off. Let it experience our rage, we say. So it was that Chichikov soon found a scapegoat who took on his shoulders everything that an aggrieved soul could unburden there. Nozdrev was the scapegoat: and he had his ribs and sides so battered that no rascally village elder or driver could ever have been better thrashed by some experienced travelling captain, or even by a general who, over and above all classical expressions, adds many new ones of his own invention. Nozdrev's lineage was thoroughly taken to pieces, and many of the members of his family in ascending line were severely handled.

But while our hero was sitting back in his hard arm-chair, the prey of uneasy thoughts and insomnia, and vigorously abusing Nozdrev and his whole kin; while a tallow candle was glimmering in front of him, on the point of going out because of the black cap of soot that had gathered round the wick; while the dark, blind night, which was about to turn into blue dawn, was staring at him through the window; while cocks were crowing in the distance and the fustian coat of some man of a class and rank unknown, and who only followed (alas!) the too well-worn path trodden by Russian tramps, was flitting through the dusk; while all this was happening, other events were occurring at the far end of the town which were destined to make our hero's position even more unpleasant.

Through the remote streets and corners of the town a strange sort of carriage was rattling along, so strange that it was difficult to find a name for it. It was not like a coach, nor a carriage, nor a chaise, but more like a plump and rounded water-melon on wheels. The cheeks of this water-melon or its doors, rather, which had traces of yellow paint on them, shut very badly owing to the shaky state of the handles and locks which were tied up with string. The water-melon was filled with chintz cushions in the shape of pouches, bolsters and simple pillows, stuffed with sacks of bread, calatches, doughnuts, and cracknels. There were even chicken-pies and fish-pies showing on the surface. On the footboard at the back stood a person who looked like a lackey, dressed in a short coat of homespun, with an unshaven chin displaying patches of grey hair; he was of the type known as a 'fellow'. The rumble and clanging of the iron clamps and the rusty screws awakened the night-watchman at the other end of the town and, gripping his halberd, he shouted with all his might: 'Who goes there?' But discovering no one and hearing only a distant rumble, he caught some sort of creature that was crawling over his collar and, approaching the lantern, forthwith executed it with his nail. He then put aside his halberd and fell asleep again according to the statutes of his order of chivalry. The horses kept stumbling because they were unshod and it was also evident that they were little familiar with the quiet cobbled streets of the town. After a few turns, the monstrous vehicle finally turned down a dark side-street past the small parish church of St. Nicholas and stopped in front of the gates of the house where lived the wife of the head priest. A girl with a kerchief on her head and wearing a warm jacket clambered out of the carriage and battered on the gate with her fists as violently as though she were pummelling a man (the 'fellow' in the homespun was then pulled down by his feet for he had been fast asleep). Dogs began barking and the gates, gaping at last, with difficulty swallowed the clumsy travelling contraption.

The carriage drove into the tightly-packed yard, which was heaped with logs, chicken-coops and all sorts of sheds.

Out of it stepped a lady. She was none other than the landowner and widow of the collegiate secretary, Korobochka. After our hero had left her, the old lady began to worry lest he might cheat her. Having spent three sleepless nights she decided to drive into town despite the fact that her horses were unshod, but she was determined to find out the current price of dead souls and to make sure that she had not been cheated in selling them, God forbid, for three times too little. The reader will learn of the consequences produced by her arrival from a conversation which took place between the two ladies when they were alone. This conversation . . . but it had better be reserved for the following chapter.

CHAPTER IX

AT an hour of the morning rather earlier than is customary for paying calls in the town of N., a lady in a flashy check cloak fluttered out of the doors of an orange-coloured wooden house with mezzanine and azure columns, followed by a footman in livery with many collars and gold braid on his round, glossy hat. With unusual celerity the lady at once fluttered up the steps, which had been let down, into the carriage that stood at the door. The footman instantly shut the carriage door, put away the steps and, grasping the straps at the back of the carriage, shouted to the coachman: 'Go!' The lady was the bearer of some news which she had only just heard, and she felt an irresistible desire to communicate it as soon as possible. Every other minute she peeped out of the carriage window only to perceive to her infinite regret that half the journey still lay ahead. Every house struck her as being longer than usual; the white stone almshouse with its narrow windows stretched on for so long and so unbearably, that she could not resist exclaiming: 'Dash that structure, there's no end to it!' Twice already the coachman had received the order: 'Drive faster, Andryushka, faster! You're dawdling to-day!' At last the goal was reached. The carriage stopped in front of a one-storied wooden house of dark grey colour: it had little white bas-reliefs over the windows, a high trellis fence right before them, and a narrow stockade enclosing some slender trees which had grown all white from endless layers of town dust. In the windows could be seen pots of flowers, a parrot with its nose hooked in a ring and swinging about in the cage, and two little dogs sleeping in the sun. The house was inhabited by a bosom friend of our lady's.

The author is in a quandary how to name these two ladies without rousing anger as on previous occasions. To invent names for them would be dangerous. However fictitious the name, there will always be someone in some out-of-the-way corner of our empire—rightly called great—who will lay some claim to it, fly into a deadly rage, and start proclaiming that the author had paid a secret visit with the express purpose of finding out who he was and what sort of sheepskin coat he wore, what Agrafena Ivanovna he visited and what food he preferred. If, Heaven forbid, any reference is made to a person's rank, the peril is even greater. Nowadays people of rank and condition are so touchy that any character in a book is at once liable to be taken for a living person; such apparently is the general mood and atmosphere. It is enough to say that there is a stupid man in some town and he is at once embodied in a living person: of a sudden, a gentleman of respectable appearance will leap out and yell: 'I am a man too, and therefore stupid!' In short, he will instantly grasp what it is all about. Therefore, to avoid all this, let us call this lady, who is about to receive her visitor, as she was wont to be called almost by everyone in the town of N., namely, a lady agreeable in all respects. She acquired this appellation quite legitimately, for she spared no effort to be obliging to the very last degree. But, of course, beneath that agreeable manner the nimble wiles of femininity were to be detected! And every now and then her amiable words had quite a sting in them! And Heaven only knows what feelings stirred in her heart against any woman who in any way pushed ahead of her. But all that was wrapped up in the most delicate and worldly manner such as is only to be found in a chief provincial town. Every movement of hers was in good taste, she even liked to read verse, and sometimes she could hold her head in a dreamy way; and everyone agreed that she certainly was a lady agreeable in all respects.

The other lady, the visitor that is, had not so complex a character, and so let us call her simply an agreeable lady. Her arrival roused the little dogs which had been sleeping in the sun: shaggy-haired Adèle always tripping over herself and spindle-legged Potpourri. Both of these barked and carried off their ringed tails into the hall where the visitor was divesting herself of her cloak; it then became apparent that she was wearing a dress of stylish cut and fashionable shade; a scent of jasmine pervaded the room. As soon as the lady agreeable in all respects learnt of the arrival of the agreeable lady, she at once came running into the hall. The ladies clutched each other by the hands, exchanged kisses and cried out as do girls from a boarding-school who happen to meet soon after their schooldays are over but before their mothers have had time to explain to them that the father of one is poorer and of lower rank than that of the other. The kisses had a smack to them and made the dogs bark again, and for this they were spanked with a handkerchief. The two ladies then passed into the drawing-room, which of course was all azure, with a sofa, an oval table and even a little screen with ivy winding round it; growling in their wake, in ran shaggy-haired Adèle and tall spindly-legged Potpourri. 'This way, this way, here's a nice corner!' the lady of the house said as she invited her guest to sit down on a corner of the sofa. 'That's right, that's right! Here is a cushion for you!' As she said that, she stuffed a cushion behind her back; on it was the figure of a knight embroidered in wool with the same effect as on canvas—the nose was a ladder and the lips a square. 'How glad I am that you . . . I heard someone driving up and I asked myself who it could be so early. Parasha said it was the vice-governor's wife and I said, "Well, the fool has come again to bore me," and I was about to tell Parasha to say I was not at home. . . .'

The visitor was just about to get down to business and impart her piece of information, but at that moment the lady agreeable in all respects gave vent to an exclamation and this suddenly diverted the trend of the conversation.

'What a gay little pattern!' exclaimed the lady agreeable in all respects, gazing at the dress of the agreeable lady.

'Yes, isn't it bright and gay! Praskofia Feodorovna, however, finds that it would have been better if the checks were smaller and the spots light blue instead of brown. I sent my sister a length of material; you have simply no idea how charming it was. Just imagine, stripes, narrow, very narrow, you couldn't imagine them narrower, a light blue background, and in between the stripes, spots and sprigs, spots and sprigs, spots and sprigs. . . . In a word, quite unique. I am sure there has been nothing like it anywhere in the world.'

'But my dear, isn't that too showy?'

'Oh no, it isn't.'

'I do think it is!'

It must be noted that the lady agreeable in all respects was somewhat of a materialist, prone to doubts and scepticism, and there were many things in life which she repudiated.

At this point, the agreeable lady explained that the material was not showy at all, and exclaimed: 'Yes, I congratulate you: flounces are no longer in fashion.'

'What do you mean, not in fashion?'

'Little festoons are being worn instead.'

'But they aren't pretty at all!'

'Little festoons are the fashion everywhere: the pelerines have festoons, sleeves have festoons, little epaulettes of festoons, festoons below, everywhere festoons.'

'All these festoons, they are not at all nice, Sofya Ivanovna.'

'They are simply charming, Anna Grigorievna. The dress can be sewn with two seams; wide slits and above . . .

But what will really surprise you, what will really make you say that . . . Well, you will be surprised now: just imagine, the under-bodice has become longer, coming to a point in front, and the busk in front is quite prominent; the skirt is gathered up all round as in the days of the old farthingale, and there is even a little padding put in at the back to make one a perfect *belle-femme*.'[8]

'Well I never!' said the lady agreeable in all respects, making a dignified movement with her head.

'But that is how it is, my dear,' replied the agreeable lady.

'As you like, but I will not take to these fashions.'

'I myself. . . . Just think what happens to fashions sometimes. . . . It's quite extraordinary! I asked my sister for a pattern just for fun; my Melanya has started to make up the dress.'

'So you have got the pattern?' exclaimed the lady agreeable in all respects, unable to conceal her excitement.

'Why, yes, my sister brought it.'

'My darling, lend it to me for the sake of all that's holy!'

'Oh, but I already promised it to Praskofia Feodorovna. Perhaps, after she has finished with it.'

'But who would wear a dress like Praskofia Feodorovna's? I must say I would find it strange if you gave preference to outsiders!'

'But, you know, she is a cousin of mine.'

'What sort of a cousin is she to you . . . only on your husband's side. . . . No, Sofya Ivanovna, I won't hear of it! You don't want to insult me, do you? It seems to me that you have tired of me and wish to bring our friendship to an end.'

Poor Sofya Ivanovna was at her wits' end to know what to do. She realized she was between the devil and the deep sea. That is what comes of boasting! That stupid tongue of hers, she was ready to bite it off.

'And how is your gallant?' asked the lady agreeable in all respects.

8. French for "beautiful lady."

'Ah, heavens! What am I doing sitting like this! I'd forgotten all about it! Do you know, Anna Grigorievna, what I came to tell you?' Here the visitor almost choked from excitement, her words were like hawks, ready to pounce on each other; and one had to be as hard-hearted as a bosom friend to venture to interrupt her.

'Praise and laud him as you will,' she said briskly, 'but I tell you straight out, and I will say this to his face too, that he is a good-for-nothing, a worthless fellow.'

'But just listen to what I have to tell you. . . .'

'They have started a rumour that he is a fine fellow, but he is not at all a fine fellow, not at all, and as for his nose . . . it's a nasty sight. . . .'

'But allow me, allow me, just to tell you . . . darling Anna Grigorievna, just allow me to tell you! It's a whole story, do you understand, a whole story, *une histoire comme on dit*,'[9] the visitor was saying with a despairing look and in a pleading voice.

It may be noted in passing that the speech of both these ladies contained a great quantity of foreign words and sometimes even whole phrases in French. But great as is the author's gratitude for the benefits rendered to Russia by the French language and for the laudable custom of our higher society in discoursing in that language at all hours of the day for reasons, of course, of deep-felt love for their country, yet he hesitates to employ a single phrase of any foreign language in this, his Russian poem. And so let us continue in Russian.

'What story?'

'Ah, my dearest Anna Grigorievna, if you can only imagine the position in which I found myself! Just think, the wife of the head priest, of Father Cyril, called on me to-day; and what do you think? Our modest fellow, our visitor, turns out to be—do you know what?'

'You don't say he's been paying court to the priest's wife?'

'Oh, Anna Grigorievna, if it were only that, it would be nothing! But just listen to what she told me. She said that Korobochka, the landowner, arrived at her place, as

9. French for "as they say, a story."

pale as death, and told her—but just listen. . . . It's quite a romance. . . . Suddenly, in the dark of the night, when everyone in the house was asleep, there was a knocking on the gate, a terrible knocking as you may imagine. . . . There were shouts of: "Open the gates, open the gates! Otherwise we shall break them down!" Now what do you think of that? Isn't that a charmer for you?'

'But what is Korobochka like? Is she young and good-looking?'

'Not in the least. She is an old crone.'

'That's a fine to do! So he has taken to hunting after old women. Well, I must compliment our ladies on their taste after that. They couldn't do better than fall in love with him!'

'But no, Anna Grigorievna, it's not at all what you think. But just imagine, here he is arriving all armed from head to foot like some Rinaldo Rinaldini[1] and demanding: "Sell to me," he says, "all the souls of the dead." Korobochka answered him very reasonably, "I can't sell them," she says, "because they are dead." "No," he says, "they are not dead, it's my business to know whether they are dead or not dead. They are not dead, not dead," he shouts, "they are not dead!" In a word, he stirred up quite a scandal: all the village folk came running round, the children were crying, everyone was shouting, nobody understood anything. It was just *horreur, horreur, horreur*! . . . But you have no idea, Anna Grigorievna, how perturbed I was when I heard all that. "Dear lady," Masha said to me, "just look at yourself in the mirror. How pale you are!" "I haven't time for the mirror," I said, "I must go along and tell Anna Grigorievna." I ordered my carriage at once: the coachman Andryushka asked me where he was to drive me, but I couldn't utter a word, I just stared at him like a fool. He must have thought that I had gone crazy. Ah, Anna Grigorievna, you have no idea how disturbed I am!'

'But that is very strange,' said the lady agreeable in all respects. 'What can be the meaning of these dead souls? I confess I am quite at a loss. This is the second time I

1. An outlaw robber, the chief character of a novel by the same name by the German writer Christian August Vulpius (1762–1827).

have heard mention of these dead souls; but my husband said that Nozdrev was lying. But there must be something in it.'

'But just imagine, Anna Grigorievna, the position I was in when I heard that. "And now," says Korobochka, "I don't know what to do. He forced me," she says, "to sign some sort of false paper and he put down fifty roubles in notes. I am a helpless, inexperienced widow," she says, "I don't know where I am. . . ." What an occurrence! But if only you knew how disturbed I am!'

'But if you allow me to say so, I don't think it's a question of dead souls. There is something else behind it.'

'I confess, I myself. . .' begged the agreeable lady, not without an air of surprise and feeling at once a strong desire to learn what else there might be concealed behind it all. She even said with deliberation: 'And what do you suppose lies behind it?'

'Well, what do you think?'

'What do I think? . . . I confess that I am at a loss.'

'But I should still like to know what you really think about it.'

But the agreeable lady found nothing to say. She only knew how to be disturbed, but she lacked the wherewithal to form any clear hypothesis, and for that reason she was in need more than others of tender friendship and counsel.

'But listen to me. What are these dead souls?' said the lady agreeable in all respects, and at these words her companion was all attention. Her ears seemed to prick up of their own accord, she sat up in her seat, almost out of it, and, although she was of heavy build, she suddenly seemed to grow thinner like a piece of down ready to float into the air at the slightest breath.

So a Russian gentleman, out hunting, might ride up to a wood, out of which a hare will leap, hard-driven by the beaters, and instantly and for a second he will become transformed, together with his horse and upraised whip, into gunpowder which might be set off by a match at any moment. With eyes scouring the darkling air he will pounce on the hunted beast and finish him off ruthlessly, however much the restless snowy steppe might strive against him, darting silver stars at his mouth, his moustaches, his eyebrows and his beaver cap.

'The dead souls . . .' said the lady agreeable in all respects.

'What? What?' her companion asked in a state of great excitement.

'The dead souls! . . .'

'For heaven's sake, tell me!'

'That's merely a fiction to conceal something else. But what is really behind it, is this: he wants to elope with the governor's daughter.'

This conclusion was quite unpredictable and in every way extraordinary. On hearing it the agreeable lady was petrified, she went as white as a sheet, and her disturbance was no joke this time.

'Good God!' she exclaimed, throwing up her arms. 'I should never have suspected that.'

'I confess that I guessed what it was all about as soon as you opened your mouth,' replied the lady agreeable in all respects.

'But what is one to say of boarding-school education after this, Anna Grigorievna! So that's their innocence!'

'Innocence indeed! I have heard her saying such things, I confess, I would not venture to repeat.'

'You know, Anna Grigorievna. Why it simply makes one's heart bleed to see depravity reach such a pitch.'

'All the men are crazy about her. As for myself, I confess that I can see nothing in her. . . . Her affectation is quite unbearable.'

'Ah, my dear Anna Grigorievna, she is a statue. Her face is quite expressionless.'

'What affectation! Oh, what affectation! Heavens, how affected she is! Who taught her that I don't know, but I've never seen such a mincing woman.'

'But, darling, she is a statue and as pale as death.'

'Don't tell me that, Sofya Ivanovna. She rouges quite brazenly.'

'How can you say that, Anna Grigorievna? She's chalk, just chalk, pure chalk.'

'My dear, I sat next to her. Her rouge was laid on as thick as a finger and it comes off in bits like plaster. Her mother must have taught her; she's a coquette herself, and the daughter will outdo the mother yet.'

'But allow me. . . . I am ready to take any oath you like. . . . I am ready to part this instant with my children, my husband, and the whole of our estate, if she uses the smallest touch, the tiniest particle, the least shade of any rouge!'

'Now what are you saying, Sofya Ivanovna!' cried the lady agreeable in all respects as she threw up her arms.

'I didn't believe you were like that, Anna Grigorievna! I am surprised!' cried the agreeable lady and also threw up her arms.

It will not strike the reader as strange that the two ladies should have disagreed about something they both happened to see at more or less the same time. There are many things in the world which have this peculiar quality, namely, that if one lady looks upon them, they will turn out to be white, but if another should happen to see them, then they will appear red—as red as cranberries.

'Now here is another proof that she is pale,' the agreeable lady continued. 'I remember quite clearly sitting beside Manilov and remarking to him, "Look, how pale she is!" It is true, however, that one must be as dense as our men-folk to admire her. And as for our charmer. . . . Oh, he struck me as being quite repulsive! You can't imagine, Anna Grigorievna, how repulsive I thought him!'

'But some of the ladies were not indifferent to him.'

'I, Anna Grigorievna? You could never say that of me, never, never!'

'But I am not talking about you. Isn't there anyone else besides you?'

'Never, never, Anna Grigorievna! Allow me to tell you that I know myself very well. That may be true of certain other ladies who pose as irreproachable.'

'I beg your pardon, Sofya Ivanovna! You must permit me to tell you that I never have been connected with any such scandals. Other people may have been, but I never, if you will permit me to tell you so.'

'Why are you angry? Other ladies were there as well.

There were even some who hastened to grab chairs near the door so as to sit close to him.'

After these words, which had been uttered by the agreeable lady, a storm might have been expected to blow up, but it was a great surprise when both ladies subsided of a sudden, and absolutely nothing ensued. The lady agreeable in all respects remembered that she had not yet received the pattern of the fashionable dress while the agreeable lady recalled that she had not yet succeeded in eliciting any details about the discovery made by her bosom friend, and as a result peace was established very quickly. However, it could not be said that either lady was by nature vicious or vindictive, and the slight urge to bite at each other arose quite spontaneously in the course of conversation. It was only a question of one of them extracting occasional pleasure from thrusting in a lively word or two: 'Here's one for you!' as it were. 'Go on, take it, swallow it!' All kinds of impulses go to fashion the hearts of men and women.

'There is only one thing I cannot understand,' said the agreeable lady. 'How could Chichikov, who was only a chance traveller, resolve on such a bold step? I cannot believe that he did not have associates.'

'And you think he did not have them?'

'And who do you suppose would have helped him?'

'Well, it might have been Nozdrev.'

'You don't say it was Nozdrev?'

'Why not? He is capable of anything. You know he once wanted to sell his father or, rather, to gamble him away at cards.'

'Good lord, what interesting things I am learning from you! I would never have supposed that Nozdrev was mixed up in this affair!'

'I always supposed it.'

'When one only thinks of what goes on in the world! Who would have supposed, when you remember Chichikov's arrival in town, that he could cause all this strange rumpus in the world. Oh, Anna Grigorievna, if you only knew how perturbed I have been! If it were not for your kindness and friendship . . . it's like being on the edge of disaster . . . where else would I turn? My Mashka has noted that I am as pale as death: "Dear lady," she says, "you are as pale as death." "Mashka," I say, "I haven't time for that now." So that is how it is! So Nozdrev is in it too, if you please!'

The agreeable lady very much wanted to elicit many more details about the elopement, such as the exact hour and the rest of it, but she was asking too much. The lady agreeable in all respects pleaded ignorance. She was incapable of lying: to suggest a hypothesis was another matter, but even then only when the supposition was based on an inner conviction. If the inner conviction had been deeply felt, then she knew how to stand up for herself, and she would have defied any barrister famed for his persuasiveness to shake her position. Such was the force of inner conviction!

There is nothing extraordinary in the fact that both ladies finally and quite definitely convinced themselves of the truth of what originally had only been a hypothesis. Our brotherhood of intelligent folk, as we call ourselves, is apt to act in a similar manner, and the proof of that lies in our learned discussions. To begin with, our savant sidles up to them like any mean fellow, he starts off shyly, discreetly, and begins by asking a most modest question: 'Was it not from there? Was it not from a particular spot that the country got its name?' or 'Does not this document date from another and later age?' or 'By such and such a people do we not really mean the other nation?' He immediately quotes this and that ancient writer, and as soon as he gets a hint, or what he simply takes to be a hint, he feels encouraged and bolder, talks to ancient writers as one man to another, sets them problems and even answers them himself, quite forgetting that he had started off with a simple hypothesis. He seems to see it already, it is all clear, and so the discussion ends with the words: 'So that is how it was!' 'So that is the people we meant!' 'So we must look at the object from this point of view!' Then he will say all this with authority, in the hearing of all, and the newly revealed truth will make its rounds of the world, collecting followers and disciples.

While the ladies were engaged in unravelling so cleverly and successfully this tangled situation, the prosecutor[2] with his unmoving countenance, bushy eyebrows and blinking eyes, walked into the drawing-room. The ladies eagerly communicated to him all the circumstances, told him about the purchase of the dead souls and the plot to elope with the governor's daughter, and threw him into such a great confusion that he remained standing as if rooted to the spot, with his left eye blinking, patting his head with a handkerchief and brushing bits of tobacco from it, but understanding absolutely nothing. In this situation the ladies left him and set off, each in her own direction, to rouse the town. This they succeeded in accomplishing within half an hour. The town was properly roused; a great unease gripped everyone but no one could make head or tail of anything. The ladies were such past-masters at throwing up a screen of fog, that everyone, and especially the officials, were for a time quite dazed. For a minute they found themselves in the position of a schoolboy who in his sleep has had a 'hussar' or a piece of paper filled with snuff thrust into his nose by his school-fellows who were awake and up before him. In his sleep he takes a deep breath and draws in all the snuff, and then, on waking, jumps up, looks round him like an idiot with bulging eyes, unable to understand where he is and what has happened to him; and only then does he begin to distinguish the walls lit up by the slanting beams of the sun, the laughter of his comrades as they lurk in the corners, and the fresh morning peeping through the window with an awakened forest ringing in a thousand warbling notes and with a glimmering river lost here and there in bright swirling turns between slender reeds, its banks crowded with naked urchins encouraging each other to plunge into the water: only after all that, he finally realizes that a 'hussar' has been inserted into his nose.

This was the situation in which the town folk and the officials found themselves at first. They stood about and

2. In Russian, *prokuror:* the official responsible for supervising the operation of government offices and the carrying out of laws and regulations; he had to approve important papers by marking them "read." See his death, page **226** below.

gaped like sheep. The dead souls, the governor's daughter, and Chichikov were all mixed in an unholy mess in their heads. After recovering from their first astonishment, they began to distinguish one thing from another, to demand an explanation, and to grow angry at the lack of any obvious logic. What sort of a parable was this? What sort of a parable were these dead souls? Where was the logic in them? How could one buy dead souls? Who would be such a fool? And what sort of money would he use for the purpose? And what would be the object and use of these dead souls? And what had the governor's daughter to do with it? If he wanted to elope with her, why did he have to buy dead souls? And if he wanted to buy dead souls, why then elope with the governor's daughter? Did he wish to make a present of them to her? What nonsense, indeed, was being talked round town! What were things coming to when stories like that were started before you had time to turn round? If there were any sense in them at least. . . . However, the stories were spread and that implied that there was some foundation to them. But what foundation was there in dead souls? There could be no foundation. It was just simply nonsense from beginning to end, just 'toil, moil and trouble'. It was just the devil knows what!

In short, it was all gossip and gossip, and the whole town was chattering about the dead souls and the governor's daughter, about Chichikov and the dead souls, about the governor's daughter and Chichikov, and all the sleeping dogs were roused. What a whirlwind swept through this once apparently drowsy town! All the 'slugs' and 'bolsters' who had been wrapped in their dressing-gowns for ages now came crawling out, putting the blame now on the shoemaker for making a pair of boots that pinched, now on the tailor or on a drunken coachman. All those who had long ceased to move in society and had intercourse, as they say, only with landowners Zavalishin and Polezhayev (well-known terms these, originating from the verbs[3] to *lie about* and to *sprawl*, which are very

3. The root of "Zavalishin" could be taken as *valyat'sya*,—"to lie" or "sprawl," "to loll, loaf"; and of "Polezhayev," *polezhat'*, also "to lie down."

popular with us in Russia, just as are the phrases 'to visit Sopikov' or 'to visit Khrapovitzky', which signify all forms of deadly sleepiness, on one's side, on one's back and in all other positions, accompanied by snores, nasal whistling and other exercises). In fact, they all emerged now, even those whom it would have been impossible to entice out of the house with a promise of a meal of a tasty fish soup worth five hundred roubles or a sturgeon two yards long, and all sorts of fish-pasties that melt in the mouth; in short, the town began to look populous and great. A Sysoy Pafnutyevich and a Macdonald Carlovich, who had never been heard of before, now appeared on the scene. A very tall, tall gentleman of a height never seen before, now also hung about the drawing-rooms. The streets were full of covered droshky and all sorts of other strange conveyances—it was a regular witches' sabbath.

At another time and in other circumstances rumours of this kind might not have attracted any attention; but the town of N. had been long cut off from any news. For the last three months there had not even been any *commérages*,[4] which are as important to a town as the timely arrival of food-supplies. It suddenly became apparent that the town had two opinions and had split into two parties—a male party and a female party. The male party, the least sensible, turned its attention to the dead souls. The female party was preoccupied exclusively with the governor's daughter and the elopement. To the honour of the ladies, let it be said, their party was more disciplined and prudent. Thus it reflected their real vocation of being good housewives and organizers. In their hands everything soon assumed a lively and definite shape, a clear and obvious form, was explained and purified, in a word, the result was a finished picture. It turned out that Chichikov had long been in love and that he had been meeting the governor's daughter in the garden by moonlight. It seemed that the governor would have given him the hand of his daughter because Chichikov was as rich as a Jew, but the obstacle proved to be his wife, whom he had abandoned (no one could tell where they

4. French for "gossip."

got the idea that Chichikov was married) and who, being in the throes of hopeless love, had written to the governor a most touching letter. On realizing that the father and mother would no longer agree, Chichikov had decided to elope. In other homes this version was recounted with slight variations. They said that Chichikov had no wife, but that being a subtle and crafty man he wished to make doubly sure of receiving the daughter's hand and, to this end, had started a secret intrigue with the mother, only later making clear his intentions with regard to the daughter; but, fearing that a sin might be committed repugnant to religion and suffering from pangs of conscience, the mother had given a categorical refusal; and this explained Chichikov's resolve to elope with the daughter. As these rumours began to circulate in the more obscure parts of the town, so they were amplified and corrected in detail. The lower classes in Russia are very fond of having a gossip about scandals in higher society, and so these affairs began to be discussed even among people who had never set eyes on Chichikov or met him; and so the details and the explanations multiplied. With every minute the theme grew more engrossing and assumed ever more definitive forms, and ultimately and in its final form it came to the ears of the governor's wife herself. As the mother of a family, as the first lady in the town, and lastly as a lady who had no suspicions of anything of the sort, the governor's wife was most indignant and quite rightly so. As a result her poor fair-haired daughter had to put up with the most painful *tête-à-tête* [5] ever endured by a girl of sixteen. On her head fell a whole torrent of questions, enquiries, rebukes, threats, reproaches, admonitions, and the girl could not contain her tears and fell to weeping without understanding a single word of what had been said. The porter was then given the strictest orders not to admit Chichikov at any time or under any pretext.

Having done their bit by the governor's wife, the ladies brought pressure to bear upon the men's party and tried to win them over to their side, affirming that the

5. Private talk of two people alone. Literally, in French, "head-to-head."

dead souls were but a red herring intended to divert suspicion and to assure the success of the elopement. Many of the men succumbed and joined the ladies' party despite the fact that they were subjected to severe censure by their friends, who apostrophized them as old women and skirts—names, as we know, most offensive to the male sex.

But however much the men might bristle and resist, their party lacked altogether the discipline of the women's. Everything about them was coarse, unfinished, not right, unsuitable, unfitting, while their heads were full of disorder, turmoil, faltering and muddled thinking; in short, there was every evidence of man's worthless character, his crude, dense nature, incapable of building a home, of sincere convictions, faithless, lazy, and the prey of endless doubts and everlasting fears. The men said it was all nonsense, that to elope with the governor's daughter was a thing that a hussar might do but not a civilian, that Chichikov would not do such a thing, that the women were lying, that a woman is like a sack—she will absorb anything you put in it, that the chief attention must be concentrated on the dead souls, not that the devil himself knew what it was all about but there was certainly something very bad and nasty about them. We shall learn at once why the men seemed to think that there was something bad and nasty about them.

A new governor-general[6] had been appointed for the province and this was an event which obviously caused some alarm among the officials: it would be followed by transfers, hauling over the coals, penalties and all the treats with which a new boss regales his subordinates! 'Well,' thought the officials, 'if he should happen to learn that these sort of rumours are floating about the town, why, he might boil over and in dead earnest.' The medical inspector went pale of a sudden: he imagined heaven knows what; that the words 'dead souls' might

---

6. The chief political and administrative official; the highest official of the first class in the administration of a province or a group of provinces *(gubernia)* in Tsarist Russia. The most trusted generals were usually appointed by the Tsar to this post.

portend those of the sick who had died off in great
numbers in the hospitals and other places of an epidemic
fever, for the prevention of which the necessary measures
had not been taken, and that Chichikov might be the
official who had been sent from the governor-general's
office to make a secret investigation. He informed the
president of his idea. The president said it was nonsense;
and then he suddenly turned pale himself as soon as he
had asked himself: 'And what if the souls purchased by
Chichikov are really dead?' And what would happen if
the governor-general happened to hear that he had
allowed the deeds of purchase to be legalized and had
even stood surety for Plyushkin? As soon as he mentioned
this possibility to one or two others, they instantly turned
pale too: fear is more contagious than the plague and is
instantly communicated. They all suddenly felt guilty
of sins they had not even committed. The words 'dead
souls' had such a vague association that there was even
some doubt as to whether they might not refer to some
corpses which had been buried in great haste as a result
of two recent incidents.

The first incident concerned some merchants from
Solvychegodsk, who had come to town for the fair and,
after clinching their deals, had thrown a party for their
friends, the merchants from Oustsysolsk—a real feast it
was in the spacious Russian manner but with some
German fancies added, like orgeats,[7] punches, balsams
and so on. The feast ended as usual in a fight. The
merchants of Solvychegodsk battered the merchants from
Oustsysolsk to death, but not without receiving some
marks and bruises on their ribs, sides, and bellies, a testimony to the outsize fists with which nature had endowed
the deceased merchants. One of the triumphant band had
his 'snout knocked off', as the champions put it, that is to
say, it was squashed to such a degree that there was
hardly a trace of it left on his face. The merchants admitted their responsibility and explained that they had
gone a bit too far; there were rumours that they slipped
across four imperial notes each when confessing. How-

7. Sweet flavoring of orange and almond.

ever, it was a very obscure case; and the result of the enquiry was that the lads from Oustsysolsk had died of charcoal fumes, and so they were buried.

The other recent incident was as follows: the Crown peasants of the village of Vshivaya-Spyess, together with like peasants from the village of Borovky, of Zadirailovo too, were charged with having swept from the face of the earth their local police force in the shape of the tax-assessor, a certain Drobyazhkin; it appeared also that the local police force, or assessor Drobyazhkin to be exact, had taken to frequenting their village too often, and his visitations were at times as bad as a plague. The cause of it all was the frailty which the local police force experienced in the region of the heart and which made him run after the village girls and women. However, all this had not been proved, although the peasants in their depositions spoke out and stated that the local police force was as lecherous as a tom-cat, that they had kept watch on him more than once and on one occasion they had even bundled him out naked from a hut into which he had strayed. Of course, the local police force deserved to be punished for its frailties of the heart, but the peasants of Vshivaya-Spyess, and Zadirailovo too, could not be condoned for taking the law into their own hands if they really had taken part in the beating to death of the police force. But it was an obscure case: the local police force was found lying in the roadway, his uniform or jacket in a worse state than any rag, and as for his physiognomy there was no way of identifying it at all. The case went the round of the courts and at last came before the higher court, where it was at first gone into in private in this sense: since it was not known which of the peasants had taken part, since there were a great many of them, since Drobyazhkin was now dead and had nothing to gain anyway even if he won his case, and since it was most important to the peasants, who were still alive, that the verdict should go in their favour, in consequence of all this, it was decided as follows: that the assessor Drobyazhkin was himself responsible for what had happened by unjustly oppressing the peasants of Vshivaya-Spyess and Zadirailovo too, and it appeared that he died in an apoplectic fit when driving back in his sledge. It looked as if the case had been well rounded off, but for no reason at all the officials now began to think that the dead souls in question had probably something to do with this case.

At this time, as if to add to the difficulties in which the officials found themselves, the governor received two simultaneous communications. One of them stated that, according to evidence and reports, there was a forger at large in the province, hiding under various aliases, and that it was imperative to make the strictest enquiries. The other communication was from the governor of a neighbouring province and referred to a bandit who had escaped from the law, and it asked that any suspicious person found without passport or proper documents should be immediately detained. These two communications produced a stupefying effect on everyone. Their previous guesses and conclusions were knocked on the head. Of course, there was no reason to suppose that these affairs had anything to do with Chichikov, and yet when each of them began to give the matter thought, when they recalled that they had no idea who Chichikov was, that even he himself had been rather vague about his past, saying, it is true, that he had suffered in the cause of justice, it was still all too vague; and when they recalled, besides, that he had confessed to having many enemies and that some of them had made attempts on his life, they began to ponder even more deeply. So his life was in danger; so he was being pursued; so he must have done something not quite right. . . . And who was he anyhow? Of course, it must not be imagined that he was a forger, to say nothing of being a bandit; he was respectable enough in appearance; but taking everything into account, who was he really? So the officials set themselves a task which they should have undertaken right from the beginning, that is, in the very first chapter of our poem. They resolved to make a few enquiries and to question those of the landowners from whom the dead souls had been bought. In this way, at least, they might find out what sort of a deal it was and what was meant by these dead souls. Perchance Chichikov might have explained or dropped a hint to someone as to his real intentions? Or he might have told someone who he was? At first they betook themselves to Korobochka, but they did not get much out of her. All she told them was that he had bought them for fifteen roubles, and that he also bought feathers and had promised to buy a lot more things, and to acquire lard for the government, and that he was very likely a rogue, for she had already come across a fellow like him who used to buy up feathers and lard for the government, but he had swindled them all, and the priest's wife had lost over a hundred roubles over it. The more she told them, the more it turned out to be a repetition of the same thing, and the officials were only driven to conclude that Korobochka was simply a silly old woman. Manilov for his part vouched for Pavel Ivanovich in whom he had implicit faith; he said that he would have sacrificed his estate to have a hundredth part of the good qualities of Pavel Ivanovich; and in general he referred to him in the most flattering terms, introducing, with eyes half-closed, a few reflections on the nature of friendship. No doubt these sentiments reflected adequately the tender emotions of his heart, but they failed to enlighten the officials. Sobakievich gave it as his opinion that Chichikov was a worthy man; he said that he had sold him the pick of his peasants and that they were a lively lot in every respect; but he could give no guarantee for the future, and if they were to die off on the road as a result of the hardships of their transplantation, it would not be his fault but only God's will, for there was no lack of plagues and mortal diseases in the world, and whole villages had been known to die out.

The officials had recourse to another and not altogether noble means, but one which is sometimes employed, namely, in devious ways and through the agency of various servants, they arranged for Chichikov's servants to be questioned about any particulars of their master's former life and circumstances; but they learnt very little. From Petrushka they only got a whiff of stale atmosphere and from Selifan, the fact that he had been in the government service, in the customs and excise, and nothing else. This sort of folk have a very strange habit. If one asks them any direct question, they will never remember the answer, they will never take it all in and will even reply that they do not know; but if you ask them about something else, they will start spinning a yarn in such detail that you have more than enough of it. As a result of all these investigations the officials concluded that they knew nothing at all about Chichikov and that yet Chichikov must certainly be somebody. They made up their minds, at last, to air this subject thoroughly and to decide at least what they were to do and how to go about it, what measures to undertake in order to determine what he was exactly, whether he was a person to be detained and arrested as an undesirable, or whether he was a person who might himself arrest and detain them as undesirables. For this purpose it was proposed that they should all assemble specially at the house of the chief of police, already known to the reader as the father and benefactor of the town.

CHAPTER X

WHEN they foregathered at the house of the chief of police, who is already known to the reader as the father and benefactor of the town, the officials had occasion to remark to one another that they had even lost weight as a result of all these alarms and excursions. The appointment of a new governor-general, the receipt of those extremely grave documents, and all those rumours, had left a clear imprint on their faces, and the dress-coats of many of them had grown perceptibly looser. There was a general deterioration: the president had lost weight, and the inspector of the medical board had lost weight, and the prosecutor had lost weight, and a certain Semyon Ivanovich, whose surname was never mentioned and who wore on his first finger a ring which he liked to show to the ladies, had also lost weight. Of course, as always happens, there were some bold spirits who had not lost courage, but they were few and far between. There was only the postmaster. He alone preserved his invariable composure and was in the habit of saying on these occasions: 'We know all about your governor-generals! They come and go, but here am I sitting pretty in one place these thirty years, my dear sir.' To which other officials would invariably reply: 'That's all right as far as you are concerned, Sprechen-Sie-Deutsch, Ivan Andreutsch; you have only to look after the post-office, a matter of receiving and expediting the mails; all the mischief you can do is to shut shop an hour earlier and overcharge some belated merchant for accepting a letter of his out of hours, or you may send off a parcel which ought not to be despatched; in such conditions anybody might be a saint. But what if the devil came twisting and turning under your nose every day, thrust temptation into your hand even when you were loath to fall for it? Of course, you have less reason to be anxious—you have only one child, and that a son; but as for me, God has been so bountiful to Praskofya Feodorovna, that she has a child every year, either a Praskushka or a Petrushka; if you were in my shoes, you'd sing a different tune.'

That was how the officials talked, but it is not the author's business to judge whether it is really possible to resist the devil. In the assembly as it was composed this time there was a notable absence of that essential thing which the run of folk call common sense. In general, for some reason, we Russians have not been created for representative institutions. In all our assemblies, from the peasant commune to every kind of learned and other committee, an unholy muddle reigns unless there is some one person to direct the proceedings. It is difficult to say why this should be so, no doubt such is the character of the people, and the most successful assemblies are those which, like clubs or pleasure gardens after the German fashion, are instituted for the purpose of sprees and dining out. And yet there is always a readiness to undertake every possible sort of thing. As the wind blows, we are suddenly capable of founding charitable and philanthropic institutions, and goodness only knows what else. The intention may be an excellent one but nothing ever comes of it. This may be due to the fact that we take too much for granted from the start and assume that everything has already been done. For instance, after launching some charitable society for the benefit of the poor and subscribing considerable sums to this end, we immediately arrange a banquet for the dignitaries of the town in order to celebrate this praiseworthy undertaking and, needless to say, this inauguration runs away with half of the money subscribed; with what is left we promptly rent a magnificent apartment, with heating laid on and porters at the door, for the use of the committee, and ultimately out of the whole sum there remains only five and a half roubles for the benefit of the poor: and even here, when it comes to distributing this sum, it will be found that not all members of the committee are agreed, and that each one of them will have a protégé of his own to recommend.

However, the present assembly was of a quite different character: its meeting was the result of necessity. It was not a question of the poor or of any strangers but one that affected every official personally; it concerned the misfortune threatening them one and all, and willy-nilly. This made for greater unanimity and contact. But in spite of it all it was a witches' brew. Quite apart from such differences of opinion as are common to all assemblies in the minds of those present there was revealed a certain incomprehensible indecision: one maintained that Chichikov was a forger of banknotes, but then corrected himself to state that maybe he was not a forger; another affirmed that he was an official of the governor-general's office, but at once added, 'The devil only knows, it is not written on his forehead.' All were up in arms against the suggestion that Chichikov was a brigand in disguise. They agreed that his appearance was entirely respectable and that there was nothing in his conversation to indicate a man of violent deeds. All at once, whether as the result of an unexpected inspiration illumining him or of something else, the postmaster, who for some minutes had been sunk in meditation, suddenly cried out: 'Gentlemen, do you know who he is?' The voice in which he uttered this was so shattering that it made everyone cry out simultaneously: 'Who?' 'Why, gentlemen, he is captain Kopeykin!' And when they all unanimously enquired, 'And who is captain Kopeykin?' the postmaster retorted, 'Don't you know who captain Kopeykin is?'

They were obliged to reply that they had not the slightest idea.

'Captain Kopeykin,' said the postmaster, holding his snuff-box only half-open for fear that someone near him might thrust his fingers inside, in whose cleanliness he had but little faith—on such occasions he was even in the habit of saying 'We know, my good sir, there is no way of telling the sort of places your fingers have been delving into, and snuff must be kept clean.'—'Captain Kopeykin,' he repeated as he took a pinch of snuff. 'Why, if one were to relate the story, it would prove an absorbing subject for some writer, a whole poem in its way.'

As everyone present was anxious to hear this story, or, as the postmaster had put it, 'this absorbing subject for a writer, a whole poem in its way,' he started his narration.

THE STORY OF CAPTAIN KOPEYKIN[8]

'After the campaign of 1812, my good sir,' so the postmaster began despite the fact that not one but six good sirs were sitting in the room, 'after the campaign of 1812, captain Kopeykin was one of the wounded to be repatriated. It is not certain where he was wounded, at Krasny or at Leipzig,[9] but, as you may imagine, he lost both an arm and a leg. Well, at that time, no arrangements had yet been made for looking after the cripples; that, so-to-speak, invalid capital fund was, as you may imagine, instituted somewhat later. Captain Kopeykin saw that he must find himself some work but the only arm he had, you will understand, was his left one. He paid his father a visit at home but the old man told him, "I can't feed you!" Just think of that. "I can barely manage my-

---

8. "Kopeykin" was a name taken by Gogol from songs and folktales about a robber and outlaw who was a Russian kind of Robin Hood. *Kopeyka* = a kopek—a penny, the hundredth part of a ruble.

9. Krasny: a battle near Smolensk, in 1812, in which Russian troops heroically resisted a French advance. Leipzig: a battle in 1813, in which Napoleon was defeated and forced to retreat into France.

self," he said to him. So captain Kopeykin decided to go to Petersburg, my good sir, in order to beg the Tsar's mercy: "That's how it is, I have in a way so to speak, sacrificed my life and spilt my blood . . ." he was going to tell the Tsar. Well, and in some way or other, getting lifts on trains of wagons or in official conveyances, in a word, sir, he at last managed to reach Petersburg. You may imagine then, how this anybody, that is to say, captain Kopeykin suddenly found himself in the capital, to which there is nothing comparable, so to speak, in the whole world! Unexpectedly there was the world in front of him as it were, a certain horizon of life, a fabulous Scheherezade.[1] Suddenly some sort of, you can fancy it, Nevsky prospect or some, you know, Gorohovaya street, the devil take it! Or some Liteynaya street—with a sort of spire there in the air; the bridges hanging in space like the very devil, as you may imagine, without any, that is to say, contact—in a word, Semiramis,[2] yes sir, there can be no argument on that point. The captain knocked about in search for a lodging, as it were, but the prices were frightfully exorbitant: curtains, blinds, all kinds of devilry you know, carpets—oriental luxury no less . . . in a word, it was like walking on capital. Well, it was just like strolling down a street with your nose literally breathing in roubles by the thousand; and, as you will understand, my captain's whole bank account was made up of no more than a dozen five-rouble pieces. Well, in the end, he did discover a room in a Revel[3] tavern for a rouble a night all included: cabbage soup and hashed beef for dinner. He saw he wouldn't be able to stick it for long. He enquired here and there where he might apply. They told him there was a sort of higher commission, an office of a kind, you know, with a general-in-chief so and so at its head. The Tsar, you must know, was not yet in the capital at the time: the troops, you see, had not yet

---

1. The heroine of the Arabian *Thousand and One Nights*, stories strung together by Scheherezade, who kept her husband from killing her by telling these stories from night to night.
2. Legendary queen of Assyria and Babylon, famous for her hanging gardens.
3. A port on the Gulf of Finland, now called Tallinn, the capital of Estonia.

returned from Paris, they were all abroad. Having got up somewhat earlier, my Kopeykin scratched his beard a bit with his left hand—the barber's fee would have meant running up an account—pulled on his uniform, and you can imagine it, dragged himself off on his wooden leg to see the head, the big shot himself. He asked the way to the house. "Over there," they said, pointing to a house on the Palace quay. It turned out to be quite a peasant's hut, you see! The window panes, only fancy, were mirrors ten feet across, so that the vases and every-thing in the rooms appeared to be on the outside—it looked as if you might have put your hand on it all; precious marbles on the walls, a display of metals, some door knob that would make you drop into a shop first of all and buy a farthing's worth of soap in order to wash your hands for two or three hours with it before you made up your mind to catch hold of it—in a word, such polish on everything as would turn you quite dizzy. The porter already looked like a Generalissimo, with his gilt stick, his aristocratic physiognomy like that of some plump well-fed pup; cambric collars, and the like knavery!... My Kopeykin just managed to drag himself up on his wooden leg as far as the waiting-room, huddled himself in a corner so as not to stick his elbow, as you can guess, into some America or India—some gilt china vase or other. Well, of course, he stood about there long enough because, as you may imagine, he had arrived at an hour when the general had, in a way, hardly got out of bed yet, while his valet had, so to speak, just brought him some silver basin or other for his various ablutions. My Kopeykin had been waiting these four hours when at last in comes the adjutant or some other officer on duty. "The general," he said, "is now coming into the waiting-room." And there were already as many folk in the waiting-room as beans on a plate. And they were not like our poor brother, they were all of the fourth or fifth grade, colonels, with here and there a fat macaroni glittering on an epaulette—a ranking general in fact. Of a sudden, you will understand, there was a barely perceptible flutter like rarified ether. A "sh-sh" was to be heard here and there and finally a terrifying silence descended. The big noise had appeared. Well, you can imagine him, a man of state! In his face, so to speak . . . well, corresponding to his rank, you see . . . with his high rank . . . just such an expression, you understand. Everyone in the waiting-room, it goes without saying, grew taut immediately, expectant, trembling, hanging on the decision, as it were, of his fate. The minister or the big noise made the rounds of this one and that: "Why have you come? Why have you come? What do you want? What is your business?" At last, my good sir, he came to Kopeykin. Gathering courage, Kopeykin reported: "This is how it is, Your Excellency: I have shed my blood, in a way lost an arm and a leg, I can do no work, I make bold to beg the imperial mercy." The minister saw before him a man with a wooden leg and an empty sleeve fastened to his uniform. "Very well," he said, "come back in a day or two." My Kopeykin left in a state almost bordering on delight: there was the fact that he had succeeded in obtaining an audience with, so to speak, a high-ranking big noise; and there was also the fact that the question of his pension would now, in a way, be decided. In this frame of mind, you will understand, he was hopping along the pavement. He dropped into the Palkinsky tavern for a glass of vodka, he dined at the London restaurant, ordered himself some cutlets with caper sauce, asked for chicken with all sorts of trimmings and a bottle of wine into the bargain; in the evening he went to the theatre, in brief he had a spree. As he was walking along the pavement he caught sight of a well-built Englishwoman, a swan so to speak. My Kopeykin, his blood, you know, began to stir, started off after her on his wooden leg, tap, tap, on the pavement. "But no," he thought, "I'll leave that for later, when I get my pension, I'm kicking over the traces too much." So, my good sir, three or four days later, my Kopeykin turned up again at the minister's and waited long enough for him to appear. "This and that," he said. "I've come," he said, "to hear Your Excellency's order relative to my illnesses and the wounds sustained. . . ." And other things in this vein and in due form. The big noise, you may imagine, recognized him at once. "Ah, very well," he said. "This time I can only tell you that you must wait until the Tsar returns to town; then doubtless orders will be issued concerning the wounded, but without the royal will, so to speak, I can do nothing." A bow, you understand, and so—farewell. As you may imagine, Kopeykin found himself in a most uncertain situation. He had thought that he would be paid out a sum of money next day. "Here you are, my dear, drink and make merry!" But instead he had been ordered to wait, and that for an indefinite time. He looked as gloomy as an owl as he went down the steps—like a poodle, you know, whom a cook has drenched in water; his tail was between his legs and his ears hung down. "Well no," he thought to himself, "I shall go there again and explain that I am eating my last morsel—if you don't help me, I must die, in a way, of hunger." In short, my good sir, he paid another visit to the Palace quay, but he was told: "You can't come in, he is not receiving, come to-morrow." The following day it was the same; the porter simply would not take any notice of him. And in the meantime, as you will understand, there was only one five-rouble piece left in his pocket. Whereas formerly he had been having cabbage soup and a bit of beef, so now he had to content himself with buying some salted herring or a salted cucumber and a halfpenny-worth of bread; in short, the poor chap was beginning to go hungry whilst his appetite grew as ravenous as a wolf's. Whenever he happened to go past any restaurant—the chef there, as you may suppose, would be a foreigner, some Frenchman with an open face, dressed in fine linen and an apron as white as snow, and he would be preparing *fines herbes* or cutlets with truffles—in fact, one would develop an appetite large enough to eat oneself even. Or if he happened to go past the Milyutinsky stores, there he would see a great salmon staring out of the window at him, cherries at five roubles apiece, a giant water-melon, a veritable stage-coach in size, would be thrust out of the window and looking, so to speak, for anyone foolish enough to pay a hundred roubles; in short, there was such temptation at every step that his mouth watered, but he only heard "to-morrow". You can conjure up therefore the position he was in: on the one side there were, so to speak, the salmon and the water-melon; and, on the other, he was being offered one and the same dish of "to-morrow". At last, the poor wretch could stand it no longer and he decided to take the fortress by storm. He hung round the doorway until another petitioner came along, and then he succeeded in squeezing his way through into the waiting-room, with his wooden leg and all, in the company of some sort of general. The big noise appeared as was his wont: "Why are you here? Why are you here! Ah!" he said, catching sight of Kopeykin. "But I've already told you that you must wait for the decision." "But Your Excellency, I beg you to consider that I haven't a piece of bread left. . . ." "What is to be done? I cannot do anything for you; try in the meantime to help yourself, try and find means for yourself." "But, Your Highness, you can to some extent judge yourself what means I can find without an arm and leg." "But you will agree," said the dignitary, "that I cannot support you, as it were, out of my own purse; I have many wounded and they all have equal rights. . . . Arm yourself with patience. The Tsar will arrive, and I can give you my word of honour that His Gracious Majesty will not forget you." "But, Your Highness, I cannot wait," said Kopeykin somewhat rudely this time. And the big noise, you will understand, began to feel aggrieved. And, indeed, here were generals all round waiting for decisions and orders; these affairs were, so to say, important, they were state affairs demanding immediate execution—a minute wasted might be fraught with importance—and here he was being pestered by a nagging devil. "Excuse me," he said, "I am busy. . . . I have to attend to more important affairs." It was a subtle way of indicating that it was time, at last, to be off. But as for my Kopeykin, hunger spurred him on, you know: "As you will, Your Highness," he said, "I shall not budge from here until you give an order." Well . . . you can picture the scene: to answer back like that to a big noise, who only has to utter a word for you to be sent flying where the devil himself will be unable to find you. . . . It is already considered rude for anything like that to be said by one official to another one rank above him. But here, just look at the gulf—between a general-in-chief and a captain Kopeykin! As ninety roubles to nought! The general, you see, did nothing more, he only glared, but his glare was like a fire-arm: there was no soul in it—it had already sunk into his heels. And, as you may imagine, my Kopeykin did not budge but stood rooted to the spot. "Well?" said the general, getting his grip on him, as it were. However, to tell the truth, he showed himself merciful enough towards him: another would have given him such a fright that for three days or so the very streets would have seemed upside down, but he only said: "Very good," he said, "if you like this place so much and do not care to await quietly in town the decisions made about your fate, then I shall have you removed at government expense. Call the guard! Have him conducted to his lodging!" And the guard was standing there already: a good six foot he was, with great big hands just fit for a coachman—in a word, he was quite a dentist.[4] . . . And so, my good sir, they caught hold of him, this poor servant of God, and thrust him into a cart, the guard accompanying him. "Well," thought Kopeykin, "at least I shan't have to pay my fare, that's something to be thankful for." And so, my good sir, off he is driven with the guard and, driving along, he argued as it were with himself: "The general told me to look for means of helping myself—all right," he said, "I will." But nothing at all is known of how he reached his destination and where exactly he was driven. And so, you will understand, rumours of captain Kopeykin were swallowed up in the river of forgetfulness, in Lethe as the poets call it. But allow me, gentlemen, for here, as we may say, begins the thread, the plot of the story. Where Kopeykin got to is not known; but just imagine it, two months had not gone by when a band of robbers appeared in the forests of

4. A slang expression for particularly brutal landlords who beat up and knocked out the teeth of their serfs.

Ryazan, and the ataman of the band, my good sir, was none other than. . . .'[5]

'But excuse me, Ivan Andreyevich,' said the chief of the police, suddenly interrupting him. 'But did you not say yourself that captain Kopeykin had lost both an arm and a leg, while Chichikov . . .'

Hereupon the postmaster gave vent to an exclamation and slapped his forehead hard, calling himself a 'calf' for all to hear as he did so. He could not understand how this circumstance had not occurred to him right from the beginning and he admitted the complete justice of the saying, 'The Russian is wise after the event.' However, a minute later he was trying to be clever and get round it, arguing that mechanical devices had been much perfected in England, that it was clear from the papers that someone had invented a pair of wooden legs, which as soon as a hidden spring was touched, would carry a man off God alone knows where, anyhow there would be no way of finding him again.

But they all doubted very much that Chichikov could be captain Kopeykin and thought that the postmaster had gone too far. However, for their part, they refused to bite the dust and, spurred on by the postmaster's witty guess, they wandered almost farther astray. Among a number of intelligent suggestions there was finally this one too, strange as it may seem, that Chichikov might be Napoleon in disguise, that the English had long been envious of the greatness and extent of Russia, that more than once telling caricatures had been published of a Russian talking to an Englishman. The Englishman was standing, holding behind him a dog on the lead, and the dog was supposed to be Napoleon! 'Look out,' he was saying, 'if you don't behave, I shall set this dog upon you!' And so, perhaps, they have let him escape from St. Helena, and he was now making his way around Russia in the guise of Chichikov, though in reality he was not Chichikov at all.

5. The censors forbade publishing various sections of the story of Captain Kopeykin because they contained criticism of those in power. "Ataman": leader of Cossacks.

Of course, they did not quite believe that official, but nevertheless they grew thoughtful and, as each one delved into the matter himself, he discovered that Chichikov's face, when he turned round and stood sideways, was indeed very like a portrait of Napoleon. The chief of police, who had served in the 1812 campaign and had personally seen Napoleon, could not but admit that he was no taller than Chichikov and that Napoleon, it might be said, was also not too stout of build, but neither was he too slight. Perhaps, some readers will think all this improbable; but, as if to make matters worse, it all happened as we relate it—which is all the more astonishing since the town was not situated in the backwoods but, on the contrary, not very far away from both capitals. However, it must be remembered that all this was taking place soon after the famous expulsion of the French. At that time all our landowners, officials, merchants, shopmen, and every sort of literate and illiterate folk, for a spell of at least eight years had turned into inveterate politicians. The *Moscow Gazette* and the *Son of the Fatherland* were perused most unmercifully and reached their ultimate reader all in shreds and quite unusable. Instead of such questions as 'For how much, father, did you sell your measure of oats?' or 'What did you do in yesterday's first fall of snow?' they used to ask: 'What are they writing in the papers? Have they let Napoleon escape from his island again?' The merchants were very afraid of this happening, for they had implicit faith in the predictions of a certain prophet who had already been sitting in jail these last three years. The prophet had appeared no one knows whence, wearing bast-shoes and an unlined sheepskin coat, and smelling terribly of stale fish; and he had announced that Napoleon was Antichrist and was kept on a stone chain, behind six walls and seven seas, but that afterwards he would break his chains and master the whole world. The prophet was very properly jailed for this prediction, but nevertheless he had done his job and set the merchants in a flutter. For a long time after, even while attending to their most profitable deals, they chattered about Antichrist on the way to the tavern for their tea. Many of the officials and members of the nobility also pondered on this subject despite themselves and, infected by the mysticism which, as we know, was then very fashionable, attached some special significance to each letter composing the word Napoleon; others even discovered in it an apocalyptical figure. Thus, there is nothing surprising in the fact that the officials of the town of N. paused to consider this point; however, they soon pulled themselves together, observing that their imagination had grown too lively and that things were not quite like that. They pondered and pondered, talked and talked, and finally decided that it would not be a bad idea to question Nozdrev thoroughly. Since he was the first to air the story of the dead souls and had been, as they say, in quite close relations with Chichikov, it followed without any doubt that he must know something of the circumstances of his life. It was therefore resolved to find out what Nozdrev had to say.

These official gentry were strange folk, as indeed are those of all other professions: they knew perfectly well that Nozdrev was a liar, that they could trust no word of his however trivial, and yet it was precisely to him that they turned. It is not easy to grasp human nature! A man may not believe in God and yet believe himself to be at death's door when the bridge of his nose itches; he will pass by the creative work of some poet, which is as clear as daylight, all bathed in harmony and the sublime wisdom of simplicity, but he will show enthusiasm for the work of some bold fellow who muddles, knots, breaks up and distorts nature, and pleased with this discovery he will cry out: 'This is it! Here is real understanding of the mysteries of the heart!' All his life he will not care a jot for any doctor but he will end by consulting some peasant woman who cures by incantations and spittle; or, better still, he will concoct for himself some mixture of heaven knows what filth which he will imagine to be just the right remedy for his malady. Of course, the really embarrassing situation in which they found themselves may serve as part excuse for these official gentry. They say that a drowning man clutches at a straw and that he has not enough presence of mind at the time to grasp that, while a fly may ride the straw, his ten or twelve stone will not; but the idea does not occur to him at the time and so he goes on clutching at the straw. So it was that our gentlemen finally clutched at Nozdrev.

The chief of police at once scribbled a note to invite him to an evening party, and a booted policeman with engagingly rosy cheeks set off that very minute, clutching his sword as he hastened along to Nozdrev's house. Nozdrev was in the thick of a very important affair; for four days he had not been out of his room, he would admit no one and his meals were handed in through the window—in a word, he had even grown thin and green. The matter in hand demanded the utmost attention: it consisted of the selection from several dozen packs of cards of the same size of a suit on which he could rely as on a trusty friend. There was still a fortnight's work ahead of him; during that time Porphyry had to keep the mastiff puppy clean, scrub his navel with a special brush and wash him in soap three times a day. Nozdrev was angry at having his solitude interrupted; his first reaction was to send the policeman to the devil, but when he had gathered from the note that some profit to him might accrue from the presence of a new-comer, he grew more amenable, quickly locked the door of his room, dressed himself anyhow and set off with him. Nozdrev's statements, testimony and suppositions formed such a contrast to those of the officials, that all their guesses were confounded. Positively Nozdrev was a person for whom doubt did not exist; and in proportion as the officials showed themselves uncertain or wavering he showed himself firm and assured. He replied to all their questions without any hesitation, declaring that Chichikov had bought several thousand roubles' worth of dead souls and that he himself had sold him some, for he could see no reason why he should not do so. In answer to the question whether or not Chichikov was a spy and was trying to nose out something, Nozdrev replied that he was a spy, that even at the school where they were educated together, he had been dubbed a sneak, and that his comrades, including himself, had given him a thrashing for that, and afterwards two hundred and forty leeches had to be applied to his temples—that is, he had intended to say forty but the two hundred had somehow slipped in. To the question of whether Chichikov was a forger, he replied that he was indeed, and launched into an anecdote about his extraordinary dexterity. To illustrate this he narrated how, when it was learnt that there were two million roubles' worth of forged banknotes in Chichikov's house, the latter was sealed up and a guard was put at each door, two soldiers every night, but when the seals were broken it was discovered that the banknotes were real. To the question whether Chichikov had or had not the intention of eloping with the governor's daughter, and whether it was true that he himself had undertaken to assist and participate in that affair, Nozdrev replied that he had helped and that, if he had not, nothing would have come of it; but as soon as he had said that he thought better of it, for he perceived that he had made a mistake in telling this lie and that he might suffer for it, but he could not hold his tongue. Besides, it was hard to do so, because of the interesting details which presented themselves and which it was impossible to pass over. He even mentioned the village by name, Trukhmachevka to be exact, containing the parish church where it was proposed to celebrate the wedding, the seventy-five roubles to be given to Father Sidor for the ceremony, the fact that the latter would not have agreed to it had he not frightened him by threatening to report him for marrying a certain corn-dealer, Michael by name, to the godmother of a child of which he was the godfather, and that he had placed his carriage at their disposal and had arranged for relays of horses at all the posting stations on the way. He got so involved in details that he was already beginning to refer to the coachmen by their Christian names.

They tried to bring the conversation back to Napoleon, but regretted it as soon as they had done so, for Nozdrev drew such a red herring across the trail that not only was there very little truth in it but all semblance of truth was lost, and sighing to themselves the officials walked away. Only the chief of police remained attentive for a while in expectation that something at least would emerge in the end, but finally he waved his hand and said: 'What the devil is this!' Everyone agreed that however much trouble might be taken with a bull there was no turning him into a milch-cow. And so the officials found themselves in an even worse plight than before, and the upshot of the matter was that they never succeeded in discovering Chichikov's identity. The nature of man grew clear as daylight: he is wise, clever and sensible in all things which pertain to others rather than to himself. What firm and prudent counsels he will offer in moments of difficulty! 'What a resourceful brain!' cries the crowd. 'What a staunch character!' But were a misfortune to befall that resourceful head, and were he himself to be confronted with difficulties, where would that staunch character be! The virile man would lose his bearings and prove a mere wretched poltroon, a weak and insignificant child, or simply a muff, as Nozdrev termed it.

For some reason, all these discussions, opinions and rumours produced their greatest effect on the poor prosecutor. They affected him to such an extent that, on returning home, he began to think and think and think, and all of a sudden, as they say, he died for no reason at all. Whether it was paralysis or something else, he fell off the chair in which he was sitting. As was customary on such occasions, gestures of despair were made and cries of 'Good God!' were heard. The doctor was fetched to bleed him, and then it became apparent that the prosecutor was but a soulless corpse. Only then was it learnt with regret that the deceased had been endowed with a soul, which out of modesty he had never shown. And meanwhile the manifestation of death was as terrible in a small man as in a great one: the man who had but recently been walking, moving about, playing whist, signing various papers and who was often to be seen, with his thick brows and his winking eye, among the officials, now lay stretched out on the table; his left eye winked no more, but one eyebrow was still raised in a sort of interrogating way. What the dead man wanted to know, why he died or why he had lived—God only knows.

But this is absurd! There is no rhyme or reason in it! It is incredible that officials should be so scared as to think such nonsense, depart so far from the truth, when even a child can see what is the matter! Many readers will say this and reproach the author for being improbable, or they will dub the poor officials fools, for men are lavish of that word, always ready to apply it twenty times a day to their next-door neighbour. It is enough to possess one stupid characteristic in ten to be labelled as a fool despite the nine remaining good ones. Judgment comes easy to readers, who look down from some nook of theirs among the peaks, whence the whole horizon becomes visible as does everything that goes on below on earth where men can only see immediate objects. And in the universal chronicle of mankind there are many whole centuries which, it seems, one might have annulled and destroyed as unnecessary. Many are the errors which have been perpetrated in the world—errors, it would seem, that even a child now would avoid repeating. What twisted, blind, narrow, impassable and devious paths have men chosen to tread in their striving to attain eternal truth when, all the time, in front of them lay a straight road—a road leading directly to the splendid halls destined to become the imperial palace. This road is broader and more resplendent than all others, illumined by the sun and lit up all night with fires; but in the unseeing dark a throng of men has flowed past it. And how often, even when they were illuminated by a heaven-sent sense, men still managed to break away and turn aside, to stray in broad daylight once again into blind alleys, to throw dust in each other's eyes and, pursuing a mirage, to reach finally the brink of a precipice, only to ask themselves then in horror how they might find a way out and get back on to the main road! The present generation now sees everything clearly, is amazed at the errors and laughs at the short-sightedness of its ancestors; it is not for nothing that this chronicle is shot through with a heavenly fire, that each letter of it screams out, that a piercing finger points from all sides—pointing at the present generation; but the present generation only laughs, and with self-assurance and pride treads a path of new errors which will prove a subject for ridicule to posterity.

Chichikov had not the slightest idea about what was going on. As though on purpose he had caught a slight chill at this time, an inflammation and swelling of the throat, a complaint very common to many of our provincial towns. To guard against the possibility of his life being cut short without posterity, he decided to spend two or three days in his room. Throughout this period he gargled his throat constantly with a mixture of milk and figs, eating the figs afterwards, and he also wore a compress of camomile and camphor against his cheek. To occupy his time he made out several new and detailed lists of all the peasants whom he had bought; he even read a volume of the Duchess de la Vallière,[6] which he dug up out of his trunk, looked over the various objects and notes which he kept in his box, once again read through one or two things, and was very bored by it all. He could not understand why it was that none of the town officials had even once called on him to enquire after his health, when only a short while before various carriages—those of the postmaster, the prosecutor, the president—were to be found frequently waiting outside his hotel. He only shrugged his shoulders as he paced about the room. At last he felt better and was greatly overjoyed at the possibility of taking some fresh air. Without delay he busied himself with his toilet, unlocked his case, poured some hot water into a glass, took out a brush and soap and prepared to shave, and it was high time that he did so, for having stroked his chin and peeped into the mirror, he exclaimed, 'H'm, quite a forest!' And true enough, forest or no forest, there was quite a thick

6. The duchess (1644–1710) was a one-time mistress of Louis XIV of France; she repented her sins, became a Carmelite nun, and wrote *Reflections on God's Compassionateness;* her letters and biography were widely read in the second half of the eighteenth century; and she was the subject of a novel by the French novelist Madame Madeleine Genlis (1746–1830), published in 1804.

growth all over his cheeks and chin. After shaving he began to dress so swiftly and rapidly that he was almost like a jack-in-the-box in his movements. At last, when he was dressed, sprinkled with eau-de-cologne and muffled up warmly, he ventured out into the street, but very prudently he still kept his cheek tied up. His coming out, like that of any person restored to health, had a festive air about it. Everything he came across—houses, passing peasants, who looked serious enough and some of whom had already had time to box one another's ears—assumed a laughing mien. He intended to pay his first call on the governor. On the way his mind was seething with all kinds of thoughts; a blonde kept recurring to his mind, his fancy even began to play pranks, and he was already beginning to jest and joke at himself. In that mood he arrived in front of the governor's residence. In the hall he was already about to take off his coat hastily when the porter completely dumbfounded him by saying unexpectedly, 'I have orders not to admit you!'

'What's this? Don't you recognize me? Have a good look at me!' Chichikov exclaimed.

'I recognize you all right! It's not the first time I'm seeing you,' answered the porter. 'But it was you and no one else that I was told not to admit.'

'Well, well! And the reason? Why?'

'Those are my orders. Evidently that's how it should be,' the porter retorted and added the word, 'Yes'. After that he stood facing Chichikov with a careless air, without any show of the attention with which he formerly used to take his overcoat. As he looked at him he seemed to be thinking: 'Aha! If the gentry are showing you the door, you must be some sort of a rogue!'

'Quite incomprehensible!' Chichikov thought to himself and set off at once to call on the president, but the president grew so embarrassed on catching sight of him that he could hardly speak, and he talked such rubbish that both of them felt guilty. However hard Chichikov tried, on leaving him, to puzzle out and grasp what was in the president's mind, and what he had intended, he could not make any sense of it. He then paid a number of other calls—on the chief of police, the vice-governor and the postmaster, but they all either refused to receive him or received him so strangely, and talked with such constraint and so incomprehensibly, and were so confused, and such a muddle resulted from it all, that he began to suspect that they were not quite right in their heads. He paid one or two more visits in the hope of discovering the cause, at least, but he could discover none. Like a sleepwalker he wandered aimlessly about the town, unable to decide whether he was mad himself or whether the officials had gone off their heads, whether all this was a dream or whether this nonsensical reality was stranger than fiction. It was already late, almost dusk, when he returned to the hotel, which he had left in such a cheerful frame of mind, and to offset his gloom he ordered tea to be brought. As he began to pour out the tea in a state of thoughtful and puzzled perplexity as to the strange situation in which he found himself, suddenly the door of his room flew open and Nozdrev made an unexpected appearance.

'As the proverb says, for the sake of a friend five miles is no distance!' Nozdrev said, taking off his cap. 'As I was going past, I saw a light in the window and I thought I would drop in. He won't be asleep yet, I thought. Ah, good, I see you've got some tea ready, I'll have some with pleasure. At dinner to-day I stuffed myself with some sort of filth and I'm beginning to feel queer already. Won't you ask me to fill a pipe? Where's your pipe?'

'I don't smoke a pipe,' Chichikov said drily.

'Nonsense! As if I didn't know that you were a smoker. Hey! What's your valet's name? Hey, Vakhramey, come here!'

'It isn't Vakhramey, but Petrushka.'

'How's that? It used to be Vakhramey.'

'I never had a man of that name.'

'You are right, Vakhramey is Derebin's man. Just fancy, the luck that's come Derebin's way: his aunt fell out with her son because he married a serf-girl and now she has left all her property to Derebin. It wouldn't be a bad idea, I thought to myself, to have an aunt like that for future reference! And what's up with you, brother? Why are you avoiding everyone and keeping away from parties? I know, of course, that you indulge sometimes in learned pursuits, that you like reading' (we cannot explain, and Chichikov still less, why Nozdrev should have concluded that our hero indulged in learned pursuits and liked reading). 'Ah, brother Chichikov, if you had only seen . . . it would have been food for your satirical mind' (there was no telling either why a satirical mind was attributed to Chichikov). 'Just fancy, brother, we were playing at cards at Likhachev's—the merchant, you know—and what fun it was! Perependev, who was there with me, "Well," he said, "if only Chichikov were here, he would be in his element! . . ."' (Chichikov was not acquainted with any Perependev.) 'But you must confess, brother, that was a low trick of yours that time when we were having a game of draughts, for it was I who won. . . . Yes, brother, you just diddled me. But the devil knows me, I can't be angry. The other day, at the president's. . . . Ah, yes! I must tell you that everyone in town has turned against you. They believe that you forge banknotes. They've been pestering me, but I put up a mountain of a defence for you, I told them that I was at school with you and knew your father; there is no denying it, I spun them a fine yarn.'

'I forge banknotes?' Chichikov exclaimed, getting up from his chair.

'Why did you frighten them so?' Nozdrev went on. 'The devil only knows, they're at their wits' end for fear; they've dressed you up as a bandit and spy. . . . And the prosecutor died of fright, his funeral's to-morrow. Will you be there? To tell the truth, they're afraid of the new governor-general in case they get into hot water over you; but my view of the governor-general is this: if he tries to be superior and important, he won't get anywhere at all with the nobility. The nobility expects to be entertained, isn't that so? One can, of course, bury oneself in one's study and not give a single ball, but what will be the result? There is nothing to be gained by that. But, Chichikov, that was a risky business you undertook.'

'A risky business? What business?' Chichikov enquired anxiously.

'Why, the governor's daughter you were going to elope with. I confess I was expecting it, honest I was! The very first time I saw you at the ball together, well, I thought to myself, it's probably not for nothing that Chichikov. . . . However, it was a pity you made that choice, I don't see anything in her. But there is one young lady, a relative of Bikusov, his sister's daughter, she's quite a girl! A walking miracle, as you might say!'

'But what are you talking about? You're mixing everything up. What do you mean, eloping with the governor's daughter?' Chichikov asked with bulging eyes.

'Don't try and pretend, brother, I know you're a close one! I will confess that I came to you with one purpose only: to help you, if you will allow it. So be it: I'll hold the wedding crown over your head, I'll see to the carriage and the relays, but only on condition that you lend me three thousand roubles. I need them more than life!'

While Nozdrev was chattering away, Chichikov rubbed his eyes several times, wishing to make sure that he was not dreaming. The charge of forgery, that of eloping with the governor's daughter, the prosecutor's death of which he was supposed to be the cause, the arrival of a governor-general—all this gave him quite a fright. 'Well if things have gone as far as this,' he thought to himself, 'there is no point in staying on. I must get out of here quick.'

He tried to get Nozdrev out of the way as expeditiously as he could, then he immediately summoned Selifan and told him to be ready at dawn so that they could leave town without fail at six o'clock; and he instructed him to check everything, to have the carriage greased, and so on, and so forth. Selifan said, 'It will be done, Pavel Ivanovich,' but remained standing in the doorway for some time, quite motionless. Chichikov then ordered Petrushka to pull the trunk out from under the bed, covered as it was already with a goodly layer of dust, and with his help he began to pack away his belongings as they came to hand—stockings, shirts, linen washed and unwashed, boot trees, a calendar. . . . All this was packed anyhow;

he particularly wanted to be ready overnight so as to avoid any delay in the morning. After standing for a couple of minutes in the doorway, Selifan at last made his exit very slowly. Very slowly, if one can only imagine how slow that can be, he descended the stairs, leaving the imprint of his muddy boots on the worn steps, and for a long time after he scratched the back of his head. What did that scratching portend? And what in general did it signify? Was it an expression of regret at the miscarriage of an outing planned for to-morrow in some licensed pot-house with a fellow coachman in a shabby sheepskin coat held together by a belt? Or had a small love-knot been tied in this new place of sojourn and was it now necessary to give up that lounging in the gateway of an evening and that politic pressure of white hands at an hour when dusk is falling on the town and a strapping lad in a red shirt twangs away on a balalaika before a gathering of house-serfs, while a mixed crowd of folk, resting from their labours, indulge in quiet talk? Or was it simply the regret at having to leave a cosy corner under a sheepskin coat by the kitchen stove in the servants' quarters, the cabbage soup and the tasty town-made pasties, in order to drag along once more through the rain and sleet, and face all the mishaps of the road? God knows—it would be hard to guess. Among the Russian people to scratch the back of one's head can signify a great many things.

CHAPTER XI

HOWEVER, nothing turned out as Chichikov had intended. To begin with, he got up later than he wanted—that was the first disagreeable thing. Once out of bed, he immediately sent a man to find out whether the horses were harnessed, but nothing was ready. That was the second disagreeable thing. In a rage, he was preparing to give our old friend Selifan something in the nature of a drubbing and waited with the greatest of impatience to hear what excuses the latter would produce to justify himself. It was not long before Selifan appeared in the doorway, and the master had the pleasure of listening to the usual sort of speech made by a servant whenever a speedy departure is essential.

'But, Pavel Ivanovich, we shall have to get the horses shod,' Selifan declared.

'Ah, you dolt! Blockhead! Why didn't you say so before? Didn't you have time?' his master cried.

'Oh I had time enough. . . . But there was the wheel also, Pavel Ivanovich, we'll have to tighten the hoop, for the road now is full of ruts, it's nasty weather this morning. . . . And if I may be allowed to report: the forepart of the chaise is quite shaky, it won't last two stages maybe.' Such was the spate of excuses.

'Scoundrel!' shouted Chichikov throwing up his arms. He went up so close to Selifan that, for fear of catching a box on the ear from his master, Selifan beat a retreat and kept at a safe distance.

'You're plotting to murder me, are you?' Chichikov yelled. 'Ah? You want to cut my throat, do you? You're going to cut my throat on the highway, are you, you highwayman, you dolt, you sea monster! Ah? Ah? Here we've been sitting three weeks, ah? And not a word did you say, you ne'er-do-well—and now, at the very last minute, you come out with it! Just when all's set and it's only a question of driving off, ah? And here you come along and make a mess of it, ah? You must have known it before! You knew it, didn't you, ah? Answer me! You knew it? Ah?'

'I did,' Selifan said, letting his head drop.

'Well, why didn't you tell me then?'

Selifan made no reply to that question, but only muttered to himself with lowered head: 'Just see how it's all turned out: I knew it all the time, but just didn't say anything.'

'Off you go now, fetch a blacksmith, and get it all done in a couple of hours. Do you hear?' Chichikov ordered. 'In two hours, everything, and if you don't I'll . . . I'll bend you in two and tie you in a knot.' Our hero was mightily angry.

Selifan turned as though to make for the door and to execute his orders, but then stopped and said:

'Another thing, sir, that piebald of ours, wouldn't it be better to sell him off, because you see, sir, he's a load of mischief. God knows, he's not a horse but a pain in the neck.'

'Ha! You think I'll go to a horse fair and try and sell him, do you?'

'Honest, sir, he only looks smart, but he really has the devil in him; nowhere is there a horse like that. . . .'

'Idiot! When I want to sell him, I will. You're starting a discussion, are you?' Chichikov shouted. 'You'll see: if you don't fetch a blacksmith at once and get everything done in two hours, I'll give you such a drubbing . . . you won't be able to recognize yourself! Go on. Get out.' Selifan departed.

Chichikov was now completely out of sorts and he threw his sword down on the floor—the sword he carried about with him when travelling to inspire due fear in whom it was necessary. It took him over a quarter of an hour to arrange things with the blacksmiths, because they were as usual out-and-out scoundrels who, having got wind of the urgency of the work, demanded just exactly six times as much as it was worth. He failed to make them see reason however much he stampeded, calling them cheats, robbers, highwaymen, and even hinting at the Day of Judgment: they lived up to their character; not only did they not lower their price, but they took a whole five and a half hours instead of two to do the work.

During that time, Chichikov experienced those pleasurable minutes, so familiar to every traveller, when all the bags are already packed and only bits of string, paper, and all sorts of rubbish left strewn about a room, when a man is neither on the road nor yet settled in some one place, and when, on looking out of the window, he sees some passers-by, who have been discussing their pennyfarthing affairs, raise their eyes in a sort of stupid curiosity at sight of him standing at the window before they proceed on their way, thus poisoning still more the already sour humour of the wretched, immobilized traveller. Everything around him, everything he sees, be it the shop opposite his windows or the head of the old hag who lives on the other side of the street, and who comes to stare through the short curtains of her window—all this revolts him, and yet he cannot tear himself away from watching. And so he stands there, now oblivious of everything, now turning his dulled attention again on everything that moves or is motionless in front of him, and in his boredom he resorts to squeezing the life out of some fly which buzzes and struggles on the window-pane beneath his fingers. But there is an end to everything, and the wished-for minute is come. At last everything was ready, the forepart of the chaise had been patched up, the wheel had a new iron hoop, the horses had been watered, and the brigand-smiths had gone off after counting over their silver roubles and bidding them a good journey. Finally the horses were harnessed to the chaise while two hot freshly bought calatches were put inside and, standing by the driver's seat, Selifan had already thrust some morsels of food into his pocket. At last our hero took his seat in the carriage while the waiter, who came out to see him off in a cut-away cotton coat, waved his peaked cap, and the tavern servants and all sorts of other footmen and coachmen gathered round to gape at the departing gentleman as they always did on such occasions. And so the chaise, which was so suited to bachelors and which had lingered so long in the town, and of which the reader may have become tired, finally drove out of the gates of the inn.

'Thank God!' thought Chichikov as he crossed himself. Selifan cracked his whip; Petrushka, who had hung for a while on the step, now clambered up beside him; and our hero, settling himself more comfortably on a Georgian rug, put a leather cushion behind his back and pressed closely against the two hot calatches, while the carriage rolled on, rumbling and romping along, thanks to the cobbled roadway which, as we all know, has a powerfully uplifting force. With a sort of vague feeling Chichikov stared at the houses, the walls, the wooden fences and the streets, which, for their part, seemed to leap up before receding slowly behind him. God alone knew whether he was ever fated to see them again in his life. At the corner of one of the streets the chaise had to come to a halt, for the whole street was taken up by an endless funeral procession. Thrusting his head out, Chichikov commanded Petrushka to enquire who was being buried and learnt that it was the prosecutor. The prey of unpleasant sensations, he at once tucked himself away in a corner, wrapped himself up in the leather covering and pulled down the curtains.

In the meantime, while the carriage was brought to a halt, Selifan and Petrushka, devoutly taking off their caps, were having a good look at this and that, and at who was driving in what, counting up how many folk there were in all, on foot and in the carriages, while their master, having ordered them not to give themselves away and not to recognize any of their lackey acquaintances, also timidly began to watch through the leather curtains: all the officials of the town were there, hatless, walking behind the coffin. He began to be afraid lest they might recognize his carriage, but their attention was elsewhere. They were not even indulging in the chit-chat which is so usual among mourners. All their thoughts at that moment were concentrated on themselves: they were asking themselves how the new governor-general would turn out, how he would go about things and how he would treat them. After the officials on foot came the carriages, and out of them ladies in mourning peeped. By the movements of their lips and their hands it was evident that they were engaged in lively conversation; perhaps they were also discussing the arrival of the new governor-general, making surmises about the balls he would give, and chattering about their everlasting frills and braids. Finally, after the carriages, a few empty cabs followed in single file; then there was nothing left, and our hero could proceed again. Pulling open the leather curtains, he sighed and exclaimed from the depths of his soul: 'Well, so that's the prosecutor! He lived and lived, and then died! And they will say in the papers that he died to the regret of his staff and all mankind, a respected citizen, a rare father, a model husband, and they will write a lot more stuff and nonsense about him; they will add, maybe, that he was mourned by widows and orphans; but if one were to investigate the matter thoroughly, it will emerge that he had nothing to him except his bushy eyebrows.' Then he ordered Selifan to drive faster, meanwhile thinking to himself: 'It was just as well to run into a funeral, it's lucky to stray on a corpse.'

By now, the chaise had turned into the more deserted streets; soon there was nothing but a stretch of long wooden fences which presaged the end of the town. Very soon the cobbled roadway came to an end, the barrier was passed, the town lay behind, and nothing remained but the journey ahead. And here he was again on the highway, with the milestones flashing past him on both sides of the road, together with posting-stations, wells, caravans, drab villages with samovars, peasant women and a rugged bearded inn-keeper, who was running out of a coaching yard with a heap of oats in his arms; a tramp in worn bast-shoes trudging along his five hundred miles; little towns, haphazardly built, with wooden stores, barrels of flour, bast-shoes, calatches and other assortments; black and white barriers, bridges under repair, endless fields and, coming and going on either side of him, antique landowners' carriages; a soldier on horseback carrying a green box full of lead peas and the name of a certain battery inscribed on it; green, yellow, and black, freshly ploughed strips flashing in the steppes; a song rising in the distance, the tops of pine-trees through the mist, the fading sound of ringing bells, crows as thick as flies and an illimitable horizon. . . . Russia! Russia! I see you now, from my wondrous, beautiful past I behold you! How wretched, dispersed and uncomfortable everything is about you; the brave wonders of nature, crowned with the daring wonders of art—cities with many-windowed lofty palaces sprouting among the crags, picturesque trees and ivy-grown houses amid the splash and eternal spray of waterfalls; you have none of these to bring you joy or to startle your eyes; your head will not be thrown back to gaze at stone rocks endlessly piled up above you; nor will any gleam pierce the dark arches massed one on top of the other in a tangle of vines, ivy and countless millions of wild roses—no gleam will pierce them of the everlasting ridges of radiant mountains jutting into the limpid silver skies. Everything about you is open, level and desert-like; your lowly towns are like dots, marks imperceptibly stuck upon your plains; there is nothing to captivate or charm the eye. But what then is that unattainable and mysterious force which draws us to you? Why does your mournful song, which is wafted over your whole plain and expanse, from sea to sea, echo and re-echo without cease in our ears? What is there in it, in that song? What is it that calls and weeps, and grips our heart? What are those sounds that caress me painfully, thrusting their way into my soul and swirling near my heart? Russia! What do you want from me? What is that unattainable and mysterious bond between us? Why do you gaze on me so? And why has everything about you turned eyes of great expectation upon me? . . . Full of perplexity, I stand there motionless, while a menacing cloud, big with rains to be, casts its shadow over my head; and when faced with your expanse, thought grows dumb. What does this boundless space presage? Is it here from you, that some illimitable thought will be born because you are boundless yourself? Will a doughty champion or *bogatyr* spring up here, where there is room for him to spread himself and stride about? Threateningly that mighty expanse enfolds me, reflecting itself with terrifying force in the depths of my soul; my eyes become illumined with unnatural power. O what a glittering, wonderful and strange expanse! Russia! . . .

'Go slow, go slow, you fool!' Chichikov was shouting to Selifan.

'I'll slash you with my sabre!' shouted a courier with moustaches a yard wide, who was galloping towards them. 'Can't you see, the devil take your soul, it's a government carriage!' And like a spectre, the *troika* vanished in thunder and dust.

What a strange, alluring, enrapturing and wonderful world it is. The highway! And how wonderful that road is in itself! A clear day, autumn leaves, a cool air . . . wrapped more tightly in our travelling coat, with the hat pulled over our ears, we shall huddle more closely and comfortably in a corner! For the last time a chill shudder runs through our limbs and in its place a pleasant warmth steals over us. The horses gallop on. . . . How tempting is the invading drowsiness, as it closes our eyelids; and already in our sleep we can hear the refrain of 'the snows are white no more', and the horses snorting, and the rumble of wheels, and already we are snoring and crushing some fellow passenger in a corner. When we awake, five stages have already been left behind and the moon is shining brightly; here is a strange town, churches with ancient wooden cupolas and darkly outlined gables, houses of dark timber and white stone. Here and there, the moonbeams look like white linen handkerchiefs hung on walls, on the roadway and on the streets; shadows black as coal fall across them slantingly; wooden roofs gleam in the moonlight like glittering metal, and there is not a soul about—everything is asleep. Perhaps there is a light somewhere glimmering in a window; some citizen may be mending his boots or a baker may be fussing round his oven. What are we to say of them? But the night, O heavens, what a night is being achieved up there on high! And the air, and the sky, lofty and remote, spreading out and boundless, clear and ringing up yonder in its unfathomable depths! But the chill breath of the night blows fragrantly upon the eyes and lulls us, and we are already asleep, oblivious and snoring and, as he feels our weight, the poor, crushed fellow traveller stirs angrily in his corner. Again we are awake—and the fields and the steppes are there again; there is nothing to be seen anywhere, only the waste lands and the open spaces. A numbered milestone flashes in your eyes; the morning kindles; a pale gold streak illumines the cold pallid skyline; the wind grows fresher and more biting: we wrap ourselves more closely in our warm coats. . . . How delicious the chill! How wonderful the drowsiness creeping over us again! A jolt—and we wake again. The sun is on the crest of the sky. 'Easy, easy!' a voice is heard saying, and a cart comes lumbering downhill: below lies a broad dam and a broad clear pond, shining like copper in the sunshine; a village with huts scattered over the slope; like a star, the cross of the village church shines apart; there is the chatter of peasants and an unbearable appetite in our inside. . . . O Lord, how splendid that long, long road can be! How often, like a drowning man, have I clung to you, and every time, great-heartedly you have succoured and saved me! And to what wonderful inventions and poetic dreams have you given birth! And what wonderful impressions you have stimulated! . . .

But at that moment our friend Chichikov was not indulging in altogether poetic dreams. Let us see how he was feeling. To begin with, he was not feeling anything at all but only looking back, wishing to make sure that he had really left the town; when he saw that the town had long ago disappeared, and that nothing was to be seen of the smithies, windmills and all those things which are to be found on the outskirts of towns, and that even the white steeples of the stone churches had long ago been buried in the earth, he concentrated only on the highway, looking only to right and left of him, and the town of N. hardly impinged on his mind, as if he had passed through it a long time ago, in his early childhood. Finally the highway ceased to hold his attention, his eyelids began to droop and his head to nod towards the cushion. The author confesses that he is quite glad this should happen, since it gives him an opportunity of talking about his hero; for up till now, as the reader has seen, he was constantly hindered from doing so either by Nozdrev, the balls, the ladies or the scandal of the town, or, in short, the thousand and one trifles which only impress one as such when they are set down in a book, whereas, in the meantime, they circulate through the world and are taken to be matters of some importance. But now let us put everything else aside and get down to business.

It is very doubtful whether the reader will like the hero of our choice. The ladies certainly will not take to him, that we can affirm, for ladies demand absolute perfection of their hero, and woe betide him if he has the slightest stain on his soul or body! However deeply an author may have penetrated into his soul, and even if he reflects the hero's image better than any mirror, the ladies will attach no value to him. The very fact that Chichikov was stout and middle-aged will be held greatly against him: they will never forgive stoutness in a hero, and a great many ladies will turn away, saying, 'Fie! What a nasty man!' Alas, the author knows all this very well, but despite it all he cannot select a virtuous man for his hero. But . . . perhaps, in this very narrative, other and hitherto undiscovered chords will resound, the infinite richness of the Russian spirit may manifest itself, a man endowed with divine virtues may pass by, or some marvellous Russian girl the like of whom you would not find in the whole wide world, a girl possessing all the wonderful beauty of a woman's soul compounded of great-hearted striving and self-sacrifice. And all the virtuous people of other nations will appear lifeless when confronted with them, just as a book is lifeless when compared with the living word. There will be an upsurge of Russian emotions . . . and then it will become apparent how deeply embedded in the Slav nature are those elements which only appear on the surface of other peoples' natures. . . . But why speak of what is still to come? It is unseemly for the author, who has long ago attained his maturity and who has been brought up in the hard school of a spiritual discipline and in the refreshing sobriety of solitude, to forget himself like any young man. There is a time and place for everything. And so my hero is not a virtuous man. And I can even explain why a virtuous hero was not chosen. Because it is time at last to give the poor virtuous man a rest; because the words, 'virtuous man', sound too vainglorious; because the virtuous man has been transformed into a horse, and there is no writer who does not ride him, flogging him on with whip and anything to hand; because they have exhausted the virtuous man to such a degree that there is not a shadow of virtue left in him, but only ribs and skin in place of a body; because they make use of the virtuous man hypocritically; because they do not respect the virtuous man. No, the time has come at last to put the rogue in harness. So let us harness the rogue!

Our hero's origin was modest and obscure. God alone knows whether his parents, who were of the nobility, were so by descent or personal merit. Facially he did not resemble them—at least, the relative who assisted at his birth, a small woman of the species usually nick-named 'lapwings',[7] exclaimed as she picked up the child, 'But he's not at all what I expected. He should have taken after his granny on the maternal side, that would have been better,' but he was born quite simply, as the pro-verb says, 'Unlike mother, unlike father, like a travelling tinker.' From the very beginning life looked sour and uncomfortable to him, it was as though a misted and frozen window-pane stood between them: as a child he had no friends or comrades. The small room with its tiny windows, which were opened neither winter nor summer, his ailing father in his long coat lined with lambswool and with knitted slippers on his bare feet, always sighing, walking up and down the room and spitting into the sand of the spittoon; the everlasting grind at his desk, pen in hand, ink all over his fingers and even on his lips; scrawled injunctions ever before his eyes: 'Speak the truth, obey your elders. Cherish virtue in your heart'; the everlasting flapping and shuffling of his father's slippers about the room; the familiar but invariably severe voice admonishing him, 'You have been fooling about again!' whenever the child, tired of the mono-tony of his task, attempted to add a flourish or tail to some letter; and the ever-familiar but always disagreeable sensation whenever his ear was tweaked most painfully as the nails of those long fingers seized hold of it from behind: such was the wretched picture of his early childhood of which he had now but the dimmest memories.

But in life everything is subject to rapid change, and one sunny day in early spring, when the snow was be-ginning to gush in torrents, the father set out with his son in a little cart drawn by a reddish piebald nag, of the kind known among horse-dealers as 'magpies'; the driver was a small hunchback, the progenitor of the only family of serfs owned by Chichikov's father, and he did

7. Small birds; here used to refer to puny, unprepossessing-looking persons.

nearly all the chores about the house. For over a day and a half they trundled along with the 'magpie'; they spent a night on the road, crossed a river, ate their meals of cold pie and roast mutton, and finally on the morning of the third day they reached town. The unexpected splendour of the city streets dazzled the boy, making him gape for a few minutes. Then the 'magpie' and the cart pitched suddenly into a ditch at the entrance of a narrow street which sloped down and was dammed by mud. It took the 'magpie' a long time, a great deal of effort and much leg-work, as well as incitement from the hunchback driver and the master himself, before it finally pulled them out into a small courtyard at the top of the slope in which two flowering apple-trees stood in front of an old house, with a garden at the back of it—a small lowly garden of elder- and rowanberry bushes with a wooden shed, covered over with bits and pieces and having a narrow opaque window, concealed in its depths. Here lived a relative of theirs, a shrunken old woman, who still did her marketing each morning and then dried her stockings by the samovar. She patted the boy on the cheeks and was impressed by their plumpness. Here he was to stay and attend the town school every day. After spending a night there, his father set off homewards the next day. The parental eye shed no tears when the time for leave-taking came; a half-rouble in copper coins was given to the boy by way of pocket-money and for sweets, and what is more important, the following ad-monition: 'Mind now, Pavlusha, be diligent, don't fool or gad about, and above all please your teachers and superiors. If you please your superiors, then you will be popular and get ahead of everyone even if you lag behind in knowledge and talent. Don't be too friendly with the other boys, they will teach you no good; but if you do make friends, cultivate those who are better off and might be useful. Don't invite or treat anyone, but conduct yourself rather in such a way as to be treated your-self, and above all, take care of and save your pennies, that is the most reliable of all things. A comrade or friend will cheat you and be the first to put all the blame on you when in a fix, but the pennies won't betray you in any difficulty. With money you can do anything in the world.' Having admonished his son thus, the father took leave of him and trundled off home on his 'magpie'. Though from that day the son never set eyes on him more, his words and admonitions had sunk deep into his soul.

As from the following day Pavlusha began to attend his classes. He revealed no special aptitude for any science; he distinguished himself mainly by his diligence and tidiness; but, on the other hand, he displayed quite a flair for the practical things of life. He suddenly had an inkling of how things are done and, putting two and two together, conducted himself towards his comrades according to the way in which they treated him. For his part he not only did not entertain them but, on the contrary, concealing sometimes some gift of sweets, he would then sell it back to them. Already as a child he knew how to deny himself things. He did not spend a kopeck of the half-rouble given him by his father; on the contrary, in the course of the year he augmented the amount, thus displaying unusual dexterity: moulding a goldfinch out of wax and painting it over, he sold it very profitably. Then for a time he indulged in other speculations of the following nature: he would buy up a supply of provisions on the market, sit down in class near the more affluent boys and as soon as he noticed that one of them was feeling queasy, a sure sign of hunger, he would as if by chance slip a gingerbread or bun to him under the desk and, having thus provoked him, he would make him pay for his appetite. For two months at home, without relaxing, he concentrated on a mouse, which he kept in a wooden cage until he had at last succeeded in teaching it to stand up on its hind legs, to lie down or to get up at his command; and he then sold it very profitably. When he had amassed five roubles, he sewed up the bag they were in and started to save up another lot. He was even more astute in his behaviour towards his superiors. No boy in class was more orderly than he. It must be noted that his master was a great lover of silence and good behaviour, and could not bear clever or perceptive boys; he was under the impression that they must infallibly be laughing at him. It was enough for the boy, who had been rebuked for wit, to stir ever so little, or inadvertently to move an eyebrow, for him to be submerged in a storm of rage. The teacher would persecute and punish him unmercifully. 'I, brother, will knock that cheek and insubordination out of you!' he would say. 'I know you through and through, better than you do yourself. I'll make you have sore knees with kneeling! And you'll learn what hunger is!' And not knowing why he was thus punished, the poor boy would wear away his knees and go hungry for days. 'Abilities and gifts? That's all rubbish,' the teacher would say; 'my criterion is conduct only. I shall give full marks in all subjects to the boy who, even if he does not know his ABC, behaves properly; but if I see a wrong and scoffing spirit in anyone, I shall give him a nought, though he be twice as wise as Solon!'[8] So said the teacher who had taken a mortal dislike to Krylov, the fabulist,[9] for saying: 'Better a drunkard who knows his business than a sober man who doesn't.' And he used to tell them, with a look of evident enjoyment in his face and eyes, that such silence reigned in the school where he had previously taught that a fly could be heard buzzing, that throughout the year not a single one of his pupils had either coughed or blown his nose, and that it was quite impossible to find out until the bell rang whether anyone was there or not. Chichikov suddenly had an inkling of his superior's idea of conduct. From now on he did not wink an eye or twitch an eyebrow in class, even though some of the boys may have been pinching him from behind; as soon as the bell went he would dash forward and be the first to hand the master his three-cornered hat (the master always wore it); having handed him the three-cornered hat, he was the first out of class, and he then tried to run across the teacher at least three times on the way, taking his cap off each time. His

---

8. An Athenian legislator (seventh and sixth centuries, B.C.), known for his wisdom.

9. Ivan Krylov (1769–1844), Russian writer famous particularly for his verse fables.

tactics were crowned with complete success. All the time he was at school he got excellent marks, and on leaving he was granted a full certificate in all subjects and a diploma, and he was presented with a book on which the following inscription was blazoned in gold letters: 'for exemplary diligence and good conduct'.

On leaving school he turned out to be a youth of fairly attractive appearance and with a chin already in need of the razor. In the meantime his father had died. All he inherited was four completely worn-out vests, two old coats lined with lambswool, and an insignificant sum of money. His father evidently was only good at giving counsel on how to save money, for he had saved very little himself. Chichikov at once sold the decrepit homestead and the wretched piece of land for a thousand roubles, and brought his family of serfs to town, proposing to settle down there and take up service. About that time the poor teacher, who loved silence and praiseworthy conduct, got the sack for stupidity or some other fault. Out of sorrow he took to drink and finally had no resources left with which to buy it: ill, quite helpless, without even a bite of bread, he lurked somewhere in an unheated and neglected hovel. Learning of his plight, his former pupils, the wits and the brains, in whom he had constantly fancied to detect insubordination and insolence, opened a subscription for him and even sold off many things which they really required: only one, Pavlusha Chichikov, pleaded lack of funds and offered a mere five kopecks in silver, which his comrades threw back at him, saying: 'Ah, you skinflint!' The poor teacher hid his face in his hands when he heard what his former pupils had done: from his dimming eyes a torrent of tears gushed forth as if he were a helpless child. 'The Lord has made me weep on the brink of the grave,' he murmured in a faint voice; and he sighed deeply when he heard about Chichikov, adding at once: 'Ah, Pavlusha! How people change! He was so well behaved, nothing rebellious about him, smooth as silk! Ah, he took me in, he took me in, he really did. . . .'

However, it cannot be said that our hero's character

was harsh and callous, or that his feelings were so blunted as to deprive him of pity or compassion. He was capable of feeling both, and he would even have liked to help so long as the sum involved was insignificant, so long as he did not have to dip into the money he had set aside; in short, he had profited by his father's admonition, 'Be careful and save!' But he had no passion for money for its own sake; he was not at the mercy of meanness and avarice. No, those were not his ruling motives; he had a vision of life full of pleasures and comforts, a well-equipped house, carriages, tasty dinners—such were the thoughts continually running through his mind. The reason why he saved up his kopecks and denied both himself and others, was that he wished to make sure of enjoying all those pleasures later, ultimately and in due course. Whenever he caught sight of a rich man driving by on a speedy and elegant droshky, drawn by thorough-bred horses in resplendent harness, he would stop as if rooted to the spot and then, as though emerging out of a profound sleep, say: 'Why, he was only an ordinary clerk once and had his hair cut in a round mop like a peasant!' Everything that suggested riches and pleasure impressed him more than he could say. On leaving school he did not even sit back and rest, so strong was his desire to tackle a job and enter the service. However, despite his flattering testimonials, it was with some difficulty that he found a niche for himself in the Courts of Justice, for even in its most out-of-the-way corners patronage was needed! The post he succeeded in securing was a quite insignificant one, with a salary of only thirty or forty roubles a year. But he resolved to devote himself whole-heartedly to his work, to overcome and vanquish all obstacles. And indeed he displayed incredible self-denial, patience and control. From early morning till late at night, without flagging in body or spirit, he went on scribbling, buried deeply in a pile of official papers; he hardly ever went home, slept on a table in the office, and supped frequently with the night-watchmen; and yet he managed to look tidy, to dress respectably, to communicate a pleasant expression to his face and even a certain dignity to his gestures.

It must be said that the officials of the Courts were all distinctly ugly and ill-favoured. Some of them had faces like badly-baked loaves of bread: one of their cheeks might be puffed out to one side and their chin to the other, while their upper lip might be blown out like a bubble, and a burst one at that—in short, it was all very ugly. They always spoke in harsh tones as though about to give someone a thrashing; they made frequent libations to Bacchus,[1] thus demonstrating that many traces of paganism still survive in the Slav nature; occasionally they came into 'presence', as they say, the worse for drink, and as a result their presence was hardly agreeable and the air anything but fragrant. In the midst of such officials Chichikov could hardly help being noticed and singled out, for he offered a complete contrast in everything to the others, whether it was in good looks, the affability of his voice or in his abstention from any strong beverages. But despite all this his path was thorny. He came under the authority of an already senile head-clerk, who might have been a model of stony callousness and indifference: he was always unassailable, unsmiling, and he was never known to greet anyone with an enquiry after their health. No change had ever been noted in his manner either in the street or at home. If only he had taken an interest in anything—even once; if only he had got drunk and burst out laughing; or if only he had given himself up to wild enjoyment, such as a bandit may indulge in when drunk; but there was not even the shade of such a possibility about him. There was absolutely nothing of that in him: neither good nor bad; and the absence of it was terrifying. His hard marble-like face, unmarred by any obvious irregularities, was unlike any other; his features had an austere harmony of their own. Only the dents and cavities of the pockmarks, which pitted his face thickly, put him in that category of people upon whose dials, as folk say, the devil threshes peas at night. It seemed beyond human power to pierce the armour of such a man and gain his favour, but Chichikov attempted it. He began by trying to please him in all sorts of trifling ways: he took care to find out how his

1. Classical god of wine.

quills were sharpened and, having prepared a few like them, he always kept them handy; he blew and swept the sand and tobacco from his table; he got hold of a new rag for his inkstand; from somewhere he dug out his cap, the worst specimen ever seen, and he always used to lay it down near him a minute or two before the end of the session; he brushed his back if there were any marks of plaster on it; but decidedly all this was of no avail, it was just as though nothing of the sort had taken place. In the end, Chichikov got wind of the old man's family life: he discovered that he had a grown-up daughter with a face that also gave one to suppose that the devil had been threshing peas on it of a night. He determined to conduct his assault from that side. He found out the church she was in the habit of frequenting on Sundays, and made a point each time of standing directly opposite her, dressed most neatly and with his shirt-front stiffly starched. His enterprise was crowned with success: the austere head-clerk wavered and invited him to tea! And before the office staff had time to look round, affairs were so arranged that Chichikov moved into the old man's house and became an indispensable person in the household, doing all the purchasing of flour and sugar, treating the daughter like a fiancée, calling the old man his 'papa' and kissing his hand; and it was assumed in the Courts that by the end of February, before Lent, the wedding would be celebrated. The unbending head-clerk took steps even to put in a word with the authorities, and in a short while Chichikov had slipped into the seat of a head-clerk as soon as a vacancy occurred. It would seem that the chief aim of his relations with the old man had consisted precisely in this, for he at once had his trunk secretly removed and on the following day he was already established in new quarters. He ceased calling the old man 'papa' and did not kiss his hands any more, while all talk of the wedding was somehow muffled up as though there had never been any question of it. Whenever he chanced to meet the old man, however, he always pressed his hand affectionately and asked him round to tea, so that despite his everlasting immobility and harsh indifference, the old man used to shake his head each time and mutter under his nose: 'He had me properly, he did, the devil!'

That had been the hardest threshold of all for Chichikov to cross. Afterwards matters went more easily and successfully. He became a person of note. He had everything that was essential for this world: an agreeable manner and behaviour, and a brisk way of dealing with affairs. By these means, in a short while, he had achieved what is called a bread-and-butter post, and made excellent use of it. About this time, it should be known, a strict investigation was launched into all cases of bribery and corruption in the service: the enquiry did not alarm him and he at once turned it to his profit, in this way displaying a really Russian inventiveness such as manifests itself only in times of stress. This is how the affair was arranged: as soon as any petitioner called and put his hand in his pocket—in order to extract therefrom the notorious 'letters of recommendation signed by Prince Hovansky,'[2] to use a current Russian expression—'No, no,' he would say with a smile, restraining him, 'you think that I . . . no, no. It is our duty, our obligation, to do everything we can without reward! You may rest assured, it will all be done by to-morrow. May I take your address, you need not bother to do anything more yourself, everything will be sent round to your home.' The charmed petitioner would return home almost in raptures, thinking to himself: 'Here at last is a real man, there should be more such! He's quite a jewel!' The petitioner waited one day, then another, the papers did not arrive, a third day also passed. Off he went to the office and discovered that his affairs had not even been started; so he applied to the 'jewel'. 'Oh, you must excuse us,' Chichikov would say very respectfully, seizing hold of both his hands, 'we had so much business on hand; but everything will be done to-morrow, to-morrow without fail. I really have it on my conscience!' And as he spoke his whole manner and

2. A jocular slang phrase for a bribe. Prince Alexander Hovansky (1771–1857), from 1818 on head of the State Banknote Bank and in charge of the issuing of all government papers and banknotes.

gestures were most ingratiating. If in the meanwhile a fold of Chichikov's coat happened to fly open, he at once attempted to put the matter right by holding it down with his hand. But still no notice of his affair reached him at home, neither the day after, nor the day after that, nor on the third day. The petitioner began to catch on: 'There must be something at the back of it.' When he ferreted it out, he was told that the copying clerks must be given something. 'Why not? I'm quite ready to give them a quarter of a rouble or so.' 'No, not a quarter, but a twenty-five-rouble note.' 'Twenty-five roubles for the copying clerks!' the petitioner exclaims. 'Why are you so excited?' they reply. 'It will all work out: the copying clerks will get their quarter, and the rest will go higher up.' The slow-witted petitioner beats on his forehead and roundly curses the new order of things, the investigation into bribery and corruption and the polite and considerate behaviour of officials. 'Formerly, at least one knew how to go about things: ten roubles to the man in charge and the affair was settled, but now one has to give twenty-five roubles and waste a whole week before tumbling to it. . . . The devil take these disinterested officials and their dignity!' The petitioner was right, of course, but, on the other hand, there were no bribe-takers now: all the men in authority were as honest and noble as may be, only the secretaries and copying clerks were rogues. Soon Chichikov's sphere of activity became much enlarged. A commission was set on foot to supervise the construction of a very large government building. He managed to get on the commission and became one of its most active members. The commission set to work at once. For six years it fussed round the building; but whether it was the fault of the climate or of the building material, whatever it was, only its foundations were laid. And in the meantime, in other parts of the town, each of the members of the commission had built himself a handsome house: apparently the soil in those parts was better. The members of the commission had begun already to prosper and to rear families. It was only then, and at this point, that Chichikov proceeded to disentangle himself a little from the austere laws of self-control and inflexible self-denial which he had imposed on himself. Only then was his lengthy fast broken at last, and it turned out that he had not always been averse from various enjoyments, from which he had known how to refrain in those years of impetuous youth when hardly any man is completely master of himself. Some superfluities crept in: he took on a *chef* of some quality and wore fine linen shirts. The cloth he bought himself could not be matched in the province, and from now on he favoured clothes of shot-brown and shot-reddish hue; already he had obtained an excellent pair of horses, and he would hold one of the reins himself, forcing the side-horse to swing round; already he was in the habit of sponging himself with water mixed with eau-de-Cologne; already the soap he bought was far from inexpensive, though very smooth on the skin. . . .

But of a sudden a new chief was sent to replace the old buffer, and he was a soldier, very strict, an enemy of corruption and everything that goes under the name of injustice. The day after his arrival he frightened the life out of one and all, demanded to see the accounts, saw the defaults and the sums missing at every step, and at once noticed the officials' handsome private residences. And so a full enquiry was ordered. Officials were relieved of their posts; the handsome private residences were confiscated by the Treasury and turned into a variety of charitable institutions and schools for soldiers' sons. Everything was blown sky-high, and Chichikov had a hotter time of it than most. God alone knows why—and sometimes no reason can be given for these things—the chief suddenly took exception to Chichikov's face, in spite of its pleasant appearance, and conceived a deadly hatred for him. But as he was a military man, after all, and therefore not acquainted with all the subtleties of civilian ways, in a while other officials wormed their way into his good graces by a superficial display of truthfulness and an ability to adapt themselves to anything, and the general was soon in the hands of even greater rogues whom he did not take to be such; he was especially satisfied at having at last made the right selection of staff, and boasted seriously of his subtle ability to distinguish aptitudes. The officials suddenly sized up his temper and character. Everyone under his authority became a rabid persecutor of injustice; in all matters everywhere they dogged its steps, just as a fisherman might hunt some white meaty salmon with a harpoon, and they persecuted injustice with such success that in a short time each of them had amassed some thousands of roubles by way of capital. By that time many of the former officials had rediscovered the path of righteousness and were once more readmitted into the service. But try as he would, Chichikov could find no way of squeezing himself in, although he had the backing of the general's secretary, who was spurred on by 'letters from Prince Hovansky' and who had succeeded in leading the general completely by the nose (though without his knowledge); but the general was so constituted that any thought which entered into his head stuck there like a nail: there was no means of knocking it out. All that the clever secretary could accomplish was the destruction of Chichikov's black service record, and this he achieved by painting in vivid colours the touching plight of Chichikov's unfortunate family which, luckily for them, did not exist.

'So be it!' said Chichikov. 'I hooked it, gave a pull, and the line broke; there is no point in crying over spilt milk. Crying won't help, it is doing things that matters.' And so he resolved once again to start on a career, once more to arm himself with patience, and to cut down his needs in everything, however pleasant it might have been to have his fling. It was now necessary for him to change towns and to make himself known elsewhere. For some reason matters did not go well. He had to give up two or three jobs within a short space of time. The jobs were of a low and degrading nature. It must be understood that, at heart, Chichikov was one of the greatest sticklers for decency who ever lived. Although in the beginning, he had to worm his way through a none-too-clean *milieu*, he was cleanly at heart and liked his offices to have polished tables and an atmosphere of dignity about them.

He never allowed any doubtful words to slip into his conversation and he was always offended at any lack of due respect for rank or calling in the conversation of others. The reader will be pleased to learn, I think, that he changed his linen every other day and every day in the summer when the hot season was at its height. He used to take exception to any smell if it were at all unpleasant. For this reason, whenever Petrushka came to undress him or take off his boots, he would always insert cloves into his nostrils, and in many other ways his nerves were as ticklish as a young girl's. It was hard on him, therefore, to find himself again in a *milieu* which smelt strongly of brandy and had no manners to speak of. Fortify as he would his spirit, he lost weight nevertheless and in times of such stress his face assumed a greenish hue. He was already beginning to fill out and acquire those rotund and respectable contours which were his when the reader first met him. Formerly, whenever he had looked at himself in a mirror, on more than one occasion many a pleasant thought would stray into his mind as he remembered his granny and his nursery, and he could not help smiling as he did so; but now, whenever he chanced to see himself, he could not help exclaiming, 'Holy mother! Haven't I grown ugly!' And for a long while after he had no wish to look at himself. But our hero bore with it all, and bore it well, bore it patiently, and—finally got a job in the customs and excise.

It must be said that this service had long been the secret object of his schemes. He was aware that customs officials disposed of a variety of stylish articles of foreign provenance, and that they used to send fine pieces of china or cambric to their godmothers, aunts and sisters. More than once he had said to himself with a sigh: 'That's where I should be: near the frontier where enlightened people live; and what fine linen I might acquire there!' I must add that his fancy strayed to a special sort of French soap which had the quality of imparting unusual whiteness to the skin and freshness to the cheeks; what it was called, God alone knows, but according to his calculations it would be available at the frontier. Thus, the customs always had an attraction for him, but he had been engrossed in the various current profits he was deriving from the building commission, and he argued very rightly that the customs was still only a stork in the sky while the commission was a bird in hand. Now he resolved to get into the customs at any cost, and this he achieved. He took to this service with extraordinary zeal. Fate itself might have destined him to be a customs official. Such agility, penetration and perspicacity had never been seen or heard of before. In three or four weeks he had mastered his job so well that he knew every aspect of it inside out; he did not even bother to weigh or measure, but could tell at sight how many yards of cloth or other material there might be in any roll: picking up a parcel, he could say straight out how many pounds it weighed. As to searching travellers, as even his colleagues admitted, he had the scent of a bloodhound: one could not help being amazed to observe the amount of patience he had in order to feel each button, and all this he performed in deadly calm, and with incredible politeness. While those who were being searched stood about impotently, losing their tempers and feeling like slapping his smug face, he exhibited no change of countenance or loss of manners, but only kept saying, 'May I ask you to take the trouble to get up?' or 'Will you be so good, Madam, as to pass into the other room? There the wife of one of our officials will see to you.' Or he would say, 'If I may, I'll just rip the lining of your coat.' And as he said that, he would pull out from it shawls and neckerchiefs as coolly as out of a trunk of his own. Even the higher officials were heard to say that he was the very devil: he discovered articles concealed in wheels, shafts, horse's ears and heaven knows where else—in places where no author would dream of penetrating and where only customs officials would think of prying. And after crossing the frontier, a wretched traveller would still be in a daze for some minutes and, wiping off the perspiration which now covered the whole of his body in small beads, he would mutter to himself, 'Well, I never!' The traveller's predicament was very much like that of a schoolboy who has just dashed out of the headmaster's study after being unexpectedly birched instead of merely reprimanded.

For a short while he made the life of the smugglers a misery. He was the menace and despair of all the Polish Jews. His honesty and incorruptibility were unassailable and almost superhuman. He did not even feather his nest from any of the variety of confiscated goods and articles, which were not passed on to the Treasury in order to avoid superfluous correspondence. Such zealous and disinterested application could not help but become the object of universal astonishment and finally be noted by the authorities. He was given a rise and promotion; he followed this up by presenting a plan for catching all smugglers, asking only to be allowed to carry it out himself. He was at once given the authority and an absolute licence to undertake any investigations. That was all he wanted. In the meantime a powerful society of smugglers had been formed and organized on the right lines: this bold venture was out to make a few millions profit. Chichikov had wind of this for some time and he had even refused to be bought, saying drily, 'the time is not yet ripe'. But when he was given full authority, he at once made it known to the society that the time was indeed ripe. The affair was a certainty. In one year he would be able to make as much as in twenty years of the most zealous service. He had not wished to establish relations with them before because he would merely have been a pawn and would have received a pittance: but now . . . that was quite another matter: he could dictate terms. To make the affair go more smoothly, he won over another official, a colleague of his, who could not resist the temptation although his hair was already grey. The terms were agreed, and the society began its operations. They made a brilliant start. The reader doubtless has heard the oft-repeated story of the ingenious subterfuge by which a flock of merino sheep crossed the frontier in double fleece, thus smuggling in a million roubles' worth of Flemish lace. That event occurred when Chichikov was serving in the customs. If he himself had not been in the know, no Jews in the wide world would have succeeded in carrying through such a scheme. After three or four such 'sheepish excursions,' the two officials had amassed some four hundred thousand roubles each by way of capital. It is said that Chichikov made over five hundred thousand because he was more pushing. God alone knows what figure these goodly sums would not have attained, had not an evil beast crossed their path. The devil set the two officials at loggerheads: quite simply the devil got into them and they quarrelled over nothing. As they were once arguing hotly, a little the worse for drink maybe, Chichikov called the other official a 'priest's son'. Although he actually was a priest's son, the other took serious offence for no reason at all, and answered him back forcefully and with unusual acerbity, in this way to be exact: 'You're lying, I'm a civil councillor, not a priest's son, but you yourself are one!' And then as a final insult he added: 'That is what you are!' Although he had got his own back by turning the tables on him, and although the expression 'That is what you are' may have been quite forcible, the official was by no means satisfied and he sent in a secret report about Chichikov. It is said that they would have quarrelled anyhow over some woman or other, a wench as strong and fresh as a lusty turnip, according to the expression used by the customs officials. It is also said that some men had even been hired to beat up our hero in a dark street one night, but that both officials were made fools of and the woman had fallen to the lot of a certain staff-captain Shamparev. God alone knows how the matter really stood; if he likes, the reader himself can invent an appropriate conclusion. The gist of the matter lay in the fact that the secret relations with the smugglers now came out into the open. Although he was disgraced himself, the civil councillor had cooked Chichikov's goose. The officials were tried, all they had was confiscated and seized, and this disaster burst over their heads like a thunderclap. Only after coming out of their daze did they realize with horror what they had done. The civil councillor could not stand up against fate and died somewhere in the wilds, but the collegiate councillor survived. He managed to hide away part of the money despite the keen scent of the investigating authorities who descended upon the scene. He employed all the subtle resources of his mind, already only too experienced and knowledgeable in human affairs, by ingratiating himself here, touching a chord there, elsewhere using the wiles of flattery which are never out of place, and by slipping a note or two into this or that palm, he worked things in such a way that, at least, he was not dishonoured as much as his colleague and escaped trial. But nothing was left of his capital and foreign wares; all these passed into other hands. All he had left was some ten thousand roubles, which he had hidden away against an evil day, and some two dozen fine linen shirts, also a smallish chaise, such as is used by bachelors, and two serfs, his coachman Selifan and his lackey Petrushka. Moreover, out of the kindness of their hearts, the customs officials left him five or six tablets of soap for the preservation of his fresh complexion. And that was all. Such then was the position in which our hero found himself! Such the immensity of the disasters that had fallen on his head! This is what he used to call 'suffering in the cause of justice'.

It might be concluded that, after such storms, trials, vicissitudes of fate and personal sorrows, he would have taken himself off with his remaining ten thousand in real money to some quiet backwater of a provincial town. There, in a satin dressing-gown, he would have settled down for the rest of his life at the window of a small one-storied house, watching the Sunday brawls of local peasants which flared up outside the windows; or for the sake of a little airing he would have taken a stroll as far as his chicken-coop in order to feel and to examine in person the chicken destined for his soup; and so he would have eked out an unexciting but not altogether useless existence. But that was not to be. We must do justice to the invincible strength of his character. After all this, which was enough to kill or, at least, to dampen and tame any man for once and all, his irresistible passion was not snuffed out. He looked sad and dejected, he grumbled at everyone and raged at the injustice of fate, he was indignant at men's injustice, and yet he could not resist making a new attempt. In short, he exhibited a patience, compared with which the blockheaded patience of a German, who is conditioned by the slow and slothful circulation of his blood, was as nothing. Chichikov's blood, on the contrary, coursed strongly, and it required a great deal of will-power to bridle everything that was struggling to burst out and to roam at liberty. He argued, and there was a certain amount of reason in his arguments, as follows: 'Why was I picked on? Why did this misfortune happen to me? Who is not doing his job now? They are all stuffing their pockets. I had made no one unhappy, I did not rob any widow, I did not turn anyone out into the street, I only profited by the extras, appropriating where anyone might have done so. If I had not profited, others would certainly have done so. Why then are the others flourishing and why must I perish like a worm? And what am I now? What am I fit for? How shall I look in the face now any respectable father of a family? How am I not to feel the pangs of conscience when I know that I am but a burden on this earth? And what will my children say afterwards? They will say, "Our father was a good-for-nothing. He left us not a bean!"'

As we know already, Chichikov was greatly preoccupied with his posterity. It was his sensitive spot! Perhaps he would not have risked so much if it had not been for the question which, for some unknown reason, suggested itself to his mind—'What will my children say?' And so the future paterfamilias[3] behaved like some cautious tomcat which, looking out of the corner of an eye to see whether the master is not in the offing, hurriedly grabs everything in sight, whether it be soap, candles, lard, or a canary if it can get its claws on it—in short, he misses nothing. Thus, while our hero grumbled and moaned his brain was busy with projects; a building was already shaping itself but it needed a final plan. He tightened his belt once more and led a hard life, denying

3. Patriarchal father, head of the family.

himself everything; once more cleanliness and a decent position were left behind while he wallowed among the garbage of low life. And pending better times he was even obliged to take up the calling of a legal agent—a calling without recognition as yet amongst us, one that was under pressure from all sides, enjoying no respect among the run of the clerks, nor even among his employers, and so he was condemned to fawn on menials in outer offices and put up with rudeness and the like; but necessity made him resolved to put up with anything. One of the jobs that came his way was to arrange for the mortgage of several hundred peasants to the Trustee Council.[4] The estate was in the last stage of ruin. It had come to this pass as a result of cattle plagues, dishonest stewards, bad harvests, infectious diseases which had carried off the best workers and, finally, of the stupidity of the land-owner himself, who had been furnishing a house in Moscow in the very latest fashion, using up all his fortune to the very last kopeck for that purpose, so that nothing was left to him even for food. As a result he had to mortgage his last remaining estate. Mortgaging to the Treasury was at that time still a novel practice to be embarked upon not without apprehension. In his capacity as a legal agent, Chichikov set about winning everyone over (as we know, without this preparatory 'oiling' no simple enquiry or verification can be put through, a bottle of Madeira, at least, must be poured down each throat concerned) and thus, having won over whom it was necessary, he then explained how matters stood and that half the peasants had died. This he did to avoid any future misunderstandings. . . . 'But they are still on the register, aren't they?' the secretary asked. 'They are,' replied Chichikov. 'Then why worry?' said the secretary. 'Some are born, others die, they all apply.' The secretary apparently could rhyme.

But in the meantime, the most inspired thought that had ever occurred to the human mind suddenly illumined our hero. 'Ah, simpleton that I am,' he said to himself, 'I'm searching for my gloves and here they are stuck in

4. A government office administering orphanages as well as mortgages and loans.

my belt! Were I to buy up all those who died before a new register is compiled, were I to collect, say, a thousand of them and, let us suppose that the Trustee Council gave me two hundred roubles for each soul, then that would already make a capital of two hundred thousand roubles! And now is a good time, there was the epidemic not long ago and quite a few of the folk died off, thank God. The landowners have been losing heavily at gambling and spending their money on sprees, and they are up to their neck in debt; they have all gone to Petersburg now in search of government jobs: they have abandoned their estates and left them to run themselves as best they can. The payment of taxes becomes more difficult each year; they will be glad to surrender their dead souls to me if only to save them paying the tax on them, and on occasion might even get an extra for my trouble. The scheme has its difficulties and bothers, of course, terrors too, for it might lead to trouble or involve me in some unpleasantness. But it's not for nothing that man is endowed with a brain. It's a fine idea and it will strike folks as so incredible that no one will believe it. It is true one can't buy or mortgage peasants without owning land. But I'll buy them for transplantation, yes, for transplantation; nowadays one can get land for nothing in the Taurida[5] and Kherson provinces if only one settles peasants on it. And that is where I shall plant them all! Kherson's the place for them! Let them live there! The plantation can be legalized in the courts, all above board. If they are in need of a certificate, I would not object. Why not? I would present them with a certificate signed by the district inspector himself. The village itself might be called Chichikov Common or the village of Pavlovsk after my Christian name.' In this fashion, this strange theme matured in our hero's head. I do not know if the readers will be grateful for it, but the author's gratitude is more difficult to express. For, say what you will, had this idea not occurred to Chichikov, this poem would not have seen the light of day.

Making the sign of the cross like any good Russian, he

5. Poetic name for the Caucasus.

set about executing it. On pretence of seeking a retreat for himself and on other pretexts, he undertook to have a peep at various corners of our empire, and at those particularly which had suffered most as a result of accidents, bad crops, high mortality and other plagues; in short, wherever it was cheapest and most convenient to buy up the sort of folk he needed. He was not indiscriminate in his choice of landowners but picked on those more to his taste, or those with whom there would be the least difficulty in negotiating such deals; and he tried first of all to establish an acquaintance and win their goodwill, so as to acquire the peasants through friendship rather than bribery. Thus, the reader must not be indignant at the author for introducing him to characters who might not be to his taste; that is Chichikov's fault, he is the master here, and we must follow him as his fancy dictates. If, however, we are justly blamed for describing such colourless and unsightly persons and characters, then we can only plead that it is never possible from the start to see the whole broad flow and scope of events. When we first come to a town or even to the capital, everything appears to us drab, grey and uniform: at first there are endless mills and factories all begrimed with smoke, and only later do we perceive the six-storied houses, the shops, the sign-boards, the immense vistas of the streets, with their belfries, columns, statues, towers, with their city glitter, noise and roar, and everything else that men's hands and thoughts have miraculously wrought. The reader has already seen how the first purchases were made. Later on he will see how Chichikov's affairs progress, what successes and failures will be his lot, how he will have to resolve and overcome more difficult obstacles, how vast images will loom, how the hidden motives of our spacious narrative will unfold and its horizon expand, and the whole of it take on a stately lyrical impetus. A long road still lies ahead of our travelling company, which is made up of a middle-aged gentleman, a chaise such as bachelors favour, the valet Petrushka, the coachman Selifan, and the *troika*, which the reader already knows so well from the Assessor to the skittish dapple-grey.

Such then is our hero, just as he is! But perhaps one final touch is lacking. What are his moral qualities? the reader will ask. It is clear that he is not a hero full of perfections and virtues. What is he then? A rogue? But why a rogue? Why be so strict towards others? There are no rogues among us now but only well-intentioned and agreeable people; of such as might exhibit their physiognomy to public shame you would find only two or three, and even they now talk of virtue. It would be most just to call him simply a proprietary and acquisitive man. Acquisitiveness is the sin behind everything: out of it arose those business affairs which the world has judged to be 'not very clean'. True, there is something repulsive in such a character, but the very reader who will entertain friendly relations with such a man in everyday life, eating and drinking, and spending a pleasant time with him, will look askance at him if he turns up as the hero of a drama or poem. But wise is the man who disdains no character, but with a searching glance explores him to the root and cause of it all. Man is subject to quick transformations; before one has had time to look around, a horrid worm has already grown up inside him, autocratically appropriating to itself all his vital sap. More than once some passion—not only an overwhelming one but an insignificant urge for some trifle—has taken hold of a man born for better deeds, forcing him to forget high and sacred duties and to see in worthless baubles something great and holy. Human passions are as numberless as the sands of the sea, and all unlike each other; fine or low, they are in the beginning all submissive to man but later grow to be terrible tyrants over him. Blessed is the man who has chosen a noble passion from among them: it grows and with every hour and minute his boundless bliss increases tenfold, and he plunges deeper and deeper into the infinite paradise of his soul. But there are passions which are not of man's choosing. They came into the world with him, and he has not the strength to deny them. They are guided by a higher destiny, and have in them something eternally challenging, never to be stilled through life. They are destined to realize themselves in the great arena of the earth: no matter whether they come as a dark image, or flash by as a bright apparition bringing joy to the world—they are called forth for some good unknown to man. And perhaps the passion that impelled Chichikov himself was not derived from within him. Perhaps his chilly existence held the secret of what would later bring him to his knees and reduce him to ashes before the wisdom of the heavens, and there is yet another mystery, that of the reason why this type of hero figures in the poem that is now seeing the light of day.

It does not worry me if readers are dissatisfied with my hero. What worries me is the conviction deeply rooted in my soul that readers may have been pleased with him. If the author had not delved deeper into his soul, if he had not stirred in his depths that which slips away and hides from the light, if he had not revealed those secret thoughts which no man confides to another, but had depicted him in the guise in which he appeared to the whole town, to Manilov and other folk, then all would have been overjoyed and would have accepted him as an interesting man. It was not essential for his face or the whole of him to be mirrored in a living image before their eyes; on the other hand, when they had finished reading, they would have felt no alarm in their soul and they could have gone back in peace to their card tables— that solace of all Russia. Yes, my good readers, you would rather not see human poverty exposed. 'Why do it?' you say. 'What for? Do we not know already that there is much of what is contemptible and stupid in life? As it is, we often have to see things which are not comforting. Better show us something beautiful and attractive. Better let us forget.' 'Why tell me, brother, that our domestic affairs are going badly?' says the landowner to his steward. 'I know it as well as you do. Haven't you got anything else to talk about? Let me forget about it, don't remind me of it, then I shall be happy.' And so the money, which might have helped to set matters right, is spent on various means of achieving oblivion. Drowsed is the mind too, which might have discovered unexpected resources; and in the meantime, the estate has been auctioned, and off goes the landowner wandering over the wide world, in his desperation tolerating inwardly base acts which formerly would have revolted him.

The author will also have to endure the censure of the so-called patriots, who sit quietly in their nooks and busy themselves with quite different affairs, piling up their capital and shaping their destiny at the expense of others; but as soon as anything happens which, in their opinion, reflects upon their country, or some book is published in which there may be an element of bitter truth, they run out of all their nooks, like spiders at the sight of a fly caught in a cobweb, and suddenly raise an unholy row: 'What's the point of bringing this to light, of making it public? Everything that is described here, all this is ours. Is that a good thing to do? And what will foreigners say? And where is the cheer in hearing oneself abused? Do they think it is not painful? Do they think we are not patriots?'

I must confess that I can find no answer to such sagacious remarks, especially when they involve the opinion of foreigners. Unless perhaps it is this. In a remote corner of Russia there lived two men. One of them was the father of a family, by name Kifa Mokievich, a mild-tempered man, who shuffled through life in a dressing-gown and slippers. He neglected his family; his existence was taken up more with cerebration and preoccupied with the following, as he called them, philosophical questions: 'Now take any beastie for example,' he used to say as he stalked about his room, 'a beastie is born naked. And why should he be born naked? Why does he not hatch out of an egg, like a bird? Very, very strange; the more one delves into it the less one understands of nature!' Such were the meditations of Kifa Mokievich. But that is not the main point. The other man, Mokyi Kifovich, was his son. And he was what they call in Russia a *bogatyr* or doughty champion; and while his father was all engrossed in the birth of the beastie, his own twenty-year-old, broad-shouldered nature was bursting to unfold itself. His was not a light touch: either someone's hand would crack in his grip or a lump would

spring up on someone's nose. At home and in the neighbourhood everyone from the domestics to the dogs took
to their heels at the sight of him; he even reduced his own
bed to splinters. Such was Mokyi Kifovich, but he was a
good-natured chap withal. But that is not the main point
either. The main point is this: 'If you please, father and
master Kifa Mokievich,' his own servants and those of
the neighbourhood would say to the father, 'what's this
for a Mokyi Kifovich you've got? There is no peace from
him, he is a regular pest!' 'Yes, he's frolicsome, frolicsome,' the father would usually answer. 'But what are
we to do? It's too late to beat him, and if I did so, I
would be accused of cruelty; and he is a man of some
ambition—if I were to reproach him in front of someone
or other, he'd come to heel, but the rumour of it, that's
the trouble! The townsfolk would get to know about it
and look on him as on a dog. And can't they imagine
how painful it would be for me? Am I not a father? And
if I am engrossed in philosophy and have little time to
spare for other things, am I less of a father? But no, I am
a father, a father, the devil take them, a father! Mokyi
Kifovich is right here in my heart!' Hereupon Kifa
Mokievich would pound his chest strongly and grow quite
passionate. 'If he is to be treated like a dog, then it is not
for me to tell them that, it is not for me to betray him.'
And having displayed his paternal feelings, he would leave
Mokyi Kifovich to continue indulging in his strong-man
antics, and turn his own attention to his favourite theme,
setting himself of a sudden some problem of this kind:
'Well, if an elephant were hatched from an egg, the shell
of it would have to be so thick that you couldn't pierce
it with a cannon-ball; one would have to invent a new
form of gun.'

And so they lived on, these two denizens who, towards
the end of our poem, peeped out unexpectedly from their
quiet retreat as from a window, to reply modestly to the
accusation levelled against them by certain ardent
patriots, until then peacefully immersed in some philosophy or some form of profitable enterprise at the expense
of the finances of their beloved country, their thoughts

concentrated not so much upon not doing wrong as upon avoiding being accused of doing wrong. But no, it is not patriotism or genuine emotion which lies at the root of these accusations; there is something else concealed there. Why be chary of the truth? Who if not the author must speak the truth and nothing but the truth? You are afraid of the deeply probing eye; you are fearful of looking too profoundly into anything yourselves; you prefer to let your unthinking eyes stray over the surface of everything. You will even laugh heartily at Chichikov, perhaps you will even praise the author, saying, 'After all he was quite smart at noting a thing or two; he must be a man of cheerful temperament!' After saying that, you will turn to yourself with twice as much pride, a self-satisfied smile will light up your face, and you will add: 'There is no disguising it, the strangest and funniest people are to be met with in some provinces, and they are quite rogues into the bargain!' And if any one of you is full of Christian humility in the solitude of his heart rather than for all the world to hear, in moments of communion with himself he will ponder this weighty question in the depths of his soul: 'Is there not a chip of Chichikov in me too?' he will ask. But of course there is! But if any acquaintance of his, neither too exalted nor too low in rank, were to pass by, he would at once nudge the person he was conversing with and say to him almost with a guffaw! 'Look, look, there is Chichikov, there goes Chichikov!' And then, like a child, quite oblivious of the respect due to age and position, he will run after him, teasing and crying out, 'Chichikov! Chichikov! Chichikov!'

But we are talking too loudly, forgetting that our hero, who was asleep while the story of his life was being unfolded, had already awakened and could easily catch his name that has been so often repeated. He is touchy enough as a man and ready to take offence when slighted. The reader does not much mind if Chichikov is angry with him or not; but the author cannot afford to quarrel with his hero in any circumstance, for they are destined yet to tramp no small distance arm in arm along the highway; two long parts of the poem are still to come, and that is no trifle.

'Hey there! What are you doing?' Chichikov cried out.

'What?' Selifan drawled back.

'What indeed?' Chichikov retorted. 'Goose that you are! What sort of driving is this? Come, get a move on!'

And, indeed, for a long time Selifan had been driving with eyes closed, only now and then flicking with the reins the flanks of the likewise drowsy horses. Petrushka's cap had fallen off long ago he knew not where, and he himself was sprawling backwards with his head tucked against Chichikov's knee, so that his master was at last obliged to give him a shove. Then, starting up, Selifan gave the dapple-grey a few switches on the back, making him set off at a trot, brandished his whip at all three horses, crying out in a thin sing-song voice as he did so, 'Don't be scared, my beauties!' The horses got into their stride and pulled the chaise along as though it were a feather. Waving his whip, Selifan kept up an encouraging 'Ech! ech! ech!' as he bounced smoothly on his box-seat while the *troika* flew up one side of a hill and down the other, along that hill-dotted highway which yet had a barely perceptible downward slope.

Chichikov was fond of fast driving, and as he rocked on the leather cushion he only smiled at the bumps. And what Russian does not love fast driving? And how should his soul not love it? For is he not prone to surrender to the sudden whirl of a spree? Is he not liable to cast discretion to the winds, saying 'the devil take it all'? And therefore is not fast driving his delight? How can he not love its magic and incantation? And is not a galloping *troika* like a mysterious force that has swept you away on its wings, so that you find yourself flying along, and everything else flying with you? The milestones fly past to meet you, the merchants in their carts are flying by, on each side of you forests of dark fir and pine trees are flying past to the thump of axes and the croaking of crows, the whole of the highway is flying on, no one knows where, into the receding distance; and there is a lurking terror in that glimmer of objects that keep flashing by rapidly and are gone before they can be identified; and only the sky overhead, the nimble clouds, and the emergent moon, appear motionless. Ah, you *troika*! Bird-like *troika*, who invented you? Surely you could only have been born among a spirited people—in a land which does not stop at jokes but has taken half the world in the embrace of its smooth plains so that one can go and count the milestones till one's head turns dizzy! Nor does it seem that much cunning was required to fabricate the sledge or carriage drawn by those three horses; it was improvised with the help of an axe and a drill by some handy Jaroslavl[6] peasant. Your driver wears no great top boots of foreign make: he is all beard and mittens, and sits perched on his seat the devil knows how; but when he stands up, cracks his whip and starts up a song, then the horses rush like a hurricane, the spokes of the wheels spin in one smooth disk, and only the road shudders beneath them while some passer-by cries out as he stops in alarm! And the *troika* is off and away, away! . . . And very soon there is only a swirl of dust on the horizon.

Russia, are you not speeding along like a fiery and matchless *troika*? Beneath you the road is smoke, the bridges thunder, and everything is left far behind. At your passage the onlooker stops amazed as by a divine miracle. 'Was that not a flash of lightning?' he asks. What is this surge so full of terror? And what is this force unknown impelling these horses never seen before? Ah, you horses, horses—what horses! Your manes are whirl-winds! And are your veins not tingling like a quick ear? Descending from above you have caught the note of the familiar song; and at once, in unison, you strain your chests of bronze and, with your hooves barely skimming the earth, you are transformed into arrows, into straight lines winging through the air, and on you rush under divine inspiration. . . . Russia, where are you flying? Answer me! There is no answer. The bells are tinkling and filling the air with their wonderful pealing; the air is torn and thundering as it turns to wind; everything on earth comes flying past and, looking askance at her, other peoples and states move aside and make way.

6. A provincial town 160 miles northwest of Moscow, the oldest town on the Volga.

PART II

CHAPTER I

WHY should we always go out of our way to describe
the wretchedness and the imperfections of our life, and
to unearth characters from wild and remote corners of
our country? But what is to be done if such is the author's
bent? What is to be done if he is sick of his own imperfections and, as a result, cannot describe anything but the
wretchedness and the imperfections of our life, or do
otherwise than keep unearthing characters from wild
and remote corners of our country? So here we are once
more in the wilds, in some out of the way corner. And
what a wilderness it is! What a remote corner!

Like the giant rampart of some endless fortress with
escarpments and turrets, the mountain peaks stretched on
and undulated for over seven hundred miles. They were
magnificently poised over endless valleys, now having
sheer walls of clay and lime, scarred by torrents and
ravines, now displaying the charm of some green and
rounded slope, covered over with young shrubs as with
lambswool, sprouting where the trees had been cut down,
now clad in dark thick forests which had, as if by a
miracle, escaped the axe. The river, keeping to its course,
twisted and turned, sometimes browsing playfully
through meadows, sometimes flashing like fire in the sunshine, sometimes plunging into thickets of birch-trees,
aspens and alders, and then, at other times, running out
of them triumphantly, pursued by bridges, water-mills
and locks, that looked as if they were trying to catch up
with it at each turning.

In one spot the steep mountain-side was wrapped more
closely in the green foliage of trees. As a result of planting,
and thanks to the broken ground of the hilly ravine, both
the northern and southern species of the vegetable kingdom were here gathered together. The oak, the fir, the

wild pear-tree, the maple, wild cherry and blackthorn, cranberry and rowanberry bushes, grown over with hops, were all there climbing up the slopes, either helping each to grow or stifling each other. At the very top, on the brow of the hill, the red roofs of the domain mingled with the green tree-tops, and behind them the curves and combs of the peasant huts showed up, as did also the upper floor of the landowner's house with its fretted wooden balcony and its large half-oval window. And above this assembly of trees and roofs the old village church towered with its five gilded cupolas. These cupolas were crowned with open-work golden crosses, fastened with gold chains, and from the distance it looked as though the air was full of sparkling, gold coins, which seemed to have no visible support. All these cupolas, roofs and crosses, were reflected upside down in the river, the banks of which were studded with monstrously contorted willows; some of these had dipped their leaves and branches in the water and got entangled in the slimy spagillas that were drifting on the surface together with yellow water-lilies; and it looked as though they were admiring the wonderful reflection in the water.

The view was a very fine one; but the view from the top, from the upper floors of the house, was even finer. No guest or visitor could stand on the balcony, and feel indifferent. He would have caught his breath in astonishment, and would have exclaimed: 'O Lord, what a view!' A boundless and illimitable horizon unfurled before him: beyond the meadows, which were sprinkled with thickets and water-mills, forests formed several belts of green; beyond the forests, in the air which was already turning a dusky hue, there was a yellow splash of sands, then more forests succeeded, glowing as blue as the sea or as a mist, and stretching far and wide; and then came more sands, paler than before, but yellow still. Chalk hills combed the far skyline, and even in bad weather they glittered whitely as though illumined by an everlasting sun. Like puffs of smoke, nebulous purple patches were to be seen scattered here and there at the foot of the blindingly white slopes which might have been made of plaster.

Those were the distant villages, which the human eye could not distinguish clearly. Only when the sun occasionally flashed on the golden cupolas of the church could one suppose that there was a populous village there. An imperturbable silence reigned, and even the voices of singing peasants, lost in the wide spaces, did not disturb it. In short, any visitor standing on the balcony and gazing on the scene for a couple of hours, could only exclaim: 'O Lord, what a spacious view!'

Who was the owner and proprietor of this village which was as unapproachable from his side as an impregnable fortress? To reach it a detour was necessary from the side where scattered oak-trees greeted the oncoming visitor with massive branches spread wide like open arms and guided him to the house itself. It was the house of which we have already caught a glimpse and its façade now came in full view, with a row of peasant, fretted huts to one side of it, and, on the other, a church with the glitter of its gold crosses and the gold lacework patterns of its air-suspended chains above it. Who was the happy man who owned this nook? None other than Andrey Ivanovich Tentetnikov, a lucky young man of thirty-two, who was a bachelor into the bargain.

Who was he? What was he? What were his qualities and characteristics? We should enquire of his neighbours. One of these who belonged to that agile and fast-vanishing race of fire-eating staff-captains, used to refer to him as follows: 'A real swine!' A general, who lived some ten miles off, used to say: 'He's not stupid, that young man, but he has too high an opinion of himself. I could be of use to him, since I am not without connections in Petersburg and even at . . .' The general never finished his sentence. The police captain turned his reply as follows: 'I shall be calling on him to-morrow to collect arrears!' When asked what his master was like, a peasant of the village made no reply. One is obliged to conclude that the general impression of him was unfavourable.

If we look at him impartially, however, it may be said that he was not a bad sort: he was simply a 'sky-gazer', an idle fellow. And since there are not a few such in the wide world who like to be gazing at the sky, why should Tentetnikov not be a sky-gazer? However, by way of a sample, here is one day from his life, a day in every respect like all his other days, and from it let the reader form his own opinion as to his character and the way in which his life corresponded with the beauty of his environment.

He was late of waking in the morning and, propping himself up in bed, he sat there for a long while rubbing his eyes. Since his eyes had the misfortune to be tiny, the rubbing of them took up an extraordinarily long time and while he was thus occupied Mihailko, his valet, stood waiting in the doorway with a basin and towel in his hands. Poor Mihailko waited thus for an hour or more, then went into the kitchen only to return again—and his master would still be rubbing his eyes and sitting up in bed. At last he would get out of bed, wash himself, put on his dressing-gown and proceed thereafter into the drawing-room to drink his tea, coffee, cocoa, and even his steamed milk, sipping a little of everything, breaking up his bread ruthlessly into crumbs and shamelessly scattering tobacco-ash everywhere. There he would sit for two hours on end over his breakfast. And that was not all: he would pick up a cup of cold tea and saunter with it to the window giving on the courtyard: and there, by the window, the following scene would recur each day.

Grigory, who served in the household in the capacity of butler, would be bawling out in these expressive terms which had some reference to Perfilievna, the housekeeper: 'You revolting creature, trash that you are! You had better keep your mouth shut, you slut!'

'A fig for you!' This trash of a Perfilievna would yell back, making the appropriate gesture. She was a hard woman in spite of her fondness for raisins, pastilles, and every sort of sweet, which she kept under lock and key.

'You'll get on the wrong side of the steward, you barnfowl!' Grigory was roaring.

'The steward is as much of a thief as you are. Do you think the master does not know about you? Why, he is here and can hear everything.'

'Where is the master?'

'Why, over there, by the window; he can see everything.'

And so it was. The master was sitting by the window and he could see everything.

To make this hullaballoo more complete one of the servants' brats was screaming for all his worth after having had his ears boxed by his mother and a borzoi was whimpering as he squatted after being scalded by the cook, who had poured some boiling water out of the kitchen doorway. In short, the din of howling and screeching was unbearable. The master saw and heard everything. And it was only when the row became so insupportable as to prevent any concentration whatsoever that he sent word for them to make less noise.

Before dinner he used to retire to his study for a couple of hours in order to apply himself seriously to a work he was engaged on, a work intended to embrace the whole of Russia from every angle—civil, political, religious, and philosophical. This work was to resolve the difficult problems and questions posed by the present age, and it was to define clearly Russia's great future; in short, all these problems were presented in a way that appeals to modern man. However, this colossal undertaking was restricted to reflection upon it: the quill pen would get nibbled, doodles would make their appearance on the paper in front of him, and then all this would be pushed aside, a book would find its way into his hands and there it would remain until dinner time. This book would be read over the soup, the sauce and the roast, over the sweet even, and as a result many of the dishes grew cold while others were removed untouched. Then a pipe was lit over coffee, and a solitary game of chess followed. . . . What happened in between until supper-time it was indeed hard to say. Probably nothing at all.

And thus it was that this young man of thirty-two spent his time, sitting about all day by himself in a dressing-gown and without a tie. He had no wish to walk or get about; he did not want to go upstairs, he was even loath to open the windows and breathe the fresh air; and the wonderful scenery, which could leave no visitor indifferent, might not have existed as far as the master of the house was concerned. From this the reader may conclude that Tentetnikov belonged to that category of people who are not yet extinct in Russia and who used to be called sluggards, lie-me-downs, bolsters, and other such names, but for whom it is now more difficult to find the right description. It is hard to say whether such characters are born or are formed as a result of sad circumstances which may impede a man's development. Instead of attempting to answer this question, we shall do better by describing the background of Tentetnikov's education and childhood.

Everything seemed to conspire to make a man of Tentetnikov. As a clever, thoughtful, and frail boy of twelve, he entered an educational establishment, the head of which was a most unusual man for his times. An idol of youth, a model of teachers, the incomparable Alexander Petrovich had the gift of sympathy and of spotting talent. . . . How well he knew the qualities of Russians! How well he knew children! How well he knew how to inspire! There was not a scamp of a boy who, after some foolish exploit, was not ready to present himself of his own accord and to confess his sins to him. The matter would not end there and he would be severely reprimanded or punished, but the scamp would leave his presence with his tail in the air rather than between his legs. There was something cheering and encouraging about Alexander Petrovich, something that implied: 'Forward! You must get on your feet again even though you have fallen!' Nor did he lecture them on good behaviour. He usually said: 'I ask you to use your minds and nothing else. Whoever wants to be brainy has no time for pranks. Prankishness must disappear quite naturally.' And so it was. The inclination to play pranks died out. Whoever did not cultivate his mind became an object of contempt for his fellows. . . . The grown-up asses and fools had to put up with the most injurious nicknames even from the junior boys, and they did not dare to lay hands on them. 'It's too much!' many of them said. 'This is going to breed arrogance among the intelligent.' 'No, it will not do that,' Alexander Petrovich used to say. 'I don't keep the less capable boys for long. I have a special course for the cleverer ones.' And so it was. The cleverer boys qualified for the alternative course. He made no attempt to check some of the boys' exuberance, for he saw in it the beginning of a spiritual development and he used to say that this was as necessary to him as symptoms to a doctor, in order that he might have a reliable way of discovering the precise nature of a person's inner content.

How the boys loved him! Never were children so attached to their parents. No, not even in the years of wild enthusiasms was inextinguishable passion so strong as the love felt by the boys towards him. To the grave, to their very last days, whenever they celebrated their birthdays, his pupils would pronounce a toast in his honour; they would close their eyes and weep for him when he was in his grave. His least word of encouragement excited them and brought joy prompting their ambition to excel. He did not keep the less capable boys for long; for them he arranged a special shorter course; but the more capable boys had to do a double course. And his highest course, the one reserved for the elect, had no parallel in other establishments. In this class only he demanded of his pupils what others illogically ask of children—that higher function of the intellect which is capable of stifling laughter, of putting up with any sarcasm, of bearing a fool without irritation, of never losing control of oneself, of not stooping to get one's own back in any circumstance, and of preserving a proud tranquillity and imperturbability of soul. Everything was brought to bear which would make for a firm character, and he was constantly experimenting in that direction. Oh, how well he knew the science of life!

He did not employ many other teachers. The majority of subjects he taught himself. He knew how to communicate the very soul of learning, so that even a junior boy would grasp it all, and he did so without any pedantic terminology or stilted theories and views. He selected only such subjects as were capable of forming the character of a man of the world. The greater part of his lectures were devoted to an account of what was in store for the young men when they left school, and he unfolded that perspective in such a way that the young man, although he was not yet apprenticed to life, lived spiritually and mentally in the atmosphere of service. He concealed nothing: he gave them a bare outline of all the disappointments and obstacles, all the trials and temptations lying ahead of them, and nothing was hidden from them. He knew everything: it was as though he was experienced in all callings and professions. Whether it was because his ambition was strongly developed or because there was something in his eyes which bade youth go 'Forward!' whatever it was, it made young men seek out the hard way and burn to go into action where difficulties abounded, where obstacles were plentiful, and where it was necessary to display great qualities of spirit. There were few who completed the course, but such as did emerged strong; they had been through fire. They succeeded in keeping their posts in circumstances of great difficulty when many others, who may have been cleverer than they were, threw up everything as a result of a trifling unpleasantness or, sinking into a morass and growing lazy, fell into the hands of corrupters and rogues. But his pupils were not to be shaken and, knowing life and mankind, and tempered with wisdom, they even exercised a strong influence on bad characters.

The impetuous heart of an ambitious boy beat faster at the very thought of joining that course. To all appearance there could have been nothing better for our Tentetnikov! But as ill luck would have it, no sooner had he joined the course of the elect, a thing he so much desired, than this extraordinary teacher prematurely died! Oh, what a blow that was for him! What a terrible first loss! Everything in the school was changed. Alexander Petrovich was succeeded by some Feodor Ivanovich. He at once concentrated on external discipline: he began to demand of children what can only be asked of grown-ups. He fancied that there was something untamed in their free and easy ways. And as though to spite his predecessor, he declared on his very first day that he set no store by intellect and success, and cared only for good conduct. Yet, strange as it may seem, good conduct was the last thing Feodor Ivanovich achieved. The boys began to indulge in all sorts of secret pranks. In the daytime everything went smoothly and in tune, but there were orgies at night.

The studies were also strangely affected. The teaching staff was changed: men of different outlook and points of view now came on the scene. They showered their pupils with new terminology and words: in their expositions they demonstrated logical connections, they pursued new discoveries, and they were carried away by their own enthusiasms. But alas, the knowledge they expounded lacked all vestiges of life. Learning was a dead letter in their mouths. In a word, everything was turned inside out. There was a loss of respect for the authorities and the powers-that-be: the pupils began to mock at their tutors and teachers; they called the head Fiedka, the bun, and various other nicknames. Depravity soon assumed anything but childlike forms: such things were set on foot that many of the pupils had to be expelled. Within two years the establishment had become quite unrecognizable.

Tentetnikov was of a quiet disposition. He was not led astray either by the nocturnal orgies of his comrades, who had a 'lady' they all visited right under the windows of the director's apartment, or by the way they scoffed at religion just because the priest happened to be none too intelligent. No, even in his dreams he had the conviction that his soul was divine. He was not to be led astray; but he did become despondent. His ambition had been roused, but there was now no suitable field of action for it. It would have been better if it had never been stimulated. He listened to the declamations of the excitable lecturers, and remembered his former tutor who had known how to be comprehensible without fuss. What subjects and what courses did he not follow! There were those of medicine, philosophy and even law: there was the universal history of mankind, a subject so broad and comprehensive, that in three years the lecturer had only succeeded in touching upon the introductory part, dealing with the development of communes in some of the German cities. God alone knows what he did not hear! But all these bits and pieces of knowledge assumed no connected form in his head. Owing to some measure of native wit he had an inkling that this was not the way to teach, but he had no idea of how it ought to be done. He frequently recalled Alexander Petrovich, and he felt so sad when he did so, that in his distress he did not know what to do.

But youth is happy in having a future. As his school days drew to a close, his heart began to pound. He said to himself: 'Why, this is not life yet: it is only a preparation for life; real life will begin in the service; that is where great deeds await me.' And, without even paying a fleeting call to that wonderful spot which so amazed every visiting guest, without paying his respects to the graves of his parents, as was the custom of all ambitious young men, he rushed off to St. Petersburg, whither, as we know, our energetic young men stream from all parts of Russia in order to serve, to shine, to gain promotion, or simply to absorb a smattering of a colourless, deceptive, social education as frigid as ice. Andrey Ivanovich's ambitious urge was cut to the root from the very beginning by his uncle, Onufry Ivanovich, an actual civil councillor. He declared that the whole point was in good handwriting and in nothing else, and that without it one could become neither a minister nor statesman. With great difficulty and with his uncle's help, Andrey Ivanovich at last found a niche for himself in a government department. When he was conducted into a bright and splendid room, with a parquet floor and polished writing desks, fit for the leading dignitaries of the realm in whose hands lay the destiny of the whole state, and when he perceived the legions of scribbling gentry who were making a rustling noise with their quills and had their heads bent sideways, and when he himself was placed at one of these tables and asked to copy, as though expressly, some paper of trifling content (the matter concerned three roubles and the correspondence had lasted six months), the inexperienced youth had a most extraordinary sensation: the gentry sitting round him reminded him of a lot of schoolboys! To complete the similarity, some of them were reading a stupid foreign novel, kept tucked away between the papers of the affair they were examining, and which they pretended to be occupied with, trembling each time their chief put his nose in at the door. It all seemed very strange to him, his former studies so much more important than his present occupation, and the preparation for service so much better than the service itself. He began to yearn for his school-days. And then of a sudden he saw Alexander Petrovich as though he were in the flesh, and he almost wept. The room whirled round the officials and the tables got all mixed up, and he just managed to avoid a momentary black-out. 'No,' he thought to himself, when he had recovered, 'I must get down to business however petty it may seem at first!' Setting his teeth spiritually and emotionally, he resolved to follow the example of the others.

Where can one not procure enjoyment? It is to be had in Petersburg in spite of the austere and gloomy appearance of that city. There is a raging thirty-degree frost crackling down its streets; that fiend of the north, that witch of a blizzard, howls along, blotting out the pavements, blinding the eyes, powdering fur collars, moustaches and the shaggy muzzles of horses, but somewhere above, on the fourth floor, a window glimmers in a friendly sort of way through the spinning snow-flakes; in a cosy room lit by stearine candles, to the noise of a hissing samovar, there is a conversation going on that warms both heart and soul, some bright page of an inspired Russian poet is being read, of a poet whom God has bestowed upon his Russia, and youthful hearts exult as they never do under a grey daylight sky.

Tentetnikov was soon at home in his new job, but instead of its becoming the aim and object of his life as he originally imagined that it would, it only proved of secondary importance to him. It was a way of spending the time and it made him treasure his spare time all the more. His uncle, the civil councillor, was already beginning to think that there was some point to his nephew when the latter of a sudden kicked over the traces. Among his friends of whom he had quite a number there were two in particular who might be described as embittered. They were of that strange restless type which could not remain indifferent not only to injustice but to anything that savoured of it. They were fundamentally kind of heart but disorderly in their behaviour, demanding indulgence for themselves but full of intolerance for others; with their fiery speech and their expressions of noble indignation against society, they influenced him a great deal. They stimulated his nerves and his spirit of irritation, forcing him to take note of trifles to which he had never paid any previous attention. Of a sudden he took a dislike to Feodor Feodorovich Lenitzin, a head of one of the departments, who had his offices in splendid quarters. He began to find fault with him. It seemed to him that in his conversation with his superiors, Lenitzin turned into a kind of syrup, but was as sour as vinegar whenever he talked to his inferiors; that following the example of all petty-minded men he chose to reprimand those who had failed to offer him their congratulations at the appropriate seasons, and to persecute those who left no visiting cards with the porter; and as a result he experienced a nervous revulsion towards him. Some evil spirit was egging him on to play an unpleasant trick on Lenitzin. He sought his opportunity with much relish and at last found it. One day he spoke to him so rudely that his chiefs gave him the ultimatum of either apologizing or resigning. He chose to resign. His uncle, the civil councillor, called on him in a state of alarm and supplication: 'For Christ's sake, Andrey Ivanovich, what are you doing? To throw up such a promising career just because you are not keen on your chief! What are you thinking about? If everyone did the like, there would be nobody left in the service. Be sensible, forget your pride and vanity, go back and have a chat with him!'

'It's not that, uncle,' the nephew replied. 'I could

easily make my excuses to him. It's my fault. He is my chief and I should not have spoken to him as I did. But there is another side to the matter. I have other work to do: I have three hundred serfs, an estate that is going to ruin, and an idiot of a steward. The government will not lose much if another man takes my place in the office to copy papers, but it will suffer a greater loss if three hundred serfs do not pay their dues. What do you think? I am . . . a landowner who has his own bit of service to do. If I concentrate on the preservation, care and improvement of the lot of those folk who are entrusted to my care, I shall have at the disposal of the government three hundred punctual, sober and hard-working subjects. In what way would my service be less valuable than that of the head of the department, Lenitzin?'

The civil councillor remained standing with his mouth open in amazement. He did not expect such a flow of words. After reflecting for a moment, he began to speak after this fashion: 'Nevertheless . . . but how is it . . . how can you bury yourself in a village? . . . Here, at least, you may come across a general or a duke walking along the street. You yourself will pass someone . . . while there . . . and of course there is gas lighting here, industrial Europe, while there, whoever you meet, it's all either peasants or peasant women. Why are you doing it? Why spoil your whole life for a few rude words?'

But the uncle's persuasive arguments had no effect on the nephew. He began to represent the village to himself as a comfortable sanctuary, a stimulant to thoughts and ideas, a unique arena of useful activity. Already he had acquired the latest books dealing with agriculture. In short, a fortnight or so after this conversation he found himself in the vicinity of the place where he had spent his childhood, not far from that wonderful spot which no visiting guest could sufficiently admire. A new emotion stirred within him. Impressions that had long lain dormant now came to the surface again. He had forgotten many of the spots and he now gazed on the wonderful scenery with fresh eyes. And suddenly, for no explicable reason, his heart began to thump. When the road sped through a narrow gorge into the thick of a vast tangled forest and he saw, above him and below him, the three-hundred-year-old oaks, as broad as three men, in between the silver firs, elm trees and black poplars, towering higher than the ordinary poplar, and when in answer to a question: 'Whose forest is this?' he was told: 'Tentetnikov's', when the road began winding up the hillside and then continued along the level top—with the, as yet, unharvested corn-fields, wheat-fields, oat-fields and barley-fields to one side—and past all the parts of the road which had already been traversed and which now appeared in foreshortened perspective on the other side; and when, gradually growing darker, the road finally passed under the shadow of the broad and branching trees, which were scattered over the green carpet until the village was reached and the fretted peasant huts and the red roofs of the landowner's buildings began to flash past, and the golden tips of the church shone out; when his pounding heart knew without question where he had arrived; then the sensations which had been accumulating within him burst out into these thunderous words: 'Well, haven't I been a fool till now? Fate decreed that I should be the owner of an earthly paradise, and I became the slave of lifeless paper, a mere scribbler! After being educated, becoming enlightened, acquiring that store of information which is essential in order to do good among those under my authority, to improve the conditions of a whole district, to fulfil all the duties of a landowner who is at the same time a judge, a manager, and a guardian of the law—how could I have entrusted this post to an ignorant steward! How could I have preferred the task of regulating the affairs of those I had never seen before, and of whose characters and qualities I knew absolutely nothing! How could I have preferred paper work to a real job! How could I have entertained the fantasy of governing provinces a thousand miles away in which I had never set foot and in which I could only commit a lot of gross errors and stupidities!'

Meanwhile he was to behold another spectacle. Learning of the arrival of their master, the peasants had gathered near the porch. He was soon in the midst of all sorts of women's head-dresses and the picturesque bushy beards of the peasants. When he heard them say, 'Our provider, you have remembered us . . .' and the old men and women, who still remembered his grandfather and great-grandfather, began to shed tears, he could not keep back his own either. And he thought to himself: 'So much love! And what for? Because I have never seen them or given any thought to them!' And he swore an oath that he would share their labours and toils.

He took matters into his own hands and began to issue orders. He cut down the amount of labour due from the peasants, decreased the numbers of days they had to work for their master, and gave them extra time for their own labours. He dismissed the fool of a steward. He started to take an interest in everything himself, to go out into the fields, to show himself on the threshing-floor, among the kilns, at the water-mills, on the quayside when the barges were being loaded, and soon even the idlers were scratching their heads. But that did not last very long. The peasants were canny: they were quick to grasp that the master, although he was alert and eager to undertake much, was yet at a loss how to go about things, and talked far too intelligently and not straightforwardly enough. The result was not so much a misunderstanding between the master and the peasant as that they just did not harmonize together, and failed to sing in tune.

Tentetnikov began to notice that his own land was giving a poorer yield than that of the peasants. His own fields were sown earlier and came up later although there seemed nothing wrong with the work. He supervised the work himself and even gave orders for a mug of vodka to be given to the peasants for their diligence. And yet the peasants' rye had already begun to shoot up, their oats had begun to spill over, their millet was growing thickly, while his own corn had barely started to sprout, and the ears of it were still to furl. In short, the master noticed that the peasants were simply up to their tricks in spite of their reduced obligations. He tried to remonstrate with them but received the following reply: 'How is it possible for us not to take the master's interests into account? You have been pleased yourself to see how we have laboured at ploughing and sowing—you even had vodka given to us.' What could he reply to that?

'But why has it turned out so badly then?' the master enquired.

'Who knows? It must have been the worms in the roots. And look what sort of a summer it is: there has been no rain at all.'

But the master could not help observing that the worms had not been eating the roots of the peasants' rye and that the rain fell in a very strange way, in some places only, bringing benefit to the peasants and none to the master.

He found it even more difficult to get on with the peasant women. They were continually asking to be given leave from work and complaining of the hardships of their labour on the master's domain. How strange it was! He had exempted them from any deliveries of home-spun linen, berries, mushrooms and nuts, he had halved their other obligatory labours, with the idea that the women would give more time to their household affairs, that they would do more sewing and dress their husbands better, that they would increase the number of vegetable plots. But nothing of the sort! The fair sex indulged in such idleness, disputes, slanders and quarrels, that their husbands were constantly coming to him with some complaint like this: 'Master, please tame this devil-of-a-woman! She's a very demon, that's what she is—there's no peace with her!'

Hardening his heart, he would have taken firmer measures. But how was he to be severe? And what a woman she turned out to be when she did come along! She squealed so much, looked so ailing and ill, wore such rags that one wondered where she had got them, with the result that he could only say: 'Be off with you! Be off! Out of my sight!' And having said that, poor Tentetnikov would then see how that ailing woman, once she was out of the gates, would start squabbling over a turnip with a neighbour of hers and would crush her ribs more effectively than any sturdy peasant would be capable of doing.

He got the idea of trying to start a school for them, but it gave rise to such confusion that he became quite despondent. He would have done better not to have dreamt about it! In dealing with cases brought before him he discovered that all those legal subtleties which had been taught him by the philosophizing professors were of no use. Both the plaintiff and the defendant would be telling lies, and the devil only could make out the rights and wrongs of it! And he came to realize that a knowledge of human nature was more essential than all the subtleties of books of law and philosophy; and he also perceived that there was something lacking in him— but what it was, God alone knew, and so, as often happens, there was no understanding between master and peasant, and between peasant and master. The peasant turned his blind side to the master, and the master his blind side to the peasant. All this helped to damp considerably the master's enthusiasm. He lost interest in the work even when he went out into the fields. He had no eyes for the scythes as they rose and fell, none for the hayricks in the making, none for the stocking of the corn, his gaze was abstracted when the work was near; and when the work was going on in the distance his eyes sought out objects nearer to hand or looked aside at some bend of the river along the banks of which some red-beaked, red-legged martin was strutting—a bird of course, not a man. He looked on with curiosity as, catching a fish and holding it in its beak, the bird seemed to be reflecting on whether to swallow it or not, and at the same time he would keep staring farther along the river where another martin was visible, a martin who had not yet caught a fish but who was in his turn staring at the bird with the catch. Or, with eyes half-closed and with head raised up towards the spacious heavens, he surrendered himself to the enjoyment of imbibing the odour of the fields and to drinking in the amazing trilling of the tuneful inhabitants of the air at those moments when from heaven and earth they join in one harmonious choir without contradicting each other. A quail is fluttering among the rye, a crake is creaking in the grass, linnets twitter and chirrup as they flit above, a lamb bleats out, a swallow trills as it vanishes in the light, and the bugle call of the raucous storks rings out as they fly in wedge-shaped formation high above. The whole of the countryside is filled with echoing sounds. . . . 'Oh, Creator! How wondrous still is your world in the depths of the country, in this country spot, far from the ghastly highways and the towns!' so he said to himself; but after a time even that began to bore him. Very soon he gave up going into the fields, stayed in the seclusion of his house, and refused even to take an interest in his overseer's reports.

Formerly some of his neighbours used to pay him calls, a retired lieutenant of the hussars who was a great pipe-smoker, or a radically-minded student who had not finished his studies and who had acquired wisdom from the perusal of contemporary pamphlets and journals. But these visitors also started to bore him. Their conversation began to impress him as being superficial, a sort of free and easy European type of relationship, with a pat on the knee, an excessive amount of kow-towing and looseness, and he came to think them far too familiar and unreserved. He decided to put an end to his acquaintanceship with all of them and to do it quite brusquely. So when one of the most agreeable of these superficial conversationalists, one of the few surviving colonel martinets who was at the same time a representative of the new advanced mode of thought, when this Varvar Nicolaievich Vishnepokromov, called on him in order to have a heart to heart talk about politics, philosophy, literature, morals and even the financial state of England—he sent out a servant to tell him that he was not at home, but as he did so he very rashly showed himself at the window. The visitor and the master of the house exchanged glances. One of them no doubt muttered through his teeth, 'What a beast!' while the other out of pique growled, 'What a swine!' On that their relations came to an end. Since that day no one had ever called on him.

But he was very glad of that, for he was giving all his time to planning a great work on Russia. The reader already knows how this plan progressed. A strange disorder became the order of the day. It cannot be said, however, that he did not have his waking moments. When the papers and journals arrived by post and he came across the familiar name of a former comrade in print, who was achieving success in some leading governmental position or who was making some notable contribution to science or world affairs, a quiet and secret nostalgia invaded his heart, and he involuntarily gave vent to a sorrowfully silent plaint at his own inaction. At those times his life appeared to him nasty and loathsome. The image of his past school days would recur with extraordinary vividness and Alexander Petrovich would appear before him as though he were alive. . . . A flood of tears would well from his eyes. . . .

What did his tears signify? Was his ailing soul revealing the sorrowful secret of its malady? The fact that his character had failed to form and affirm itself? The fact that, unaccustomed from youth to face and overcome difficulties, he had failed to get preferment and to grow tempered by overcoming obstacles and difficulties? The fact that, smelted like steel, the rich store of his thoughts and feelings had not been properly tempered? The fact that his rare teacher had died too soon, and that there was no one now who had the power to restore the force that was sapped by constant wavering and by impotent inelastic will-power, no one who might rouse the soul with the encouraging cry of 'Forward'—that call for which the Russian of all conditions, callings, and professions is everywhere thirsting?

Where is the man who will know how to utter that omnipotent word 'Forward', and address it to the Russian soul in its native language? Where is he that, knowing all the strength and qualities, all the depths of our nature, could direct us with one motion towards a higher life? With what tears and love would grateful Russians repay him! But centuries succeed one another, and there is only shameful idleness and the senseless activity of immature youth. . . . And still no one comes forward who can utter that word!

There was one circumstance which nearly shook him

out of his drowsiness and almost revolutionized his character: it was an event very much like love. But even this came to nothing. In the neighbourhood, some seven miles from his village, there lived a general who, as we have already seen, was not too well inclined towards Tentetnikov. The general lived a general's life, entertaining; he liked his neighbours to call on him and pay their respects; he himself did not return their visits, talked in a husky voice, and had a daughter, a strange and exceptional creature. She was the very personification of life.

Her name was Ulinka. She had had a strange upbringing. She had been taught by an English governess who spoke no word of Russian. Her mother had already died when she was a child. The father had no time to occupy himself with her. However, as he loved his daughter passionately, he could only have spoilt her. She was self-willed, like any child who is brought up on freedom. If anyone had caught sight of her as a severe frown puckered her fine brow when in a rage or as she argued heatedly with her father, he might have assumed that she was a most capricious creature. But her anger was kindled only when she heard of some injustice or some evil act no matter who was responsible. She never quarrelled on her own account or justified herself. Her anger would have vanished instantly if she had seen the object of her rage in trouble. At the least request for charity she was ready to hand over her purse and all it contained without any further argument or calculation. She was impulsive by nature. Whenever she spoke her whole being seemed to surge in the wake of her thoughts —the expression of her face, the tone of her conversation, the gestures of her hands; the very folds of her dress seemed to billow in the same direction and she looked as though she might herself fly away in the wake of her words. She was anything but secretive. She would not have been afraid to disclose her thoughts in front of any one, and no force could have compelled her to keep quiet when she wished to say anything. Her enchanting and very individual bearing had so much unruffled ease about it when she was walking that everyone involuntarily gave way before her. An ill-intentioned person was cowed and struck numb by her; a deft and lively talker would be at a loss in conversation with her; while a shy person might talk to her as with no one else, and right from the beginning of their conversation it would seem to him that he had known her before, had seen those features on some previous occasion—in the days of immemorial childhood perhaps, in some relative's house, on some joyful evening, in the midst of jolly games and playing children, and for a long time afterwards the years of discretion would seem dull and boring to him.

That is what happened between her and Tentetnikov. A new and inexpressible feeling stirred his soul. His dull life was instantly illumined.

At first the general used to receive Tentetnikov gladly and reasonably well; but they could not get on together. Their conversation usually ended in disputes which made them both feel uncomfortable, for the general disliked to be contradicted and opposed, and Tentetnikov was also a most sensitive person. Of course, for the sake of the daughter much was forgiven to the father, and there was no breach of the peace until some relatives came to stay with the general: these were the countess Boldyrev and the princess Youzyakin, who had been maids of honour at the court during the last reign, but who still had some court connections, for which reason the general showed himself a little too obsequious in their presence. As soon as they arrived, Tentetnikov seemed to notice a certain cooling off in the general's manner towards him; the general did not seem to notice him and treated him somehow impersonally; he referred to him slightingly as 'my dear fellow', 'my dear chap', and even familiarly as 'thou'. This at last roused him to fury. He set his heart and gritted his teeth, but he had the presence of mind to say in an unusually soft and polite voice while red spots appeared on his face and he boiled inwardly: 'I thank you, general, for your good disposition towards me. By calling me "thou" you have indicated a desire for a close friendship between us, and you oblige me to respond by calling you "thou" also. But the difference in our years is an obstacle to such familiarity between us.' The general grew confused. Collecting his thoughts and words, he began to say, though without much logic, that he had not pronounced the word 'thou' in that sense, and that it was sometimes permissible for an old man to say 'thou' to a young man (he did not say a word about his rank).

It goes without saying that their acquaintance came to an end after that, and love was nipped in the bud. The light which had flashed for a second before his eyes was now extinguished, and the succeeding dusk was even more gloomy. Everything drove him to indulge in the sort of life which the reader has already had occasion to observe—a life of dawdling and inaction. Disorder and dirt made their appearance in the household. The brush and the dust would be found lying in the middle of a room for a whole day. His trousers even found their way into the drawing-room. A pair of greasy braces lay on a smart table in front of the sofa as though they had been served up as part of a guest's entertainment, and his life became so drowsy and insignificant that not only did his domestics cease to respect him but the very chickens almost pecked at him. Pen in hand, he would doodle for hours on end, drawing squiggles, little houses, huts, carts, *troikas*. But sometimes, quite unconsciously, his pen scribbled away without its master's knowledge, tracing a small head with fine features, with a quick penetrating glance and a raised lock of hair, and he would then be surprised to discover the semblance of her whose portrait no artist could have drawn. And this made him feel even more sad and, convinced that there was no happiness on earth, he plunged into ever greater gloom and despondency.

Such was the state of Tentetnikov's mind. As he sat by the window according to his habit, in order to stare at whatever might be going on, he was surprised to hear neither Grigory nor Parfilievna but only a slight commotion in the courtyard instead. The kitchen boy and the woman who washed the floors were running to open the gates. Framed in the gates, three horses appeared just as though they had been sculptured on a triumphal arch: one head to the left, another to the right, and the third in the middle. A coachman and footman were sitting above them, the latter dressed in a frock-coat tied round with a handkerchief. Behind them sat a gentleman in a cap and greatcoat, with a brightly coloured shawl wrapped round his shoulders. When the carriage finally pulled up at the porch it turned out to be a light chaise on springs. A gentleman of unusually respectable appearance jumped out on the steps displaying almost the agility and speed of a smart officer.

Tentetnikov had a moment of fear: he thought it might be a government official. Here we must note that in his youth he was once mixed up in a risky affair. Two philosophizing hussars who had been stuffing themselves with every sort of pamphlet, an aesthetician who had not finished his studies and an inveterate gambler, had started up between them a philanthropic society under the ultimate and sole direction of an old rogue, mason and gambler, but who was a most eloquent man. The society was formed with a very broad aim—that of bringing enduring happiness to the whole of mankind, from the banks of the Thames as far as Kamchatka.[7] Vast funds were required for this project; incredible sums were collected from generous members. But only their supreme chief knew what happened to all these funds. Tentetnikov was drawn into this society by two of his friends, who belonged to the category of embittered people, kind enough folk at heart but who had turned into regular drunkards from having to pronounce too many toasts in the name of science, enlightenment and future progress. Tentetnikov soon saw daylight and abandoned this circle. But the society had already managed to get entangled in various affairs, some of which were not quite respectable for a member of the nobility to be involved in, and afterwards the matter came to the notice of the police. . . . No wonder then that Tentetnikov was a little nervous even

7. A large, remote peninsula in northeastern Siberia, projecting into the Pacific between the Bering strait and the Sea of Okhotsk.

though he had quitted the society and broken off all relations with it; his conscience was not quite at ease. It was not without alarm therefore that he now stared at the door which was being swung open.

His fear however quickly vanished as soon as the visitor had made his bows with incredible agility, keeping his head respectfully poised and bent slightly to one side, and had explained in short but definitive words that he had long been voyaging through Russia both for reasons of necessity and of curiosity. He added that our empire was rich in remarkable objects to say nothing of the variety of trades and the diversity of soils; that he had been attracted by the picturesque situation of the village; that he would not have dared to disturb him by his untimely arrival despite the wonderful situation, if the spring floods and the bad roads had not caused his carriage to have a slight accident which necessitated a helping hand from blacksmiths and wheelwrights; and that, taking everything into account, even if his chaise had not had an accident, he would still not have been able to deny himself the pleasure of personally paying his respects to him.

On terminating his speech, the visitor scraped his foot back with disarming courtesy; the foot was clad in a smart half-boot of patent leather with mother-of-pearl buttons; and having done this, despite the roundness of his body, he immediately leapt backwards with the lightness of a rubber ball.

Tentetnikov was now reassured, and he concluded that his visitor must be some learned professor, who was doing a tour of Russia in order to collect specimens of vegetation or to engage in archaeological research. He at once expressed his readiness to be of help to him; he offered him his skilled workers, wheelwrights and blacksmiths; he begged him to make himself at home; he made him sit down in a roomy Voltairean armchair, and he got ready to hear him discourse on the natural sciences.

The visitor, however, turned the conversation on to themes of a more intimate nature. He compared his life to a ship at sea driven on by treacherous winds; he referred to the fact that he had tried many different professions, that he had suffered much in the cause of justice, that even his life had been endangered more than once by enemies, and he spoke of many other things which denoted that he was a man of a practical turn of mind. On concluding his speech he blew his nose so loudly into a white cambric handkerchief that Tentetnikov had never heard anything like it.

Sometimes such a strumpet of a trumpet is to be met with in an orchestra, and when it emits a blast, it seems as though the sound is vibrating not in the orchestra but right in your ear. Such was the sound that broke the quiet of the sleeping house, and it was immediately followed by a whiff of fragrant eau-de-Cologne, which was invisibly wafted on its way by a deft wave of the cambric handkerchief.

The reader will have divined perhaps that the visitor was none other than our respected and long-absent friend, Pavel Ivanovich Chichikov. He looked a trifle older: it was evident that this period had not been without its strains and stresses. It seemed as though his tailed coat had grown a little faded, while the chaise, the coachman, the footman, the horses, and the harness, had all grown more worn and ragged. It even looked as though his finances were not in the most enviable condition. But there was no change in the expression of his face, his decorum and his manners. If anything, his approach and turns of phrase were even more agreeable, and he crossed his legs more smartly than ever when sitting down in an armchair. He was even more soft-spoken and cautious in his utterance, and he had acquired a greater sense of tact. His collar and shirt-front were whiter than snow and, although he had just been travelling, there was not a particle of dust to be seen on his swallow-tailed coat; he might have been a guest arriving for a birthday party. His cheeks and chin were shaved so smoothly that only a blind man could have failed to admire their pleasant, rounded curves.

The house was at once transfigured. The portion of it that had hitherto been shuttered and confined to darkness, was now illumined and lit up. Chichikov's belongings were brought into these bright rooms, and they were soon arranged in the following fashion: everything he required for the night was put into the room which was to serve as a bedroom; as for the room which was set aside as a study . . . but we must note first of all that this room had three tables, a writing desk in front of the sofa, a card-table in between the windows and in front of a mirror, and a corner table placed between the door leading into the bedroom and the door leading into an uninhabited room stacked with invalid furniture where no one ever ventured. The corner table had now spread on it those articles of clothing which had been unpacked and which consisted of a pair of evening trousers, a pair of new trousers, a pair of grey trousers, two velvet waistcoats, two satin waistcoats, and a frock-coat. All these articles were placed one on top of the other in the form of a pyramid, and they were covered over with a silk handkerchief. In another corner, between the door and the window, various pairs of boots had been set out; some of them were not altogether new, others were quite new, some were patent leather half-boots, others were slippers. They were also shyly curtained off with a silk handkerchief to make it appear that they were not there. On the writing desk another assortment of articles had been put out: a box, a casket with eau-de-Cologne, a calendar, and two novels, both of which were second volumes. The clean linen was put into a dressing-table which was already in the bedroom; the soiled linen was tied in a bundle and thrust under the bed. The sword which accompanied him in his travels as a warning to bandits was now also brought into the bedroom and hung on a nail near the bed. Everything looked unusually clean and tidy. There was not a scrap of paper, a feather or a speck of dust to be seen anywhere. The very air seemed to have become purer; it had now the agreeable odour of a fresh healthy man, who changed his linen frequently, visited the baths and sponged himself down on Sundays. The odour of his footman, Petrushka, tried to consolidate itself in the hall, but not for long, for Petrushka was moved into the kitchen quarters as was fitting.

For the first few days Tentetnikov had fears for his independence: he was afraid lest his guest might constrict him, disturb his way of life or upset the daily programme which he had so successfully instituted for himself. But these apprehensions were groundless. Chichikov showed himself extraordinarily adaptable to everything. He approved of his host's philosophical and unhurried life, and he commented that it would surely help him to reach the age of a hundred. He found some happy things to say about his host's secluded habits and added that they fostered great thoughts. Glancing at his host's collection of books and saying a few words in praise of books in general, he remarked that they saved men from idleness. He did not say much but what he said had weight. He was even more considerate in his actions. He arrived on time and left at the right moment; he refrained from assailing his host with questions when the latter was not in a talkative mood; he took pleasure in playing chess with him and was quite content to remain silent. While one of them smoked his pipe and emitted curly clouds of smoke, the other did not smoke but indulged in some corresponding activity. He would, for example, pull out a black and silver snuff-box and, holding it between two fingers of his left hand, spin it round with a finger of his right hand somewhat in the manner in which the earth turns round on its axis; or he would drum on it and whistle an accompaniment. In short, he was no trouble to his host. 'It's the first time I have come across a man with whom I can live,' Tentetnikov said to himself. 'On the whole that art is sadly lacking among us. We have plenty of clever, educated, and good people, but I doubt if there are many to be found who are of an equable temper and with whom it would be possible to live for a long time without quarrelling. This is the first man like that whom I have met.' Such was Tentetnikov's opinion of his guest.

Chichikov, for his part, was very glad to find himself installed for a time in the house of such a mild and gentle host. He was weary of his wandering gypsy life. To spend a month at least in a lovely village, within sight of the fields when spring was beginning, was useful even from the point of view of his piles.

It would have been hard to find a better spot for repose. The spring, which had been retarded by frosts, suddenly blossomed in all its beauty and, on all sides, there was a pulsing of life. The forest glades were already beginning to be covered with azure, dandelions shimmered on the early emerald green, and pink lilac anemones were bowing their tender heads. Swarms of midges and other insects appeared over the swamps; water-spiders were already engaged in pursuit of them; and birds of all sorts were gathering in the dry bulrushes. They were all assembling to have a look at each other. Of a sudden the earth was populous, the forests were wide awake, the meadows loud. The folk in the village had already started their dancing and singing. There was room enough for this merriment. How bright was the green! What freshness in the air! What twittering of birds in the orchards! What a paradise it was! What joy and exultation in everything! The countryside sang and chanted as at a wedding feast.

Chichikov did a lot of walking. There was no end to the promenades and enjoyments. Sometimes he would direct his steps along the flat top of the hillside, overlooking the plains spread out below where large lakes still remained after the floods had receded, with islands showing among them formed by the as yet leafless trees; at other times, he would penetrate into the thickets, into wooded ravines, where trees grew thickly loaded with birds' nests and where croaking ravens darkened the sky as they crossed each other in flight. When the ground had dried it was possible to make one's way to the quayside, from which the first barges were unmoored, loaded with peas, barley and wheat, while at the same time, with a deafening roar, the water gushed towards the wheel of the water-mill which was just resuming its work. He used to go and watch the first spring labours in the fields; he looked on as the plough cut a dark strip through the green grass and a peasant, tapping on the sieve which was slung from his neck on a level with his chest, scattered equal handfuls of seeds to left and right of him.

Chichikov went everywhere. He had his talks and discussions with the steward, the peasants, and the miller. He got to know everything, every little detail, how this was done and how that, how the estate was managed, how much they asked for their flour, how much they charged for grinding the corn in spring and autumn, and he found out the names of all the peasants, all their family relations, where they had bought their cows, what they fed their pigs on—in short, he got to know everything. He also learned how many peasants had died off; there were not very many. As an intelligent observer he could not help noticing soon that Tentetnikov's affairs were not being managed very efficiently: there was a great deal of waste, neglect, thieving, and quite a lot of drunkenness among the peasantry. And he thought to himself: 'All the same, what a pig this Tentetnikov is, to neglect his estate like this! He could be getting an income of fifty thousand a year from it!'

More than once in the course of his walks it occurred to him that he might—not just now, of course, but later on when he would have achieved his aim and had acquired the necessary resources—himself become the peaceful proprietor of such a domain. Then he would immediately picture to himself some fresh-complexioned young woman of the merchant class or some other well-to-do section of society, who would even be able to play the piano. He also envisaged a younger generation which was destined to perpetuate the Chichikov family: a frolicsome boy and a stunning daughter, or even two boys and two or three girls, so that everyone should know that he really existed and had not passed over the earth as a mere shadow or spectre; in fact, so that he should not be ashamed to look his country in the face. Then he even began to imagine that it would not be a bad idea for him to have some addition to his rank—that of a civil councillor, for example, an honoured and respected rank, would suit him perfectly. . . . What only does not come into a man's head when he is out walking! Things that often allow him to escape from the boring present, that rouse, stimulate and excite the imagination! And it all gives pleasure even when a man is not convinced that these things will ever come to pass!

Chichikov's servants also took a liking to the village. Like him, they became acclimatized. Petrushka was soon on the best of terms with Grigory, the kitchen boy, although at first they were unbearably uppish with each other. Petrushka took the wind out of Grigory by his account of his travels; Grigory at once floored him by claiming to know Petersburg, a place Petrushka had never visited. The latter attempted to recover his prestige by enumerating all the distant places he had passed through, but Grigory named a spot that could not be found on any map and counted up to twenty-five thousand miles or more, so that Chichikov's footman was quite flabbergasted and became the laughing-stock of the servants' quarters. This rivalry however ended in the closest of friendships. At one end of the village, Bald Pimen, the uncle of all the peasants, kept a gin-shop which was known by the name of 'Akulka'. The friends were to be seen in this establishment at all hours of the day. There, their friendship ripened and they became what folk call 'regulars'.

Selifan had other fish to fry. Almost every evening in the village songs were being sung and folk-dancing was in swing. He was forced to stand gaping for hours at the well-built village girls of good stock, such as are not to be found often in large villages these days. It was hard to decide which of them was fairer: they were all white-breasted, white-necked, they all had eyes like turnips— languishing eyes, they moved like peacocks and had plaits hanging down to their waist. When he held them by their white hands on each side of him, when he moved round slowly with them in the dance, or when he advanced upon them with other lads, like a wall, and when the girls, who were also moving in a wall towards them, sang out loudly: 'Boyars, show us the bridegroom!' as dusk softly settled on the countryside and the echo of the refrain was wafted sadly back from far beyond the river, Selifan did not know what was happening to him. In his sleep as well as when awake, in the morning as well as at dusk, he kept fancying that he was holding those white hands in both of his, and that he was moving round in the dance.

Chichikov's horses also took to their new home. The shaft-horse, the Assessor, and the dapple-grey, found their sojourn at Tentetnikov's anything but dull, the oats were excellent and the stables unusually comfortable. Each of them had a stall to himself and, though it was partitioned off, it was yet possible to see other horses, so that if any one of them took it into his head to neigh suddenly, it was possible to pay him back in the same coin.

In a word, everyone felt at home. As for the necessity which drove Chichikov to travel through the wide spaces of Russia, that is, the bait of the dead souls, he had now become very careful and tactful in broaching the subject even when he had to do with complete fools. But Tentetnikov went on quite blissfully reading his books, philosophizing, and trying to clarify for himself the various causes of everything—the why and wherefore of it all? 'No, I had better try the other way round,' Chichikov thought to himself. From his frequent chats with the domestics he had learnt among other things that their master had formerly used to frequent a neighbouring general, that the general had a daughter, and that their master had a liking for her which was reciprocated . . . but then for some reason they had fallen out and had stopped meeting. He had himself noticed that Tentetnikov was continually drawing with pen and pencil some sort of girlish heads, all as alike as two peas.

One day, after dinner, as he was making the silver snuff-box rotate as usual on its axis, he spoke as follows: 'You have everything, Tentetnikov, but one thing is lacking.'

'What?' the latter enquired as he blew out a puff of curly smoke.

'A life-partner,' said Chichikov.

Tentetnikov made no reply to this. On that the conversation ended.

Chichikov was not put out. He picked another opportunity, this time before supper, and, while talking of

this and that, he suddenly said: 'You know, Tentetnikov, it would not be a bad thing if you got married.'

But not a word did Tentetnikov utter. It was as though
any reference to the subject was disagreeable to him.

Chichikov was not put out. He picked another opportunity, after supper this time, and spoke thus: 'And yet,
however much I consider your circumstances, I am still
convinced that you must marry. You are falling into a
hypochondria.'

Whether it was that Chichikov's words were more
convincing this time, or whether he was more disposed to
be frank that day, Tentetnikov sighed and replied as he
puffed out a cloud of smoke: 'One has to be born lucky,
Pavel Ivanovich,' and he told Chichikov the whole story
of his acquaintanceship with the general and the reason
for their quarrel.

When Chichikov had heard the story word for word
and had realized that the whole misunderstanding had
come about from the use of the word 'thou', he was
dumbfounded. For a whole minute he stared fixedly at
Tentetnikov, undecided what to make of him: was he an
utter idiot or merely a fool?

'Andrey Ivanovich! I ask you!' he said, clasping
Tentetnikov's hands in his. 'But what sort of insult is that?
What is there insulting about the word "thou"?'

'There is nothing insulting in the word itself,' said
Tentetnikov, 'but there was in the sense in which the
word was used and in the tone in which it was spoken.
Thou! I took that to mean, "You must remember that
you are not worth much: I am receiving you only because
there is no one better around; but when a princess
Youzyakin visits me, then you must know your place and
stay in the background." That's what I take it to mean.'
As he said this, Tentetnikov's mild and gentle eyes
flashed; and his voice had a note in it of irritation and
offended feeling.

'But even if he had meant it in that sense, what is there
to take offence at?' said Chichikov.

'What! You expect me to continue seeing him after
such behaviour?'

'But what did he do? It can't even be called behaviour,' Chichikov said coolly.

'What do you mean? Not behaviour?' Tentetnikov asked with astonishment.

'Oh, it's not behaviour but just a general's habit: they all say "thou",' Chichikov replied. 'And besides, why shouldn't a worthy and respectable gentleman be allowed to say it?'

'That's a different question,' Tentetnikov said. 'If he were an old man and poor, neither proud nor boastful, and if he were not a general, then I would have allowed him to call me "thou" and I would even have respected him.'

'He's an utter idiot,' Chichikov thought to himself. 'To allow a beggar to say what he would not allow to a general.' 'All right!' he went on aloud. 'Let us suppose that he did insult you, but you have got your own back. You returned the compliment. To quarrel like that to the detriment of your personal affairs, that is, if you will excuse me, something I don't. . . . If you have once fixed on a goal, you must go through with it at any cost. Why bother if a man is condescending! Men are always snarling at each other, that's just human nature. You wouldn't find anyone in the whole wide world who wasn't like that.'

'What a strange man this Chichikov is!' Tentetnikov said to himself in perplexity, very worried by his statement.

'What an eccentric this Tentetnikov is!' Chichikov thought to himself in the meantime.

'Andrey Ivanovich! May I speak to you as a brother?' Chichikov now addressed himself to Tentetnikov. 'You lack experience. Allow me to arrange this matter for you. I shall call on His Excellency and explain to him it was all a misunderstanding due to your youth and the lack of knowledge of people and the world.'

'I have no intention of crawling before him!' Tentetnikov declared, taking offence. 'Nor can I authorize you to do as you suggest.'

'I am not capable of crawling before anyone,' Chichikov exclaimed, taking offence in his turn. 'I may err in other ways since human nature is frail, but I am incapable of meanness—never. . . . You must excuse me, Andrey Ivanovich, for my good intentions; I did not expect you to put such an offensive interpretation on my words.' Chichikov said all this with a great feeling of dignity.

'It's my fault, you must excuse me!' Tentetnikov was touched, and he spoke hurriedly as he took Chichikov's hands in his. 'I had no intention of offending you. I am ready to swear that I value your kind intervention! But let us stop talking about this matter. Let us never broach it again!'

'In that case I shall pay a call on the general anyway.'

'Why?' Tentetnikov asked, looking into his eyes in a perplexed sort of way.

'Oh, just to pay my respects.'

'What a strange man this Chichikov is!' Tentetnikov thought.

'What a strange man this Tentetnikov is!' Chichikov thought.

'I shall drive out to see him to-morrow at about ten o'clock in the morning,' Chichikov said. 'In my opinion, the sooner one pays one's respects the better. Since my chaise has not yet been put right, may I take one of your carriages? I should like to drive out and see him at about ten to-morrow morning.'

'But certainly. What a request! You are master here. The carriage and everything else are at your disposal.'

Following that conversation, they took leave of each other and went off to bed, but not without reflecting upon each other's eccentricities.

But how strange! On the following day, when the carriage was brought round and Chichikov had leapt into it with almost the agility of a smart officer, dressed as he was in a new frock-coat, a white tie and a white waistcoat, and when he had rolled off to pay his respects to the general, a feeling of agitation such as he had not experienced for a long time seized hold of Tentetnikov. The whole course of his drowsy and rusty thoughts was transformed into an agitated flow. A state of nervous indignation took hold of him and all the emotions of a hitherto slothful dreamer, who spent his days in mindless languor, now came to the surface. He would sit down on the sofa, then get up and go to the window, then he would pick up a book, or he would try to think, but it was all in vain! He could not concentrate his thoughts. And he even found it useless to try and not think about anything! Fragments of thoughts, bits and ends of thoughts, these, indeed, came pouring in from all sides and stuck in his head. 'A strange state of affairs!' he said to himself as he moved nearer the window and stared out at the road, cut through a grove of oaks; at the end of it could be seen a cloud of dust which had not yet had time to settle. But let us leave Tentetnikov and follow Chichikov.

CHAPTER II

In just over half an hour the good horses had transported Chichikov over a distance of seven miles, at first through an oak grove, then by cornfields just beginning to turn green in the midst of freshly ploughed land, then through hilly country with frequent views of the open fields, and at last through a broad avenue of lime-trees which brought him straight into the middle of the village. The avenue of lime-trees took a turning to the right and, becoming transformed into a street of poplars protected at their base by wicker boxes, ran alongside the open-work iron-wrought gates through which could be seen the richly ornate façade of the general's house with its eight Corinthian columns. Everywhere there was a smell of oil-paint with which everything had been newly refreshed so that nothing was allowed to fade. The yard was as clean as a parquet floor. Chichikov climbed out of the chaise with a feeling of respect, ordered his arrival to be reported to the general and was taken straight into his study.

The general's majestic appearance astonished him. He was attired in a crimson quilted-satin dressing-gown. He had an open and virile countenance, moustaches, and large, grizzled whiskers; his hair was closely cropped, and his neck was a thick one, in three storeys or three

folds as they say, with a crease across the middle of it—
he was one of those picturesque generals who were so
plentiful in the famous year of 1812. General Betrishchev,
like most of us, had many good qualities and many failings.
As is usual with Russians, these were all mixed in colour-
ful profusion. In critical moments he was magnanimous,
brave, boundlessly generous and quite sagacious; but he
was also capricious, ambitious, vain and had other such
petty characteristics as no Russian lacks when he lives in
idleness. He disliked everyone who had got promotion
ahead of him in the service, and he referred to them in
biting and sarcastic epigrams. He was particularly bitter
in his references to a former colleague of his, whom he
regarded as inferior to himself in mind and ability, but
who had nevertheless outdistanced him and was already
the governor-general of two provinces and, to make it
worse, of the province in which he had his estate, so that
he found himself in a sense dependent on his former
colleague. By way of revenge general Betrishchev jeered
at him, censured all his orders and saw only the height
of folly in all his acts and measures. Among his many
peculiarities was the question of enlightenment, of which
he was a champion and zealot; he liked to be informed
about things of which other people were ignorant, and he
disliked people who knew something he did not know. In
short, he loved to parade his knowledge. Although his
education had been half foreign, he wanted at the same
time to play the part of a Russian landed gentleman. In
view of his uneven character and the innate and obvious
contradictions of his nature, it is not surprising that he
was inevitably involved in many unpleasant situations in
the service, and that he had retired as a result of them,
putting the blame on some hostile party and lacking the
magnanimity to hold himself responsible for anything at
all. In his retirement he preserved his picturesque and
majestic carriage. He made the same impression whether
he was wearing a jacket, a tailed-coat, or a dressing-gown.
Everything about him, from his voice to his slightest
movement, was commanding, dominating, and inspiring
of at least awe, if not respect, from his inferiors.

He inspired Chichikov with both awe and respect. Bending his head sideways respectfully and holding out his hands as though about to raise a tray loaded with cups, Chichikov bowed from the waist with amazing agility and said: 'I thought it my duty to pay my compliments to Your Excellency. Respecting as I do the bravery of the men who saved our country on the field of battle, I thought it my duty to present myself personally to Your Excellency.'

The general evidently did not dislike this approach. With a benevolent nod of his head he said: 'Very glad to meet you. Will you please take a seat. Where have you served?'

'My career in the service,' said Chichikov, sitting down not in the middle but on the edge of the armchair, and grasping the arm of it with one hand, 'My service career began in the Treasury, Your Excellency. I was in various other posts later on: I have been in the Imperial Court, in the Building Commission and in the Customs and Excise. My life may be compared to a ship in stormy seas, Your Excellency. It may be said that I am woven of or wrapped in patience; I represent, so to speak, a personification of patience. . . . And what have I not suffered from enemies who have even made attempts on my life! Neither words, nor colours, nor even a painter's brush itself could convey it, and so in my declining years I am searching for a nook where I might spend the rest of my days. In the meantime I am staying with a near neighbour of Your Excellency's.'

'And who is it?'

'Tentetnikov, Your Excellency.'

The general frowned.

'Oh, Your Excellency, he is most sorry for the disrespect he showed you . . .'

'Disrespect for what?'

'For Your Excellency's great merits,' Chichikov replied. 'He can't find words. . . . He says, "If I only could make it up . . ." he says. "I know how to appreciate men who have saved our country," he says.'

'I pray you, what is it all about? I am not angry with

him,' said the general, relenting. 'At heart I am quite fond of him and I am positive that in time he will become a most useful person.'

'You have expressed yourself most aptly, Your Excellency. Yes, indeed, a most useful man. He has the gift of words and a mastery of the pen.'

'But I expect he writes trifling stuff—verses?'

'No, Your Excellency, not trifling stuff. . . . He has got a serious work in hand. . . . He is writing . . . a history, Your Excellency.'

'A history? What of?'

'A history . . .' At this point Chichikov paused, and either because a general was sitting in front of him or simply because he wished to give more weight to his theme, he added: 'A history of generals, Your Excellency.'

'How do you mean of generals? Of what generals?'

'Of generals in general, Your Excellency. That is to say, more precisely of patriotic generals.'

Chichikov was becoming involved and confused. He almost spat out as he said to himself: 'Oh Lord, what nonsense I am blabbing!'

'But excuse me, I don't quite understand. . . . What is it going to be? A history of a given period or a series of individual biographies? And in the latter case, will it be that of all generals or only of those who took part in the patriotic campaign of 1812?'

'Exactly so, Your Excellency, of those who took part in the war of 1812!' Having said that he thought to himself: 'You might kill me but I haven't the foggiest notion where I am!'

'Then why doesn't he call on me? I could furnish him with a great deal of quite interesting material.'

'He's too diffident, Your Excellency.'

'Nonsense! Just because of a silly word uttered by chance when we last met. . . . I am not that sort of person. I wouldn't mind calling on him myself.'

'He wouldn't dream of letting you do that, he will call on you himself,' said Chichikov, who had now quite recovered and become cheerful. And he thought to himself: 'What luck! These generals have come in handy although it was quite by chance that I mentioned them.'

There was suddenly a rustling sound in the study. The walnut door of a carved cupboard flew open, and on the other side of it a slender, living figure appeared with one hand on the brass knob of the door. If an oil-painting had suddenly been lit up from behind and made transparent, it would not have caused as much surprise as the apparition of this figure. It was apparent that it had come to say something to the general, but on seeing a complete stranger. . . . It was as though it had brought a ray of sunshine with it and the general's frowning study had burst into laughter. For a minute Chichikov could not explain to himself what it was precisely that he had in front of him. It was hard to say of what land she was the native. It would have been impossible to find anywhere except perhaps on ancient cameos such pure and noble features. Straight and light as an arrow, she seemed to dominate everyone in height. But that was only an illusion. She was not really tall. It was the result of the extraordinary symmetry of all the parts of her body. Her dress fitted her so perfectly that it gave one the impression that the best of dressmakers had consulted together how to adorn her. But that also was an illusion. It was as though her dress fitted her naturally: a few stitches of the needle and an uncut piece of material had draped her in such tucks and folds that, if she were to be painted in her dress, all the fashionably attired young ladies would have seemed like popinjays or something from the rag and bone shop by comparison. And if she were to be chiselled in marble, with all her tucks and folds, the sculpture would have been pronounced a work of genius. She had only one defect: she was too thin and slender.

'May I present my spoilt darling?' said the general, turning to Chichikov. 'But what is your surname, Christian name and patronymic?'

'But why should you bother about the name of one who has no great achievements to boast of?' Chichikov answered modestly, bending his head slightly to one side.

'But of course we must know it. . . .'

'Pavel Ivanovich, Your Excellency,' said Chichikov, bowing almost as smartly as an officer and leaping backwards with all the ease of a rubber ball.

'Ulinka!' said the general, turning to his daughter. 'Pavel Ivanovich has just told me an interesting piece of news. Our neighbour Tentetnikov is not quite the fool we took him to be. He is engaged on a work of some importance—a history of the generals of the campaign of 1812.'

'But who ever believed that he was a fool?' she said quickly. 'Only Vishnepokromov perhaps, whom you trust although he is feather-brained and contemptible as a person.'

'Why contemptible? But feather-brained, yes, he is that,' said the general.

'He's not only feather-brained but mean and revolting,' Ulinka said. 'Anyone is a revolting person who treats his brothers so abominably and turns his own sister out of the house.'

'But that's only rumour.'

'People wouldn't say things like that if there was nothing behind it. I don't understand, father, that a man with a heart of gold like yours can go on receiving a person who is poles apart from you and whom you yourself know to be a bad character.'

'So you see now,' said the general, laughing. 'We are always quarrelling like this.' And turning to his quarrelsome daughter he continued:

'But, my love, I couldn't send him packing, could I?'

'No need to send him packing! But why be so attentive to him? Why be fond of him?'

At this stage Chichikov thought it was timely to insert a word of his own.

'Everyone expects to be loved, miss,' said Chichikov. 'What's to be done? Even a cow loves to be stroked and will thrust its muzzle out at you from a stall. "Here, stroke me!" it will say.'

The general burst out laughing. 'Exactly so. It will thrust out its muzzle: "stroke me!" . . . Ha, ha, ha! Not only is the fellow's face all plastered with soot but he's entirely covered in it, and yet he asks, as they say, to be encouraged. . . . Ha, ha, ha!' The general's body began to shake with laughter. His shoulders, which once carried thick epaulettes, were quivering as if the epaulettes were still there.

Chichikov also ventured to laugh, but out of respect for the general he pitched his laughter in a lower key. He, he, he, he! And his body also began to shake, although for want of thick epaulettes his shoulders did not quiver.

'He'll clean out the Treasury, the rogue, and then expect a reward into the bargain! "I can't do without encouragement," he will say. "I did my best. . . ." Ha, ha, ha, ha!'

A painful expression crossed the girl's noble face. 'Oh, papa! How can you laugh like that! Such dishonesty depresses me, that's all. Whenever I see deceit being perpetrated in the sight of all and those responsible escape the contempt of all, I do not know what happens to me but I grow spiteful and even vicious: I think, think. . . .' And she almost burst out crying.

'But only please don't be angry with us,' said the general. 'We are not to blame. Isn't that so?' he said, turning to Chichikov. 'Now come, give me a kiss and go back to your room. I shall begin dressing for dinner in a moment.' And turning to Chichikov and looking him straight in the eyes he said, quite familiarly this time: 'And you, I hope, will stay for dinner?'

'Your Excellency, if only that is not . . .'

'Without ceremony. Thank God. I can still entertain my guests. There is some cabbage soup.'

Chichikov dropped his arms smartly and bowed with such gratitude and respect that for a time all the objects in the room vanished from his sight and he could only see the tips of his own boots. When, after keeping his head in that respectful position for some time, he raised his head once more, he did not see Ulinka. She had disappeared. In her place a giant of a butler had appeared, with thick moustaches and whiskers, holding a silver wash-basin in his hands.

'You don't mind if I dress in front of you?'

'Your Excellency may not only dress but do whatever he thinks fit in front of me,' said Chichikov.

Slipping off his dressing-gown and rolling up the sleeves of his shirt over his heroic arms, the general began to wash himself, splashing and snorting like a duck. The soapy water flew in all directions.

'They love, indeed, they love to be encouraged,' said the general as he dried his neck. . . . 'Stroke him, yes, stroke him! Why, without encouragement he would not even steal! Ha, ha, ha!'

Chichikov was in indescribably good spirits. Suddenly he had an inspiration. 'The general is a merry soul and a kind fellow—why not try?' he thought to himself and, noticing that the butler had gone out, he exclaimed: 'Your Excellency! Since you are so kind to every one and attentive, I have a great favour to ask you.'

'What is it?'

Chichikov first looked round him.

'There is a decayed old man, a sort of uncle I have who owns about three hundred souls . . . and I am the only heir. He's so gaga that he can't manage the estate himself, but he won't let me do it either. And this is the strange reason he gives for it: "I don't know my nephew very well," he says. "He may be no good. Let him prove first of all that he is a reliable fellow: let him acquire three hundred serfs for himself first; and then I will leave him my three hundred souls."'

'Is he crazy or what?' said the general.

'I wouldn't mind that, Your Excellency, as long as he held on to his property. But judge my position, Your Excellency! The old man has now got a housekeeper living with him and she has children. If I'm not careful he will leave it all to them.'

'He's out of his senses, the old man, that's all there is to it,' said the general. 'But I don't see how I can help,' he said, looking with surprise at Chichikov.

'I have an idea,' Chichikov replied. 'Now if you were to transfer to me all your dead peasants, Your Excellency, so that it looked as if they were still alive in the deed of purchase, I could then show this deed to the old man, and he would leave me his property.'

At this the general burst out into such laughter as had never been heard before. He even collapsed into an armchair. The whole house was alarmed. The butler came on the scene. The daughter ran in with a startled look on her face.

'Father, what is the matter?' she asked in alarm, gazing into his eyes with perplexity.

But for a long while the general could utter no sound.

'Nothing, nothing, my dear,' he gasped out at last. 'Don't worry. Go back to your room: we shall come in for dinner in a moment. Don't be alarmed. Ha, ha, ha!'

Fighting for breath, the general once more burst into uncontrollable laughter which echoed through the whole house. Chichikov was becoming uneasy.

'What an uncle, what an uncle! What a fool he will be made to look! Ha, ha, ha! And he will get a lot of dead folk instead of real peasants! Ha, ha!'

'He's off again!' thought Chichikov to himself. 'Blast him, how ticklish he is! He might burst!'

'Ha, ha, ha!' the general continued. 'What an ass he is! What an idea to get into his head: let him acquire first of all three hundred souls himself, then I will let him have three hundred of my own! What an ass!'

'An ass, Your Excellency!'

'And then your idea of placating the old man with these dead souls. Ha, ha, ha! I'd give God knows what to be present and to see you hand over the deed of purchase. Well, and what is he like? What sort of an old man is he? Is he very old?'

'About eighty.'

'But still he gets about, doesn't he? In good health, is he? He must be hearty still to have a housekeeper living with him? . . .'

'He's as strong as a horse, Your Excellency!'

'What a fool! He is a fool, isn't he?'

'A fool, Your Excellency.'

'But he still drives about? He still pays his social calls, doesn't he? He's still steady on his feet, isn't he?'

'Not too steady, Your Excellency.'

'What a fool! But he is still quite strong, isn't he? Has he any teeth left?'

'Only two teeth, Your Excellency.'

'What an ass! You musn't be angry with me. . . . He may be your uncle but he is an ass all the same.'

'An ass, Your Excellency. Although he is a relative of mine and it is hard for me to confess it, but he is!'

Chichikov was of course lying: it was not hard at all for him to make that confession, especially as it is unlikely that he ever had an uncle.

'So, Your Excellency, you will let me have them. . . .'

'The dead souls? Yes, for such an idea I'd be ready to give them to you with the land and houses thrown in! You may take the whole cemetery! Ha, ha, ha! What an old man! Ha, ha, ha, ha! What a fool you will make of him! Ha, ha, ha!'

And the general's laughter went on echoing through the whole house.

(*The rest of this chapter is missing in the manuscript.*)

CHAPTER III

'IF colonel Koshkaryov is as mad as they say he is, that's not at all a bad thing,' Chichikov said to himself as they drove once more through the open fields after they had left everything behind them and there was only the firmament, with two clouds floating in it, above them.

'Selifan, did you make sure of the way to colonel Koshkaryov's?' he asked his coachman.

'I was so busy attending to the chaise, your honour, I didn't have time. But Petrushka asked the other coachman.'

'You are a fool! Didn't I tell you not to rely on Petrushka!' Chichikov exclaimed. 'Petrushka is a blockhead! Petrushka is stupid! I'm sure Petrushka has had a drop too much!'

'One might think great learning was required!' Petrushka said as he swung half round looking sulkily.

'There is nothing in it except to go downhill and then turn through the meadows.'

'I see you haven't tasted anything but cheap brandy! You're a fine fellow, that's obvious! One can really say that you have astonished Europe by the beauty of your looks!' Having said that Chichikov stroked his chin and thought to himself: 'What a gulf there is after all between an enlightened citizen's face and a coarse footman's physiognomy!'

Meanwhile the chaise began to go downhill. They were now driving through fields and open spaces studded here and there with groves of aspen trees. With an occasional gentle shudder of its springs the carriage continued to roll down the almost imperceptible slope until, finally, it was driving over the fields again past windmills, swaying gently over the yielding ground of the plain. There were no tree stumps and no bumps. Their progress was as smooth as could be!

As they drove quickly past bushes, slender alder-trees and silvery poplars, the branches brushed against Selifan and Petrushka, who were sitting on the driver's seat. Petrushka had his cap swept off more than once. The sulky footman would jump down, swear at the tree and at whoever had planted it, but he refused to tie on his cap or even to hold it with his hand, hoping that each time it fell off would be the last. Soon birch-trees and fir-trees also came on the scene, their bases thickly overgrown with grass, sweet-rush and tulips. The forest grew as dark as though night were descending. But of a sudden glimmers of light, like bright mirrors, flashed from all sides through the branches and tree-trunks. The trees thinned out, the glimmers became brighter, and there, in front of them, lay a lake, an expanse of water some three miles across. On the other side of the lake, on the slope above it, the wooden huts of a village could be seen. A noise of shouting was coming from the lake: some twenty men, up to their waists, shoulders or necks in the water, were dragging a net to the opposite shore. There had been an accident. A stout man, as broad as he was long, and very like a water-melon or barrel in appearance, had got entangled in the net together with the fish. He was in a desperate fix and was shouting for all he was worth: 'Denis, hand over to Kozma! Kozma, grab the end from Denis! Don't tug so hard, Foma the Big! Go and join Foma the Little! Ah, the devils! I tell you, you will break the net!' The water-melon man was evidently not apprehensive on his own account: he was so stout that he could not drown, and however much he might plunge and dive he would have floated to the surface in any case; even if two men had sat on his back he would still have remained on the surface like an obstinate bubble, only puffing a little under them and blowing bubbles out of his nose. But he was very much afraid lest the net might burst and the fish escape and, in order to avoid that, he had been secured by ropes while several men on shore pulled him in and others tugged at the net.

'That must be the master, colonel Koshkaryov,' Selifan said.

'Why do you think that?' Chichikov asked.

'Because his body, as you can see, is whiter than that of the others, and he is quite respectably stout, like you, sir,' Selifan replied.

Meanwhile the entangled gentleman had been pulled in much nearer the shore. Feeling that he could reach the bottom he stood up at last and, as he did so, perceived the carriage rolling over the dam with Chichikov sitting in it.

'Have you dined?' the gentleman shouted, making his way on shore, still entangled in the net together with fish. He resembled a lady's hand encased in a light, open-work glove such as is worn in summer. With one hand he shielded his eyes from the sun; the other he held like Botticelli's[8] Venus emerging from the sea.

'No, I haven't,' Chichikov replied, raising his cap and bowing as he sat in the carriage.

'Well then, you may thank God!'

'And why should I do that?' Chichikov enquired with curiosity as he held his cap above his head.

'That's why!' the gentleman replied. 'Foma the Little,

8. Sandro Botticelli (1445–1510), famous Italian painter.

let go the net and show us the sturgeon! Go and help him, Kozma!'

The two fishermen lifted up a monstrous head. 'Look at the prince! He must have swum in from the river!' the stout gentleman was shouting. 'Now you must drive on to the house! Coachman, will you take the road lower down, the one through the orchard! Run along, Foma the Big, and take down the hurdle! He'll show you the way. I'll catch up with you. . . .'

The long-legged Foma the Big, barefoot as he was and wearing only a shirt, ran ahead of the carriage the length of the whole village, in which each hut had nets and fishes' heads hanging out in front of them, for all the inhabitants were fishermen; then he moved aside a hurdle, which barred the way into an orchard, and the carriage went driving through until it reached a square in the vicinity of a wooden church. Farther on, beyond the church, could be seen the roofs of the master's houses.

'This Koshkaryov is an eccentric,' Chichikov thought to himself.

'And here am I,' a voice beside him announced. Chichikov looked round. The gentleman was driving close to him; he had already had time to dress; he was wearing yellow trousers and a grass-green nankeen jacket, but his shirt was open at the neck like Cupid's. He was sitting sideways on the droshky, filling it completely. Chichikov was about to say something to him but the stout gentleman had already vanished. The droshky reappeared on the spot where they were pulling out the net, and once more his voice could be heard calling out: 'Foma the Big and Foma the Little! Kozma and Denis!' But when Chichikov was driving up to the porch of the master's house, he saw to his great surprise that the stout gentleman was already standing on the steps and there he embraced him. Chichikov could not make out how he had managed to get ahead of him. They kissed each other thrice according to the old Russian custom: the gentleman was of the old school.

'I have brought you greetings from His Excellency,' Chichikov announced.

'From which Excellency?' the other enquired.

'From your relative, general Alexander Dmitrievich.'

'Who is this Alexander Dmitrievich?'

'General Betrishchev,' Chichikov replied with some surprise.

'I don't know him,' the gentleman said, equally surprised.

Chichikov was now positively astonished.

'How's that? . . . I hope that I have at least the pleasure of talking to colonel Koshkaryov?'

'No, don't hope that. You are not in his house but in mine. Pyotr Petrovich Petukh,[9] that's my name! Petukh, Pyotr Petrovich,' the host hurried to add.

Chichikov was dumbfounded. 'How is that?' he said, turning to Selifan and Petrushka, who were gaping with their mouths wide open, the one as he sat on the driver's seat and the other as he stood by the door of the carriage. 'You fools, what have you been doing? Didn't I tell you to drive to colonel Koshkaryov's. . . . But this gentleman here is Pyotr Petrovich Petukh. . . .'

'Your servants have done excellently! Now off with you to the kitchen. You'll be given some vodka there,' said Petukh. 'Unharness the horses first and then go at once to the servants' quarters!'

'I feel very embarrassed,' said Chichikov. 'It was a mistake, it was quite unexpected.'

'No mistake at all. You must taste the dinner first and then decide whether it was a mistake or not. Will you please come along?'; and as he said that Petukh took Chichikov by the arm and led him inside. There they were met by two youths in summer suits, both of them as thin as a rake; they were each a foot or two taller than their father.

'Here are my sons. They are on their holidays from the gymnasium[1] . . . Nikolasha, will you stay with the guest; and you, Aleksasha, come with me.' Having said that, the host disappeared.

Chichikov now occupied himself with Nikolasha. It

9. *Petukh* means "rooster" in Russian.   1. Secondary school.

looked to him as though Nikolasha would turn out to be a good-for-nothing. He told Chichikov at once that there was not much point in studying at a provincial gymnasium and that he and his brother wished to go to Petersburg because the provinces were not worth living in. . . .

'I understand,' Chichikov thought to himself. 'I know how it will all end—with tea-shops and the boulevards . . .' 'And how are affairs on your father's estate?' he enquired aloud.

'Mortgaged,' replied the father himself, who had returned in the meantime to the drawing-room. 'Mortgaged!'

'Very bad,' Chichikov thought to himself. 'At that rate there will be no estates left soon. I must make haste.' 'A pity, a great pity,' he said aloud in a sympathetic tone. 'You were in a hurry to mortgage it.'

'Oh, it doesn't matter,' said Petukh. 'They say it's profitable. Every one is mortgaging his estate. Why should I lag behind? And besides I have always lived here. Why shouldn't I try and live in Moscow for a change? My sons too are persuading me to live there, they want all the enlightenment that a city can give.'

'What a fool, what a fool!' thought Chichikov. 'To waste his substance and to make ne'er-do-wells out of his sons! He's got quite a respectable estate. The peasants look well off and their masters are not badly off either. But when they start enlightening themselves in restaurants and theatres, then all this will go to the devil. He should stay in the country, the trout!'

'I know what you are thinking,' Petukh said.

'What?' Chichikov asked, abashed.

'You are thinking, "That Petukh is a fool, a fool. He asked me to dinner and the dinner has not yet been served." But it will be ready, my dear sir, it will. In less time than it takes a cropped wench to plait her hair it will all be ready.'

'Father! Platon Mikhailovich is coming!' Aleksasha cried out, looking out of the window.

'Where? Where?' Petukh shouted as he went up to the window.

'Who is Platon Mikhailovich?' Chichikov asked Aleksasha.

'A neighbour of ours, Platon Mikhailovich Platonov, an excellent person, a really excellent person,' Petukh himself replied.

Meanwhile Platonov himself entered the room. He was a handsome and well-built man with light-reddish, curly hair. A great big monstrous dog, called Yarb, stalked in after him, wearing a brass collar that made a rattling noise.

'Have you dined?' the host enquired.

'Yes, I have.'

'Have you come to mock at me then? What's the use of you after you have dined?'

The visitor smiled and replied: 'If it's any comfort to you, then I have not eaten: I simply have no appetite.'

'You should have seen the catch! What a sturgeon we caught! And you should just see the shell-fish!'

'It makes me sad to hear you talking like that!' the visitor said. 'Why are you always so jolly?'

'And why should I be sad, I ask you?' the host enquired.

'What do you mean, why be sad? Because life's boring,' the visitor replied.

'You eat too little, that what's wrong with you,' the host declared. 'Now you must try and dine well. This boredom of yours is a recent invention: no one was ever sad in the old days.'

'That's enough of your boasting!' the visitor exclaimed. 'You can't tell me you have never been bored?'

'Never! I don't know what it's like, I just haven't time to be bored. As soon as I wake up the cook is already asking me what I shall have for dinner. Then it's teatime, then the steward comes along, then there's the fishing, and then it's dinner-time. I haven't a moment for a snooze after dinner but the cook is back again asking what I shall have for supper. And then there is tomorrow's dinner to think about. . . . When have I time for being bored?'

During this conversation Chichikov was scrutinizing Platonov, who astonished him by his unusually handsome appearance, by his picturesque build and size, by the freshness of his unexhausted youthfulness, and by the maidenly purity of his face which was unblemished by a single pimple. Neither passion nor sadness, nor anything resembling agitation or restlessness, would have as much as dared to cross his virgin face and leave on it the imprint of a frown; nor would they have enlivened it. For despite an occasional ironic smile Platonov's face somehow managed to preserve a drowsy look.

'If you will allow me to say so, I also fail to understand how you can feel bored, with an appearance such as you have got,' Chichikov said. 'Of course you may be short of money or you may have enemies who think nothing of attempting your life. . . .'

'Believe me,' the handsome visitor interrupted him, 'for the sake of variety I would sometimes willingly be frightened. If only somebody would put me in a rage, but even that never happens. I only feel bored and nothing else.'

'Then probably you have too little land on your estate? Or too few peasants?' Chichikov said.

'No, that's not it. My brother and I between us have thirty thousand acres and over a thousand peasants,' Platonov replied.

'How strange! I don't understand. But perhaps you've been suffering from bad crops and epidemics? Perhaps a lot of your male serfs have died off?' Chichikov enquired.

'On the contrary,' Platonov said. 'Things could not be better, and my brother is an excellent manager.'

'And yet you feel bored! I don't understand it,' Chichikov said and shrugged his shoulders.

'And now we shall send boredom packing,' the host said. 'Run along quickly Aleksasha to the kitchen and tell the cook to send up some savouries as soon as possible. And where is that dawdler Emilyan and that thief of an Antoshka? Why aren't they serving the snacks?'

But the door opened. Emilyan the dawdler and Antoshka the thief appeared with the napkins, laid the table, and set down a tray with six decanters of various coloured home-brewed wines. A necklet of plates with every kind of tempting savoury on them was soon surrounding the trays and decanters. The servants moved about smartly, bringing in covered plates which gave off a sizzling sound of melted butter. Dawdling Emilyan and the thieving Antoshka were coping splendidly with their task. Their nicknames had been given them only for the sake of encouragement. Their master was no bully, he was kind of heart; but a Russian cannot do without spice in his conversation. He needs it to help his digestion as much as a glass of vodka. What is to be done? Such is his nature: he is not fond of anything stale.

After the snacks came the dinner. Here the good-natured host let himself go. As soon as he noticed that a guest had only one piece of anything left, he immediately helped him to another, saying as he did so: 'Neither men nor birds can survive without pairing.' If anyone had two morsels left, he added a third, saying: 'Two doesn't go far. God favours the Trinity.' If a guest had three morsels, the host would say to him: 'Where have you seen a cart on three wheels? Or a house with three corners?' He had an apt phrase for four morsels, and for five also. Chichikov had already eaten almost twelve morsels and was thinking to himself: 'Well, now that's floored him.' But nothing of the sort: without a word the host helped him to some veal chops grilled on a spit, with kidneys thrown in. And what veal chops they were too!

'I reared that calf for two years on milk,' Petukh said. 'I looked after him as I would after my own son.'

'I really couldn't manage any more,' said Chichikov.

'But you must try it first and then say you "can't".'

'I've no room left,' Chichikov replied.

'There was no room in church, but when the mayor came in room was found all right,' the host retorted. 'And there was such a crush that there wasn't even room for an apple to fall. Just try—that's the mayor's morsel.'

Chichikov applied himself: and the morsel did indeed prove something in the nature of a mayor. It squeezed into a space where there seemed no space left. 'Now

how will such a man survive in Petersburg or Moscow?'
Chichikov asked himself. 'With such a hospitable nature
he would ruin himself within three years!' But Chichikov
did not know what has since become a commonplace,
that one can ruin oneself not in three years but in three
months without indulging even in hospitality.

The host kept filling their glasses: whatever was left
over he passed to Aleksasha and Nikolasha, who downed
one glass after another; it was already obvious on what
branch of human endeavour they would concentrate
when they reached the capital. The guests by now could
hardly stir: they barely managed to drag themselves on
to the balcony and it was with difficulty that they sank
into their armchairs. The host sank back into his own
four-seater armchair and dozed off at once. His massive
person, transformed now into a bellows, began to give
forth by means of his open mouth and his nasal outlets
such sounds as could rarely be imagined by any writer;
they partook at once of a drum, a flute and an intermit-
tent roar not unlike the barking of dogs.

'Blast him, how he whistles!' Platonov said.

Chichikov burst out laughing.

'No wonder he doesn't feel bored after such a sumptuous repast!' Platonov continued. 'Anyone would feel
sleepy after it, wouldn't he?'

'Yes. But if you will excuse me, I still cannot understand how one can feel so bored,' Chichikov said. 'There
are so many ways of warding off boredom.'

'What are they?' Platonov asked.

'A young man would find many ways,' Chichikov
replied. 'There is dancing, the mastery of some musical
instrument . . . or marriage, of course.'

'With whom?'

'Aren't there plenty of rich and beautiful brides in the
locality?' Chichikov asked.

'No, there aren't.'

'Well then, one could look for them elsewhere. One
might do a little travelling.' A fruitful idea suddenly
occurred to Chichikov. 'Yes, that is a marvellous way!'
he exclaimed, looking straight into Platonov's eyes.

'What is it?'

'Why, travelling of course,' Chichikov replied.

'Where would one go?'

'Well, if you are at liberty to do so, why not come along with me?' Chichikov said, thinking to himself as he looked at Platonov: 'That would be an excellent thing. We could share expenses, and he could foot the whole bill for the repairs of the carriage.'

'And where are you going?' Platonov enquired.

'For the time being I am travelling not so much for my own sake as out of an obligation I have for another person. General Betrishchev, a close friend of mine and, I may also say, a benefactor, begged me to visit a number of his relatives. . . . Of course, relatives are just relatives, but at the same time there is some pleasure to be got out of it for oneself, one sees the world, how people live and, whatever you may say, it's all like a book come to life, a second science.' And as he said that Chichikov was thinking to himself: 'It would really be an excellent idea. I might even get him to foot all the expenses, and even make use of his horses while mine could stay behind in his village and find some proper nourishment.'

'And why shouldn't I do a little travelling?' Platonov was thinking to himself in the meantime. 'There is nothing for me to do at home, my brother manages the estate; therefore there would be no upset. Why shouldn't I do a little travelling?' Aloud he said: 'And would you agree to spend a day or two at my brother's? Otherwise he would not let me go.'

'With the greatest of pleasure. Even three days if you like.'

'Fine! It's agreed then! Let's travel!' Platonov decided, brightening up.

They shook hands. 'Let us be off!' they both cried.

'Where are you off to, where?' the host shouted, waking up and gaping at them. 'No, my dear sirs! I ordered the wheels of your carriage to be removed and as for your horse, Platonov, he's pasturing ten miles from here. No, you will spend the night here with me, but you may depart to-morrow after an early lunch.'

What could they do with Petukh? There was nothing left but to stay the night. They were rewarded, however, by a wonderful spring evening. The host arranged an outing on the river. Twelve rowers with two oars apiece, singing as they rowed, swept them over the smooth surface of the glassy lake. From the lake they were rowed into the river, which flowed on endlessly between sloping banks, frequently having to pass under cables which had been stretched across the river as an aid to fishing. There was not a ripple on the water; one view succeeded another in silence and one grove after another consoled their gaze with its varied compositions of trees. Plying their two dozen oars the rowers would of a sudden raise them all and, like a bird, the boat would skim the still surface of the glassy waters. The choir leader, a hefty broad-shouldered lad, who was number three in the boat, would make his pure ringing voice heard, issuing as from a nightingale's throat as he intoned the initial refrains of a song; five more would take him up, six others would chime in, and the song would come pouring out as illimitable as Russia itself. And as though shaking his wings, cock-like, Petukh added his hoarse note whenever the choir flagged; and even Chichikov felt himself to be a Russian. Platonov was the only one to say to himself: 'What's the point of this monotonous song? It only makes one feel sadder.'

It was already dusk when they were returning. Blindly the oars struck the water which no longer reflected the sky. It was quite dark when they reached the shore along which several fires were blazing: over these, tripods had been set, and the fishermen were preparing a soup for themselves out of fresh and still quivering fish they had just caught. Everything else had already turned in. The geese and the chickens, the cows and the horses, had already been locked up; the dust they had raised had had time to settle; and the shepherds who had driven the cattle home were waiting by the gates for their jug of milk and to be invited to partake of the fishermen's soup. The quiet hum of conversation, and the barking of dogs in other villages, resounded through the twilight air. The moon was ascending and beginning to light up the shadowy neighbourhood. Then suddenly everything was brightly illumined. What wonderful scenes those were! But there was no one to admire them. Instead of galloping past them on their two spirited horses, Nikolasha and Aleksasha were dreaming of Moscow, the tea-shops and the theatres of which they had heard their fill from a visiting cadet; their father was pondering how he might fatten his guests; Platonov kept yawning. Chichikov was livelier than any of them. 'Really, I must get myself a village!' he said to himself as he pictured his future wife and a brood of Chichicks.

They gorged themselves again over supper. When Chichikov at last repaired to his bedroom he put his hand on his belly as he got into bed: 'A real drum!' he said to himself. 'No mayor could get into it now!' As though by coincidence their host's study turned out to be next door. The wall was a thin one and through it one could hear everything that was being said there. Under the pretext of an early lunch the host was ordering the cook to get ready a veritable banquet. And the way he was ordering it would have revived a dead man's appetite!

'Make the fish-pie a four-cornered one,' he was saying as he sucked in his breath. 'In one corner put the cheeks and dried spine of sturgeon, in another some buckwheat, and some mushrooms and onions, and some soft roe, yes, and some brains, and something else as well. . . . Yes, and see to it that the crust is well browned on one side and a trifle less on the other. And see to the underside . . . see that it is baked so that it's quite . . . not to the point of crumbling but so that it might melt in the mouth like snow and make no crunching sound.' Petukh smacked his lips as he spoke.

'The devil take him! He won't let me sleep,' Chichikov thought to himself and he tucked his head under the quilt in order to stop listening. But even through the quilt he could hear his host saying:

'And by way of a lining for the sturgeon put in some beetroot, smelts, mushrooms and, you know, some turnip, carrots, beans, then add something else, I leave it to you, so that it should be richly garnished and have plenty of stuffing. And as for the pig's belly, stuffed with minced meat and buckwheat, put a little ice in it to make it swell up properly.'

Petukh ordered many another dish. He could be heard urging the cook to 'fry it well', to 'roast it right', to 'stew it properly'. By the time Chichikov fell asleep the talk was of a turkey.

The following day the guests had gorged themselves so much that Platonov was incapable of mounting his horse, which had to be ridden by a stable boy instead. At last they were in the carriage. The big-headed dog padded lazily after it, for he had also gorged himself to the full.

'It's too much,' Chichikov said when they had driven out of the courtyard.

'And yet he is not bored with it!' Platonov exclaimed. 'What a pity!'

'If I had seventy thousand roubles a year by way of an income as you have,' Chichkikov thought to himself, 'I would not allow even the shadow of boredom to fall upon me. Now that contractor Mourazov is worth ten million, if you please. . . . What a windfall!'

'Do you mind if we pay a call on the way?' Platonov asked. 'I'd like to visit my sister and brother-in-law.'

'With the greatest of pleasure,' Chichikov replied.

'He's our prize landowner and estate manager. He succeeds, my dear sir, in getting an income of two hundred thousand from an estate which eight years ago hardly brought in twenty thousand.'

'Oh, he must be a remarkable man! It will be interesting to make his acquaintance. Of course it will. Yes, he is, so to say. . . . But what is his name?'

'Kostanzhonglo.'

'And what is his Christian name and patronymic?'

'Konstantin Feodorovich.'

'Konstantin Feodorovich Kostanzhonglo,' Chichikov said. 'I shall be very interested to make his acquaintance, it will be most informative to meet such a person.'

Platonov then took Selifan in hand. It was high time,

for the coachman could hardly sit straight in his seat. Petrushka had already twice tumbled out of the carriage, and it was at last found necessary to tie him to his seat. 'What a beast!' Chichikov kept repeating to himself.

'Now look over there! That's where my brother-in-law's estate begins,' Platonov said. 'It looks quite different from the others.'

And so it did. A wood had been planted in one of the fields, and all the trees were of the same height and as straight as poles; then came another wood of young trees, a little taller this time; then an old forest, and each succeeding forest was taller than the last. And in this fashion the newly planted strips of forest alternated with the older ones. As if through the gates of a wall they drove through three such woods. 'He's grown all that within some eight or ten years. Another landowner would have taken twenty or more.'

'How did he manage to do it?' Chichikov enquired.

'You had better ask him. He's an expert agriculturist, nothing goes to waste with him,' Platonov replied. 'It's not enough for him to know all about the soil, he knows all the rotations and what trees to plant next to a particular crop as well. Everything on his estate serves three or four purposes. His woods, for example, not only provide the timber but are planted in a particular spot in order to collect moisture for the fields, to help to manure them with their fallen leaves, and to bring shade to them. . . . When there is drought all round, he has none; when there are bad harvests in the vicinity, his are normal. It's a pity I know so little about these things, I can't give you all the details, but he is up to all the tricks. . . . And yet it's all so boring. . . .'

'He really must be a remarkable person,' Chichikov thought. 'It's a great shame this young man is so superficial and can't tell me more.'

At last they came in sight of Kostanzhonglo's village. Its numerous houses were scattered over three hills like a town; each of the hills was crowned with a church, and the village was fenced in on all sides by gigantic stacks of corn and hayricks. 'Yes,' Chichikov thought to himself, 'this is the domain of an ace of landowners.' The peasant huts looked well built; the village streets were solidly laid out; if a cart was standing anywhere, it was a new and strongly made one; the peasants they met all looked intelligent; the cattle was pedigree; even the common pigs had the air of aristocrats. It was obvious that here dwelt peasants who, as the saying goes, 'shovelled silver with a spade'. There were no English parks or lawns here with all their fancies; instead, as of old, there was a vista of barns and workshops and these stretched right up to the proprietor's house, making it possible for the master of the domain to see everything that was going on around him. The high roof-top of the house was topped by the turret of an observation post; it was not there for adornment or for the sake of the view alone, but to allow the master to keep an eye on the work that was going on in the distant fields. As they drove up to the porch they were greeted by servants, who were quite unlike the drunken Petrushka, even though they wore no frock-coats but only cossack coats of blue homespun cloth.

The lady of the house came running out herself on the steps. She had the freshest of complexions; she was as pretty as a fair day; and she was as like Platonov as two drops of water, though with none of his listlessness, for she was animated and gay.

'How are you, brother? I'm so glad you have come,' she said. 'Konstantin is not at home, but he will be back soon.'

'Where is he then?' the brother enquired.

'He has some business to transact with dealers in the village,' she replied as she led the visitors into the house.

With curiosity, Chichikov looked round the house of this remarkable man, who had an income of two hundred thousand, and he expected it to reflect some of the qualities of its owner, just as it is possible to judge from a shell whether it had been inhabited by an oyster or a snail. But in this case it was difficult to arrive at any conclusion. The rooms were plain and empty enough: they contained no frescoes, pictures, bronze ornaments, flowers, or shelves loaded with china; nor were there any books to be seen. In short, everything went to show that the main portion of the life of its inhabitant was not spent within the four walls of a room but in the open fields, and that his ideas were not thought out in Sybarite fashion in a comfortable armchair by the fireplace, but wherever business had to be transacted, and wherever the ideas occurred there they were put into action. It did not escape Chichikov, however, that the rooms bore some trace of a busy housekeeper: planks of fresh maple-wood had been laid out on the chairs and tables, and on them were heaped the petals of some species of flowers for drying. . . .

'What's all this rubbish, sister, you have lying about here?' Platonov asked.

'Rubbish!' the lady of the house retorted. 'It's the best remedy there is against fever. Last year we cured all the peasants with it; these herbs here are for flavouring home-made wines and those over there are for flavouring jam. You are always laughing at the jam-making and the salting of vegetables we do, but you praise the results when you taste them.'

Platonov went up to the piano and began to turn over the sheets of music.

'Oh Lord! What ancient stuff this is!' he said. 'Aren't you ashamed of it, sister?'

'That may be, brother, but I haven't had time for music for a long while,' she replied. 'My daughter is eight now and I have to teach her. I wouldn't dream of putting her in the hands of a foreign governess in order to have more time myself for music. No, brother, I wouldn't do that.'

'How boring you have grown!' the brother said and went up to the window. 'There he is! He's coming, he's coming!' Platonov cried.

Chichikov also made for the window. A man of some forty years of age, brisk in his manner and swarthy in appearance, and wearing a jacket of camel hair, was approaching the house. He was not particular about his appearance: he had on a serge cap. He was accompanied on either side of him by two men of a lower class who were holding their caps in their hands: one of them was a

simple peasant and the other a visiting *kulak* in a blue
Siberian coat; and they were all engrossed in conversation. As they came to a stop near the steps, their conversation could be heard in the house.

'Now this is what you had better do: buy yourselves
off from your master,' Kostanzhonglo was saying. 'I may
give you a loan: you can work it off later.'

'No, Konstantin Feodorovich, why should we buy our
freedom? Take us over. There is so much to learn from
you. It would be difficult to find anywhere another man
as clever as you are. The way things are these days one
only just manages to keep one's head above water. The
gin-shops are selling such wines that one glass is enough
to scorch your belly and make you drink a whole bucket
of water afterwards. Before you know where you are,
you have brought it all up. There is too much temptation. Maybe it's the devil who is pulling the strings, I
wouldn't be surprised! Everything is done to lead the
peasants by the nose: now take tobacco and all the other
things. . . . What is to be done, Konstantin Feodorovich?
We are human, we couldn't hold out.'

'Now listen. This is how it is,' Kostanzhonglo argued.
'You would not be so free if I did take you over. True, you
would get a cow and a horse at once; but then I ask more
of my peasants than anyone else. With me work comes
first; I allow neither myself nor anyone else to dawdle. I
myself work like an ox, and my peasants too, for I know
by experience that all this nonsense comes into people's
heads only because they don't work. So you had better
think it all over in peace and discuss it among yourselves.'

'We have discussed it already, Konstantin Feodorovich.
The old men say the same. What more can we say? Every
one of your peasants is well off, that is no accident; and
your priests are conscientious. But with us even they have
gone the way of all flesh and there is no one left even to
bury the dead.'

'All the same you had better go and talk it over,'
Kostanzhonglo said.

'Very well, I will,' the peasant replied.

'Now, Konstantin Ivanovich, won't you do me a

favour and . . . knock down your price a little?' said the visiting *kulak* in the blue Siberian coat who was walking on the other side of Kostanzhonglo.

'But didn't I tell you already that I do not like bargaining,' Kostanzhonglo replied. 'I'm not like your ordinary landowner to whom you can come and buy from him cheaply just when the interest on his mortgage falls due and he is about to pawn his belongings. I know you all: you keep lists of them all and know when they have to pay up. What's the point of it? A landowner like that is in a hurry and so he lets you have it cheap. But what do I want with your money? I don't mind if my produce lies in store for three years: I don't have to pay any interest.'

'That is so, Konstantin Ivanovich,' the *kulak* replied. 'I was only suggesting it, so to say, because we are going to have dealings in the future, and not out of any sense of greed. Will you please accept these three thousand roubles by way of an advance.' Hereupon the *kulak* pulled out a wad of dirty notes which Kostanzhonglo took from him and, without counting them, stuffed them into the back pocket of his jacket.

'H'm!' Chichikov thought to himself. 'He treats them as though they were a handkerchief!' Then Kostanzhonglo appeared in the doorway of the drawing-room. This time Chichikov was struck even more by the swarthy tint of his face, the wiry quality of his black and prematurely grizzled hair, the lively expression of his eyes and his somewhat bilious aura which was no doubt due to his ardent southern origin. He was not quite Russian; but he himself did not know where his ancestors had come from. He was not interested in his genealogy and believed it to be quite superfluous from the point of view of his interests. But he did consider himself a Russian, and besides he knew no other language.

Platonov then introduced Chichikov. They embraced.

'To cure myself of my spleen, I have decided to make a tour of the various provinces,' said Platonov. 'And Pavel Ivanovich here has kindly suggested that I should accompany him.'

'An excellent idea!' Kostanzhonglo said. 'And where are you going?' he continued, turning to Chichikov in a friendly manner. 'What places do you propose to visit?'

'I confess that I am not travelling only on my own account,' Chichikov replied with a friendly inclination of his head and stroking at the same time the arm of his chair. 'General Betrishchev, who is an intimate friend of mine and a benefactor into the bargain, has asked me to visit some relatives of his. However, relatives are only relative, and there is also some personal advantage to be gained from a trip like this: besides the good it will do my digestion, I shall see a bit of the world, how people live, and that is, so to say, a living book, a second science.'

'Yes, it's not a bad idea to see some places,' Kostanzhonglo said.

'A most excellent observation: it really is not at all a bad idea. One will see things one would not otherwise have seen: and one will meet people one would not otherwise have met. To hear some people talk is like handling real minted gold, just like the chance of meeting you. . . . I appeal to you, my dear Konstantin Feodorovich, give me the benefit of your wisdom, teach me, quench my thirst for truth. Like manna, I await your sweet words.'

'But what can I say? What can I teach you!' Kostanzhonglo said, growing confused. 'I myself learnt all there is to be learnt by handling coppers.'

'You can teach wisdom, my dear sir, wisdom—the ability to manage such an awkward thing as an estate, the wisdom of being able to ensure an income from it, and to acquire real rather than imaginary property, thus fulfilling one's duty as a citizen and winning the respect of one's compatriots.'

'Do you know what?' Kostanzhonglo said, looking at him and reflecting. 'Why not stay a day or two with me? I will show you round the estate and show you how it is managed. As you will see, there is no particular wisdom involved.'

'Yes, do stay,' the lady of the house exclaimed and, turning to her brother, she added: 'Do stay with us, brother. Why be in such a hurry?'

'I don't mind if I do,' the brother replied. 'What does Pavel Ivanovich think about it?'

'I should like to, yes, with the greatest of pleasure. . . .' Chichikov replied. 'There's only one thing, general Betrishchev's relative, a certain colonel Koshkaryov. . . .'

'But he's mad.'

'I believe he is. But general Betrishchev is a good friend of mine and also, so to speak, a benefactor. . . .'

'In that case, do you know what?' Kostanzhonglo said. 'Drive out and see him at once. He lives not seven miles from here. One of my droshkys is all ready, so go and visit him. You'll be back in time for tea.'

'An excellent idea!' Chichikov exclaimed, picking up his hat.

The droshky was brought round and in half an hour he was at the colonel's. The colonel's village looked all higgledy-piggledy: all kinds of structures littered the streets, which were also heaped with piles of lime, brick and timber. Some of these structures looked like government offices. One of them had inscribed on it in gold letters: *Depot for Agricultural Implements*; another was called, *Principal Counting House*; others were respectively entitled, *Committee for Rural Affairs, School of Elementary Education for Villagers*. In short, only the devil could make head or tail of it!

He discovered the colonel at a desk in one of the offices, holding a pen between his teeth. He greeted Chichikov quite affectionately. In appearance he was the kindest and most considerate of mortals: he began to tell Chichikov how much labour it had cost him to bring the estate to its present state of prosperity. He complained feelingly of the difficulty he had found in making the peasants understand that there are higher pleasures to be derived from enlightened luxury and art; that he had been unable to date to oblige the peasant women to wear corsets, whereas, when he was in Germany with his regiment in 1814, he had met the daughter of a miller who could play the piano; and that, nevertheless, despite all the obstinacy he had encountered on the part of the ignorant, he would not fail to achieve a state of affairs in which his peasants, while continuing to plough, would read a book about Franklin's lightning conductors, Virgil's *Georgics*[2] or some work on the Chemical Properties of the Soil.

'Yes, it all sounds very fine!' Chichikov thought to himself. 'But I haven't had time yet to read my volume by the Duchess de la Vallière.'

The colonel had a great deal more to say about how he was going to make his folk happier. He attached great importance to dress: he said that he was ready to stake his head that the level of culture and trade would rise, and that a Golden Age would dawn in Russia as soon as half the Russian peasants had donned German trousers.

Chichikov listened and listened to him, looking straight into his eyes, and finally said to himself: 'There is no point in standing on ceremony with this man.' And he at once explained to him that he had need of some dead souls and the completion of a deed of purchase with all due formalities.

'As far as I can judge from what you say,' the colonel replied without any signs of confusion, 'you have in fact made a request, isn't that so?'

'Exactly.'

'In that case you must put it down in writing. Your request will then be passed on to the *Bureau of Reports and Petitions*. The Bureau will pass it back to me with its comments, and I shall send it on to the *Committee for Rural Affairs*. With their comments it will be passed on to the steward. And the steward will deal with it together with the secretary. . . . .'

'But excuse me!' Chichikov exclaimed aghast. 'In this way the affair will drag on, God knows how long! It's not the usual sort of transaction. . . . The souls are to some extent . . . dead ones.'

'Very well,' the colonel replied. 'You will put that down in writing, that the souls are to some extent dead.'

'But they are dead,' Chichikov said. 'Though one can't say so. Although they are dead they must appear to be living.'

2. Poetical work on farming by the Latin poet (70 to 19 B.C.).

'Very well,' the colonel replied. 'You will put that down also: "it is not necessary, or it is required, or it is desired, or it would be best that it should appear that they are living". Without putting it down on paper it will be impossible to do anything. Look at the example of England and even of Napoleon. I shall detach a commissionaire to conduct you wherever you may have to go.'

He pressed a bell. A man appeared.

'Secretary! Will you call the commissionaire.' The commissionaire then presented himself; it was difficult to say whether he was a peasant or an official. 'He will conduct you wherever you need,' the colonel said.

What could one do with the colonel? Out of curiosity Chichikov decided to go with the commissionaire and to inspect all the essential offices. The *Bureau for Reports and Petitions* existed only in name, the doors of it were shut. Khrulyov, the official in charge, had been transferred to the newly formed *Committee for Rural Construction*. His place had been taken by Berezovsky, the valet; but he also had been seconded to the Committee. They tried the *Department for Rural Affairs*—it was in the process of transformation. They woke up a man who was lying drunk and asleep on the premises, but they could get no sense out of him. 'There's no order anywhere,' the commissionaire at last said to Chichikov. 'Our master is being led by the nose. The *Committee for Construction* is bossing it over everyone and despatching whomever it wants wherever it wants. It alone gets things done.' He was apparently dissatisfied with the Committee. But Chichikov had had enough, he did not want to see any more. Returning, he told the colonel straight out that everything was in a mess, that he could get no sense out of anyone, and that the *Committee for Reports and Petitions* was non-existent.

The colonel boiled over with noble indignation and shook Chichikov warmly by the hand in sign of gratitude. He then grabbed a sheet of paper and set down eight very searching questions: 'Why had the *Committee for Construction*,' he asked, 'acted so autocratically and taken over the officials of another department? How could the official in charge of the Bureau go off without leaving anyone in charge? And how could the *Committee for Rural Affairs* be indifferent to the fact that the *Bureau for Reports and Petitions* did not exist at all?'

'That's started a hullabaloo!' Chichikov thought to himself, and he made to take his leave.

'No, I shan't let you go,' the colonel said. 'My self-respect is now involved. I'll show you how an estate should be run organically and properly. I shall entrust your affair to a man who is worth the whole lot of them put together: he has a university degree. That's the sort of serfs I have! So that you may not waste your time, I beg of you to wait in the library,' the colonel said, open-ing a side door. 'Here are books, papers, pens, pencils, everything you want. Make use of them, make use of everything: you're master here. Enlightenment should be available to everyone.'

So said the colonel as he introduced Chichikov into the library. It was a vast room, lined with books from floor to ceiling. There were even some stuffed animals. The books covered every subject: there were books on forestry, on cattle-rearing, pig-breeding, and gardening; there were specialist journals on every topic, such as are subscribed for but never read. Realizing that all these books were not intended to afford pleasure, Chichikov turned towards another book-case, and landed from the frying pan into the fire: these were all books of philosophy. Six enormous volumes arrested his attention: they were entitled, *A Preliminary Introduction to the Theory of Thought in its General Aspect as a whole, and in its Application to the Interpretation of the Organic Principles of the Mutual Distribu-tion of Social Productivity*. On every page Chichikov came across such expressions as 'manifestation', 'development', 'abstract', 'inherence and coherence', and the devil knows what else! 'That's not my cup of tea,' Chichikov said as he turned to face the third book-case which contained books dealing with the arts. He then pulled out a large volume illustrated with immodest mythological drawings and began to examine them. Drawings of this sort afford pleasure to middle-aged bachelors, and sometimes also to old men who regale themselves on the ballet and other such spiced entertainments. When he had finished examining one volume, Chichikov was about to pass on to another of the same kind, but at that moment colonel Koshkaryov appeared, looking pleased with himself and carrying a sheaf of papers.

'Everything's done, and excellently too!' he exclaimed. 'The man I told you about is positively a genius. For this I shall promote him above all the others and shall institute a new department for his benefit. Just look what a clear head he has and how he has resolved this problem in a few minutes.'

'Well, thank God!' Chichikov thought to himself and got ready to listen. The colonel began to read:

'Referring to the commission that your honour has seen fit to entrust to me, I have the honour to report as follows:

1. To begin with, the request made by the collegiate councillor and cavalier, Pavel Ivanovich Chichikov, is based on a misunderstanding, for he has mistakenly described the census souls as "dead." By this he no doubt intended to indicate those who were near death rather than those who were dead. To have described them thus already denotes a stage of empirical studies not exceeding that imparted by the parish school, for the soul is known to be immortal.'

'The rascal!' the colonel exclaimed with evident relish when he had stopped reading. 'That's a slight dig at you. But you must confess that he has a lively pen!' The colonel then resumed his reading:

'2. There are no unmortgaged census souls on the estate either near to death or otherwise, for not only are all the souls already mortgaged but they have been mortgaged twice over, which has brought in an additional fifty roubles per soul—all with the exception of those to be found in the small village of Gourmailovka, the position of which is not clear owing to the lawsuit with the landowner Predistchev, and for this reason the village has been impounded as was stated in an advertisement which appeared in the *Moscow Gazette* No. 42.'

'Then why didn't you tell me about that before? Why did you keep me here for nothing?' Chichikov exclaimed heatedly.

'Yes. But it was necessary for you to see all this on paper,' the colonel replied. 'It would not have been right otherwise. Any fool is capable of grasping something unconsciously, but the whole point is to appreciate the position consciously.'

In his anger Chichikov grabbed his hat and, casting all ceremony to the winds, made for the door at a run. The coachman had the droshky ready, for he knew well that there was no point in unharnessing the horses since the feeding of them would have required the filling up of numerous forms and the resolution to issue a ration of oats would not have been completed until the following day. The colonel, however, also ran out of the house; he shook Chichikov forcibly by the hand, pressed him to his heart and thanked him for giving him the opportunity of showing him his system in operation. The colonel added that, as a result of his visit, he would have to tighten up his administration, otherwise his staff might fall asleep and the springs of his administrative system might rust and grow weak. He added that the happy idea had now occurred to him to found a new committee which might be called the *Committee for Inspecting the Construction Committee*, and that this would preclude the possibility of any more filching.

Chichikov returned in an angry and dissatisfied frame of mind. He was late and the candles had already been lit.

'What kept you so late?' Kostanzhonglo asked him as soon as he appeared in the doorway.

'What were you discussing with him for so long?' Platonov asked.

'I've never come across such a fool in the whole of my life,' Chichikov replied.

'That's nothing,' Kostanzhonglo said. 'Koshkaryov is a comforting phenomenon. A necessary one too. He is the epitome and caricature of the stupidities of all our smart thinkers—of all our bright thinkers who, instead of learning their job on the spot, make a point of stocking themselves with all sorts of rubbish abroad. That's the sort of landowner that flourishes nowadays; they have started up offices, factories, schools and committees, and the devil knows what else! That's the sort of smarties they are! I thought they had settled down after the French invasion of 1812, but now they have started up-setting the apple-cart again. They are doing more damage than the French even, and the result is that your Pyotr Petrovich Petukh is a good landowner by comparison.'

'But he has also mortgaged his estate,' Chichikov exclaimed.

'Yes, he has mortgaged everything and everything will be mortgaged.' As he was saying that Kostanzhonglo began to grow angry. 'There are landowners who are starting up factories for making hats and candles; one of them has imported candlemakers from London. They are all becoming tradesmen! A landowner's is a respectable calling, but as for all these industrialists and factory-owners. . . . Just think of it! They are setting up spinning machines to make fal-lals for the city wenches and the village girls. . . .'

'But you have set up factories yourself,' Platonov observed.

'And who set them up? They came into being themselves! I had so much wool piled up, there was no getting rid of it—so I began to weave cloth, plain thick cloth at a cheap price and to sell it on the local market. The peasants need it, my peasants buy it. For six years traders had been dumping fish refuse on my bank of the river. Well, what was I to do with it? I began to make glue and it brought me in forty thousand roubles. That's the way I go about things.'

'He's a real devil!' Chichikov thought to himself as he looked straight into his face. 'He just rakes it in!'

'Yes, and the reason why I did it was because it was a hungry year and, thanks to all these factory owners who had neglected their crops, a lot of jobless hands had wandered into the district. I have many such factories, brother. Every year I start another one depending on what I have left over and on the waste there is available.

Now if you were to look closely at your own estate, you'd find you might be able to make a profit on all sorts of rubbish, so much so that you would cry "Halt!" That's why I don't build myself palaces with columns and façades.'

'That's amazing. . . . And the most amazing thing of all is that every sort of rubbish brings in a profit,' Chichikov exclaimed.

'Yes, indeed! It's a question of the simple approach, of seeing things as they are; but to-day everyone tries to be a mechanic; they do not want to open a coffer simply but with some gadget. And they go off specially to England for that purpose. That's what's wrong! Fools that they are!' Kostanzhonglo spat out as he said that. 'And when they return from abroad they will be a hundred times more stupid!'

'Ah, Konstantin! You are in a temper again,' his wife said uneasily. 'You know it's bad for your health.'

'How can I not lose my temper? If it were someone else's property I wouldn't worry, but it is I who have a close interest in it all. How sad it is that the Russian character is getting spoilt! There is a quixoticism about the Russian character now which it never had before! If a Russian gets a bee in his bonnet about enlightenment he immediately becomes a Don Quixote: he will set up schools such as even a fool would not dream of founding! And that school will produce the type of man who is good for nothing, fit neither for the city nor the village, a drunkard only and yet full of his own importance. He will turn philanthropist—a Don Quixote of philanthropy: he will build a million roubles' worth of senseless hospitals and institutions ornamented with columns, then he will go bust and loose his patients on the world. That's philanthropy for you!'

Chichikov was not interested in enlightenment. He wanted to question his host in detail as to the way in which profit could be made from all sorts of waste and rubbish; but Kostanzhonglo did not give him a chance to put in a word. Choleric phrases kept pouring out of his mouth and he could no longer contain himself.

'The way they think they can enlighten the peasant. . . . They should make him a good and prosperous farmer first, and then he would learn himself all that is to be learnt. How stupid the world has grown lately! One just can't believe it! The things these scribblers write nowadays! One of them publishes a book and everyone wants to read it! . . . This is the sort of thing they are saying now: "The peasant leads too simple a life; he must be introduced to articles of luxury, and the demand must be created in him for things above his means. . . ." Thanks to all this luxury, they have themselves become like rags rather than like men. The devil knows what diseases they have already contracted, and there is not an eighteen-year-old lad who does not know too much: his teeth have gone and he is already as bald as a balloon, and yet they want to infect him even more. . . . But the Lord be thanked, there remains at least one healthy layer of the population which has been spared these fancies! We should thank God for that! Yes, our tillers of the soil are the worthiest of all. Why then touch them? May the Lord grant that everyone be like them!'

'You think then that it is more profitable to be a tiller of the soil?' Chichikov asked.

'Right rather than more profitable. "Till the land in the sweat of thy brow," that is the saying. There is no room for fancy there. The experience of the ages has proved that when he is on the land man is morally purer, nobler and higher. I don't mean to say that men should not do other things as well, but the land is the foundation of it all. That's how I see it! The factories will spring up of their own accord, proper factories, for providing what man needs on the spot instead of stimulating all sorts of artificial demands such as have undermined the present generation. They would not be factories like those that, in order to keep going and to sell their wares, use every sort of abominable means, depraving and disintegrating the unfortunate people. However much you may try and persuade me, even though you may argue that it is for their benefit, I refuse to set up any of those manufactures which stimulate increased demands, such as those for tobacco or sugar. No, not if I lost a million as a result. If depravity is gaining ground it will not be with my help! My conscience at least will be clean. . . . I have been living these twenty years among the people and I know where it all leads.'

'The thing that amazes me most of all is how, with good management, one can make a profit from all sorts of waste and rubbish,' Chichikov interjected.

'H'm! Political economists!' Kostanzhonglo continued with a bitterly sarcastic expression on his face and without heeding Chichikov. 'Fine political economists they are! One fool on top of another, one fool trying to catch up with another, but they don't see farther than their nose! He may be an ass and yet he will get up on a platform and put on his spectacles. . . . Idiots!' and in his rage Kostanzhonglo spat out.

'It's all as you say, very right, only please don't get angry,' his wife exclaimed. 'Can't you talk about these things without losing your temper?'

'Listening to you, Konstantin Feodorovich,' Chichikov said, 'one begins to understand the meaning of life, one feels the very kernel of the whole business. But leaving aside for the moment the universal aspect of things, may I draw your attention to a personal matter. Let us suppose that I became a landowner and entertained the idea of growing rich in a short space of time, so that I might, so to speak, fulfil my duty as a citizen, how should I go about it?'

'How go about it to get rich?' Kostanzhonglo picked him up. 'This is how. . .'

'Let's go and sup,' the lady of the house interrupted, getting up from the sofa and walking into the middle of the room, and as she did so, she wrapped a shawl round her youthful shoulders which were feeling the chill.

Chichikov leapt up from his chair almost as smartly as an officer, offered her his arm, and conducted her ceremoniously into the dining-room where a soup tureen was already standing on the table with its lid off, exhaling the agreeable aroma of a soup full of spring

greens. They all sat down to table. The servants promptly
set down all the dishes with the lids on them, and everything else that was required, and departed at once:
Kostanzhonglo did not like his servants to overhear his
conversation at table and still less did he like them to
stare at him as he was eating.

Having finished his soup and drunk a glass of excellent
wine that had some affinity to Tokay, Chichikov addressed
his host as follows: 'Allow me, Konstantin Feodorovich,
to bring you back to the theme of our interrupted conversation. I was asking you to tell me how to go about it.
How should I best apply myself?'[3]

'If he asked me to pay him forty thousand for that
estate, I would give it to him right away.'[4]

'H'm!' Chichikov reflected. 'Then why don't you
acquire it yourself!' he said with some diffidence.

'Well, there is a limit,' Kostanzhonglo replied. 'I have
plenty of worries as it is with my own estates. And besides,
the local gentry are already agitating; they accuse me of
taking advantage of their difficulties and of buying up
the land from them for a song. I have had enough of that.'

'How can people be so ill-spoken!' Chichikov exclaimed.

'If it comes to that, you have no idea what our province is like: they never call me anything but a codger
and a prize-skinflint,' Kostanzhonglo said. 'As for themselves, they find all sorts of excuses. "I have ruined
myself, of course," one of them will say, "but it was
because I lived up to the highest standards, encouraged
industrialists, rogues, that is to say. . . . If I had not done
so, I might have lived a pig's life, like Kostanzhonglo."'

'I should like to be such a pig,' Chichikov exclaimed.

'What nonsense it all is!' Kostanzhonglo said. 'What
higher standard? Whom do they think they are bluffing?
And even though they set up a library of books, do they
ever read them? It all ends in card-play and. . . . And
they talk about me like that because I do not invite them

3. Two pages of the manuscript are
missing here [*Translator's note*].
4. The following comment is to be
found in the first Russian edition of
Part II: 'It may be assumed that

Kostanzhonglo had suggested that
Chichikov should acquire the estate
of his neighbour, Khlobuyev' [*Translator's note*].

to banquets and do not lend them money. I don't invite them to banquets because that would bore me. I am not used to it. But if anyone calls on me and partakes of my fare, he is very welcome. What they say about my not lending money is absolute nonsense. If a really needy person came along to me and explained the circumstances and the way he would use my money, and if he convinced me that he would use the money wisely and to some profit, then I would not refuse him and I would not even charge interest on it.'

'I must make a note of that,' Chichikov thought.

'I never refuse in such cases,' Kostanzhonglo continued. 'But I am not going to chuck my money away either. No, thank you! The devil take it! When one of them plans a dinner for his mistress or goes mad over the furnishing of his house, or goes to a masquerade, or arranges a jubilee to celebrate the fact that he has lived for age without doing a stroke of work, and then expects me to lend him money!'

At this point Kostanzhonglo spat and almost let drop some unseemly and violent words in the presence of his wife. The austere shadow of a gloomy melancholy fell upon his face. The lines which now creased his forehead vertically and horizontally were evidence of his rising spleen.

'Allow me, my dear Konstantin Feodorovich, to remind you again of the theme we had broached but not finished,' Chichikov said as he drank another glass of raspberry cordial, which was really excellent. 'Let us suppose that I did acquire the estate which you were pleased to mention, how long would it take me to grow rich enough to. . . .'

'If you want to get rich quickly,' Kostanzhonglo broke in impetuously and severely, for he was in bad spirits, 'then you will never grow rich. But if you want to grow rich without worrying about time, then you will grow rich quickly.'

'So that's how it is!' Chichikov exclaimed.

'Yes,' Kostanzhonglo rapped out as though he were angry with Chichikov. 'You must be fond of work: without that there is nothing doing. You must love your estate, yes! And believe me it is not at all boring. They say that country life is a bore . . . but I would die if I spent one day in town in the sort of way they do, in their stupid clubs, taverns and theatres. Fools that they are! A generation of idiots and asses! The master of an estate cannot have and has no time for boredom. His life is not empty, not even an eighth of an inch empty. On the contrary, it is very full. The very variety of occupations, and what occupations!—occupations that really exalt the spirit. Whatever you may say, here man walks hand in hand with nature, with the seasons, he takes part and shares in everything that goes on in creation. Now look at the cycle of work: what expectancy and preparation there is before the coming of spring! The seeds are got ready, everything is checked, the corn stacked in the granaries is measured and dried, the holdings are redistributed. Everything is gone into and calculated in advance. And when the ice breaks up and the rivers start moving, and when everything dries and the earth begins to be turned up, then the spades are digging up orchard and garden, the plough and harrow are working in the fields, and the planting and sowing are in full swing. Do you understand what that means? They call it idleness! But it is the next harvest that is being sown! It is happiness that is being sown! It is the sustenance of millions that is being assured! Summer comes and then the mowing starts. . . . And then the harvest time is upon one: the rye is ready, the wheat follows, and then the barley and the oats. Everything is a hive of activity; there is not a minute to be lost; if one had twenty eyes there would be work for them all. And when all these labours are rounded off with feasting, and when all the harvest has been piled on the threshing-floor and stacked up, and when the winter crops have been sown and the barns repaired for the winter, and when the women have completed all their work, and when one draws up a balance sheet of it all and realizes what has been done, why then . . . And winter is no time of idleness either! There is the threshing and milling, and the carting of the corn from the floors to the barns. Then one goes round the mills and the factories, one has a look at the workshops, one drops in to see the peasants and to find out how they are getting on. As far as I am concerned, if a carpenter is a master of his axe I can stand watching him for two hours on end, such is the pleasure I derive from his work. And when you realize that all this work is being done with a purpose, and that everything around you is multiplying over and over again, bringing both fruits and profit, why I cannot describe the feeling that possesses one. And it is not because you make more money in the process—money is just money—but because it is all your own handi-work, because you see that you are the mainspring of it all, that you are a creator, one of the magi scattering benefits and abundance all around you. Now where would you find any pleasure to equal this?' So spoke Kostan-zhonglo, and the lines had vanished from his face which he held uplifted. 'Yes, nowhere in the world would you find anything to equal this delight! It is here that man is most like God! The task of creation is God's highest pleasure, and He asks man also to be a creator and to work for prosperity all around him. And they call that a boring occupation! . . .'

Chichikov was listening to his host's sweet-sounding phrases as to the singing of a bird of paradise. His mouth watered as he drank in the words. Even his eyes grew moist and sweet as he continued to listen.

'Konstantin! It's time we left the table,' the lady of the house said as she got up from her chair. They all followed suit. Offering her his arm, Chichikov conducted her back to the drawing-room, but his movements lacked some of their wonted smartness because his thoughts were else-where.

'Whatever you may say, I still find it very boring,' said Platonov who was walking behind them.

'Our guest is not stupid,' the host thought to himself. 'He is attentive, measured in his words, and no scribbler.' And as he thought this he grew more cheerful; it was as though his own words had warmed him up and he was celebrating the discovery of a person who was ready to heed wise counsels.

When at last they had settled down in a comfortable room, lit with candles and facing a balcony and a glass door giving on the garden, and when they saw the stars glimmering over the tree-tops of the sleeping garden, Chichikov had a cosy feeling such as he had not experienced for a long while. He felt as though he was at last under a homely roof after prolonged wanderings and had everything he wanted, having thrown away his wanderer's staff and said: 'I've had enough of it.' Such was the delightful state of mind into which his host's conversation had plunged him. There are certain phrases which are nearer and dearer to all of us than all others. It often happens that one may unexpectedly meet a man in some remote and quite deserted out-of-the-way corner, whose conversation has that warming quality which will make one forget oneself, the endless road, the discomfort of wayside lodgings, the pointlessness of contemporary life, and the deceitfulness of the illusions leading men astray. And the lively memory of an evening thus spent will imprint itself for ever on the mind in all its details: one will remember who was there and who sat where, what he was holding in his hands and what the colour of the walls was like.

So it was that evening; Chichikov noted every little trifle. He memorized the charming and plainly furnished room, the good-natured expression which had appeared on the face of his wise host, the pattern on the wall-paper ... the pipe with the amber mouthpiece which had been offered to Platonov, the smoke which he then began to puff out into Yarb's big muzzle, the way Yarb snorted, the hostess's charming laugh and the way she said, 'Don't torment him!' the gay candles, the cricket in the corner, the glass door, and the spring night outside, which looked down on them, leaning on the tree-tops, all spangled with stars and loud with the singing of nightingales as they trilled their melodies in the depths of the green-branched thickets.

'Sweet are your words to me, my dear Konstantin Feodorovich!' Chichikov said at last. 'I must say that in the whole of Russia I have never met anyone as intelligent as you.'

Kostanzhonglo smiled. He himself was conscious of the injustice of this remark. 'No,' he said, 'if you want to meet a really intelligent person, then we have one such man here who may really be called intelligent—and I am not worth the sole of his old shoe.'

'Who can that be?' Chichikov asked in surprise.

'Mourazov, our contractor.'

'It's the second time I've heard him mentioned,' Chichikov said.

'He is a man who could manage not only an estate but a whole state,' Kostanzhonglo said. 'If I were the ruler of a state, I would at once make him my Minister of Finance.'

'And they say that he is a man who has broken all the laws of probability,' Chichikov said. 'They say he has made ten million.'

'Ten is only a flea-bite! Kostanzhonglo replied. 'They say he has made over forty million. Half of Russia will soon be in his hands.'

'You don't mean that?' Chichikov exclaimed, gaping at him and opening his mouth.

'It's inevitable. It's quite clear,' Kostanzhonglo said. 'A man who has a few hundred thousand is slow to get rich, but one that has millions has a greater radius of action: whatever he takes up increases twofold or three-fold despite himself. His field of action, his arena, is too wide: he has no rivals left. There is no one to take up the cudgels against him. There is no arguing with him what-ever price he cares to name: there is no one to bid against him.'

'Oh Lord, Oh Lord!' Chichikov exclaimed, making the sign of the cross. He was staring straight into Kostan-zhonglo's eyes—he caught his breath. 'The imagination can't grasp it. Thought is petrified at the very idea! When we examine a beetle, we are amazed at the wisdom of Providence. But I am more amazed at the fact that such vast sums may be concentrated in the hands of a single mortal. May I ask you one thing? I assume that all this has not, of course, been acquired without sin?'

'In the most impeccable way and by the justest means,' Kostanzhonglo replied.

'I don't believe it! It's incredible! Thousands yes, but millions. . . .'

'On the contrary,' Kostanzhonglo replied. 'It is

difficult to acquire thousands without sin, but millions can be easily made. A millionaire has no need to be crooked: he has a straight road ahead of him; it is only a question of going and taking whatever lies in front of him. Another would not pick it up; it's not everyone would have the strength to do so; but the millionaire has no competitors. His radius of action is great. As I told you, whatever he takes up increases twofold or threefold. . . . As for thousands, they only bring in ten or twenty per cent.'

'But what I find difficult to grasp,' Chichikov said, is that it all begins with a copper or two.'

'It is never otherwise. That is the law,' Kostanzhonglo said. 'Whoever is born with thousands, and has been brought up on them, will acquire no more; he has formed his habits and many another thing! One must begin at the beginning and not in the middle, with a penny and not a shilling, at the bottom and not at the top. That is the only way of getting to know both the common folk and their life, for it is among them that you will have to twist and turn. When you have tried this and that on your own skin, and when you get to know that every penny must be cherished before you can treble it, when you have passed through all the trials, then you will be so schooled and wise that you will not trip up in any undertaking. That is the honest truth, believe me. You must begin at the beginning and not in the middle. I would not believe anyone who said to me, "Give me a hundred thousand and I shall at once grow rich!" He would be merely taking his chance and not backing a sure thing. He must work up from a penny.'

'In that case, I shall make a fortune,' Chichikov said, involuntarily turning his thoughts to the dead souls. 'For I am really starting from scratch.'

'Konstantin, it's time to give Pavel Ivanovich a chance to rest and sleep,' the lady of the house said. 'And here you are still talking.'

'Of course you will make a fortune,' Kostanzhonglo went on, without heeding his wife. 'Rivers of gold will flow into your hands. You will not know what to do with your income.'

Chichikov sat there as though enchanted in a golden sphere of looming dreams and projects. His thoughts were spinning madly. His excited imagination was embroidering gold patterns on a golden carpet, and in his ears there was the echo of the words, 'Rivers of gold will flow. . . .'

'Really, Konstantin,' his wife said, 'it is time for Pavel Ivanovich to go to bed.'

'Why need you worry? Go off to bed if you feel like it,' the host said and then stopped, for at that moment the sound of Platonov's snoring resounded in the room, and immediately after, Yarb could be heard snoring even more loudly. Realizing that it was really time for bed, the host woke Platonov, saying to him, 'That's enough of your snoring!' and he then wished Chichikov goodnight. They went their ways and were soon asleep in their beds.

Chichikov alone did not feel like sleeping. His thoughts were uppermost. He was pondering on how to become the proprietor not of an imaginary but a real estate. After his host's conversation it was all so clear! The possibility of making a fortune seemed so obvious! The whole difficult business of management now looked easy and comprehensible, and so much part of his character! It only remained to mortgage the dead souls and to acquire a non-imaginary estate! He already saw himself acting and managing his affairs in the way Kostanzhonglo had propounded, that is, carefully and efficiently, embarking on no new project without thoroughly investigating all the old methods, keeping an eye on everything oneself, getting to know all the peasants, renouncing all superfluous things, and devoting oneself wholly to work and the management of the estate. He already experienced a foretaste of the pleasure he would feel when he had established a stable system and when all the springs of his household machine would be working smoothly and busily activating each other. The work would hum and, just as a mill quickly grinds wheat to flour, so cash would be ground out from every kind of filth and rubbish. The image of Kostanzhonglo, that ideal proprietor, haunted his thoughts. He was the only man in the whole of Russia for whom he felt a personal respect. Until then he had respected people only for their rank or for their large fortune. Until then he had respected no one for his intelligence; Kostanzhonglo was the exception. Chichikov realized that there was no point in trying any tricks on him. He was now absorbed in another project—that of buying Khlobuyev's estate. He had ten thousand roubles of his own; he might try and borrow fifteen thousand from Kostanzhonglo, for the latter had declared that he was ready to help anyone wishing to better himself; as for the remainder, he would get hold of it anyhow, either by mortgaging or by making Khlobuyev wait. That too was possible and the latter would hardly go to court about it! For a long time he turned this over in his mind. At last slumber, after already holding the rest of the house in its embrace for four hours, put its arms round Chichikov, and he fell asleep like a log.

CHAPTER IV

THE next day things could not have turned out better. So ready was Kostanzhonglo to help anyone to improve his position that he was delighted to lend Chichikov ten thousand roubles without interest or security, simply upon a signed receipt. But that was not all; he undertook to introduce Chichikov to Khlobuyev and to look over the estate with him. Chichikov was in the best of spirits. After a satisfying breakfast they set off, all three of them, in Chichikov's carriage; their host's empty droshky followed after them. Yarb ran on ahead chasing the birds off the road. For ten miles they drove through the forests and the arable land belonging to Kostanzhonglo. As soon as his domain came to an end, they were faced with quite a different landscape: the corn looked sparse and there were only stumps where forests should have been. Although beautifully situated, from far off Khlobuyev's village showed signs of neglect. Then they caught sight of an uninhabited stone house which had never been quite completed and behind it of another one, this time inhabited. They discovered the master of the house at home, all dishevelled and drowsy, for he had just got out of bed. He was some forty years of age; his tie was all askew; his jacket had a patch on it and one of his boots had a hole in it.

He seemed boundlessly delighted to see the visitors; it was as though he were welcoming back his own brothers from whom he had long been parted.

'Konstantin Feodorovich! Platon Mikhailovich!' he cried. 'Your visit is a godsend! Just let me rub my eyes! Here I have been thinking that no one would ever visit me again. Everyone avoids me like the plague; they think I shall ask them for a loan. Ah, it's a hard life, a hard life, Konstantin Feodorovich! I know that I am myself to blame. But what am I to do? I'm leading a pig's life, I know. You must excuse me, gentlemen, for receiving you in this attire; my boots, as you see, have holes in them. What will you have to eat and drink?'

'Don't let us be ceremonious. We have come on business,' Kostanzhonglo said. 'Here is Pavel Ivanovich Chichikov, who would like to buy your estate.'

'I am delighted to make your acquaintance,' Khlobuyev said. 'Allow me to shake you by the hand.'

Chichikov held out both hands.

'I shall be delighted, my dear Pavel Ivanovich, to show you my estate, which is deserving of attention. . . . But, gentlemen, may I enquire whether you have dined?'

'We have, we have,' Kostanzhonglo said, wishing to get out of it. 'Don't let us waste time but go round the estate at once.'

'In that case, let us go.' Khlobuyev picked up his cap. 'Let us inspect all the disorder and confusion for which I am responsible.'

The visitors donned their caps and they all set off through one of the village streets. On either side of them they saw blind hovels with tiny windows stuffed with rags.

'Let us go and inspect all the disorder and confusion for which I am responsible,' Khlobuyev repeated. 'Of course it was just as well that you dined beforehand. Would you believe it, Konstantin Feodorovich, I haven't a chicken left in my yard—that's what I've come to!'

Khlobuyev sighed, and sensing that he would get little sympathy from Kostanzhonglo took Platonov by the arm and went on ahead with him, pressing him tightly to him. Kostanzhonglo and Chichikov were left behind and, arm in arm, followed them at a distance.

'It's a hard life, a hard life!' Khlobuyev was saying to Platonov. 'You cannot imagine how hard it all is! No money, no bread, no boots. For you that is just a foreign language. It would be a mere trifle if I were young and alone. But when all these misfortunes begin to make you ache in your old age and when one has a wife and five children, then one feels a bit sad, quite sad despite oneself.'

'Well, but you will sell your village, and that will put you right, won't it?' Platonov asked.

'Put me right!' Khlobuyev cried, with a wave of his hand. 'It will all go to pay off my debts. I shan't have a thousand roubles left.'

'What will you do then?' Platonov enquired.

'God knows.'

'Why don't you do something to get out of this mess?'

'What can I do?' Khlobuyev asked.

'Why don't you accept some sort of post?'

'I am a provincial secretary you know. What sort of a post would I get? Only an insignificant one. How could I accept a salary of, say, five hundred a month? I have a wife and five children.'

'Why not try and become a steward?'

'But who would entrust their estate to me? I have ruined my own,' Khlobuyev replied.

'Well, but when faced with hunger and death, you must do something,' Platonov said. 'I shall ask my brother if he can get somebody in town to hunt up some sort of a job for you.'

'No, Platon Mikhailovich,' Khlobuyev replied with a sigh, pressing him warmly by the hand. 'I'm not fit for anything now. I've grown decrepit before my time; my former sins are making my back ache and I've got rheumatism in my shoulder. I'm not fit for it! Why waste public money? As it is, there is a spate of job-hunters.

The Lord preserve me from making my salary add to the burden of the taxation imposed upon the poorer classes!'

'So here we have the fruits of a disorderly life!' Platonov thought to himself. 'It's worse than my lethargy.'

While they were thus conversing, Kostanzhonglo was beside himself with indignation as he walked along with Chichikov behind him.

'Just look at that,' Kostanzhonglo said, pointing with his finger. 'The way he has reduced his peasantry to poverty! There isn't a cart or a horse to be seen. Why, if there is a cattle plague, one can't just look to one's own property: one must sell what one has and furnish the peasant with cattle, so that he does not remain a day without means of working. But now it will take years to put this right. And the peasants too will have lost the habit of work, they will all have become idlers and drunkards. The very fact of leaving a peasant without any work to do for a whole year will have spoilt him forever: he will have got used to wearing rags and leading a beggar's life. And look at the state of the ground, just look at it!' Kostanzhonglo went on, pointing to the meadows which were now visible behind the huts. 'It's all been under water! I'd sow flax there and make five thousand roubles from the flax alone: I'd sow turnips too and make about four thousand. And look at the rye over there on the slope—it's not worth much. And I know that he did not grow any corn this year. And look at the ravines over there. . . . I'd plant such forests there that a raven wouldn't fly as high as the tree-tops. And to think he has neglected this treasure of a land! Well, if he had nothing with which to plough, he might at least have used the spade and made it into a vegetable plot. He could have taken a spade himself, and made his wife, children and all his servant folk do the digging. Yes, he should have died working. If he had killed himself while doing it, he would at least have been doing his duty instead of gorging himself like a pig at some dinner or other!' Kostanzhonglo spat as he said that, and a cloud of gloom spread over his face.

When they came nearer and stood above the ravine

which had grown over with yellow acacia, when they saw the glittering bend of the river and the cliffs in the distance, and when they perceived a part of general Betrishchev's house hidden among the thickets, and beyond it a wooded hill which looked a dusty blue in the distance, Chichikov suddenly divined that that must be Tentetnikov's estate and said: 'If one were to plant forests here, the view would be more beautiful than . . .'

'So you are an amateur of views!' said Kostanzhonglo, looking severely at him. 'You'd better be careful. If you start chasing after views, you will remain without bread and without views. Look to what is useful and not at beauty. Beauty will come of its own accord. Let towns serve you as an example: the best and most beautiful are those which have grown naturally, in which everyone built according to his needs and tastes, rather than those which have been constructed according to a formula and where there is nothing but barracks and barracks. . . . Beauty can wait! attend to what is useful. . . .'

'It's a pity one has to wait so long. One would like to see it all as one would wish . . .' Chichikov began.

'But are you a youth of twenty-five? . . . A Petersburg official? . . .' Kostanzhonglo interrupted. 'Patience! Work hard for six years on end, plant, sow, dig the earth, without giving yourself rest. It's hard, I know, very hard. But then afterwards, when you have churned up the earth, it will begin to help you, and that will be no ordinary thing . . . no, my dear sir, besides your seventy labourers you will have seven hundred other invisible ones assisting you. You will get everything tenfold! I don't have to move a finger now, everything happens by itself. Yes, nature loves patience; and that is a law given it by God Himself, Who glorified the meek.'

'I grow stronger as I listen to you. I feel my spirits rise,' Chichikov exclaimed.

'Look at the way that soil is ploughed!' Kostanzhonglo cried bitterly, pointing to the slope. 'I can't bear to stay here any longer. It's death for me to see all this disorder and neglect. You can now conclude your business with him without my help. He only spoils what God has given him.' As he said this Kostanzhonglo looked even gloomier, he took his leave of Chichikov and catching up with their host began to say good-bye to him.

'But how is this, Konstantin Feodorovich?' the astonished host was saying. 'You have only just arrived and now you are off again.'

'I can't stay. I must absolutely get back home,' Kostanzhonglo replied. He said good-bye, got into his droshky and drove away.

It seemed as though Khlobuyev understood the reason for his hurried departure.

'Konstantin Feodorovich can't stand it,' he said. 'It's depressing for such a fine landowner as he is to see the mess I am in. Believe me, Pavel Ivanovich, I did not even sow any corn this year. Honest truth! I had no seeds, to say nothing of ploughs. They say that your brother, Platon Mikhailovich, is an excellent manager. As for Konstantin Feodorovich, what is there to say about him! He is a Napoleon at his job. I ask myself often enough why one man should have so much brains. If only I had a small share of them in my stupid head. Now, you must be careful here, gentlemen, or the bridge will collapse into the water. I gave orders for it to be repaired in the spring. . . . I am sorry most of all for the poor peasants. They need an example. But what sort of an example can I give them? What is to be done? Take them, Pavel Ivanovich, under your wing. How can I teach them to be orderly when I am so disorderly myself? I would have given them their freedom long ago, but that would not improve matters. I realize that they must be taught how to live first of all. They need some stern and just man over them, somebody who would live among them for a long while and inspire them by the example of his own inde-fatigable activity. . . . Judging by myself, I can see that a Russian cannot go on without a taskmaster. Otherwise he will only drowse off and stagnate.'

'It's strange,' Platonov said. 'Why is a Russian so prone to doze off and stagnate? Why is it that if you do not keep an eye on the ordinary man he will turn into a drunkard or a rogue?'

'It's because of his lack of enlightenment,' Chichikov exclaimed.

'God knows why it is! Here are we who have been enlightened and have been to the University, and yet what are we worth? Now, what have I learnt?' said Platonov. 'Not only did I not learn how to live in orderly fashion but I learnt the art of spending money on all sorts of refinements of comfort, and to think of all sorts of objects which require a lot of money. Was it because I learnt stupidly?' He paused and then went on. 'No, my fellow students were in the same boat. Two or three of them got some real profit out of it, but that was perhaps because they were clever to start with. As for the others, they tried their hardest to learn everything that undermines the health and empties the pockets. That's the truth of the matter. And what do I think about it all? At times it seems to me that a Russian is a lost soul. You want to do everything for him and nothing comes of it. You keep thinking that you will start a new life as from to-morrow, that you will start a new diet to-morrow, but nothing of the sort happens: by the evening of that same day you have gorged yourself so much that you can only blink and lose the power of speech, and you sit there like an owl, blinking at everyone, really you do! And that is all there is to it!'

'Yes,' Chichikov said with a smile, 'that happens often enough.'

'We were not born to be sensible,' Platonov went on. 'I don't believe that any one of us has any sense. If I see any one of us living reasonably well and saving money, I can't even believe it. The devil is sure to lead him astray in his old age: he will suddenly let it all go. And it's true of everyone, whether enlightened or not. No, there is something else missing there, but what it is I do not know.'

The scenes they saw as they walked back were very similar. An untidy disorder reared its ugly head everywhere. They came across a fresh puddle in the middle of the street. The peasants' property as well as the master's showed every sign of neglect. An angry peasant woman in a greasy sack-cloth dress was beating a poor little girl almost to death and was letting rip at some third person, swearing by all the devils as she did it. Standing to one side two peasants were looking on apathetically at this drunken woman. One of them was scratching his backside while the other was yawning. The very buildings looked drowsy and the roofs seemed to yawn. As he looked round him, Platonov could not restrain a yawn. There were patches on everything. One of the huts had a wooden gate resting on top of it by way of a roof: the sagging windows were propped up with beams pinched from one of the master's barns. It was obvious that the system in vogue was that of Trishkin's kaftan:[5] the cuffs and facings were trimmed to mend the elbows.

'Yours is not a very attractive property,' Chichikov said after they had finished their inspection and had reached the house again. . . . Inside they saw an amazing mixture of poverty and glittering bric-a-brac in the latest fashion. There was a statuette of Shakespeare on the inkstand and an ivory hand for scratching one's back lay on the table. The lady of the house was dressed fashionably and with taste, and she chatted about the town and the new theatre which had just opened. The children were frisky and gay. The boys and girls were excellently dressed—very appropriately and in good taste. But it would have been better if they had worn plain homespun shirts and bright peasant skirts in the peasant fashion, and had run about in the open. Very soon a friend of the lady of the house paid a call: she was an empty-headed chatterbox. The ladies retired to their quarters and the children ran after them. The men were left alone.

'And what is your price?' Chichikov enquired. 'I am asking you, I confess, to name your final price, for the property is in a worse state than I expected.'

'Yes, indeed, it is in a bad state,' Khlobuyev agreed. 'And that is not all. I shall not hide from you the fact that out of the hundred souls down on the census register only fifty are alive: cholera took a good many and some of them have run away, and you may as well consider them

---

5. Proverbial for something the improvement of which leads to the worsening of something else.

dead; if you were to take the matter to court you would only use up the whole of the estate to pay the costs. For that reason I shall only ask you for thirty-five thousand roubles.'

Chichikov began, of course, to bargain.

'But how is that? Thirty-five thousand? Thirty-five thousand for such a property!' he said. 'My offer is twenty-five.'

Platonov grew ashamed of this bargaining. 'Buy it as it stands, Pavel Ivanovich,' he said. 'An estate is always worth that price. If you don't give him thirty-five thousand, my brother and I will go halves and buy it for ourselves.'

'Very well, I agree,' Chichikov said, alarmed. 'Very well, only on condition that I pay you half the amount in a year's time.'

'No, Pavel Ivanovich! I cannot agree to that,' Khlobuyev replied. 'You must pay me half of it now and the rest within a reasonable period. . . . I could of course raise that money by mortgaging, but. . . .'

'I really don't know what to do,' Chichikov said. 'I have only ten thousand at my disposal now.' Chichikov was lying, for he had in all twenty thousand, including the money borrowed from Kostanzhonglo. But he was reluctant to part with so much money at once.

'No, Pavel Ivanovich, that won't do!' Khlobuyev exclaimed. 'It is absolutely essential for me to have fifteen thousand at once.'

'I shall lend you five thousand,' Platonov said.

'Perhaps that would be the best thing!' Chichikov said, and he thought to himself: 'That loan will come in handy.' His box was brought along from the carriage and the ten thousand roubles were at once taken out of it and handed over to Khlobuyev: the remaining five thousand he promised to bring along the next day, and the balance in a day or two, inwardly resolving to delay payment if he could possibly contrive it. Chichikov had a particular dislike for letting money out of his hands. Even though it might be an urgent case, he always preferred to pay up to-morrow rather than to-day. In short, he acted as any of us would do. For we get a kick out of making the needy wait: 'Let him rub his back on the doorpost,' we say. As though he cannot wait a bit! What business is it of ours that he finds every hour precious and that his affairs suffer from the delay? 'Come along to-morrow, brother,' we say, 'we have no time to-day.'

'And where do you intend to live afterwards?' Platonov asked Khlobuyev. 'Have you another property handy?'

'Yes, I shall have to live in town. I have a house there,' Khlobuyev replied. 'I should have had to do this in any case both for my own sake and the children's. They need to be taught scripture, music and dancing. You could not get that for any money in the country.'

'He hasn't a bite of bread, and yet he wants his children to learn dancing!' Chichikov exclaimed to himself.

'Strange!' Platonov thought.

'However, we must celebrate our deal,' Khlobuyev said. 'Hey, Kiryiushka! Bring us a bottle of champagne.'

'He hasn't a bite of bread but he has champagne,' Chichikov thought.

Platonov did not know what to think. Khlobuyev had got a stock of champagne out of necessity. He had sent to town for it. The village shop would not let him have *kvas* on credit, but drink he must. The Frenchman who had recently arrived with wines from Petersburg gave credit to everyone. And so there was nothing to be done: he had to have the champagne.

The champagne was brought in. They drank two or three glasses of it and became quite cheerful. Khlobuyev grew talkative: he turned out to be quite witty and full of anecdotes. His talk revealed that he had a great knowledge of people and the world! He saw so many things in the right perspective, in a few brief phrases he was able to sum up correctly and precisely his fellow landowners; he had a clear notion of all their failings and mistakes and was intimately acquainted with the history of all the ruined gentry; he knew why, and how, and for what reasons, they had ruined themselves; he was able to mime their habits with such originality and humour that Platonov and Chichikov were both enchanted at his talk, and they were ready to admit that he was the most intelligent of men.

'I am astonished,' Chichikov said, 'that with all your intelligence you cannot find means and ways of resolving your difficulties?'

'There are ways and means,' Khlobuyev said, and he at once unloaded a heap of projects on them. But they were all so stupid and fantastic, they depended so little on a knowledge of men and of the world, that one could only shrug one's shoulders and say: 'O lord! What a gulf there is between a knowledge of the world and the ability to make use of that knowledge!' With him everything depended on being able to get hold of a hundred or two hundred thousand roubles. Then it seemed to him that everything could be arranged as it should be and that the estate would pay for itself, that his past mistakes would be wiped out, that the income could be quadrupled, and that he could then pay off all his debts. And he ended his discourse thus: 'But what would you have me do? There just isn't a benefactor to be found who would give me two hundred or at least a hundred thousand roubles by way of a loan. It looks as though God is against me.'

'No wonder,' Chichikov thought. 'As if God would send that fool two hundred thousand!'

'I have an aunt worth three millions,' Khlobuyev continued. 'She's very religious. She gives away a lot to the churches and monasteries, but she is not very forthcoming with her relatives. She is an aunt of the old school, she's worth seeing. She has at least four hundred canaries, to say nothing of pug-dogs, hangers-on and servants such as you would not find anywhere else these days. Her youngest servant is about sixty, and she calls him: "Boy!" If any of her guests misbehave at dinner, she will instruct the servant to stop serving him, and how! That's the sort she is!'

Platonov smiled.

'What is her name and where does she live?' Chichikov enquired.

'She lives in our town, and her name is Alexandra Ivanovna Hanasarova.'

'Why don't you ask her to help you?' Platonov said sympathetically. 'It seems to me that, if she were to acquaint herself with your circumstances, she could not refuse to help you.'

'Oh yes, she could. She has a tough character. She is quite a skinflint! And besides, there are a lot of others who are trying to cadge from her. One of them is even aiming at becoming the governor: he claims to be a relation of hers. . . . Will you do me a favour?' Khlobuyev said suddenly, turning to Platonov. 'Next week I am giving a banquet for all the notables of the town. I should like your company.'

Platonov gaped at him. He did not know as yet that in the towns and capitals of Russia there are many such wise men whose life is a complete and inexplicable enigma. To all appearances such a one has spent all he had, he is up to his ears in debt, he has nowhere to turn for money, and yet he will give a banquet; and all his guests will tell each other that it is his last fling and that he will end up in prison the following day. Then ten years go by, and still this smart fellow holds his place in society, he is still deeper in debt, and still giving banquets which his guests believe to be the last, all just as convinced as ever that he will be put in jail to-morrow.

Khlobuyev's town house was a remarkable institution. One day a priest in all his vestments would be celebrating mass there; the next a troupe of French actors would be rehearsing in it. One day there would not be a bite of bread to eat; the next all the actors and artists of the town would be entertained and it would be open house. At times he was in such difficulties that another man would have shot or hanged himself; but his religious turn of mind prevented him from doing so, surprising though it was to find this co-existing with his inept way of life. In his bitter moments he used to read the lives of the saints and martyrs, and thus fortify his spirit against despair. At these times his soul would melt, his spirit would overflow with humility, and his eyes would be full of tears. He would pray, and—strange thing—almost invariably he received help from some unexpected quarter: either one of his old friends would remember him and send him money; or some strange lady, who happened to be passing through the town, and who had heard tell of him by chance, would send him a rich gift on the impulse of a generous heart; or again some affair of his, of which he had not even heard, would unexpectedly bear fruit. He would then reverently admit the inexhaustible charity of Providence, order a thanksgiving mass to be celebrated, and once again embark upon his irregular life.

'I have a great pity for him, really I have,' Platonov said to Chichikov when they had bidden their host goodbye and were driving away from the house.

'He's a prodigal son,' Chichikov said. 'There is no point in pitying such men.'

Very soon they had ceased to think about him. Platonov forgot him because he was in the habit of looking at people as well as everything else in the world in a lazy and drowsy sort of way. At the sight of suffering in others he felt sore and compassionate at heart, but these impressions did not leave a deep imprint on his soul. At the end of a few minutes he had stopped thinking about Khlobuyev. He did not think about him because he did not think about himself. Chichikov, on the other hand, did not think about him because all his thoughts were concentrated on the purchase he had just effected. However, having of a sudden become not an imaginary but a real proprietor of a non-imaginary estate, he grew pensive, and his thoughts and suppositions became more sober and brought a significant expression to his face. 'Patience and work!' he said to himself. 'That is not so difficult. I have grown to know them, if I may say so, ever since I wore baby clothes. They are nothing new as far as I am concerned! But shall I be able to show as much patience now as I could when I was a young man?' However much he turned it over in his mind, from whatever angle he examined his purchase, he could not help concluding that it was a profitable investment. He thought of all the possibilities. He might mortgage the estate after selling off the best portions of the land or he might manage it himself and become a landowner after the example of Kostanzhonglo, relying on his advice as that of a neighbour and benefactor. He might even resell the estate (if he did not wish to manage it himself, of course), keeping only the dead souls and the runaway serfs for himself. Then another profitable possibility occurred to him: he might do a bolt and get out of repaying Kostanzhonglo's loan. A strange thought that was! Not that Chichikov himself conceived it, but it rose up before him of its own accord, teasing and mocking him, blinking at him. What a skittish, profligate thought! Who is the creator of these suddenly assailing thoughts? ... He was feeling pleased with himself—pleased at being a landowner at last, not an imaginary one but a real landowner, who now had in his possession lands, property, and serfs, not imaginary serfs but real existing ones. After a little while he began to jump up and down on his seat and to rub his hands; he winked at himself and, putting his fist to his mouth, blew a march on it as on a bugle, and he even said aloud a few encouraging words to himself, something in the nature of 'You little mug!' and 'You little capon!' But then, remembering suddenly that he was not alone, he grew quiet and tried to smother his uncertain impulse of delight; and so, when Platonov, who had interpreted some of these ejaculations as words addressed to him, asked him: 'What?' he replied 'Nothing.'

It was only then that, casting a glance round him, he noticed that they had long been driving through a very beautiful grove: the charming hedge of birch-trees stretched on and on to either side of them. Glittering like a snow-covered palisade the white trunks of the birch-trees and aspen-trees lifted up lightly in the air the green of their newly fledged leaves. The nightingales sang loudly and intermittently in the thickets. Forest tulips glowed yellow in the grass. Chichikov could not imagine how he had got there, in that beautiful spot, after being in the open fields but a short while ago. Then through the trees he caught a glimpse of a white stone church and, on the other side, a grating could be seen. As they finally drove into a street, a gentleman appeared walking towards them, wearing a cap and carrying a stick. An English hound, on long and slender legs, was running ahead of him.

'That is my brother,' Platonov cried. 'Coachman, stop!'

Platonov got out of the carriage and Chichikov followed him. The dogs had already had time to kiss each other. The quick slender-legged Azor licked Yarb on his nose with his nimble tongue; he then licked Platonov's hand and, leaping up on Chichikov, licked his ear. The brothers embraced.

'Now, Platon, what have you been up to?' said the brother, who was called Vassily.

'What do you mean?' Platonov asked him apathetically.

'Yes, what have you been up to? There has been no news of you these three days! The stable boy brought in your stallion from Petukhov's. "He's gone off," he said, "with a gentleman." If you had only sent a message to say where you were going, and why, and for how long! How can you act in such a way? And I, God knows, what didn't I think all these days!'

'Well, what's to be done? I forgot,' Platonov replied. 'We paid a visit to Konstantin Feodorovich: he sends you his greetings, our sister also. This is Pavel Ivanovich, a good friend. And that is my brother Vassily. Brother Vassily! This is Pavel Ivanovich Chichikov.'

The two persons, who were thus introduced, shook hands and, taking off their caps, kissed each other.

'Who is this Chichikov?' brother Vassily thought to himself. 'My brother, Platon, is not very discriminating about making friends.' And he scrutinized Chichikov as closely as was consistent with good manners, and perceived that he was to all appearances a respectable person.

For his part, Chichikov also scrutinized brother Vassily as closely as was consistent with good manners, and he perceived that the brother was shorter than Platonov, had darker hair and was far from being as handsome, but his features were far more animated and showed traces of a more generous disposition. It was apparent that he slept less. But Chichikov paid less attention to that side of him.

'I have decided, brother, to travel together with Pavel Ivanovich through saintly Russia, maybe that will do away with my spleen.'

'What do you mean you have just decided?' asked brother Vassily in perplexity. He almost added: 'And to set out with a man whom you have only just met and who may turn out to be a worthless fellow or the devil knows what!' Filled with suspicion, he looked sideways at Chichikov but only saw a person of astonishing respectability.

They turned right and entered through the gateway. The courtyard was an ancient one, the sort that is no longer built, with eaves jutting out from under a high roof. Two immense lime-trees were growing in the middle of the courtyard and cast their shade over almost the half of it. Beneath them there was an array of wooden benches. Flowering lilac and elder bushes ringed the fence round the courtyard in a necklace of beads, and completely hid it beneath their flowers and leaves. The manor house was completely concealed from view except for the windows and the door, which peeped out through the branches and looked charming. In between the straight upstanding trees the kitchens, storehouses and cellars could be made out. All these buildings were hidden among bushes. The nightingales sang loudly, making the thickets ring with their trilling. Involuntarily the soul was invaded with a peaceful and agreeable feeling. Everything reminded one of those easy days when everyone lived to his heart's content, simply and without complications. Brother Vassily invited Chichikov to sit down. They sat down on the benches under the lime-trees.

A lad of about seventeen, in a handsome pink shirt, brought along and set down before them several decanters filled with fruit waters and *kvases* of various kinds and of different colours, some of them as thick as butter, others as fizzy as lemonade. Having set down the decanters, the lad picked up a spade, which was propped against a tree, and went off with it into the garden. Like Kostanzhonglo, the brothers Platonov kept no personal servants: the latter fulfilled the function of gardener as well, and all the household staff took their turn at gardening. Brother Vassily argued that being a servant was not an occupation: anyone could serve at table, and it was not worth while having a special category of people for that job. He maintained that Russian folk were able and alert, and no idlers, only as long as they wore their traditional shirts and peasant coats; but that as soon as they donned a German suit they would suddenly become awkward, stupid and lazy, forgetting to change their shirts or to visit the baths, and that they would sleep in their suit, begetting under their German cut cloth bugs and fleas in numberless quantities. In that he may have been right. In the Platonovs' village the folk dressed extra smartly: the women's head-dresses were fringed with gold while the sleeves of their blouses were like the edging on a Turkish shawl.

'Our house is long famous for its *kvases*,' brother Vassily said.

Chichikov poured himself a glass from the first decanter. It was like the mead he had once tasted in Poland; it bubbled like champagne and its gaseous effects communicated themselves rapidly from mouth to nose. 'This is nectar!' he said. He tried another glass, filling it up from the next decanter. It was better still.

'It's the drink of drinks!' Chichikov exclaimed. 'I can claim to have sampled a most excellent cordial at the house of your brother-in-law, and here am I now tasting your own exquisite *kvas*.'

'The cordial is ours too; it was my sister who made it. Now tell me, what part of the country and what spots do you propose to visit?' brother Vassily asked.

'I am journeying not so much on my own account as on that of another,' Chichikov replied, rocking on the bench, stroking his knee and bending forward. 'General Betrishchev is a close friend of mine and, I may say, a benefactor, and he asked me to visit some relatives of his.

Relatives are, of course, just relatives, but I am also, so to speak, travelling on my own account; to say nothing of the benefit to my digestion, and the possibility of seeing the world and how people live, travelling is in itself, as it were, a living book and a second science.'

Brother Vassily pondered. 'He's a bit florid in his speech but there is some truth in what he says,' he thought. After a moment's silence he turned to Platonov and said: 'I am beginning to think that a journey might shake you up. Your trouble is a sleepy soul. You have quite simply fallen asleep—and you have fallen asleep not out of any satiety or weariness, but from the lack of any vivid impressions and sensations. Now I, for example, am quite different. I should prefer to feel less acutely and not to take to heart so much everything that happens.'

'Why do you take everything so much to heart?' Platon asked. 'You always look for trouble and cause yourself needless anxieties.'

'What need have I to invent trouble when there is unpleasantness at every step?' Vassily retorted. 'You haven't heard the trick that Lyenitzin played us while you were away? He has seized the common land where we celebrate the "Red Hill."[6] In the first place, I would not have parted with that common for any money in the world. . . . There my peasants have celebrated the "Red Hill" every spring, and all the traditions of the village are bound up with it; and I look on custom as a sacred thing, and am ready to sacrifice everything for it.'

'He doesn't know about it, that's why he grabbed it,' Platon said. 'He's a new man, fresh from Petersburg; one should explain it all to him and talk it over.'

'He knows all right. I sent him a message, but he returned a rude answer,' the brother replied.

'You should have called on him yourself and talked it over,' Platon said. 'You yourself should have a talk with him.'

'No, I won't. He's too stuck up. I shan't call on him. If you like, you can call on him.'

'I'd go willingly, but you know I don't interfere in your

6. The first week after Easter.

affairs. . . .' Platon replied. 'He might trick and deceive me.'

'If you like, I can go,' Chichikov chimed in. 'But you will have to tell me what it's all about.'

Vassily glanced at him and thought to himself: 'He really seems to be fond of travelling!'

'Only you must give me an idea as to the sort of man he is,' said Chichikov. 'And you must also tell me what it's all about.'

'I am ashamed to burden you with such a disagreeable commission. As a person I think he is just trash: he is one of the smaller nobles of our province, who has been in the service in Petersburg, has got married there to somebody's natural daughter,[7] and has now put on airs. He is setting the tone. But the folk round here are not so stupid: fashion is not an edict for us, and Petersburg is not sacrosanct.'

'Of course,' Chichikov said. 'But what is it all about?'

'This is it. He needs land of course. If he did not act as he does, I would willingly have given some in another place, without charging him anything. . . . But as things are, that uppish man will think. . . .'

'In my opinion, it is better to talk it over with him,' Chichikov said. 'Maybe the matter is . . . I have been entrusted with negotiations before and no one has ever regretted it. Now take general Betrishchev, for example. . . .'

'But I am ashamed that you should have to talk to a man like that,' the brother said.

'. . .[8] and taking every care that it should be kept secret,' Chichikov said. 'For it is not so much the crime as the temptation that is harmful.'

'That is so, that is so,' Lyenitzin said, bending his head completely to one side.

'How nice it is to find that we think alike!' Chichikov continued. 'I am engaged in an enterprise that is both legal and illegal: it is illegal only in appearance, in sub-

---

7. Illegitimate daughter.
8. In the manuscript the two pages preceding this word were found to be cut out [*Translator's note*].

stance it is quite legal. Being in need of a mortgage, I am disinclined to involve anyone in the risk of paying two roubles for a living soul. Anything might happen, I might go bust—God preserve me from it!—it would be unpleasant for the owner: so I decided to make use of runaway serfs and dead souls, those that have not yet been struck out of the census list, thus acting like a Christian and relieving the poor owner of the burden of malities and make out a deed of purchase as for living souls.'

'It's all very strange,' Lyenitzin thought to himself as he moved his chair back a little. 'Yes, the affair is a bit . . .', he began.

'And there need be no temptation since it will be a secret,' Chichikov replied. 'And besides it will be a transaction between people who are well disposed to each other.'

'But nevertheless . . . however . . . the affair is. . . .'

'There need be no temptation,' Chichikov replied quite frankly and straightforwardly. 'We have talked over the transaction: it will be just between us, and since we are well disposed to each other, of reasonable age, of good rank, it will remain a secret.' And saying that he looked frankly and nobly into Lyenitzin's eyes.

However resourceful Lyenitzin was, however skilful in all kinds of transactions, he was now quite perplexed, especially as he felt that he had in some strange way got entangled in his own net. He was quite incapable of unjust actions and he had no wish to be unjust even in secret. 'This is a nice pickle!' he thought to himself. 'Here is a fine friendship! There's a nut for you to crack.'

But fate and circumstances seemed to favour Chichikov. As though to assist him in this difficult situation, in came the lady of the house, Lyenitzin's young wife, a pale, thin, short woman, who was yet dressed in Petersburg fashion and had a snobbish liking for all people who were *comme il faut*.[9] A nanny followed her carrying a first-born infant, the fruit of the tender love of the newly

9. French expression meaning "proper."

wedded couple. Tripping forward smartly, his head to one side, Chichikov completely enchanted the lady from Petersburg and then the infant. The latter began by howling but Chichikov succeeded, by the use of the words 'Agoo, agoo, little darling!', by snapping his fingers and dangling the cornelian seal on his watch-chain, in luring him into his arms. Then he began to lift up the infant towards the ceiling, evoking a pleasant smile from him, at which both parents were exceedingly delighted. But either from some sudden pleasure or from some other cause, the infant misbehaved himself.

'Oh, heavens!' Madame Lyenitzin exclaimed. 'He has ruined your coat!'

Chichikov looked down: the sleeve of his new dress-coat was completely spoilt. 'May you choke, you little devil!' he thought in his heart.

The master and mistress of the house and the nanny all ran out to fetch the eau-de-Cologne. Then they began to rub him from all sides.

'It's nothing, nothing, nothing at all!' Chichikov kept saying, trying to impart to his face, as far as he could, a gay expression. 'Can an infant spoil anything in his golden age?' he kept repeating. But at the same time he thought to himself: 'What a little beast! May the wolves devour him! He's put me in a fix, the cursed little rascal!'

This apparently insignificant circumstance completely won the master of the house over to Chichikov's side. How could he refuse anything to a guest who had shown such affection for the tiny tot and had magnanimously paid for it with his coat? So, in order to avoid setting a bad example, they decided to settle the affair secretly, for it was not the affair itself but the temptation that was harmful.

'In return for the favour you have done me, allow me to repay you likewise with a favour,' Chichikov said. 'I should like to act as a referee between you and the brothers Platonov. You want land, don't you? . . .'

(*The rest of this chapter is missing in the manuscript.*)

CHAPTER V[1]

EVERYONE makes the most of his opportunities. 'Need is a spur', as the proverb says. The exploration through the trunks was brought to a successful conclusion, and something left over from that investigation remained to be put away in Chichikov's private box. In short, everything was sensibly arranged. Chichikov did not so much steal as profit by whatever came to hand. Every one of us profits in this way at some time or another: some by government timber, others by judicious saving from public funds; some steal from their children for the sake of an actress who may be passing through the town, others strip their peasants in order to acquire fashionable furniture or the latest type of carriage. What is to be done if the world is grown so full of temptations? What is to be done if there are lavishly expensive restaurants, masked balls, all sorts of excursions and gypsy dancing? It is hard to keep a check on oneself if everyone else indulges in these whims and fashion dictates it. Just try and control yourself in such circumstances! Chichikov should have already set out but the weather had made travelling difficult. Meanwhile the town was getting ready for another market fair—an aristocratic one this time. The previous fair had been mainly one of cattle, horses and raw materials, as well as of such peasant produce as was bought up wholesale by merchants and *kulaks*. The present fair was to be devoted to all such genteel goods as had been purchased by middlemen at the Nizhny-Novgorod[2] fair and then transported here. This was the chance for all the exploiters of Russian purses to congregate, Frenchmen and their madames, and Frenchwomen in fashionable hats, all exploiters of money earned by sweat and blood—that swarm of Egyptian locusts, as Kostanzhonglo used to call them, which would not even leave their eggs behind them but bury them deep in the ground after gobbling up everything in their path.

1. This chapter was not numbered by the author [*Translator's note*].

2. A town on the Volga, famous for its fairs, now called Gorky.

Only the failure of their crops kept many of the land-owners in their villages. But the officials, who were not subject to these vagaries of nature, turned up in full force: to make matters worse their wives did likewise. Having read a great many books recently published with the purpose of stimulating all sorts of new needs, they were all obsessed by an extraordinary thirst to absorb all these new delights. A Frenchman opened a new establishment unheard of till then in the countryside, a vauxhall or garden where suppers were served at extraordinarily low prices and half on credit. . . . A desire to show off their equipages and coachmen possessed the inhabitants of the town. There was great competition among the classes over this enjoyment. Despite the filthy weather and the mud, there was a rapid coming and going of smart carriages. God knows where they all came from, but they would not have disgraced the streets of Petersburg. . . . Smartly doffing their hats, the dealers and shop-assistants overcharged the ladies. Bearded men in shaggy fur caps were hardly to be seen: everyone looked European, the men's chins were shaved, and they had rotten teeth. 'This way. This way! Please come into this shop, sir!' the shop-boys were bawling in places.

But they were contemptuously ignored by those of the dealers who were versed in European ways; with a feeling of dignity they sometimes said to a prospective customer: 'Here we have materials claire and black.'

'Have you any sprigged cloth of a cranberry colour?' Chichikov asked.

'We have very fine materials,' the merchant said, raising his cap with one hand and pointing to his shop with the other. Chichikov went into the shop. The shopkeeper raised the counter-flap and emerged on the other side of it, with his back to the goods which were piled up in rolls to the ceiling, and stood there facing his customer. With both his hands propped smartly against the counter and rocking his body slightly, he enquired: 'What sort of cloth would you like to see?'

'Sprigged, olive or bottle-coloured, on a ground as near as possible to cranberry,' Chichikov replied.

'I can assure you that our cloth is first-class, you would not find anything better except in the most enlightened capitals. Boy, fetch down that material from above, the one that is under number thirty-four! That's not the one! Why are you always getting above your sphere, like the proletariat? Throw it down here. Here is the material, sir!' And unrolling it from the other end, the merchant stuck it right under Chichikov's nose, so that the latter was able not only to stroke the silky, glossy material but also to smell it.

'It's very good, but not quite what I want,' Chichikov told him. 'I have served in the customs and I am used to having the very best quality. Besides, I should like to have a cloth of a redder hue, as near as possible to a cranberry.'

'I understand,' the merchant replied. 'You would really like a colour that is just coming into fashion. I have a most excellent cloth here. But I must warn you that, although it is of the highest quality, it is rather expensive.'

The 'European' clambered up. A roll of cloth fell down. He unrolled it with all the art of bygone days, oblivious for a time of the fact that he belonged to a later generation. He raised the cloth to the light and even went out into the open air in order to display it all the better and, with eyes half shut in the light, he exclaimed: 'An excellent colour this! A cloth of smoke and flame.'

Chichikov liked the cloth and they agreed on a price although, as the merchant asserted, it had a *prix fixe*.[3] Thereupon a deft pulling and tugging with both hands took place. The piece of cloth was then wrapped in paper, Russian fashion, with incredible speed. The parcel spun beneath a string which gripped it in a quivering knot. The string was then cut with scissors, the packet was at once put into the carriage, and the merchant was doffing his cap. Chichikov had just pulled out some money to pay for his purchase when a voice rang out:

'Will you show me some black cloth?' it said.

'The devil take it! It's Khlobuyev,' Chichikov mut-

3. A firm price that cannot be reduced by bargaining.

tered to himself and turned his back upon him, deciding that it would be unwise to enter into any discussion with him about the inheritance. But Khlobuyev had already spotted him.

'What's the meaning of this, Pavel Ivanovich? Are you avoiding me on purpose?' he asked. 'I could not find you anywhere, but in view of the state of our affairs we must have a serious talk.'

'My dear sir!' Chichikov said as he shook him by the hand. 'Believe me, I have wanted to have a chat with you, but I couldn't find time.' To himself he thought: 'The devil take you!' And then he suddenly saw Mourazov entering the shop. 'Heavens! it is you, Afanasy Vassilievich! How are you?' Chichikov exclaimed.

'And how are you?' Mourazov said, taking off his hat. The merchant and Khlobuyev also doffed their hats.

'I have an ache in my back and I am not sleeping too well,' Chichikov replied. 'I don't know whether it is due to lack of exercise. . . .'

But instead of probing into the cause of Chichikov's ailments, Mourazov turned to Khlobuyev and said: 'I saw you go into the shop and followed you. I have a few matters to discuss with you. Would you mind coming to my house?'

'Of course, of course!' Khlobuyev exclaimed hurriedly, going out with him.

'I wonder what's in the wind?' Chichikov thought to himself.

'Mr. Mourazov is a very worthy and clever man,' the merchant said. 'He knows his business, but he lacks enlightenment. A merchant,' he went on sententiously, 'is not just a merchant, but a negotiator. In that capacity the budget and reaction are combined, for otherwise the result would be pauperism.' Chichikov only waved his hand at this rigmarole.

'Pavel Ivanovich, I have been looking for you everywhere,' a voice behind him exclaimed. It was Lyenitzin. The merchant respectfully doffed his hat.

'Ah, is that you, Feodor Ivanovich!' Chichikov exclaimed.

'For God's sake, come along to my house. I must have a word with you,' Lyenitzin said. Chichikov glanced at him and perceived that he was out of countenance. Settling with the merchant, he walked out of the shop with Lyenitzin.

'Ah, there you are at last,' Mourazov said as Khlobuyev came in. 'Please come into my room.' And he conducted Khlobuyev into the room which is already familiar to the reader. An official living on a salary of seven hundred roubles a year could not have had a less cosy room.

'Tell me now, I assume that your circumstances have improved?' Mourazov asked. 'Your aunt did leave you something, didn't she?'

'What am I to say, Afanasy Vassilievich?' Khlobuyev replied. 'I'm not sure if my circumstances have improved. My share was only five hundred serfs and thirty thousand in cash, and out of that I ought to pay off part of my debts. When I have done that I shall have nothing left. But the most important part of the whole business is that the will was anything but above-board. There has been any amount of trickery involved! I shall tell you all about it now, and you will see for yourself what has been happening. That Chichikov. . . .'

'If you will allow me, let us first of all talk about yourself before we pass on to that Chichikov,' Mourazov said. 'Tell me now: how much do you calculate would suffice and satisfy you in order to put right all your affairs?'

'My circumstances are complicated,' Khlobuyev replied. 'In order to put my affairs right, to pay off my debts, and to have the possibility of existing in a very modest way, I should need at least a hundred thousand roubles, if not more—in short, I don't see how it would be possible to do it.'

'But supposing you had that amount, what sort of life would you lead then?' Mourazov enquired.

'Well, in that case I should rent a small apartment and busy myself with my children's education,' Khlobuyev replied. 'There is no point in thinking about myself any longer: my career is ended. I can't take on a job: I am not fit for anything.'

'But in that case your life would still be one of idleness,' Mourazov declared. 'And idleness gives rise to temptations such as would not occur to anyone who had any work to do.'

'I can't do it. I'm not fit for anything: I have grown stupid and my back aches,' Khlobuyev replied.

'But how can you live without work? How can you exist without a job or position?' Mourazov asked. 'I ask you! Just look at any of God's creatures: each one of them performs some sort of service, each one of them is guided by a purpose. A stone even has its uses; and it wouldn't do at all for man, who is the most reasonable of creatures, to be of no use.'

'But I won't be altogether without an occupation,' Khlobuyev protested. 'I can attend to my children's education.'

'No, Khlobuyev, no! That is the most difficult thing of all,' Mourazov went on. 'How can anyone who has not educated himself undertake to educate children? The only way to educate children is by personal example. And is your life a proper model for them? It would only encourage them to be idle, and to spend their time playing cards. No, Khlobuyev, let me take over your children: you yourself would only spoil them. Just think it over seriously: idleness has been your downfall—you must fight against it. How can anyone live without a firm foundation? Someone has to do his duty. A labourer also does service in his own way. He may exist on a farthing's worth of bread, but he earns it and has the interest of his occupation at heart.

'Honest to God, Afanasy Vassilievich, I have tried to overcome my weakness!' Khlobuyev said. 'But what is to be done? I have grown old and incapable. What am I to do? Must I take up service again? At forty-five am I to sit at the same desk with junior clerks? And besides I am incapable of taking bribes—I would only be an obstacle to myself and to others as well. Officials have their own caste system. No, Afanasy Vassilievich, I have thought about it, I have tried, I have examined all the possible positions—I just wouldn't fit in. I'm only fit for the workhouse. . . .'

'A workhouse is all right for those who have worked; but for those who have done nothing but enjoy themselves in their youth the answer is, as the ant said to the cricket: "Go and dance for it!" And in any case there is work to be done in a workhouse too, they don't play whist there,' Mourazov retorted as he stared fixedly at Khlobuyev. 'You are only deceiving yourself and me into the bargain.'

Mourazov continued to stare at him fixedly; but poor Khlobuyev could find nothing to reply. Mourazov took pity on him.

'Listen, Khlobuyev,' he said. 'You are a man who prays and goes to Church. I know that you never miss either morning or evening service. You may not like getting up early, but you do get up and go along to mass all the same. Sometimes you even go to mass at four o'clock in the morning when no one else is up.'

'That's another thing, Afanasy Vassilievich,' Khlobuyev replied. 'I know that what I am doing then is not for man but for the sake of Him who created us all. What's to be done? I believe that He is merciful to me, that however vile or abhorrent I may be, He might yet forgive me and accept me, while people might only kick me aside and even my best friend might betray me and justify it, moreover, by saying that he had betrayed me for a good cause.'

An expression of distress came over Khlobuyev's face as he said this. There were even tears in his eyes.

'Then serve Him Who is so merciful to you,' Mourazov replied. 'Work is as acceptable to Him as prayer. Take any job you like, but do your work as though it were for His sake and not for that of men. You may pound water in a mortar if you like, but you must think that you are doing it for Him. The profit you will get from it is that you will have no time left for evil—for gambling away your money, for fancy banquets and society life. Ah, Khlobuyev! Do you know Ivan Potapich?'

'Yes, I do, and I respect him very much.'

'He used to be a good merchant, worth half a million roubles; but when he saw that everything was bringing him profit, he eased up,' Mourazov went on. 'He had his son taught French and married his daughter to a general. And whether one met him in the shop or on the Exchange, he would always drag a friend off to a tavern for a cup of tea; he used to spend whole days drinking tea, and as a result he went bankrupt. And then there was a misfortune into the bargain: his son . . . But now, you see, Potapich is serving as one of my clerks. He has started again from scratch. His affairs are in order now. He could do trade again to the amount of five hundred thousand roubles if he wanted, but he says now, "I have been a clerk and I want to die one. Now my health has improved and I feel rejuvenated, whereas formerly my stomach used to give me trouble and had a touch of dropsy. No!" That's what he said. And now he doesn't even drink tea: his only fare is cabbage soup and buckwheat. Yes, that's how it is! And he says his prayers like no one else; he also assists the poor more than any of us. Another man might wish to help, but when he came to doing so he might find that he had frittered away all his money.'

Poor Khlobuyev grew thoughtful. Mourazov took both his hands in his. 'Listen Khlobuyev,' he said. 'If you only knew how much I pity you! I have been thinking about you all the time. Now listen to me. You know that there is an anchorite in the local monastery who sees no one. He is a man of great, very great intellect. He does not usually speak, but if he does give one counsel, then . . . I began telling him that I had a friend—I did not mention his name—and that he was suffering from a particular complaint. He listened to me and then suddenly interrupted me with the following words: "God's business comes before one's own. They are building a church but there is not enough money. Funds must be collected." He said that and banged the door. "What does he mean?" I thought to myself. "He is evidently unwilling to advise me." So I dropped in to see the archimandrite.[4] I hadn't crossed the threshold before he asked me if I did not know anyone who might be entrusted with organizing a collection for the church, anyone of the nobility or of the merchant class who had a superior

4. Abbot; head of a monastery.

education and who would look on his task as a matter of personal salvation. The thought struck me at once and I paused: "Heavens!" I said to myself. "That ascetic has destined this task for Khlobuyev. It would be a good cure for him. As he makes the rounds of landowners, peasants and town-folk, he will not only find out how differently people live and what each of them lacks, but he will also have been round several provinces and will get to know the locality and countryside better than all those people who dwell in towns. . . ." And such men are now required. The prince was telling me recently that he would give a lot to have an official who had a practical and not a paper knowledge of affairs, because it seems that they can no longer make head or tail of their papers—they have all got mixed up.'

'You have thrown me into complete confusion, Afanasy Vassilievich,' Khlobuyev exclaimed, looking at him in amazement. 'I cannot even believe that you are really proposing this to me; a mission like that requires an energetic and businesslike person. Besides, how can I abandon my wife and children who will have nothing to eat without me?'

'Don't worry about your wife and children. I shall take them under my care, and I shall get tutors for the children,' Mourazov replied. 'Rather than wander about with a wallet and beg charity for yourself, it would be nobler and better of you to go begging for the sake of the Almighty. I shall give you a plain tilt-cart. Don't be frightened of the shaking, it will be good for your health. I shall also give you money for the journey, so that you can dispense charity on the way to those who are in greatest need. You will be able to do many a good deed: you will make no mistake, and whoever will receive from you will deserve it. In this way, travelling about, you will get to know all those who . . . That will be a very different kettle of fish from any ordinary official, who intimidates everyone and from whom nothing is to be expected; but, knowing that you are collecting money for the building of a church, people will open their hearts to you.'

'I see,' Khlobuyev said. 'It is an excellent idea. I

should very much like to fulfil even a part of the task, but it really seems to me beyond my powers.'

'Above your powers?' Mourazov exclaimed. 'There is nothing within our powers; everything is above our powers. Without help from on high nothing is possible. But prayer helps to concentrate our strength. Crossing himself, a man will say: "Oh Lord, have mercy on me!" He pulls at his oars and reaches the other shore. There is no need to ponder long on it; one must simply accept it as God's will. I shall have the tilt-cart ready for you at once; and you had better run and see the archimandrite and get his blessing, then you can set off.'

'I shall heed you and treat this as a sign from heaven,' Khlobuyev said. 'Bless me, O Lord!' he exclaimed inwardly, and felt at once strength and cheerfulness welling into his soul. Even his mind began to be roused with hope at this escape from his sad and hopeless plight. But now there was a glimmer of light on the horizon. . . .

But let us now leave Khlobuyev and return to Chichikov.

Meanwhile petition on petition was being presented to the courts. New relatives came forward of whom no one had ever heard before. Like carrion birds swooping down on a carcass, they all gathered round the large fortune left by the old lady: they made secret denunciations against Chichikov, they contested the will, claiming that it was a false one, and they produced evidence of theft and of the misappropriation of certain sums. There were even denunciations of Chichikov on the ground that he had dealt in dead souls and had indulged in contraband activities when he was serving in the customs. All the facts about him came to light and his past history became known. God knows how they managed to get on the scent of it all: evidence was even brought forward about matters which Chichikov believed to be a secret between himself and the four walls. For the time being all this was known only to the legal authorities and did not come to Chichikov's ears, but the note which he soon received from his solicitor gave him some idea of what was cooking. The note was brief and read as follows: 'I hasten to inform you that your case promises to be troublesome, but I would remind you that there is no cause for anxiety. The chief thing is to preserve your calm. We shall fix it all up.' This note completely reassured Chichikov. 'That solicitor's a real genius,' he said. To crown the good news, the tailor brought him his new suit on time. He was seized with an irresistible desire to see himself in his new frock-coat of smoke and flame. He pulled on the trousers which fitted him so beautifully that they might have been a work of art. They brought out the lines of his thighs and calves perfectly, imparting to them quite a youthful appearance. The cloth sat on him so well that it revealed his slightest parts and gave them even greater elasticity. When he tightened the strap behind, his belly looked like a drum. Thereupon he slapped it with a brush, adding: 'What a fool he is! and yet he makes a good picture as a whole.' The frock-coat seemed even better made than the trousers, it had no wrinkles, fitted closely round the ribs, went in at the waist and displayed all his curves. In reply to Chichikov's remark that the coat was a trifle tight under the right armpit, the tailor only smiled: according to him that made the coat sit better round the waist. 'You needn't worry about the work,' he said in evident triumph. 'You won't get such a cut anywhere else except Petersburg.' The tailor himself came from Petersburg but his signboard read: 'A Foreigner from London and Paris.' He did not like joking and he wished to ram these two towns at once down the throats of all the other tailors, so that in future not one of them might claim that provenance, though they might of course write 'Karlsruhe' or 'Kopenhagen' on their signboards.

Chichikov generously settled the tailor's bill and, when he was left alone, started to examine himself at leisure in the mirror, like an artist overflowing with aesthetic feeling, and *con amore*.[5] Everything appeared to him an improvement on what had gone before; his cheeks looked

---

5. Italian for "with love," "with passion."

more attractive, his chin more enticing, his white collar set off his cheeks, his blue satin tie set off his collar, his ornate velvet waistcoat set off his shirt-front and his frock-coat of smoke and flame, as glossy as silk, set off everything else. When he turned sideways to the right he looked perfect! When he turned sideways to the left, he looked still better! His waist was like that of a chamberlain or the sort of gentleman who itches away in French and who, even when he is in a rage, does not venture to swear in Russian but will get heated in French dialect— such his tact! Bending his head a little to the side, Chichikov tried to assume a pose such as he might adopt if he were addressing a lady of middle age and of up-to-date enlightenment: it was quite a *tableau*.⁶ Painter take up thy brush and paint! In his delight Chichikov executed a light leap in the manner of an *entrechat*. The dressing-table shook and a flask of eau-de-Cologne fell to the floor, but that did not bother him at all. As was fitting, he branded the stupid flask a 'fool' and thought to himself: 'Whom shall I visit first? It had better be . . .'

But suddenly there was a trampling of boots and a clinking of spurs in the hall, and a fully armed gendarme appeared in the doorway as though personifying a whole army. He said: 'You are commanded to appear immediately before the governor-general!' Chichikov was dumbfounded. Confronting him was the scarecrow with huge moustaches, a horse's tail on his head, a shoulder belt to the right of him and another to the left, an immense sword dangling at his side. Chichikov seemed to see a rifle too, and the devil only knows what else on the other side: the gendarme loomed before him like a whole army! He made as though to protest but the scarecrow rudely retorted: 'The orders are that you go at once!' Through the door leading into the hall, Chichikov saw another such scarecrow; he glanced out of the window and perceived a carriage drawn up outside. What was he to do? He was obliged to get into the carriage as he was, in his suit of smoke and flame and, trembling in all his limbs, to set off to the governor-general's, accompanied by the gendarmes.

6. A picture, scene.

As soon as he arrived there, he was given no time to collect his wits. 'Proceed! The prince is already waiting for you,' he was told by the official on duty. As in a mist he passed through the ante-room which was thronged with couriers who were being given sealed envelopes, then through a large room, thinking all the while: 'He'll seize hold of me and send me straight to Siberia without trial!' His heart started pounding as strongly as that of a lover in an excess of jealousy. Then at last the fateful door was flung open and before him loomed the governor's study with its brief-cases, cupboards, bookcases, and the prince himself, who looked the personification of rage.

'He's my destroyer!' Chichikov thought to himself. 'He'll finish me off like a wolf would a lamb.'

'I spared you and allowed you to stay in the town when you should have gone to jail,' the prince exclaimed. 'And you have once more disgraced yourself by the most dishonest piece of roguery that a man is capable of!' The prince's lips were trembling with rage.

'What have I done, Your Highness? What dishonest deed and what roguery do you accuse me of?' Chichikov asked, trembling.

'The woman,' the prince said, as he advanced upon Chichikov staring him straight in the eyes, 'the woman who signed the will at your dictation has been arrested and will be confronted with you.'

Chichikov's eyes grew dim.

'Your Highness,' he exclaimed, 'I shall tell you the whole truth. I am guilty: but I am not altogether guilty; my enemies have been my downfall.'

'No one is to blame for your downfall,' the prince retorted, 'because you are more full of vileness than the most notorious liar. I believe that all through your life you have never been anything but dishonest. Every penny you own has been obtained by the most dishonest means, as a result of theft and trickery, for which you deserve to be punished by the knout and Siberia[7]! No, you've had your fling! You will be put in prison immediately and there, with the lowest scum and bandits, you will have to await

---

7. Typical Russian punishments: "knout"—a whip; "Siberia"—exile, forced labor, imprisonment.

your sentence. And that is merciful because you are several degrees worse than the others: because most of them are peasants in peasant dress while you . . .' Here the prince glanced at Chichikov's dress-coat of smoke and flame and then, pulling the cord, rang the bell.

'Your Highness,' Chichikov cried out, 'have mercy on me! You are the father of a family. Spare my old mother at least if not myself!'

'That's another lie!' the prince angrily exclaimed. 'Just as once before you begged me to take pity on you for the sake of your wife and children, which you never had, so now you talk of your mother.'

'Your Highness! I am a scoundrel and a rogue,' Chichikov gasped . . . 'I did indeed tell you a lie, I have no children or family; but as God is my witness, I have always wished to possess a wife and to do my duty as a man and citizen, so as to earn eventually the respect of my fellow citizens and the authorities. . . . But what a wretched concatenation of circumstances there has been! Your Highness! I had to sweat blood to earn my daily bread. At every step there were trials and temptations . . . enemies bent on exploiting and ruining me. My whole life was like a whirlwind or a ship tossed among the waves at the mercy of the winds. I am—a human being, Your Highness!'

Tears suddenly streamed from his eyes. He fell at the feet of the prince, just as he was, in his frock-coat of smoke and flame, in his velvet waistcoat and satin tie, in his perfectly tailored trousers and with his hair exquisitely brushed and giving off the sweet scent of superior eau-de-Cologne—thus dressed and scented he fell at the prince's feet and struck the floor with his forehead.

'Go away! I won't have you near me!' the prince exclaimed. 'Soldier, call the guard to remove him!' the prince cried to the first person who opened the door.

'Your Highness!' Chichikov was shouting, as he gripped one of the prince's boots with both his hands.

A shudder ran through the prince's veins.

'Go away, I tell you!' he cried, attempting to free his foot from Chichikov's embrace.

'Your Highness! I shall not leave this place until you will show me mercy,' Chichikov cried without letting go the prince's boot and trailing with it over the floor, dressed as he was in his coat of smoke and flame.

'Go, I tell you!' the prince exclaimed with that inexplicable feeling of revulsion a man feels at the sight of a hideous insect, which he yet lacks the spirit to crush underfoot. The prince gave a violent shake with his leg so that Chichikov felt his boot strike him on the nose, lips and rounded chin, but he did not let go his hold and clung on with all his might. It took two hefty gendarmes to pull him away and, grasping him by the arms, they led him out of the study through all the adjacent rooms. He looked terribly pale and worn out, in a state of semiconsciousness such as comes over a man when confronted with black and inevitable death—that monster repugnant to our nature.

In the doorway giving on the main staircase they ran into Mourazov. Chichikov suddenly saw a glimmer of hope. In an instant, with superhuman strength he had torn himself from the gendarmes' grip and cast himself at the feet of the astonished old gentleman.

'Heavens, Pavel Ivanovich!' Mourazov cried. 'What is the matter with you?'

'Save me!' Chichikov shouted. 'They are taking me to prison, to death. . . .' Then the gendarmes seized hold of him and led him away without letting him even be heard.

A rank and raw hole of a room, smelling strongly of soldiers' boots and puttees, a plain wooden table, two rickety chairs, a barred window, and a cracked stove which only let smoke escape through its chinks and gave no heat—such was our hero's new abode. There he was already beginning to taste the joys of life again and to attract the attention of his fellow prisoners by his stylish dress of smoke and flame. He had not even been given time to fetch some of his essential things, his box for example, which contained all his cash. His papers, the deeds of purchase for the dead souls—all these were now in the hands of officials. He had slumped down on the ground and a hopeless dejection wound itself round his heart like a carnivorous worm. With ever greater speed it began to gnaw away at that defenceless heart. Another such day of gloom and Chichikov would have ceased to exist on this earth. But someone's all-saving hand was not idle. An hour later the doors of the prison were flung open and in came Mourazov.

If someone had poured a stream of clear spring water into the parched throat of an emaciated and exhausted traveller, tormented by a raging thirst and covered with the grime and dust of the road, he would not have been so refreshed or quickened as poor Chichikov at the sight of the old gentleman.

'My saviour!' he exclaimed, suddenly seizing Mourazov's hand, kissing it and pressing it to his breast, as he still knelt there on the floor where he had fallen in his dejection. 'The Lord will reward you for thus visiting a wretch.'

He burst into tears. The old gentleman stared at him with a pained expression and kept repeating: 'Ah, Pavel Ivanovich, Pavel Ivanovich, what have you done?'

'I can't help it now! That cursed woman cooked my goose! I lost my head: I didn't know where to stop,' Chichikov exclaimed. 'Satan himself seduced me, enticing me beyond the bounds of sense and human reason. I have transgressed, indeed I have!' Chichikov cried. 'But then how can they treat me so? To throw a nobleman, a nobleman, into prison without any preliminary investigation or trial! . . . A nobleman, Afanasy Vassilievich! How could they act so and not give me time to go home and make some arrangements about my belongings? All my things have remained behind at everyone's mercy. The box, Afanasy Vassilievich, the box, the whole of my property is in it! Everything I have gained by sweat and blood, in the course of years of toil and privation. . . . My box, Afanasy Vassilievich! They will rifle it and steal everything! Oh, heavens.'

And, failing to restrain the wave of sadness mounting to his heart, Chichikov burst out sobbing in a voice that pierced the thick walls of the prison-house and re-echoed dully in the distance, tore off his satin tie and, tugging at his collar, split his frock-coat of smoke and flame.

'Ah, Pavel Ivanovich!' Mourazov exclaimed. 'How the idea of property has blinded you! For the sake of it you lost sight of the terrible position into which you had got yourself.'

'Benefactor, save me, save me!' poor Chichikov cried out in despair, falling at Mourazov's feet. 'The prince loves you, he would do anything for you.'

'No, Pavel Ivanovich, I can't do that, however much I should like to do so,' Mourazov replied. 'You are now in the grip of an inexorable law and not in the power of any one person.'

'Ah, the tempter, accursed Satan, that monster of the human species!' Chichikov cried out.

He knocked his head against the wall, and then banged the table so hard with his fist that he made it bleed, but he felt no pain in his head and no hurt in his fist.

'Pavel Ivanovich, calm yourself!' Mourazov urged him. 'You must think how to make your peace with God rather than with men. You must think of your soul!'

'But consider my fate, Afanasy Vassilievich!' Chichikov went on. 'Has such a fate ever befallen any other person? I can claim that I earned my pennies with blood-sweating patience, by labour and toil; I did not gain them by robbery or by absconding with public money as some people do. And why did I save up my pennies? In order to spend the remainder of my days in comfort—in order to be able to leave something to my wife and children whom it was my intention to acquire for the good of my country. That is why I wished to have them! I have been a little crooked, I won't deny it, I have been crooked. . . . That can't be helped now. But I took the wrong turning only when I saw that I could not get anywhere along the straight road, and that the crooked road led more directly to the goal. But I did toil and use my wits. If I did take what did not belong to me, I did so from the rich. And what about all those scoundrels who hang round the courts, taking in thousands from the coffers of the Treasury, robbing the poor, stripping the last penny from those who have nothing! . . . What is this ill-luck, tell me, what is it that weighs me down? Each time I am just on the point of plucking the fruit and, so to speak, putting my hand on it, suddenly a storm bursts or a submerged rock comes in the way, and the whole of my ship breaks into splinters. Now I did have just under three hundred thousand roubles by way of capital; I already had a three-storied house and twice I have bought myself a village. . . . Ah, Afanasy Vassilievich! How have I deserved . . .? Why these blows? Was my life not already like a ship in a stormy sea even without this? Where is the justice of heaven? Where is the reward of patience, of unexampled perseverance? Did I not start again three times from scratch? Having lost everything, I started again and worked my way up from a penny whilst another man in despair would have long ago taken to drink and would have gone to rot in a gin-shop. The struggles I had and the sufferings I endured! All my spiritual energies went into each penny I earned! . . . Let us suppose that others made their way easily, mine was the hard path: each penny counted and one made two, as the proverb says, but to achieve this, as God is my witness, I had to exercise iron and unflagging will-power. . . .'

The pain was too much for Chichikov: he sobbed out loudly and, falling back into a chair, tore off the rent and dangling strip of his frock-coat and threw it away. Thrusting both his hands into his hair, which he had formerly taken such pains to keep tidy, he was tearing at it mercilessly. This pain brought him satisfaction, for it deadened the inextinguishable pangs of his heart.

For a long time Mourazov sat facing him, staring at this extraordinary sight which he was witnessing for the first time. And beside himself, the wretched man, who had but recently fluttered with all the easy elegance of a man about town or a smart officer, was now rushing about with a dishevelled and disreputable appearance, in a torn frock-coat and unbuttoned trousers, waving a bruised and bloody fist, and pouring out a spate of abuse against the hostile forces frustrating mankind.

'Ah, Pavel Ivanovich, Pavel Ivanovich!' Mourazov

exclaimed. 'What a man you would have made if you had turned all that energy and patience of yours to good account and had some worthy object! Heavens, how much good you could have done! If only any one of those people, who love to do good, were to use as much effort to their end as you did to earn your pennies, and knew how to sacrifice their vanity and ambition for the sake of good, without sparing themselves, just as you did not spare yourself when earning your pennies—Oh, Lord, how our earth would prosper! . . . Pavel Ivanovich, Pavel Ivanovich! The pity of it is not that you are guilty in the eyes of others but rather that you are guilty before yourself—before those rich gifts and forces which were your portion. Your destiny was to have been a great man, but you wasted your energies and destroyed yourself.'

There are secrets of the soul: however far a man may stray from the direct path, however hard of feeling an inveterate criminal may become, however set in the ways of his corrupted life, yet if you reproach him by drawing his attention to himself, to his own good qualities which he has besmirched, he will involuntarily waver and be shaken.

'Afanasy Vassilievich,' poor Chichikov gasped, catching hold of both his hands in his. 'Oh, if I could only be set free and have my property restored, I swear to you that I would then lead quite a different life! Save me, benefactor, save me!'

'But what can I do?' Mourazov asked. 'I would have to fight against the law. Let us suppose even that I resolved to do so, the prince is a just man—he would not go back on his decision.'

'Benefactor! You can do anything,' Chichikov exclaimed. 'It is not the law I am frightened of—I can find means of getting round it—but it is the fact that I have been imprisoned without cause, that I shall perish here like a dog, and that my property, papers and the box will . . . Save me!'

He threw his arms round the old gentleman's legs and drenched them with tears.

'Ah, Pavel Ivanovich, Pavel Ivanovich!' Mourazov

repeated, shaking his head. 'How that property of yours has blinded you! Because of it you have grown deaf to the voice of your soul.'

'I will think of my soul too,' Chichikov cried, 'but save me first.'

'Pavel Ivanovich! . . .' Mourazov began to say and then stopped. After a pause he went on. 'To save you is not in my power—you can see that for yourself. But I will do my best, everything I can, to make your predicament lighter and to have you set free. I do not know if I shall succeed in achieving this but I shall try. However, if I do succeed, contrary to expectation, I shall ask you to reward me for my trouble—I shall ask you to give up this striving of yours after profit. I tell you on my word of honour that if I were deprived of all my possessions—and I have more of them than you—I would not shed a tear over them. The gist of the matter is not in the property which might be confiscated from me but in that which no one can steal or take away! You have lived long enough in the world to know that! You yourself have compared your life to a ship in a stormy sea. You have already enough to live on for the rest of your days. Find a quiet retreat for yourself somewhere, as near as possible to a church and a community of simple, kindly folk; or if you have a strong itch to found a family, marry some not too wealthy kind-hearted girl, who knows measure in all things and will be able to run a simple household. Forget this noisy world and all its whims and temptations. Let it forget you too: there will be no peace for you in it. As you see, everything worldly is your enemy, a tempter and a betrayer.'

'I will, I will!' Chichikov cried. 'It was my wish, my intention already, to lead a proper life. I wanted to attend to my estate and to change my life. But the demon, the tempter, led me astray. . . . Satan, the devil, the monster!'

Chichikov now felt welling up in him hitherto unfamiliar and inexplicable feelings; it was as though something was striving to come to light, something remote and out of the depths—something belonging to his childhood years which had been repressed by the harsh and formal upbringing he had received, by the unaffectionate and sad character of his childhood years, by the desert-like emptiness of his home life, by the isolation of his family life which was poor and beggarly in its initial impressions. . . . And it was as though that repressed something, long daunted by the harsh glance of fate, which had stared gloomily at him through a misty snow-strewn window, was now striving to set itself free. A moan burst from his lips and he brought out in a sorrowful voice: 'It's true, it's true!'

'All your knowledge of men and experience did not help you once you had embarked upon this illegal path,' Mourazov said. 'But if there had been a lawful purpose behind your activity! . . . Ah, Pavel Ivanovich, why did you destroy yourself? Rouse yourself: it is not too late yet, there is time still. . . .'

'No, it is too late, too late!' Chichikov groaned in a voice that made Mourazov's heart bleed. 'I am beginning to realize, to hear, that I have been walking on the wrong path, that I have strayed far from the straight road, but I can't do anything about it! My father inculcated morality into me, beat me, forced me to copy the ten commandments, but at the same time he thieved wood from his neighbours and even obliged me to help him do so. He started an unlawful liaison; and he seduced an orphan girl whose guardian he was. Example is more potent than all the commandments. I can see and feel, Afanasy Vassilievich, that I am leading the wrong sort of life, but I feel no great revulsion to vice. My nature has grown blunted; I feel no love for good, for that fine propensity to do good deeds pleasing to God, which becomes natural, a habit. . . . I do not experience the same desire to struggle for good as I do to improve my material circumstances. I am telling you the truth—what is to be done?'

Mourazov gave vent to a deep sigh.

'Pavel Ivanovich! You have so much will-power, so much patience,' he said. 'Medicine is bitter to the taste, but a sick man takes it, for he knows that otherwise he will not get well. If you have no love for good—then you must force yourself to do good even though you feel no love for it. That will count even more in your favour than the doing of good out of love for it. Force yourself to do it, only you must do it more than once, and then love will come with it. Believe me, it can be done. 'The kingdom forces', that's the saying. Only you must strive towards it forcibly . . . you must compel yourself to achieve it, you must take it by force. Ah, Pavel Ivanovich, you have the strength to do it such as others do not possess. You have iron patience—and why should you not conquer? It seems to me you might be a champion, a *bogatyr*. For nowadays folk have no will-power, they are all flabby.'

It could be seen that these words pierced into the depths of Chichikov's soul and stirred the ambition hidden in its core. His eyes flashed if not with a look of decision, at least with something strongly resembling it.

'Afanasy Vassilievich!' he said firmly. 'If only you succeed in having me pardoned and in making it possible for me to leave this place with some of my belongings, I give you my word of honour that I shall start a new life: I shall buy myself a village, I shall save up money not for myself but in order to help others, I shall devote all my energies to doing good. I shall forget about myself and all the banqueting and meals that come of living in cities; I shall lead a simple and sober life.'

'God will strengthen your resolve!' Mourazov replied, overjoyed. 'I shall do everything I can to get the prince to set you free. God alone knows whether I shall succeed or not. In any case, your lot will probably be made easier. Ah, heavens! Embrace me, allow me to embrace you also. You have really made me glad! Well, God be with you, I shall go and see the prince at once.'

Mourazov went out, leaving Chichikov alone.

He was shaken to the core of his being and melted too. Platinum, the hardest of metals, the one most resistant to fire, can be smelted too! When the fire of the forge needs intensifying the bellows are pumped and an unbearable heat radiates, and then the obstinate metal turns white and finally liquefies. The strongest of men also yield in the furnace of misfortune, when, growing ever more intense, its unbearable fire burns through his crusted nature. . . .

'I do not know what it feels like, but I shall employ all my energies to make others feel it; I am a bad man myself, I know, but I shall do all in my power to inspire the others; I am the worst of Christians, but I shall use all my endeavour to avoid setting a bad example,' Chichikov said to himself. 'I shall work hard, I shall sweat on my land, and I shall perform my tasks honestly so as to set a good example. I am not quite useless yet! I have a knack for management; I am careful, energetic and reasonable, I am even capable of constancy. I have only to make up my mind. . . .'

So thought Chichikov and it seemed that he was beginning to grasp at something with the just awakening forces of his soul. It seemed as though a dark intuition of his nature was beginning to realize that there is a duty which man must perform on earth, which he can fulfil anywhere, in any corner of the world, despite all impeding circumstances, all confusion or change taking place in his environment—that he can do his duty wherever he is. And the image of a hard-working life, removed from the bustle of cities and those temptations which man invented for himself out of idleness, began to imprint itself so strongly on his mind that he almost forgot the very unpleasant situation in which he found himself and, maybe, he was even ready to thank Providence for the heavy blow it had dealt him, provided he was set free and given back at least a part of what belonged to him. . . .

But at that moment the door of his filthy cell was flung open and an official personage came in—a certain Samosvistov, who was an epicurean, a boisterous fellow with shoulders a yard wide, and a regular beast of a man, as his comrades called him. In war-time this man would have worked miracles: he could have been sent to infiltrate into the most impassable and dangerous positions and could have stolen a gun right under the nose of the enemy—it would all have been in a day's work for him. But for want of a war-like arena to spend his energies and make himself into an honest man, he now turned his hand to any dirty job. Inexplicable thing! He had the strangest of convictions and principles: he was honest with his friends, betrayed none of them and kept his word to them; but he looked upon the authorities above him as something in the nature of an enemy battery which he had to infiltrate, taking advantage of every weak spot, gap, or lack of vigilance.

'We all know about your plight, we have all heard about it!' he said as soon as he made sure that the door was shut securely behind him. 'But it's nothing, nothing! Don't lose courage: everything will be put right. We shall all pull strings for you—we are at your service. Thirty thousand roubles for the lot—that is all that's required.'

'You don't mean that?' Chichikov cried out. 'And I shall be found not guilty?'

'But of course! You will even get compensation for the loss you have sustained,' Samosvistov exclaimed.

'And what will it cost?' Chichikov enquired.

'Thirty thousand. That's all included—our fellows, the governor-general's and the secretary,' Samosvistov replied.

'But how can I do it?' Chichikov asked. 'All my things, and my box . . . they are all sealed now and taken over. . . .'

'I shall deliver them to you within an hour,' Samosvistov replied. 'Is it agreed?'

Chichikov shook hands with him; his heart was thumping, and he did not believe it possible.

'Well, bye-bye for the time being!' Samosvistov said. 'Our mutual friend asked me to tell you that the main thing is peace of mind.'

'H'm!' Chichikov thought to himself. 'I understand. It's my solicitor at work.'

Samosvistov disappeared. Left alone, Chichikov found it hard to credit what he had heard, but in less than an hour following the conversation his box was delivered to him. The papers, the money, and everything else in it, were in the best of order. Samosvistov had turned up at Chichikov's lodgings as one who gave orders: he reprimanded the sentinels for their lack of vigilance, ordered the sergeant to increase the number of soldiers on duty, then took not only the box but also all such papers as might compromise Chichikov, tied them all together, sealed them and commanded one of the sentinels to take them immediately to Chichikov wrapped up in essential articles of night attire, so that Chichikov received, together with his documents, also all the warm things which he needed to cover his frail body. This prompt delivery gladdened him immeasurably. Hope was returning to him and he began to indulge in some dreams of amusements such as an evening at the theatre and the dancing girl he had run after. The village and country quiet began to pale, while the city and its bustle began to grow brighter and more vivid . . . Oh, Life!

In the meantime the affair had assumed unheard-of proportions in the courts of justice. The clerks were busy copying papers and, in between pinches of snuff, legal heads were cerebrating and, like artists, admiring many a copyist's squiggle. Like one of the secret magi, Chichikov's solicitor was invisibly manipulating the whole mechanism; he had succeeded in getting everyone entangled in his mesh before they had time to look round. The confusion grew worse. Samosvistov excelled himself by his unexampled boldness and temerity. On discovering where the arrested woman was kept under guard, he went straight there and put up such a brave and commanding show that the sentinel stood to attention and saluted him. 'Have you been long on duty?' he asked the sentinel. 'Since the morning, your honour,' the sentinel replied. 'When will you be relieved?' he pursued. 'In three hours' time, your honour,' the sentinel replied. 'I shall need you,' Samosvistov told him. 'I shall tell the officer in charge to send a substitute.' 'Right, your honour,' the sentinel barked out. And driving home, without losing a moment, so as to involve no one else and take the responsibility on himself, he disguised himself as a gendarme with moustaches and whiskers, and even the devil himself would not have recognized him. Arriving at the house where Chichikov was incarcerated and grabbing hold of the first woman prisoner he came across, he handed her over to two young officials, bright lads too, and himself went off with his moustaches and a rifle all in order, and presented himself before the sentinel: 'Beat it! The commander has sent me to replace you.' They changed guard and Samosvistov took up his post. That was all that was required. Meanwhile, in place of the original woman prisoner, another had been substituted who did not know or understand anything of what was going on. The original woman was put away so efficiently out of sight that there was even no way of finding her afterwards.

While Samosvistov was executing his military manœuvres, the solicitor was performing miracles in the civil arena: he hinted to the governor that the prosecutor was writing a denunciation against him; he informed the official of the gendarmerie that an inspector, who was staying secretly in town, was sending in reports about him: he assured this secret inspector that there was yet a more secret official who was reporting about him; and he reduced everyone to such a state of alarm and confusion that they all had to turn to him for advice. The result was complete confusion: denunciation followed denunciation, and such a state of affairs began to be revealed as had never been seen under the light of the sun, and there were even revelations of non-existent things. Everything came in handy: who was the illegitimate son of whom, his origin and profession, who had a mistress, and whose wife was unfaithful with whom. Scandal followed on scandal, and they were soon so inextricably mixed up with Chichikov's affair, and with the dead souls, that there was no way of telling which of them was the more arrant nonsense: they were more or less of a piece.

When at last the papers began to be put before the governor-general, the poor prince could not make head nor tail of them. A clever and energetic official, who was appointed to sum up the position, almost went mad: for the life of him he could not pick out the thread of the matter. In the meantime the prince had become preoccupied with a multitude of other affairs, one more unpleasant than the other. In one part of the province there was a famine. The officials who had been sent to distribute the bread had apparently not acted as they should have. In another part of the province dissenters became restive. Someone had started a rumour among them that a new Antichrist had appeared who did not even leave the dead in peace but bought up dead souls. In another place the peasants had revolted against their masters and the police captains. Some tramps had spread the rumour among them that the time had come when peasants should become landowners themselves and must wear frock-coats, while the landowners would don peasant coats and turn peasants—and as a result a whole district, without reflecting on the fact that there would then be too many landowners and police captains and too few peasants, refused to pay the taxes. The authorities had to resort to forcible measures. The poor prince was very much upset by all these events. It was then reported to him that the contractor Mourazov had arrived to see him. 'Let him come in,' the prince said. Mourazov entered.

'What do you think of your Chichikov now?' the prince exclaimed. 'You stood up for him and defended him, but now he has been caught out over an affair which even the most hardened thief would not attempt.'

'May I inform you, Your Highness,' Mourazov replied, 'that I do not understand this affair very well.'

'The forgery of a will, and what a forgery!' the prince exclaimed. 'A public flogging is the right punishment for that.'

'Your Highness, may I venture to say the following— not with any idea of defending Chichikov but to get the affair in proper perspective—his guilt has not yet been proved,' Mourazov said. 'The case has not yet been made out.'

'We have the best of evidence,' the prince said. 'The woman who was dressed up to take the place of the dead woman has been arrested. I should like to question her expressly in your presence'; the prince rang the bell and gave orders for the woman to be brought in.

Mourazov kept silent.

'It's a most disgraceful affair,' the prince continued. 'And to their shame some of the leading officials in the town are involved in it, including the governor himself. He should not mix in such company with thieves and idle folk!' The prince spoke heatedly.

'After all the governor is an heir of hers; he had the right to expect something,' Mourazov said. 'But the fact that all the others came running along from all directions, that is just human nature. A rich woman dies without making any good and sensible arrangements; the birds of prey come flocking from all sides—yes, that's all very human. . . .'

'But why do such vile things? . . . The scoundrels!' the prince exclaimed with indignation. 'I haven't a single honest official under me: they are all rogues!'

'Your Highness, but which of us is as good as he should be?' Mourazov replied. 'All the officials of our town are human beings, having qualities of their own and many of them know their job to perfection. But everyone is apt to sin.'

'Listen to me, Afanasy Vassilievich,' the prince went on. 'Now tell me—you are the only honest person I know here—what is this passion you have for defending every sort of scoundrel?'

'Your Highness,' Mourazov replied, 'whoever he may be whom you call a scoundrel, he is still a human being. And why not defend a human being when one knows that half the mischief he does is the result of his coarse upbringing and ignorance? We commit injustices at every step and every minute we are the cause of somebody else's misfortune, even when it is not our intention. For, Your Highness, you have also done a great injustice.'

'How?' the prince exclaimed in astonishment, completely taken aback by this unexpected turn in the conversation.

Mourazov paused, kept silent for a moment as though reflecting and then at last said: 'Well, let us take the case of Derpennikov.'

'Afanasy Vassilievich,' the prince exclaimed. 'His was a crime against the fundamental laws of the state, it was equivalent to betraying one's country.'

'I am not trying to justify him,' Mourazov went on. 'But was it just to condemn that youth, who was led astray by his inexperience and the prompting of others, as severely as you would one of the ringleaders? For Derpennikov got as big a sentence as some Voronoy-Dryaniy, but their guilt was not the same.'

'For God's sake . . .' the prince exclaimed in evident agitation. 'Do you know anything about that affair? If so tell me. Only recently I sent a petition direct to Petersburg, asking for mitigation in his case.'

'No, Your Highness, I am not telling you this because I know something more about the case than you,' Mourazov replied. 'But to be precise, there is one circumstance which might serve him in good stead, though he would hardly agree to it since it would bring suffering to another person. I am only asking myself whether you did not see fit to hurry the proceedings overmuch? You must excuse me, Your Highness, I am judging merely in accordance with my weak powers of reasoning. You commanded me several times to speak frankly to you on all matters. When I was a chief, I had many workers of all sorts under me, good and bad. One should take into account a man's past life because, if one does not weigh all the circumstances impartially, and only shouts one's accusations from the very start, then one will only frighten the accused and elicit no real confession from him. But if you were to question him sympathetically as you might a brother, then he will tell you everything and will not even ask for a lighter sentence; and there will be no bitterness left, because he will see clearly that it is not you who are punishing him but the law.'

The prince grew thoughtful. In the meantime a young official entered with a brief-case and stopped in front of him respectfully. His youthful and as yet fresh-complexioned face showed signs of worry and preoccupation. It was evident that he took his job of one engaged in secret missions seriously. He was one of the few who did their work *con amore*. Impelled neither by vanity nor by the desire for profit, not striving to imitate anyone, he served only because he was convinced that his place was here and not anywhere else, and that that was the purpose of his life. His job was to investigate, to unravel and, picking out the threads of the most tangled affair, to clarify it and resolve it into its component parts. His labour, efforts and sleepless nights, were bountifully rewarded if the affair he was tackling began at last to grow clear and the mainsprings of it became revealed; and he felt that he could then sum it up in a few words, clearly and precisely, so that it would become obvious and comprehensible to everyone. It can be said that no pupil rejoiced more, when analysing a difficult sentence and extracting from it the real meaning of a great author's thought, than did he when he succeeded in disentangling a most complex affair. However [8] . . .

'. . . bread in places where there is a famine: I know that locality better than the officials. I shall look into the matter myself, and find out who needs what,' Mourazov was saying. 'And if you will allow me, Your Highness, I shall have a talk with the dissenters. They will be more willing to speak out when they have to do with one of their own folk, with a simple man, and maybe, God grant it, I may be able to help and arrange this affair peaceably. The officials would not be able to do that: they will only start a correspondence and as it is they have got so involved in their papers that they cannot see the wood for the trees. As for the money, I shall not take any from you because, as God is my witness, it would be a shame to think of profit for myself at a moment like this when people are dying of hunger. I have a stock of flour; just recently I have been sending some to Siberia; and by next summer I shall be able to replenish it.'

'Only God himself could reward you for such service, Afanasy Vassilievich,' the prince said. 'I shall not venture to thank you because—as you can feel yourself—words would be ineffective. But if you will allow me, I shall say a word about the request you made. Now tell me frankly: do you think I have the right to ignore that matter? And would it be just or honest of me to pardon those scoundrels?'

'Your Highness, honest to God, I would not call them

8. There is a gap in the manuscript here [*Translator's note*].

that, especially as many of them are very worthy people,'
Mourazov replied. 'At times man's predicament is very,
very complex, Your Highness. There are times when it
may look as though everything points to a man being
guilty; but when one goes into the matter, then it turns
out that he was not guilty at all.'

'But what will they say themselves if I let the matter
drop?' the prince asked, and then went on: 'There are
among them such as would raise up their heads and even
say that they had frightened me. They will be the first to
lose respect. . . .'

'Your Highness, may I tell you what I really think you
should do,' Mourazov replied. 'I would call them all together, tell them all you know, and put your predicament before them just as you have been good enough to
confide in me, and ask them for their advice. Ask each
one of them what he would do in your place?'

'So you think that they are capable of nobler impulses
than just intrigue and profit-making?' the prince asked.
'Believe me they will just laugh in my face.'

'I don't think so, Your Highness,' Mourazov replied.
'Men have a sense of justice—even those who are the bad
eggs. A Jew, perhaps, might lack it but not a Russian. . . .
No, Your Highness, you have nothing to hide. Speak to
them exactly as you have spoken to me. They will be
slandering you as a proud man, who will not hear anything and who is convinced in his own mind—well then,
let them see what you are really like. Why worry? You
have justice on your side. Speak to them as though you
were not speaking to them but were confessing before
God.'

'Afanasy Vassilievich,' the prince said thoughtfully, 'I
shall think it over. In the meantime I should like to thank
you very much for your advice.'

'And, Your Highness, you will give orders to have
Chichikov released?' Mourazov said.

'Tell that Chichikov of yours to get out of the town as
quickly as possible and the farther off he goes the better,'
the prince replied. 'I should never have pardoned him.'

Mourazov bowed and set off at once to see Chichikov.
He found him in better spirits, quietly preoccupied with

doing justice to quite a decent dinner, which had been brought to him on china plates from some quite respectable kitchen. From the very first words they exchanged Mourazov noticed at once that Chichikov had already succeeded in getting in touch with some of the law-court officials. He even grasped that the invisible influence of Chichikov's solicitor was already at work here.

'Now listen to me, Pavel Ivanovich,' Mourazov said to him. 'I have brought you your freedom on condition you leave town at once. Collect your belongings—and be off with you. God speed. Don't delay a minute, for the affair is even worse than I expected. I know there is a man plotting against you; I am telling you in secret that there is another charge about to be levelled against you, and that nothing would then save you. The man in question enjoys knocking out others for fun and the affair is coming to a head. I left you in a good mood—in a better one than you are now. My advice to you is no joke. Yes, yes, the gist of the matter is not in property, for the sake of which people quarrel and cut each other's throats as though it were possible to arrange life on earth without thought of the next life. Believe me, Pavel Ivanovich, until people give up all that for the sake of which they snarl at and gobble each other here on earth and begin thinking of the good ordering of their spiritual properties, there will be no harmony on earth. A time of famine and poverty will come, as among the common folk, so there will be division in every . . . That's clear. Whatever you may say, the body depends on the soul. How then would you have things properly arranged? Stop thinking of dead souls and think rather of your living one, and God speed you on a new road! I also am setting out to-morrow. Now hurry up! Otherwise, when I am away, you will get into trouble.'

Having said that, Mourazov went out. Chichikov pondered for a moment. Life again seemed unimportant to him. 'Mourazov is right,' he said to himself. 'It's time to take a new road.' Having said that, he walked out of the prison. The sentinel carried the box behind him. . . .

Selifan and Petrushka were overjoyed to see their master liberated they knew not how. 'Well my good fellows,' Chichikov said to them kindly, 'we must pack and be off.'

'We'll roll along, Pavel Ivanovich,' Selifan replied. 'It looks like the road has set: enough snow has fallen for that. It's time, it is, to get out of this town. I'm so fed up with it I don't want to look at it any more.'

'Go along to the coachmaker and get him to put our carriage on runners,' Chichikov said to Selifan, and then he went into town, but he had no wish to pay any farewell visits. After the late events it would have been embarrassing to do so, especially as all sorts of unpleasant rumours were circulating about him.

He avoided meeting people, but he did call on the merchant from whom he had bought the cloth of smoke and flame and, having purchased an additional four yards of it, enough to make him a frock-coat and a pair of trousers, he then dropped in to see the tailor. For twice the price, the tailor agreed to increase his tempo and got his assistants to sit up all night by candlelight, with their needles, irons and teeth, and the suit was ready by the morning with only a slight delay. The horses were already harnessed. Chichikov, however, insisted on trying on the suit. It turned out to be a splendid piece of workmanship, exactly like the last one. But alas, he noticed a shiny smooth spot on his head, and he muttered sadly to himself: 'Why did I give way so much to despair? And I should never have torn my hair!' Having settled the tailor's bill, he at last drove out of the town feeling a bit odd. He was no longer the former Chichikov. The inner state of his soul might be compared with a building that had been taken to pieces for the purpose of reconstructing it; but the new building had not yet been started because the definite plan had not been received from the architect and all the labourers had been left perplexed. An hour ahead of him the old man Mourazov had set out in a tilt-cart covered with matting, accompanied by Potapich; and an hour after Chichikov's departure the order was issued that the prince, on the occasion of his departure for Petersburg, desired to see all the officials assembled together.

In the large room of the governor-general's house there gathered the whole body of the officials of the town, beginning with the governor and ending with the titular councillors. Chiefs of departments, administrators, councillors, assessors; Kisloyedov, Krasnonosov, Samosvistov; those who accepted bribes and those who did not; those who played crooked, half-crooked, or not crooked at all; all these were present. Not without some emotion and agitation they all waited for the governor-general to appear. When the prince emerged at last, he looked neither gloomy nor cheerful: his expression was as firm as his step. All the officials bowed, some of them to their waist. Responding with a slight bow, the prince began his address:

'Before departing for Petersburg I have thought it proper to meet you all and even partly to explain to you the reason for the meeting. We have recently been involved in a very disturbing affair. I assume that many of those present know what I have in mind. That affair led to the discovery of other no less dishonest affairs in which have been involved persons whom I had until then considered honest. I am even aware of the secret attempt to confuse all these affairs so as to make it impossible to disentangle them formally. I even know who was chiefly responsible for that and whose secret . . . although he has very ingeniously covered up his tracks. But the point I want to make is that I am resolved to investigate this case not by ordinary legal procedure and through files, but by resorting to a court martial as in time of war, and I trust that the Emperor will grant me that privilege when I put the matter before him. In such cases, when there is no possibility of conducting the investigation in the usual civilian manner, when cabinets of files are burnt, and when, finally, there are attempts to obscure an already dark affair by too many irrelevant and false denunciations, I assume that a court martial is the only means left of arriving at the truth, and I should like to have your opinion on this matter.'

The prince paused as though expecting a reply. Everyone stood with their eyes fixed on the ground. Many of those present had turned pale.

'I am also aware of another affair, although the persons responsible for it are fully convinced that it cannot be known to anyone. The investigation of this affair will not follow the routine procedure, because I myself will be the petitioner and shall bring forward convincing evidence.'

Someone in that crowd of officials shuddered. Some of the more timid also grew confused.

'It naturally follows,' the prince went on, 'that the ringleaders will be deprived of their ranks and property, while the rest will lose their positions. It goes without saying that among those who will suffer will be a number of innocent persons. What is to be done? The affair is far too dishonest and cries to heaven for justice. Although I know that this will not even serve as a lesson to others, since in the place of those dismissed others will come, and those who had hitherto been honest will become dishonest, and those who were considered worthy of trust will deceive and betray—despite my awareness of this, I must act harshly because justice demands it. I know that I shall be accused of harshness and cruelty, but I also know that . . . I must forge of them all an impartial sword of justice which will descend on their heads . . . .'

Involuntarily a shudder ran over the faces of those assembled. The prince was calm. His features expressed neither anger nor indignation.

'Now he who has the fate of many in his hands and whom no prayers can mollify, he now asks of you all a favour. Everything will be forgotten, erased and forgiven; I shall myself plead for you all if you execute my request. Here it is. I know that it is impossible to eradicate lies by any means, by any threats or punishments: they are too deeply ingrained in us. The dishonest practice of accepting bribes has become an essential and necessary part of the lives even of those persons who were not born to be dishonest. I know that it is almost impossible for many of you to go against the general current. But I must now— as in a decisive and sacred moment when the salvation of our country is at stake, when each citizen contributes and sacrifices all he has—I must now appeal to you, to those of you at least who have a Russian heart beating in their breasts and who still understand the meaning of the word "nobility." There is no point in discussing which of us is the most guilty! Maybe it is I who am the most guilty of you all; perhaps I treated you all too coldly in the beginning; perhaps by being over-suspicious I repulsed those of you who sincerely wished to be of use to me, although I for my part might also have made use of you. . . . If they really loved the justice and goodness implicit in their country, they should not have been offended by my arrogant behaviour, they should have controlled their personal vanity and sacrificed their personality. I could not have failed to notice their self-denial and their great love of goodness and to have accepted in the end their useful and wise counsels. All the same it is rather for a subordinate to adapt himself to the temper of his chief than for the chief to adapt himself to the temper of his subordinate. That at least is more in the order of things and easier, because subordinates have only one chief, while a chief has many subordinates. But let us now leave aside this question of who is most guilty. The point is that the time has come to try and save our country. Our country is in danger of perishing not from the invasion of twenty foreign tribes but from ourselves; for besides the lawful rulers, other rulers have set themselves up, far stronger than any lawful ruler. These rulers have established their own conditions, values, and have even made their price generally known. And no governor, though he be wiser than all other lawgivers and rulers, is strong enough to correct this evil, whatever controls he may exercise over the actions of bad officials by appointing other officials to supervise them. It will all come to nothing until each one of us feels that, as in the age of the revolt of the peoples, he arms himself against. . . . So each one of us must rise up against these lies. As a Russian bound to you by ties of common blood, I appeal to you now. I appeal to those of you who have any inkling of what nobility of thought signifies. I invite you to remember the duty that is each man's burden wherever he may be. I invite you to examine your conscience more closely as well as the obligations of your earthly occupation, because that is something we can all picture to ourselves, and we are hardly . . .'[9]

9. Here the manuscript finally breaks off [*Translator's note*].

Backgrounds and Sources

A Chronology of Gogol's Life

1809   *Apr. 1* Born in town of Sorochintsy, near Mirgorod, in the Ukraine. His father is a small landowner.

1821–28   Studies at high school *(gymnaziia)* in Nezhin.

1825   His father dies.

1828   Goes to Petersburg. Looks for a job and writes poetry.

1829   Brief trip to Lübeck and Hamburg, North Germany. Returns to Petersburg and enters civil service.

1830   Begins publishing stories on Ukrainian subjects.

1831   Teaches history in girls' institute. Meets the great poet Pushkin.
Sept. Publishes first collection of stories, *Evenings on a Farm near Dikanka.*

1832   *Mar.* Publishes second volume of Ukrainian stories.
June Visits Moscow.

1834   Appointed adjunct professor of general history, University of Petersburg.

1835   Resigns his professorship and devotes himself fully to writing. Publishes two volumes of stories, *Arabesques and Mirgorod.* Becomes recognized as the leading literary figure in Russia.

1836   The play *The Inspector General* is produced in Petersburg and Moscow.
June Leaves for Switzerland, Paris, Rome. Spends most of next twelve years abroad.

1839–40   *Sept.–May* Temporary return to Russia.

1840–41   *June–Sept.* Back in Italy.

1841–42   *Oct.–May* Back in Russia again.

1842   *May* Publishes first volume of *Dead Souls.*
June Begins six years of extensive travel.

1847   *Selected Passages from Correspondence with Friends* published. Some conservatives delighted; radicals outraged.

1848   *Jan.–Apr.* Pilgrimage to the Holy Land.
Apr.–May Returns to Russia.

1848–52   Lives in Moscow, Odessa, Petersburg. Often sick; visits monasteries; religious interests intensify.

1852   *Feb.* Very sick. Burns manuscripts of second volume of *Dead Souls.*
Mar. 4 Dies.

Gogol's "Four Letters to Divers Persons Apropos *Dead Souls*"†

I

You are wrong to be indignant at the intemperate tone of some of the attacks on *Dead Souls*. There is a good side to it. Sometimes it is necessary to have embittered people against oneself. He who is captivated by the beauty of things does not see the faults in them and forgives everything; but he who is embittered does his utmost to unearth all the rottenness in us and bring it into the open so glaringly that you see it in spite of yourself. It so rarely befalls us to hear the Truth that for one grain of it we can forgive all the abusive voices by which it was pronounced. There is much justice in the criticisms of Bulgarin, Se(n)kowski, and Polevoi,[1] beginning with the advice given to me first to learn how to read and write in Russian and only then to write. It is true, if I had not been in a hurry to publish the manuscript and had kept it for a year, I would then have seen myself that it should not appear in the world in such a slovenly condition. Indeed, the very epigrams and the ridicules aimed at me were necessary to me, even though at first they cut me to the quick. Oh, how we need these continual nips and this abusive tone, and these sarcastic jibes which pierce us through! So much pettiness is hidden in the depths of our soul, so much paltry self-love, so much touchy, nasty vanity, that at every moment we ought to be pricked, struck, beaten by all possible arms, and we must every moment thank the hand striking us.

I would have wished, however, for a little more criticism, not on the part of men of letters, but on the part

† These four "letters" were published in 1847, as chapter 18 of Gogol's book *Selected Passages from Correspondence with Friends*. This volume, the last of Gogol's works to be published during his lifetime, presents in letter form his chief religious, moral, and aesthetic views. Between 1842 and 1847 (five years before his death in 1852), the two things that chiefly preoccupied him were the composition of *Selected Passages* and the continuation of *Dead Souls*. Reprinted from Nikolai Gogol, *Selected Passages from Correspondence with Friends*, trans.

Jesse Zeldin (Nashville, Tenn.: Vanderbilt University Press, 1969), pp. 96–110.

1. T. V. Bulgarin (1789–1859) and N. A. Polevoy (1796–1846), both writers, journalists, and literary critics, had long been antagonists of Gogol's. O. I. Senkowski (1800–1858) was a professor of Oriental languages at the University of Petersburg, editor of the journal *Library for Reading*, and the target of Gogol's attack in 1835 article. Both he and Bulgarin were Poles by birth. Senkowski was influential as a scathing journalist.

of people of busy lives, on the part of practical people; as ill luck would have it, except for the men of letters nobody answered.

Meanwhile, *Dead Souls* made a great deal of noise, aroused much grumbling, cut many to the quick by its jibes, by its truth and justice, and by its caricature; it discussed an order of things which we all daily have before our eyes; it is full of blunders, anachronisms, and obvious ignorance of many subjects; indeed, cutting and offensive things were designedly placed in it: perhaps some one will rate me properly and in swearing and wrath tell me the truth of what I have attained.

If one soul had raised his voice! Anyone could have. And sensibly! The working bureaucrat could have clearly proven to me, in the sight of everyone, the improbability of the events I had depicted, by adducing two or three facts which have really occurred, thus refuting me better than in words, or he could have done it so as to support and justify the fairness of my account. The adducing of facts that have occurred is a better proof than mere words and literary verbiage. The businessman and the land-owner could have done the same—in short, any literate person, whether he does not stir from his place or roams far and wide across all the face of the Russian land. Besides his personal point of view, every man, whatever be his place and rank in society, has an opportunity to see things from an angle from which no one but he can see them. On the occasion of *Dead Souls,* another incomparably more interesting book than *Dead Souls* could have been written by a mass of readers, and it could have taught not only me but the readers themselves, because— nothing may conceal this sin—we all know Russia very badly.

And if but one soul had begun to speak out in public! It was exactly as though everything had died out, as though Russia in fact was inhabited not by living but by *Dead Souls.* And they reproach me for knowing Russia badly! As though, by the strength of the Holy Spirit, I ought unfailingly to know everything that is done in all its corners—to learn it without having been taught! But by what means could I learn, I, a writer, already condemned by the vocation of a writer to a sedentary, secluded life, I, who am sick besides, and therefore compelled to live far from Russia, by what means could I learn? I could not learn from men of letters and journalists who are themselves secluded desk people. For a writer there is only one teacher—his readers. But the readers refused to teach me. I know that I will have a terrible account to render to God for not having performed my work as I should have, but I also know that others will render an account for me. And I do not speak in vain. God sees that I do not speak in vain!

1843

II

I had a presentiment that all the lyrical digressions in the poem would be taken in a false sense. They are so vague, they are so little in accord with the objects passing before the eyes of the reader, so irrelevant to the form and manner of the work as a whole, that they led both adversaries and defenders astray. All the passages in which I vaguely mentioned a writer were laid to my account; I even blushed at explanations of them in my favor. It serves me right! In no case should I have published a work which, even though not badly made, was sewn with white threads, like a dress a dressmaker has only brought for a fitting. I only marveled that I was so little reproached in regard to my art and creative knowledge. The angry temper of my critics was disturbed by this, unaccustomed as they are to close examination of how a work is built. One would have to show them how the monstrously long parts are connected with the others where the writer betrayed himself by not sustaining the tone he had adopted as his very own. No one even noticed that the last half of the book is less worked over than the first, that there are great gaps in it, that capital and important events have been condensed and abbreviated, unimportant and tangential ones spread out, and instead of the inner spirit of the whole work appearing, the mixed character of the parts and its scrappiness strike the eye. In short, it would have been possible to raise incomparably more efficient attacks, to rebuke me much more than I am now rebuked, and to rebuke to the point. But there was no talk of that. The talk was of the lyrical digressions, which the journalists in particular have attacked, seeing in them signs of presumption, of a boasting and a pride until now unheard of in any writer. I mean that passage in the last chapter where, having described the departure of Chichikov from the town, the writer, for a time abandoning his hero in the middle of the high road, puts himself in his place and, struck by the tedious monotony of the landscape, by our uninhabited, shelterless spaces and the sorrowful songs arising from every feature of the Russian land from sea to sea, in a lyrical appeal addresses himself to Russia herself, asking her for an explanation of this incomprehensible feeling with which he is filled, that is: wherefore and why does it seem to him as though everything in her, from inanimate things to animate, fixes its eyes on him and expects something from him? These words were taken for a pride and boasting unheard of till now, while they are neither the one nor the other. They are simply an awkward expression of a real feeling. It seems the same to me now. I have never been able to bear the doleful, lacerating sounds of our songs which rush across all of boundless Russian space. These sounds eat into my heart, and I marvel that everyone is not aware of the same thing. Whoever at the sight of these uninhabited, empty spaces unrelieved by village or home does not feel depressed, whoever in the doleful sounds of our songs does not hear painful rebukes to himself—indeed, to himself—either has fulfilled his duty as he should, or is not a Russian in his soul. Things must be seen as they are. Almost 150 years have elapsed since our sovereign Peter I cleared our eyes by the purgatory of European enlightenment; he put in our hands all the means and instruments of action, and still our spaces remain just as empty, sorrowful, and unpeopled, just as homeless and unfriendly all around us; just as though we still have no home, no roof of our own but somewhere homeless pause on a public road and breathe from Russia not the hearty natal air which welcomes brothers but a kind of cold chill at a post station where only a guard indifferent to everything is seen, stalely responding: "No horses!"

What then? Who is to blame? We or the government? But the government all this time acted ceaselessly. In witness whereof there are whole tomes of enactments, statutes, and institutions, a great number of houses built, a great number of books published, a great number of institutions of all kinds instituted—educational, philanthropic, religious, and, in short, such as the government of no other state has set up. It is from on high that the demands resound, the responses from below. Sometimes demands resound from on high that testify to the chivalric and magnanimous operations of many sovereigns acting even to the detriment of their own interests. But how was all this responded to from below? It is a matter, you see, of adapting and applying whatever idea it may be in such a way that it is accepted by and lodged within us. An edict, as well-considered and precise as it may be, is no more than a formal statement, if there is no sincere desire below to put it into practice in the proper way, as it must and should be and as only he who has an enlightened understanding of divine rather than human justice will be able to see clearly. Otherwise, everything is turned into evil. The proof of it is all our subtle swindlers and grafters who know how to bypass all decrees, for whom a new decree is only a new source of profit, a new way to encumber the exercise of business with greater complications, a new way to trip people up. In short, wherever I turn, I see that expediency is at fault, that is, our colleagues: either the fault is that they are in a hurry, desiring too soon to become famous and to grab a decoration; or the fault is that they rush forward too heatedly, desiring, in the Russian way, to give proof of their self-sacrifice; without any appeal to reason, without any reflection, in the heat of the affair they take over as though they are experts, and then suddenly, still in the Russian way, they grow cold witnessing their defeat. Or the fault, finally, is that, because of a slight insult to their vanity, they throw up their place, which they had once pursued so nobly, cede it to the first rogue who comes along—let him rob the people. In short, rare is he among us whose love of the good is sufficient for him to resolve to sacrifice his ambition and vanity to it, together with all the easily irritated details of his egoism, and lay down for himself one definite rule—to serve his country and not himself, every moment remembering that he accepted his place for the happiness of others and not for his own. On the contrary, these latter days, as though on purpose, Russians have attempted openly to exhibit all the shabby details of their irritated vanity. I do not know whether there are many among us who have done all that they ought to have done, who could openly say before the whole world that Russia has nothing to reproach them with, that not one soulless object in its empty spaces gazes at them reproachfully, that all are contented with them and nothing is expected of them. I only know that I have heard this reproach. And I hear it now. And that in my career as a writer, modest as it may be, it may be possible to do something more useful and more durable. What has resulted because the desire for the good has always dwelt in my heart and I took up the pen uniquely because of it? Have I fulfilled it? This my work which has just appeared under the title *Dead Souls*—has it produced the impression that it would have produced if it had been written as it should have been? My personal thoughts, simple, unpuzzling thoughts, I did not know how to transmit, and I myself gave grounds for these misinterpretations, and on the harmful rather than the useful side. Whose fault? Can I really say that the petitions of my friends urged me on, or the impatient desires of elegant amateurs charmed by empty, transitory sounds? Can I really say that circumstances squeezed me and, desiring to procure the money necessary for my subsistence, I had to hasten to premature issue of my book? No, no circumstances can shake one who has resolved to fulfill his task honestly; he will stretch out his hand and ask for alms if it comes to that, but he will ignore passing censures as well as the vain social niceties of the world. He who corrupts a task necessary to his country for the vain social niceties of the world does not love his country. I recognized the contemptible weakness of my character, my mean cowardice, the impotence of my love, and that is why I heard the painful reproach addressed to me by all those things missing in Russia. But a higher power raised me: it was not irreparable faults, not even the empty spaces which had inflicted melancholy on my soul, ravishing me by the great scope of their space, by their wide field of action. From my soul this appeal was uttered to Russia: "How could one not be your hero when there is a place for him to display himself?" This was not said for the sake of the picture or as a boast: I really felt it; I feel it now.

In Russia, now, it is possible to make oneself a hero at every step. Every rank and place demands heroism. Each of us has so disgraced the holiness of his rank and position (all positions are holy) that heroic powers are necessary to lift them to their legitimate height. I perceive

that great vocation which is not now possible for any
other people, which is possible for the Russians alone,
because before them alone is there such scope and their
soul alone is acquainted with heroism—that is why that
exclamation was wrenched out of me, and it was taken
for vainglory and presumption!

1843

III

You, you who are such an expert and knowledgeable
man, you are inclined to set me the same empty questions which others know how to set. Half of them are concerned with things that are still in the future. What is
the use of a curiosity like this? One question alone is wise
and worthy of you, and I wish that others had set it to
me, although I do not know whether I can answer it
wisely. Here is the question: Why are the heroes of my
last works, and especially those of *Dead Souls,* although
far from being portraits of real persons, although their
characteristics are so unattractive, close to the soul, without anyone's knowing why, just as though some sort of
spiritual circumstance had participated in their composition? A year ago it would have been awkward for me to
answer on this point, even to you. Now I say everything
directly: my heroes are close to the soul because they
come from the soul; all my last works are the story of
my own soul. In order to explain all this better, I will
define myself to you as a writer.

I have been much interpreted, most of my facets discussed, but no one has defined my principal essence.
Only Pushkin perceived it. He always told me that no
other writer has the gift of representing the banality of
life so clearly, of knowing how to depict the banality of
a banal man with such force that all the *petty details*
which escape the eyes *gleam large* in the eyes. That is
my principal virtue, belonging to me alone, precisely that
which is in no other writer. Only afterwards was it
deepened in me by its union with some spiritual circumstance. But I was in no condition to reveal it then, even
to Pushkin.

This characteristic appeared with greater strength in
Dead Souls. Dead Souls did not frighten Russia and make
such a noise in it because it laid bare some of its wounds

or its internal sicknesses, nor even because it presented a shocking picture of evil triumphant and innocence conquered. Not at all. My heroes are not at all villains; if I had only added one good feature to any one of them the reader would have been reconciled with them all. But the banality of all of them frightened my readers. What frightened them is that my heroes follow one after the other, one more banal than the other, that there is not one consoling scene, that there is nowhere for the poor reader to rest and take a breath, and, after having read the whole book, it seems exactly as though he were emerging from some stifling cellar into God's light. I would sooner have been forgiven if I had presented pictures of monsters: but banality I was not forgiven. The Russian is more frightened of his insignificance than of all his vices and shortcomings. A splendid event! A capital fear! Whoever is strongly disgusted at his insignificance probably has everything opposite to insignificance. Thus, this is my principal virtue; but this virtue, I say again, would not have developed in me with such strength if my own spiritual circumstance and my own spiritual history had not been united with it. None of my readers knew that while laughing at my heroes, he was laughing at me.

There was not one overpowering vice in me which appeared more visibly than all my other vices, just as there was not one picturesque virtue which could have given me a picturesque appearance: but rather, instead of that, in me was a collection of all possible abominations, a little of each, and besides, in such numbers as I have thus far not encountered in any individual. God has given me a many-sided nature. He has also inspired in me, since my birth, some good characteristics; but best of them all, for which I do not know how to thank Him, was *the desire to be better.* I have never loved my bad qualities, and if God's divine love had not commanded that they be revealed to me gradually, a little at a time, instead of being revealed suddenly and immediately before my eyes, at a time when I still had no understanding of His infinite mercy, I would have hanged myself. In proportion to the rate at which they were revealed, the desire to be delivered of them was strengthened in me by a wonderful impulse from on high; by an extraordinary spiritual event, I was driven to transfer them to my heroes. What the nature of that event was you may not know: if I had seen any use in it for anyone, I would already have announced it. From that moment on, I began to provide my heroes with my own rottenness in addition to their abominations. This is how it was done: taking one of my bad qualities, I pursued it under another name and in another field, I tried to represent it as a mortal enemy who had inflicted the worst outrage on me, I pursued it in anger, with sarcasm and anything else that fell to my hand. If anyone had seen the monsters which first issued from my pen, he would promptly have shuddered for me. It is enough for me to tell you that when I began to read the first chapters of *Dead Souls* to Pushkin, in the form in which they formerly were, Pushkin, who always laughed at my readings (he loved laughter), slowly became gloomier and gloomier, and finally he was completely somber. When the reading was finished, he uttered in an anguished voice: "God, how sad is our Russia!" This amazed me. Pushkin, who knew Russia so well, had not noticed that it was all a caricature and my own invention! Then I saw what something whose spring is the soul and is a spiritual truth means, how frightening a sight it can be to a man when he is presented with shadows, and how much more threatening is *the absence of light*. From this time forward I began to think only of how to mitigate the painful impression which *Dead Souls* had produced. I have seen that many abominations are not worth anger; it is better to show all their insignificance, which must be their fate forever. Besides, I wanted to test what a normal Russian would say if he should be regaled with his own banality. Since the plan of *Dead Souls* had been adopted long before, for the first part I needed worthless people. These worthless people, however, are not simply portraits of worthless people; on the contrary, assembled in them are the traits of those who consider themselves better than others, like generals degraded to the ranks. Here, besides my own, are the traits of many of my friends, and yours too. I will prove this to you later in case you find it necessary; until then it is my secret. I had to pick up from all the fine people I know everything banal and nasty that they had caught accidentally and to restore it to its legitimate owners. Do not ask why all the first part had to be *banality* and why every person in it had to be banal: the other volumes will give you the answer—and that is all! The first part, despite all its imperfections, has done the chief thing: in everyone it has inspired a loathing for my heroes and their worthlessness; it has caused me a certain necessary melancholy at the sight of it all. For the moment, this is enough for me; I am after nothing else. Of course, it would all have been more substantial if I had been less in a hurry to publish it and had polished it better. My heroes were still not completely detached from me, and therefore did not receive independence. I had still not lodged them firmly in the land where they were to exist, they had still not entered into the round of our customs, furnished with all the circumstances of real Russian life. The entire book is still no more than a prematurely born child; but its spirit is already invisibly spread abroad, and even its premature appearance may be useful to me in that it will force my readers to point out all my blunders concerning social legislation and particular usages in Russia. So if you, instead of posing empty questions to me (with which half your letter was stuffed, and which had no end other than the satisfaction of an idle curiosity), if you had instead assembled sensible observations on my book, both yours and those of other intelligent people, busy, like you, with experience and a sensible life, if you had been able to adjoin accounts of events and anecdotes such as have occurred either in your immediate neighborhood or throughout the province, in confirmation or denial of what is in my book, so that it would have been possible for me to tidy up tens of them on every page—then you would have done a good deed, and I would have given you hearty thanks. How my horizon would have been enlarged! How my mind would have been refreshed and how successfully my work would have gone forward! But what I ask no one fulfills; no one considers my questions important but only esteems his own; and some even demand sincerity and frankness of me, not understanding what it is they demand. And why this idle curiosity to know beforehand, and this idle haste without object and without goal which I notice is already beginning to infect you? See how in nature everything is performed decorously and wisely, by harmonious law, and how reasonably everything proceeds, one thing from another! Only we, God knows why, are confounded. Everyone is in a hurry. Everyone is feverish. Well, have you thoroughly weighed your words, "A second volume is now vitally necessary"? Solely because of the general displeasure with me I should hurry the second volume as foolishly as I hurried the first. Have I really gone entirely out of my mind? I need this displeasure; it is in his displeasure that a man will express something to me. And what led you to the conclusion that a second volume is necessary right now? Have you really stolen into my head? Have you sensed the existence of a second volume? For you it is needed now, but for me not for two or three years, because of the rapid movement of circumstances and times. Which of us is right? He who already has the second volume in his head or he who does not even know of what the second volume will consist? What a strange fashion has now been established in Rus! The very man who is indolent, too lazy for the matter at hand, hurries someone else, exactly as though the someone else should be overjoyed by his friend's indolence. Hardly is a man seriously occupied with something before he is immediately pressed on all sides and given a good rating if he does something foolish; they do not say to him, "Why all the hurry?"

But I have finished my sermon. I have answered your intelligent question and even said more than I have said to anyone else. Do not think, however, after these confessions, that I am just such a monster as my heroes. No, I do not resemble them. I love the good, and I search for it and burn with it; but I do not love my abominations and I do not hold their hands, as my heroes do; I do not love those meannesses of mine which separate me from the good. I struggle, and will struggle, with them, and with the help of God I will expel them. What the foolish, clever men of the world turn out is nonsense, professing that a man may be educated only in school and that afterwards it is not possible for his features to be changed: such a foolish idea could only be formed in a foolish, worldly noodle. I have already got rid of many of my abominations by transmitting them to my heroes, I have turned them to ridicule in them and compelled others to laugh at them as well. I tore myself away from many things because, having deprived them of the fine airs and chivalrous masks under which our loathsomeness struts, I put them beside all the abominations which are apparent to everyone. When I confess myself before Him Who commanded me to come into the world and free myself from my faults, I see many vices in myself; but they are already not such as they were but a year ago: a holy power has helped me to tear myself away from them.

I advise you not to ignore these words but, after having read my letter, to remain alone for a few minutes and, far away from everyone, look at yourself thoroughly, passing all your life in review in order to verify the truth of my words. In my answers you will find an answer also to other questions, if you look more intently. It will also explain to you why up to now I have not offered the reader consoling scenes and have not chosen virtuous people for my heroes. They are not invented by the mind. As long as you still somewhat resemble them, as long as you have not acquired constancy and firmly established some good qualities in your soul—all that your pen writes will be a dead thing, as far from truth as earth is from Heaven. As for inventing nightmares, I have not invented any either; these nightmares weigh on my soul: what was in my soul is what issued forth from it.

1843

IV

The second part of *Dead Souls* was burned because it was necessary. "Lest the seed die, it will not live again," says the Apostle. It is first necessary to die in order to be resurrected. It was not easy to burn the work of five years, produced with such painful effort, where each line was the result of a shock, where was much of what had constituted my best thoughts and had occupied my soul. But all has been burned, and, further, at that very time when, seeing my own death before me, I desired so much to leave after me something which would be a better reminiscence of myself. I thank God for having given me the strength to do it. Immediately that the flame had carried away the last pages of my book, its content suddenly was resurrected in a purified and lucid form, like the Phoenix from the pyre, and I suddenly saw in what disorder was what I had considered ordered and harmonious. The appearance of the second volume in the form in which it was would sooner have done harm than good. It is necessary to consider not the enjoyment of some lovers of art and men of letters, but all the readers for whom *Dead Souls* was written. To describe some fine characters who are supposed to demonstrate the nobility of our race would lead to nothing. It would only arouse empty pride and vanity. Many of us today, especially among the young, have begun to pride themselves immeasurably on our Russian virtues and do not in the least think of deepening and cultivating them in themselves, but rather of putting them up for show and saying to Europe, "Look, foreigners; we are better than you!" This boasting is the destroyer of everything. It irritates others and will cause harm to the boaster himself. The best deed may be turned to dirt if you simply boast of it and swagger about it. And among us, even before something is done, it is boasted of! Boasted of in anticipation! No, in my opinion a temporary despondency and melancholy is better than presumption. In the first case, a man at least sees how contemptible he is, sees his base insignificance, and, in spite of himself, he remembers God who draws all things out of the depths of nothingness; in the second case, he runs away from himself straight into the arms of the devil, the father of presumption who deludes man by illusions of his own virtues. No, there are times when it is not possible to turn society, or even one generation, towards the beautiful, so long as it is not shown the depths of its present abasement; there are times when one may not even speak of the sublime and the beautiful, if the way and roads to it for everyone are not shown clear as day. This last circumstance was badly and weakly developed in the second volume of *Dead Souls*, where it should have been the chief thing, and therefore it was burned. Do not judge me and do not draw conclusions: you would be in error, like those of my friends who, having made their ideal writer out of me, according to their idea of a writer, began to demand that I answer to their created ideal. God created me and did not hide my purpose from me. I was not at all born to produce an epoch in the sphere of literature. My business is simpler and lower: my business is above all what every man must think about, not just myself. My business is *the soul and the durable things in life*. That is why the form of my actions must be firm, and what I write must be firm. There is no need for me to hurry; let others hurry! I burn when it is necessary to burn, and, probably, I act as I must, because I never start anything without prayers. Your apprehensions concerning my weak health, which would not perhaps allow me to write a second volume, are pointless. It is true that my health is very weak; at times it weighs so heavily upon me that without God I could not bear it. To the exhaustion of my strength is added so much sensitivity to cold that

I do not know how I will ever get warm: I should move about a good deal—I have not the strength. I hardly have an hour in the day for work, and I am not always fresh for it. But my hope is not a bit diminished. It is He Who by pride, ailments, and obstacles has quickened the development of my powers and my thoughts, without which I would never have conceived my work, it is He Who has formed the greater half of it in my brain, it is He Who will give me the strength to accomplish the rest—and put it down on paper. I am decrepit in body but not in soul. In my soul, on the contrary, everything is getting stronger and becoming firmer; my body also will get stronger. I believe that, if the right time comes, in several weeks I will accomplish that on which I have spent five sick years.

1846

From Gogol's Letters†

To A. S. Pushkin.[1] October 7, 1835. St. Petersburg.

* * * I have begun to write *Dead Souls*.[2] The plot has stretched out into a very long novel, and it will, I think, be extremely amusing. But now I've stopped it on the third chapter. I'm hunting for a good slanderer with whom one can become intimate. I want to show all Russia— at least from one side—in this novel.

Do me a favor and give me some plot;[3] whether it's amusing or not amusing doesn't matter as long as it's a purely Russian anecdote. * * *

To V. A. Zhukovsky.[4] November 12, 1836. Paris.

. . . Having roamed around the spas during the summer, I moved over to Switzerland for the fall. I wanted to settle

† From Carl R. Proffer, ed., *Letters of Nikolai Gogol*, trans. Carl R. Proffer in collaboration with Vera Krivoshein (Ann Arbor, Mich.: The University of Michigan Press, 1967), 52, 62–64, 99–100, 105–7, 112, 113, 115–18, 159–60, 161–62. Except where indicated differently, notes are by Carl R. Proffer.
1. Alexander Pushkin (1799–1837), generally considered Russia's greatest poet [*Editor*].
2. This is the first reference to *Dead Souls* in Gogol's letters.
3. According to Gogol, Pushkin did suggest a plot, and the result was *The Inspector General*.
4. Vasily Andreevich Zhukovsky (1783–1852), dulcet-tongued, sentimental poet, influenced strongly by German romantics; talented translator [and adaptor] of everything from *The Odyssey* to "Leonore" and "The Prisoner of Chillon"; friend and protector of Pushkin and Gogol; tutor of the Tsar's children. * * *

down some place faster and get to work; for this I lodged in a little house outside of Geneva. There I undertook to reread Molière, Shakespeare, and Walter Scott. I read until it got so cold that all desire to read disappeared. The cold spells and winds in Geneva drove me to Vevey. . . .

At last a fine autumn set in in Vevey, almost summer. It became warm in my room, and I took up *Dead Souls* which I had just begun in Petersburg. I re-did anew everything that had been started, considered the whole plan more thoroughly; and now I am carrying it forward calmly, like a chronicle. Switzerland has become more agreeable to me since then; its grey-lilac-light-and-dark-blue-pink mountains are lighter and airier. If I accomplish this work as it should be accomplished then . . . what a huge, what an original topic! What a varied heap! All of Russia will appear in it! This will be my first decent thing, something which will make my name endure. Every morning, in addition to my breakfast, I added three pages to my epic poem, and I had enough laughter from these pages to sweeten my solitary day. But finally it got very cold in Vevey too. My room was not warm at all; I couldn't find a better one. Then I imagined Petersburg, our warm houses; then I imagined you more vividly—just as you met me when I came to see you and you took me by the hand and were glad of my arrival . . . and I felt terrible melancholy, my *Dead Souls* didn't cheer me up; I didn't even have enough cheer in reserve to continue it. My doctor found symptoms of hypochondria in me, resulting from the hemorrhoids; and he advised me to amuse myself; but seeing that I was in no condition to do that, he advised me to move somewhere else. Until then my intention had been to spend the winter in Italy. But the cholera was raging in Italy in a terrible way; quarantines covered it like locusts. With no hope of amusing myself in Italy, I set off for Paris where I had had no intention at all of going. . . .

Paris is not as bad as I imagined; and what is best of all for me, there is a multitude of places for walks—just the Tuileries gardens and the Elysée fields are enough for a whole day's walking. Without noticing it I get a very decent amount of exercise—which is essential to me now. Here God has stretched his protection over me and He performed a miracle: He pointed out to me a warm apartment in the sun, with a stove; and I am blissful, again I am happy. The Dead Ones flow in a lively way, more freshly and briskly than in Vevey; and it seems to me exactly as

if I were in Russia; before me are all our people, our landowners, our civil servants, our officers, our peasants, our
huts, in a word—all Orthodox Russia. It even amuses me
when I think that I am writing *Dead Souls* in Paris. Another leviathan is being undertaken. A holy trembling
runs through me beforehand when I just think about it;
from it I perceive something. . . . I will experience divine
moments . . . but . . . now I am completely engrossed in
Dead Souls. Vastly great is my creation, and not soon will
it be finished. Still new classes and many people of all kinds
will rise up against me, but what am I to do! It is my fate
to be at war with my countrymen. *Patience!* Someone invisible writes before me with a mighty rod. I know that
after my death my name will be luckier than I am, and
that the descendants of these same countrymen of mine,
perhaps with moist eyes, will pronounce reconciliation for
my shade. . . .

Can you imagine any tangles that might result from
the purchase of dead souls. This would be a fine thing
for me; because, whatever it is like, your imagination will
surely see that which mine will not. Inform Pushkin about
this, maybe he will find something on his part. I want
terribly much to exhaust this plot from all sides. I have
many things that I would on no account have imagined
formerly, but nevertheless you can still tell me much that
is new, for each head has its own intellect. Don't tell anyone what *Dead Souls* is about. You may announce the title
to everyone. Only three people—Pushkin, Pletnev,[5] and
you—should know the real thing. . . .

To S. T. Aksakov.[6] December 28, 1840. Rome.

* * *

Another circumstance which can give hope for my return is my work. I am now preparing the first volume of
Dead Souls for the final revision. I am changing, polishing,
and completely reworking many things, and I see that its
publication cannot get by without my presence. Meanwhile, its further continuation is being elucidated more

5. Peter Alexandrovich Pletnev
(1792–1865), close friend and literary
agent of Pushkin, editor of *The Contemporary* after Pushkin's death.
Critic, poet of small talent, professor
of Russian literature, member of the
Russian Academy.

6. Sergei Aksakov (1791–1859), the
late-blooming author of one of Russia's greatest classics, *A Family Chronicle* (1846–56), a work begun partly
at Gogol's urging. * * * Gogol was
idolized by Aksakov's family.

clearly and majestically in my mind, and now I see that with time it can be something colossal if only my weak powers permit. At least, surely, a few people know to what powerful thoughts and deep phenomena an insignificant plot, the first innocent and modest chapters of which you already know, can lead. My sickness took a lot of time away from me; but now, praise God, at times I even feel the freshness which is very necessary to me. I ascribe this partly to the cold water which I have begun to drink on the advice of the doctor, whom God bless for this and who thinks this cold treatment should help me. The air is wonderful in Rome now, clear. But the summer (this I have already experienced), I must certainly spend the summer on the road. I hurt myself very much by prolonging my stay in suffocating Vienna. But what was I to do? I confess I did not then have the means to undertake a journey; everything I had was too closely budgeted. Oh, if only I had the opportunity to take some distant road every summer! The road is amazingly salubrious for me. . . . But let's turn to the beginning. In my trip to see you, the significance of which even I didn't understand in the beginning, there was much, much for me. Yes, I perceive the feeling of love for Russia is strong within me. Much that formerly seemed unpleasant and unbearable to me, now seems to have sunk into its triviality and insignificance; and I, calm and steady, am surprised that I could ever have taken them close to heart. * * *

To P. A. Pletnev. January 7, 1842. Moscow.

Shattered both in body and in spirit I write to you. I would like very much to go to Petersburg now; it is necessary for me, I know, but nevertheless I cannot. Illness has never turned up in me as inopportunely as now. Now its attacks have assumed such strange forms . . . but forget about them; I must talk about the censorship now, not about illness. It is a blow which was in no way unexpected for me—the entire manuscript has been forbidden.[7] First I gave it to the censor Snegirev who is somewhat more sensible than the others so that if he found any passage leading to doubt in his mind, he would inform me straightaway, and then I would send it to Petersburg. In two days Snegirev solemnly informed me that he found the manuscript completely loyal both in relation to its purpose

7. *Dead Souls.*

and in relation to the impression produced on the reader, and that except for one insignificant place—the change of two or three names (I immediately agreed and changed them)—there was nothing which could incur the suspicion of the strictest censorship. He declared the same thing to others as well. All of a sudden someone got him muddled, and I found out that he had presented my manuscript to the committee. The committee received it as if they had been prepared in advance and were all set to enact a comedy, for the accusations without exception were comedy in the highest degree. No sooner had Golokhvastov, the acting president, heard the title than he shouted in the voice of an ancient Roman: *"Dead Souls!* No, I will never allow this—the soul is immortal, there cannot be any dead soul; the author is taking up arms against immortality." Only with some effort, finally, could the intelligent president understand that it was about serfs not yet taken from the tax rolls. No sooner had he understood and along with him the other censors understood that "dead" means souls not yet removed from the tax rolls than an ever greater mess was made. "No," cried the chairman and after him half of the censors, "even more that cannot be allowed, even if in the manuscript there were nothing else, but only the words 'tax-roll soul'—even this alone cannot be allowed; this means it is against serfdom." Finally, Snegirev himself, seeing that things had already gone far afield, began to assure the censors that he had read the manuscript and there were not even any hints about serfdom, that there were not even any of the usual slaps in the face of serfs which resound in many stories, that this was about something completely different, that the main concern was based on the amusing misunderstanding of the sellers and subtle ruses of the buyer and on the general hodgepodge that this strange purchase caused, that this was a series of characters, the internal mode of life of Russia and a few ordinary inhabitants, a collection of scenes which were not at all scandalous. But nothing helped.

"Chichikov's undertaking," they all began to shout, "is in itself a criminal offense." "But nevertheless, the author does not justify him," observed my censor. "Yes, he doesn't justify him! But here he shows him off now, and others will go take his example and buy dead souls." That's the kind of views! Those are the views of the censor-Asians, i.e., of old people who have curried favor and are now sitting at home. Now follow the views of the censor-

Europeans, young people who have just returned from abroad. "Whatever you say, the price that Chichikov gives (said one of these censors, to be specific, Krylov), the price of two and a half rubles which he gives for a soul makes the soul indignant. Human feeling cries out against this, although, of course, this price is given for the name alone, written on paper; but, nevertheless, this name is a soul, a human soul, it lived, existed. This couldn't be allowed in France, England, or anywhere. Why after that not one foreigner would come to our country." These are the central points upon which the prohibition of the manuscript was based. I won't tell you about the other minor observations—e.g.: in one place it is said that one landowner ruined himself decorating his Moscow house in the fashionable taste. "Why isn't it so that even the Tsar is building a palace in Moscow!" said a censor (Kachenovsky). A conversation unique in the world began among the censors about this. Then there were other observations which I'm ashamed even to repeat, and finally the affair ended by the manuscript being declared forbidden, even though the committee had read only three or four passages. There's the whole story for you. It's almost unbelievable, and besides that, for me it's suspicious. One couldn't suppose such stupidity existed in man. The censors are not all stupid to such a degree. I think that someone is against me. However, this matter is too important for me. I have a hangover from their comedies and intrigues. You yourself know that my entire existence and all my means are included in my poem.[8] The affair is coming to the point of taking away from me my last piece of bread, earned by seven years of selfless labor, seclusion from the world and all its advantages; I cannot undertake anything else for my existence. My growing propensity for illness and my ailments even deprive me of the possibility of continuing further the work which has been begun. I don't have very many bright moments, but now my hands are simply paralysed. I no longer even remember what I have written you; I think you won't be able to make out my handwriting at all. Here's what must be done. Now you must act by joining forces and get the manuscript to His

---

8. In his correspondence Gogol is inconsistent about the genre of *Dead Souls*, sometimes calling it a novel, sometimes a "poem"; but on the fanciful skull and scroll-embellished title page he created for the first edi- tion, the title itself is dwarfed by the genre-specification *POÈMA* — a Russian term usually applied only to rather long works in verse. See a reproduction of this illustration on p. ix of this volume [*Editor*].

Majesty. I am writing to Alexandra Osipovna Smirnova[9] about this. I asked her to act through the grand duchesses or by other means, that's your task, you have a conference about that together. Ask A. O. to read you my letter. Prince Odoevsky has my manuscript. Read it together, three or four people, no more. This case should not attract any publicity. Only those who really love me should know. I rely firmly on your friendship and on your soul, and we must not waste words any more! I embrace you firmly, and God bless you! If the manuscript is allowed to pass and it is necessary to give it to a censor only as a formality, I think it is better to give it to Ochkin to sign it, however, do as you find best. I have no more strength to write.

To N. Ya. Prokopovich.[1] April 9, 1842. Moscow.

The manuscript was received April 5. The delay took place at the Censorship Committee, not at the post office. The Censorship Committee lied in telling Pletnev it was forwarded on March 7, because it wasn't signed by the censor until the ninth. They threw out my whole episode about Kopeikin, which is very necessary for me, even more than they think. I have decided not to give it up no matter what. Now I have redone it so that no censorship could carp. I threw out the generals and all and am sending it to Pletnev for delivery to the censor. Please go to his place and find out about this. . . .

To A. V. Nikitenko.[2] April 10, 1842. Moscow.

I thank you for your letter. In it one can see much concern, much honesty, much of everything that beauti-

9. Alexandra Osipovna Smirnova (née Rosset—or Rozetti) 1809–82. Beautiful lady-in-waiting of the Empress. A friend of Zhukovsky, Vyazemsky, and Lermontov. Like other poets, Pushkin (who introduced her to Gogol) had written poems to her. Her husband was a rich diplomat to whom she was indifferent (in her memoirs she wrote, "I sold myself for 6000 souls for my brothers"). She frequently acted as *"notre dame aux bons secours"* when her literary friends ran afoul of the censorship. After a rather rowdy youth, her moral development (in the forties) took the same direction as Gogol's. He became her very close spiritual friend.

1. Nikolai Prokopovich was a school chum of Gogol's [*Editor*].

2. Alexander Vasilevich Nikitenko, a censor. In a letter to Pletnev (February 17, 1842) Gogol says: "Besides his views on the censor's duty, he understands the calling of the censor in the sense of the ancient Roman censors, i.e., watchers after purity of morals; and therefore many of my expressions will suffer greatly from him."

fully and nobly excites a man. Yes, I cannot complain about the censorship; it was condescending to me, and I know how to be grateful. But, I confess, the destruction of Kopeikin disturbed me a great deal. It is one of the best parts. There is no way I can patch up the hole which is visible in my poem. You yourself, gifted with aesthetic taste which is so well reflected in your letter, you yourself can see that this piece is essential not for the connection of events, but in order to distract the reader for a moment, to replace one impression with another; and he who is an artist in his soul will understand that without it a large hole is left. It occurred to me that perhaps the censorship was afraid of the generals. I redid Kopeikin; I threw out everything, even the minister, even the word "excellency." In the absence of everyone a temporary committee remains in Petersburg. I drew out the character of Kopeikin more sharply, so that now it is clear that he himself is the cause of his actions—and not a lack of compassion in others. The Head of the Commission even treats him very well. In a word, now everything is in a form such as no strict censorship, in my opinion, can find anything reprehensible in any respect. I entreat you to return this passage to me—and as quickly as possible in order not to delay the printing. Get the manuscript from Pletnev and return it to him afterwards for forwarding to me. I will not say anything more to you, for you yourself said in your letter that you understand me, and therefore you will also understand my gratitude.

To A. S. Danilevsky.[3] *May 9, 1842. Moscow*

. . . I don't expect to receive an answer to this letter in Moscow, because in a week and a half I am leaving. This will be my last and perhaps my most prolonged stay away from the fatherland: my return is possible only by way of Jerusalem.[4] That is all I can tell you. . . .

Within a week after this letter you will receive the printed *Dead Souls*—the rather pale threshold of the great poem which is being *formed* within me and which will finally solve the riddle of my existence. But enough. . . .

3. Alexander Semenovich Danilevsky (1809–88), one of Gogol's closest friends throughout his life, from Vasilevka and Nezhin to Petersburg and Paris.

4. Before leaving Russia in 1842 Gogol solemnly announced a forthcoming pilgrimage to the Holy Land. He did not make the trip until 1848.

To V. Zhukovsky. June 26, 1842. Berlin.

* * * I recall how, desiring to convey to you something of the bliss of my soul, I didn't find words in conversation with you, I uttered only incoherent noises resembling the delirium of madness and perhaps until now perplexity has remained in your soul about whom to take me for and what strange thing took place within me. But even now I won't tell you anything—and what is there to talk about? I will say only that with each day and hour it becomes more radiant and triumphant in my soul, that my journeys, eloignments, and separations from the world were not without meaning or goal, that in them the education of my soul has taken place unseen, that I became far better than the man who was imprinted in the memory (which is sacred for me) of my friends, that my spiritual tears permit solemnity more and more often, and that in my soul there lives a deep and irresistible faith that the divine power will help me ascend the ladder which stands before me, although I am standing on its lowest and first steps. There is much labor and road and spiritual education ahead yet! My soul must be purer than the celestial snows and more radiant than the heavens, and only then will I acquire the strength to begin heroic deeds and the great pursuit, only then will the riddle of my existence be solved.

That is all that I can tell you! And also I bless you with the strength of my aspirations, the strength of tears, the strength of spiritual thirst to be worthy of this. This blessing is not powerless, therefore accept it with faith. About the everyday trifles of my life I say nothing to you; there are almost none of them, and incidentally, thank God I do not even feel or perceive them. I am sending you *Dead Souls*. This is the first part. By the assurance of the local postmaster you will receive it by mail along with a letter in three days. I have changed it in many ways since the time I read you the first chapters, but nevertheless I cannot help seeing its insignificance in comparison with the other parts which will follow it. In relation to them it still seems to me like an entrance portico attached to a palace planned to be constructed on a huge scale by a provincial architect—and without doubt now quite a few of the shortcomings which I still do not see have accumulated in it. For the sake of God, inform me of your ob-

servations. Be as severe and merciless as possible. You yourself know how essential this is for me. Don't even be seduced by a felicitous expression, although at first glance
it seems enough to make up for a slip. Don't read without
a pencil and paper, and immediately write your observations on little scraps of paper. Next, after reading each
chapter, make two or three observations in general about
the entire chapter. Next, about the interrelations of all the
chapters, and then after reading the whole book, in general
about the whole book. Gather together all these observations, both the general and the specific, seal them in a
package, and send it to me. In no respect is it possible to
make a better gift to me now. . . .

Addressee unknown. About July 20, 1842. Gastein.

. . . In gratitude you must saw a few words to me about
Dead Souls. I don't at all demand a definition of its merit
and significance, but here is what I do demand of you: You
imagine that I am an innkeeper in some European hotel
and I have a table for everyone or a *table d'hôte.* There
are twenty dishes on my table and perhaps more. Naturally,
not all these dishes are identically good or, at least, it goes
without saying that everyone will choose for himself and
eat only the dishes he likes—and concerning this he can
tell the host frankly, "You have such-and-such dishes, but
I like these here; they were more to my taste," and this
will not offend the host in the least. So I am only asking
you to say this: "This is what is more to my taste in your
work, these places here." This you can say! . . . Incidentally,
here is one of my important character traits for you. I have
lived through the years of youth, gotten over the attraction
to love of fame, and moved far away from society in order
to educate myself for others in the depths of my soul;
and it is still a long way to the end of my education. I have
long been indifferent to what tickles with fame, I look at
myself as at an outsider, and now there is no result more
desirable or beautiful to me than to see my mistakes, shortcomings, errors. When he has seen his shortcomings and
errors, a man is already above himself. There is no evil
which cannot be corrected, but it is necessary to see just
what this evil consists of. I tell you this sincerely, right
from the depth, and you will understand that this cannot

be insincere. My creations differ from other works in that everyone can be a judge of them, all the readers from one to the next—because the subjects are taken from the life which turns around each person. I know many opinions in advance. I know in advance what will be said about me in print in such-and-such a journal; but the opinions of people who are deeply practical, who know life, who have much experience and intelligence, who have turned everything to their use, are more valuable to me than book theories which I know by heart. That is why I have importuned you. . . .

To S. T. Aksakov. August 18, 1842. Gastein.

. . . All of your news, everything included in your letter, everything to the last word and line was interesting and equally pleasant for me—beginning with the way you spend your time, the fishing in ponds and streams, down to your news about *Dead Souls*. Its first impression on the public was precisely that which I suspected beforehand. Indeterminate comments, quick haste to read, and dissatisfied emptiness after the reading. Annoyance at the continual triviality of the events of life, triviality which involuntarily becomes a sneer and a reproach. All this I knew in advance. The poor reader avidly grabbed the book in his hands to read it like an entertaining and fascinating novel and, exhausted, he dropped his head and hands, having encountered completely unforeseen boredom. I knew all this. . . .

Your opinion that there is no one who would understand *Dead Souls* the first time through is absolutely correct and should be spread around to everyone, because much can be comprehensible to me alone. Don't even be afraid of your first impression that the exaltation in many passages seemed to you to have reached the point of ridiculous excess. It is true, because the full meaning of the lyrical hints can only be elucidated when the last part is published. . . .

My long and difficult journey[5] frightens you. You say you cannot understand the reasons for it. . . .

How can you not want for there to be engendered in the breast of one who has experienced the elevated mo-

5. His projected trip to the Holy Land.

ments of a heavenly life, who has experienced love, the desire to look at the land where passed the steps of Him who first said the word of this love to men, the land whence it flowed into the world? We are moved by gratitude to a poet who, with his works, has gifted us with pleasures of the soul; we hurry to bring him the tribute of respect; we hurry to visit his grave, and no one is surprised by such an act, feeling that even his great ashes are worthy of respect. A son hurries to his father's grave, and no one asks him the reason why, feeling that the gifts of life and upbringing deserve gratitude. It is only considered somehow strange to worship at the very place of the earthy wanderings of the one who brought down the paradise of bliss to earth, who is the cause of all elevated aspirations. At least if anyone from our circle undertakes such a journey we somehow goggle at him, measure him from head to foot as if asking if he's a sanctimonious hypocrite, if he is crazy. Admit it, it seemed strange to you when I announced such an intention to you the first time. My character, appearance, way of thinking, the stamp of my intellect and what I say and my life—in a word, everything that goes to make up my character seems unfitting for such a thing. For a man who bears neither cowl nor miter, who has made and is making people laugh, who until now has considered it an important matter to display unimportant matters and the emptiness of life—for such a person, isn't it so, it is strange to undertake such a journey? But aren't there strange things in nature? Wasn't it strange for you to meet lyrical exaltation in a work like *Dead Souls*? Didn't it seem amusing to you at first, and didn't you become reconciled to it afterwards, even though you still hadn't discovered its full significance? Thus, perhaps, you will become reconciled to this lyrical tendency of the author himself later. And how can we say that what seems to us a momentary inspiration, a revelation that has unexpectedly flown from the heavens, has not been put in our very nature by the omnipotent will of God and developed in us unseen by others? And can one know that there is not perhaps a secret connection between this distant journey and this work of mine which rattled out into the world through a dark low wicket and not through victorious triumphal gates accompanied by the thunder of horns and solemn sounds? And how can we know that there is not a deep and marvelous connection between all this and all my life and the future which approaches us unseen and which none of us perceives? Reverence to Providence! * * *

To A. O. Smirnova. July 25, 1845. Karlsbad.

. . . You touched on *Dead Souls* and ask me not to get angry at the truth, saying that you are full of compassion for what you formerly laughed at.[6] My friend, I do not love my former works which have been printed up until now, especially *Dead Souls*. But you will be wrong if you are going to condemn the author for them because you take the ridiculing of the provinces for a caricature—just as you were wrong to praise him before. The subject of *Dead Souls* is not at all the provinces, and not a few ugly landowners, and not that which people ascribe to it. For the meantime it is still a secret which all at once, to the surprise of everyone (for not a soul among the readers has guessed), was to have been revealed in the following volumes—if it had pleased God to lengthen my life and bless my future work. Again I repeat to you that it is a secret, and for now the key to it is only in the soul of the author. Much, even much of what was apparently directed to me myself was taken in a completely wrong sense. I did really have some pride, but not for my *present*, not for the attributes I possessed; the pride for the *future* stirred in my breast—for what stood ahead of me, the happy discovery by which, as a consequence of God's grace, to illumine my soul. In the discovery that one can be far *better* than man is, that there are means, and that for love. . . . But I have started talking at the wrong time about what does not yet exist. Believe me, I know very well that I am too much rubbish. And I have always more or less felt

6. Smirnova had written: "I recall your *Dead Souls* often, but unfortunately I can no longer laugh at these shortcomings; now they arouse only pity in me." There are passages in her letters to him in late 1844 which show her attitude toward Gogol: "Pray for Russia, for all those who need your prayers, and for me, a sinful woman who loves you very, very much and with living gratitude. You have made life easy for me; it had lain on my shoulders like a Tyrolese waggon. And should I confess my sins to you? I don't pray at all except on Sundays. . . . You know the heart well—look into mine more deeply and tell me whether some baseness is nesting there. . . ." "I am bored and sad. Bored because there is not a soul with whom I could think and feel aloud as with you; bored because I have become accustomed to having Nikolai Vasilevich with me and because there is no such person here, and one isn't likely to find another Nikolai Vasilevich in life. . . ."

that in my *present* state I am rubbish, and that everything that has been done by me is rubbish, except what it pleased God to inspire me to do—and I did that in a way far from the way I should have.—But my hand grows tired. My friend, let us strengthen ourselves in spirit! . . .

To N. M. Yazykov.[7] *May 5, 1846. Rome.*

. . . Thank you for the excerpts from the introduction to the German translation of *Dead Souls.* The German judges things rather sensibly.[8] It is the best view which a foreigner could have on these things. In spite of that it is extremely unpleasant that *Dead Souls* has been translated. However, what happened did not happen without the will of God. God only grant the strength to finish and publish the second volume. Then they will discover that we Russians have much that they never even guessed about, and that we ourselves do not want to recognize—if only it will please God to give me the strength amid infirmities and illnesses to fulfill the task honorably and devoutly.

* * *

Ranks in Tsarist Russia

In order to understand Gogol (and other nineteenth-century Russian writers), it helps to be aware of the importance of Russian civil service (and military) ranks. Russia was a most hierarchical country. Titles, honorifics, orders of precedence (i.e., in going through a door and in seating at the table at ceremonial and other occasions), awards, and decorations (military and civilian orders) carried much weight in prestige, material benefits, and power.

Most Russian titles in the civil service can be traced back to 1722, when Peter the Great set up a schedule of fourteen official ranks, known as the Table of Ranks. Their order was as follows, from the highest (class 1) to the lowest:

7. Nikolai Mikhailovich Yazykov (1801–46), primarily an elegist, was one of the most important poets of the period. Later, Gogol considered Yazykov a kindred soul, but Yazykov's own letters are full of nasty remarks ridiculing Gogol. His "Earthquake" was Gogol's favorite poem.

8. *Dead Souls* was translated by Phillip Loebenstein and published in Leipzig in 1846.

Class	Civilian Rank	Military Equivalent (after 1884)
1	Chancellor	Field Marshall
2	Actual Privy Councillor	General
3	Privy Councillor	Lieutenant-General
4	Actual State Councillor	Major-General
5	State Councillor	——
6	Collegiate Councillor	Colonel
7	Court Councillor	Lieutenant-Colonel
8	Collegiate Assessor	Captain
9	Titular Councillor	Staff Captain
10	Collegiate Secretary	Lieutenant
11	Ship's Secretary (abandoned after 18th century)	——
12	Provincial (*gubernsky*) Secretary	Sub-Lieutenant
13	Provincial (*provintsialny*) Secretary (abandoned after 18th century)	——
14	Collegiate Registrar	——

Each rank had a special title by which holders were supposed to be addressed. Thus the top two classes were to be addressed as "Your Supreme Excellency," three to five as "Your Excellency," six to eight as "Your Supreme Honor," the others as merely "Your Honor." Each civil service rank corresponded to a certain rank in military service, what we would call "assimilated" ranks.

The pecking order involved much kowtowing, bullying, one-upmanship, and tyrannizing. Each rank—not only in the military and navy but also in the civil service—had its uniforms and insignia of rank (epaulettes, stripes on trousers, braid, etc.).

Essays in Criticism

ROBERT A. MAGUIRE

[The Legacy of Gogol Criticism]†

I

"It always seemed to me," Gogol wrote toward the end of his life, "that I would become well known, that a wide range of activities was awaiting me, and that I would even do something for the general good." [1] As a nineteen-year-old graduate of an obscure secondary school in the Ukraine, Nikolay Vasilievich Gogol set out for St. Petersburg in December 1828, to follow up his hunch. He did not know just where it would take him: literature was only one possibility; government service and the theater were others. His debut as a writer would have discouraged anyone with a feebler sense of destiny. In May 1829, he published, at his own expense, a long "idyll in scenes" cast in meters borrowed from Pushkin and entitled *Hanz Küchelgarten*. Only two critics took notice; both consigned it to oblivion. Gogol complied: he bought up all the copies he could find and burned them. That was the end of his career as a poet, and the end of "V. Alov," the pseudonym he had adopted. He then switched to prose fiction, began to publish—now under his own name, and no longer at his own expense—stories of Ukrainian life, and in 1831 and 1832 put out a two-volume collection entitled *Evenings on a Farm Near Dikanka*. With their blend of lyricism, humor, folklore, the supernatural, and the demonic, these stories fed the public appetite for "romantic" treatments of subjects then considered "exotic." Now the critics spoke of a fresh and promising talent, and Gogol was suddenly a celebrity.

Had he died just then, he would have rated a footnote in literary histories as one of the better representatives of a populous breed of local colorists active at the time. It was only with the appearance, in 1835, of two new volumes of stories—*Arabesques* and *Mirgorod*—and the production, a year later, of the play *The Inspector General*, that he

† From *Gogol from the Twentieth Century*, sel. ed., and trans. by Robert A. Maguire (Princeton, N.J.: Princeton University Press, 1974), pp. 3–16.
1. "Avtorskaya ispoved," PSS, VIII, 1952, 438. This work was written in 1847, but published posthumously (1855). Actually, the manuscript bears no title; that was added by S. P. Shevyryov for the publication.

was established as a major writer who marked a decisive turn in the direction of Russian literature. Vissarion Belinsky, who was just beginning a career that would make him the most important critic of the time, even ranked him beside Pushkin. The death of Pushkin in 1837 made it seem likely that Gogol was now the greatest living Russian writer; the death of Lermontov and the publication of *Dead Souls* in 1842 made it a certainty.

The appeal of Gogol's works certainly did not depend on their story line, which by and large was rudimentary or—in the case of *The Inspector General* and *Dead Souls*—already familiar to the public in the form of anecdotes. His settings and stylish mannerisms, though striking, were not entirely strange to readers either. He began to write at a time when a new esthetic was developing in Russian literature, one that set prose fiction above poetry, focused on the lower orders of society, saw man as a communal animal, found dirt and evil prevalent in the world, and mixed an olio of modes and genres within a single work. Most of the devotees of this new style—it would come to be called realism or naturalism—had been hacks, toiling away in the lesser journals but admirably documenting (as mediocrities tends to do) the changes that were in progress. But in Gogol, Russia found a writer capable of turning this style into an artistic achievement of such power as to signal the onset of a new literary age.

As heirs to the German romantic movement, young Russians of the 1830s were intensely concerned with the problem of nationality. There was a strong feeling that a great writer, a "Russian Homer," must arise to give expression to the soul of the restless and burgeoning *narod,* or "people." Neither Vasily Zhukovsky (1783–1852) nor Alexander Pushkin (1799–1837) quite qualified: though acknowledged as great poets, both came out of the eighteenth century, and were therefore considered beholden to the literary values of Western Europe. The point was made graphically and querulously by Belinsky, who stated that, as of 1834, *"we have no literature."* A year later, however, the appearance of *Arabesques* and *Mirgorod* prompted him to hope that in Gogol Russia had produced a writer who would create a truly national literature, independent of foreign models.[2]

2. The quotation (Belinsky's italics) comes from "Literaturnye mechtaniya," as in *Polnoe sobranie sochinenii,* I, Moscow, 1953, 23; the opinions on *Mirgorod* and *Arabesques* are found in "O russkoi povesti i povestyakh g. Gogolya ('Arabeski' i 'Mirgorod')," *Polnoe sobranie sochinenii,*

The fact that Gogol began his career when Pushkin was at the height of his powers helped define his originality. In the eyes of contemporaries, no two writers could have been less alike. To be sure, Pushkin had written prose fiction, and had also cultivated many of the mannerisms of the new style, as any reader of *Eugene Onegin* was aware. But in the public mind he was above all an aristocrat and a poet, who represented the "classical" values of balance, clarity, and elegant simplicity, was indifferent to topical social problems, and even seemed vaguely "foreign" in his intimate knowledge of French and English literature. Gogol was regarded as his opposite in every important respect. The contrast at first served merely to define a change in literary generations. But before long it took deep root and branched out to cover the whole of Russian literature. "Pushkin" and "Gogol" came to stand for two "schools" of writing, each thoroughly national, but each very different; and Russians have been classifying their literature accordingly ever since. To the "Pushkin" school are assigned mainly poets, such as Afanasy Fet, Anna Akhmatova, and the later Pasternak, as well as a few prose writers like Tolstoy and Turgenev. To the "Gogol" school belong most of the better novelists, such as Dostoevsky, Saltykov-Shchedrin, Bely, and Nabokov. At issue here is not the validity of the contrast (which is familiar to every schoolchild), but its persistence as a truism in the national mind, and its effect on the ways Russians read their writers, including, of course, Gogol.

Other clusters of themes, just as striking and insistent, soon began to form; they were to recur, in various guises, over the course of a century and a half. They concerned: (1) Gogol's subject matter, and his approach to it; (2) the

---

I, Moscow, 1953, 259–307.

The fact that Gogol was Ukrainian by origin did not bother Belinsky; he regarded this as a variant of Russian nationality. In families of the middle gentry, like Gogol's, Ukrainian was spoken with the peasants. Gogol's father, an amateur writer, turned out comedies in Ukrainian. But the moment anything "serious" arose, such as business dealings, education, or government service, Russian was used. And anyone who aspired to more than local celebrity as an author had to write in Russian as Gogol always did. Over the decades there has been much speculation about the influence of the Ukrainian language on Gogol's often peculiar Russian. See, e.g., V. V. Vinogradov, "Yazyk Gogolya," in *N. V. Gogol': Materialy i issledovaniya*, II, ed. V. V. Gippius, Moscow-Leningrad, 1936, 281–376. The literature in Russian on the problem of "nationality" (*narodnost'*) is vast. For an especially interesting discussion as it concerns Gogol, see D. A. Ovsyaniko-Kulikovsky, *Gogol' (Sobranie sochinenii*, IX), 4th ed., St. Petersburg, 1912, 140–42, 157–63.

social and political implications of his works; (3) his own
life and personality.

Discussions of the first point turned around Gogol's
"realism," or, as it was usually put, around the accuracy of
his portraits of Russian life. Since those portraits, from
1835 on, were largely of a gloomy and sordid nature, more
than mere theory was at stake. Two opposing views were
advanced. One saw Gogol's settings, characters, and language as faithful copies of originals: Russia therefore was
a nasty and depressing land. The other insisted that reality
cannot be entirely negative: the absence of ennobling elements in Gogol's works therefore robbed them of any claim
to realism, and made them "dirty" and "low" caricatures.
Somewhere in between stood Belinsky. He thought that
literary realism neither mirrors nor caricatures, but rather
"reflects [life's] various phenomena from one point of view,
as if in a convex glass, selecting those aspects which are
needed for the formulation of a full, live, and unified
image." The result, in Gogol's work, was a typical picture
of Russia.[3]

The next question arose naturally from the first. Did all
these scenes of venality, stupidity, filth, fear, and despair
serve purely esthetic purposes? A few critics apparently
thought so, in their insistence that Gogol's works were
nothing more than farces aimed at providing harmless
entertainment. A greater number believed that Gogol was
trying to convey some serious message of moral uplift, but
insisted that it bore on individual vices and not on society
as a whole. Most commentators, however, did seem to
regard Gogol as a social satirist who was bent on pointing
up the discrepancies between the real and the ideal world.
His humor, in Pushkin's famous phrase, amounted to
"laughter through tears,"[4] and it was supposed to provoke
indignation and reform.

It was Gogol's personality, however, which exerted the
strongest pull on the minds of his contemporaries. He was
one of the most bizarre figures of an age that prized eccen-
tricity. To be sure, his external biography was unremark-
able. He was born in 1809 into a family of small landowners near Dikanka, in the Ukraine. After a thoroughly
indulged childhood, he was sent to the school at Nezhin

3. "O russkoi povesti i povestyakh g.
Gogolya ('Arabeski' i 'Mirgorod'),"
Polnoe sobranie sochinenii, I, Moscow, 1953, 267.
4. Review of second edition of *Eve-*

nings on a Farm Near Dikanka, published in *Sovremennik*, No. 1, 1836.
Gogol himself later used the same
formulation in *Dead Souls* (Part I,
ch. 7).

in 1821. There he remained seven years, and then traveled to St. Petersburg in search of his "mission." He failed as an actor; he failed as a poet; he failed as a civil servant. *Evenings on a Farm Near Dikanka* brought him fame, and connected him with the literary luminaries of the capital, among them Zhukovsky and Pushkin. Between 1832 and 1836 he put in a brief and disastrous stretch as a teacher of history at St. Petersburg University, conceived the ideas for virtually all the works of fiction he would ever write, and completed *Mirgorod, Arabesques,* and *The Inspector General.* In 1836, he went abroad, where he remained— mostly in Rome—for twelve years, with only two brief trips back to Russia. During the 1840's he finished off the first volume of *Dead Souls* and worked away at the second; but he was becoming more and more preoccupied with a quest for religious verities and self-perfection, which he documented in obsessive letter-writing and tried to formulate definitively in *Selected Passages from Correspondence with Friends* (1847). A pilgrimage to the Holy Land in 1848 failed to bring the spiritual invigoration he had hoped for; in 1851 he returned to Russia, settled in Moscow, and lived there, increasingly self-critical, for the one year that remained to him. He could not make the continuation of *Dead Souls* say what he wished it to; and, repeating what he had done twice before—with an earlier version of this same work, and with *Hanz Küchelgarten*—he threw the manuscript into the fire. Part of it was rescued; but this was, in effect, his farewell to life. A few weeks later he died, largely from self-willed malnutrition and general debilitation. The date was February 22, 1852; he was just short of forty-three.[5]

Though not exciting in outline, Gogol's life did make a pattern that was suggestive to sensibilities nourished on romanticism. As a Ukrainian, he came from an area that Russians regarded as "romantic." With the city of St. Petersburg he demonstrated a love-hate relationship that was characteristically romantic. He was a rootless man, who never married, never had a love affair, found friendships difficult, and chronically complained of being mis-

5. For fuller accounts in English of Gogol's life, see: David Magarshack, *Gogol*, London, 1957; Vsevolod Setchkarev, *Gogol—His Life and Works*, New York, 1965; Victor Erlich, *Gogol*, New Haven and London, 1969; V. V. Gippius, *Gogol*, ed. and trans. by R. A. Maguire, Ann Arbor, Mich., 1981. Gogol's letters also provide much valuable information; an anthology is now available in English (*Letters of Nikolai Gogol*, sel. and ed. by Carl R. Proffer, Ann Arbor, Mich., 1967).

understood. His wedge-shaped face, his long nose, and his evasive ways all suggested demonic mystery. He exiled himself from Russia and settled into a fashionably impoverished life in Rome—one of the more romantic cities in what was of course the most romantic country in Europe. His death amounted to suicide and was regarded by many as an act of protest against the world.

There was also a political dimension to the reading public's conception of the romantic artist, in Russia as in the West. He was regarded as a champion of man's free spirit and therefore as an opponent (conscious or not) of the established order. The point had particular validity in a country like Russia, which was ruled by an autocrat and had a long history of censorship of the written word— sometimes benevolent, but often draconian: Radishchev had been condemned to death, Pushkin had been exiled to the south, Polezhayev had been conscripted into the army as a common soldier. Minor encounters with the censors were a routine occupational hazard; Gogol knew that from the church scene in "The Nose," which the censor pronounced blasphemous, and from the title of *Dead Souls,* which was taken as an impermissible denial of immortality. Such encounters no doubt encouraged many writers to view themselves as practitioners of a "liberal" profession. They could make no plainly subversive political statements in their works; but readers of a certain inclination—helped by like-minded critics—could always find them there. And when pictures of political corruption and social stagnation were presented in Gogol's vivid manner, it was not hard for younger critics with radical leanings to see them as thinly disguised protests against the political establishment.

The publication, in 1847, of *Selected Passages from Correspondence with Friends* came as a shock to such readers. This book grew out of Gogol's long and intensifying preoccupation with the problem of evil. He hoped to make Russians aware of the maladies of their country, and to prescribe remedies. In the thirty-two articles, most of which were based on actual letters to acquaintances, Gogol ranged over the major areas of life in Russia—religious, political, social, economic, and literary—as well as the state of his own soul. He called for moral regeneration through a scrupulous observance of Christian humility within the existing structure of "everything our Church and our gov-

ernment have decreed for us by law." [6] He considered
Selected Passages his most important work, and with it he
hoped to "atone for the uselessness" of all his earlier writings, which had "led almost everyone into error with regard
to their true meaning," a meaning he now insisted was
moral, not social.[7]

Late in life Gogol asserted that his political and social
views had never basically changed. No doubt he was right.
Those views had always been conservative, and, like his
spiritual struggles, had been amply documented in a volu-
minous correspondence. Why, then, did *Selected Passages*
stir up such a fuss? Even Gogol's conservative friends were
shocked by what they took to be arrogance, spiritual pride,
false humility, and plain bad taste: the book read virtually
like a parody of their own preoccupations. Officials of the
church and the government resented Gogol's passion for
lecturing them about their own business. Among younger
readers of radical mind, however, it was the ideas that
excited the greatest indignation. Belinsky spoke most eloquently for them in a letter to Gogol that was an acknowl-
edgment of deep disappointment, if not virtually heart-
break. "Why, if you had made an attempt on my life, even
then I would not have hated you more than I do for these
shameful lines." For "I loved you with all the passion
with which a man bound to his country by blood ties is
capable of loving that country's hope, honor, glory, and
one of its great leaders on the road of reason, self-awareness,
development, and progress." But now, Belinsky said, Gogol
had lost the right to such love. He had refused to see that
Russia was ruled by "huge corporations of sundry official
thieves and robbers," and instead had come forth as "the
advocate of the knout, the apostle of ignorance, the champion of obscurantism and benightedness, the panegyrist of
Tartar morals," who was trying to pass off "lies and im-
morality as truth and virtue." [8]

6. Letter to P. A. Pletnyov, October
20, 1846.
7. "Predislovie," *Vybrannye mesta iz
perepiski s druz'yami*, PSS, VIII, 1952,
215, 216. The first English translation of this book, by Jesse Zeldin,
appeared in 1969 (Nashville, Ten-
nessee).
8. "(Pis'mo k N. V. Gogolyu)," *Polnoe sobranie sochinenii*, X, Moscow,
1956, 212, 213, 214. This letter is
reproduced in the Academy of
Sciences edition of Gogol's works
(PSS, VIII), presumably as a kind of
antidote to *Selected Passages*, which
appears in the same volume. Gogol
returned a wounded but relatively
gentle reply (August 10, 1847), after
tearing up his first version, which
was savage and often incoherent.

This letter immediately became radical scripture. For many years it was considered subversive by the government, and existed only in manuscript (finally being published in 1872). One of the charges brought against Dostoevsky at the time of his arrest in 1849 was that he had helped to circulate it. But it is perhaps more interesting as evidence of the crumbling of a myth that had been created in defiance of the evidence. *Selected Passages,* in its way, was as revolutionary as anything Belinsky envisaged; but that way was certainly not his.

The question of motives naturally arose at once. Why should Gogol apparently have betrayed all his earlier work? The possibility of sincere religious conversion was allowed only by a few like-minded friends. Some people suggested mental derangement (his letters are a litany of sundry disabilities, emotional and physical). Some suspected that he might be trying to tap a few conservative roubles (the book expressed gratitude to the Emperor for a stipend). But the interpretation put forth by Belinsky was destined to have the longest life and the strongest influence on later critical opinion. Faced with the apparently hopeless contradiction between *Selected Passages* and everything else Gogol had written, Belinsky simply decided that the new book was unimportant: Gogol's place in Russian literature rested on his earlier work, which remained unaffected by this unfortunate and incomprehensible aberration.[9]

This distinction was already implicit in a view of the mind that was widely held in Gogol's time. According to Belinsky's version of it, the mind is made up of two large areas: one contains the creative process and is responsible for art; the other contains the faculties of logical thinking, and produces scholarship, science, and criticism. The main difference lies in the means by which each process operates: "One [the rational] *proves* and the other [the creative] *shows,* and both *convince*—the one, however, by logical arguments, the other by pictures [images]."[1] Ideally, these two sides are in harmony; the great artist should also be a great thinker. But Gogol's career indicated that this was not necessarily so. He was, in effect, split into two entirely different persons. One, the artist, was a towering genius, and therefore served the highest humanitarian (and political) ideals; the other, the thinker, lacked intelligence, common sense, even decency, and must therefore be ignored.

9. "Otvet 'Moskvityaninu,'" *Polnoe sobranie sochinenii,* X, Moscow, 1956, 227.

1. "Vzglyad na russkuyu literaturu 1847 goda," *Polnoe sobranie sochinenii,* X, Moscow, 1956, 311.

This idea of "two Gogols" had been put forth earlier by other critics; it was implicit in romantic esthetics, which thrived on dualities, such as the real versus the ideal. Belinsky's version, however, has proved to be the most enduring. Many critics have taken exception to it, but exceptions depend, of course, on the recognition of rules. It was the last of the truisms about Gogol to be formulated in his lifetime, and it has been perhaps the hardiest of them all.

These early critics set out all the major themes that future generations would honor: realism, typicality, nationality, humor, satire, the two Gogols, and so on.[2] They regarded good art primarily as the vehicle of good ideas, and emphasized the duties and responsibilities of the artist to society. Along with a tendency to moralize about art went an indifference to style, or, rather, a subsumption of style under moralizing criteria too: hence the discussions of Gogol's language in terms of "high" and "low," or the speculations on how "national" in spirit his odd linguistic usages might be. Most of these critics were keenly aware that Gogol's work did not readily fit into the literary systems of the past; but they found it difficult to throw off the hold of those systems and articulate what was new and unique in Gogol. It is easy, however, to indulge in disparagement more than a century later. We may find much of this criticism shallow and unreadable now, but it ought to be judged in the context of its own time. As a later distinguished critic of Gogol pointed out, the important thing is what Gogol "seemed to be to his *audience,* his contemporaries, his readers."[3] And Gogol's own view of the nature of art virtually coincided with that of the majority of his contemporaries. He had always seen himself as being entrusted with a mission to serve Russia and be useful to society. His obsession with self-purification in the 1840s was entirely consistent witht this view. Its terms were not Belinsky's, but both men agreed on the principle of service as the artist's highest obligation.

This body of commentary on Gogol could never have acquired the weight of a living tradition if literary criticism, in those years, had not come to occupy a position in Russian culture that in prestige and power was almost the

2. For a useful survey of critical opinions about Gogol in his own time, see Paul Debreczeny, *Nikolay Gogol and His Contemporary Critics,* Philadelphia, *Transactions of the American Philosophical Society,* New Series, Vol. 56, Part 3, 1966.
3. Vasily Rozanov, "Gogolevskie dni v Moskve," *Sredi khudozhnikov,* St. Petersburg, 1914, p. 261.

equal of the writer's. For criticism had to do with more than mere "literature." Or better, the conception of literature reached out beyond the text itself to society as a whole, as an entity to be not merely depicted, but guided and instructed as well. The critic saw it as his duty to clarify what he considered implicit in the text, to translate the language of art into the language of usable ideas. This view of the role of criticism is exemplified in the career of Vissarion Belinsky, the first fully professional critic in Russia. His rise to eminence made it plain that, by the 1840s, literary criticism was one of the few "intellectual" occupations outside government service open to young men from the lower reaches of society: he himself was the son of an obscure ship's doctor.

Gogol always took a keen interest in the opinions of his critics, or, at least, he professed to do so. Like most writers, he constantly complained of being misunderstood. In his later years, particularly after the spectacular fiasco of *Selected Passages,* his letters were filled with appeals for *negative* criticism; this, he felt, would help him steer a truer course in his quest for self-perfection, and thereby enable him to bring the troublesome second volume of *Dead Souls* to a "positive" conclusion. The pathological implications of such an attitude aside, the parallel careers of Gogol and Belinsky are striking testimony to the close link that existed between belles-lettres and criticism and brought them together under the larger heading of "literature." The two men achieved prominence at about the same time, wrote all their major works contemporaneously, and climaxed their careers in 1847, with Belinsky's final illness (he died the following year) and Gogol's *Selected Passages.* It is absurd to suggest, as some critics have done, that Gogol was virtually the creation of an intensive publicity campaign waged by Belinsky. But Belinsky did manage to make him the measure of all new Russian literature for decades; to this day, most Russians (whether school children or professional critics) cannot think of one without thinking of the other.

II

Gogol's death in 1852 opened a new phase of criticism, which lasted until nearly the end of the century. The basic themes established in the earlier period now put down deeper roots. But critics began to approach Gogol with a fundamentally different attitude.

It was Nikolay Chernyshevsky, the most influential critic of the 1860s, who set the tone. He insisted that the "two Gogols" theory was false. *Selected Passages,* however regrettable its ideas—and, as a radical, Chernyshevsky found them repellent—was nonetheless the sincere utterance of "an honest enthusiast" who was only endeavoring to "perform the duty imposed on him by his conscience," and who remained "one of the noblest people of our century." [4] The book represented no deviation from the earlier period (as Belinsky had thought) but grew organically from it. Despite apparent contradictions, all Gogol's life and work formed a pattern, and the job of the critic was to uncover it. He must put moralizing aside and ask *why* Gogol had acted as he did. The answers would be found not in speculation on Gogol's intentions or motivations, but in a close examination of his milieu. All men, in Chernyshevsky's view, were basically the same in their instincts and desires; differences were accountable to environment, which either promoted or hindered (usually the latter) the right use of inborn qualities. Study a society, therefore, and you know the men who lived in it.

Chernyshevsky's Gogol was a representative man in nearly all respects: typical of a society intellectually no more advanced than he; typical of a self-educated man who sees life as merely a series of disconnected, patternless phenomena; typical of any human being in his desire to associate with the rich and the famous. Unique to him was "only a tormenting dissatisfaction with himself and his character . . . an extraordinarily energetic desire to minister to social defects and to his own weaknesses"— and the mysterious spark of genius.[5] Yet, even here, he was a representative genius: like Pushkin and Lermontov, his nature was too lofty for the society in which he had to live. Had he been born twenty years later (that is, in Chernyshevsky's own time), he would have been more enlightened, and therefore presumably a better writer.

Chernyshevsky was asserting, then, that the "enigma" of Gogol was only apparent; everything could be explained. From now on, Gogol was placed at one remove from the sort of moralizing criticism that had been practiced by

4. Review of *Zapiski o zhizni Nikolaya Vasil'evicha Gogolya,* ed. P. A. Kulish, St. Petersburg, 1856, *Sovremennik,* No. 5, 1856 (as in *Polnoe sobranie sochinenii,* III, Moscow, 1947, 535).

5. Review of *Sochineniya i pis'ma N. V. Gogolya,* ed. P. A. Kulish, 6 vols., St. Petersburg, 1857, *Sovremennik,* No. 8, 1857 (as in *Polnoe sobranie sochinenii,* IV, Moscow, 1948, 610).

most of his contemporaries. Increasingly he came to be regarded as an object of study. In this second period, vigorous efforts were made to gather information on every conceivable aspect of his life and activity. Memoirs and letters came out in a steady flow until the end of the century. New editions of the works (none of them complete) appeared in the 1850s and 1890s. Shortly after Gogol's death, P. A. Kulish published two essays in biography, but they were hesitant and fragmentary. The Academy of Sciences commissioned S. P. Shevyryov, a first-rate critic with conservative views, to prepare a full-scale life of Gogol; but he died before he could get under way. Otherwise, no significant attempt was made for the next forty years to synthesize a growing body of material. That was surprising, considering that critics, scholars, and the general public continued to take an intense interest in Gogol's life and work: there was virtually none of the decline in popularity which major writers so often undergo for decades after their death (Pushkin being a case in point). Perhaps his personality was still too puzzling to an age that honored the verities of science and positivism.[6] In any event, it was only in 1892 that V. I. Shenrok's *Materials for a Biography of Gogol* began to appear.[7] This four-volume work sets forth, in paraphrase and luxuriant citation, virtually everything that was then known about Gogol. Actually, the title is too modest. Although the book does not represent a finished piece of writing (Shenrok intended to produce that later, but never did), it organizes its materials

6. A political factor seems to have been at work too. For all his conservatism, Gogol was regarded with suspicion by many officials of the government. Vasily Gippius suggests that the reason for this was the belief, among radicals, that Gogol had contributed to the development of a revolutionary state of mind in Russia. He cites as an example Alexander Herzen's book *On the Development of Revolutionary Ideas in Russia*, first published in German in Bremen the year before Gogol's death; it circulated illegally in Russian for years thereafter. Gippius says that the government was "even more disturbed" by the "demonstration of popular affection for Gogol," as shown by the huge turnout at his funeral, and that it resorted to "repressive measures"—forbidding the publication of a new edition of Gogol's works, and also forbidding this fact to be mentioned in print for three years (V. V. Gippius, "N. V. Gogol'," introductory essay to Vol. 1 of the complete works, PSS, 1940, 55, 57). Ivan Turgenev was also arrested and exiled to his country estate for an obituary notice, which was published in Moscow, where the censor did not know that it had been proscribed in St. Petersburg. The notice is utterly innocuous. Turgenev himself believed that the real reasons for the government's action were the publication of *A Sportsman's Sketches* (widely regarded as a protest against serfdom), and the fact that he had put something over on the censor.
7. *Materialy dlya biografi Gogolya*, 4 vols., Moscow, 1892–97.

around a theme, and thereby attains a certain unity.

The approach owes much to Chernyshevsky, and the conclusions are similar to his, although they are buttressed, of course, by far more elaborate detail. Like Chernyshevsky, Shenrok assumes that Gogol's life and work, from start to finish, constitute a unity, which can be discerned through scrupulous attention to all the evidence, especially the letters. The investigator must work from "external biographical facts" to reach an understanding of the "inner intimate life." [8] The picture that takes shape here, as in Chernyshevsky, is one of an essentially passive personality: Gogol wrote by way of involuntary response to an irresistible need; but the forms his writing took were fashioned by upbringing, environment, and the literary tradition. Shenrok offered no really new interpretations; in effect, he was consolidating the findings of four decades. But his book was a landmark. It put an end to a long period of mere data-gathering, and indicated that the time for interpretation had now come. In suggesting how such interpretations might run, Shenrok prefigured nearly all the directions that the critics of the twentieth century would follow.

V. G. BELINSKY

Chichikov's Adventures, or *Dead Souls:* Gogol's Epic Poem†

Gogol's complete renunciation of the Ukrainian[1] element in *Dead Souls* was an important step forward for his talent, one by which he became a Russian national poet in the full sense of the word. At each word of his poem the reader can say:

Here is the Russian spirit, here it smells of Russia.[2]

8. Materialy . . . , II (1893), V.

† Vissarion Belinsky (1811–48) was probably the most influential Russian critic of the age of Gogol. He was the leading spirit behind the radical, revolutionary movement. The extracts printed here come from his 1842 article in the magazine *Fatherland Notes.* The translation by Thomas Seifrid is based on the text in S. Mashinsky, ed., *N. V. Gogol v*

russkoy kritike i vospominaniakh sovremennikov [N. V. Gogol in Russian criticism and recollections of contemporaries] (Moscow, 1951), pp. 85–90 and 105–6.

1. Many of Gogol's earlier works dealt with themes and folklore of the Ukraine.

2. A line from Pushkin's introduction to his long narrative poem *Ruslan and Lyudmila* (1820).

This Russian spirit is felt in the humor, the irony, the author's expression, the sweeping power of the emotions, the lyricism of the digressions, and the pathos of the whole poem. It is felt in the personalities of the characters, from Chichikov and Selifan to the roguish dapple-gray horse; in Petrushka, who carries with him his own peculiar air; and in the night watchman, who in the light of his lantern executes a creature with his nail, then again falls asleep. I know this will offend the prim sensibilities of many readers, who will take offense in print at that which is so substantively characteristic of them in life and will call obscene such caprices as the creature executed with the nail. But to do so would mean not understanding the poem, which is based on the pathos of everyday life as it really is. If you portray the petty, philistine life of the Germans, you will have to mention (be it in praise or in mockery) the pedantry of their neatness. To mention the life of the simple Russian peasantry (which is not, as is well known, distinguished by excessive cleanliness) without noting that not only in the villages do women sit in the afternoon by the gate zealously executing creatures on their children (thus displaying tenderness and care), but that in the cities as well cabmen at their cabstands and workmen on the streets render similar services to one another, solely out of an unselfish love of such pursuits, would be to omit one of its most characteristic features. I know in advance that our hack writers and critics will not miss this opportunity to make use of the primness of many readers and their tendency to see in themselves the refinement of high society in order to demonstrate their own knowledge of the decorum of high society. Attacking the author of *Dead Souls* for the obscenity of his poem, they will cry out with grief-stricken hearts that not even a decent lackey would express himself as do Gogol's loyal and repectable officials. But enough of them, these scribblers and carpers so privy to the mysteries of high society. Let them fuss over that which they do not understand and stand up for that which they have never seen and do not wish to know.

Dead Souls will be read by all, but obviously not all will like it. Among the many reasons for this is that *Dead Souls* does not meet the crowd's notion of the novel as a fairy tale in which the characters fall in love, part, and later get married and become rich and happy. Gogol's poem can be enjoyed only by those to whom the thought and the artistic execution of a work are accessible, for whom content and not "the story" is important. For the enjoyment of the others, there remain only certain passages and details. Furthermore, like any great work, *Dead Souls* does not reveal itself completely upon a first reading, even to an intelligent person: Reading it a second time is just as if one were reading a new, hitherto unseen work. *Dead Souls* requires study. It also bears repetition that humor is accessible only to the deep and greatly developed soul; the crowd neither understands nor appreciates it. We have all sorts of hack writers who rack their brains to portray violent passions and strong characters (copying them, of course, from themselves and their acquaintances). They think it offensive to descend to the comic, which they hate by instinct, as a mouse a cat. The "comic" and "humor" are understood by the majority in Russia as clownish, as caricature. And I am sure that many will seriously, with cunning grins of satisfaction at their own perspicacity, claim that Gogol called his novel a poem in jest. And it really is so! Why, Gogol is a great wit and joker, and goodness! what a merry fellow he is! He himself laughs incessantly and makes others laugh as well. Yes, you really have guessed it, you brilliant people. . . .

As far as I am concerned, not considering it within my rights to discuss in print the personality of a living author, I will only say that Gogol was not joking when he named his novel a "poem," and that by this he does not mean a comic poem. This much I gain not from the author, but from his book. I see nothing joking or funny about it. In not one of the author's words do I detect any intention of making the reader laugh: All is serious, calm, genuine, and profound. Do not forget that this book is but the exposition, the introduction, to the poem, and that the author promises two more books of the same length in which we will again meet Chichikov and will encounter new persons in whom the other side of Russia will be expressed. One could not look more erroneously on *Dead Souls* or understand it more crudely than to see in it a satire.[3]

* * *

It is sad to think that this lofty, lyrical pathos, these resounding, singing dithyrambs of a blissful national self-awareness, worthy of a great Russian poet, will by no means be accessible to all, to think that good-natured ignorance from the heart will laugh at that which makes the hairs

3. Here Belinsky goes on to quote six of the last pages of Part I of *Dead Souls*.

stand up on the head of another in holy fear. Yet so it is and can be no other way. This lofty, inspired poem will pass for the majority as "an incredibly funny joke." There will also be patriots (of whom Gogol speaks in his poem) who with characteristic acumen will find *Dead Souls* a harsh satire, the product of coldness and a dislike of the native and patriotic (they who have it so cozy in all the houses and even villages they have accumulated, the fruits of their loyal and diligent service . . .). I suppose they will also raise a clamor about personalities. Still, in one sense this is good: It will be the best critical evaluation of the poem. On the other hand, as far as I am concerned, I would sooner blame the author for the overabundance of feelings that have not been subjected to calm, judicious contemplation (which in places are too distracting, in a puerile way) than for any lack of love or fervor for the native and patriotic. I am speaking of certain places, fortunately few but unfortunately abrupt, where the author too lightly judges the national characters of other peoples and with too little humility lends himself to dreams about the superiority of the Slavs over them. It would seem better to leave to each his own and, recognizing one's own merits, be able to respect the merits of others as well.

* * *

Having been led astray by the title, "poem," that Gogol gives his work, Konstantin Aksakov [4] would call all the characters portrayed in it fine people. He believes that this means understanding Gogol's humor. Regardless of what he says, it is evident from his tone and from the entire article itself that he sees in *Dead Souls* a Russian *Iliad*. To do so would be to understand Gogol's poem inside-out. All these Manilovs and those like him are amusing only in a book—God forbid meeting them in real life. Yet not to meet them is impossible, since there are a fair number of them in real life, and consequently they are representatives of some part of it. A fine *Iliad,* with reality as its hero, a reality with such representatives as that! Only a poem in which a substantial segment of national life, in all the richness of its inner content, serves as subject matter, in which this life is *presented* and not *rejected,* can evoke the *Iliad*. A genuine criticism of *Dead Souls* should consist not of ecstatic cries about Homer and

4. Konstantin Aksakov (1817–60) had published an article arguing that *Dead Souls* had qualities similar to those of Homer's Greek epic *The Iliad*. Belinsky contested this view repeatedly.

Shakespeare, nor about the act of creation, nor about the merits of Manilov's or Selifan's unspoiled Russian nature, nor about the troika and the chaise. No, genuine criticism should reveal the poem's inspiration, which consists of the contradiction between the social forms of Russian life and their deep substantive principle. Hitherto this principle had remained mysterious, unexposed to self-awareness and elusive of all definition. This criticism must then take up the bases and causes of these forms and must resolve a multitude of apparently simple but essentially important questions, such as the following: Why is the beautiful blonde railed at until she cries, when she does not even understand what she is being scolded for? Why does the provincial town of N. turn out to be populous and crowded, while the gossip about Chichikov is instigated by the lively assistance of "a lady agreeable in all respects" and "a simply agreeable lady"? Why does Chichikov's appearance seem "loyal" to the governor and all the officials of the town of N.? What does "loyal" mean in bureaucratic jargon? Why does the author consider the necessary appurtenances of a long and boring journey to be not only chills (which occur on all sorts of journeys), but sleet, mud, stoppages, the altercations of blacksmiths and all sorts of riffraff on the road? Why does Sobakievich include Elizaveta Vorobey in his list? Why is the prosecutor's coachman considered an experienced fellow for driving with one hand while supporting his master with the other? Why do the merchants from Solvychegodsk give a feast for the merchants from Oustsysolsk that results in their deaths, themselves receiving marks and bruises on the ribs, sides, and bellies, calling all of this "having gone a bit too far"? One could pose many such questions. Many will consider them trifling; but *Dead Souls* is great precisely in that it lays bare and dissects life down to its trivialities, and these trivialities acquire a general significance. Of course, an Ivan Antonovich with a snout like a jug is both very funny in Gogol's book and a very trivial phenomenon in real life— but if you ever have any business with him, you will lose all desire to laugh at him and will not find him trivial. Why can he prove so important to you in real life—there's a question! Gogol brilliantly, by nonsense and trivialities, elucidates the mystery of how Chichikov turned into such an "acquirer." It is this that constitutes his poetic greatness, and not some imaginary resemblance to Homer and Shakespeare.

ALEXANDER I. HERZEN

Diary Entries on *Dead Souls*†

I

Gogol's *Dead Souls* is a remarkable book, a bitter reproach to contemporary Russia, but not a hopeless one. Where his glance manages to pierce through the mist emanating from dirty manure piles, he perceives a nation full of bold, strong spirit. His portraits are remarkably good, and life is preserved in all its fullness. These are not abstract types, but kind people whom each of us has seen a hundred times. It is just as somber in Chichikov's world as it is somber in our real life; both here and there the one consolation is faith and a hope in the future. This faith cannot be negated and is not simply some romantic hope *ins Blaue*.[1] It has a realistic basis: Somehow a Russian's blood circulates well through his breast.

II

Talk of *Dead Souls* . . . There are words of reconciliation; there are premonitions and hopes for a future full and triumphant; but this does not prevent the present from being reflected in all its repulsive actuality. In passing from a Sobakievich to a Plyushkin, one is gripped with horror. One bogs down with every step, sinking deeper. Suddenly a lyrical passage springs to life, shedding light, only to be replaced by a picture that reminds one all the more clearly which moat of hell we are in and how Dante longed to cease seeing and hearing—and the humorous words of the *merry* author resound. *Dead Souls* is a poem to be profoundly suffered through. *Dead Souls*—the title itself bears something that evokes horror. Gogol could not name it otherwise; not the dead serf-souls, but all these Nozdrevs, Manilovs, and all the others like them—these

---

† Alexander Herzen was an outstanding writer, political figure, journalist, and author of the remarkable memoirs *My Past and Thoughts*. He spent most of his life as an emigré in London. The passages translated here by Thomas Seifrid were entries in Herzen's diaries for 11 and 29 June 1842. The translation is based on pp. 171–72 in the same Russian collection from which the Belinsky comments have been translated.

1. German for "in the blue," "in the sky," "the heavens."

458

are the dead souls, and we meet them at every turn. And where are the common and keen interests for which all the dead souls breathing around us live? Do we not after our youth in one way or another all lead the life of one of Gogol's heroes? This one stops at Manilov's vacant dreaminess; another raises Cain *à la Nosdreff;* a third is a Plyushkin; and so forth. There is one active person— Chichikov—and he is a narrow-minded cheat. Why does he not encounter a moral landowner like "Kind-heart" and "True-think"?[2] . . . How could such an abnormal person fall into this maelstrom, and how could he be a type? In *Eugene Onegin* Pushkin presented a delightful human phenomenon in Vladimir Lensky,[3] then shot him— and for good reason. What else could he do but die, in order to remain a noble and beautiful phenomenon? In ten years he would have finished his learning and would have become more intelligent, but he would still have been a Manilov.

DONALD FANGER

Dead Souls: The Mirror and the Road†

* * *

Gogol's novel is organized and dominated by the road.[1] It begins with an arrival and ends with a departure; its concluding lines are a panegyric to the road. Lotman has shown how the road in *Dead Souls* involves all the varieties of "Gogolian space" as they have appeared in the earlier works—from boundlessness through fragmentation to domestic warmth—thereby providing an index of the way it confers amplitude and orders the several levels on which the narrative functions.[2] Literally the instrument of Chichikov's quest on the level of story, it leads him to planned and unplanned encounters, and so stands for experience,

2. Names of type characters from moralistic Russian works of the eighteenth century.

3. A Romantic poet, a character in Pushkin's long narrative poem *Eugene Onegin* (1823–31).

† From Donald Fanger, *The Creation of Nikolai Gogol* (Cambridge, Mass.: Harvard University Press, 1979), pp. 169–91.

1. Appropriately enough, its earliest textual beginnings have been traced to the travel notes he made in the summer of 1835, when he journeyed from Petersburg to his Ukrainian family home.

2. In an article, parts of which are translated in this volume, pp. 577–83 [*Editor*].

perspective, movement, change, life. "How much there is," Gogol writes in the last chapter, "of the strange, and the alluring, and the transporting, and the wonderful in the word: road! And how wondrous it is itself, this road." For all that, the road here serves neither as pretext nor as occasion for adventures. It affords *views*—of landscapes, characters, and routines, presented through "those trivia which seem trivia only when they are put into a book." The mirror moving down this road is, in the first place, Chichikov himself, the featureless hero ("neither handsome nor of displeasing exterior, neither too plump nor too thin," not exactly old "but not any too young"). Like a mirror, he is all surface: "Whatever the subject of conversation, he could always keep it going: if the talk was about stud farming; if it was about good dogs, here too he would contribute very weighty observations; if [the company] discoursed on the investigation carried out by the Treasury office, he showed that he was not uninformed about courtroom tricks; if there was a dissertation on billiard playing, he was up on billiards too; if the subject was virtue, he discoursed very well about virtue, even with tears in his eyes. . . . He spoke neither loudly nor softly but just in the right way. . . . The governor expressed the conviction that he was a reliable man; the prosecutor, that he was a sensible man; the colonel of police said that he was a learned man." His successive encounters are less interactions than evocations of those whom he meets, and when the gallery of transitory images is complete, the mirror moves on ("Occupied exclusively with the road, he glanced only to the right and the left, and it was as if the town of N. did not exist in his memory"—though not before turning opaque and becoming an object in its own right. This process begins in Chapter 9, when the town officials ask themselves "the question they should have asked in the beginning, that is, in the first chapter of our *poema*": "Who was he in fact?"—only to conclude that though "they did not know for certain what Chichikov was, nonetheless Chichikov must without fail be something."

The opacity conferred at the end by giving Chichikov biographical dimensionality is meant to explain his enterprise and so prepare the next stage of his road, on which the events of this novel have been only a way station. But it has a deeper function in making clear, retrospectively, that what was presented as Chichikov's mirroring of the characters has in fact been mutual. Manilov now appears as a hyperbolic parody of Chichikov's main quality, decorum; Korobochka represents a naive variant of his suspicious canniness in bargaining; Nozdryov shows more than comparable resourcefulness in prevarication, though his is instinctive and motiveless; Sobakevich manifests the calculating side of Chichikov, with its implicit misanthropy laid bare; and Plyushkin represents the passionate side of his acquisitiveness, showing how, unchecked, it can destroy the family life to which Chichikov so eagerly looks forward. Even Petrushka, the lackey, with his indiscriminate taste for reading ("It wasn't what he read about that pleased him, but more the reading itself, or, more precisely, the process of reading itself") parodies his master, who is shown in the first chapter tearing down a theatrical poster, the better to scrutinize it at leisure (he reads all the actors' names, "got down even to the price of orchestra seats and learned that the poster had been printed in the shop of the provincial administration; then he turned it over to see whether there might not be something on the other side, but finding nothing wiped his eyes, folded it neatly, and put it in his traveling box, where he had the habit of storing everything that came his way").

The portrait gallery of the book is thus a gallery of mirrors as well—to which, in the process of presentation, the narrator adds his own generalizing reflections. Only the author, whose voice emerges distinctly from that of the narrator at times, remains above this process, in the role of self-justifying commentator and ultimately of creator. Having, so to speak, gone through the looking glass to reveal Chichikov's scheme and its relation to his biography, he comments: "Had the author not looked more deeply into [Chichikov's] soul, had he not stirred at the bottom what slinks away and hides from the light, had he not revealed the most secret thoughts that one man never confides to another, but rather shown him as he appeared to the whole town . . . [readers] would be happy with him and would take him for an interesting person." But then, he adds—evincing the didactic note that separates the world of this work from that of *The Inspector General*—the reader's soul would have gone undisturbed and he might simply turn again to the card table, "the consoler of all Russia."

Presentation is the work of the narrator; it embraces the

projections and perceptions of the characters and offers them, embellished and in a new perspective, to be registered by the reader. The author, by contrast, appears as such, hinting at a larger enterprise of his own, as enigmatic as Chichikov's, and likening his own task to a journey. The passages where his voice dominates might collectively bear the title given Gogol's posthumous "Author's Confession," constituting as they do crucial passages in the tale of his authorship. They are all keyed to the question: why? (See Chapter 3: "But why be concerned so long with Korobochka? Whether it's Korobochka or Manilov, a thrifty life or unthrifty—let us leave them behind!" The author himself is a creature of the road; at the beginning of Chapter 6 he recalls his youthful curiosity in approaching new places; at the beginning of Chapter 7 he envies the traveler returning home and contrasts him with the writer whose mission it is to confront all the repulsive phenomena "with which our earthly, sometimes bitter and dull road seethes."

Dead Souls, as Sinyavsky[3] observes, is to a considerable extent "a book written about how it is written." The apologetic passages regularly follow the pattern of the seventh chapter, where confession breaks off: "Back to the road! to the road! Away with the wrinkle that has settled on the brow and the severe gloom on the visage! Let us plunge suddenly and wholly into life . . . and see what Chichikov is up to." Into life? Yes, for in Gogol's reversible terms "the world is a living book, and the road he proclaims himself fated to travel "for a long time yet hand in hand with my strange hero" a means of salvation: "My God, how good you are at times, you long, long road! How often like one perishing and drowning have I clutched at you, and each time you have magnanimously delivered and saved me! And how many wondrous ideas, poetic dreams have been born, how many marvelous impressions felt while traveling you!". This author's voice is seldom ironic; it contains the *norms* on which the purely narrative ironies rest, thus differentiating the method of *Dead Souls* from that of "The Overcoat" and showing a new openness in articulating his fundamental themes—Gogol's vision (in the double sense) of Russia, and of himself as writer— which come together in the last chapter, in the famous

3. Andrei Sinyavsky, a contemporary Russian critic and writer, formerly from Moscow, now living in France, author of a Russian book on Gogol [*Editor*].

lyrical passage beginning, "Russia! Russia! I see thee; from my wondrous, beautiful far-off place I see thee," and culminate in the demand: "Russia! what wouldst thou have of me? What ineffable, hidden bond unites us? Why dost thou gaze at me so, and why has everything in thee turned its eyes, full of anticipation, on me?"

This grandiloquence has few precedents in Gogol's published writing, though it appears in many letters and in such intimate fragments as "1834" and "Nights at a Villa." It is what he took to be the immediate language of his soul, and he was to offer it increasingly to his public as the conviction strengthened in him that "poetry is the pure confession of the soul and not the product of artifice or of human desiring; poetry is the truth of the soul, and therefore can be equally accessible to all." (Fortunately, *Dead Souls* as a whole displays, though for the last time, another sort of poetry, continually productive of sudden glory, the work of a language "boundless and alive as life," a language "which is in and of itself already a poet.") Here was a corrective to art's liability to misinterpretation of the kind he had experienced with his play, and all the more attractive since he expected *Dead Souls* to sell "better than any other book" and looked beyond the upper-class public for his readership. The authorial interpolations in *Dead Souls*—as opposed to narrative comment—are confessions and admonishments, pleas for sympathy and defiant complaints about probable misunderstanding. Testimony to a new conception of the writer's function, they parallel the programmatic revisions of "The Portrait" and "After the Play." But they remain outside the world of the novel, like the scattered fragments of an introduction the author feared his readers might otherwise pass by.[4]

The world of that novel is the weedlike culture on the Russian heartland, conceived abstractly from a distance and bodied forth in disconcerting closeups, with absences commanding the same meticulous attention as presences and thereby assuming a like status; this verbal world takes its weird consistency from such ontological mixing and

4. Nabokov suggests a formal function for the "lyrical outbursts [which are not] really parts of the solid pattern of the book. . . ." They represent, he says, "those natural interspaces without which the pattern would not be what it is." *Nikolai Gogol* (Norfolk, Conn.: New Directions, 1944), p. 107. [See the translation of parts of Nabokov's book in this volume, pp. 531–41 *Editor.*]

implies its own relation to other worlds simply by existing as it does. The oddness of the first paragraph alone (the first seven in Bernard Guerney's translation, which also makes an even twelve chapters out of Gogol's odd eleven) has been well analyzed by Nabokov in English and by Irakly Andronikov in Russian. Both see its blurring of essentials and sharp etching of irrelevancies as typical of the presented world of *Dead Souls,* semantically malproportioned to produce an effect of comic grotesquerie. Indeed this feature is recapitulated three paragraphs later in the description of Chichikov's room at the inn, which concludes: "In short, the same thing you find everywhere, with the sole difference that one of the paintings depicted a nymph with such enormous breasts as the reader, most probably, has never beheld." Gogol's phrase for this is "a sport of nature *(igra prirody)*": that phrase defines the look of the town[5] as well as its life and has an emblematic meaning that extends throughout a narrative in which nature figures prominently.[6] Our first view of it comes in Chapter 2, as Chichikov sets out on the first of his forays into the countryside:

> Hardly had the town retreated when (quite the usual thing among us) there unrolled on both sides of the road vistas of a wild preposterousness: hummocks, fire groves, small, squat, sparse undergrowths of young pines, charred stumps of old ones, wild heather, and such-like nonsensical rubbish. One came upon villages all strung out in a single line, with huts that looked like weather-beaten woodpiles, covered over with gray roofs, the wooden fretwork decorations underneath them resembling hanging towels with embroidered designs. A few muzhiks in short sheepskin jackets were, as usual, yawning as they squatted on benches placed before the gates; countrywives, with stout faces and their breasts caught up by shawls, were looking out of the upper windows; out of a lower window a calf would peer, or a sow might be poking its unseeing snout. In brief, the sights were of a thoroughly familiar nature. (Guerney translation)

Out of this flat miscellaneousness crystallizing into colorful incongruities, Gogol shows how each of the five landowners Chichikov visits—solipsists all—has arranged a particular landscape reflecting his own dominant qualites. Thus the rough and solid order of Sobakevich's estate is matched by the master himself, whose very face is described as one of

---

5. A hatter's shop-sign announces "Vasily Fyodorov, Foreigner", for example.

6. Yuri Mann makes somewhat different use of the phrase; see his article, pp. 482–89 below.

those on which nature took few pains, but simply hacked away from the shoulder with an ax, "and set him into the world unplaned, saying: 'It lives!'" This technique is so artfully handled and so subtly sustained as to preclude brief citation; avoiding the allegorical consistency it threatens, Gogol manages to suggest the variety of nature through the range of his observation and the modulation of his emphases. The symbolic high point of all this is the long description of Plyushkin's garden in Chapter 6, singled out by Nabokov as an example of the epoch-making novelty of Gogol's painterly rendition of landscape.[7] The concluding lines as he translates them summarize:

> In a word all was as beautiful as neither nature nor art can contrive, beautiful as it is only when these two come together, with nature giving the final touch of her chisel to the work of man (that more often than not he has piled up anyhow), alleviating its bulky agglomeration and suppressing both its crudely obvious regularity and the miserable gaps through which its stark background clearly showed and casting a wonderful warmth over all that had been evolved in the bleakness of measured neatness and propriety.

A larger point was made by Pletnyov in one of the first reviews of the book. Citing the same passage, he observed that Gogol had "with astonishing clarity set forth in these few words his whole esthetic theory. . . . *His whole book is like this garden.*"[8] This corner of Plyushkin's estate is unique—"It alone lent freshness to this extensive settlement and it alone was fully picturesque in its pictorial desolation"—and it represents a norm by which to judge the eccentricities both of the presented world and of the presentation itself. No less remarkable in this respect is the companion passage in the same chapter, where narrative digression creates a scene so minute as to seem observed rather than imagined, one that similarly suggests a perspective from outside the suffocating world of the book. Chichikov is standing before Plyushkin:

> And so, that's the sort of landowner who was standing before Chichikov! It must be said that the like is only rarely to be met with in Russia, where everything would rather expand than contract, and such a phenomenon is all the more striking since right next door a landowner may turn up who carouses

---

7. See Nabokov's comment and translation in his *Gogol*, pp. 86–89.
8. "Čičikov ili *Mertvye Duši* Gogolija" [Chichikov, or Gogol's *Dead*

Souls], 1842, reprinted in P. A. Pletnyov, *Sočineniia i perepiska* [Works and correspondences] (St. Petersburg, 1885), p. 493.

as only the reckless Russian gentry can, burning his candle, as they say, at both ends. The unfamiliar traveler will stop in astonishment at the sight of his dwelling, wondering what sovereign prince has suddenly surfaced amid these small and insignificant proprietors: Like palaces do his white stone buildings gaze out with an infinity of chimneys, belvederes, weathervanes, and all sorts of outbuildings for the house guests. What doesn't he have there? Theatricals, balls—all night, set about with lights and lampions and live with music, his garden glows. Half the province in their best finery promenade gaily beneath the trees—no one sees anything wild or threatening in this forced illumination—when from the arboreal thickness a branch leaps out, suffused with counterfeit light, stripped of its bright verdancy, while above, darker and sterner and twenty times more dreadful for that the night sky looms and, rustling their leaves on high, disappearing deeper into the impenetrable dark, the austere treetops make their indignant protest at this tinselly glitter which has lit up their roots from below.

The world of *Dead Souls* is a world of detail natural and fictive, familiar and strange—and all subtly out of joint. Even at its sharpest, this detail contributes to the general impression of indeterminacy: What time of year can it be when the peasant men sit in sheepskin coats, their women are up to their knees in a pond, Korobochka comments on a snowstorm, and the fruit trees are covered with a net to keep off the crows? [9] Thus Biely is led to conclude that "there is no plot in *Dead Souls* outside of the details," just as there is nothing except "the bare carcass of Gogol's dissertations" outside the ubiquitous nuance. The people themselves become features of the landscape—Plyushkin a "rip," Sobakevich a bear, the unidentified woman in Sobakevich's house "one of those persons who exist in the world not as objects, but as foreign specks or spots on objects." Korobochka is exemplary in the way, at the end of her interview with Chichikov, she fades back into the details of which she seems less the mistress than the emanation: "Reassured, [she] had already begun to examine everything that was in her yard; she stared at the housekeeper who was bringing a wooden flagon of honey out of the store-room, at the peasant who had appeared at the gate, and little by little settled back entirely into the life of her household."

How these details relate to each other and cohere to fulfill a serious intention is as difficult to formulate as it is easy to feel in the reading. Paraphrase misses the sus-

9. On these seasonal anomalies see Yuri Mann and Andrei Bely [pp. 482–89 and 517–31 in this volume—*Editor*].

taining magic of the language—Gogol's triumph here—
and so deadens. Analysis freezes the essential movement of
the text, which is not lineal, thus risking arbitrariness, not
to mention endlessness. Summary supposes, fatally, that
plot provides a meaningful pattern. There is no single locus
or level of significance adequate to account for this text in
which speech events rival human events (even *generate*
them), and characters who stumble momentarily into the
narrative through hearsay or are invited in to make up a
simile,[1] share a quality of enigmatic, stubborn "thereness"
with those whose presence is demanded by Chichikov's
scheme or the narrator's *sententiae*. All of which doubtless
accounts for the fact that in the more than a century and
a quarter since *Dead Souls* was published and proclaimed
a masterpiece, scarcely a single serious critical monograph
has been devoted to it. One looks for links and finds instead shifting fields of force; one isolates levels and discovers that their effectiveness rests on the rhythms of their
discontinuity. *Dead Souls,* that strange reflection on the
static and the confined, seethes with energy; even the ending is motion. The writing that indicts the mere semblance
of life seems itself possessed of a disconcerting vitality.
Sinyavsky explains the paradox behind this elusiveness:

> The plot here is devoured by the portraits and swamped by the
> details. From an engaging story the accent is shifted to the char-
> acters; but in the characters (or portraits) the accent is shifted
> to details of setting. The novel slips into landscape—roadside or
> domestic; the estates with their owners are countries, islands
> in an ocean; each house is sketched as a self-confined ambience
> with its own specific local color; as is appropriate in journeys,
> the geographical principle comes to the fore, character being
> rendered primarily as a relief arising out of the environment.
> As interior, the interior forms a cosmos, woven out of the ma-
> terial of objects . . . the material of objects, blending with ma-
> terial of speech, produces the illusion of spatial form proper;
> the *poema* in Gogol's usage converges with the spatial concept
> of a panorama. The lyrical theme of Russia, which does not
> arise formally from the characters and events of the foreground,
> is joined with the idea of space, maximally accentuated, and
> is inserted not into the plot but into the purview of Gogol's
> prose. The formlessness and superabundance of the prose be-
> come a quality of the earth.[2]

1. Nabokov writes splendidly of this
auxiliary population, but turning
from his pages to the text itself one
may be nonplussed to discover that
the examples he implies to be everywhere are in fact a good deal sparser,
leaving vast stretches of the writing
unaccounted for.
2. Abram Terc [Andrei Sinyavsky], *V
teni Gogolja* [In Gogol's shadow]
(London: Collins, 1975), pp. 378–79.

The matter of *Dead Souls* is so difficult to handle because it is so peculiarly, materially verbal. The interpolated "Tale of Captain Kopeikin" in Chapter 10 offers an extended and crucial example. A masterpiece of *skaz* (mannered narration in which the speaker unwittingly vies with his story for attention and vivid manner overshadows ostensible matter), it consists largely of fillers, malapropisms and colorfully misdirected hyperbole. " 'After the campaign of 1812, my fine gentleman'—thus the postmaster began, despite the fact that not one gentleman but a whole six were sitting in the room—'after the campaign of 1812 among those sent back with the wounded was Captain Kopeikin. Whether it was at Krasnoe or at Leipzig, anyway, just image, his arm and leg had been blown off. Well, at that time they hadn't yet made any, you know, provisions for the wounded; any sort of veterans' fund was already established, as you can imagine, so to speak, much later.' " The postmaster's purpose in telling the story is to suggest that Chichikov is really Captain Kopeikin; six pages later the police chief interrupts to point out that Chichikov has all his limbs—as indeed he could have done after the second sentence. Had the tale been meant merely to cap the absurd series of rumors about Chichikov, to demonstrate the absentmindedness of the teller or the density of the listeners, it might have been cut or summarized when the censor objected to it as politically inflammatory. Gogol, however, made a desperate plea for its necessity—in terms of form:

> This is one of the best passages. And I am unable in any way to patch the hole [which its excision would leave] visible in my *poema*. . . . The piece is essential, not for the connection of the events, but to distract the reader for a moment. . . . It has occurred to me that perhaps the censorship took fright at [the mention of] generals. I have reworked Kopeikin and thrown out all of that, even the minister, even the word "Excellency. . . . " I have drawn the character of Kopeikin more sharply so that it is now clear that he himself is the cause of his behavior, and not any lack of compassion in others. . . . In a word, it is all in such a form now that even the strictest censorship, in my opinion, cannot find anything in any wise reprehensible.

The care Gogol lavished on the rhythm of his texts is a matter of record; but there is more than distraction involved here. The whole tale is one of those irrelevant details on which the novel rests, and despite its irrelevance there is something in it. For one thing, it brings the provinces into relation with Petersburg yet again—an important element in Gogol's perspectivism. But its uniqueness lies in the way it parodically mirrors the larger text of which it is a part. Gogol makes this clear when, introducing it, he quotes the postmaster's claim that if the tale be told, the result would be "a sort of whole *poema*, and a fascinating one for some writer." The tale, in other words, exists not only to present in new focus a narration that is a performance, a colloquial stylization replete with outlandish words, functional irrelevancies, alternating sharpness and blur; and not only to make the largest addition to the enormous cast of supernumerary presences. Beyond manner, it parodies the form of *Dead Souls* by ending precisely at the point where the teller announces "the beginning, one may say, the thread, the start (*zavjazka*) of a novel."

The universe of *Dead Souls* expands and contracts in the reader's consciousness—from metaphysical intuition to densely enigmatic vocables. That is why if we pause at any point in our reading, the whole appears as an ontological puzzle. The smallest and so most apparently tractable elements—the words themselves—may call language as such into question, to such an extent can they appear freed not only from clear referential meaning but from single specifiable relevance.[3] In this connection, the title itself is central: Biely declared that he could write dozens of pages on the tricks of narration that arise from the ambiguity of both words.

Souls in this novel are absent, displaced, or atrophied. Sobakevich pinpoints the ambiguities when he assures Chichikov that "some other crook would deceive you, sell you rubbish, and not souls"; his dead souls are select merchandise, each one "either a skilled workman or some healthy peasant." And he gives the concept its larger extension in replying to Chichikov's objection that he is itemizing the qualities of a population that is, after all, dead:

> "Yes, of course they're dead," said Sobakevich, as if reflecting and recalling that they were in fact already dead; then he added: "But for that matter you could also say what good are the people that are now numbered among the living? What sort of people are they? They're flies, and not people."

3. Cf. A. De Jonge, "Gogol," in John Fennell, ed., *Nineteenth-Century Russian Literature: Studies of Ten Russian Writers* (London: Faber & Faber, 1973), pp. 124–25.

The objection echoes with a stubborn plausibility despite the fact that the speaker himself gives the appearance of being a body with no soul in it—"or, if there was one, then by no means in the place where it should have been." For truths issue eccentrically in this book; there is no privileged source among the characters. Sobakevich's point is borne out by Chichikov's heartfelt (*"ot duši";* literally, from the soul) reaction to the only death in the book: "There's the public prosecutor for you! He lived and lived, then up and died! And now they'll be printing in the papers that, to the grief of his subordinates and all humanity there passed away a respected citizen, a rare father, an exemplary spouse, and all sorts of things. . . . But if one were actually to look into the matter carefully . . . all there really was to you was your bushy eyebrows." The narrator himself both takes and denies this view, reporting sardonically that only when the prosecutor had become a soulless corpse did those around him discover "that the deceased had in fact had a soul, though in his modesty he had never shown it. But for all that the appearance of death was as awful in a little man as it is awful in a great: he who not so long before had walked, moved, played whist, signed various papers and been seen so often among the officials with his thick eyebrows and winking eye now lay on the table; his left eye no longer winked at all, but one eyebrow was still raised with a sort of interrogative expression. What the deceased was asking about—why he had died or why he had lived—God alone knows."

This is a reprise of the way the death of Akaky Akakievich had been registered, and it can produce a similar uneasiness in readers who, like Rozanov, deny Gogol the right to regard his characters as occasions for solemnity when he has already mocked them in the very act of creating them. In the broader context of *Dead Souls,* however, where the refrain of *ne to* ("not that"—not the thing supposed or intended or required) is so constantly and variously sounded, the prosecutor's death is as large a symbolic event as the tale of Captain Kopeikin, and any uneasiness on the reader's part simply proves that the point has been taken: "How the inanity and impotent idleness of a life are replaced by a murky death which says nothing. How this awful event is accomplished senselessly. No one is moved. Death strikes an unmoving world. All the more strongly thereby should the dead insensibility of life be brought home to the reader" (Gogol's notes to Volume One)

In these words the fundamental paradox of the novel is laid bare: Living people and dead ones may be clearly distinguished in the action, but the cumulative sense of the text denies this distinction, as it denies the autonomy of comedy. Bergson shrewdly locates the originality of a comic artist in "the special kind of life he imparts to a mere puppet"; but when, in Vyazemsky's phrase, *Dead Souls* turns into a Holbein-like dance of death, the comedy turns painful, revealing the poles of the spectrum shown not as death and life, but as death and death-in-life.[4] Here is a clue to the "special kind of life" in question, and it suggests that the terms of Gogol's presentation are not so much skewed as incomplete. Annensky explained the matter this way. In each of us there are two persons, one of them visible and tangible, the other "enigmatic and secret" —the carrier of an indivisible, incommunicable, primordial selfhood. The first strives above all to be a type—that is, to assume a social identification; the second alone creates individuality. "The first eats, sleeps, shaves, and ceases to breathe; you can lock it in a jail or nail it up in a coffin." But it is only the second that can be reproached, loved, or respond to moral demands. Gogol, he finds, "sundered the first of these two persons fused together by life from the second, and made him so incandescently typical . . . so stunningly corporeal, that that second person proved utterly effaced. He even became outright unnecessary, so that the first, the tangible one, now answered for both."[5]

Here is the best answer to Sobakevich's question about what sort of people the living are in this book. The landowners Chichikov visits do not, as Biely claims, represent a progressively greater degree of deadness; the individuating moral principle in each is *equally* absent. What they rather represent are differing degrees (and kinds) of *aliveness*—an aliveness that reaches its apogee in Sobakevich and Nozdryov, the one impressing his selfhood on everything around him and so reifying it, the other making everything a possession (or attribute) of himself and so

4. Henri Bergson, "Laughter," in Wylie Sypher, ed., (Garden City, N.Y.: Doubleday Anchor Books, 1956), p. 80.
5. An English version of Annensky's article, entitled "The Aesthetics of Gogol's *Dead Souls* and Its Legacy," may be found in Victor Erlich, ed., *Twentieth-Century Russian Literary Criticism* (New Haven and London: Yale University Press, 1975).

perpetually dispersing that selfhood. Nozdryov, as Annensky puts it epigrammatically, "is not at all a liar" but "some uncontrollable, some insane abundance," "the cheerful indifference of nature." The same passionate miscellaneousness (though the ruling passions give it different contours) can be seen in Plyushkin, in Manilov—and in Chichikov himself. These figures may exist on the level of humors but, like Panurge and Falstaff, they are perfectly individuated, and profoundly nuanced in expression. To generalize the quality of any of them, one has to use his name, no common noun will do; in that sense these creations are at the same time *discoveries*.

Chichikov and the landowners are the major characters of *Dead Souls*, and the major instances of Russian character; hence the narrative reminders that all have their counterparts in the capital. But they are more than exhibits. In Chapters 2 through 6, they lay the groundwork for the comedy of attribution which will turn collective in Chapters 7 through 10. Each of them, in his interview with Chichikov, can be seen projecting his peculiar fantasies onto the void of the "real" world—as if their society were a conspiracy of silence to permit this.[6] When in Chapter 8 Chichikov has taken possession of his ambiguous capital (consisting only of words on paper: the mortgageable lists of the dead serfs he has bought), the scene shifts back to the town, and the portraiture becomes satirical as general attention focuses on him and his putative wealth. Now it is the ladies of the town who begin investing Chichikov with new qualities. These ladies, Gogol notes, "were by no means fortune-hunters: the word 'millionaire' was to blame for it all—not the millionaire himself but just the word alone." [7] Nor does discovery of the truth halt this process. When Nozdryov and after him Korobochka finally make known the nature of Chichikov's purchases, the whole town begins collectively to explain him

6. Pletnyov, whose review so pleased Gogol that he copied it verbatim in his own hand, saw this, noting the absence in the book of "what we do not yet meet in our life—a serious social interest."

7. The independent life of words as such in this book has been examined in English by Nabokov and, more broadly, by Simon Karlinsky, whose observation this is; see the latter's "Portrait of Gogol as a Word Glutton, with Rabelais, Sterne, and Gertrude Stein as Background Figures," *California Slavic Studies* 1 (1970): 169–86. Karlinsky marshals the evidence so well that I have not sought to go over the same ground here. His emphasis, however, is more on Gogol's verbal "appetite" than on questions of rationale and function. [See pp. 546–58, below—*Editor*.]

and his enterprise—once more by attribution. He is Napoleon, Rinaldo Rinaldini, the devil, Captain Kopeikin. The text of Gogol's fiction swells with internally generated fictions: the mutual mirroring now gives way to the effect of an amusement-park hall of mirrors—from which Chichikov simply escapes, to vanish on the last page in the last of the book's optical illusions and the last of its changes of level.

Dead Souls exploits the narrative voices and devices worked out in the most Gogolian of his earlier comic writings; the text abounds with parallels, at times almost citations, from "Shponka," "Old-World Landowners," the story of the two Ivans, "The Nose," "The Carriage," all five of the Petersburg Tales, *The Inspector General*. It is his last, most inclusive, and most intentional performance in that special mode of his own devising—half monologue, half story—by which he creates a world whose status with relation to ordinary experience remains, like the implied personality of the narrator, teasingly elusive. The world of *Dead Souls* differs only in this because it is more ample, it shows a greater consistency, the very discontinuities suggesting a pattern, the several levels echoing each other to signal a controlling perspective over the whole design. Technique itself does not simply carry but becomes a part of theme; the humblest details take on a thematic charge.

That theme at its broadest is the amorphousness, characterlessness, purposelessness, senselessness, alternately ludicrous and ominous, of life—specifically Russian life in the first place—as material for a novelist. "Well," Chichikov ruminates after the ball in a passage reminiscent of the last scene of *The Inspector General*, "what if some writer, say, took it into his head to describe this whole scene as it is? Why, even there, even in a book, it would be just as senseless as it is in nature. What kind of scene is it? Moral? Immoral? The devil alone knows what! You'd just spit, and then close the book." Compare Gogol's draft notes to Volume One:

> The whole town with the whole whirlwind of rumors embodies the idleness [8] (*bezdel'nost'*) of the life of all mankind in the mass. . . .

8. A letter of 1846 provides a gloss on the concept in question. "The world in which you are now moving," Gogol writes Samarin, "is not corrupt in its root or essence but corrupt out of depression and boredom, morbidly listless and, from having nothing to do, vacuous and stupid."

How bring all the sorts of idleness in the world down to a resemblance with the town's idleness? And how elevate the town's idleness to the level of an embodiment of the world's? To manage it, include all the similarities and introduce a graduated progression.

This notion of a tiered significance suggests in the first place all those passages which insist on Petersburg variant of the same local phenomena; but the symbolic intention, so generally expressed, goes beyond this. Gogol's concern is with levels of interpretation, and he might well have had in mind Dante's classic assertion that

> books can be understood, and ought to be explained, in four principal senses. One is called *literal,* and . . . goes no further than the letter, such as the simple narration of the thing of which you treat. . . . The second is called *allegorical,* and this is the meaning hidden under the cloak of fables, and is a truth concealed beneath a fair fiction. . . . The third sense is called *moral;* and this readers should carefully gather from all writings, for the benefit of themselves and their descendants. . . . The fourth sense is called *anagogical* [or mystical], that is, beyond sense; and this is when a book is spiritually expounded.[9]

I do not mean to suggest that *Dead Souls* should be tortured into strict conformity with these medieval categories, but only that some comparable scheme was demonstrably a part of Gogol's intention and can in fact be fruitfully applied to this (and only this) text of his.

How are such levels of serious significance incorporated into a comic novel? Some examples may make this clear, but a broad answer can be ventured in advance. It is that Gogol found a key to the most puzzling of his inherent tendencies when he took contemporary Russia as his theme. Even on the strategic authorial level, that is, *Dead Souls* remains a comedy of attribution. It is a symbolic statement of what it means to live (as Gogol claimed he had written previously) without controlling consciousness, without asking "why?" and "to what end?" Here was a license for derision, or rather a serious warrant for the most ingeniously unserious presentation. No oddity, no irrelevance, no absurdity but could—given the unflagging genius of the language—contribute to the painful because concrete sense of an absence.

9. "Letter to Can Grande della Scala," in George Rice Carpenter, ed., *A Translation of Dante's Eleven Letters . . . by Charles Sterrett Latham* (Boston and New York. Houghton Mifflin, 1891), p. 194 n1.

On the first page, for example, the contextless conversation about the wheel on Chichikov's carriage is conducted by "two Russian muzhiks"—a pleonasm roughly comparable to speaking of "two American cowboys." Many Russian readers have noted this as a lapse and seen in it an unconscious reflection of Gogol's Ukrainian foreignness to Russian phenomena or a sign of his distant (Roman) perspective at the time of writing. But the very amount of attention to the single word, "Russian," proves the functional validity of the phrase, as one scholar inadvertently acknowledged in referring to this "definition which defines nothing." [1] It is a perspectival cue,[2] warning the reader that nothing is to be taken for granted in this examination of "everything that is every minute before our eyes but is unseen by indifferent eyes." It is, in other words, a cue to the particular kind of "making-strange" that informs the book, one element in the emphasis on *ne to*. As such it manifests in little what distinguishes such fantastic-atmospheric passages as the remarkable one that brings Chichikov back to the town of N. at the end of Chapter 6:

The twilight was already deep when they drove up to the town. Light and shadow were utterly mixed up, and it seemed that the very objects were mixed up as well. The striped toll-gate had taken on some indeterminate hue; the mustaches of the sentry on duty there seemed to be on his forehead and much higher than his eyes, while his nose was as if altogether absent. . . . The streetlamps had not yet been lit; only here and there were lights beginning to appear in the windows of the houses; and in the alleys and byways scenes and conversations were taking place of a sort inseparable from this time of day in all towns where there are many soldiers, cabbies, workmen, and beings of a special sort in the guise of ladies with red shawls and shoes without stockings who dart like bats about the intersections. Chichikov did not notice them, and even failed to notice the many slender clerks with little canes who were, probably, returning home after having taken a stroll out of town. Occasionally certain exclamations, apparently female, came to his hearing: "That's a lie, you drunkard! I never al-

1. S. A. Vengerov, *Pisatel' graždanin. Gogol'* [Gogol, the citizen writer] (St. Petersburg, 1913), p. 139. On this phrase see also Yuri Mann [pp. 482 – 89 in this volume—*Editor*].
2. See Gogol's defense of *The Inspector General* in his "After the Play": To one spectator's objection that a comedy "should be a picture and mirror of our social life . . . [and]

reflect it with complete fidelity," Gogol responds that "this comedy is not at all a picture, but rather a frontispiece. You can see that the stage and the place of the action are ideal. Otherwise the author would not have allowed himself obvious inaccuracies and anachronisms. . . . This is a composite place."

lowed him such rudeness!", or: "Don't you try to fight, you
ignoramus, just come down to the station, I'll prove it to you
there! . . ." In short, such words as will suddenly scald some
dreaming twenty-year-old youth returning from the theater. . . .
He is in heaven, he has dropped in to visit Schiller—when
suddenly, like thunder, the fateful words resound above him
and he sees that he has come to once more on earth, and even
on Haymarket Square, and even in the vicinity of a tavern,
and everyday life has once more started to strut its stuff before
him.

This marvel of quiet anomaly and subtle progression would
repay careful analysis; I cite it here merely as one striking
instance of the way Gogol makes a scene at once specific
and enigmatically general, confounds the everyday with
the near-surrealistic, and fosters a sense of *huis clos* that
hangs over the entire narrative.

Related to this in its functional superfluity is the introduction of Manilov in Chapter 2. The passage is remarkable in the first place for its slippery logic and its self-
canceling conclusion, which make it the overwhelmingly
present sign of an absence:

> [With such characters] a forcible harnessing of the attention
> is necessary while you compel all their subtle, almost invisible
> traits to stand out before you, and in general even an eye
> already educated and disciplined in science must be forced to
> its uttermost penetration.
>
> God alone might be able to say what kind of character Mani-
> lov's was. There is a class of people known as so-so, neither-
> this-nor-that, neither fish nor fowl, as the proverb has it. It is
> among them, perhaps, that Manilov should be numbered. . . .
> During the first minute of conversation with him you couldn't
> help saying, "What a pleasant and kind man!" The next
> minute after that you wouldn't say anything at all; while the
> minute after that you'd say, "The devil knows what this is
> about!"—and you'd get as far away as possible. . . . No amount
> of patience could get you any lively or even emphatic word
> out of him, of the kind you can hear from almost anybody if
> you touch on a subject close to his heart. Everyone has some
> passion of his own: the passion of one man may have turned to
> wolfhounds; another fancies himself a great lover of music and
> amazingly sensitive to all its profundites; a third is a master at
> valiant dining, a fourth at playing a role ever so slightly higher
> than the one assigned to him; a fifth, with a more limited desire,
> sleeps and dreams of how he might be seen strolling with an
> aide-de-camp for the benefit of his friends, acquaintances, and
> even those who don't know him at all; a sixth is already gifted
> with a hand preternaturally impelled to bet on some ace or
> deuce of diamonds, while the hand of a seventh just itches to
> set things right somewhere . . . in short, everyone has something
> all his own, but Manilov didn't have a thing.

Reminiscent in its anticlimax of the passage in "The Overcoat" describing Akaky Akakievich's lack of recreation, this two-tiered noncharacterization operates in still other ways. It reinforces the sense of a closed world by the reversibility of its items: the seven hypothetical individuals not only assert Manilov's minimal position on the ladder of human being; they are, morally speaking, seven sleepers, representing a range of trivial preoccupation that will be exemplified throughout the book.

None of this is strictly necessary, since the impression of Manilov that emerges from his slow-motion dealings with Chichikov makes the point indelibly. But it and similar passages are absolutely necessary as contributions to the reader's complicity with the narrator, that clever and sardonic fellow. Sharing his perspective and judgments, we are all the more likely to accept his generalizations about Russian habits, the Russian word, Russian character—and so to credit (even when we cannot follow) his insistence that there is a sober sense to all this luminous nonsense. The angle of vision, reinforced by overt comment, supplies a level of consciousness which the denizens of the novel are so consistently denied.

What are conventionally called the lyrical digressions in *Dead Souls* thus need to be distinguished in terms of two distinct tendencies. One set enriches the presentation by growing out of it, directly or through association; these fall within the range—an extraordinarily ample one—of what I have called the narrative voice. The other set—the work of the authorial voice—comments on the novel as an artifact in process of creation, emphasizing its dignity, its uniqueness, and its difficulty. Alternately open confessions and defiant manifestos, these are self-justifying, self-encouraging, sometimes self-pitying excrescences in the narrowly artistic sense, but uniquely valuable evidence of a new writerly consciousness.

Gogol speaks of the difficulty of his task in two principal connections. One is vis-à-vis his public. Throughout the text he anticipates and rebuts objections: to his use of "low" colloquial language, his taking a "scoundrel" as hero, his exclusion of love intrigue, and so on. These amount to an attack on the conventional novels of his time and on the expectations of their readers (whom he treats in this respect as dangerously enfeebled if not actually dead souls themselves). At the same time, he contrasts the happy lot of the popular writer with that of the writer who has dared to call forth all that is constantly before our eyes but which indifferent eyes remark not—all the terrible, shocking slime of trivia that have encumbered our life, all the depth of cold, fragmented, everyday characters with which our earthly, at times bitter and dull road teems. . . . The court of contemporary judgment, the hypócritically unfeeling court of contemporary judgment, which brands as low and insignificant the creations he has cherished, will allot him a despised corner in the ranks of writers who have insulted humanity, will attribute to him the qualities of the characters he himself has depicted, will strip him of heart and soul and the divine flame of talent. For that court of contemporary judgment does not recognize that equally wondrous are the lenses used for viewing suns and for revealing the movements of insects unobservable by the naked eye; for that court of contemporary judgment does not recognize that a great deal of spiritual depth is required to illumine a picture taken from a despised stratum of life and raise it into a pearl of perfection; for that court of contemporary opinion does not recognize that lofty, rapturous laughter is worthy to stand alongside a lofty lyricism and that a whole gulf divides it from the affected posturing of a fairground entertainer.

It is the desire for a lofty lyricism, baffled and diverted, that produces a kind of comedy which has too loosely been said to border on or overlie tragedy. Thus Gogol's comedy at its most characteristic may stand to the world of his heart's desire as a photographic negative, in which all the bright spots show up as black and only the rhythm— the mysterious, varying, perfect tact of his narrative units— gives evidence of the lyricism that he has transfigured not for purposes of parody but in obedience to an obscure inner prompting, a powerfully ambivalent mixture of love and contempt.

The word "love" is another red herring in traditional Russian writing on Gogol. He himself used it with some frequency, particularly after 1836 when he embraced comic writing as a mission, and sympathetic critics at the time and since have recurred to the word as a way of insisting on a positive aspect often denied him. What is at issue, of course, is love not as a biographical experience but as an impulse perceptible in the text, and here the best formulation is, again, Annensky's when he speaks of Gogol's "ecstatic love for existence—not for life, but precisely for existence." The distinction is crucial: Gogol's primary attachment is a travesty of Spinoza's *amor intellectualis,* a love that motivates the close observation of miscellaneous and insignificant things and finds its justification by transmuting them into art. As such it is parodied in the fragment, "Semyon Semyonovich Batyushek," used in "Shponka," confessed in "Old-World Landowners," incarnated in Akaky Akakievich—and commented upon at the very center of *Dead Souls,* in that most personal of authorial digressions which opens Chapter 6 and introduces the theme of time into the novel.

In that passage Gogol recalls how every new place, however drab, used to reveal "a great deal that was curious" to his "childishly curious glance": "Nothing escaped my fresh, subtle attention, and thrusting my nose out of my traveling carriage I would gaze at the never-before-seen cut of some frock coat, and at wooden boxes with nails, with sulphur gleaming yellow in the distance, with raisins and soap that could be glimpsed through the doors of a vegetable shop together with jars of dried Moscow sweets; I would gaze as well at the infantry officer walking alongside, translated from God knows what province into this local tedium, and at the merchant in his Siberian caftan flashing by in his racing carriage, and I would pursue them in thought into their paltry life." Now, however, such sights inspire only indifference, "and what would in previous years have awakened liveliness in my face, laughter and endless talk, now glides past and my motionless lips preserve an apathetic silence. Oh my youth! Oh my freshness!"

"Freshness" (*svežest'*) is a word that occurs periodically throughout Gogol's text. It denotes a condition—openness to inspiration, creative capacity—which is exclusively reserved to the author, the very ground of his existence as such. When the authorial digressions shift from the public's ability to understand what he has done to his own continuing ability to do it, they signal the only consequential drama in the book—an interlinear one. Hence the relevance of those confessions of uncertainty which dot the manuscripts.[3]

3. In Chapter 10, one of the nodal passages that connects Chichikov's progress with Gogol's and with humanity's contained in draft the following italicized words: "How many times, led by a sense vouchsafed from heaven, have [people] nonetheless contrived to stumble and veer off to the side, contrived in broad daylight to land in impassable thickets . . . [and] reach the edge of an abyss, only then with horror to ask each other: 'Where is the way out? Where is the road?' *And the lofty soul becomes miserable, overcome with illness . . . and the tears are ready to gush forth.*" A comparable note appears even more clearly in the opening lines of the first chapter of Volume Two.

The lament over the passing of youth and freshness thus participates simultaneously in two contexts—the drama of authorship and the antidrama of Chichikov's adventures— making its appearance doubly appropriate in the chapter that introduces Plyushkin. With Plyushkin, time enters the narrative. What we are told about the earlier lives of Manilov and Korobochka makes clear that time is not a constitutive factor there. But Plyushkin is shown to have *become* what he is, not a "dead" but a deadened soul. Gogol details the process and discusses it in monitory terms ("To such insignificance, pettiness, vileness could a man sink! could a man so change!! Does all this have verisimilitude? All this has verisimilitude, all this can befall a man"). A rejected draft shows even more explicitly the awareness that troubled Gogol and was intended eventually to save Chichikov: "He had forgotten that he was already at that fateful stage of life when everything turns more sluggish in a man, when he needs to be constantly roused lest he go to sleep forever." He was oblivious, Gogol notes, to the way a person beginning to age "is insensibly and almost imperceptibly taken over by the vulgar habits of society . . . which at length so encumber and envelop him that no self remains in him, but only a heap of conditionings and reflexes that belong to the world. And when you try to break through to the soul, it's no longer there."

Bringing time into the novel—through Plyushkin and through the biographical sketch in the last chapter that puts Chichikov, too, on the level of becoming—brought cause for mortal apprehension in the artistic sense as well as the moral. Gogol's fateful error lay in accepting and repeating Pushkin's remark that his gift was for "divining a man" on the basis of a few observed traits. It was never that. Accuracy (as the few examples show) was never in question; the gift alluded to was for *creating* a plausible and amusing portrait, one more gratuitous item in the collection of what he came here to label as dead souls. His genius lay always in eccentric but lifelike attribution—a kind that tempts one to add "expressionist" to the other anachronistic labels (symbolist, surrealist, absurdist) that fit his work better than any current in his own time. So long as Chichikov remained an enigmatic vehicle for this process of creation and exhibition, he served his author's genius perfectly by sharing Gogol's freedom of arbitrary movement at the expense of the static population of his book.

Indeed, Chichikov's very quest for nonexistent merchandise that would, all the same, have impact in his world parallels Gogol's quest to render an absence that would, by the force of the rendering, change the historical consciousness of his Russia. Both aim at "creation out of nothing," the literal dead souls of the title being at once a pretext and a pre-text—as were the lyrical digressions, in Gogol's view. "The full meaning of the lyrical hints," he declared, could be grasped "only when the last part comes out."

It may well be, as one Russian critic cruelly observed, that Gogol's last act as a great writer was to burn the sequel to this book shortly before his death. By so doing he left a monument to his own ambivalent feeling for existence— immutable, fragmentary, pregnant with an undeclared meaning, and made precious by the demonstration that "the word for a thing may be more precious than the thing itself." For, as Sinyavsky has pointed out, it is not things that Gogol makes attractive but only his redeeming and transfiguring account of them. If the pleasure of the text is "value shifted to the sumptuous rank of the signifier," *Dead Souls* provides it in the fullest measure.[4] That explains Gogol's twentieth-century appeal; we are most comfortable with texts that are paradoxes and puzzles. At the same time, it explains the novel's earlier appeal and influence. As an entity at once polished and open-ended, *Dead Souls* brought together in literary form a flux of attitudes and tendencies, sights and sounds—the raw material of an unborn national self-consciousness. Fixing that flux between the covers of a book, Gogol made it an object of contemplation, and Annensky was right to see something portentous and heroic in this. "What would have become of our literature," he asks, "if [Gogol] alone and for all of us had not shouldered that burden and that torment and immersed in fathomless physicality our still-so-timid language . . . ?"

At this remove in time and space, we might alter the stress, noting the extent to which the deeply subjective medium that holds the pieces of this mosaic holds them fast. Ideas cannot be disengaged and discussed outside the unique form that gives them their being as literary ideas. Thus the profound truth of Gogol's claim that he never sought to be a mirror of the reality around him. In the last

4. Roland Barthes, *The Pleasure of the Text,* trans. Richard Miller (New York: Hill and Wang, 1975), p. 65.

chapter of *Dead Souls* a view of the bleak Russian plain
appears to prompt a question ("Russia! What is it you
would have of me? What ineffable bond mysteriously connects us? . . . What does this boundless space prophesy?")—
but the view, obeying the peculiar laws of Gogolian space
("The mighty expanse awesomely enfolds me, having been
reflected with fearsome power in my very depths"), is really
a vision, and at one with the question. The palpable mis-
cellany of the book has coalesced into an abstraction, which
can be questioned only rhetorically. The famous final paragraph consists almost entirely of such questions, most of
them, strictly speaking, senseless: a phantom interrogation
of a phantom symbol. What more fitting close to a novel
that demonstrates with unprecedented brilliance the power
of form without content and action without resolution—
a work that finally does invite comparison with Cervantes'
in the subtlety of its comedy and the depth of its symbol-
ism, mimicking the emptiness of life no less resourcefully
than the *Quixote* had mimicked life's fullness? [5]

YURI MANN

On the Two Opposing Structural Principles of
Dead Souls†

[Gogol's main task] took shape with the beginning of
work on *Dead Souls,* that is, in the mid-thirties despite the
fact that a detailed "plan" of the poem, and even more its
following parts, remained unclear to him.

Toward the mid-thirties, a crisis occurred in Gogol's
work. Later, in "An Author's Confession," Gogol was inclined to define this crisis on the basis of an attitude toward
laughter and the purposefulness of the comic: "I saw that
I was laughing *in vain* and *to no purpose* in my works,
without knowing why myself. If one is to laugh, then it's
better to laugh *powerfully*, and at something which is

---

5. See Americo Castro's seminal essay,
"Incarnation in *Don Quixote*," with
its argument that "the basic theme
of *Don Quixote* is life as a process
creative of itself," in Stephen Gilman
and Edmund King, eds., *An Idea of
History: Selected Essays of Americo
Castro* (Columbus, Ohio: Ohio State
University Press, 1977). Castro's work
contains invaluable material for the
serious comparative study of the two

books that still remains to be written.
† Translated by Robert Sorenson from
the article "*O poetike 'Myortvykh
dush'* " [The poetics of *Dead Souls*],
pp. 193–99 in D. Ustiuzhanin, ed.,
Russkaya klassicheskaya literatura
[Russian classical literature] (Moscow,
1969), an anthology of critical essays
about various individual masterpieces
of Russian literature.

really worthy of universal ridicule." The contrast in these words, however, is excessively categorical; this is explained by the later Gogol's stern and lofty approach to his early pieces. Even before 1835, of course, Gogol did not merely laugh "in vain" and "to no purpose"! A more just contrast is that based on the feature that Gogol approaches at the end of the citation above, that of "universal ridicule."

Even earlier, Gogol's artistic thought had striven for broad generalizations. Hence his attraction to collective images—Dikanka, Mirgorod, Nevsky Prospect [1]—which go beyond the framework of geographical or territorial names and signify whole continents on the map of the universe, as it were. At first, however, Gogol tried to approach these "continents" now from one side, now from another, fracturing the picture of the whole into many fragments. The title *Arabesques,* for one of the collections of Gogol's works, was not at all coincidental, of course.

However, Gogol persistently sought the kind of representational method in which the whole would appear not in parts or "arabesques," but as a whole. In one year, 1835, the writer began work on three compositions that would show, as he expressed it later, "the deviation of the *whole society,* from the straight path." One of these works was the unfinished historical drama *Alfred.* Another was *The Inspector General.* The third was *Dead Souls.* Among these projects, a special, higher meaning was ascribed to *Dead Souls.*

As early as a year after he had begun work on *Dead Souls,* Gogol wrote: "If I finish this creation the way it must be finished, then . . . what an immense, what an original subject! What a variegated mass! *All Russia* will appear in it!"

In *The Inspector General,* the broad, "all-Russian" scale arose largely because of the similarity between Gogol's city and many other Russian "cities," and not, of course, isolated cities (state and provincial capitals, and so on). Gogol called the city in *The Inspector General* a "composite one." This was the representation of a living organism through one of its cells, which involuntarily imitated the vital activity of the whole (that is, of the whole Russian Empire).

In *Dead Souls,* Gogol expanded this scale widely. Not

1. Dikanka and Mirgorod are place-names of small localities used by Gogol as titles of collections of some of his short works; Nevsky Prospect, a large boulevard in Petersburg, is the title of one of Gogol's stories [*Editor*].

only did he set himself the task, soon after he began work, of also portraying in his poem the positive phenomena of Russian life, which had not appeared in *The Inspector General* (although the real meaning and capacity of these phenomena were still unclear to Gogol), but the plot and method of narration were also important: Gogol was preparing to travel "throughout Russia" together with his hero. In other words, the generalization of *Dead Souls* was not so confined as in *The Inspector General*; it presupposed an extended period of maturation for the design, which was to be viewed through the "crystal ball" of time and acquired experience. Generalization in the poem presupposed a successive inclusion of more and more sides of Russian life.

As for the causes that influenced Gogol's new creative orientations and the formation of the large scale of both *The Inspector General* and *Dead Souls,* we must first of all name Gogol's historical and scholarly pursuits. They directly preceded the artistic projects mentioned above and imparted that quest for a "universal idea," for conformity with universal laws, which Gogol considered obligatory for both artist and historian from about the mid-thirties on:

> All the events in the world must be as closely connected with each other and linked together, as the links of a chain. If one link is torn away, the chain breaks. The connection must not be taken in a literal sense. It is not that visible, material connection, by which occurrences are often forcibly linked, or a system created in the mind without regard to facts, to which events in the world are then willfully drawn. This connection must consist in one universal idea. . . .

In this passage, Gogol has the task of the historian and scholar in view, but he also here characterizes, in a certain sense, the principles of his artistic thought. In *Dead Souls,* Gogol calls himself "the *historian* of the events presented." This self-definition is not entirely ironic. Besides the breadth of his task (which we mentioned above), a strictly "historical" consistency of exposition was refracted in its own way in Gogol's artistic manner, as was the attempt to lay bare all the secret "springs" of actions and intentions and to motivate, by means of the characters' circumstances and psychology, any change in the action or turn in the plot. There is no direct analogy here, of course. But the kinship between Gogol's scientific and artistic principles is indubitable.

From this very kinship comes a certain rationalism in

the overall "plan" of *Dead Souls,* at least of the completed first part. Each chapter is, as it were, thematically completed, with its own task and its own "subject." The first chapter is Chichikov's arrival and his acquaintance with the city; the second through sixth chapters present visits to landowners, a separate chapter being devoted to each of them; the seventh chapter gives the registration of the purchase deeds; and so on. Everything is logical; everything occurs in strict, consistent succession. "If one link is torn away, the chain breaks. . . ." And now it turns out that alongside this tendency in *Dead Souls,* another, opposing one develops. Counterbalancing the author's attraction to logic, an illogical strain appears strikingly here and there. The attempt to explain facts and phenomena at every step collides with what reason can neither explain nor control. Consistency and rationality are "violated" by the inconsistency of the very subject portrayed—the actions, intentions, and even the "things" described.

We begin with the style of the poem, with several descriptions.

The inn where Chichikov has taken lodgings does not present any special features. The common hall is like those everywhere. "Every traveler knows very well what these common halls are like." (By the way, here again among the concrete "details" we find a purposefully generalized form of description that evokes associations.) "In a word, everything was just the same as it is everywhere: the only differences being, that on one picture a nymph was portrayed, with such enormous breasts that the reader has probably never seen their like." This would seem to be a random comic detail. But it is not thrown in without reason. The motif of a strange "play of nature," as Gogol says, is woven into the whole artistic fabric of the poem.

We observe the same "play of nature" in Nozdrev's house: "Some *Turkish* daggers were shown, on one of which "Master *Saveli Sibiriakov*" was engraved *by mistake.* Then a barrel-organ was shown to the guests. . . . The barrel-organ did not play unpleasantly, but in the middle, it seems, something happened, for the mazurka ended with the song 'Malbrouke va-t-en guerre,' and 'Malbrouke va-t-en guerre' unexpectedly ended with some long-familiar waltz." The unusual, the unexpected digression from the rule—these are Gogol's favorite motifs. All the people in the portraits hanging in Sobakievich's house were healthy: "They were all handsome youngsters, all Greek commanders, engraved at full length. . . ." But "among the strong Greeks, *for an unknown reason and purpose*, was Bagration, *gaunt, thin*, with little banners and cannon below and in a very narrow frame."

The same unexpected digression from the rule appears in the finery of the provincial ladies: Everything is proper; everything is well thought out; but "suddenly some kind of headdress *never seen on earth* stuck out, or even some kind of feather, almost a peacock's, *against all fashion*. . . . But of course one couldn't get by without that; such is the nature of a provincial city: Somewhere it has got to fall on its face."

The "play of nature" appears not only in domestic utensils, pictures, and attire, but in the actions and thoughts of the characters.

Chichikov, as we know, has the habit of blowing his nose "remarkably loudly": "His nose sounded like a trumpet." "This apparently quite innocent distinction earned for him, however, great respect from the tavern servant, so that every time he heard the sound he tossed back his hair, straightened up more respectfully, and, bowing his head from on high, asked, "Would you like anything?" Why the tavern servant reacted to Chichikov blowing his nose in just such a way is quite as inexplicable as how Bagration was placed in Sobakievich's gallery of Greek military leaders.

Illogicality blooms into a luxurious flower in the last chapters of the poem, where the reaction of the city's inhabitants to the Chichikov affair is described. Here there is an absurdity at every step; each new "thought" is more rib-tickling than the last. The woman pleasant in all respects concludes from the story about Chichikov that he "wants to carry off the governor's daughter." This version is then taken up by the whole feminine half of the town. The postmaster concludes that Chichikov is Captain Kopeykin, having *forgotten* that the latter "lacked an arm and a leg." [2] The officials, despite all the arguments of common sense, turn to Nozdrev for help, which allows Gogol to draw a broad conclusion: "These officials are *strange people*, and after them *all other occupations* as well: They knew very well that Nozdrev was a liar, that you could not believe a word he said, not in the tiniest trifle,

---

2. Of course, the artistic functions of the "Tale of Captain Kopeikin" are not exhausted by this. One of them is the interjection of the Petersburg capital plane into the "provincial" plane —the inclusion of the higher, capital spheres of Russian life in the plot of the poem.

but meanwhile it was to him they ran for help."

And Chichikov's very "negotiations" are fundamentally illogical: Chichikov is trading in nothing, buying nothing ("An object, after all, is simply rubbish"). At the same time, this operation promises him real, tangible wealth.

The dead souls on the tax-lists arise as though out of non-being. And it is not only Chichikov who treats them almost as living people. Although Korobochka agrees with the arguments that they are simply "dust," she still entertains the thought: "But perhaps they'll be of use in running the place, by some chance." Sobakievich actually begins to praise the deceased with enthusiasm: "Some other scoun-drel would cheat you, and sell you trash and not souls; mine are like nuts with large kernels, all selected. . . ." It would be a mistake to think that Sobakievich is merely being crafty; to some extent he actually believes what he says. Dead souls, having become an object of trade, for sale, acquire in his eyes the worth of living people.[3] The por-trayal continually splits in two: A reflection of a kind of phantasmagoria, of a strange "play of nature," falls upon real objects and phenomena.

"Chichikov's purchases became a subject of conversation in town." People begin to discuss how the peasants will be transported to the southern provinces.

> "Of course," some said, "it's just so, there's no quarrel with that: The land in the southern provinces is, just so, good and fertile, but how will it be for *Chichikov's peasants* without water?"
>
> "But Ivan Grigorievich, you've forgotten to account for one important thing: You haven't asked what kind of peasant Chichikov has got. You've forgotten that a landowner won't sell a good man; I'll lay my head on the line that if Chichikov's peasant isn't a thief and an absolute drunkard, then he's an idler and doesn't behave himself."

The mass of opinions snowballs, but it grows out of noth-ing, out of the fiction made up by Chichikov's peasants. It is not that there is a lazy and shiftless peasant behind it: There is not a living soul. (Gogol continually "plays" with the possibility of placing real people behind the fiction. This is one of the sources of the inimitable comedy of *Dead Souls,* and at the same time of its transition into sadness, "tears," and the tragic.)

---

3. Nikolai Chernyshevsky, in debating Shevyryov's opinion that Sobakievich could not have "praised his dead souls," writes: "It really is surprising, how the coldest, coarsest people come to life and become eloquent when it is a matter of buying and selling."

The consequences of Chichikov's "negotiations" are not limited to rumor and discussion. The affair does not go by without a death—the death of the prosecutor. The appearance of death, says Gogol, is "just as terrible in a small as it is in a great man." If, say, a fantastic dénouement arose out of real events in "The Overcoat," in *Dead Souls* results completely palpable in their real tragedy arise out of a somewhat unusual event, portrayed in fantastic shades (the acquisition of "dead souls").

In fending off a reproach about the unlikeliness of the events depicted ("It's impossible that officials could frighten themselves so . . . could stray so far from the truth"), Gogol appeals to genuine facts, to the historical experience of humanity: "What crooked, blind, narrow, impassable roads, leading far off to one side, humanity has chosen for itself in striving to attain *eternal truth,* when the *direct path* lay open before them. And how many times, already started off by the sense that came down from heaven, have they managed to step back and lose the path . . . managed again to lower an impenetrable fog into each other's eyes and, dragging off after will-o'-the-wisps, managed to find their way to a precipice, in order to ask each other in horror, 'Where is the exit? *Where is the road?* '" Everything in this lyrical "digression" is significant: the fact that Gogol consistently uses Enlightenment categories ("road," "eternal truth"),[4] and that in using them he sees a monstrous deviation of humanity from the straight path. In the final analysis, the duality of the structural principles in *Dead Souls* originates in this anomaly.

The early Gogol felt the contradictions of the "mercantile age" more sharply and plainly. The anomaly of reality sometimes intruded directly and dictatorially into Gogol's artistic world, evoking a turbulent play of fantasy and the collision of strange, unreal powers. One of the ways the crisis in his work in the mid-thirties was expressed was in the subjection of fantasy to a strict accounting; he placed in the foreground the principle of synthesis, a sober and complete inclusion of the whole, the portrayal of human destinies in their interrelation with the main "road" of history. But the principle of the grotesque did not disappear from Gogol's poetics; it merely sank into the depths.

4. Also Gogol on the purpose of comedy: Comedy demonstrates "the deviation of the whole society from the *straight path (road)*." Or from a letter to P. Annenkov: ". . . We are all going to the same goal, but we each have our own road." In "An Author's Confession": "The world is on the road, not in a haven."

It could not disappear, because it was nourished by the anomaly of Russian reality (and not only Russian: Gogol did not appeal to the experience of all human history by chance). The writer analytically dissected that reality and investigated it with artistic sobriety, almost scientifically.

In his book *Gogol*, Voronsky notes quite justly: "After 'Viy,' the fantastic in Gogol almost disappears. But this is a strange and wondrous matter: Reality itself turns somehow transparent and from time to time appears to be fantastic. This fantastic character gives reality its frightening faces, its pig's snouts, the mixture of the inanimate with the human, its revolting refuse." [5] We need only to add, speaking of *Dead Souls*, that the fantastic begins with the style itself, with the illogicality of the descriptions and the alternating levels. It develops with the very plot of the poem, the history of Chichikov's "negotiations" and the attitude of the province's inhabitants to his dealings.

The rational and the grotesque form two poles of the poem, between which its whole artistic system unfolds. In *Dead Souls*, which in general is constructed by contrast, there are also other poles: the epic and the lyric (condensed, in particular, in the so-called lyric digressions); satire and comedy, and tragedy. I dwell in detail only on the first "contrast," because it is especially important for the whole structure of the poem and because the other two have been more or less fully explicated in the literature on Gogol.

V. V. GIPPIUS

An Introduction to *Dead Souls*†

I

Dead Souls was not an ordinary, run-of-the-mill work for Gogol. It was conceived as a work of exceptional significance: for the scope of life depicted in it ("All Russia will

5. *Novy Mir*, no. 8, 1964, p. 229. Voronsky's book *Gogol*, which came out in the mid-1930s in the series "The Lives of Remarkable People," exists in only a few copies. I cite from the excerpts in *Novy Mir*. [Alexander Voronsky was a Soviet critic and magazine editor who was influential in the 1920s. He was purged in 1928, arrested in 1937, and died in 1943, probably in a prison camp—*Editor*.]
† Translated by Thomas Seifrid from *Ot Pushkina do Bloka* [From Pushkin to Blok] (Moscow-Leningrad, 1966), pp. 123–45. Vasily Gippius, born in 1890, was professor of literary history at Perm University in 1922 and later worked at the Institute of Russian Literature in Leningrad. His book on Gogol was published in 1924. It has been called "one of the very best things ever written about Gogol" (Donald Fanger). Gippius is reported to have died during the Nazi siege of Leningrad in World War II.

appear in it"); for its place among Gogol's works ("This will be my first decent creation"); and, perhaps, for its place in Russian literature in general. As Gogol himself attested in his *Author's Confession,* it was Pushkin who led him to the idea of writing a "grand work." The example cited by Pushkin—Cervantes' [1] literary fate before and after writing *Don Quixote*—shows that the meaning of his advice pertained not to the size of the work alone, but also to the significance of its contents: Pushkin was requiring of Gogol a Russian epic equivalent to *Don Quixote.* This is how Gogol took the advice ("This time I myself have become seriously pensive"). The very subject of speculating in dead souls (suggested by the realities of serfdom) Pushkin "gave away" to Gogol as one that would allow him "the full freedom to traverse all of Russia with his hero and depict a multitude of the most varied characters." Continued Gogol: "I was going to begin writing without setting myself any detailed plan, without having taken into account what, precisely, the hero himself should be. I simply thought the humorous project that Chichikov undertakes would in itself lead me to varied persons and characters and that the very desire to laugh, originating within me, would itself create a multitude of humorous phenomena, which I intended to blend with touching ones." This design can have pertained only to the earliest stages of the work. A trace of it remtains in Gogol's letter to Pushkin of 7 October 1835 (prior to the writing of *The Inspector General*): "I have begun writing *Dead Souls.* The subject has stretched itself into a most lengthy novel and, it seems, will be tremendously funny. But now I have stopped it at the third chapter. I am looking for a good informer with whom I could share a brief intimacy: In this novel I want to show all of Russia, at least from one side." Obviously, neither the size, nor the plan, nor the scope of the contents, nor the general tone of the work was completely clear to the author himself in 1835. The design unfolded gradually. In the letter to Pushkin, Gogol speaks only of the "humorous subject," but in the *Author's Confession* he continued his reminiscence thus: "After *The Inspector General* I felt more than ever before the need to write a full work, which would contain not only that which deserves laughter." In the letter to Pushkin, the portrayal of Russia "at least from one side" was conceived; in the

1. Miguel Cervantes (1547–1616), Spanish author of the novel *Don Quixote* [*Editor*].

letters of 1836 written from abroad (to Zhukovsky and Pogodin), it is stated without this reservation that "all Russia" will be reflected in *Dead Souls*. In general, the letters written in 1836 during Gogol's journey already re-sound with an awareness of the whole immensity of the work he had undertaken. They make clear both the social content of the design and its denunciatory nature, which promised an unavoidable conflict ("The new social classes and many various people will rise up against me—but what am I to do! It is my fate to be at enmity with my fellow countrymen!"). The letters also make clear the pecu-liar genre of the work—neither a tale nor a novel, but a poem (the letter to Pogodin from Paris, 18 November 1836).

The early version of *Dead Souls* begun in Petersburg and continued in Switzerland and Paris has not survived to our day (at least, not completely). Of the first chapters of this version, we know only what Gogol wrote in his *"Four Letters to Divers Persons Apropos Dead Souls."* Ac-cording to Gogol, in them he prosecuted "with malice, mockery, and whatever came to hand" the stupid human traits of people of various "callings" and "walks of life." [2] Here, evidently, the satirical demands took precedence over those of objective description. In a later self-evaluation this satire became a "caricature" and "my own invention." But these very satirical images struck Pushkin as onerous and caused him to proclaim, "God, how dreary is our Russia!" One might tentatively compare with this early, sharply satirical plan portions of the last chapters of the earliest-known version. They are distinguished by a par-ticularly personal tone, and the author, speaking of himself in the first person and entering into spontaneous conver-sation with the reader, in fact frequently shifts from an ironic tone to one of anger ("I'm stubborn, and don't want to look at those kinds of faces one should spit at"). At times the satirical portrayals of people have an intentionally gro-tesque character ("How many there are of the sort who do not at all look like people! This one is a perfect dog dressed up in tails," and so forth).

2. In "Four Letters to Divers Persons Apropos *Dead Souls*," this method is connected with the need to rid one's own self of bad traits. It should be recalled that Gogol wrote the *Four Letters* under the influence of his later ideas and moods, and it is pos-sible that he subjected his own past to stylization. But even here the poem's denunciatory content is not completely derived from self-denunci-ation: ". . . I began to endow my characters with my own rubbish, in addition to their own filth." [These letters appear on pp. 411—24 of this volume—*Editor*.]

After recounting Pushkin's reaction, Gogol continues: "From that time I began to think how I might assuage that onerous impression *Dead Souls* was capable of producing. I saw that many of the foul things did not deserve malice— better to show their utter paltriness." The words "from that time" cannot be considered exact, but the nature of the change in Gogol's plan is faithfully conveyed: The basic content of *Dead Souls* became precisely the portrayal of "paltriness" or, using the expression of the same article, of "the vulgarity of a vulgar man." But this in general was the basic feature of Gogol's works: Gogol's own definition covers not only *Dead Souls,* but also *The Inspector General, Marriage,* the tales of everyday life in *Mirgorod,* and the Petersburg tales.

In the process of its composition, the first volume of *Dead Souls* was stylistically reworked several times, but neither the general plan nor the descriptions of the characters underwent any significant changes. It was not the plan of the first volume that evolved substantially from 1836 to 1841, but that of the entire poem. The sequel began to assume more and more significance for Gogol; this is reflected in part in the text of the first volume, especially in the text of the aesthetic declaration at the beginning of chapter 7 (on the two types of writers.) A revealing piece of evidence of Gogol's work on *Dead Souls* is contained in a letter written from Rome to S. T. Aksakov on 28 December 1840: "I am now preparing the first volume of *Dead Souls* for a complete cleaning. I rearrange, I polish, much of it I rework. At the same time its further continuation emerges more purely and majestically in my mind, and I now see that with time perhaps something colossal will come of it, if only my weak powers permit it. At any rate, surely there are few who know to what powerful thoughts and profound revelations one can be led by an insignificant subject, the first innocent and humble chapters of which you already know." Even as the first volume was being published, Gogol still more decisively wrote to Zhukovsky (on 36 June 1842) that the first volume seemed to him only the porch, hastily added to the palace, "which is intended to be built in colossal dimensions." Promises of two further volumes found their way into the text of the first; these were to contain yet "unstruck chords" and the portrayal of radiant scenes and positive heroes.

All this led Gogol's contemporaries to the idea of searching the design of *Dead Souls* for parallels to that of the *Divine Comedy*. Herzen compared the first volume with the *Inferno* (in his diary for 1842)[3]; later, Viazemsky wrote of the two parts of the sequel as the corresponding *Purgatorio* and *Paradiso*.[4] By no means can this parallel, which subsequently became popular, be fully accepted. In general it has no relation whatsoever to Gogol's original plan. Only later did the moralistic idea of a "purgatory" dominate Gogol's consciousness. But in the second part of the poem, know to us in fragments, there is nothing resembling a "purgatory" for Gogol's characters. The plan for a "purgatory" can be linked only with the projected, but unwritten, third part.

Neither can an objectively historical evaluation of *Dead Souls* accept Gogol's definition of the first volume as only the "porch" to the poem's sequel. We perceive the first volume of Dead Souls as a complete and unified work that may be discussed independently of the further plan, all the more so since this volume was the only one to become a living literary event in its time. The second volume, on which Gogol worked after his self-avowed "abrupt turnabout," requires special examination in relation to the ideas later formulated by Gogol and to his later works.

II

Gogol defined his conception of *Dead Souls* and its place in the development of his creative work in the following words: "The new social classes will rise up against me" and "All Russia will appear in it." "New social classes" meant primarily landowners; perhaps in the original plan for the sequel, other "social classes" were intended as well. Society in Gogol's consciousness fell precisely into "social classes," not according to any judicial features, nor according to any genuine features of class, but according to those of cultural *milieu* and everyday life. In this sense, the high society of the nobility, the noble officials, and the noble landowners were for him separate social classes. He particularly singles out the "middle class . . . which lives on its salary" (in the article "The Petersburg Stage"). But in Gogol's plan "all Russia" meant not simply the sum of various social classes. Gogol strove not only for the variety of everyday life, but first and foremost for generalizations.

3. Passages from Herzen's diaries are translated above, pp.458–59 [*Editor*].   4. *Russky Arkhiv*, VII, 1866.

Dead Souls became a poem about "all Russia" first because all the separate depictions are given in their relation to the whole—to Russia—whereby the artistic image of Russia is formed; second, because the poem reflects the basic social contradiction of Gogol's contemporary reality: serfdom. *Dead Souls* is a poem about the Russia of serfdom and its ruling class, the serf-owning landowners. Here the Russia of landowners and peasants is revealed at its foundations; and neither the absence from the poem of sociological questions in the narrow sense of the word (i.e., the questioning of the institution of serfdom) nor the author's primary attention to depicting the landowners in any way contradicts this. By means of his entire artistic method, including both realistic analysis and synthesis, humor and lyricism, Gogol succeeded in unmasking the Russia of serfdom. In *Dead Souls,* as in *The Inspector General,* Gogol did not succeed in reaching the roots of social life; in those years neither as theoretician nor as artist did he pose the question of these roots. But as in *The Inspector General,* in *Dead Souls* the most progressive solutions to the social problems broached in the poem are supported by the entire structure of the poem's artistic means. Gogol had every reason to believe that after *Dead Souls* the "new social classes will rise up" against him.

Gogol constructs his poem according to two plans. The first and most evident is the psychological: the task of "depicting a multitude of the most varied characters." All the major characters are attached to the *milieu* of the landowners. But the significance of Gogol's characters outstrips their original social categorization. Manilovism, Nozdrevism, and Chichikovism (as well as Khlestakovism) acquire significance as broad, typifying generalities. This is not only the result of historical reevaluation; the generalized nature of the types was foreseen in the author's original plan. Gogol mentions this in relation to nearly all of his characters.

The Gogolian method of typifying generalities has nothing in common with that of abstract, psychological schematization. Those human traits first discovered by Gogol (such as Khlestakovism, Manilovism, Chichikovism, etc.) were originally discovered by him in concrete, everyday social conditions. For the characters of *Dead Souls,* these are the conditions of the everyday lives of remotely provincial, serf-owning landowners (while at the same time each character possesses a distinctly individual background). But it was clear to Gogol that reality produces variations of the types he had discovered—in conditions that are not exactly the same, but similar for each variant. This is made particularly clear in the chapter on Sobakievich, where he, with his power over peasants, is compared to a Petersburg bureaucrat who has power over other bureaucrats. All the possible parallels to the main characters, both those directly pointed out and those merely suggested, significantly expand the content of the poem and include in it whole stretches of Russian life.

The second plan according to which the poem is built (which includes the first, psychological plan) is the historical one. Each of Gogol's character types is historical because each is marked with the features of its age. Along with enduring historical phenomena, all of them reflect newly arisen phenomena (Chichikov, for example, is the acquisitive man of the new type). The whole Gogolian image of Russia, composed by combining and interpreting specific images, is placed in the perspective of historical development. Gogol had only the development of Russia in mind; but independent of his intentions, his images acquired an enduring historical significance, not only on a national but on an international scale as well. Chernyshevsky aptly indicated the existence of German Manilovs and English Chichikovs.

The tasks Gogol set himself could not have found full expression in the form of a novel, be it a novel of travel, a novel of picaresque adventures, or a novel of manners. All these elements entered the plot design to varying degrees, but neither separately nor collectively did they exhaust it. The novel, even in the latest broad and encompassing form that had at that time been developed by European literatures (of the kind written by Sir Walter Scott), inevitably remained within the boundaries of a portrayal of persons and events. There was no place in it for a generalized image of a people and a country, nor for an image of the author as a versatile yet deeply subjective poet who pronounces his judgments and his meditations with his evaluation of the present and his dream of the future. Proceeding from these tasks (which did not repudiate but included an intensified portrayal of real life), it was necessary to create a special genre: a large epic form broader than the novel. Gogol did call *Dead Souls* a poem, and by no means in jest, as hostile critics claimed. It is no coincidence that on the cover of *Dead Souls* drawn by Gogol himself the word "poem" is set in especially large letters.[5]

Gogol's intentions are made clearer by the theoretical meditations in his *Textbook of Literature* [*for Russian Youth*]. Here it is directly stated that "the novel does not take in all of life, but a remarkable event in life." In Gogol's understanding the novel approaches drama in its principles of selection and the distribution of its material: In the novel, persons and events are united around the fate of the hero and "that which flies past the scene" finds no place in it.

Different problems are posed by the epic, which "embraces not just certain features, but an entire epoch of time in which there acts a hero with the type of thoughts, beliefs, and even confessions that mankind made at that time." The epic requires a hero of historical significance. There may also arise, on the other hand, "minor epic genres" without this condition. Under this rubric Gogol wrote:

> In modern times there has emerged a type of narrative work that constitutes a sort of middle ground between the novel and the epic, the hero of which is a private and insignificant figure, but one who is nonetheless significant in many respects for the observer of the human soul. The author leads his life through a chain of adventures and changes in order to present, along with a hero, a true-to-life picture of that which is significant in the traits and mores of the time he has chosen: that earthy, almost statistically grasped picture of shortcomings, abuses, faults, and all he has noticed in the chosen epoch and time. . . . Such phenomena have appeared from time to time among many peoples. Many of these incidents, though written in prose, may nonetheless be considered poetic works. It is not the whole world that is portrayed, but there is often a full epic range of remarkable individual phenomena.

There can be no doubt that these lines, written after the completion of the first volume of *Dead Souls* and during work on the second, represent Gogol's own commentary on his poem. He names Ariosto[6] and Cervantes as authors of the "minor epic genres." Both these authors are mentioned in the early versions of *Dead Souls* as Gogol's literary mentors, along with Shakespeare, Fielding, and Pushkin, with a general characterization of all five

---

5. This cover, or frontispiece, drawn by Gogol himself, is reproduced on p. ix , above [*Editor*].

6. Ludovico Ariosto (1474–1533), Italian author of the epic *Orlando Furioso* and other works [*Editor*].

authors: He speaks of them as having "reflected nature as it is." Thus as early as the first conception of *Dead Souls,* Cervantes' *Don Quixote* was Gogol's model.

A "full epic range" demanded that Gogol draw together diverse material. For Gogol this task of achieving completeness and "faithfulness" was characteristically associated with unmasking: First place among the "traits and mores of the time" is occupied by "shortcomings, abuses, and faults." The author not only depicts but evaluates the depicted as well. His methods of evaluation are multifarious. First among them, as in the earlier tales and comedies, is the method of humor: The vulgar is presented as humorous. But the more substantial the side of life portrayed, the more complex the forms in which the author's humor appears and the more his laughter is "diluted by bitterness" (as Belinsky noted regarding "The Diary of a Madman"). While in the objective depictions the author maintains a tone of calm, epic humor and his tears remain, as Gogol expressed it, "unseen," the author reserves the freedom to alternate whenever necessary from the tone of narrator and ironic commntator to the personal tone of a lyrical poet. In doing so he correspondingly varies all the linguistic means, changing from the language of everyday conversation in the variety of its dialects to that of the elevated lyric and the sermon. The form of a "minor epic genre" allows this lyrical-epic variety of tones. The image of the author, who is narrator and poet in one person, is the carrier of this variety.

III

Character types should naturally occupy the primary (though not the only) place in the design of a poem of "full epic range." That the creation of typical characters was Gogol's conscious task is evident from the structure of the poem. Of its eleven chapters, six represent sketches of particular characters; moreover, beginning with the second chapter, the poem presents what amounts to a "portrait gallery," with accentuated attention given to each portrait individually. It is natural that in a denunciatory poem about the Russia of serfdom, the character types of serf-owning landowners take precedence. This is what Gogol does, presenting, after the first chapter of general exposition, five consecutive chapters on Manilov, Korobochka, Nozdrev, Sobakievich, and Plyushkin.

Gogol steadfastly uses the same method he used in creating the character Khlestakov.[7] He rejects typicality in its usual meaning—in the sense of reproducing "from nature" actually existing persons who are taken as models, if only for their characteristic traits, i.e., for the frequency of those traits' occurrence. Still more decidedly does he reject the method of schematization, of constructing a character from one feature. The great innovative significance of Gogol's method of character portrayal lies precisely in his not portraying the character on the basis of certain "traits," but discovering new human attributes.

The first detailed description in the poem begins with an ironic but declarative introduction on the difficulty of characterizing such "gentlemen" as Manilov, and on the necessity of a special method, a special "science of extraction" in order to catch "all the fine, nearly invisible features." The creation of a large, typical generalization from the depiction of a person who is "neither one thing nor the other," of a person "without any temperament," of a person of the minutest psychological dimension was one of Gogol's most remarkable achievements. This could be accomplished only by a principled refusal to build characters from "traits." Of course, even Manilov has his particular negative attributes: He is a do-nothing, an idle dreamer, a cloying phrasemonger. But these are all traits derived from his general social characterization. Using Gogol's notions and even his expressions, one may define this social basis as "the emptiness and impotent idleness of life," a "stagnant world." Historically, the same notions may be interpreted as a social inertia arising from the parasitism of serfdom. Not only do Manilov's affairs "somehow get along on their own," but even his personal behavior is defined by none other than social inertia. Analyzing the impression produced by Manilov, Gogol with subtlest humor distinguishes three moments: "In the first minute of conversation you cannot but say, 'What a pleasant and kind man!' The next minute you say nothing, and the third you say, 'What the hell is this?' and back away from him; and if you don't back away you'll feel mortal boredom." This scheme is supported by the entire contents of the chapter. The impression of pleasantness is connected with that form of everyday culture in which the image of Manilov

7. The central character of Gogol's stage comedy *The Inspector General* (1836) [*Editor*].

appears. It is a shallow but inoffensive form of sentimental imitation that has passed from literature into everyday life, reaching even the provincial estates. This provincial sentimentalism is expressed not only in the "temples of solitude" and idle daydreaming most frequently associated with Manilovism (of course, this is because this trait has turned out to be the most enduring). Very characteristic is the whole tender "friendship" between Manilov and Chichikov, with its high-flown phrases ("a saint's-day of the heart") and tears "glimmering" in their eyes. All this parodies not so much literary sentimentalism as sentimentalism in everyday life.

The sensitive nature of the character Manilov turns out to be an empty shell. This is revealed in the second minute of acquaintance: "You say nothing," because the essence of this character is emptiness, "neither one thing nor the other." But in the third minute repulsive traits are discovered behind this lack of any personality and at its base: an eagerness to agree with anything at all, to move from any push in any direction—all precisely the result of an inherent lack of content.

One variation of this aspect of Manilovism is the character Mizhnev. Mizhnev's outer wrapping is different—he has the temper of a debator—but behind it one discovers the same essence. It is said of people like Mizhnev that they always "agree to what they had repudiated: The stupid man they will call clever and then go tripping merrily to another man's tune; in short, they will start on the level and end up on the crook."

Of all the typifying generalizations created by Gogol, besides the notion of Khlestakovism, that of Manilovism has entered the general consciousness and the Russian language itself in a particularly lasting way. Manilovism, unmasked by Gogol in its most organic surroundings (amidst the parasitic idleness of the landowners' estates), remains for us to this day a symbol of human attributes that thwart productive labor from within.

Korobochka's character is endowed with less generalizing power. It is a remarkable image of a petty, backwater landlady, in all the concreteness of her everyday life, notions, habits, and of the attributes of a primitive businesslike nature and simpleminded fear of the new and of unclean spirits. Korobochka's image is necessary to the poem not only for its own sake, but also for connections and comparisons. Her simpleminded lack of culture sets off Manilov's pretensions to culturedness, as well as other false glitters of culture, such as the lady aristocrat who awaits behind her unfinished book "the visit of some witty society caller." Korobochka's "blockheaded" obstinacy also turns into an occasion for a brief portrait of "another respectable and official personage." But in drawing all these parallels and having the author pose the question of "whether Korobochka's place in life is really so low in the infinite scale of human perfection," Gogol refrains from accentuating those of Korobochka's qualities and positive traits to which there are hints in one of the drafts. Gogol was particularly inclined to these by the Slavophile Shevyrev.[8] He rejected this idea, limiting Korobochka's "attributes" to purely negative traits and preserving the unity of a denunciatory tone for the images of all his landowners.

In Nozdrev's image Gogol again touched on the theme of Khlestakovism, not only in that both characters lie, but also in that both are capable of acting as if they are unaccountable to anyone. In Nozdrev this Khlestakovian quality is developed to the extreme: not only does he lie "completely without any necessity," but he plays dirty tricks on his closest friends "without any good reason for it." Nozdrevism differs from Khlestakovism in that, in *Dead Souls* as opposed to in *The Inspector General,* the theme of a person's behavior is generally more complex and intensified. *The Inspector General* is constructed around an isolated incident that forces the collective of officials to band together in self-defense; Khlestakov passively submits to this general excitement. In *Dead Souls* the characters are presented in epic manner, and nuances of character may be found in each of them. Manilov and Korobochka differ in the cultural features of their everyday lives, but they absorb equally passively the norms of social life. Nozdrev's social behavior is reflected energetically and with contradictions: The elemental instinct to associate with other people appears in his case in wild, essentially antisocial forms. Nozdrev is humorous in that he embodies in its most superficial and completely debased form the leaven of an old, grand-scale feudal lord, greedy for feasts and even battles. The feasts are replaced by an elementary drunkenness and prodigality; and the battles by "birching

8. Stepan Shevyrev (1806–64), a Slavophile literary critic and historian, professor at the University of Moscow [*Editor*].

the landowner Maximov while he was drunk," by his attempt at beating up Chichikov, and so on. It is characteristic that Nozdrev's "vassals," the houseserfs Porfiry and Pavlushka, take part in his reprisals. Only rarely does the anarchical, feudal element show up in violent outbursts; in the new social conditions Nozdrev easily becomes a "historical person"—a common scoundrel and a cheat.

Nozdrev's character is dependent on his social profile, which is that of a landowner of the transitional era. But the author also indicates the most important of Nozdrev's "anarchical," antisocial features, his ability inexplicably to "play dirty tricks on his closest friends" in the wider sphere of the society of serfowners, mentioning how vile the behavior of a "person of rank . . . with a star on his breast" can be. He also mentions in general that Nozdrev is "everywhere in our midst, though, perhaps, in a different suit; but imperceptive people are thoughtless, and a man in a different suit seems to them a different man." That Nozdrev is prodigal and predatory in his own affairs thus is far from being the most characteristic of his traits; here, as elsewhere, the condition of the nobility's estates is not the basic theme of the poem.

Sobakievich contrasts with Nozdrev, though his character is every bit as monstrous. But Sobakievich's monstrousness does not exceed that which in the everyday life of serfdom passes for "normal." In his "animallike" appearance there is not one human feature, save his practical sense (which is, incidentally, so elementary and utilitarian that it does not affect the nature of his character). Nozdrev's antisocial features are moderated by a sort of vague social instinct; Sobakievich is portrayed as a convinced misanthrope. The exception he makes for Chichikov is motivated in the poem by the attributes of Chichikov himself—his peculiar talent for being "pleasant." Sobakievich's inordinate gluttony is presented, of course, not as a traditional, one-dimensional literary type of mask, but as a feature indicative of his generally animal quality. This impression of something inhumanly soulless is intensified by the comparison made with a piece of wood to which "nature has paid little heed," that is, with an object of the setting, and intensified especially by the comparison with a bear. The comparison of Sobakievich with a bear is widely known; less attention has been paid to one of its particular details: At the moment of his deal with Chichikov, Sobakievich is compared to a bear "who had been trained in the art of turning somersaults and doing various tricks." This qualification refers to Sobakievich's external manners, to a "certain deftness," but this deftness is given a psychological basis: Sobakievich is deft when it comes to profit. And if his basic bearlike qualities correspond to the stagnant everyday life of the feudal estate, then his "deftness," bearlike as it may be, in itself reveals a knack for adapting naturally to the conditions of the new "mercantile" age.

Sobakievich's animalistic, bearlike qualities also have their variations: There are Sobakieviches outside the backwater provincial estates. Chichikov thinks of this after they conclude their bargain. He prefers a bear of a village *kulak* [9] to that of a clerk in the capital who "snaps his fingers at his inferiors or dips into the public funds." In one of the drafts for the novel, Gogol himself agrees with this, noting that "the scoundrel Sobakievich, who is far from being noble in spirit or emotions, at least did not ruin his peasants or make lazybones or drunkards out of them." However, it was precisely Chichikov whom Gogol convincingly had discover Sobakievich's purely utilitarian motives ("they belong to you, and you would be worse off if you did maltreat them.")

The distortion of human appearance is portrayed statically in Nozdrev and Chichikov. In Plyushkin it is portrayed in its development. Up until his sudden change Plyushkin is "merely . . . a thrifty proprietor" with the qualities of "a mind, experience, a knowledge of the world," "industriousness," and "wise stinginess." These qualities by themselves would not be so far from those of Sobakievich, but in Plyushkin's case it becomes possible for the first time to raise the question of human emotions. Precisely that—only to raise it. Even earlier Plyushkin's feelings were neither weak nor strong ("No great intensity of feeling was observable in his face," and "With every minute the human feelings, of which he had never had a great store, diminished"). The most natural feelings "diminish" in him: With ease he curses first his daughter, then his son, having ceased to have any interest in them. He has wholeheartedly submitted to the inertia of material cares, which have grown up into miserliness and petty predation, to the extent of robbing his peasants of insignificant items. This path is shown as the gradual loss

9. Russian for "rich peasant" (literally, "fist") [*Editor*].

of everything human, as the degradation of a man. Here are given the psychological and even the thematic premises for Shchedrin's [1] Gogolian chronicle.

Plyushkin's is the most depressing portrait in the Gogolian gallery of ugly landowners; here the comic depiction passes over into the tragicomic grotesque. Here Gogol no longer draws lines to other social variants; on the contrary, he speaks of the "rarity" in Russian life of such a phenomenon as Plyushkin. But, of course, if Plyushkin is an exception, then (to use Kliuchevsky's expression)[2] he is a "typical exception": Plyushkin's degradation, his complete falling away from social ties, and the entire psychology that arises on the basis of that degradation are natural to the life of a serfowner. The image of Plyushkin is especially carefully surrounded with the details of social and everyday life. Not only is he characterized by his talk of the peasants who have died of hunger, not only does he himself speak of his fugitive souls, but in the scenes with Proshka and Mavra he is graphically shown to be an oppressor. These scenes are all the more striking because they are presented as regular scenes of everyday life.

In creating the character of Plyushkin, Gogol followed the path of least resistance by addressing the theme of stinginess. He gave a new, very significant solution to this theme. Plyushkin's stinginess is not a congenital trait, but the result of his personal and social fate; it is not an inherent but a derived characteristic, which is all the more indicative of the process of degradation portrayed in him. The struggle within Plyushkin between his habitual stinginess and the remnants of other feelings is shown with great subtlety. Thus, not even to Plyushkin can one apply a definition of the Gogolian method as one of moral sententiousness, of reducing each character type to one feature.

Chichikov is not simply one portrait in a series of others, but the one conceived as the poem's central image. This complicates an analysis of his character type: in the first place, because he is frequently given the auxiliary role of uniting the poem's elements (though sometimes the role of the author's surrogate seems utterly impossible for him); in the second place, because it is announced in the first volume that his image is not yet complete. But since the

1. Mikhail Saltykov-Shchedrin (1826–89), author of *The Golovlyovs* and other works of fiction satirizing the corruption of nineteenth-century Russian characters [*Editor*].

2. Vasily Kliuchevsky (1841–1911), famous historian, author of a five-volume history of Russia [*Editor*].

first volume is to a certain degree artistically complete, one may discuss Chichikov on the basis of its material. This is all the more true because the material in the second volume does not contradict the image in the first, and the meager information given about the novel's projected sequel contradicts the data of both the first and the second volumes so strikingly as to require special explanation in regard to Gogol's further literary evolution.

Special attention falls, of course, on Chichikov. The basic outline of his portrait is already sketched out in the first chapter; what follows develops and fills it in. Finally, to Chichikov is dedicated a special monographic chapter, the eleventh. In the first chapter Chichikov is revealed more by his generic than by his individual characteristics: For the time being, he is one of Gogol's many inert beings, whose emptiness is covered with an outer gloss. Revealing details of behavior and everyday life portray this emptiness (the day's routine, the torn poster, the contents of the trunk). These are all new variations on the portrayals in the Mirgorod and Petersburg tales. But Chichikov's outer gloss differs significantly from those of Khlestakov and Kovalev,[3] and even of Manilov, who is depicted at the beginning of the same chapter. Here Gogol has not simply applied a veneer of everyday traditions for fashion's sake, but he has expertly constructed a mask. As early as the first chapter, Chichikov appears endowed with the traits of a particularly flexible adaptability and at the same time with a persistence, behind the two of which hides his later revealed "passion." It is these combinations that set Chichikov's portrait apart from the others in Gogol's series.

These qualities are connected with Chichikov's social profile and social behavior. Chichikov's family tree, discovered in the eleventh chapter (his parents were of the nobility, but "God alone knows whether they were so by descent or by personal merit"), is not as important as the entire portrait of him and its whole function in the poem. Chichikov, the owner of two living souls and a few hundred dead ones, is a foreign body in the landowners' milieu, an imposter who does nothing but strive for and dream about the social norm. Gogol used the individual character of Chichikov as a symptom of large social changes that he was diagnosing, as an indication that "all has long ago changed

---

3. Character in Gogol's comical-fantastical story *The Nose* (1835), who temporarily loses his nose [*Editor*].

in society," that among the movers of society the "electricity" of monetary capital occupies first place (the article "After the Theater"). With great social perspicacity, Gogol made the clash of two social phenomena the basis of his poem: the old foundations of the serf-owning estate and the new "electricity" of capital. This motif of conflict anticipates the comic content of the plot. This is natural, since the conflict is shown in its early stages, in unripe and therefore paradoxical forms. Chichikov's character combines the comic nature of an innovation that has yet to take shape with that of an antiquity that has outlived its time. The Chichikovs of this world bring nothing essentially new into everyday life, nor into psychology, still less into ideology. Each new scene promises only a new variant of the "dark kingdom" of the landowners. Thus through this image of a hero of base gain and in the theme of Chichikov's speculation, Gogol anticipates the character types of Derunov and Razuvaev and the theme of *The Refuge Mon Repos*.[4]

The social and historical particulars of Chichikov's character determine also his personal traits. As opposed to those characters who either do not act at all or who act "completely . . . without any reason for it," Chichikov acts consciously and with an exact goal. As opposed to those "with no temperament whatsoever" or with a senseless temperament, in Chichikov there is "a passion which draws him on." This passion is a base one, incapable of making Chichikov a positive hero even in part; but taken abstractly, such attributes as "energy" and "activity" appear positive. It is this contradiction that complicates the image of Chichikov in chapter 11, where the author enigmatically hints that "perhaps the passion that impelled Chichikov himself was not derived from within him" and hints at "yet another mystery, that of the reason why this type of hero figures in the poem that is now seeing the light of day." This "mystery" is partly explained by one of Gogol's biographers, who heard from Gogol himself that the poem was to conclude with "Chichikov's first sigh" of longing for a new

---

4. *The Refuge Mon Repos (Ube-zhishche Monrepo)* (1878–79) is a satirical work by Mikhail Saltykov-Shchedrin. *Mon Repos* is French for "My Rest" or "My Repose," a banal name for a cottage. Derunov (cognate with the Russian root for "skinning," hence something like Mr. Skinner) and Razuvaev (cognate with the word for "strip" or "take off shoes," hence something like Mr. Strip-them) are names of two of Saltykov-Shchedrin's typed characters, through whom he satirized the greed, selfishness, and cruelty of merchants and other nouveau-riche Russians [*Editor*].

life. This was written in the last years of Gogol's life, at a time when his religious moralism was becoming more intense; whether or not this finale was in accordance with the original plan for the poem, we do not know. This motif of rebirth does not fit in with the image of Chichikov in the first volume: There is no foreshadowing of it. True, in the same eleventh chapter (in the episode with the sick teacher), the author explains that his hero's nature is not so severe and callous, nor his feelings so dulled, that he should know neither pity nor sympathy. But, as is clear from what follows, this explanation is ironic, its meaning being that "nature" is impotent before the influences of one's environment and the habits of social behavior. Nowhere does Gogol base his hero's behavior on "nature" alone, nor does he do so here. The paternal instruction to "guard" every kopeck and fawn upon the rich; the passion for "life in all its enjoyments," supported by the examples of plebeians who have made it rich (the rich clerk); the experience of having served in positions of varying caliber; and, finally, the general atmosphere of Russian bureaucracy and serfdom: All this turns out to have a greater effect on Chichikov than his "nature," which is furthermore characterized only negatively, as the absence of "severity" and "callousness." In the novel's main plot, Chichikov appears completely "callous," beyond any human sympathies whatsoever. The single, intentional exception is Chichikov's nervousness at the ball upon meeting the governor's daughter; but the subtle analysis made in this episode requires special reservation, even to the point of renaming common human emotions: "It cannot be said with any certainty that our hero was overcome by the feeling of love; it is even doubtful whether gentry of that sort, that is to say, those who are neither too fat nor yet too thin, are capable of love, but taking everything into consideration, there was something strange here, something of a nature he could hardly explain."

Gogol firmly and convincingly binds Chichikov's character to his social biography. But, as in other instances, this does not impoverish the meaning of the character type. Chichikovism is defined by a passion for "life in all its enjoyments" and a readiness to use any means to achieve this goal, from common adaptability to eccentric speculations. In the end Chichikovism is defined by the process of capitalization. The power of money and its psychological results could have been revealed in various social and biographical variants, though they would have been less revealing than Chichikov's biography. Gogol himself underscores the general meaning of Chichikovism: "And who among you . . . will ponder this weighty question in the depths of his soul: 'Is there not a chip of Chichikov in me too?'"

In the chapter on Korobochka a parallel is drawn from typical bureaucratic relations to Chichikov's character and to the motif of his adaptability: "Ivan Petrovich" (also a typifying generalization) is an eagle among his inferiors, but a chicken in the office of his superior. Chichikov himself is also shown as an official wholly typical of bureaucratic Russia: the Chichikov of chapter 11 is a direct variant of the characters in *The Inspector General,* but he is more refined than the simpleminded provincial powers depicted there. In Chichikov the traits of an experienced bribe-taking official are combined with those of an adventurer of the new type, but he dreams of becoming a landowner, at first (in part 1) in name, then (in part 2) in reality. All this makes Chichikov the synthesizing figure in the denunciatory plan of *Dead Souls.*

IV

The six especially emphasized portraits present the concentration of the basic "denunciatory material" and the basic social-psychological problems raised in the novel. This is the foreground, behind which there are several more planes; the poem's genre allows free arrangment of this material.

The characters next on the scale of attention paid them by the author are Chichikov's servants, Selifan and Petrushka. For Gogol to turn immediately from Petrushka to Selifan requires ironic excuses, that special device of authorial "lapsing into silence" ("But knowing as he does by experience how unwilling they are to acquaint themselves with low society, the author hesitates in taking up so much of the reader's time with people of base origin"). Gogol also uses this method later, where he finds it necessary to break abruptly with tradition. Indeed, literature of the nobility traditionally either excluded servants or presented them with the intention of idealizing them morally or, on the contrary, caricaturing them. Not bowing to tradition, Gogol simply made Selifan a good-natured *raisonneur,* and Petrushka a distinctive parallel to Chichikov, both by contrast and similarity: Chichikov's cultural level is not far from that of Petrushka; as "readers" they closely resemble one another, and only in neatness does the collegiate assessor surpass his serf.

Gogol repeats the ironic method of "lapsing into silence" when he proceeds to the provincial ladies. With them it was necessary for him to break with the traditions of the society tale and the novel in still another regard, by deflating and debunking the cliché of the genteel heroine. New apologies preface the remarkable images of the two ladies, Anna Grigorievna, the lady pleasant in all respects, and Sofia Ivanovna, the simply pleasant lady. Despite their episodic roles, these two feminine types have become nominal; their generalized labels, which have stuck to them better than their first names and patronymics, of course, contribute to this. Provincial grande dames and gossips had been satirized a hundred times over in eighteen-century satire, but didactic satire was unable to lend any lifelike character to these types. Gogol does this, not only by masterfully reproducing their peculiar "dialect," but also by creating complete characters. Sofia Ivanovna, in spreading the news brought by Korobochka, is herself a variant of Korobochka ("She only knew how to be disturbed, but she lacked the wherewithal to form any clear hypothesis"); while Anna Grigorievna, in reaching "with her own mind" the conclusion that upsets "the whole town," is a variation of the know-it-alls and gossips in *The Inspector General.*

The overall picture of the provincial town recedes somewhat into the background. Here, where the theme of "all Russia" appears, it would be inappropriate to lend primary importance to a picture of the town and a characterization of its inhabitants. The collective portrait of society is more vivid than any separate portraits because of the major attention paid to "mores" instead of to separate persons. Relatively greater attention is paid to the chief of police, Aleksei Ivanovich, as to a type indicative of the whole life of the provincial town. A curious parallel to the town's governor, this "wonder-worker" and uniquely "kind bribe-taker," beloved of the citizens for being "not proud," makes one recall Gogol's words that "my characters are by no means villains: If I but add one kind feature to any one of them, the reader will make peace with all of them." This experiment (which could hardly be called possible for "any one of them") was realized in this episodic figure.

The postmaster, Ivan Andreich, also occupies a place close to the foreground, not so much because of the way he is characterized (he is a variation on Liapkin-Tiapkin,[5] that lover of "enlightenment," mystic, and author of rash hypotheses), as because it is precisely he who narrates the "Tale of Captain Kopeikin." This tale plays a more significant role than that commonly played by the novellas that, in the tradition of biographical and travel novels, were inserted to lend variety to the narration or to elucidate the author's ideas. The scenes in the capital, such as the torments of the starving invalid as he journeys from one ministry's reception room to the next, the episode with the former soldiers turned robbers, and, finally, the letter from the robber-chief to the Tsar: All this belongs in a poem about Russia and expands its social range. Moreover, Gogol finds a completely organic way to include in the poem this material that seems foreign only at first glance. In the postmaster's comic tale, the reader divines and recreates its genuine, poignantly real content through its paradoxical linguistic and psychological form.

Under the pressure of censorship, however, Gogol was forced to sacrifice the acrimony of his social satire. This acrimony is gradually weakened in the three versions of the tale known to us. The details of the thieves who rob only from public funds are dropped, as well as those of negotiations with the Tsar, and, finally, those of the bureaucracy's soullessness toward a defender of the homeland. In the censored version Kopeikin is made guilty of his own misfortunes. Though he agreed to these compromises, Gogol was not willing to cut out the tale itself. Thus there were artistic reasons for keeping the tale, independent even of the details of the hero's psychology and the degree of denunciatory acrimony. The stylistic completeness of the oral narrative style may have been one of these reasons, but probably not the decisive one. More essential was the compositional role of the tale.

The second part of the first volume represents a parodic and almost comic use of the motifs of adventure. Gogol's contemporaries likened this picture of an "excited town" to the plot of *The Inspector General*; the difference between them, however, is substantial. The mistake of the officials in *The Inspector General* unwittingly discloses their true mores and natures, including those of Khlestakov.

5. The character of a judge in Gogol's play *The Inspector General* (1836) [*Editor*].

In *Dead Souls* false rumors pile up one on top of the other, revealing for the most part stupidity and narrow-mindedness, the lack of culture in provincial society. The chain of hypotheses grows, becoming stronger with every link; but none of the characters can grasp the real Chichikov, although it would seem that each holds the key in his own hands; Chichikov steals away the governor's daughter; he is a robber; and, finally, he is a gang leader, moreover one who is missing an arm and a leg. Here absurdity reaches such extremes that even the provincial society is aware of it, but this unmasked absurdity only leads them to replace it with an even worse one: that Chichikov is Napoleon in disguise! Had the tale been omitted, this chain of absurdities would have been broken and with it the definitive collective characterization of provincial society.

The awaited arrival of the new governor-general intensifies the town's commotion, and this evokes a direct return to the motifs of *The Inspector General:* the officials' fear and the recollection of "peccadillos" resulting in the accumulation of new material for satire. The whipped noncommissioned officer is paralleled in two concisely alluded-to plots, which are tragicomically told by the author and are more horrifying than humorous: the beating of the merchants and the peasants' mock trial of the assessor Dobriazhkin. The officials themselves speak of bribes with the same faith in their social stability that is exhibited in *The Inspector General*. The scenes in the courthouse in chapter 7 also are close to a "physiological sketch" [6] about the everyday life in government offices. All these episodes and allusions, however, seem mere echoes of and variations on *The Inspector Generals* The same themes are developed much more energetically in Chichikov's biography in chapter 2. Here Gogol not only portrays the subtle methods of bribe-taking, but continues, as it were, the very plot of *The Inspector General:* An honest official turns out, unbeknownst to himself, to be deftly ensnared.

Thus, the poem's basic material is the everyday lives of the serf-owners, supplemented by bureaucratic material not new to Gogol's works. The satirical themes of arbitrary rule, lawlessness, and self-interest enter the poem on all levels of the bureaucratic ladder—from the petty clerks to the minister.

6. A term applied to short prose essays or character sketches describing people in various, mostly low, occupations; a genre popular in the 1840s in Russia (as well as France) [*Editor*].

V

By adopting the stance of an epic poet, Gogol found still more opportunities for including diverse material in the poem. In the course of narration, the author is able to introduce images only distantly related to the plot, and sometimes not related at all. Subordinated to the general epic composition of the poem, all these images become commensurate elements of the whole. This is the basis of Gogol's unique method of painting in miniature.

From the first chapter to the last, *Dead Souls* is strewn with such miniature portraits. In some instances, the miniature is based on some detail of plot or even on some secondary plot element that unexpectedly grows to the proportions that suit the author. Chichikov buys up dead and fugitive souls; he has the lists in his hands. The plot should progress farther, to the closing of his deed of purchase. But these dead and fugitive souls have independent meaning in the general design of the poem. Chichikov's adventure is built on the fates of men, both living and dead. Their character types, their exemplary and revealing biographies, become necessary to the internal meaning of the poem. Thus do the remarkable portraits of Stepan Probka, Maxim Telyatnikov, Popov the house serf, and Abakum Fyrov arise. These portraits are attributed in part to Chichikov (in one of the drafts, where, however, certain apologies are made for the intervention of the author himself); in part they are taken over by the author—in those places that require a more profoundly lyrical intonation. The peasant theme of the poem is not only expanded in the miniatures of the seventh chapter, but acquires substantially new emotional nuances.

In other instances the plot provides occasion for generalized portraits of entire social groups and types. The digression on "the thin and the fat" in chapter 1 and the generalization portrait of stewards belong to this type of miniature. The latter is particularly important in that the typifying portrait is followed by a typifying generalization of peasant life: "Having become a steward, he of course conducted himself as do all stewards: He consorted and kept company with the village folk who were better off and augmented the taxes levied on the poorer households. . . ." The miniatures include parallels to the main characters, as mentioned above. Korobochka evokes the image of an obstinate employee of the state and of an aristocratic lady with "rigid ideas." Nozdrev evokes the image of "a person with a medal," who loves to play dirty tricks on his close friends. Sobakievich evokes the image of an official who robs the till. These miniature portraits and their like not only lend overtones to the original characters, but expand the "epic range" as well, indicating the pertinent social variations of the main characters.

A completely special type of miniature is that found in similes. The device of extended similes, a bold variation of Homer's epic similes, fulfills a complex epic function in *Dead Souls*. Their obvious function is to create models of the elevated and beautiful out of the details of everyday, typically comic life. But by this route, which lies completely beyond the plot, vital material also penetrates into the poem. Here is a characteristic example from chapter 5: "As he drove up to the porch, he noticed two faces which were peeping out of the window almost simultaneously: one was a woman's, long and narrow as a cucumber, crowned with a cap; the other a man's, broad and round as the Moldavian pumpkins which go by the name of *gorlyanki* from which Russians make balalaikas—light two-stringed balalaikas, the boast and joy of some smart twenty-year-old lad, saucy-eyed and jaunty, winking an eye and whistling at the white-breasted and white-throated maidens who gather round to listen to his soft-stringed twanging." From the comic comparison of Sobakievich's face with a pumpkin there arises, by capricious association, the lively and charming image of the balalaika player, a merry lad from among the peasants, an image that has no relation whatsoever to the plot, but is included by the author's fiat in the general picture of "all Russia."

There are instances, finally, when the author does not even require external connections with the poem's basic material: The miniatures may arise in the composition of his "broad digressions." Thus, the sixth chapter begins with a lyrical reminiscence of youth, and the author introduces the town and estate scenes, the portraits of the provincial official and the landowner, only to serve as examples of youthful powers of observation and ability to "figure a person out."

Thus the poem is expanded by every means of epic narration. It is filled, even within the bounds of the first volume, with the broadest possible subject matter, from sentinel and deserter to minister and Tsar, including the provincial capital, the estate, landowners and peasants, officials of all ranks, and—episodically or in miniatures—the aristocracy, the merchant class, the officer class (Kopeikin), and the intelligentsia (in the mocking of the scholarly historian).

But Russia is revealed in *Dead Souls* not only through social types. In the final chapter, which is in many respects a summary, the narration is interrupted by pictures of nature that acquire generalized character: Chichikov's journey is conveyed by a selection of details, whence a shift is made to a generalization of all Russia. This occurs first with regard to Russia's nature: "Russia! Russia! I see you now, from my wondrous, beautiful past I behold you! How wretched, dispersed and uncomfortable everything is about you. . . ." The shift from here to the Russian song, which is presented as an expression of the Russian spirit, and then to Russia's future, returns us to the ideas of the *Arabesques*,[7] in particular to the old idea of the link between geography and history. But what sounds like an abstract thought in the *Arabesques* finds its artistic fulfillment in *Dead Souls*: The ideas of Russia and of history in general influenced the creation of the central image of Gogol's poem—that of Russia.

The image of Russia in her development enters the poem in the so-called lyrical digressions, which first interrupt, then conclude the last chapter of part 1. Russia is a "bird-like troika," flying "in a surge full of terror," Russia, to whom the poet addresses his burning question, "Where are you flying?" This is a romantic generalization, evoked by the writer's deep and long-standing faith in "Russian man in his development," mentioned as early as the article on Pushkin. This image was meant to be indefinite: The roads down which his native land "flies" have no distinct outlines for the poet, and the question "Where are you flying?" is followed by the insignificant words: "There is no answer." The profoundly progressive nature of *Dead Souls* consists precisely of its simultaneous, very concrete, realistic unmasking of the actual Russia and its romantic faith in the possible, future Russia. The poem's pathos, along with its definitive image of Russia, is composed of the contrast between the gloomy present on one hand and the possibilities of the future and a faith in the nation's strengths on the other. While Gogol was still working on

7. Gogol's third book, published in 1835, containing stories as well as essays [*Editor*].

Dead Souls, Belinsky wrote (in a letter to Botkin, 13 June 1840): "All that is substantial in our people is great and immense, but its definition is vile, filthy, and base." This could be a translation, as it were, of the basic content of *Dead Souls* into the language of philosophical formulas. It is not surprising that Belinsky reacted to Gogol's poem as to the appearance of an ally.

But Gogol's attitude toward the positive possibilities of the Russian people was expressed not only in romantic lyricism and not only in the image of Russia as a troika. He viewed these possibilities in living Russian men, but—very characteristically—not among the characters who are landowners. He found them among the folk characters portrayed in chapter 7, in the miniature portraits that enter the "meditations" on the list of peasants. Here the author is tolerant and gentle even in humorous scenes; but where he speaks of the barge haulers who trade "the rampages of a boisterous life" for "toil and sweat," his voice is pierced with lyrical animation. It is significant that for none of the characters of part 1, other than the peasants, does Gogol find lyrical intonations similar to those that resound throughout the poem for the generalized image of his native land.

VI

The current expression "lyrical digression" is not accurate in its application to the lyrical passages of *Dead Souls*, because the latter are all necessary links in the whole epic. In particular, the appeals to Russia not only do not "digress" from the poem's basic content, but on the contrary concentrate it within themselves, since it is the image of Russia that organizes and provides a basis for the content.

The second organizing image in the poem is that of the narrating author. In the poem's design, the "author" is not simply a conventional figure who draws together separate elements, but a unified personality. The author openly evaluates all that he himself has narrated, with his own clearly expressed view of things: The whole objective material of the poem, all its images and the image of Russia that unites them, are shown through the author's subjectivity. They are drawn, in Belinsky's words, "through his own *living soul*." The profound originality of Gogol's poem arises from the combination of an epic method of narration with an emotionally heightened and lyrical method. Moreover, not only man in general is revealed in the author, but a militant writer as well. The poem's very design represents a literary polemic—its novelty is underscored. This is why neither the separate polemical comments on artistic creation scattered throughout the poem nor the beginning of the seventh chapter, which unites them (the remarkable parallel of the two writers), can be called "digressions."

The beginning of the seventh chapter bears more significance than any other of Gogol's literary declarations. Here Gogol resolutely contrasts the happy and universally recognized writer, who "has never pitched his lyre in a lower key," idealizing reality by composing images "remote from the earth," the writer of Schiller's type, with the Gogolian type, unrecognized, reflecting real life with its "mess of trifling things." In formulas that are accurate despite their metaphoric form, Gogol characterizes the essence and tasks of the realistic method of fiction (but without pronouncing the words themselves). This method is primarily the task of "bringing into the open what is ever before men's eyes, all those things which the indifferent gaze fails to perceive, the whole horrid and shocking slimy mess of trifling things which have clogged our life, the whole depth of those chilly, split-up, everyday characters who swarm upon our bitter and dreary path on earth . . ." Here Gogol intensifies those theses earlier expressed in his article on Pushkin (the author's justification for selecting common material) and now asserts the predominance in life of "trifling things"; these are not only ineffective but repulsive—but precisely this makes them important to art. Not only is the artist able to include trivial things in the material of art, but his task lies precisely in the unmasking of trivial things, since the mess of trifling things has clogged life. Here, as in *The Inspector General,* the problems of aesthetics are inseparable from those of social morality. Here everyday characters ("chilly, split-up") are contrasted with "characters who embody the highest values of humanity," the "few exceptions," those chosen by the "happy" writer. By "chilly, split-up" everyday characters, of course, Gogol means what in "Four Letters to Divers Persons Apropos *Dead Souls*" is called "the vulgarity of a vulgar man." Thus the "unrecognized writer" is distinguished first of all by the very material he writes about—human vulgarity. But the portrayal of vulgarity requires its own method: Vulgarity must be uncovered and denounced; it requires extensive analysis, the "science of extraction" mentioned in chapter 2, the exposure of the imperceptible and "invisible" ("For . . . the telescope pointed at the sun and the microscope recording the movements of unnoticed insects are equally wonderful"). Then a different task is set before him: ". . . and with the firm power of a relentless chisel to dare and present them roundly and clearly for the benefit of all." The method of analysis is complemented by that of synthesis, the creation of integral images, "round" and "clear" in both their outer and inner aspects, the creation of typifying generalities.

One of Gogol's most important aesthetic formulas is expressed in the words: "Contemporary judgment does not recognize that great spiritual depth is required to illuminate a picture drawn from despised life and to make of it the pearl of creation." The essence of the problem and the indication of a method are important here. The appeal to "despised life" for Gogol meant not the "destruction of aesthetics," but the widening of aesthetic content. The beautiful coincides neither with the elevated nor with the comely. From this thesis, adopted by the majority of the Romantics and by whole Romantic schools of art, Gogol made the logical, realistic conclusions that "despised life" must give the artist his material. In the revised version of "The Portrait," written simultaneously with *Dead Souls,* this is expressed in the words "for him [i.e., the artist] nature contains no base objects." The parallels between *Dead Souls* and "The Portrait" also help to explain the expression "illuminate . . . and make of it the pearl of creation." Reality must be "illuminated" by the author's subjectivity; the "soulless" imitation of nature alone cannot be called the creation of art. These words about "illumination" and "being made the pearl of creation" are connected with the subsequent aesthetic formula, "for contemporary judgment does not allow the high laughter of delight a worthy place side by side with lofty lyrical emotion." In "After the Play" and other articles on the theater, Gogol finds the "illuminating" sources precisely in laughter. But the laughter of comedy is none other than the author's subjective point of view. "Laughter" is one of the possibilities of "illumination," the comprehension of reality. It is not the only possibility, but in Gogol's aesthetics it is the most essential, since the unmasking of vulgarity comes about primarily through the methods of humor and satire.

The "microscopic" analysis of vulgarity, the synthetic creation of generalized images, the "illumination" of those images with laughter and, in general, with the author's subjectivity—these were Gogol's guiding principles as he opened the way for critical realism in Russian literature.

ANDREI BELY

The Figure of Fiction in *Dead Souls*†

The chief technical device in the writing of *Dead Souls* is the clearcut, precise development of the "figure of fiction." This figure, of which I shall have more to say in the following pages, may be defined essentially by the following: In the subject matter of the novel—in the particular form that the novel imposes on it—there is nothing besides an indefinite delimitation of two categories: "everything" and "nothing." A given object is characterized by its distance on one side from "everything," and on the other from "nothing." This distance "from" is not a true characterization; rather, it is a parody of a characterization. The subject is an empty, generalized space, within which a fiction is inscribed: The value of the fiction may not be greater than one or less than zero. The particles "not" and "no" generate an entire series of fractions, which is neither "this" nor "that"—"that" being located at a certain distance from "everything," and "this," from "nothing." The subject (person or thing), overgrown with indefinite characteristics, becomes, by means of a system of repulsion from empty categories, the image of a "something" located at the midpoint of the "everything"-to-"nothing" line. This midpoint is itself spontaneous and direct, like $\infty/2$; and from this develops a "fiction of convexity"—a fiction possessing a sort of three-dimensional reality.

If zero is taken to symbolize "nothing," and one, "everything," the figure of fiction then may be represented: $\frac{0+1}{2} = \frac{1}{2}$. The universe of half-finished entities depicted in *Dead Souls* appears as a positive equilibrium. Yet at the same time the sought-after subject—stand-in for the figure of fiction—may be objectively represented best

† Translated by Geoffrey Packer from pp. 80–88 of Andrei Bely's book on Gogol, *Masterstvo Gogolia* [Gogol's art and craft], first published by OGIZ in Moscow-Leningrad in 1934. Bely was a prolific symbolist poet and prose writer.

as $\dfrac{1}{0}$; that is, as an infinite number of definitions. Thus, raging gales of contradictory concepts underlie this evasive equilibrium. Every minute brings with it a fresh surprise.

Definitions made by means of "some" (how much?), "not a lot, not a little," "to a certain degree" (to what degree?) do not define precisely. A slithering "form" crawls into the "positive" figure of Chichikov, a "form" that is similar to the force that has slipped into the being of the sorcerer.[1] This strange force pokes through all vague, gauzy definitions with its nose, which in profile is reminiscent of the nose of Napoleon. Chichikov is by no means and in no way well-balanced; yet he gives the impression of being so.

It is this that the figure of fiction consists of.

* * *

From the standpoint of everyday reality, *Dead Souls* presents a somewhat different case: Here delimitation is not carried out by the boundaries of the category "all"; "nothing" is also delimited (in the sorcerer's case, it is not delimited). "Nothing" is bounded in by "something" and by "something to a certain degree." These mutual limitations are defined—but only in principle. Chichikov does not fall away into "nothing." His journeys between "everything" and "nothing" may be schematized as a variety of open figure eights. Indeed, he intrigues us no less than does the sorcerer. The sorcerer is terrifying; Chichikov is pleasantly respectable. Fear of the sorcerer is annulled by the sorcerer's fear, while the decorous Chichikov harbors a strange "something" that causes the sudden death of the public prosecutor (and of how many others?). The sorcerer founders; Chichikov, even in prison, continues to hope for "something": Murazov will rescue him. Spread out before Chichikov is "New Russia," from which, with the help of Gogol, he will worry out his own dead soul; this is something more terrible than all the sorcerer's murders: The sorcerer destroys the body, but Chichikov smothers the soul. It is capitalist Russia, cocooned within Chichikov, that suddenly becomes, in the guise of his own nonexistent troika, a symbol of Russia. Gogol does not respond overtly to the question of what precisely Chichikov's troika is, only approaching the subject sidelong in such phrases as "presented itself dimly" and "we hardly"—phrases that tear

1. A reference to Gogol's story "A Terrible Vengeance" (1832), in which the heroine's father is an evil sorcerer.

Dead Souls asunder, just as they did Gogol's own life. The figure of fiction ends by casting Gogol out of literature . . . and out of life itself.

Chichikov appears in the first chapter as something impersonal, a round, featureless area concealed in a *brichka*.[2] The *brichka* calls attention to itself; it seems to be something of a particular sort (while its owner does not); but the "something," here, is a fiction. It is in *brichkas* such as this that "all those referred to as gentlemen of an average sort" set forth on journeys. Now this "of an average sort" is not a proper definition at all: It has a certain meaning for some people and quite a different meaning for others. A single, concrete meaning cannot be pinned down.

In the *brichka* is sitting something of an ordinary variety, something "neither dashingly handsome nor ugly; neither too stout nor too slender," of whom "it cannot be said that he is old; however, he is no longer young." A something whose "arrival did not make . . . any sort of a stir and was not accompanied by any event of particular interest."

The same "no"s and "not"s are associated with the sorcerer, but there they have a different effect. They serve to set the sorcerer distinctly apart from everyday existence; he exists, as it were, in an abyss in the midst of the ordinary, an abyss whose bounds are set by the mountain Krivan. Every "not" affixed to the sorcerer serves to estrange him, to place him within that abyss. On the other hand, the owner of the *brichka* in *Dead Souls* merges, with the aid of "not" and "no," with the whole of everyday existence. Chichikov has no distinguishing characteristics; no pit is hollowed out for him. Quite the contrary, in fact: The rough patches separating him from everyday existence are planed away to the point that an affinity, even a close resemblance, may be detected between Chichikov and the governor. Chichikov likewise moves toward merger with the average sort of *brichka*. The quintessential feature of a *brichka,* or any carriage, is the wheel; and all of the wheels exist on the same level, all are round. A couple of peasants take note of a wheel as the *brichka* passes by: "Looky there," says one of the peasants, "What a wheel that is! D'ye think, if it came to that, it would go as far as Moscow, or not?" "It would make it to Moscow," the other peasant replies. "But likely not all the way to Kazan, eh?" "No, not to Kazan."

2. A light coach; a buggy.

Here the wheel is defined in terms of the distance of Moscow and of Kazan from some unknown town.

Thus, one is led from traveler to *brichka,* from *brichka* to its wheel: The wheel is not defined in any way. As for the "two *Russian* peasants" standing at the door of a tavern: Why "Russian peasants"? What else but Russian could they possibly be? After all, the action does not take place in Australia!

Nothing has really been said; and yet, it seems that *something* has been said.

The focus now shifts from the "hero" of the poem to someone strolling by, someone who vanishes almost immediately. This person is dressed "in very tight-fitting white duck trousers, a dress coat with pretensions to the fashionable and under which a shirt-front is visible; this latter is held in place by a stickpin of Tula make, which has a head in the form of a bronze pistol."

What is this passerby doing here?

He is here to distract attention from the man in the *brichka.*

"The gentleman was received . . . by a servant, or waiter, as they are called"; "it was impossible to get a good look at his face": An impersonal figure meets another impersonal figure. "The inn was of a well-known type; that is, it was just the way inns usually are." The room assigned to the traveler is, once again, "of that well-known type." The traveler makes his way to the common room: "Everyone knows quite well what these common rooms are like." The pictures on the walls have been brought in "at an unknown time, by persons unknown." The traveler takes off a scarf "of all different colors," of the sort "made by wives for their spouses," and is regaled with "various dishes of the sort one gets in inns." After dinner, the traveler asks the servant some "not entirely pointless questions."

A stream of settled events flows smoothly by: In the wake of the impersonal traveler come *brichka,* wheel, servant, inn, bedroom, common room, dinner—all presented in general, nonindividual terms. This pervasive obscurity of the surroundings stems from a corresponding dullness in the perceptions of the traveler: "The same walls . . . the same . . . ceiling; the same candelabrum . . .; in short, everything just the same as it is everywhere else."

The sensibilities are bombarded by a sort of active vagueness.

In place of an authorial sketch of Chichikov's personal characteristics, one is provided with a small piece of paper, an information form filled out by travelers for the local police: "Collegiate Advisor Pavel Ivanovich Chichikov, landowner, on private business. . . ." Now "on private business" does not create any sort of picture. A passport is a fiction of an individual; the title *Dead Souls* is a fiction as well, one for which Gogol had to pay a price. The soul either does not exist, or it is immortal: What then can a "dead soul" be?

The next morning, Chichikov makes a round of calls. An enumeration of the people whom he visits is begun, but it is never completed: "It is rather difficult to keep in mind all the mighty ones of the world." Chichikov says something flattering to each host or hostess, speaking somewhat offhandedly. He talks about himself and adds "some sort of general commentary . . ."; he slips in some bookish phrases: For instance, he says that he is "an insignificant worm in this great world." Here the word "worm" *is* significant: "Before one has time to look around, a terrible worm has sprung up inside one . . . and . . . in . . . Chichikov there was a passion, a force from without, which led him on irresistibly; there is something in the essential nature of man that will sooner or later bring him to his knees, and turn him to ashes . . . and the reason that this worm appears is still a mystery."

In view of the future importance of Chichikov—of the fictional figure of Chichikov and his word about himself—and of the generally illusive quality of "photographically realistic" description—a sort of etching on water with a pitchfork, it is evident that Gogol, at the time of the writing of *Dead Souls,* was unfamiliar with the Russian provincial town: nor was he acquainted with the Russian village.

The governor who receives Chichikov is, like Chichikov himself, "neither stout nor thin"; "he had been awarded an order . . . he did embroidery on tulle." Later on he will be pictured with a card in one hand and a lapdog in the other. At first he receives Chichikov; later he refuses to see him. In the words of Manilov, the governor is "most distinguished and extraordinarily amiable"; while, according to Sobakievich, the man is "a thieving rascal of the worst sort" who would "cut your throat for a kopeck." However, the "honorable scoundrel" who emerges here is a fiction.

At the governor's residence, "everything is as it should be." Here, "as everywhere else," there are men "of two sorts": Some are slender; others are stout. Of the slender sort one is informed, much later, that they are "nothing more than something on the order of a bunch of tooth-picks." And one learns that the stout men "do not fit into tight corners," and that their wives often refer to them as "dumplings," "piggy-banks," and "pot-bellies." But the gov-ernor, that honorable scoundrel, is neither slender nor stout.

A complete and total fiction!

Chichikov, like the governor neither fat nor thin, in the course of the dinner party pays the latter a compliment "suitable for a middle-aged gentleman who holds a rank neither too high nor too low." Chichikov makes his bows "not without a certain agreeableness"; he argues "pleas-antly"; he "somehow manages always to be in the middle of things"; and he speaks "neither loudly nor softly, but in just the way he ought" about the glue factory, philan-thropists, judicial proceedings, local administrators, and hot claret.

It soon becomes evident that Chichikov is not really interested in these conversations: His essential position in social situations is mirrored by the position of his double, his lackey Petrushka, in regard to reading. It is all one to Petrushka what it is that he is reading: a romantic ad-venture tale, a primer, or a prayer book; he is enthralled by the way "that, look'ee here, these here letters come together to make up some sort of a word." For Chichikov, then, people are letters; from these letters something will make itself up. People are merely a buzzing cluster of flies: The comparison of the guests at the governor's evening party with flies is not coincidental.

In the second chapter, Chichikov's visit to Manilov's estate is described. Manilov's personality is not one of Gogol's major concerns. Manilov is sketched in vague terms; no sooner has he been presented than smoke begins to billow from his *chibouk*: [3] "The *chibouk* rattled and wheezed, and that was all."

A similar haze of vagueness envelops the environs of the town. "They set out to depict, according to our custom [to what custom?], the assorted odds and ends that lined both sides of the road." The items are enumerated in the

3. A Turkish long-stemmed clay pipe.

text: "a fir grove . . . shrubbery . . . stalks and tree trunks . . . heather; and all that sort of rubbish." The environs of the town are gray; the time of year is unknown. Peasants are sitting around "in . . . sheepskin jackets" as their womenfolk "muck about in the ponds." That same night, Korobochka cries out: "What a blizzard it is." But the fruit trees are covered with nets—to keep the magpies away.

At a certain time of year, Chichikov sets off for a certain place: "Manilovka, perhaps, or Zamanilovka." Some place or other, then, is located at some distance or other from this place: "Go on straight ahead . . . a verst or so . . . , then . . . turn right." They went on two versts, "and three, and four": still no sign of Manilovka. In the same vein: "If . . . they tell you . . . it's fifteen versts . . . , that means . . . it's a good thirty."

The distances are unrealistic. Chichikov, after having traveled the thirty versts or so to Manilovka, and having spent the whole day there, dined, and indulged to his heart's content in after-dinner chat, sets out for Korobochka. He loses his way and discovers, at last, that he is some sixty versts from the town. How far did he travel alogether? It appears that he must have covered at least seventy-five versts, and this after spending the day and evening at Manilov's estate: This is unrealistic in terms both of plot consistency and of the realistic capabilities of horses. On the following day, Chichikov drops in on Nozdrev, who lives nearby. On the third day, after spending a rather tempestuous morning with Nozdrev, and then getting mired in the mud on the road, he still manages to eat a hearty supper at Sobakievich's; travel to Plyushkin's, where he transacts some business; and reach town by dusk: The town is a good distance from Plyushkin's estate. The fact of the inordinate length of this third day's journey is unquestionable when one takes into account the locations of the various estates.

Gogol is not concerned with precision; for him, it is sufficient to say: at a certain time, at a certain distance.

The day itself is of just such a fictive nature: "neither clear nor overcast; some sort of shiny-gray."

Some further characteristics of Manilov: "There is a certain type of person . . . the man of a middling sort, neither fish nor fowl, neither the urban Bogdan nor the rustic Selifan." A most precise beginning! Farther on, one learns that Manilov is "the devil knows what!": that is, an

unknown quantity. "To each his own, but Manilov had
nothing that was peculiar to himself." "It cannot be said
that he occupied himself" with husbandry and agriculture
(although he did draw up agricultural projects, so that
it also cannot be said that he did not occupy himself with
husbandry and agriculture). Whenever the steward said
that it would be a good idea "to do this or that," Manilov
would reply: "Yes, that's not a bad idea." The furniture
in the room of this not unpleasant person is "not cheap"
(it is not stated straight out that it is expensive); but two
of the armchairs are not completely covered: "They haven't
been finished yet." Manilov's study is "not without a certain
pleasing quality," the walls have been painted "some sort
of lightish blue, rather grayish." Although everything in
the room is dusted over with tobacco ash, there are also
small mounds of ash "arranged not without an effort at
being attractive." The Manilovs, husband and wife, are
"what is spoken of as being happy."

Everything that concerns Manilov is vague, ill-defined;
everything is a fiction, a fusion of "not without something"
and "not without nothing." This fusion may be expressed
as the merging of —0.01 and —0.02, and as zero plus an
infinitely small quantity—"nothing; not without something." There are as well the two precise sketch-lines: "He
smokes a *chibouk;* his eyes [which he screws up coyly]
are like sugar." The screwing up of the eyes diffuses itself
throughout the first volume of *Dead Souls* and commingles
with the hoarse gurglings of the ash-choked, "not sweet"
chibouk. Here, again, one finds a fiction rather than a
definition: sugar plus ash, divided by two. The gestural
repetition discloses nothing of the essential Manilov, of a
man who most likely contains a "worm." But Gogol does
not focus on Manilov's inner man, does not disturb this
particular "worm." Only take Manilov's estate away and
cast him into the midst of St. Petersburg; who, then, could
tell what worm would emerge, what sort of "Spanish
King" [4] he would turn into?

Every one of Gogol's type characters is, in the author's
own words, full of "an elusive individuality": "These gentlemen are terribly difficult to make portraits of"; and,
indeed, Gogol gives not a portrait but a sort of expressive
sketch, which he sets up like a screen; or, rather, as camou-
flage.

4. The chief character of Gogol's story "Diary of a Madman" (1835),
in which a mad office clerk imagines himself to be the exiled king of Spain.

The fiction creates three-dimension-like portraits, never-theless; the characters in *Dead Souls* are reductions of a multitude of possibilities. One or two characters are created with the aid of the habitual gesture; for instance, Sobakie-vich, from his first appearance on, steps on people's toes; then, with head bent, he falls silent, swears under his breath, and finally says, "Pardon me." One seems to recog-nize the type of rascal; one believes in him: And yet he does not exist. He is like the signboard, "Vasili Fyodorov, Foreigner," like the "honorable scoundrel," like "ashen sugar" and "dead souls."

The stock-in-trade of these fictions is dust and ashes: little mounds of ashes "not without beauty"; Plyushkin's crumbling sheets and his haystacks that are in a state of "rot not without ripe kernels:" The details of the exposi-tion of plot are given in markedly indefinite terms: "It would not be superfluous to make the acquaintance of . . ." (not simply "one ought to"); "although these personages are not so noteworthy" (not simply "not noteworthy"); "the author likes very much . . . to be thorough in every-thing, despite the fact that he is a Russian. . . . Here, how-ever, such thoroughness does not require a great deal of time [instead of simply 'a little'], because not much need be added to the characterization of Petrushka" (of whom little has yet been said). It appears that the author does *not* have a great liking for thoroughness; he even refuses to bring Petrushka's thoughts to light: "It is difficult to know just what a house serf is thinking . . . when his master is giving him instructions." It is still more difficult to know what the author is thinking as he weaves his subterfuges and circumlocutions into the texture of the work: "In a word, a well-known variety."

But this variety is, in fact, not at all well known.

This, then, is the device that, obliquely and sideways, through "not this" and "not that," carries on the hidden theme. This "oblique, sideways move" of Chichikov is his stereotyped, cliché gesture, as he sits in ambush in a thicket of grayish equilibrium: $\dfrac{0+1}{2} = \dfrac{1}{2}$ (in fact, $\dfrac{1}{0} = \infty$).

Chichikov spends his time, "as the saying goes," agree-ably (was it really agreeably?) traveling about in "the well-known" *brichka* (which has not been described at all). He says curtly to Petrushka: "What the devil, sir, don't you know . . ."; he does not say straight out "you stink." He even "perceived, not without a certain joy," the crossing-gate, and approaches the swing-arm of the gate "not without satisfaction"; he even becomes a bit muddled from the feeling (which is to be expected). He asserts that: "I have neither a great name nor even an important rank." Manilov corrects him: "All the same, you know, you do have all that, and a bit more besides." Chichikov is a resounding name, and collegiate assessor is a significant rank. This agreeable indefiniteness continues to grow: "Please, if you will, make yourself comfortable in . . . the armchair."—"If you will, I'll just sit on this chair."—"If *you* will, you shall not." Chichikov sits down and reflects: "There is much in nature that even the widely-ranging mind cannot grasp." The demonstration of agreeable indefiniteness referred to above is followed immediately by an unpleasant vagueness: Manilov "became restive and embarrassed," while "Chichikov, for some unknown reason, stared straight ahead" and delivered himself of a speech about the purchase of serfs: "How would you like to buy the peasants? With or without land?"—"It's not exactly just plain peasants that I want. . . . Actually, I'm after dead ones. . . . Could you possibly . . . not actually alive, you see, but alive according to legal form . . . make them over to me, or whatever you think best. . . ."

After which Manilov asks: "Can it be that here . . . in what you just said . . . something completely different is hidden?"

But the function of the figure of fiction is precisely to indicate hidden realities that are obscured by superficial images, to point up the unseen underlying the seen. This is illustrated in Chichikov's proposal to finalize the purchase of the dead souls. The proposal is a fraud: "We'll put down that they are alive. . . . I am accustomed never to step even an inch outside of the law. . . . Duty is something sacred to me. . . . I bow down before the law."

Is the law here a forgery? Or is this forgery a law? What does Manilov make of all this? But "the *chibouk* gurgled hoarsely, and that was all."

Finally Manilov speaks up: "Isn't it true that . . . this transaction might be more, so to speak, as they say . . . more in accordance with the long-range interests of Russia?"

Certainly, forgery is a very bad thing; still, the government will reap tax benefits from it—this is certainly just as good. So, here the juxtaposed values "not very good" and "not very not good" yield "good."

Again, a certain vagueness emerges: This trifling business deal is unrelated to the long-range interests of Russia. Although neither the long-range interests of the country nor the more concrete and localized interests of individuals are brought to the fore, it is clear that the transaction hinges on the latter, as well as on the more immediate interests of Russia itself: "The government will even make a profit, since it gets all the legal taxes. . . . And I think that this is a good thing."

Is Manilov a sincere person? Sincere with himself—no; with the inhabitants of the town—we do not know. It certainly cannot be said that he was deceitful through ignorance, after he had begun to have suspicions; nor can it be supposed that the fiction of lulling-into-calmness had lulled him into calmness. For why then was he "so mixed up and confused," and why did he glance back over his shoulder, and, after Chichikov had left, why did the thought of the little deal just completed somehow "not set right with him"; this despite his warm friendship for Chichikov?

Now Chichikov has disclosed a new side of his nature, something rather antisocial and slimy (the goal toward which this "sliminess" is directed is no longer hidden in the second chapter). Even Chichikov's desire to be agreeable may now be viewed as the superficial offshoot of a deeper desire: to do whatever must be done to reach the ultimate goal. However, "nothing of that sort was visible. . . . His expression was even unusually composed. . . . His eyes . . . were clear; there was no sort of savage fire in them; everything was as it should be, in good order." This shift back to facade lasts up to the time of Chichikov's departure. He says to Manilov's small child, jokingly, "I'll bring you a drum . . . such a drum . . . it will go toorrrooo, tra-ta-ta, ta-ta-ta. . . . Goodbye for now, little darling." Then he "turned to Manilov . . . with a faint smile on his face, the kind of smile with which children are accustomed to greet their parents."

In the second chapter, the fiction is conveyed through details. The fiction establishes a central point in this chapter, from which a long line extends in two opposing directions; such a central point does not exist in the first chapter. This extended line is not the line of the fictive plot; rather, it is the dot on the "i"—as if the author had suddenly whispered to us that everything displayed on the surface is a blind, a decoy.

The author's position is transmitted through the utterance of Manilov: "Perhaps here . . . in the explanation you just gave . . . something else is hidden!"

I shall limit myself to this brief discussion of the technique of the first two chapters in order not to weary the reader. I would only add that the figure of fiction is the hub, the generating core of each of the eleven chapters of *Dead Souls.* * * *

As we shall see below, the most frequently appearing colors in the first volume of *Dead Souls* are white, black, gray, and yellow, as well as an increasingly significant percentage of light blue. The colors gray, yellow, and light blue are not commonly found in literary works of the first phase. The colors that appear in *Dead Souls* are immanent in that device that generates the fictive "something" in the form of a balanced "everything plus nothing": "Everything" is refracted into a color spectrum just as is a shining, *white* ray of light. "Nothing" here corresponds to darkness (black). The fusion of black and white produces gray—the color that accompanies the fictive equilibrium of the figures in *Dead Souls* (their pseudonaturalism, so to speak): *gray* villages, *gray* wallpaper, abbreviated *gray* days, and so on. Both yellow and light blue have roles in Goethe's theory of colors: Yellow is the opaque medium (darkness) cast upon light, the glimpsed sparkling of "everything" through "nothing"; light blue is light thrown onto darkness, "nothing" glimpsed through a chink in "everything."

Gogol's categories "nothing" and "everything," together with their offshoots ("in a certain way"; "similar to"; "something"; and so forth) may be taken as the subject matter of *Dead Souls,* and the color spectrum is immanent in the book's subject matter: "everything"—white; "nothing"—black; "neither this nor that"—gray. "Something," "in a certain way," "so to speak," and like expressions generate graduated spectra of yellowish and dark-brownish shades; while expressions such as "not without" give rise to a grayish–light blue shading—the color of Manilov's wallpaper.

The spectrum of the first volume of *Dead Souls* is a powerful means to make the plot concrete. "Everything" and "nothing" are, in the indefiniteness of their counterposed limitations, not only hyperboles; they are also a means of supplying ideas and didactic tendentiousness. That which ruins the second volume of *Dead Souls* is an effective artistic device in the first volume. It is reflected in the style, in the art of depiction and in the action itself.

Chichikov

The circle is an equilibrium; but there are two different types of circularity: the all-embracing roundness of Platon Karataev [5] and the self-enclosed roundness of Chichikov. The *brichka's* wheel, its spokes blurred by its own motion, ushers in Chichikov in a vignette captioned, "Pavel Ivanovich Chichikov, landowner, on private business."

A man "neither old nor young," "respectably middle-aged," "not exactly handsome, but by no means ugly; neither too stout nor too thin." Of Napoleon, in the same vein: "It cannot be said that he was fat; on the other hand, he was not at all thin." Chichikov makes his bows "to the sound of vague noises which sounded something like French"; "he was vague when speaking about himself": "However, I still don't know your given name and patronymic." "Is it necessary to know the name of someone who has not exactly covered himself with glory?"—"Nevertheless . . ."—"Well, then, Pavel Ivanovich, Your Excellency." People come to realize that they "still do not know Chichikov at all"; "still, he *must* be somebody or other." Chichikov speaks "as one speaks in public places," "neither loudly nor softly, always just as the situation required." He speaks "in general about the entire Russian Empire" and is "loud in his praises of its vast expanses."

From out of the pervasive vagueness crawls the newly hatched motif of roundness: "a round face"; "like a bulldog or a plump little capon"; "the chin: completely round"; "roundness of the body"; "a full, round belly"; also, round, full cheeks. This overall solidity is also manifested in a general quality of weightiness: "He was a heavy fellow"; "rather heavy"; "a round little belly like a ram's." And when Chichikov appears and makes his little *entrechat,* "the commode trembled, and a small glass filled with eau-de-Cologne was dashed to the floor"; again, "the commode shook, and a brush fell from it." Chichikov breaks out in a light sweat: "He was all sweated up"; "sweat broke out on his forehead."

The motif of roundness is associated with pleasantness and neatness: "an amiable . . . appearance"; "any way you look at it, a thoroughly decent man"; "from childhood on, affectionate, polite, not the least bit excitable—simply,

5. A character in Leo Tolstoy's *War and Peace.* Karataev is a wise peasant, whose "roundness" is emphasized by Tolstoy as though it is connected with the harmoniousness of the peasant's spirit.

smooth as silk." Chichikov never utters an indecent word.
"There was a kind of solidity . . . in his manner"; "he was
able to envelop everything around him in a sort of slow-
motion atmosphere"; "he made his bows to the left and
to the right," and said that "he would esteem it a sacred
obligation . . . to pay his respects," and "the sooner, the
better." "He positively charmed a lady from St. Petersburg." Chichikov generally makes himself necessary: "He
could flatter anyone." In discussions he displays a fundamental "soundness." He rolls his words out "with fitting
weight." When the general bursts out with a "ha-ha" of
laughter, Chichikov "lets loose a hearty 'he-he' of laughter."
Once, Chichikov even turned down a proffered bribe: "The
very word 'bribe' offended his sensibilities and outraged
his sense of decency." He is "a sensitive and fussily exacting person": He "carried around a snuff-box with violets
on the bottom"; he is very fond of eau-de-Cologne and in-
hales with relish the scent of a miniature carnation; a
"stream of sweet-smelling exhalations" wafts from his hair;
he changes his linen often, and pats wine-moistened lips
dry with a napkin. "After fussing around inside his mouth
with his tongue, Chichikov spent a long time soaping and
scrubbing his cheeks"; then "taking the towel from his
shoulder, he rubbed himself dry, beginning behind the
ears, and snorted twice." He has "snow-white cheeks," which
are "genuine silk," and to which "his white collars gave a
real tone." In short: "an unusually pleasing exterior."
Even Chichikov's feet are ensconced in "dandyish lacquered
half-boots with mother-of-pearl fastenings." To round out
the picture: "a sky-blue neck-cloth . . . the latest word in
false shirt-fronts . . . a velvet waistcoat"; an enamelled
silver snuffbox; and, finally, "a cranberry-colored dress coat
with spangles." "He held forth as though he were at court
—such tact and decorum."

As is written in the second volume of *Dead Souls*, "Artist,
take up thy brush and paint."

The image of Chichikov is both vivid and multifaceted.
Chichikov appears vividly in our collection of quotations,
which all illustrate one particular facet: This is a sort of
vividness in the depiction of a nonentity. Like the governor, the figure of Chichikov is neither saint nor scoundrel; like Napoleon, he is neither stout nor thin. Just where
does this "Chichikov" fit in? Somewhere in between the
general run of stout men and thin men; with Napoleon

and the governor—with predator and with prey. "Chichikov" is a tidy, pleasant, generalized space without progeny: a bubble in the flood.

VLADIMIR NABOKOV

Our Mr. Chichikov†

* * *

The Russian language is able to express by means of one pitiless word the idea of a certain widespread defect for which the other three European languages I happen to know possess no special term. The absence of a particular expression in the vocabulary of a nation does not necessarily coincide with the absence of the corresponding notion but it certainly impairs the fullness and readiness of the latter's perception. Various aspects of the idea which Russians concisely express by the term *poshlost* (the stress-accent is on the puff-ball of the first syllable, and the final "t" has a moist softness that is hardly equaled by the French "t" in such words as "restiez" or "émoustillant") are split among several English words and thus do not form a definite whole. On second thought, I find it preferable to transcribe that fat brute of a word thus: *poshlust*—which renders in a somewhat more adequate manner the dull sound of the second, neutral "o." Inversely the first "o" is as big as the plop of an elephant falling into a muddy pond and as round as the bosom of a bathing beauty on a German picture postcard.

English words expressing several, although by no means all aspects of *poshlust* are for instance: "cheap, sham, common, smutty, pink-and-blue, high falutin', in bad taste." My little assistant, *Roget's Thesaurus*, (which incidentally lists "rats, mice" under "Insects"—see page 21 of Revised Edition) supplies me moreover with "inferior, sorry, trashy, scurvy, tawdry, gimcrack" and others under "cheapness." All these however suggest merely certain false values for the detection of which no particular shrewdness is required. In fact they tend, these words, to supply an obvious classification of values at a given period of human history; but what Russians call *poshlust* is beautifully timeless and so

† From Vladimir Nabokov, *Nikolai Gogol* (Norfolk, Conn.: New Directions, 1944), pp. 63–78.

cleverly painted all over with protective tints that its presense (in a book, in a soul, in an institution, in a thousand other places) often escapes detection.

Ever since Russia began to think, and up to the time that her mind went blank under the influence of the extraordinary regime she has been enduring for these last twenty-five years, educated, sensitive and free-minded Russians were acutely aware of the furtive and clammy touch of *poshlust*. Among the nations with which we came into contact, Germany had always seemed to us a country where *poshlust*, instead of being mocked, was one of the essential parts of the national spirit, habits, traditions and general atmosphere, although at the same time well-meaning Russian intellectuals of a more romantic type readily, too readily, adopted the legend of the greatness of German philosophy and literature; for it takes a super-Russian to admit that there is a dreadful streak of *poshlust* running through Goethe's *Faust*.

To exaggerate the worthlessness of a country at the awkward moment when one is at war with it—and would like to see it destroyed to the last beer-mug and last forget-me-not,—means walking dangerously close to that abyss of *poshlust* which yawns so universally at times of revolution or war. But if what one demurely murmurs is but a mild pre-war truth, even with something old-fashioned about it, the abyss is perhaps avoidable. Thus, a hundred years ago, while civic-minded publicists in St. Petersburg were mixing heady cocktails of Hegel and Schlegel (with a dash of Feuerbach), Gogol, in a chance story he told, expressed the immortal spirit of *poshlust* pervading the German nation and expressed it with all the vigor of his genius.

The conversation around him had turned upon the subject of Germany, and after listening awhile, Gogol said: "Yes, generally speaking the average German is not too pleasant a creature, but it is impossible to imagine anything more unpleasant than a German Lothario, a German who tries to be winsome. . . . One day in Germany I happened to run across such a gallant. The dwelling place of the maiden whom he had long been courting without success stood on the bank of some lake or other, and there she would be every evening sitting on her balcony and doing two things at once: knitting a stocking and enjoying the view. My German gallant being sick of the futility of his pursuit finally devised an unfailing means

whereby to conquer the heart of his cruel (
evening he would take off his clothes, plun
and, as he swam there, right under the eye
he would keep embracing a couple of s
been specially prepared by him for that
quite know what those swans were supposed to sy...
but I do know that for several evenings on end he did
nothing but float about and assume pretty postures with
his birds under that precious balcony. Perhaps he fancied
there was something poetically antique and mythological
in such frolics, but whatever notion he had, the result
proved favorable to his intentions: the lady's heart was
conquered just as he thought it would be, and soon they
were happily married."

Here you have *poshlust* in its ideal form, and it is clear
that the terms trivial, trashy, smug and so on do not cover
the aspect it takes in this epic of the blond swimmer and
the two swans he fondled. Neither is it necessary to travel
so far both in space and time to obtain good examples.
Open the first magazine at hand and you are sure to find
something of the following kind: a radio set (or a car, or
a refrigerator, or table silver—anything will do) has just
come to the family: mother clasps her hands in dazed
delight, the children crowd around, all agog, Junior and
the dog strain up to the edge of the table where the Idol
is enthroned; even Grandma of the beaming wrinkles peeps
out somewhere in the background (forgetful, we presume,
of the terrific row she has had that very morning with her
daughter-in-law); and somewhat apart, his thumbs glee-
fully inserted in the armpits of his waistcoat, legs a-straddle
and eyes a-twinkle, stands triumphant Pop, the Proud
Donor.

The rich *poshlust* emanating from advertisements of this
kind is due not to their exaggerating (or inventing) the
glory of this or that serviceable article but to suggesting
that the acme of human happiness is purchasable and that
its purchase somehow ennobles the purchaser. Of course,
the world they create is pretty harmless in itself because
everybody knows that it is made up by the seller with
the understanding that the buyer will join in the make-
believe. The amusing part is not that it is a world where
nothing spiritual remains except the ecstatic smiles of
people serving or eating celestial cereals or a world where
the game of the senses is played according to bourgeois

les ("bourgeois" in the Flaubertian, *not* in the Marxist sense) but that it is a kind of satellite shadow world in the actual existence of which neither sellers nor buyers really believe in their heart of hearts—especially in this wise quiet country.

If a commercial artist wishes to depict a nice little boy he will grace him with freckles (which incidentally assume a horrible rash-like aspect in the humbler funnies). Here *poshlust* is directly connected with a forgotten convention of a faintly racial type. Kind people send our lonely soldiers silk hosed dummy legs modeled on those of Hollywood lovelies and stuffed with candies and safety razor blades— at least I have seen a picture of a person preparing such a leg in a certain periodical which is a world-famous pur-veyor of *poshlust*. Propaganda (which could not exist with-out a generous supply of and demand for *poshlust*) fills booklets with lovely Kolkhos maidens and windswept clouds. I select my examples hurriedly and at random— the "Encyclopédie des Idées Reçues" which Flaubert dreamt of writing one day was a more ambitious work.

Literature is one of its best breeding places and by *poshlust-literature* I do not mean the kind of thing which is termed "pulp" or which in England used to go under the name of "penny dreadfuls" and in Russia under that of "yellow literature." Obvious trash, curiously enough, con-tains sometimes a wholesome ingredient, readily appreci-ated by children and simple souls. Superman is undoubtable *poshlust,* but it is *poshlust* in such a mild, unpretentious form that it is not worthwhile talking about; and the fairy tales of yore contained, for that matter, as much trivial sentiment and naive vulgarity as these yarns about modern Giant Killers. *Poshlust,* it should be repeated, is especially vigorous and vicious when the sham is *not* obvious and when the values it mimics are considered, rightly or wrongly, to belong to the very highest level of art, thought or emotion. It is those books which are so *poshlustily* re-viewed in the literary supplement of daily papers—the best sellers, the "stirring, profound and beautiful" novels; it is these "elevated and powerful" books that contain and dis-till the very essence of *poshlust*. I happen to have upon my desk a copy of a paper with a whole page advertising a certain novel, which novel is a fake from beginning to end and by its style, its ponderous gambols around elevated ideas, and absolute ignorance of what authentic literature was, is and always will be, strangely reminds one of the swan-fondling swimmer depicted by Gogol. "You lose yourself in it completely,"—says one reviewer;—"When the last page is turned you come back to the world of everyday a little thoughtful, as after a great experience" (note the coy "a little" and the perfectly automatic "as after a great"). "A singing book, compact of grace and light and ecstasy, a book of pearly radiance,"—whispers another (that swimmer was also "compact of grace," and the swans had a "pearly radiance," too). "The work of a master psychologist who can skillfully probe the very inner recesses of men's souls." This "inner" (mind you—not "outer"), and the other two or three delightful details already mentioned are in exact conformity to the true value of the book. In fact, this praise is perfectly adequate: the "beautiful" novel is "beautifully" reviewed and the circle of *poshlust* is complete—or would be complete had not words taken a subtle revenge of their own and smuggled the truth in by secretly forming most nonsensical and most damning combinations while the reviewer and publisher are quite sure that they are praising the book, "which the reading public has made a [here follows an enormous figure apparently meaning the quantity of copies sold] triumph." For in the kingdom of *poshlust* it is not the book that "makes a triumph" but the "reading public" which laps it up, blurb and all.

The particular novel referred to here may have been a perfectly honest and sincere (as the saying goes) attempt on the author's part to write something he felt strongly about—and very possibly no commercial aspirations assisted him in that unfortunate process. The trouble is that sincerity, honesty and even true kindness of heart cannot prevent the demon of *poshlust* from possessing himself of an author's typewriter when the man lacks genius and when the "reading public" is what publishers think it is. The dreadful thing about *poshlust* is that one finds it so difficult to explain to people why a particular book which seems chock-full of noble emotion and compassion, and can hold the reader's attention "on a theme far removed from the discordant events of the day" is far, far worse than the kind of literature which *everybody* admits is cheap.

From the various examples collected here it will be I hope clear that *poshlust* is not only the obviously trashy but also the falsely important, the falsely beautiful, the falsely clever, the falsely attractive. A list of literary characters personifying *poshlust* (and thus namable in Russian *poshlyaki* in the case of males and *poshlyáchki* in the case of females—and rhyming with "key" and "latchkey" respectively) will include Polonius and the royal pair in Hamlet, Flaubert's Rodolphe and Homais, Laevsky in Chekhov's *Duel,* Joyce's Marion Bloom, young Bloch in *A la Recherche du Temps Perdu,* Maupassant's "Bel Ami," Anna Karenina's husband, Berg in *War and Peace* and numerous other figures in universal fiction. Socially minded Russian critics saw in *Dead Souls* and in *The Government Inspector* a condemnation of the social *poshlust* emanating from serf-owning bureaucratic provincial Russia and thus missed the true point. Gogol's heroes merely happen to be Russian squires and officials; their imagined surroundings and social conditions are perfectly unimportant factors—just as Monsieur Homais might be a business man in Chicago or Mrs. Bloom the wife of a schoolmaster in Vyshny-Volochok. Moreover their surroundings and conditions, whatever they might have been in "real life," underwent such a thorough permutation and reconstruction in the laboratory of Gogol's peculiar genius that (as has been observed already in connection with *The Government Inspector*) it is as useless to look in *Dead Souls* for an authentic Russian background as it would be to try and form a conception of Denmark on the basis of that little affair in cloudy Elsinor. And if you want "facts," then let us inquire what experience had Gogol of provincial Russia. Eight hours in a Podolsk inn, a week in Kursk, the rest he had seen from the window of his traveling carriage, and to this he had added the memories of his essentially Ukrainian youth spent in Mirgorod, Nejin, Poltava—all of which towns lay far outside Chichikov's itinerary. What seems true however is that *Dead Souls* provides an attentive reader with a collection of bloated dead souls belonging to *poshlyaki* and *poshlyáchki* described with that Gogolian gusto and wealth of weird detail which lift the whole thing to the level of a tremendous epic poem; and "poem" is in fact the subtle subtitle appended by Gogol to *Dead Souls.* There is something sleek and plump about *poshlust,* and this gloss, these smooth curves, attracted the artist in Gogol. The immense spherical *poshlyak* (singular of the word) Paul Chichikov eating the fig at the bottom of the milk which he drinks to mellow his throat, or dancing in his nightgown in the middle of the room while things on shelves rock in response to his ponderous jig (which ends in his ecstatically hitting his chubby behind— his real face—with the pink heel of his bare foot, thus propelling himself into the true paradise of dead souls) these are visions which transcend the lesser varieties of *poshlust* discernible in humdrum provincial surroundings or in the petty iniquities of petty officials. But a *poshlyak* even of Chichikov's colossal dimensions inevitably has somewhere in him a hole, a chink through which you see the worm, the little shriveled foot that lies all huddled up in the depth of the *poshlust*-painted vacuum. There was something fainty silly from the very start about that idea of buying up dead souls,—souls of serfs who had died since the last census and for whom their owners continued to pay the poll-tax, thus endowing them with a kind of abstract existence which however was quite concretely felt by the squire's pocket and could be just as "concretely" exploited by Chichikov, the buyer of such phantasma. This faint but rather sickening silliness was for a certain time concealed by the maze of complex machinations. *Morally* Chichikov was hardly guilty of any special crime in attempting to buy up dead men in a country where live men were lawfully purchased and pawned. If I paint my face with homemade Prussian Blue instead of applying the Prussian Blue which is sold by the state and cannot be manufactured by private persons, my crime will be hardly worth a passing smile and no writer will make of it a Prussian Tragedy. But if I have surrounded the whole business with a good deal of mystery and flaunted a cleverness that presupposed most intricate difficulties in perpetrating a crime of that kind, and if owing to my letting a garrulous neighbor peep at my pots of home-brew paint I get arrested and am roughly handled by men with authentic blue faces, then the laugh for what it is worth is on me. In spite of Chichikov's fundamental irreality in a fundamentally unreal world, the fool in him is apparent because from the very start he commits blunder upon blunder. It was silly to try to buy dead souls from an old woman who was afraid of ghosts; it was an incredible lapse of acumen to suggest such a Queer Street deal to the braggard and bully Nozdrev. I repeat however for the benefit of those who like books to provide them with "real people" and "real crime" and a "message" (that horror of horrors borrowed from the jargon of quack reformers) that *Dead Souls* will get them nowhere. Chichikov's guilt being a purely conventional matter, his destiny can hardly provoke any emotional reaction on our part. This is an additional reason why the view taken by Russian readers and critics, who saw in *Dead Souls* a matter-of-fact description of existing conditions, seems so utterly and ludicrously wrong. But when the legendary *Poshlyak* Chichikov is considered as he ought to be, i.e., as a creature of Gogol's special brand moving in a special kind of Gogolian coil, the abstract notion of swindling in this serf-pawning business takes on strange flesh and begins to mean much more than it did when we considered it in the light of social conditions peculiar to Russia a hundred years ago. The dead souls he is buying are not merely names on a slip of paper. They are the dead souls that fill the air of Gogol's world with their leathery flutter, the clumsy animula of Manilov or of Korobochka, of the housewives of the town of N., of countless other little people bobbing throughout the book. Chichikov himself is merely the ill-paid representative of the Devil, a traveling salesman from Hades, "our Mr. Chichikov" as the Satan & Co. firm may be imagined calling their easy-going, healthy-looking but inwardly shivering and rotting agent. The *poshlust* which Chichikov personifies is one of the main attributes of the Devil, in whose existence, let it be added, Gogol believed far more seriously than he did in that of God. The chink in Chichikov's armor, that rusty chink emitting a faint but dreadful smell (a punctured can of conserved lobster tampered with and forgotten by some meddling fool in the pantry) is the organic aperture in the devil's armor. It is the essential stupidity of universal *poshlust*.

Chichikov is doomed from the start and he rolls to that doom with a slight wobble in his gait which only the *poshlyaki* and *poshlyáchkis* of the town of N. are capable of finding genteel and pleasant. At important moments when he launches upon one of those sententious speeches (with a slight break in his juicy voice—the tremolo of "dear brethren"), that are meant to drown his real intentions in a treacle of pathos, he applies to himself the words "despicable worm" and, curiously enough, a real worm is gnawing at his vitals and becomes suddenly visible if we squint a little when peering at his rotundity. I am reminded of a certain poster in old Europe that advertised automobile tires and featured something like a human being entirely made of concentric rings of rubber; and likewise, rotund Chichikov may be said to be formed of the tight folds of a huge flesh-colored worm.

If the special gruesome character attending the main theme of the book has been conveyed and if the different aspects of *poshlust* which I have noted at random have become connected in such a way as to form an artistic phenomenon (its Gogolian leitmotiv being the "roundness" of *poshlust*), then *Dead Souls* will cease to mimic a humorous tale or a social indictment and henceforth may be adequately discussed. So let us look at the pattern a little more closely.

> The gates of the hostelry in the governmental town of N. [so the book begins] admitted a smallish fairly elegant *britzka* on springs, of the sort used by bachelors such as retired colonels, staff-captains, country squires who own about a hundred souls of peasants—in short by all those who are dubbed "gentlemen of the medium quality." Sitting in the *britzka* was a gentleman whose countenance could not be termed handsome, yet neither was he ill-favored: he was not too stout, nor was he too thin; you could not call him old, just as you could not say that he was still youthful. His arrival produced no stir whatever in the town and was not accompanied by anything unusual; alone two Russian *muzhiks* who were standing at the door of a dram-shop opposite the inn made certain remarks which however referred more to the carriage than to the person seated therein. "Look at that wheel there," said one. "Now what do you think—would that wheel hold out as far as Moscow if need be, or would it not?" "It would," answered the other. "And what about Kazan—I think it would not last that far?" "It would not,"—answered the other. Upon this the conversation came to a close. And moreover, as the carriage drove up to the inn, a young man chanced to pass wearing white twill trousers that were very tight and short and a swallow-tail coat with claims to fashion from under which a shirtfront was visible fastened with a Tula bronze pin in the shape of a pistol. The young man turned his head, looked back at the carriage, caught hold of his cap, which the wind was about to blow off, and then went his way.

The conversation of the two "Russian *muzhiks*" (a typical Gogolian pleonasm) is purely speculative—a point which the abominable Fisher Unwin and Thomas Y. Crowell translations of course miss. It is a kind of to-be-or-not-to-be meditation in a primitive form. The speakers do not know whether the *britzka* is going to Moscow or not, just as Hamlet did not trouble to look whether, perhaps, he had not mislaid his bodkin. The *muzhiks* are not interested in the question of the precise itinerary that the *britzka* will follow; what fascinates them is solely the ideal problem of fixing the imaginary instability of a wheel in terms of imaginary distances; and this problem is raised to the level of sublime abstraction by their not knowing the exact distance from N., (an imaginary point) to Moscow, Kazan or Timbuctoo—and caring less. They impersonate the remarkable creative faculty of Russians, so beautifully disclosed by Gogol's own inspiration, of working in a void. Fancy is fertile only when it is futile. The speculation of the two *muzhiks* is based on nothing tangible and leads to no material results; but philosophy and poetry are born that way; meddlesome critics looking for a moral might conjecture that the rotundity of Chichikov is bound to come to grief, being symbolized by the rotundity of that doubtful wheel. Andrey Bely, who was a meddler of genius, saw in fact the whole first volume of *Dead Souls* as a closed circle whirling on its axle and blurring the spokes, with the theme of the wheel cropping up at each new revolution on round Chichikov's part.[1] Another special touch is exemplified by the chance passer-by—that young man portrayed with a sudden and wholly irrelevant wealth of detail: he comes there as if he was going to stay in the book (as so many of Gogol's homunculi seem intent to do—and do not). With any other writer of his day the next paragraph would have been bound to begin: "Ivan, for that was the young man's name" . . . But no: a gust of wind interrupts his stare and he passes, never to be mentioned again. The faceless saloon-walker in the next passage (whose movements are so quick as he welcomes the newcomers that you cannot discern his features) is again seen a minute later coming down from Chichikov's room and spelling out the name on a slip of paper as he walks down the steps. "Pa-vel I-va-no-vich Chi-chi-kov"; and these syllables have a taxonomic value for the identification of that particular staircase.

When speaking of *The Government Inspector* I found pleasure in rounding up those peripheral characters that enliven the texture of its background. Such characters in *Dead Souls* as the inn-servant or Chichikov's valet (who had a special smell of his own which he imparted at once to his variable lodgings) do not quite belong to that class

1. See the translation in this volume of a portion of Bely's book on Gogol, pp. 517–31 [*Editor*].

of Little People. With Chichikov himself and the country squires he meets they share the front stage of the book although they speak little and have no visible influence upon the course of Chichikov's adventures. Technically speaking, the creation of peripheral personages in the play was mainly dependent upon this or that character alluding to people who never emerged from the wings. In a novel the lack of action or speech on the part of secondary characters would not have been sufficient to endow them with that kind of backstage existence, there being no footlights to stress their actual absence from the front place. Gogol however had another trick up his sleeve. The peripheral characters of his novel are engendered by the subordinate clauses of its various metaphors, comparisons and lyrical outbursts. We are faced by the remarkable phenomenon of mere forms of speech directly giving rise to live creatures. This is perhaps the most typical example of how this happens.

"Even the weather had obligingly accommodated itself to the setting: the day was neither bright nor gloomy but of a kind of blue-grey tint such as is found only upon the worn-out uniforms of garrison soldiers, for the rest a peaceful class of warriors except for their being somewhat inebriate on Sundays."

It is not easy to render the curves of this life-generating syntax in plain English so as to bridge the logical, or rather biological, hiatus between a dim landscape under a dull sky and a groggy old soldier accosting the reader with a rich hiccup on the festive ouskirts of the very same sentence. Gogol's trick consists in using as a link the word *"vprochem"* ("for the rest," "otherwise," *"d'ailleurs"*) which is a connection only in the grammatical sense but mimics a logical link, the word "soldiers" alone affording a faint pretext for the juxtaposition of "peaceful"; and as soon as this false bridge of *"vprochem"* has accomplished its magical work these mild warriors cross over, staggering and singing themselves into that peripheral existence with which we are already familiar.

* * *

EDMUND WILSON

Gogol: The Demon in the Overgrown Garden†

* * *

Gogol's style is a variety of that viscous prose which—
for reasons rather difficult to understand—was so popular
in the early nineteenth century. The plum cake of Charles
Lamb [1] is a typical example; so, in a different field, is the
maddeningly impeded narrative style of a Hawthorne or a
Herman Melville. This style allows no rapid progression.
A paragraph seems a mere clot of words, which might
almost as well be read backward as forward and in which
the contrived rhythms have the air of being ends in themselves, since they are always forcing the reader to stop and
pay attention to them instead of carrying him along. This
style must have been due to some very strong pressures,
for it is shared by a relatively careless writer who worked
on a big scale, like Balzac; [2] and even by a popular writer,
like Scott,[3] who did want to tell a story. The settings of
the stage in Balzac, the antiquarian preliminaries of Scott,
are often mare's-nests of this littered non-functional style,
which combines the facetious with the pompous, clumsily
handled actualities with jaunty mythological allusions.
Now, Gogol is the master of the mare's-nest. Though he
may seem to be merely stirring round and round his thick
and nutritious pages, as if they were the strawberry boiled
preserve, or the *kasha* [4] to be eaten with currants or honey,
or the dough full of hazelnuts and poppyseeds for one of
the fancier forms of the rich polymorphous Ukrainian
bread that his country people are always eating, this invariably results in a finished dish, which contributes to a
well-arranged dinner. The Russian genius for movement,
which is one of the great features of Russian literature—
I make no apology in this connection for continually changing the metaphor—never allows Gogol's prose to get really
stuck; there is always a drama on foot that you know will
not let you down, and in the meantime the rhapsodies,

† From *The Nation*, December 6,
1952, pp. 521 and 523–23. All notes
are by the editor.
1. English essayist, 1775–1834.
2. Honoré de Balzac (1799–1810),

masterly, prolific French novelist.
3. Sir Walter Scott (1771–1832), Scottish author of historical novels.
4. A common Russian dish; buckwheat gruel.

the inventories, the interpolated anecdotes, and the huge, Homeric similes that are whole short stories in themselves are managed with a great sense of rhetoric, so that they do not hold anything up, and they always become in some curious way organic parts of the story. With so much that might be stifling or stagnant, like the life that Gogol depicts, there is always something else that creates suspense—an element of the passionate, the *detraqué*,[5] that may startle us at any moment. In these pages, which in style resemble the tangled forests and the overgrown gardens that are a recurrent motif in Gogol's work, from his earliest goblin tales to Plyushkin's estate in *Dead Souls*, astounding transformations take place: a devil will suddenly appear at the turn of a paragraph, a treasure will be revealed—though the treasures are mirages arranged by the devils—but, as is not always the case with the Gothic novels or the Hoffmannesque [6] tales from which Gogol derived, these visions have a force of emotion, an intense identity and life of their own, that make even Poe seem cerebral and such fancies of Hawthorne's [7] as the Minister's Black Veil and the Black Sabbath of Young Goodman Brown mere phantoms of woven words.

* * *

From *Dead Souls* all the glory has departed of ancient Ukrainian legend as well as the amusing mythology of Ukrainian peasant lore, and even the gentleness and decency of the comfortable "old-world landowners." We are submerged in the messy and stuffy and smelly and run-to-seed life of landowners who are drunken and quarrelsome, moping and ineffective, brutal and self-assertive or crazily acquisitive or stupidly grasping. After an opening almost Pickwickian,[8] with a man putting up at an inn, this strange book, which never ceases to be humorous, leads us into a domain of horror: another and ranker jungle that is also a stagnant morass. Gogol wallows, like his characters, in the paragraphs of a cluttered, apparently phlegmatic style that has now been brought to perfection; yet this style has a persistent undercurrent of sadness, of disgust, of chagrin;

5. French for "derailed," "mad."
6. E. T. A. Hoffmann (1776–1822), German author of romantic stories of the grotesque and fantastic.
7. Nathaniel Hawthorne (1804–64), American novelist, author of *The Scarlet Letter* (1850) and many other works. The Minister and Goodman Brown are characters in his fiction.
8. *The Pickwick Papers* (1836–37), a series of humorous sketches by Charles Dickens (1812–70), English novelist.

it condemns and it undermines. There is still the same queer suspense that is sometimes disrupted by violence but is never completely relieved. What, we ask ourselves, is meant by this chronicle of Chichikov, the empty soul, who buys up the names of serfs (referred to as "souls" in old Russia) and have died since the last census, in order to pretend he owns them and borrow money on them? Are not the souls of their masters also dead? Are these landowners really devils who appear to Chichikov or is he himself a devil who has come for *them?* Exposed in the district he has been working, he is last seen driving away in his carriage. There is a moment of respite and open horizons—the troika dashing off with its cheerfull bells. In this torpid and moldy Russia, something has been set in motion, and Gogol has a moment of exaltation. Bùt where is it going? he asks, and the horizon returns no answer. Nor is he able to escape from this world that is tedious as well as mad; nor has he power to redeem his hero through the Purgatory he plans to succeed this Hell. In the fragments that have come to us of the Second Part, the adventurer Chichikov, though sent to jail, seems to emerge just as much of a scoundrel, and the supposedly virtuous characters are the victims of obsessions like those of the First.

* * *

The typical situation in Gogol is the sudden falling-out of the bottom of some impressive construction that we have watched being elaborately built. You have, thus, the dissolution of the old-world landowners; the loss of Taras Bulba's sons; the explosion between the two Ivans; the theft of the overcoat in the famous later story; the cataclysmic discoveries, too late, in the plays, of the large-scale imposture of "The Inspector General" and of the confidence game in "The Gamblers," the abject jumping out the window of the fiancé of *Marriage* at the moment when, with infinite difficulty, his betrothal has been achieved; the breakdown of Chichikov's fraudulent traffic just in his hour of triumph when he is feted as the toast of the town. So Gogol and his great book, at the moment when Turgenev says that all attention in Russia was centered on him and it, unexpectedly collapsed together.

Gogol presents an unusual case of a frustrating impasse of the spirit, a hopeless neurotic deadlock, combined with a gusto for life, an enormous artistic vitality. So vigorous and so rich is this talent that it must have been difficult for his friends and his readers to foresee that it was doomed to be choked. Lavrin suggests that the trouble may be traced to an Oedipus complex, an explanation suggested so often that it is coming to seem rather suspect. There is, however, no doubt that Gogol's defeat was bound up with his lifelong failure to arrive at any satisfactory sexual life. Fear of marriage is made the comic theme of the story of "Shponka and His Aunt," deliberately left unfinished, and of the rather inferior comedy "Marriage," and Gogol's difficulties in this connection appear in another kind of theme, which he never succeeds in developing: that of the ideal woman, seen briefly and adored from afar—the maidenly *pensionnaire* who makes such an impression on Chichikov; the Italian beauty who gleams in the crowd for the hero of the projected novel on Rome. The magnificent opening of this novel has far more of positive inspiration than anything that has survived from the Second Part of *Dead Souls*. Gogol's longing for a feudal world becomes somewhat more sympathetic when it is dramatized in the person of an Italian prince returning from impoverished exile to discover for the first time his native Rome, but at the moment when it at last becomes necessary, after the long, the monumental buildup, to bring the prince into direct relations with the dazzling Annunziata, the story abruptly breaks off. In "Viy," of the Mirgorod series, the traveler and the beauty—both Gogol and his heroes are always traveling—do engage, but with a fatal result, and that this fatal result was inevitable to Gogol's vision of life is shown by the turn that he seems to have given to the folk tale from which he derived the story. This is a version of the vampire legend in which a young man must stand watch for three nights by the body of a dead woman, who at midnight comes to life and attacks him. Gogol says that he has followed the folk tale exactly, but in the versions of this story included in the collection of Afanasiev, the Russian Grimm,[9] the young man is always able to defend himself with the Psalter and the sign of the cross, and finally defeats the witch; and, from these and from the habits of folk tales in general, we may assume that it is Gogol himself—the solid Ukrainian background, more or less realistically presented, is certainly very much Gogol's—

9. The Grimm brothers—Jakob (1785–1863) and Wilhelm (1786–1859)—collected German folktales; Alexander Afanasiev (1826–71) was the chief nineteenth-century Russian student, collector, and editor of Russian fairy tales.

who is responsible for making his student succumb at the third vigil and fall dead with fright when the vampire calls in the reinforcements of Hell (just as, in "Taras Bulba," the young Andrey is destroyed through the irresistible spell that has been cast on him by the Polish princess). It should be noted that the girl is revenging herself. She had fastened herself first on the student in the shape of an old hag, and he had only got rid of her by beating her to death, at which point she had been forced to reveal herself as the typical Gogolian beauty, intimidating and unattainable. In a final ironic scene, the boy's former companions on the walking trip that has had for him this tragic end— back in college now and warming over their cups—are discussing his fate at their ease. Not having had to share his ordeal, they decide that if he had not been yellow, the witch could have done him no harm: "You've only got to cross yourself and spit on her tail, and nothing can happen to you!" But this rite had never worked for Gogol. It was always the Devil who appeared to him, never the Savior he hoped for, and when the feminine apparition toward whom he aspired comes at all close to any of his heroes, she proves to be a devil, too.

It was only to Dostoevsky, in the next generation, that the Christian revelation came. It is one of the striking features of the continuity of Russian literature that Dostoevsky should not only show strongly the literary influence of Gogol but that he should even give somewhat the impression of being haunted by Gogol's devils and even of saving Gogol's soul.

SIMON KARLINSKY

[Portrait of Gogol as a Word Glutton]†

No one who reads *Dead Souls* attentively should fail to notice Gogol's overwhelming interest in language in general, in its phonetic aspects and in various other linguistic phenomena and problems. This interest is so general and all-embracing that it begins even before the stage where actual verbalization is reached on that pre-verbal level

† Abridged version of the article "Portrait of Gogol as a Word Glutton, with Rabelais, Sterne, and Gertrude Stein as Background Figures," *California Slavic Studies* V (1970): pp. 169–86.

where tone or pitch alone can convey the meaning, that is the vocal rather than the verbal kind of communication which animals also use.

Thus, at one point Plyushkin, the miser, mutters something unintelligible to Chichikov, and Gogol tells us that the tone of this muttering conveyed the message decipherable as: "May the devil take you and your respects." Similarly, the gobbling of the tom turkey in Mme. Korobochka's barnyard is interpreted by Gogol to mean "Bless you, sir!" The entire novel *Dead Souls* is permeated with remarks or formulae that call our attention to the verbal side of things —such qualifying expressions as: "spending his time, as they say, very pleasantly," or "as these are called in Russian inns," or "as the French say," or "according to a wonderful expression used by Russian peasants."

Throughout the book, Gogol never quite recovers from his fascination with the way language works. He examines the problems of tone and diction in his commentary on the conversation between Chichikov and Mrs. Korobochka on the morning after he had spent the night at her estate. Gogol points out that the tone used by Chichikov on that occasion was far less respectful than the tone he used when speaking to Manilov and this observation is followed by a detailed discussion of various degrees of respect or servility that it is possible to express in Russian in various social situations. At the end of part one, chapter 3, there is the commentary on the comparative virtues of the English, French, German, and Russian languages and on their suitability to express the respective national character of each nation. And when Chichikov, in his meditations at the governor's ball, uses one single word that may be considered substandard or sub-literary (*galantërnyj*), Gogol seizes this pretext to launch on a page-long examination of various lexical usages in the literary Russian of his day and of the various current attitudes to literary and sub-literary strata existing in the language.

Although he has no term to describe it, Gogol is clearly aware of what we today call the phonemic systems peculiar to various languages. For instance, while preparing to go to the ball, Chichikov emits various sounds which we are told sounded like French even though he did not know any French. Elsewhere in the novel, Gogol says that in order to pronounce English correctly one has to make a birdlike face. If we discount the humor of this statement, what remains is evidence of Gogol's understanding of the type of articulation required by the phonemic system of a language which uses sounds that do not exist in Russian. * * *

When we come to individual separate words, we note that a particular word may play a key role in Gogol's plots, which goes far beyond its inherent meaning. * * * In *Dead Souls,* we see Chichikov toppled from his earlier position of wealth and power because on one single occasion he called his partner in crime *popovič*.[1] In the unfinished second part of the novel, the love affair between Tentetnikov and the ideal girl Ulenka collapses because of the brief word *ty* [2] used by Ulenka's father General Betrishchev when addressing his daughter's suitor. Gogol points out such ability of a word to acquire a significance and a momentum beyond its original meaning when he comments on the sudden popularity of Chichikov with the ladies after his purchase of the serfs becomes known: "The word 'millionaire' was to blame—not the millionaire himself but just the word alone."

Here we see what is usually taken to be Gogol's social criticism operating as it always does on two levels: while seemingly investigating a social phenomenon, Gogol is also investigating how words work and how he can play with them. * * *

From this preoccupation with verbal power there is only a step to the concept of the word as a magical spell or incantation. This concept is very much present both in Gogol's work and in his general mentality. * * * Even in the supposedly realistic *Dead Souls,* part two, after describing Tentetnikov's inactivity and his need to be awakened by someone who will come and say "forward" to him, Gogol extends Tentetnikov's predicament to the whole of Russia and says that all his country needs is a statesman who will command the whole of Russia to arise by uttering this all-powerful single word "forward!" Lest we take this for an allegory, we should remember that Gogol seriously expected the whole of Russia to experience a profound moral regeneration the moment Zhukovsky's [3] translation of *The Odyssey* was published and read by all social classes; that

1. The son of a priest [*Editor*].
2. The familiar second-person pronoun, as distinguished from the more formal and polite *vy* [*Editor*].

3. Vasily Zhukovsky (1783–1852), great Russian Romantic poet, whose translation of Homer's *Odyssey* was published in 1849 [*Editor*].

he expected deep-going social reactions to result from publication of some new poems by Yazykov; [4] that in his *Selected Passages from Correspondence with Friends* he recom-
mends the landowners to use certain designated swearwords
on their serfs that should immediately change these serfs'
character and outlook; and, finally, we may recall the
passages in his private letters where he warns people that
his own words are divinely inspired and that misfortune
awaits those who would not heed his prophetic words.

Gogol does not have as great an interest in the graphic
side of language as does Laurence Sterne,[5] with his typo-
graphical tricks, lines full of asterisks, and blank pages.
But even this aspect of language does not escape Gogol's
attention entirely and in *Dead Souls* we get the charming
vignette of the valet Petrushka who reads any sort of book
whatsoever because his main interest is the reading process
itself and the curious fact that the separate letters on the
printed page are always sure to form some word or other.

Gogol shares with Rabelais,[6] Sterne, and Stein [7] an interest in an aspect of the speech act of which most other
writers are not even aware. When Chichikov, immersed in
his checkers game, absentmindedly reiterates the same sentence three times, and Nozdrev, equally absorbed in his
cheating, repeats his answer twice, we are given a sample
of speech that has nothing to communicate beyond asserting
the presence of the speaker. Chichikov's horses, we are told,
also require such communication for its own sake. The
thing that pleases these animals most about Tentetnikov's
stables is that any horse can neigh at any other horse there
and receive a reply. Anton Chekhov [8] was later to develop
such non-communicating verbalization to the level of a
full-fledged dramatic device in his plays.

* * *

Persons who study Russian complain frequently that they
find Gogol impossible to read in the original. Indeed, the
prose of Gogol presents to a foreign reader difficulties that

4. Nikolai Yazykov (1803–46), Russian poet famous in the 1820s, praised
for the rush of words as well as
for cool restraint; Yazykov was Gogol's favorite poet [*Editor*].

5. English author (1713–68) of the
whimsical, humorous novels *A Senti-
mental Journey* and *Tristram Shandy*
(1760–67) [*Editor*].

6. François Rabelais (1494–1553),

French writer, author of *Gargantua
and Pantagruel* [*Editor*].

7. Gertrude Stein (1874–1946),
American writer who lived in Paris
for the last forty-three years of her
life. She greatly influenced Heming-
way and other modern writers [*Editor*].

8. Russian playright and short story-
writer, 1860–1904 [Editor].

he would never encounter in Pushkin, Tolstoy, or Chekhov. I have not seen any statistics on the subject, but it seems likely that Gogol used one of the largest and most varied vocabularies among nineteenth-century Russian writers. He made use of almost the entire lexical range of spoken and written Russian of his time, from the most elevated philosophical and theological vocabulary rooted in Old Church Slavic to the most vulgar and crude slang he could find, not to mention the rich admixture of Ukrainian in his early stories.

In matters of vocabulary, the position of Gogol in Russian literature is exactly analogous to that of Rabelais in French literature. Like Rabelais three hundred years before him, Gogol found the standard literary vocabulary insufficient and resorted to dialectal forms, to special vocabularies, and took to inventing his own words. Andrey Bely's masterful study of Gogol's style demonstrates the wide use of regional, colloquial, rare, and invented verbs in *Dead Souls*.[9] The special and professional vocabularies used in *Dead Souls,* such as agricultural terminology, the slang of hunters and dog-breeders, bureaucratic language, military slang that Nozdrev had picked up from his officer friends, and special culinary terminology are described in detail by Bely and by V. V. Vinogradov. The lists of Nozdrev's dogs (part one, chapter 4) and Korobochka's cakes (part one, chapter 3) show that Gogol revels in difficult and rare words, many of which could not be easily understood by the Russian reader of his time and are even less accessible today.

The character in *Dead Souls* whose vocabulary shows the greatest verbal invention and variety is Nozdrev. L. A. Bulakhovsky sees in his speech a sort of compendium of bad speech habits of his age. Here we get a mixture of slangy

9. [See extract from Bely's study of Gogol, pp. 517–31, below—*Editor.*] The lengths to which Gogol could go in order to use rare and unusual verbs can be seen in part two, chapter 1, where after the passage about Tentetnikov's difficulties with the peasants, we are treated to a nature description in which six species of birds are mentioned, so that Gogol can introduce six strange verbs that denote birdcalls. One of these birds is called *barašek*, which also means "lamb" (it appears in Derzhavin's "Life at Zvanka" [1807]; and S. T. Aksakov discuses this bird in his *Memoirs of a Hunter,* where he relates its name to the bleating sound it makes). The *barašek* completely confused David Magarshack, who, in his translation of *Dead Souls* (Baltimore, 1961), thought Gogol meant a real lamb. Stopping short at the idea of an airborne ungulate, Magarshack translated *podnjavšijsja na vozdukh barašek* as "a lamb was bleating as it skipped in the meadow."

expressions of varied derivation, and it is curious to note that the verbal imagination of his character seems to stimulate Gogol to a verbal inventiveness of his own, even in the descriptive passages. In the next chapter, devoted to the miser Plyushkin, the method is visual rather than verbal, in keeping with the verbal paucity of Plyushkin himself, and the descriptive passages are accordingly toned down.

The postmaster, who tells the story of Captain Kopeykin, shares with Nozdrev the predilection for the macaronic mixture of French and Russian. In this, Gogol is not unique in the Russian literature of his time. We know from other writers the important role of the French language in Russian society of the first half of the nineteenth century. Griboedov [1] objected to the mixing of French "with the dialect of Nizhny-Novgorod" and Pushkin obtained humorous effects by having a character in *Dubrovskij* conjugate a Russian verb in accordance with French grammar. In 1840, there appeared a long satirical macaronic poem *Sensacii i zamečanija gospoži Kurdjukovoj za granicej dan l'ètranže* by Ivan Myatlev which had a considerable popular success. The method of Myatlev is that of Gogol's two ladies, the simply pleasant one and the one pleasant in every respect: the Russian is sprinkled with French words and phrases, but without doing any actual violence to either language. What Nozdrev and the postmaster do to French on the other hand is similar to what Rabelais often does with Latin, especially in the speech of the Limousin scholar whom Pantagruel meets (book two, Chapter 6). French words are russified with Slavic prefixes and suffixes: *bezeška* from *baiser, razuspé-delicatesse, burdaška* for *Bordeaux*.

The macaronic neologisms of the postmaster represent only a small portion of the coined and invented words Gogol uses in *Dead Souls*. Eighteenth-century Russian writers invented words because there was a practical need for new words. Dostoevsky introduced new words to convey new shades of meaning and some of his coinages have entered the language permanently. Gogol, like Rabelais and like Sterne in the tale of the abbess and Margarita,[2] invents words that he needs only for one particular occasion. At the simplest level. he follows the earlier tradition much used by Tredyakovsky, the quasi-Homeric double

---

1. Alexander Griboedov (1795–1829), Russian playwright, author of *Woe from Wit* [*Editor*].

2. In *Tristram Shandy* [*Editor*].

adjective: *umno-khudoščavoe slovo, vsespasajuščaja ruka.*
These are easily intelligible and so are many of the strange
new verbs Gogol coins from existing nouns (*omedvedit'*, "to
make someone like a bear"; *oščelivat'*, "to cover with cracks
or slits"), or nouns from unexpected verbs (*vospoitel'nica,*
"female nourisher, who gave drink"). The reader has to
make contextual guesses when Nozdrev coins a verb from
a non-existent noun (*poddeljulit'*) or when Gogol himself
comes up with a verbal noun like *vzbutetenivanie* in a descriptive passage. Vinogradov, in line with the Soviet view
of Gogol as critical realist and ethnographer, treats Gogol's
coinages as genuine regional or slangy terms which Gogol
had overheard and faithfully recorded. He cites the cardplayers' slang as an example. Vladimir Nabokov is probably
nearer the truth when he conjectures that the odd coinages
in the passage quoted by Vinogradov are actually Gogol's
own invention.[3]

The proper names of his characters constitute the area in
which Gogol gives his extraordinary verbal inventiveness a
completely free rein. As Andrey Bely puts it: "Family
names are Gogol's delirium;" or, even more imaginatively:
"His need to gush forth in whistling sounds runs amok in
a squadron of names." In *Dead Souls,* this applies less to
the names of the principals than to minor and episodic
characters. There have been attempts to explain such names
as Chichikov and Plyushkin as having specific significance,
but their semantic suggestivity is too vague and indefinite
for any precise identification. Gogol's method has nothing
to do with the eighteenth-century Russian comedy of Fonvizin and Kapnist[4] where the name was used to designate the
type of character. As far as concrete significance goes, Bely
makes a convincing case for Korobochka being the double
of Chichikov's cassette (*škatulka*): the fact that she catches

3. Vladimir Nabokov, *Nikolai Gogol* (New York, 1961), passim. For the benefit of those who know the passage on the cardplayers from versions such as Magarshack's ("Heart! Heart-ache! Spades! Spadefulls! Spade-a-little-lady! or simply Speedy!"), it is instructive to quote a part of Nabo-kov's exegesis of the same passage. "*Piki*—'spades'—French—*piques*—turn into *pikentia*, that is, assume a jocular dog-Latin ending; or they produce such variations as *pikendias* (false

Greek ending) or *pichura* (a faint ornithological shade), sometimes magnified into *pichurishchuk* (the bird turning as it were into an ante-diluvian lizard, thus reversing the order of natural evolution)" (*Nikolai Gogol*, p. 85). It can be seen what riches are inevitably lost in any trans-lation of Gogol, no matter how excellent.
4. Denis Fonvizin (1745–92), Russian playwright; and Vasily Kapnist (1757–1823), poet and playwright [*Editor*].

him with the cassette open, the similarity of the description of the insides of the cassette and the insides of her coach, the danger that her arrival in town constitutes to his most precious possession. As Bely puts it, she is the very opposite of the fairy-godmother even if she does travel in a pumpkin-like conveyance. In fact, Korobochka is not only the double but also the nemesis of the cassette. One might also venture to suggest that there is a strange reversal of names between Sobakevich ("dog's son") and Nozdrev ("of nostrils"). It is Nozdrev who is constantly surrounded by dogs, while *his* name suggests the ring through the nostrils by which the trained Russian bears, to whom Sobakevich is compared, are led about.

Once we move away from the principals, the names of Gogolian characters seem to have but one purpose: to be as subtly unusual and unexpected as possible. There is a broad humor in the names of the dead serfs that Chichikov buys, all those Korovy-Kirpich ("Cow's brick"), Elizaveta Vorobey ("Elizabeth the sparrow"), Neuvazhay-Koryto (nicely rendered by Mrs. Garnett as "Never mind the trough!"). Episodic characters are invented merely in order to bring in absolutely impossible, unlikely names, such as that strange Russian Scot Macdonald Karovich. The urge for name-giving extends to objects and animals.

The publication of Gogol's complete notebooks for *Dead Souls* in the 1951 Soviet Academy of Sciences edition of his Collected Works provides us with a number of new insights into Gogol's verbal preoccupations. In his researches into the rural life of central Russia (with which he had had little first-hand contact), Gogol was aided by P. M. Yazykov, the brother of the poet Nikolay Yazykov (for whom Gogol conceived a passionate emotional attachment when he was writing *Dead Souls*). Of the long lists of local Simbirsk proper names, professions, household utensils, birds, bird-calls, etc., provided by P. M. Yazykov (an amateur ethnographer of sorts), Gogol inevitably selected the most bizarre and outlandish items, many of which found their way into the first or the second part of his novel. Much of the dog-lore displayed in the description of Nozdrev's kennel, Korobochka's pastries, the waterfowl in the second part, are all traceable to Yazykov's lists. In every case, Gogol, the supposed realist, chooses the more whimsical items and then adds some particular verbal invention of his own that is not found in the notebooks.

Thus, of the six names of rural saloons listed by Yazykov, Gogol selects the rather unexpected name Agashka (the pejorative diminutive of Agafya or Agatha). By the time this name found its way into the second part of *Dead Souls,* Gogol had transformed it in a way that provides a one-word illustration of the difference between raw ethnography and artistic creation. The name of the tavern that appears in the novel is Akulka, the derogatory form of Akulina.

The noble Roman name of Aquiline had undergone a strange degeneration in Russia and became the symbol of everything low and common. In the household of Sobake-vich, Akulka is the name of the kitchen maid who takes out the slops. To show the prosaic turn Tatyana's mother took after a long residence in the country, Pushkin (in *Eugene Onegin*) tells us that she took to calling a servant she had formerly addressed as Celina by her real name of Akulka, the two names presumably representing the greatest possible contrast in terms of elegance and vulgarity. A hundred years later, Vladimir Nabokov, in translating *Alice in Wonderland,* rendered Lewis Carroll's "will speak in contemptuous tones of the shark" as "he addresses the shark (*akula*) as Akulka." Agashka as a tavern name was bizarre, but Akulka is so outlandish as to merit the twentieth-century term "surrealistic."

* * *

The names in *Dead Souls* have been examined by Bely, who lists the strangest ones; by Kasack, who explains their etymologies, occasionally in rather farfetched ways; by Ermakov, who tried to treat these names in Freudian terms; and by Vladimir Nabokov, who commented on the humorous use to which these names are put by Gogol. None of these investigators seem to have noticed that Gogol amuses himself by arranging his strange names into definite patterns. In this respect, the practice of Gogol again has close parallels in Rabelais and in Gertrude Stein.

The simplest arrangement in Gogol involves two closely similar names usually with a rhyming effect: Uncle Mityay and Uncle Minyay; Foma the Elder and Foma the Younger; Father Carp and Father Polycarp; Moky Kifovich and Kifa Mokievich. The rhyming pair can also be hidden inside a longer list: among the landowners enumerated for Chichikov by Korobochka, the pair Kharpkin and Trepakin are surrounded by four other names. The next morning the innkeeper located a few versts from Korobochka's estate comes up with an entirely different set of neighbors and this time the point of the joke is the squire with the sudsy name of Myl'noy ("soapy"), inoffensively hidden among four other comparatively reasonable names.

The most usual form taken by the longer listings of names in *Dead Souls* is a sort of musical composition, with several minor climaxes and the final culmination in a blast of absurdity at the very end. The pattern can be seen in its basic form when some of the serfs that Plyushkin sold to Chichikov are enumerated (part one, chapter 6): "Paramonov and Pimenov and Panteleymonov, and even a certain Grigory Doezzhay-ne-doedesh." The reader is at first lulled by the alliterative series of names derived from Greek Orthodox saints, only to be suddenly jolted by the completely impossible name which contains two mutually contradictory statements: "go right up to it" and "you will not get there."

This is also the essential pattern of the extended list of young ladies of whom Chichikov happens to think when he runs out of conversation with the governor's daughter at the ball (part one, chapter 8). This is the passage which most English translators of Gogol either delete or abbreviate and simplify beyond recognition. Vladimir Nabokov quotes it in its entirely, comments on it and explains some of the names. In terms of a musical crescendo, we might note that the first minor climax in this list occurs when we learn that a name very rare in Russia is represented in the same family in both its French and German versions (Adelaide and Adelheid); the second and lesser one is connected with sisters Roza Feodorovna and Emilia Feodorovna. The final cymbal crash of absudity occurs at the very end of the list with the appearance of Maklatura Aleksandrovna, "maklatura" (more usually spelled "*makulatura*") being no name at all, but a technical term meaning "paper pulp" or "worthless paper."

Still more sophisticated is the list of Nozdrev's dogs (part one, chapter 4). In the first part of the list Gogol merely embroiders on the technical kennel terms he obtained from P. M. Yazykov. The dog names listed by Yazykov were often imperative forms of verbs—a widespread nineteenth-century Russian custom (dogs with names in the imperative also figure in the hunting scenes of Tolstoy's *War and Peace* and in Chekhov's farce *The Marriage Proposal*). Gogol uses some very rare Simbirsk area regional terms in this list. (His translators should have consulted an etymological dictionary to learn that *skosyr'*, which looks like an imperative of some obscure verb, is really a northern Russian word meaning "fop" or "insolent one," and that *severga* is a dialectal term meaning "impatient one" and not "northerner," as Mr. Guerney has wrongly guessed.) The effect of the list is one of crudity and vigor, but the last item comes from an entirely different lexical stratum, an elegant word that suggests a stately and aristocratic dowager (*popečitel'nica*, i.e., "a patroness of charitable activities"). Here again, the whole point seems to be the careful preparation of the final surprise. By placing his own invention against the ethnographic background provided by his informant, Gogol again achieves an effect of surreal fantasy.

* * *

Names are the most frequent item that Gogol arranges into lists, but there are many others. When Tolstoy lists objects, as he does in the first of the Sebastopol stories, he does so to convey the impression of the scene and the verbal side of the list is of no interest to him: "you go to the wharf—a peculiar odor of coal, manure, dampness and of beef strikes you; thousands of objects of all sorts—wood, meat, gabions, flour, iron, and so forth lie in heaps about the wharf." [5] Tolstoy lists only five objects out of the thousand and then breaks the list off with "and so forth," knowing that he had created the impression he needed. Gogol, however, at the very idea of the things Nozdrev *could have* bought at the fair if he had the money, lists nineteen hypothetical purchases, most of them with a modifying adjective. The lists of foodstuffs in *Dead Souls* can compete with anything in Rabelais, including the list of delicacies that make up the anatomy of the King Caremeprenant. Bely counts eighty-six various dishes mentioned in *Dead Souls*, the comedies and the Petersburg tales and comments "Not an Iliad but a Gobble-iad (*Zratv-iada*)." Wolfgang Kasack points out that many of these food lists constitute an important means of characterization. And indeed, the foods served by Nozdrev, Korobochka, and Sobakevich definitely contribute to their general characterization. A very interesting proof of this can be seen in the case of Korobochka. She offers Chichikov mostly baked things and meat pies

5. English version quoted from L. Tolstoy, *Sebastopol*, trans. by Isabel F. Hapgood (New York, 1888), p. 6.

during his visit in chapter 3. Five chapters later we recognize her before her name is ever mentioned as the mysterious traveler in the watermelon carriage by the baked items in her luggage. The identification is made even though only one item is repeated from the earlier list: *skordumki* (translated by Nabokov as "Skoro-dumplings"). Gogol had some more bakery goods to enumerate and he was not going to miss his chance.

Once we realize Gogol's love for words, his need to play with them in every imaginable way, we can see the origin of some of his stylistic extravagances and understand their odd resemblance to similar aspects in the style of writers seemingly so different from Gogol. In Gertrude Stein or Rabelais, as in *Dead Souls,* we encounter the wide use of tautology, of repetition of all sorts, of recapitulation and parallel syntactic constructions. * * *

Gogol's powerful visual imagination joins his verbal exuberance to produce his famous developed comparisons, such as the likening of the men at the ball to flies or Korobochka's dogs to a church choir. A very striking one occurs at the end of chapter 4, when Nozdrev, who is attacking Chichikov, is likened to a desperate young lieutenant about to take a fortress. After developing this comparison, Gogol withdraws the visual props but keeps the verbal ones by referring to Chichikov as the fortress for a few more sentences. A comically unexpected effect is produced at this point because due to the gender of the word "fortress" (*krepost'*) Chichikov is suddenly spoken of in the feminine.

There are other verbally exuberant qualities in Gogol's style: his elaborate sentence structure, analyzed in detail by Bely, who speaks of Gogol's "exploded sentence, scattered about in splinters of subordinate clauses" and the devices which Pereverzev in his chapter on Gogol's style calls amplification and self-interruption.[6] The best example of the use of amplification is the "Tale of Captain Kopeykin," a good early illustration of what later came to be called *skaz.* The narrative manner of the postmaster who tells this story is announced in chapter 8; the auxiliary expressions he uses to stretch out and amplify the tale occupy roughly half of the text, and if we were to blue-pencil the extraneous matter and the repetitions, the story could probably be cut down to about one-third of its length.

6. Valerian Pereverzev (1882–1968), a Soviet Marxist literary critic active in the 1920s, arrested and imprisoned from 1938 to 1956 [*Editor*].

The suspended logic of the "Tale of Captain Kopeykin" (the man who is suspected of being Chichikov, we are told at the very beginning, is without an arm and a leg) has a close parallel in Rabelais, when Master Janotus de Bragmardo is made to plead with Gargantua at great length for the return of the church bells which had been returned earlier (Book one, chapters 18, 19, 20). In such passages, the humor is in the explicitly absurd situation and the verbal humor plays an auxiliary role.

A related technique, peculiarly Gogol's, depends on the tacit assumption of an absurd proposition that is never verbalized. In the parable of Kifa Mokievich and Moky Kifovich, the really absurd idea is not that elephants hatch from an egg, but the tacit assumption that people go hunting bird eggs with rifles. Here we might again use the word surrealism. Another prime example of verbal surrealism in *Dead Souls* is the direct quotation from the dapple horse, a member of Chichikov's *troika* (all three horses are developed as very individual human characters). The odd thing is not that the horse thinks or speaks, but that it uses the language of an uneducated Russian peasant. This social and educational characteristic of the horse is what we may term Gogol's realism squared, super-realism, with the typical telescoped logic which is now called surrealism.

* * *

DMITRY ČIŽEVSKY

Gogol: Artist and Thinker†

* * *

The clearest instance in Gogol of a phantasmal reality concealed behind the concrete world is his device of *realization of metaphor*. Reality proves to be concealed behind a metaphor or simile or else simply turns into one. After beginning a simile Gogol seems to forget about it, and a strange process takes place: a *sbitenshchik* (a vendor of hot mead) turns into a samovar, Chichikov into a fortress, and Petr Petrovich Petukh into a watermelon.

A *sbitenshchik* was standing at the window with a ruddy copper samovar and a face as ruddy as the samovar, so that from a

† From the Annals of the Ukrainian Academy of Arts and Sciences in the U.S. II (Spring 1952): 272–78.

distance you might have thought there were *two samovars* in the window if one of *them* had not had a beard as black as pitch.

Nozdrev . . . looked the part of a lieutenant storming a fortress, desperate and at his wit's end. . . . *The fortress* he was attacking [Chichikov] looked anything but impregnable. On the contrary, the *fortress* was in such a fright that *its* soul hid in its very heels.

Along with the fish a round sort of man had got entangled [in the net], a man as wide as he was tall, a perfect watermelon or barrel. He was in a desperate situation and was shouting at the top of his lungs. . . . *The watermelon* was evidently not afraid on its own account. . . .

[Korobochka's carriage enters the town at night.] A very strange vehicle, which inspired doubts as to what one should call it. It was . . . rather like a fat-cheeked, swollen watermelon on wheels. The cheeks *of this watermelon,* that is, its doors, . . . were very hard to close. . . . *The watermelon* was filled with chintz pillows, . . . crammed full of bags of bread loaves, twisted rolls, rusks, biscuits, and pretzels of scalded dough. . . .

The sidewalk rushed along beneath him, the carriages with their galloping horses seemed motionless, the bridge stretched and broke at its arch, a house stood upside down, a sentry-box was rushing toward him, and the sentry's halberd together with the gilt letters of a signboard seemed to glisten on his very eyelash. And all this was brought about by a single glance, a single turn of a pretty head.

Thus the world distintegrates and dissolves into nothing; everything proves to be something other than it is; real objects pass through complete metamorphoses: Sobakevich is a "medium-sized bear"; Plyushkin is a "tear on the cloth of humanity"; a nobleman is a "bandit"; a nose is a "Counsellor of State," "a gentleman in a uniform . . . sewn in gold, with a high stand-up collar, wearing suede trousers and carrying a sword at his side." But this fantastic world is described by Gogol so vividly, so graphically, so plastically, and in such bright colors that its equal is hardly to be found in any literature.

Thus the "nothingness" of this world is revealed by techniques once used exclusively to scale the heights of "true being," with its *coincidentio oppositorum,* seemingly unattainable and inexpressible. The world dissolves into nothing; its deceptiveness is disclosed by the mere fact that everything in it proves to be like something else. Moreover, the likeness is usually to something "lower" than itself; Gogol's metaphors are very frequently "downward metaphors," i.e., comparison of a higher order of being to a lower—in particular of human beings to animals or even objects. Does not Gogol's work thus become much more negative and destructive than his nineteenth-century critics supposed? For they regarded him as a realistic satirist who used his art to scourge society, to lay bare the evils of the "Nicolaian [1] Russian" of his time. But does not his satire in reality appear to be directed against the world itself?

Such a conclusion is tempting, but at bottom erroneous. Gogol did not regard destruction and negation as the aim of art or of literary art in particular. Art is called upon not to destroy, but to create: art must be an "imperceptible step toward Christianity." And for Gogol this means not destruction, but amelioration; not annihilation, but transformation of existing reality:

> My friend, in this world we are called upon not to destroy and demolish, but . . . *to turn everything to good ends,* even that which man has corrupted and turned to evil.

For Gogol the central idea in Christian doctrine is precisely this notion of "transformation," of "turning things to good ends." No matter how insignificant this mundane world may be, it is merely corrupt, but not fundamentally evil. In all the "nastiness," "swindlers," "bribe-takers" and "scoundrels" Gogol feels a primary responsibility to seek out the good that lies there hidden and disfigured.

> If you consider a swindler not merely as a swindler, but as a man as well, if you consider all the spiritual powers given him for good, which he has turned to evil or left unused . . . only then will you feel how noble our species can be . . . even in a swindler.

And knowledge of "nastiness" helps to show us the way out of this world, where the good is corrupted and disfigured. We

> have forgotten that the paths and the roads to this bright future lie hidden here in this dark and tangled present. . . . Since I began looking deeper into the nastiness around me, the light has shone forth in my spirit: before my eyes ways of egress, means, and paths begin to be revealed.

The principal method is love for mankind:

> Perhaps this man was not born utterly dishonest. . . . Perhaps a single drop of love would be sufficient to set him back on the path of righteousness.

1. Those of the age of Tsar Nicholas I, 1825–55 [*Editor*].

It may well be that the concrete means of salvation Gogol proposed in his "strange book," *Selected Passages From My Correspondence With My Friends,* are very naive, unsatisfactory, and unconvincing. In fact, their chief weakness is that they are too concrete. Concreteness is the greatest defect of all utopias. And, by accompanying his outline for a moral and religious utopia with bits of concrete advice on what should be done in the concrete historical situation of Russia under Nicholas I, Gogol himself weakened the efficacy and attractiveness of his utopia. He is a paradoxical figure, this Gogol, divided in his allegiances and striving to reconcile the opposites in his work and combine them into a single moral and religious doctrine. He was by no means a one-sided eulogist of his time, as many passages from this same "reactionary" book make clear. Often he considers the Russia of his time simply as a country "of the past":

> On the ship of duty and service each one of us must now be borne out of the slough. Each one of us must now serve, not as he used to serve in the Russia *of the past,* but in another, heavenly realm, the head of which is Christ Himself.

And Gogol even considers the possibilities of the utopian socialism of that time in the most ecstatic—and probably most successful—essay in the book, *The Glorious Resurrection*:

> How fitting this day would be, I thought, for this nineteenth century of ours, when thoughts about the happiness of mankind have become the favorite thoughts of everyone, . . . when many are dreaming about how to *transform all mankind,* . . . when people have even begun to say that *everything should be held in common*—houses and lands.

Of course, this is not an expression of sympathy for socialism, but it indicates a hope that Gogol's utopia might satisfy the socialists too; he does not even attempt to brand their ideal with any negative epithet.[2]

But the main thing for Gogol is not an external, juridical, social transformation of the world, but the transformation of each individual man, that "renascence" which

2. V. Gippius called attention to this passage in his brilliant book *Gogol'* (Leningrad, 1924, p. 184). Gippius's book contains a number of excellent observations on Gogol's ethics, but unfortunately "for reasons of censorship" he was obliged to be very timid in his references to the central religious motifs in Gogol's philosophy. [A translation of a section of an article by Gippius is included in the present volume, pp.489–517 above—Editor.]

was to have been the theme of the later parts of *Dead Souls*. The theme is hinted at even in the first part:

> Human passions are as numberless as the sands of the sea, and all are different from one another, and all of them, base and noble alike, all begin as man's servants and only later become his terrible masters. . . . But there are passions the selection of which comes not from man. . . . They are inscribed in us from on high, and in them there is something which summons us incessantly our whole life long. They are destined to accomplish great things on this earth: no matter whether they pass by in an image of gloom or a vision of light, bringing joy to the world—they are equally sent us to perform good works unknown to man. And perhaps in Chichikov himself his driving passion springs not from him, and in his cold existence these is something hidden which will then cause men to fall on their knees in the dust before the wisdom of the heavens.

This fragment, which usually passes unnoticed by most readers of *Dead Souls,* contains the central nucleus of Gogol's philosophy. It likewise helps to explain the fundamental peculiarity of Gogol's writings: the combination of satire and utopianism, of affirmation and denial, of pessimism and optimism, of "laughter visible to the world through unseen ˙and unknown tears." Laughter is used to lay bare the insignificance of this world. Gogol's tears are shed for a world created beautiful by God, yet now corrupted and disfigured. If the artist's glance causes the world virtually to dissolve and disintegrate into nothing, what lies behind this deceptive veil of corporeity and everyday reality is not Nothing, but, on the contrary, true reality, the realm of grace:

> Merely glance at the world: it is filled with God's grace. . . .
> All events, especially unexpected and extraordinary ones, are God's messages to us.
> The darkened firmament is the herald of a bright and triumphant dawn.

Gogol was perhaps too optimistic about the means of attaining this world of grace; he believed that if people only recognized the utter insignificance of this world, the gates of "Supreme Eternal Beauty" or "Heavenly Beauty," as he calls the Divine Reality, would open before them, and not after this life, but during it. Gogol believed, as we have seen, in the possibility of morally transforming each individual man. He also believed that in this life one could live "another life":

Blessed is he who in *this* life lives by the happiness of *another* life.

Is not every striving by which noble souls seek one another, loving only the other's divine, and not his earthly attributes— is this not a striving toward Christ?

Wherever God manifests Himself, there nothing remains in equilibrium, but marches forward, ever striving to become better and better.

As cosmic satirist, Gogol conceived his function as a means of aiding the reader to recognize the insignificance of this insignificant world and thus further the destruction of demonic deception and unreal illusion; in this way he opens up the path to the world of "Supreme Eternal Beauty." This process is reinforced by his function as preacher: in his private letters, in the *Selected Passages From My Correspondence With My Friends,* the *Author's Confession,* the *Interpretation of the Divine Liturgy,* and of course in personal conversation with persons who regarded him not only as an "accuser" of the contemporary world, but as a guide to Eternity. In a literary sense, at least, Gogol's attempt to propagate his ideas among a wider circle of readers was by and large a failure. The reasons for this failure are various and complex: Gogol's "positive" work did not possess the same straightforwardness and solidity he had revealed as a satirist; his capacity for expressing and formulating his positive ideals proved inadequate to the requirements of his age. He was too far removed from the spiritual needs of his contemporaries— Westernizers and Slavophiles and all the other schools of the period—to be able not only to rebuke them, but also to give them encouragement and faith. It was difficult to find words to touch their hearts. And in general there were no "words" capable of doing this, if one considers the state of the Russian literary language in Gogol's time: the 1840s marked the beginning of a period of extreme decline in the tradition of homiletic and "sacral" language. The succeeding generation took an ironic attitude toward Gogol's sermons, regarding them as a set of utterly pointless "letters to a Kaluga governess." Gogol did not succeed in "singing a hymn to Heavenly Beauty," and what he said about "Supreme Eternal Beauty" evoked almost no response in that spiritual desert.

But Gogol's failure does not give us the right to forget

his importance as a thinker and to consider only one aspect of his work. We must not allow the artist to blot out the thinker.

VIKTOR SHKLOVSKY

The Literary Genre of *Dead Souls*†

Gogol's "Poem" Rejects the Poetics of the Domestic Novel

Gogol's description of the commotion in town following the disclosure of Chichikov's purchases of dead souls is something of a parody: The wives of the local officials invent a whole romantic tale to fit the circumstances, puzzling out the hero's actions while always remaining inside the bounds of contemporary literary convention and taste. This "lady's novel" is similar to traditional novels of the time; of course, it is by no means realistic.

It may be that this passage is a parody on literary tradition; in any case, one finds here the direct juxtaposition of an erroneous interpretation and the true explanation of the affair:

> The men's faction, the more scatter-brained of the two, looked into the matter of the dead souls. The women's faction busied itself exclusively with the kidnapping of the governor's daughter. The latter group, to the honor of women be it said, acted with infinitely more decorum and circumspection. Clearly, this was related to their abilities as good housewives and manageresses. For them, everything immediately assumed the most definite features; everything came to the surface clearcut and overt; each detail was explained, dusted, polished to a mirror gleam; in short, a final picture of events was produced. As it turns out (according to this version of events), Chichikov has been in love for quite some time, and there have been lover's meetings in the gardens, by moonlight. . . .

The male segment of society puts forward its own explanation of Chichikov's behavior; after this, the postmaster recounts the "Tale of Captain Kopeykin," which deals with the adventures of a war-disabled bandit chief. This "tale" contains many details of day-to-day life in St. Petersburg; the city and its seductions are described here in a way that

† Translated by Geoffrey Packer from Viktor Shklovsky, *Povesti o proze* [Tales about prose] (Moscow, 1966), pp. 127–35.

closely recalls portions of one of Gogol's own St. Petersburg "tales": "Nevsky Avenue." In both cases, the city of the wealthy is seen through the eyes of a poor man.

The key to the riddle of Chichikov is given in chapter 11, the final chapter of the first volume of *Dead Souls,* in the extended passage beginning with the words: "The origins of our hero are humble and obscure."

Such an ordering of plot is entirely new.

Gogol discloses the "secret" of the novel in a completely different way: The strange adventures of his hero are explained, after the fact, by the ordinariness, even pettiness of his earlier life, and by the constant, unwavering, and passionate desire of the hero to become just like any other member of the landed aristocracy.

After all fancy speeches have been spoken and all romantic allusions made, it turns out that Chichikov is only a petty predator of the most ordinary sort. Here, the reader cannot fail to be disenchanted with the hero. Gogol emphatically states: "The very paunchiness and middle-agedness of Chichikov does much to spoil his 'heroic' image: A pot belly is something that no reader will forgive in a literary hero. . . ."

Chichikov is rather handsome and not devoid of character; but these things do not exalt him, do not give him the outlines of a "positive" figure. Chichikov's outer man lowers the standard of the traditional "positive hero."

> Among the variegated throng of witticisms (and would-be witticisms) there was one that would have it—strange as this may seem—that Chichikov might well be Napoleon in disguise, that the English, so long envious of the size and power of the Russian Empire . . . had quite likely freed Napoleon from his exile on the island of St. Helena, and that he was now making his way across Russia; and Chichikov was not really Chichikov at all.
>
> Of course, the local officials were far from swallowing all this; still they mulled it over, each according to his lights, and found that Chichikov's face, in profile, did indeed look very much like the portraits of Napoleon. Some readers may call this improbable. . . . Nonetheless, everything happened just the way it has been set down.

Chichikov, the petty predator, moves about in a land that Gogol describes in singing cadences. Gogol senses, justly values, and extols the vast latent forces within Russia—the land of the valiant warrior-heroes; his lyrical digressions arise from this attitude. Gogol writes:

But a higher power raised me up: The offences were not incorrigible; the same deserted expanses that had once filled me with such anguish now exalted me with the vastness of their onward sweep—with their promise of a far-flung field of possibilities.

The Gogolian Definition of Genre

The word "poem," set apart from the rest of the title, testifies not only to the wide-ranging scope of the work, but also to a renunciation of the traditional novelistic conventions. This renunciation is made quite intentionally, on the basis of Gogol's own analysis and understanding of the novelistic and epic genres.

In "A Textbook of Russian Philology" (1840) Gogol introduces his concept of "lesser forms of the epic." He writes there:

In the past few centuries a new type of artistic composition has arisen, which, as it were, takes the middle road between the novel and the epic. The hero of this new gentre is, although an isolated, insignificant figure, nevertheless meaningful in many respects for the observer of the human soul. The author leads this central figure through a connected series of adventures and changes, in order to present, together with a true, living picture of everything significant in the features and mores of the time that he has selected, a mundane, almost statistically charted view of inadequacies, ill-usage, sins, and all else that he has noticed in the selected time period that is worthy of attracting the regard of any attentive contemporary seeking in the fabulous past living lessons for the present.

Gogol considers Ariosto's *Orlando Furioso* and Cervantes' *Don Quixote* to be examples of this special type of epic. He contrasts the novel with the epic and asserts that the greatest inadequacy of the former is its conventionality of plot. "Like the drama," writes Gogol of the novel,

it is too fixed and static a form of composition. It also employs a strictly and calculatingly contrived beginning. All of the characters whom it is intended to include in the action, or, better, among whom the action must develop, must be taken up in advance by the author, who is necessarily preoccupied with the destiny of each of his characters; he is thus unable to push along and shift around these characters rapidly and in large quantities, as if they were fleeting phenomena. The advent of each character, at first apparently without any particular significance, is nonetheless a proclamation of his future participation in the novel's action. Everything is presented only through the necessity of its direct relation to the hero's destiny.

Here, as in the drama, all that is permitted is an overly compressed interaction of characters; every one of the distant relations between them, every one of those encounters that is not completely and immediately necessary, is a defect in the novel and renders it prolix and dull.

To Gogol, the novel is a work with a conventional, artificial plot strictly limited by the scope of the particular novelistic world; while the epic "poem" offers a wide scope and a realistically accurate depiction of reality.

The term "lesser" applied to the epic binds together Cervantes' novel and Ariosto's epic poem. *Don Quixote* is thus removed from the ranks of ordinary novels.

In the "lesser epic" genre, Gogol envisioned the possibility of telling a story in many different ways without using the conventional novelistic framework. When Gogol writes that everything in the novel is "too much tied up with the fate of the hero," he is expressing the same objections against the novelistic genre as Tolstoy did in later years.

Tolstoy insists upon the "necessity of linking characters, scenes, and thoughts by means of one dominant idea."

In *Dead Souls,* Gogol gives a typical picture of his times. He writes: ". . . the town was comparable to other provincial centers"; or, "the gentleman made his way to the common room. Every traveler knows very well what these common rooms are like"; or else, "the room was full of all the old, familiar things that one finds in every small wooden inn—the sort of inn that has sprung up all along our highways in such large numbers. . . ." There follows a description of the inn's decor. Here, in his description of the utterly commonplace, Gogol manages to give refreshing glimpses of that which underlies the stale crust of habituation; the commonplace is made to shadow forth in genuine essence.

The "buying up of dead souls" is an improbable, and yet a typical, undertaking, one which may exist, in various guises, anywhere where men and men's labor are commodities.

The strained "improbability" of the undertaking permits the artist to reveal the typical features of his times.

Sobakievich is more than simply a *kulak* [1] whom provincial life has rendered bearlike. Gogol says: "But only unbend one or two fingers of that fist, and things will turn

1. A rich peasant [*Editor*].

out even more badly." And one imagines Sobakievich in St. Petersburg, Sobakievich issuing decrees, Sobakievich in the Academy of Sciences—and so on, ad infinitum.

In the same vein, Gogol says of Korobochka: ". . . yet, wait a moment; is it quite true that Korobochka stands so low on the endless staircase of human perfectability?" And the writer follows this up with a quick sketch of Korobochka as the owner of an aristocratic mansion.

The heroes of the first volume of *Dead Souls* have almost all become bywords.

The title itself, *Dead Souls,* is an acute and original pun. On January 7, 1842, Gogol writes to Pletnev:

> Someone suddenly got Snegirev all twisted around, and I now discover that he is presenting my manuscript to the committee. The committee is receiving it as if the issue had been decided in advance, and all that remains now is to play out the comedy; for all the charges without exception were comic to the highest degree. As soon as Golokhvastov, who was presiding, heard the title *Dead Souls,* he bellowed in stentorian tones: "No, this I will never permit: the soul is immortal; the author is taking up arms against immortality." They were finally able to get it through the wise chairman's head that the "souls" in question were "revisionary souls"—serfs. When he and all his fellow censors had all finally come to understand this point, there arose almost immediately a still bigger fuss. "No," cried the chairman and, in his wake, half of his colleagues, "the thing would be inadmissible even if only the term "revisionary souls" were involved—this certainly cannot be passed; it is clearly against the institution of serfdom.

This dispute points up more than just the stupidity of the censors. It need not be assumed that Gogol is writing an objective account of events: He is exercising his right to the creation of satire.

Gogol introduces this same argument over the title into the second volume of *Dead Souls.* The censor's comments are forwarded to Colonel Koshkarev's smug clerk. The colonel compels Chichikov to submit a written application regarding the purchase of the dead souls. In response to his application, Chichikov receives the following official communication:

> With reference to deliberations concerning the instructions with which your Honor has furnished me, I have the honor herewith to inform you as regards the subject: 1.) In the very request of Chichikov, Pavel Ivanovich, the honorable collegiate assessor, there is evident a misapprehension; this in the fact that the "revisionary souls" are referred to there, most imprudently, as "dead." By this, evidently, it is meant that these souls

are close to death or dying, not that they are in fact deceased. What is more, such a term as "dead souls" points to a sort of superficial erudition probably limited by the instruction of a parish grammar school, since the soul is immortal.

The upshot of Gogol's argument with the censors was that the sharp and biting title *Dead Souls* was watered down with the addition of a more traditional title: *The Adventures of Chichikov*. However, on the overleaf (which Gogol himself designed)² the words *Dead Souls* are twice as large as the words *The Adventures of Chichikov*.

M. M. BAKHTIN

Verbal Art and the Folk Culture of Laughter†

In our book on Rabelais¹ we strove to show that the basic artistic principles of that great writer were defined by a historic folk culture of laughter. One of the significant shortcomings of modern literary criticism is its attempt to place all literature, that of the Renaissance in particular, into the framework of official culture. The works of Rabelais, however, may be understood in actuality only within the stream of folk culture, which always, at all stages of its development, opposes official culture and develops its own peculiar view of the world and its own peculiar forms for depicting that world in imagery.

Literary criticism and aesthetics usually proceed from the narrow and impoverished manifestations of laughter found in the literature of the last three centuries. They attempt to squeeze the laughter of the Renaissance into these narrow conceptions of laughter and the comical as well. However, these conceptions are hardly adequate, even for an understanding of Molière.²

Rabelais was the heir and crown of millennia of folk

2. This overleaf or cover design by Gogol is reproduced on p. ix above [*Editor*].

† A translation by Thomas Seifrid of some parts of M. M. Bakhtin, *Iskusstvo slova i narodnaya kul'tura (Rabelais i Gogol')* [Verbal art and folk culture (Rabelais and Gogol)], pp. 248–59 in *Kontekst 1972* (Moscow: Nauka, 1973).

1. The present article was a section in Bakhtin's doctoral dissertation on Rabelais, which was not included in his later book on Rabelais, *Tvorchestvo François Rabelais i narodnaya kultura srednevekovaya i Renessanca* (Moscow, 1965). This book was translated into English by Hélène Iswolsky as *Rabelais and His World* (Cambridge, Mass.: M.I.T. Press, 1968) [*Editor*].

2. Famous French dramatist (1622–73), author of many comedies [*Editor*].

laughter. His works are an irreplaceable key to the whole of the European culture of laughter in its strongest, most profound, and original manifestations.

Here we will discuss the most significant appearance of the literature of laughter in the modern era: the works of N. V. Gogol. We are concerned only with those elements of the folk culture of laughter that are found in his works.

* * *

A careful analysis would reveal the basis of *Dead Souls* to be the forms of a merry (carnival) journey through the underworld, through the land of death. *Dead Souls* presents a most interesting parallel to Rabelais' Fourth Book, that is, to Pantagruel's journey. The theme of the world beyond the grave is present in the very conception and title of Gogol's novel, *Dead Souls,* for a good reason. The world of *Dead Souls* is that of a merry underworld. Externally, it more resembles the underworld of Quevedo y Villegas,[3] but its inner essence resembles the world of Rabelais' Fourth Book. In it we find the rabble and trash of a carnival "hell" and a whole series of images are abusive metaphors made literal. Here a careful analysis would reveal many of the traditional elements of a carnival underworld, of the depths of earthly and freshly existence. The very type of Chichikov's "journey" ("traveling through purgatory") is a chronotopic[4] type of movement. This traditional basis of *Dead Souls* is enriched and complicated, of course, by a large amount of material of a different order and of different traditions.

In Gogol's works we find nearly all the elements of festive folk culture. Gogol possessed a carnival view of the world, though it is true that in most cases it was tinged with romanticism. He expresses this view in various forms. We mention here only the remarkable, purely carnival way he characterizes fast driving and the Russian man: "For what Russian does not love to drive fast? Is it for his soul—

3. C. D. Quevedo y Villegas' *Los sueños* [Visions], written between 1607 and 1613 and published in 1627, in which the representatives of various classes, professions, and various faults and human weaknesses pass through Hell. The satire is almost completely lacking in profound and genuine ambivalence [*Editor*].

4. "Chronotope" is a technical term coined and popularized by Bakhtin.

It is derived from a combination of the Greek words for time and space, and refers to the spatialized time frame of a literary work. Bakhtin believes that such "time-space" or chronotope underlies every conceptualization of reality and is endowed with the capacity to determine the kinds of events that can happen within its borders.

which loves to whirl, carouse, and sometimes say: 'To hell with it all!'—is it for his soul not to love fast driving?" And somewhat farther on: "The whole road flies God knows where into the receding distance, and something awesome is contained in this swift rush, where one does not even have time to make out the objects as they fly past. . . ." We emphasize this destruction of all the static boundaries between phenomena. The particular feeling for "the road" so often expressed by Gogol also has a purely carnival nature.

Neither was a grotesque conception of the body foreign to Gogol. This draft for the first volume of *Dead Souls* is very characteristic:

> And really, what sorts of faces aren't there on this earth! No matter what mug you pick, none are alike. The nose is the commanding presence on the face of one, for another it's the lips, for a third it's cheeks which have so enlarged their domain as to make even the nose look no bigger than a vest button; another has such a large chin that he has to keep it covered with a handkerchief to keep from spitting on it. . . . And how many there are who do not look like people at all. This one is a perfect dog dressed up in tails, such that you're surprised to see him carrying a walking stick: it looks like the first person he meets would snatch it away.

In Gogol we also find an extremely consistent system for converting proper names into nicknames. Gogol's name for the town in the second volume of *Dead Souls* reveals with nearly theoretical precision the very essence of the ambivalent nickname, which at once praises and damns: *Tfuslavl!* [5] We also find other vivid examples of such familiar combinations of praise and abuse (in the form of a rapt damnation that blesses), like "Damn you, steppes! How beautiful you are!"

Gogol was profoundly aware of the philosophical and universal nature of his laughter, yet at the same time could find nothing similar, no theoretical substantiation for or illumination of such laughter, in the conditions of "serious" nineteenth-century culture. When discussing the reasons for his laughter he obviously did not dare to reveal fully its nature, its universal, all-encompassing folk character. He often justified his laughter by the limited morality of his time. In these justifications, which Gogol aimed at the

---

5. A made-up word combining a syllable meaning "phooey" and one meaning "praise be" or "glory"— hence, something like "phooeyglory" [*Editor*].

level of understanding of those to whom they were addressed, he unintentionally reduces, limits, and sometimes even tries to fit into an official framework that tremendous transforming force that leaps out of his humorous works. By causing irritation and toppling over familiar notions, the first external, negative effect of "mockery" prevented the immediate observers of this force from seeing its positive essence. "Why then is my heart despondent?" asks Gogol in his article "After the Theater" (1842), and he answers, "No one noticed the honest person who was in my play." Later he reveals that "this honest, noble person is *laughter*," and continues, "He is noble because he decided to appear regardless of the low meaning attributed to him by society."

This "low," earthy folk-meaning also lends laughter, as Gogol puts it, "a noble face"; he might as well have added "a divine face," since that is how the gods laugh in the folk element of laughter in ancient folk comedies. None of the then existing or possible explanations could accommodate this laughter (the very fact of it as a character, a dramatis persona).

"Laughter is significant and more profound than people think," Gogol wrote in the same article.

> Not that laughter born of a temporary irritability or a peevish, ill disposition, and not even that laughter that serves as the idle entertainment and amusement of men—but that laughter that flies forth whole from bright human nature, flies forth from it because at its bottom lies "its eternally flowing spring . . ." No, they are wrong who say that laughter arouses anger. Only that which is gloomy arouses anger, and laughter is bright. There is much that would anger a man if seen in its nakedness; but illuminated with the force of laughter it even brings reconciliation into his soul. . . . But they don't hear the mighty force of such laughter: "that which is funny is base," says society. Only that pronounced in a severe and tense voice do they call elevated.

Gogol's "positive," "bright," and "elevated" laughter, which arose on the basis of the folk culture of laughter, was not understood (to this day much of it has not been). This laughter, incompatible with that of the satirist, defines what is most important in Gogol's works. One could say that his inner nature led him to laugh "like the gods," but that he felt it necessary to justify his laughter with the limited human morality of his time.

This laughter is, on the other hand, completely revealed in Gogol's poetics, in the very structure of his language.

His language abounds in elements of folk verbal life that have not been made literary (its nonliterary strata). Gogol uses the unpublished spheres of speech. His notebooks are literally filled with exotic, enigmatic, and semantically and phonetically ambivalent words. He even indicates his intentions of publishing his own *Explanatory Dictionary of the Russian Language,* in the foreword to which he asserts that "such a dictionary seems all the more necessary to me because in the life our society lives abroad, which shares so little in common with the spirit of the earth and of the folk, the direct, genuine meaning of native Russian words is perverted—some obtain a different meaning, others are forgotten altogether." Gogol sharply felt the need for this folk element of speech to struggle against the dead, externalizing strata of language. The characteristic absence from Renaissance thought of any single, authoritative, indisputable language is evoked in his works by the organization of a complete interaction in laughter among the spheres of speech. Hence in his language we observe a continual liberation of forgotten or forbidden meanings.

These forgotten meanings lost in the past begin to communicate with one another, to emerge from their shells and seek application and conjunction with other meanings. Under these conditions, it becomes possible for those semantic links extant only in the context of certain utterances, within the bounds of certain centers of speech that are inseparably connected to their accompanying situations, to be reborn, to join in a renewed life. Otherwise they would remain invisible, as if having ceased to exist. As a rule they would not be preserved, would not be fixed in any abstract semantic contexts (those developed in written and printed speech), as if having fallen by the wayside forever, barely having taken shape for the expression of some living and unique situation. In an abstract, normative language they would have no right to enter the *system* of a worldview, because they represent not a system of conceptual meanings but of *life itself speaking.* Because they are usually expressions that are outside of literary, business, or serious situations (in general, when people laugh, sing, curse, celebrate, and feast they break out of the usual rut), they can make no claim to representation in serious official language. However, these situations and turns of speech do not die, though the literary language may forget or even avoid them.

Because of this, a return to living folk speech is necessary; it has already made itself felt by all in the works of such a genius at expressing the folk consciousness as Gogol. This contradicts the primitive impression of some sort of linear forward progress commonly held in normative circles. Clearly, every truly significant step forward is accompanied by a *return to origins* ("primordiality"), or more exactly by a *renewal of origins*. Only *memory* can go forward, not forgetfulness. Memory returns to origins and renews them. Of course, the terms "forward" and "backward" themselves become less exclusively absolute in this sense and instead reveal by their mutual interaction that living, paradoxical nature of motion that has been studied and variously interpreted by philosophers (from the pre-Socratic to Bergson). In its application to language, such a return signifies the restoration of the language's active accumulated memory in its full semantic range. The folk culture of laughter so vividly portrayed by Gogol also serves as one of the means of this restoration and renewal.

Gogol so organizes the humorous word that its goal becomes not the simple indication of certain negative phenomena, but the revelation of a special aspect of the world as a whole.

In this sense, for Gogol the zone of laughter becomes one of contact. Here the contradictory and the incompatible unite: A bond is revived. Words entail total impressions of contacts between genres of speech that are nearly always far removed from literature. In this context the simple chatter (of a lady) sounds like a verbal problem, like meaning that must step through a litter of speech that would seem to have no meaning.

This language continually exceeds the literary norms of its age and correlates with other realities that shatter the direct, official, "decorous" surface of the word. The process of eating and in general various manifestations of material and corporeal life (an oddly formed nose, a bump, etc.) all require their own language for signification, new twists of speech and agreements. They demand a conflict with the necessity of expressing oneself neatly and without offending canon; at the same time, it is clear that they cannot but offend it. This gives rise to splintering, a semantic skipping from one extreme to another, a striving to maintain balance and simultaneous disruptions: The word is comically travestied, revealing its multidimensional nature and showing the path to its renewal.

The same end is served by unruly dances, animalistic

features appearing in a man, and so forth. Gogol pays particular attention to the gesticulatory and invective resources of language, neglecting none of the specific peculiarities of humorous folk speech. Life outside of uniforms and ranks exerts an unusually strong attraction on him, though in his youth he dreamed of a uniform and rank. The trampled rights of laughter find their defender and spokesman in him, although all his life he thought about serious, tragic, and moralistic literature.

Thus we see the collision and interaction of two worlds: the completely legalized, official world shaped by ranks and uniforms, vividly portrayed in the dream of "life in the capital," and the world where all is funny and nonserious, where only laughter is taken seriously. The nonsense and absurdities introduced by this world seem, on the contrary, to be the genuine, unifying inner source of the other, external world. This is the _merry_ absurdity of folk sources, which contain the multitude of speech correlations accurately recorded by Gogol.

The Gogolian world, consequently, always inhabits the zone of contact (as do all humorous portrayals). All things in this zone obtain a renewed tangibility: A meal presented by the means of speech becomes capable of creating an appetite, and it becomes possible to depict separate movements analytically without losing their wholeness. All becomes extant, contemporary, and actually present.

It is characteristic that Gogol does not convey anything substantial in the zone of reminiscences. Chichikov's past, for example, is related in a distant zone, a different plane of speech than that of his quest for "dead souls": There is no laughter. In the quest, however, his character is truly revealed, and it is there that the element of laughter acts— unifying, conflicting, and contacting all that surrounds it.

It is important that this world of laughter be continuously open to new interactions. Here the usual, traditional notion of the whole and of the _element_ that obtains its meaning only in that whole must be reexamined and considered in somewhat more depth. The fact is that every such element simultaneously represents some other whole (for example, folk culture) in which it above all receives its primary meaning. The wholeness of the Gogolian world is thus on principle unclosed and unself-satisfied.

Only because of folk culture does Gogol's time become a part of "large-scale time."

Folk culture lends depth and coherence to Gogol's car-

nivalized images of collectives—Nevsky Prospect, official-
dom, chancellaries, the department (which at the beginning of "The Overcoat" is abusively called "the department
of dirty tricks and nonsense," etc.). It comprehends only
merry ruin, the kind of merry deaths we find in Gogol
(Taras Bulba, who loses his pipe), and merry heroism (the
transformation of Akaky Akakievich, his madness before
death, with its cursing and rebelliousness, and his travels
beyond the grave).[6] Folk laughter in essence removes these
carnivalized collectives from "real," "serious" life "as it
should be." There is no serious point of view that opposes
laughter. Laughter is "the only positive hero."

The grotesque in Gogol is consequently not a simple
violation of the norm but a negation of all kinds of abstract, immobile norms that claim to be absolute and
eternal. Gogol rejects obvious appearances and the world
of the self-evident, for the sake of unexpectedness and the
unpredictability of truth. It is as if he were saying that
good must be expected not from the firm and familiar,
but from "miracles," which embody the folk idea of renewal and the affirmation of life.

In this sense, the buying up of dead souls and the various
reactions to Chichikov's propositions may also be viewed
as belonging to the folk conception of the bond between
life and death, to carnivalized ridicule. There is also an
element of carnival play with death and the boundaries
between life and death (for instance, Sobakievich's musings
on the relative uselessness of the dead, Korobochka's fear
of the dead, and the saying that "one should at least fasten
the gate against the dead," etc.). There is carnival play
when the base clashes with the serious and frightening
and in the carnival playing up of the notions of infinity
and eternity (infinite court cases, infinite absurdities, etc.).
So also does Chichikov's journey remain *uncompleted*.

The juxtapositions of real images and the subplots concerning the system of serfdom (the buying and selling of
men) also appear more clearly in this perspective. These
images and plots end with the end of serfdom. But Gogol's
images and plot situations are immortal: They reside in
large-scale time. A phenomenon that belongs to small-scale
time may be purely negative or even hateful, but in large-
scale time it is ambivalent and always pleasant, as a part

6. Bakhtin here refers to various
works by Gogol. "Nevsky Prospect"
and "Taras Bulba" are stories published in 1835; Akaky Akakievich is
the chief character in the story "The
Overcoat" (1842) [*Editor*].

of objective reality. All these Plyushkins, Sobakieviches, and their like have passed from that plane where they deserve only ruin and hatred, or must merely be tolerated, from that plane where they exist no more, into a plane where they remain eternally, where they are shown as participants in an eternally becoming, undying existence.

The mocking satirist is never merry. At best he is sullen and gloomy. But for Gogol laughter conquers all; in particular, he creates a certain *catharsis* of vulgarity.

The problem of Gogolian laughter may be correctly formulated and resolved only on the basis of studying the folk culture of laughter.

YURI M. LOTMAN

The Problem of Artistic Space in Gogol's Prose†

The tendency toward cyclicization distinctly manifested in Gogol's prose at all stages of his development as a writer has an interesting aspect: Gogol places some side of Russian reality (and human existence) at the basis of his representation and gives a territorial attribute to that which he represents (Mirgorod, Petersburg). Thus an aspect of life acquires the attribute of a part of Russia's territory; partitive significance is activated.

Dead Souls was conceived from the beginning as a work about a certain artistic *universum,* about all sides of life and all of Russia. Because of this, all the types of artistic space that had previously been interwoven through Gogol's prose were synthesized in it into a unified system.

Not the opposition "limited—unlimited," but the opposition "directed—nondirected" became the basic differentiating feature of space in *Dead Souls.* The tendency to spread out aimlessly in all directions and that to enclose oneself inside a pint-sized shell are equally perceived as variants of nondirected, and consequently *immobile*, space.[1]

† Translated by Thomas Seifrid from pp. 45–50 of Yuri Lotman's article "Problema khudozhest'vennogo prostranstva v proze Gogolia" [The problem of artistic space in Gogol's prose], in *Uchennye zapiski, Tartu Gos. Universitet, Trudy po russkoi i slavianskoi filologii: literaturovedenie, 1968,* XI: fascicle 209.

1. The nondirectionality of space is equivalent to the aimlessness of the existence of the person who inhabits it: "He became somehow livelier, even firmer of character, like a man who has already defined and set himself a goal. Doubt, indecision, in a word, all his wavering and ill-defined features had disappeared of their own accord from his face and his actions."

Gogol speaks of these possibilities as reciprocally equivalent with regard to Plyushkin: "It must be said that the like of him is to be rarely met in Russia, where everything tends to expand rather than to contract."

Sobakievich and Korobochka "contract," and in Plyushkin this spatial contraction causes a "rent"—emptiness. But Nozdrev, like Plyushkin's neighbor, who "spreads himself out to the full breadth of Russian rashness and lordly ways and, as they say, scorches his way through life," "tends to expand." A tendency to cross the boundaries of propriety, of rules of play, and of any norms of behavior is the basis of Nozdrev's character. This also is expressed in spatial terms. Almost immediately following Chichikov's appearance in Nozdrev's village, the latter takes him out to inspect "the boundaries of my lands." It is significant that Gogol has none of the other landowners do this. In Nozdrev's imagination, these boundaries turn out to be an extremely loose concept, encompassing the whole horizon: " 'Here is the boundary!' Nozdrev announced. 'Everything that you see on this side, all of it is mine, and everything on the far side, that whole dark-blue forest over there and also everything behind the forest, all that is mine.' " The identity of spatial antonyms ("expand—contract") is underscored here by the absurd attempt to make limitlessness "one's own."

We find the same tendency to identify previously opposed types of space in the description of the provincial town. On the one hand, the town belongs to a world of dead particularities that has been fragmented to the point of nonspatiality. The formula of Gogol's rough sketch for the plan is striking: "The idea of a town. Emptiness appearing in the highest degree." The properties of this emptiness are immobility ("They do not stir. Death strikes an unstirring world") and disjointedness ("occupied with disconnected idleness"). But the same town is portrayed as a space of blurred boundaries and, almost in the spirit of "Viy," [2] of cancelled oppositions: "It was already dusk when they reached town. The light and shadows were so intermingled now that the very objects seemed fused. The black and white barrier assumed a nebulous color; the sentinel's whiskers seemed to grow out of his forehead above his eyes and he did not appear to have a nose at all."

2. A story by Gogol (1835) about a pseudofolklore, fantastic creature [*Editor*].

What was new in *Dead Souls* was that this world of blurred boundaries that could be both good and evil seemed base and antipoetic. It is populated not by the witches of "Viy," nor by the brunettes of "Nevsky Prospect," but by "creatures of a special kind in the shape of ladies, in red shawls and boots worn on stockingless legs, who flit about the crossroads like bats" and pronounce "the sort of phrases which would scald some dreamy twenty-year-old youth. . . . He is high in heaven and is paying a call on Schiller—when suddenly, like thunder, the fatal words are uttered above his head, and he discovers that he is treading the earth again, somewhere near Haymarket Square or some low tavern; and so once more he is sucked back into the round of everyday life."

In and of itself, spaciousness in *Dead Souls* becomes completely ambivalent—it may be united with both grandeur and vulgarity. It becomes possible to unite this image with the author's irony, which had earlier been decidely opposed to it. Thus, it is mentioned that the beauty of the Madonna is "rarely to be found in Russia, where everything tends to be spacious—everything there is, whether it be the hills, the forests and the steppes, or faces, lips, and feet." The civil councillor, when he does not know how to engage the ladies in conversation, "will say that Russia is a very spacious country." The officials, having decided Chichikov is Napoleon in disguise, among "a number of intelligent suggestions" give the reason that "the English had long been envious of the greatness and extent of Russia." Even the author himself, complaining that there will always be some "smart reader" living "in some out-of-the-way corner of our empire," notes that that empire is "rightly called great."

In order to become elevated, space must not only be vast (or unbounded), but also directional: Those located in it must *move toward a goal*. It must be a *road*. The "road" is one of the basic spatial forms that organize the text of *Dead Souls*. All the characters, ideas, and images are divided into those that belong to the road—aspiring, having a goal, moving—and those that are static and aimless.

We have used the concepts "road" and "journey" as synonyms; it is now appropriate to differentiate them. "Road" is a certain type of artistic space, while "journey" is the movement of a literary character in that space.

"Journey" is the realization (complete or incomplete) or the nonrealization of the "road." In *Dead Souls* the road becomes the universal form for organizing space. It includes all the forms of Gogolian space, since it passes through them: infinity ("crows like flies and an endless horizon"), base fragmentation ("with its chills, slush, filth, drowsy stationmasters . . . and all sorts of riff-raff on the road"), domestic warmth ("beholds at last the familiar roof and the glimmer of lights rushing to meet him"; "wrapped more tightly in our traveling coat, with the hat pulled over our ears, we shall huddle more closely and comfortably in a corner"), and others. One peculiarity must be emphasized. The image of the road attracts Gogol because it presents, as he imagines it, an isomorphic picture of life. It is not an accident that it is possible to trace mentions of "the whole vast movement of life" and "our bitter and dreary journey on earth" through the whole work. "But let us be off! Let us be off! Away with invading wrinkles and the harsh twilight that falls upon a face! Without hesitation let us plunge into life with all its hollow noise [3] and jingle of bells. . . ." Though encompassing all forms of Gogolian space, the "road" belongs to none of them: It passes through them. Correspondingly, neither does the "hero of the road" belong to any environment.

G. A. Gukovsky's profound observation of the link between character and surroundings in realistic art has been too often taken as absolute, so that the given, historically concrete, artistic form appears as an extratemporal absolute. Moreover, the norm turns out to be not Gogol and not even Pushkin, but that which links both writers with the general tenets of the Natural School.[4] As a result there occurs an inordinate narrowing of our understanding of artistic thought in nineteenth-century Russian literature. For Gogol, determining whether or not a character belongs to a given space (more narrowly, surroundings) is organically connected with the question, "How does he make his way out of his surroundings?" It is precisely the correlation of these problems that marks nineteenth-century Russian

3. Cf. the drafts for "Viy": "The corpse with its soft, almost boneless leg hollowly thumped on the floor"; "This sound was emitted completely soundlessly."
4. A term applied in Russian literary scholarship to the realistic writings of Gogol, Nekrasov, Grigorovich, and others, especially around the mid-1840s, characterized by the effort to describe everyday details (the "physiognomy") of life in a large city (particularly Petersburg) [*Editor*].

literature. It should be noted that the unqualified inclusion of a character in a certain world that surrounds him, assuming that world's predominance over him, obviates the questions of moral responsibility and of a person's individual active participation in causes that were so crucial to nineteenth-century literature. The artistic modeling of these questions was most often achieved through the language of spatial dislocations (it is significant that Turgenev's novels, the heroes of which do not change but express certain deep essences—social, psychological, and of worldwide importance—are spatially fixed, thus profoundly differing from the novels of Tolstoy and Dostoevsky).

With the appearance of the image of the road as a spatial form there also develops the idea of the journey as a norm for the lives of men, nations, and humanity. Characters are sharply divided into those in motion ("heroes of the journey") and those immobile. The character in motion has a goal. Even if it is a shallow, self-seeking one (and consequently his trajectory is brief, and upon reaching his desired point he comes to a stop), the author all the same distinguishes him from the world of immobile puppets. The hero who can come to a stop can also not come to a stop; he has not yet become frozen, and the author hopes to turn his temporary and egoistical movement into an unbroken and organic one. "No, the time has come to put the rogue in harness. So let us harness the rogue!" Related to this are the author's hopes for Chichikov's rebirth. Plyushkin's fugitives are hardly ideals, but they also belong to the "mobile" world, and this sharply sets them off from Uncle Minyai and Uncle Mityai.

[There is a] difference between the journeys of Gogol's heroes and the interpretation given this question by the Enlightenment (including here the Tolstoyan interpretation). For the adherent of the Enlightenment with his idea of the innate anthropological features of human nature, the journey cannot be endless. It is bounded on one side by the beautiful aspects of human nature: Man cannot become better than the moral norm inherent in children, who are unspoiled nature itself. But neither can perversion be endless: If all the innate positive traits are inverted, one obtains the limits of evil. Good is always the preservation of, or return to, what is given by nature; evil is departure from it. Any journey of a hero of the Enlightenment lies between these two boundaries.

For Gogol the journey has the same form as the road and is as a matter of principle unbounded at both ends. It may consist of infinite ascent or infinite fall. Gogol more than once emphasized the idea of infinity in good and evil itself, though since he expounded his views at times in the meta-language of the theories of the Enlightenment and at times in that of the theories of Romanticism, he was not always consistent. Thus, speaking of Plyushkin, he discusses his fall as a loss, purely in the spirit of the Enlightenment: "Take with you all those human emotions which you will never recover once you leave them behind!" Clearly, one can lose only that which exists: evil is the loss of original good and thus cannot be boundless. But in the very same passage, Gogol insists precisely on the boundlessness of the human journey: "To what depths can man fall to be so low, petty and nasty! How he can alter! And is this really true? *There is truth in everything and man can become anything.*"

But there is yet another interesting peculiarity to the spatial structure of *Dead Souls*: It is hierarchical in one extremely interesting regard. The characters, the reader, and the author belong to different types of that particular space that constitutes a knowledge of the laws of life. The characters are on earth; their horizon is obscured by objects; they know nothing except practical, everyday life, strikingly nearsighted considerations. The reader's point of view is more elevated—he sees widely about him and can have knowledge of the characters, of their past and future, and can observe several of them simultaneously. He may change position within this space, and the author's words "Let us go over to" or "Let us see what so-and-so is doing" are commonly directed to him. Gogol directly interprets in spatial terms this difference between the reader, to whom the connections hidden from the characters are revealed, and the novel's characters themselves: "Judgment comes easy to readers, who look down from some nook of theirs among the peaks, whence the whole horizon becomes visible as does everything that goes on below on earth where men can only see immediate objects."

But the reader, seeing the whole expanse of plot connections, does not know the moral solution, to which Gogol also lends a spatial image: "Where is the way out? Where is the road?" This is seen by the man of the journey— the author. It is because of this that everything in Russia "turns" on him "eyes of great expectation."

The author is a man of the journey like all prophets—from comic folk prophet on the level of uncles Minyai and Mityai, who "had appeared no one knows whence, wearing bast-shoes and an unlined sheepskin coat, and smelling terribly of stale fish; and he had announced that Napoleon was Antichrist and was kept on a stone chain, behind six walls and seven seas, but that afterwards he would break his chains and master the whole world," to the image of the narrator created by the entire text of the first volume. Another peculiarity is connected with this: The Gogolian prophet cannot proclaim a program, but preaches *movement in infinity*. In this sense, the second volume of *Dead Souls* presents a completely different scheme of spatial relations, which is sharply distinct from all the prose that precedes it and is essentially non-Gogolian, although separate fragments of the text are built on the artistic language familiar to us from the first volume.

* * *

The language of spatial relations, as we have stated, is not the only means of artistic modeling; but it is important, since it is a primary and basic one. Even temporal modeling frequently represents a secondary superstructure of spatial language. Gogol was, perhaps, the first to reveal the full artistic power of spatial models to Russian literature. He defined much for the artistic language of Russian literature from Tolstoy, Dostoevsky, and Saltykov-Shchedrin, to Mikhail Bulgakov and Yuri Tynianov.[5]

5. Bulgakov (1891–1940), Russian author of plays and fiction, known particularly for his *Master and Margarita;* Tynianov (1893–1943), Russian formalist literary critic, scholar, theorist, and novelist [*Editor*].

Selected Bibliography

Articles included in this volume are omitted from this bibliography.

Annenkov, Pavel. Trans. by Irwin R. Titunik. *The Extraordinary Decade: Literary Memoirs by P. V. Annenkov.* Ann Arbor, Mich., 1968.

Debreczeny, Paul. *Nikolay Gogol and His Contemporary Critics.* Transactions of the American Philosophical Society, n.s., 56, pt. 3. Philadelphia, Pa., April 1966.

Driessen, F. *Gogol as a Short Story–Writer: A Study of His Technique of Composition.* Slavistic Printings and Reprintings, 57. The Hague, 1965.

Erlich, Victor. *Gogol.* New Haven, Conn., 1969.

Erlich, Victor, ed. *Twentieth-Century Russian Literary Criticism.* New Haven, Conn., 1975.

Franz, Philip, ed. *Gogol Bibliography.* Ann Arbor, Mich., 1983.

Gippius, V. V. *Gogol.* Ed. and trans. by Robert A. Maguire. Ann Arbor, Mich., 1981.

Karlinsky, Simon. *The Sexual Labyrinth of Nikolai Gogol.* Cambridge, Mass., 1976.

Lindstrom, Thais. *Nikolay Gogol.* New York, 1974.

McLean, Hugh. "Gogol and the Whirling Telescope," in Legters, L. H., ed. *Russia: Essays in History and Literature.* Seattle, Wash. 1972, pp. 79–99.

Magarshack, David. *Gogol: A Life.* New York, 1969.

Maguire, Robert A., ed. *Gogol from the Twentieth Century: Eleven Essays.* Princeton, N.J., 1974.

Meyer, Priscilla, and Stephen Rudy, eds. and trans. *Dostoevsky and Gogol: Texts and Criticism.* Ann Arbor, Mich., 1979.

Mirsky, D. S. *A History of Russian Literature, pp.* 149–62. New York, 1958.

Muchnic, Helen. *The Unhappy Consciousness: Gogol, Poe, Baudelaire.* Baltimore, Md., 1967.

Peace, Richard Arthur. *The Enigma of Gogol.* Cambridge, Eng. and New York, 1981.

Poggioli, Renato. "Realism in Russia," *Comparative Literature,* III, pp. 253–67.

Proffer, Carl R. *The Simile and Gogol's Dead Souls.* The Hague, 1967.

Reeve, F. D. "Dead Souls." In his *The Russian Novel,* pp. 64–102. New York, 1966.

Rowe, William Woodrin. *Through Gogol's Looking Glass: Reverse Vision, False Focus, and Precarious Logic.* New York, 1976.

Setschkareff, Vsevolod. *Gogol—His Life and Works.* New York, 1965.

Troyat, Henri. *Divided Soul: The Life of Gogol.* Trans. by Nancy Amphoux. Garden City, N.Y., 1973.

Woodward, James B. *Gogol's Dead Souls.* Princeton, N.J., 1978.

Zeldin, Jesse. *Nikolai Gogol's Quest for Beauty: An Exploration into His Works.* Lawrence, Kans., 1978.

NORTON CRITICAL EDITIONS

AUSTEN   *Emma*   edited by Stephen M. Parrish

AUSTEN   *Pride and Prejudice*   edited by Donald J. Gray

Beowulf   (the Donaldson translation)   edited by Joseph M. Tuso

Blake's Poetry and Designs   selected and edited by Mary Lynn Johnson and
      John E. Grant

BOCCACCIO   *The Decameron*   selected, translated, and edited by Mark Musa and
      Peter E. Bondanella

BRONTË, CHARLOTTE   *Jane Eyre*   edited by Richard J. Dunn

BRONTË, EMILY   *Wuthering Heights*   edited by William M. Sale, Jr.
      Second Edition

Robert Browning's Poetry   selected and edited by James F. Loucks

Byron's Poetry   selected and edited by Frank D. McConnell

CARROLL   *Alice in Wonderland*   selected and edited by Donald J. Gray

CERVANTES   *Don Quixote*   (the Ormsby translation, substantially
      revised)   edited by Joseph R. Jones and Kenneth Douglas

Anton Chekhov's Plays   translated and edited by Eugene K. Bristow

Anton Chekhov's Short Stories   selected and edited by Ralph E. Matlaw

CHOPIN   *The Awakening*   edited by Margaret Culley

CLEMENS   *Adventures of Huckleberry Finn*   edited by Sculley Bradley,
      Richmond Croom Beatty, E. Hudson Long, and Thomas Cooley
      Second Edition

CLEMENS   *A Connecticut Yankee in King Arthur's Court*   edited by
      Allison R. Ensor

CLEMENS   *Pudd'nhead Wilson* and *Those Extraordinary Twins*   edited by
      Sidney E. Berger

CONRAD   *Heart of Darkness*   edited by Robert Kimbrough   *Second Edition*

CONRAD   *Lord Jim*   edited by Thomas Moser

CONRAD   *The Nigger of the "Narcissus"*   edited by Robert Kimbrough

CRANE   *Maggie: A Girl of the Streets*   edited by Thomas A. Gullason

CRANE   *The Red Badge of Courage*   edited by Sculley Bradley, Richmond
      Croom Beatty, E. Hudson Long, and Donald Pizer   *Second Edition*

Darwin   edited by Philip Appleman   *Second Edition*

DEFOE   *Moll Flanders*   edited by Edward Kelly

DEFOE   *Robinson Crusoe*   edited by Michael Shinagel

DICKENS   *Bleak House*   edited by George Ford and Sylvère Monod

DICKENS   *Hard Times*   edited by George Ford and Sylvère Monod

John Donne's Poetry   selected and edited by A. L. Clements

DOSTOEVSKY   *Crime and Punishment* (the Coulson translation)   edited by
      George Gibian   *Second Edition*

DOSTOEVSKY   *The Brothers Karamazov* (the Garnett translation revised by
      Ralph E. Matlaw)   edited by Ralph E. Matlaw

DREISER   *Sister Carrie*   edited by Donald Pizer

ELIOT   *Middlemarch*   edited by Bert G. Hornback

FIELDING   *Tom Jones*   edited by Sheridan Baker

FLAUBERT   *Madame Bovary*   edited with a substantially new translation by
      Paul de Man

GOETHE   *Faust*   translated by Walter Arndt and edited by Cyrus Hamlin

HARDY   *Jude the Obscure*   edited by Norman Page

HARDY   *The Mayor of Casterbridge*   edited by James K. Robinson

HARDY   *The Return of the Native*   edited by James Gindin

HARDY   *Tess of the d'Urbervilles*   edited by Scott Elledge   *Second Edition*

HAWTHORNE   *The Blithedale Romance*   edited by Seymour Gross and
      Rosalie Murphy

HAWTHORNE   *The House of the Seven Gables*   edited by Seymour Gross

HAWTHORNE   *The Scarlet Letter*   edited by Sculley Bradley, Richmond Croom
      Beatty, E. Hudson Long, and Seymour Gross   *Second Edition*

George Herbert and the Seventeenth-Century Religious Poets   selected and
      edited by Mario A. Di Cesare

HOMER *The Odyssey* translated and edited by Albert Cook
HOWELLS *The Rise of Silas Lapham* edited by Don L. Cook
IBSEN *The Wild Duck* translated and edited by Dounia B. Christiani
JAMES *The Ambassadors* edited by S. P. Rosenbaum
JAMES *The American* edited by James A. Tuttleton
JAMES *The Portrait of a Lady* edited by Robert D. Bamberg
JAMES *The Turn of the Screw* edited by Robert Kimbrough
JAMES *The Wings of the Dove* edited by J. Donald Crowley and
    Richard A. Hocks
Ben Jonson and the Cavalier Poets selected and edited by Hugh Maclean
Ben Jonson's Plays and Masques selected and edited by Robert M. Adams
MACHIAVELLI *The Prince* translated and edited by Robert M. Adams
MALTHUS *An Essay on the Principle of Population* edited by Philip Appleman
MELVILLE *The Confidence-Man* edited by Hershel Parker
MELVILLE *Moby-Dick* edited by Harrison Hayford and Hershel Parker
MEREDITH *The Egoist* edited by Robert M. Adams
MILL *On Liberty* edited by David Spitz
MILTON *Paradise Lost* edited by Scott Elledge
MORE *Utopia* translated and edited by Robert M. Adams
NEWMAN *Apologia Pro Vita Sua* edited by David J. DeLaura
NORRIS *McTeague* edited by Donald Pizer
Adrienne Rich's Poetry selected and edited by Barbara Charlesworth Gelpi and
    Albert Gelpi
The Writings of St. Paul edited by Wayne A. Meeks
SHAKESPEARE *Hamlet* edited by Cyrus Hoy
SHAKESPEARE *Henry IV, Part I* edited by James J. Sanderson *Second Edition*
Bernard Shaw's Plays selected and edited by Warren Sylvester Smith
Shelley's Poetry and Prose edited by Donald H. Reiman and Sharon B. Powers
SOPHOCLES *Oedipus Tyrannus* translated and edited by Luci Berkowitz and
    Theodore F. Brunner
SMOLLET *The Expedition of Humphry Clinker* edited by James Thorson
SPENSER *Edmund Spenser's Poetry* selected and edited by Hugh Maclean
    Second Edition
STENDHAL *Red and Black* translated and edited by Robert M. Adams
STERNE *Tristram Shandy* edited by Howard Anderson
SWIFT *Gulliver's Travels* edited by Robert A. Greenberg *Revised Edition*
The Writings of Jonathan Swift edited by Robert A. Greenberg and
    William B. Piper
TENNYSON *In Memoriam* edited by Robert Ross
Tennyson's Poetry selected and edited by Robert W. Hill, Jr.
THOREAU *Walden and Civil Disobedience* edited by Owen Thomas
TOLSTOY *Anna Karenina* (the Maude translation) edited by George Gibian
TOLSTOY *War and Peace* (the Maude translation) edited by George Gibian
TURGENEV *Fathers and Sons* edited with a substantially new translation by
    Ralph E. Matlaw
VOLTAIRE *Candide* translated and edited by Robert M. Adams
WATSON *The Double Helix* edited by Gunther S. Stent
WHITMAN *Leaves of Grass* edited by Sculley Bradley and Harold W. Blodgett
WOLLSTONECRAFT *A Vindication of the Rights of Woman* edited by
    Carol H. Poston
WORDSWORTH *The Prelude: 1799, 1805, 1850* edited by Jonathan Wordsworth,
    M. H. Abrams, and Stephen Gill
Middle English Lyrics selected and edited by Maxwell S. Luria and
    Richard L. Hoffman
Modern Drama edited by Anthony Caputi
Restoration and Eighteenth-Century Comedy edited by Scott McMillin